Neurobiology

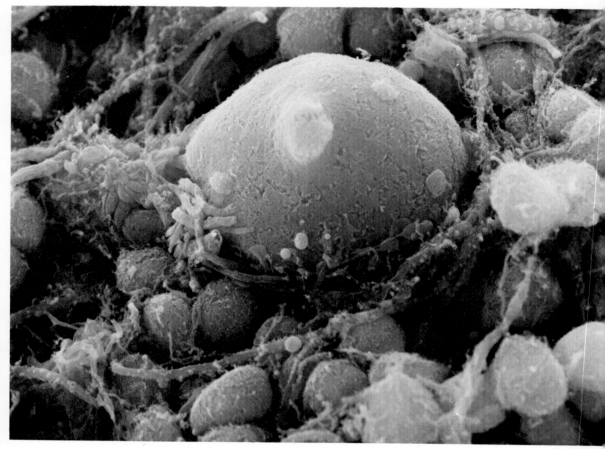

Scanning electronmicrograph of a large egg-shaped Purkinje cell body in the rat cerebellum. On its surface are small button-like synaptic terminals from basket cell axons; surrounding it are several long nerve fibers, and numerous small spherical cell bodies of granule cells. The tissue was prepared by chemical digestion in osmium and drying, after which the slices were gently pulled apart to expose the nerve cells and fibers. Magnification × 4030. (Courtesy of Bonnie Reese, Dennis Landis, and Thomas Reese, National Institutes of Health and Harvard Medical School)

NEUROBIOLOGY

GORDON M. SHEPHERD, M.D., D. Phil.
Professor of Neuroscience
Yale University

New York   Oxford
OXFORD UNIVERSITY PRESS
1983

Library of Congress Cataloging in Publication Data
Shepherd, Gordon M.
Neurobiology.
Bibliography: p.   Includes index.
1. Neurobiology.   I. Title.   [DNLM: 1. Behavior.
2. Neurophysiology.   3. Psychophysiology.   WL 102 S548n]
QP355.2.S52   1983   599.01′88   82-7938
ISBN 0-19-503054-0   AACR2
ISBN 0-19-503055-9 (pbk.)

Printed in the United States of America

Printing (last digit): 9 8 7 6 5 4 3 2

For my Parents

Preface

This book is written as an introduction to the field of neurobiology. It aims to summarize modern knowledge about nerve cells and their organization into functional circuits, and show how this relates to animal behavior.

The book had its origins several years ago in conversations with Jeffrey House of Oxford University Press, and our mutual feeling that although there were a number of excellent texts covering many parts of neurobiology, there was none that adequately covered the whole field in a systematic way. An informal survey of a dozen or so undergraduate courses in neurobiology was accordingly carried out, and the response of course directors at colleges and universities throughout the United States very much confirmed our feeling. I studied and collated the course outlines provided by this survey, and used this as a basis for organizing the material. I should like to record my thanks to all the course directors who responded to this survey and discussed their particular needs and generously offered detailed comments and suggestions on our proposal.

The format of the book is meant to be adaptable to several learning modes. The primary aim of the book is to serve the needs of the undergraduate student who is meeting the subject for the first time. Modern studies of the nervous system now touch on so much of animal life that some colleges are beginning to offer a broadly based course in neurobiology and behavior in parallel with the traditional sequence of introductory biology followed by upper level neurobiology. The present book can be adapted to both situations. The beginning student will focus mainly on the narrative account, whereas the upper level student will want to study details of the text, figures, and figure legends, and pursue the references to more specialized subjects. The 31 chapters can be taken in weekly steps for a full year course; the pace may be quickened, or a selection made of certain chapters, for shorter courses lasting a quarter or a semester. Although the book is not primarily aimed at medical school or graduate school students, it does cover a good deal of material, much of it very recent, not available at present in textbooks at those levels, and it may be useful therefore in those settings as a core or supplemental text.

In addition to being organized for effective learning and teaching, the material builds on some fundamental concepts about the ways that nervous systems themselves are organized. One of these concepts is the idea that any given region or system contains successive levels of organization, beginning with ions and molecules, and building up through cells and their circuits to behavior. Although the work of identifying these different levels and their specific functions is at an early stage, it seems to me important that we begin to think about organization in these terms, and try to correlate the different levels within a region in a coherent way. A related concept is the idea that different regions contain more or less corresponding levels, and that a full understanding of one region rests to a certain extent on our ability to relate its levels of organization to those of other regions. These concepts seem to me crucial to the task of developing common principles that apply to all nervous systems. Colleagues in the field will recognize that these are concerns that have been coming to the fore in recent years. There is a growing realization that we are in an era in which experimental results are pouring in much faster than we can fashion concepts that give them meaning. I hope the present effort will serve to some extent as a contribution toward the goal of synthesizing a body of basic principles for the functional organization of all nervous systems.

With regard to the main sections of the book, I felt it important to begin with an overview of invertebrate and vertebrate animals, as a basis for the comparative approach which underlies the later accounts of different systems. It helps to emphasize the evolutionary context within which nervous systems and the behaviors they mediate need to be evaluated. It also, incidentally, introduces some of the terms relating to the classification of different species which many students—myself included—find difficult to remember! The section on cellular mechanisms reflects the widely shared view of the cell as the fundamental building block of the nervous system. The sections on sensory and mo-

tor systems reflect a logical division of these subjects. However, the more centrally one proceeds, the more artificial is this division, and the present simplified accounts do not do justice to the extent of descending, motor, or centrifugal control of sensory systems; or of ascending, sensory, or internal feedback control of motor systems. Beyond sensory and motor systems, most textbooks tend to roam over a landscape populated by miscellaneous "higher functions." I decided to group all of these together in a section on Central Systems. As will be seen, this forces a definition of central systems, as specifically concerned with mediating global behavior patterns, that sets them apart from specific sensory and motor systems. This definition is heuristically useful for the teacher and the student, and I believe also reflects crucial distinctions between these types of systems and their levels of organization in relation to behavior. These distinctions are necessary, as will be shown, in defining and discussing global behaviors such as waking, emotion, learning, and memory.

Because the entire book is written as one continuous narrative, I have had an opportunity to attempt a wider integration of many aspects of neurobiology than is usually the case. One of my discoveries as the writing progressed was the extent to which a given subject is never isolated, but needs to be discussed in many contexts. The sensory hair of insects may be cited as an example. Its development is discussed in Chap. 10, the chemosensory types mediating taste and smell in Chap. 12, the tactile variety in Chap. 13, the type subserving the sense of balance in Chap. 15, the role in sensorimotor control of the proboscis of the fly in Chap. 24, and the role in control of feeding behavior in Chap. 27. Similarly, synaptic plasticity, in its molecular and cellular aspects, is discussed in the early chapters on basic cellular mechanisms; it is referred to in several subsequent chapters on specific sensory and motor systems; it is at the core of the discussion of learning and memory in Chap. 30, and it is also important in the cellular basis of human cortical function in Chap. 31. I have made a particular effort to cross-reference related aspects of subjects such as these as they arise in the text, so that the reader can follow through on specific topics. The importance of understanding a given neuronal property or type of circuit in all its functional and behavioral contexts is one of the key messages I hope to convey to the student of neurobiology by this means.

The systematic nature of this account brings in material that may be unfamiliar to some readers. For example, the chemical senses—taste and smell—are regarded as minor senses in most accounts, and are even left out completely in some textbooks. However, cell biologists know that chemosensitivity involves molecular interactions that are of great interest with regard to basic membrane mechanisms, and ethologists know that these senses have dominant roles in the behavioral and social organization of most animal life. I have tried to show how this chemical sensitivity may be integrated into the principles of neurobiology. Another subject that is almost completely ignored in modern textbooks is the vocal mechanism of human speech. This puzzling neglect of one of our highest and most important faculties seems no longer supportable to me, and I have tried to rectify it by including an account that describes this function from a perspective of sound production in both invertebrates and vertebrates. These are just two among a number of subjects which are included in this book, and which I believe must be incorporated into our thinking from the start of our studies if we are to build a truly valid and coherent view of neurobiology based on first principles.

The present account, though extensive, is by no means exhaustive, and there are many subjects which are absent or covered only skimpily. Any account of this vast field must be selective, and I hope that this attempt can serve as a framework so that the student or teacher can add other material or explore other subjects in a logical way.

My interest in writing a book of this nature has evolved out of my own work in two main areas: the principles of organization of synaptic circuits, and the mapping of activity in those circuits in the awake behaving animal. The idea that these two levels—synaptic circuits and natural behavior—could be joined in a way that would allow one to begin to build the neural basis of behavior was first instilled in me by Niko Tinbergen, through his early writings and through a conversation we had while I was a graduate student at Oxford in 1960. This goal seemed remote to my own work until the early 1970s, when James Sprague at Philadelphia encouraged me to start thinking again of synaptic organization in terms of its behavioral significance. In the synthesis of ideas that has ensued, I was stimulated by Eric Kandel to include invertebrates equally with vertebrates, and by Tomas Hökfelt to incorporate the new findings of neurochemistry.

The neural basis of behavior is a central concern of modern neurobiology and of this book, and deserves further comment. Many workers in recent years have studied synaptic properties and circuits and their correlations with simple behaviors; what is still needed is an understanding of how, beginning at the single synapse, one builds up successive levels of synaptic circuits of increasing extent to mediate complex naturally occurring behaviors. The synaptic circuits within different regions have only been revealed in their correct details in recent years; surprisingly, it is at these intermediate levels of circuit organization that common principles are emerging very clearly, as is documented in many chapters of this book. From all this work one can see that complex naturally occurring behaviors, such as feeding and mating, are just what nervous circuits are primarily designed for. One can summarize this in a proposition, paraphrasing the well-known aphorism of Theodosius Dobzhansky about biology and evolution, that "Nothing in neurobiology makes sense except in the light of behavior."

In view of these considerations, it was important in this book not to describe neural circuits and mechanisms in isolation from the kinds of behavior that they mediate. What is accomplished if the student is asked to learn the neural mechanisms that control manipulation, for example, without a clear picture of what the organs of manipulation look like, how they function, and how they compare with other organs of similar or related function? I have therefore extended the usual scope of a neurobiology text, and have included treatment of anatomical structure, comparative physiology, and different kinds of social behavior, wherever it seemed to help illuminate the text or simply bring out the precision or beauty (too often forgotten) of the behavior involved. This extension of scope should help the student pursue further, using the references provided, those topics that overlap with other fields.

Many parts of the text have grown directly out of my teaching experiences here at Yale and at other institutions. In addition to medical and graduate courses, they include a Pierson College seminar course for undergraduates on "Man and his Brain" at Yale. I am indebted to Kurt Schlesinger and Herb Alpern for their kind invitation to give a mini-course on synaptic organization in the Department of Psychology at the University of Colorado in 1981, and for stimulating discussions there which helped in formulating some of the ideas relating to Central Systems in Section V. Chapter 24 includes material I have used as a guest lecturer in the Master Class for Vocal Music, under Blake Stern, the noted tenor, at the Yale Music Festival in Norfolk, Connecticut; I thank Mr. Stern and George Shepherd for stimulating discussions about the singing voice. Parts of the book draw on material from the second edition of my book, *The Synaptic Or-*

ganization of the Brain, published by Oxford University Press in 1979. These include especially Chaps. 8 and 9, as well as excerpts and figures scattered in Chaps. 4–7, 9, 12, and 17. Much of this material is concerned with basic principles of cells and synapses, and is more appropriate now in the present context.

One of the major concerns of this book is a comparison between the circuits of invertebrates and vertebrates for each major functional system, and one of the major themes is the extraordinary degree to which the circuits appear to be built on similar organizational principles. In pursuing these comparisons I have been led into many areas of invertebrate neurobiology with which I have no first-hand experimental knowledge. Many colleagues have helped me, with stimulating discussions and criticisms, and clarification of innumerable items of detail. Among them I am especially indebted to Jurgen Boeckh, John Hildebrand, Steve Matsumoto, Malcolm Burrows, Keir Pearson, Brian Bush, Alan Roberts, Jeffrey Wine, Simon Laughlin, John Miller, Robert Wyman, Melvin Cohen, and John Nicholls.

A great number of colleagues have helped with parts of the text and with specific illustrations. Those to whom I am most indebted include Marilyn Farquhar, Amiram Grinvald, Raymond Murray, Linda Bartoshuk, Robert LaMotte, Carole LaMotte, Melvin Cohen, Daniel Alkon, Simon Laughlin, Pasko Rakic, Patricia Goldman-Rakic, Stephen Smith, Rich Aldrich, Lynn Landmesser, Robert Wyman, Jeffrey Wine, Richard Day, Charles Bradford, Albert Beveridge, Ralph Norgren, Alan Peters, Bonnie Reese, Tom Reese, Stephen Kitai, Dennis Lincoln, William Schwartz, Kent Morest, Mahlon DeLong, Aage Moller, Fred Naftolin, Tom Thach, Peter Strick, Edmund Crelin, Damien Kuffler, William Miller, and Victor Wilson.

The parts of the book that are drawn from my own research reflect the results of the combined efforts of many students and co-workers with whom it has been my privilege to be associated in recent years. It is a pleasure to record my special indebtedness in this respect to Lewis Haberly, Lanay Land, Thomas Getchell, John Kauer, Frank Sharp, William Stewart, Martha Nowycky, Neil Krieger, Ulrich Waldow, Kensaku Mori, Charles Greer, Doron Lancet, Norbert Halasz, Burton Slotnick, Patricia Pedersen, Thane Benson, Leona Masukawa, Paul Greengard, and Tomas Hökfelt. Our work has been generously supported by research grants from the National Institute of Neurological and Communicative Disorders and Stroke, and from the National Science Foundation.

Several colleagues graciously consented to take time from their busy schedules to read entire sections of the book while it was at the manuscript stage. These were Sol Erulkar (Section II), Albert Hudspeth (Section III), Keir Pearson (Section IV), and Alan Epstein (Section V). They have corrected many errors of detail, and made a number of valuable suggestions about organization and emphasis. The faults which remain are mine, not theirs.

Particular care has been taken with the illustrations. A number of these are composites of several figures, which help the student to correlate different levels of organization or function. Many are original illustrations, which constitute new interpretations of recent findings. I apologize to colleagues whose work in this regard has been oversimplified in the interests of clarity or meaning for the introductory student. For these, my pencil drawings have been put into final form by Virginia Simon, of the Medical Illustration Department at Yale, and her associates, Linda Seigneur, Wendolyn Hill, and Beverly Pope. I am grateful to them for their beautiful artwork, to Thomas Coughlan for expert photography, and to all of them for their considerable efforts in seeing over 400 illustrations to completion in a limited period of time.

Each author of an original illustration is credited in the figure legend, and is cited under References at the end of that Chapter. The citation is either to the original publication, or, in some cases, to a later publication which would be more accessible or relevant to an introductory student, or in which the original illustration has been updated or otherwise modified. Authors referred to in the text are also cited in the References. In resolutely keeping the account at an introductory level, I have held the number of references to an absolute minimum, which has meant leaving out much work that deserves equal mention; I hope my colleagues will be understanding in this regard. Even at that, there are some 500 references, many of them within the past several years. I thank the many authors and publishers who have kindly granted permission to reproduce copyrighted material.

The writing has been done on evenings, weekends, and holidays, and this has placed great burdens on my family. I am not only deeply grateful to my wife, Grethe, and to Gordon, Kirsten, and Lisbet, for their understanding and support, but also for their assistance in typing, editing, copying, and reading the text, and helping with several of the illustrations.

From first to last, Jeffrey House has given unstinting support. He has maintained his belief in a single-author text during the hard times when my faith was wavering, and he deserves much of the credit for seeing the project through to completion. The editing of text and figures within the time available was a demanding job, which Brenda Jones has performed with efficiency, and a tactful indulgence in my idiosyncracies.

I dedicate this book to my parents, Eleanor and Geoff Shepherd, who have taught me by word and deed to explore life carefully, write about it as clearly as possible—and retain a gentle sense of humor.

Hamden, Connecticut G. M. S.
June 1982

Contents

III   SENSORY SYSTEMS

IV   MOTOR SYSTEMS

V   CENTRAL SYSTEMS

I
Introduction

1

The Cellular Basis
of Neurobiology

What Is Neurobiology?

There are many reasons for studying the nervous system. Perhaps the most obvious is that we all have some curiosity about how our own brains function. Growing up, we acquire skills and knowledge and experience the difficulties and rewards of living with ourselves and others. If we ask how it is that we learn to throw a ball with one hand and not the other, or why we feel anger when frustrated, or how we construct a visual image of the world about us, we are essentially asking questions about how the human brain functions. We may also grow philosophical and ask: what is consciousness? or, who am I? For answers we are ultimately brought back to the nature of the organ through which these questions are posed.

For similar reasons, many studies in specialized fields of knowledge lead to the nervous system. In biology, for example, one cannot learn about the different forms of animal life and their amazing diversity of behavior without soon realizing that these behaviors all depend on a corresponding diversity of nervous systems. The study of behavior patterns in animals in their natural habitats is known as ethology, and the correlation of these patterns

with nervous mechanisms is called neuroethology. The testing of animals under controlled laboratory conditions is called physiological psychology or animal behaviorism. If, on the other hand, one is interested in general psychology, relevant studies will raise many questions about the brain mechanisms that underlie human behavior. The same can be said of psychophysics, which is concerned with the quantitative analysis of sensory perception. And there are fields of the social sciences, such as anthropology, which raise fascinating questions about how our brains have grown more complex through evolution and in correlation with the emergence of human cultures.

Another avenue of approach is through physics and chemistry. Many students with an interest in the fundamental nature of matter or the molecular basis of life find themselves drawn to the special study of these subjects as they apply to nerve cells. Traditionally this has been carried out in the fields of biophysics and biochemistry, and the subspecialty of neurochemistry. Recently, a vast new armamentarium of techniques from the fields of molecular biology and molecular genetics has become available to neuroscientists. These new methodologies are responsible for many recent advances in our knowledge of the nervous system, and they promise new breakthroughs in our understanding of the molecular and genetic mechanisms controlling nerve cells.

A very important area of research is in medicine. Anyone who has seen a child undergoing an epileptic seizure, or has known an older person who suffers from Parkinson's disease or a stroke, is aware of how devastating a disease of the nervous system can be. Medical students begin with studies of the structure of the brain in neuroanatomy, and its functions in neurophysiology. In neuropharmacology they learn about the effects of drugs on the nervous system, and what is known about the molecular and cellular basis of drug actions. This knowledge is applied in clinics and hospitals in the specialty fields of neurology, in which patients are treated with drugs, and neurosurgery, in which patients are treated by surgery or other instrumental means. As more is learned about the nervous system, there is growing evidence that some mental disorders, such as schizophrenia, which have traditionally been treated by psychiatrists, may have a physical basis, and thus be treated like other neurological disorders.

Thus, many fields of learning involve the nervous system. We may think of them as overlapping spheres of interest, and where they overlap defines the field of *neurobiology* or *neuroscience* (Fig. 1.1). Some of its features may be pointed out immediately. It is a relatively *new* field, reflecting the fact that many of its component disciplines had not advanced far enough to intersect significantly until very recently. It is obviously a *multidisciplinary* field; this means that no one approach has a corner on the truth, and we need to correlate the results from several methods in order to understand any particular brain function. Finally, it is a field *without distinct boundaries*. Just as students in other fields may be drawn to the nervous system, so,

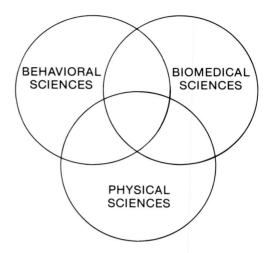

Fig. 1.1. The fields of science that contribute to neurobiology.

when investigators start with a problem in the nervous system, they soon find themselves dealing with fundamental aspects of other fields.

A field that is new, multidisciplinary, and without boundaries may seem too broad to admit definition, and this certainly presents a problem. What is needed is a framework or a point of view that helps organize the different kinds of knowledge. Such a framework is in fact to be found in the concept that all living matter is composed of *cells*. Just as we study the organization and function of other organs of the body, such as the heart or the lungs, in terms of their cellular structure and function, so can we best understand the nervous system in terms of its cellular organization. For our purposes, therefore, we will define the subject matter as follows: *Neurobiology is the study of nerve cells, and the ways in which they are organized to form nervous systems which mediate animal behavior.*

The Cellular Basis of Neurobiology: a Brief History

The idea that living organisms are composed of cells was first formulated in 1838

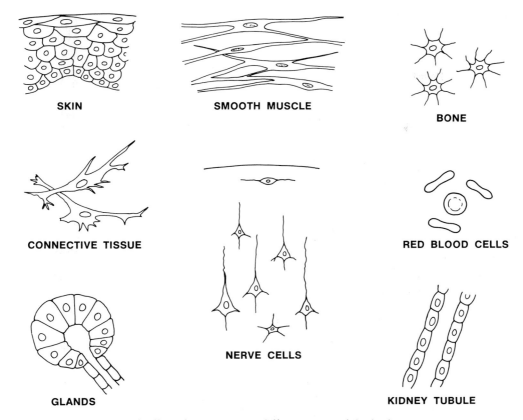

Fig. 1.2. Arrangements of cells to form tissues in different parts of the body.

by Matthias Schleiden in Berlin, based on his studies of plants, in which the cells, with their heavy cellulose walls, could be relatively easily distinguished with the primitive microscopical techniques of that time. The idea was extended by his friend, Theodor Schwann, in 1839, to animals as well. Although his original concept of how cells form was inaccurate, his belief that "there exists one general principle for the formation of organisms . . . (which) may be comprised under the term *cell theory*" gave the age its name. There quickly gathered widespread support from studies of all the different organs of the body—all, that is, except the nervous system. The cellular structure of the nervous system could not be visualized adequately with the histological methods then available. Part of this was due to the fact that nervous

tissue is difficult to fix (harden) and stain, and part was due to the fact that nerve cells, by their nature, have long, thin processes that are difficult to visualize even with the best of methods. These problems in fact, have continued to complicate the study of nerve cells right down to the present day.

Figure 1.2 presents a comparison of cells in different types of tissue, using some of the common stains for light microscopy. Note that in most tissues the cells have simple shapes that reflect in large part their particular functions. Thus, the cells of the skin form layers, the cells of the kidney form tubules, the cells of the glands form ducts to carry their secretions, and muscle cells form fibers that can contract and elongate. Nerve cells, however, give off fibers, trunks, and branches in various di-

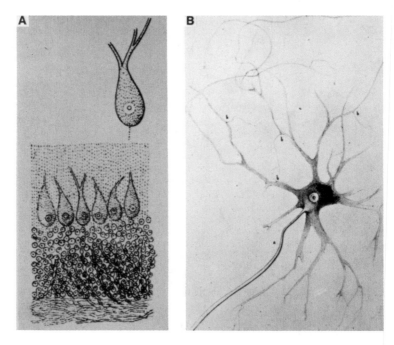

Fig. 1.3. **A.** Nerve cells in the cerebellum, as observed by Purkinje in 1837. **B.** A large motoneuron in the spinal cord, as observed by Deiters in 1865. (From Liddell, 1960)

rections, and these processes seem to disappear in the surround. Very little, therefore, can be deduced about nerve cell function from the structures seen with routine staining procedures.

From these considerations it can be appreciated why debate continued for many years about whether the cell theory applied to the nervous system. Scientists from many European nations contributed to this debate, which continued through much of the nineteenth century. As early as 1836 Jan Purkinje, the great Czech anatomist, had published observations of cells (which later would bear his name) in the cerebellum, but, as can be seen in Fig. 1.3, these showed little more than the nucleus and surrounding cytoplasm. An important advance was made in 1865, when the observations of Otto Deiters were published posthumously. He was a brilliant young scientist of Bonn who died prematurely in 1863 at the age of 29. In his diagram of a large motor neuron of the spinal cord he distinguished between two kinds of fiber

arising from the cell body. One kind consisted of a number of branches which appeared to be extensions of the cell body, and which he termed "protoplasmic prolongations", *protoplasm* being the traditional term for the living substance of the cell. The other kind consisted of a single, unbranched, tubular process, or "axis cylinder," which arose from a small, conical mound on the cell body, and in turn became the fiber which left the spinal cord and entered the peripheral nerve that supplied the muscles. The protoplasmic prolongations came eventually to be called "dendrites", a term borrowed from botany, meaning, simply, branches. The axis cylinder came to be called "axon". In Chap. 4 we will consider the varieties of these processes in more detail.

Despite these advances, a single nerve cell had not yet been seen in its entirety. One could therefore only speculate as to how nerve cells were organized. Many believed that, when an axon split up into fine branches within the brain, those branches

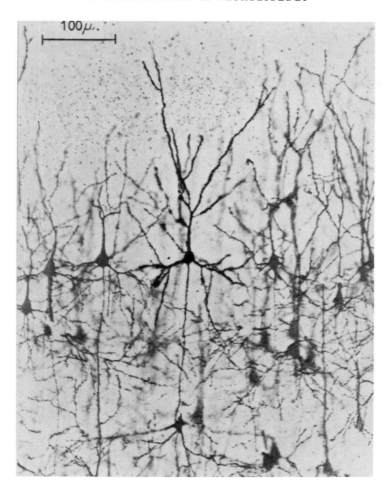

Fig. 1.4. Neurons in the visual cortex of the cat impregnated by the Golgi method. (From Sholl, 1956)

became continuous with the finest branches of dendrites of other cells, in much the same way that the smallest arteries and veins in the body communicate through capillaries. This became known as the "reticular theory" of nervous organization, in opposition to the cell theory, in which each nerve cell was conceived of as a separate entity whose branches terminate in "free nerve endings".

It seemed almost impossible to resolve this issue, because even if a method could be found that made it possible to stain the finest branches, they would be obscured by the thousands of other branches around them. What was needed was a method that would stain only a few percent of the cells, but stain them in their entirety. And that

is exactly what happened! In 1873, an impoverished doctor, Camillo Golgi of Pavia, was carrying out experiments by candlelight in his kitchen, trying to find a better way to visualize nerve cells. Among the many different methods he tried was a combination of potassium dichromate fixation and silver impregnation. To his astonishment, in nervous tissue this method revealed, here and there, a few cells with their cell bodies and dendrites stained completely black, out to the finest terminal branches. Golgi applied his method to a number of different parts of the nervous system, and published his results in 1885, in a comprehensive work in Italian. At first it aroused little interest among anatomists, and the full implications of the results were not realized until a Spanish histologist, Santiago Ramón y Cajal, working in a small laboratory in Barcelona, stumbled on the method in 1888. The effect of this new vision of the nervous system is best described in his own words (as translated by Sherrington, 1935):

Against a clear background stood black threadlets, some slender and smooth, some thick and thorny, in a pattern punctuated by small dense spots, stellate or fusiform. All was sharp as a sketch with Chinese ink on transparent Japan-paper. And to think that that was the same tissue which when stained with carmine or logwood left the eye in a tangled thicket where sight may stare and grope for ever fruitlessly, baffled in its effort to unravel confusion and lost for ever in a twilit doubt. Here, on the contrary, all was clear and plain as a diagram. A look was enough. Dumbfounded, I could not take my eye from the microscope.

Cajal worked feverishly, developing the Golgi method and applying it to many parts of the nervous system in many animal species. Figure 1.4 gives examples of cells in the cerebral cortex. Cajal had the genius to realize that the entity stained by the method was, in fact, the entire nerve cell, and that this procedure provided the long-sought proof that each nerve cell is an entity, separate from the others. He also deduced the basic principles that nervous signals pass through the dendrites as well as the axon of a cell, and that transmission between cells takes place where their axons and dendrites contact each other.

Cajal's outpouring of publications between 1888 and 1891 attracted a number of other anatomists, and most of them agreed with his interpretations. These ideas also fit with conclusions that had been reached from studies of the embryological development of nerve cells by Wilhelm His, of Leipzig, in 1887, and of the way that nerve cells respond individually to injury by August Forel, of Zurich, in 1888. It only remained for someone to assemble all the evidence in a convincing way, and this was done by Wilhelm Waldeyer, a distinguished professor of anatomy and pathol-

ogy in Berlin, in 1891. Waldeyer's extensive review in a German medical journal finally showed, after a 50 year delay, that the cell theory applied to the nervous system, too. Waldeyer suggested the term "neuron" for the nerve cell, and the cell theory as applied to the nervous system became known as the "neuron doctrine". Cajal, for his part, never quite forgave Waldeyer for being credited with the doctrine he considered his own. Ironically, Golgi himself never accepted the individuality of the nerve cell, clinging bitterly to the reticular theory even on the occasion of his Nobel lecture when he and Cajal shared the award in 1906.

Although the neuron doctrine became widely accepted, final proof required a method that could demonstrate that nerve cell membranes remain everywhere distinct from each other. This is beyond the power of resolution of the light microscope, and the question awaited the advent of the electron microscope. This instrument was first applied to physical materials in the 1940's, and to biological tissues around 1950. Its application to the nervous system was delayed by the same problems of fixing and staining the tissue that we have already noted. However, the early investigations of David Robertson in London, Eduardo de Robertis in Argentina, and Sanford Palay and George Palade in New York, in the mid-1950's, showed that the nerve cell membrane resembles the basic "unit membrane" of other cells, and that it appears to be continuous around each nerve cell (see Fig. 1.5). This supported the neuron theory in its proposition that each nerve cell is a genetic and anatomical unit like other cells of the body, and its corollary that nervous tissue consists of populations of these units organized into functional systems.

The Functional Building Blocks of the Nervous System

Recognition that the nervous system is composed of cells does not reveal how the

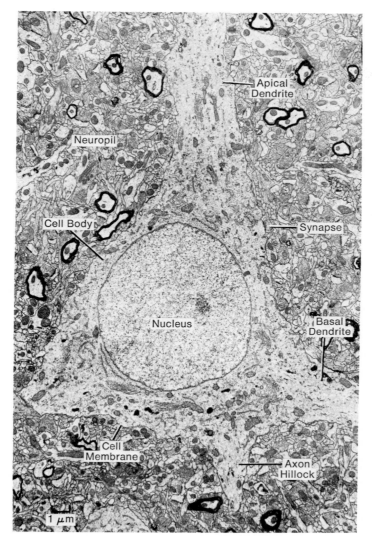

Fig. 1.5. Electron micrograph of a pyramidal cell in the visual cortex of the rat. (Courtesy of Steven Hersch and Alan Peters)

nervous system works. It is in fact only the starting point. As the second part of our definition of neurobiology makes explicit, the problem is to understand how nerve cells are organized into functional systems. Let us, for comparison, glance back at Fig. 1.2 and consider again the organization of cells in other body tissues. In glandular organs, like the liver, the main functions are to be found in the metabolic activity and secretions of the individual cells; the spatial relations between cells are

important only for the transport of substances between the cells and the blood vessels. In other tissues, like skin, muscle, and bone, mechanical factors are of primary importance. Organs like the lung or kidney combine both metabolic and mechanical functions.

In the nervous system, as in other organs, the cells carry out a variety of metabolic functions, and they must also satisfy certain mechanical constraints. However, the nervous system differs in one key aspect: *nerve cells process informa-tion.* To do this they must be organized to pass information along specific pathways and combine different kinds of information together in specific ways, as stressed in the second part of our definition of the subject matter of neurobiology.

At the cellular level we can identify several properties that are important or necessary for nerve cells to fulfill these functions. First, a nerve cell, like most cells, is involved in exchanges of chemical substances with its environment; these range from ions and metabolites to peptides and hormones. Many of these substances have actions that tend to affect the cell as a whole and occur over long periods of time. Second, there must in addition be sites for rapid transmission of signals between nerve cells. These sites are called *synapses.* Third, there must be mechanisms for the actions at those sites. These actions may be mediated by electrical current, or, more commonly, by chemical transmitter substances. Fourth, there must be responses of cells to the synaptic actions. These responses are termed synaptic potentials, and are graded in intensity depending on the amount of electrical or chemical synaptic activity. And finally, there must be means for conducting activity within a cell. This occurs over short distances through local potentials or electrotonic potentials, which are graded in intensity with the amount of synaptic activity, or it can take place by means of impulses, all-or-nothing signals which are conducted over both short and long distances. On logical grounds we can expect these properties to be the minimum necessary to provide for the functional organization of nerve cells. They may thus be regarded as the elementary properties of nerve cells, and the functional building blocks of the nervous system.

The properties we have named above are those most closely related to the *transmission* of information, and that is the function that we understand best. However, this is only one of the things that nervous systems do. Recent research is beginning

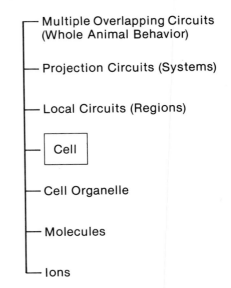

Fig. 1.6. Levels of organization in the nervous system.

to provide us with evidence of how nerve cells *generate* information themselves, and how they *store* and *retrieve* information. These are crucial functions that all nervous systems must provide for.

The cell is a useful focus in studying neurobiology for an additional reason, and that is because, on a scale of organization, it stands at an intermediate level (see Fig. 1.6). Below are the cell organelles and, below them, the molecular mechanisms that control the interactions of cells. Above are the multineuronal circuits through which individual cells are organized to carry out specific functions, like visual reception or feeding, and above that are the multiple overlapping circuits that are brought into play during behaviors of the whole organism, such as sleeping, emotion, and thought.

In this book special emphasis will be placed on the ways in which nerve cells are connected through their synapses to form functional circuits. The synaptic circuit will be shown to be a key concept in enabling us to understand how nerve cells are organized to mediate behavior. We will see that this requires certain modifications in the classical concept of the neuron as an independent unit. For example, many

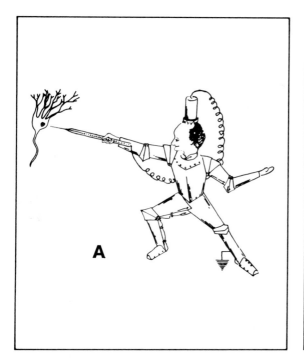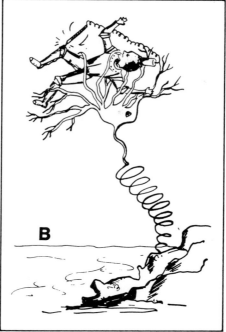

Fig. 1.7. An affectionate view of Stephen Kuffler from the early years of modern neurobiology. Armed with his trusty microelectrode, Don Quixote seeks the secrets of the neuron (**A**), but finds that the neuron fights back (**B**). (From Kuffler, 1958)

neurons, like many other cells, have the continuity of their plasma membrane interrupted by gap junctions (electrical synapses), which allow small molecules to pass freely between cells. It has been argued that "It is the coupled cell ensemble, and not the single cell, that is the functional compartmental unit for the smaller cytoplasmic molecules" (Loewenstein, 1981). Studies of chemical synapses have similarly changed our views. In place of the old idea that each neuron is a simple functional unit, receiving synaptic inputs in its dendrites and emitting signals through its axon, is an enlarged view in which the neuron can provide multiple sites for input–output units in both its dendrites and axon. In this view, it is synaptic units, organized into multineuronal circuits and assemblies, that provide the basis for nervous organization (Shepherd, 1972). One of the main purposes of this book is to identify these circuits that underlie different behaviors.

A second purpose of this book is to compare the circuits in invertebrates and vertebrates, in order to identify basic principles of organization. For those pursuing biology in its broadest aspects, the invertebrates represent solutions to adaptation that are of interest in their own right, quite apart from their relevance to vertebrates. Those who are primarily interested in the vertebrates should heed the warning of E. J. W. Barrington:

Vertebrate studies by themselves . . . tell us little, if anything of the origin of vertebrates, or of the origin of the principles of biological organization that have determined the course of their adaptive evolution. Indeed, the appeal that the vertebrates make to our anthropocentric tendencies can be dangerously deceptive. It can easily lead to over-optimistic generalization from limited data, obtained from some laboratory mammal that has nothing to recommend it for the purposes other than its convenience and its compliant behaviour. If, therefore, we are to evaluate and exploit the dramatic advances of contemporary biology . . . we need as one essential condition the widest possible extension of our understanding of the principles of animal organization.

And finally, those whose interests are confined mainly to humans will see, when we come to consider higher mental functions in the final chapters, that our understanding is drawn from a wide perspective on the principles of organization of neuronal circuits that has been built up in the preceding chapters.

We will therefore begin with a brief overview of invertebrate and vertebrate nervous systems, in the remainder of this section. The following section will deal with the elementary properties mentioned above that are common to all nerve cells. This paves the way for discussions of how these properties provide for the organization of functional systems. For each system, we will compare examples in invertebrates and vertebrates, and finish by discussing humans. We consider first the processing of sensory information, then the control of motor output, and finally central systems for the generation and control of behavior.

REFERENCES

The References at the end of each chapter list the sources that are cited in the text or figures of the chapter. In later chapters, if a source is listed that has been cited previously, the chapter in which it is first cited is indicated in brackets []. The References are followed by Additional Reading, covering further background material or related topics.

Barrington, E. J. W. 1979. *Invertebrate Structure and Function.* New York: Wiley.

Haymaker, W. (ed). 1953. *The Founders of Neurology.* Springfield, Ill.: Charles C. Thomas.
Entertaining capsule summaries of historical figures.

Kuffler, S. W. 1958. Synaptic inhibitory mechanisms. Properties of dendrites and problems of excitation in isolated sensory nerve cells. *Exptl. cell Res.,* *Suppl. 5:* 493–519.

Liddell, E. G. T. 1960. *The Discovery of Reflexes.* Oxford: Oxford University Press.

Loewenstein, W. R. 1981. Junctional intercellular communication: The cell-to-cell membrane channel. *Physiol. Rev.* 61: 829–913.

Locy, W. A. 1915. *Biology and Its Makers.* New York: Henry Holt.

Peters, A. S. L. Palay, and H. de F. Webster. 1976. *The Fine Structure of the Nervous System.* New York: Harper & Row. Background on the modern evidence for the neuron theory, and definitive electronmicrographs of nervous tissue.

Shepherd, G. M. 1972. The neuron doctrine: a revision of functional concepts. *Yale J. Biol. Med.* 45: 584–599.

Sherrington, C. S. 1935. Santiago Ramón y Cajal. 1852–1934. *Obituary Notices of the Roy. Soc. of London, no. 4:* 425–441.

Sholl, D. A. 1956. *The Organization of the Cerebral Cortex.* London: Methuen.

Waldeyer, W. 1891. Über einige neuere Forschungen in Gebiete der Anatomie des Centralnervensystems. *Deutsche Med. Woch.* 1352–1356.
It is here that the word "neuron" was introduced.

Additional Reading

Boring, E. G. 1950. A History of Experimental Psychology. New York: Appleton.
Somewhat out-dated, but good background reading.

Cajal, S. Ramón y. 1937. *Recollections of my Life.* Trans. by E. H. Craigie and J. Cano. Philadelphia: University of Pennsylvania.
A vivid autobiography by one of the greatest neuroanatomists.

Granit, R. 1967. *Charles Scott Sherrington. An Appraisal.* New York: Doubleday.
An affectionate account of one of the greatest neurophysiologists.

Tower, D. B. 1958. Origins and development of neurochemistry. *Neurology 8, Suppl. 1:* 3–31.
A historical account up to the onset of the modern era.

2
A Comparative Overview
of the Invertebrates

It has been estimated that there are approximately 2 million different species of animals living in the world today. In the study of neurobiology, as in other specialty fields of biology, the student soon learns that this enormous number reflects two competing tendencies in the evolution of living organisms. One is the tendency for animals to develop specializations or *differentiations* of cells, tissues, and organs that enable them to find living spaces in almost every conceivable niche and corner of the earth's environment. The other is the tendency for every organism to maintain itself as an *integrated* whole despite the extremes of specialization and in the face of the pressures of competition from other species.

Each species has solved these two problems in different ways, and these differences are reflected in the structures and functions of the various organs, including the nervous system. As neurobiologists, we should, in principle, be interested in nervous organization in all its manifestations throughout the animal kingdom, but in practice our interests are usually much narrower. A biologist, for example, may be mainly interested in an insect or a fish, a molecular biologist in a worm, while a

medical student is naturally interested in humans. The neurobiology student may well feel that there is more than enough complexity involved in any one species without having to learn about many others; also, to some extent, any one species expresses general principles that apply to most or all of the others. However, a given species represents only one solution to the problems of differentiation and integration mentioned above, and we would be seriously limiting our understanding of these mechanisms and their behavioral significance by holding ourselves to the study of only one or a few organisms.

There is another reason why it is important to learn about different kinds of nervous systems, and that is because each species varies in how accessible it is to experimental investigation. To take an example, let us suppose we want to understand the mechanism of the nerve impulse. As we will see in Chap. 7, such an experiment requires making recordings with a very fine-tipped microelectrode inside an individual axon. Now it should be immediately obvious that the human is a very inappropriate subject for such an experiment; the axons in our nervous system are relatively thin (the largest have only the thickness of a human hair); penetrations even with an ultra fine microelectrode would be extremely difficult to manage; and not many people would happily agree to the prolonged anesthesia, surgical removal of parts of their skull, and insertion of electrodes into their brain that would be required. In contrast, there are "giant axons" in certain animals, such as the earthworm and the squid, which have diameters of up to 1 mm (as thick as a pencil lead), and thus are easy to dissect and penetrate with relatively large electrodes. Consequently, the detailed analysis of the nerve impulse was first carried out in these giant axons, and then extended to the axons of other animals.

This is in fact a common strategy in biology, as anyone knows who is familiar with modern concepts of molecular genetics, which have been based to such a large extent on experiments on simple organisms like bacteria, fungi, and viruses. A similar strategy lies behind the use of the simple nervous systems of invertebrates and lower vertebrates for the study of cellular mechanisms involved in many aspects of behavior, as we will see in later chapters.

The study of neurobiology therefore ranges over the whole breadth of animal life, seeking answers where it can find them, and assembling the puzzle of nervous organization with a variety of interlocking pieces. In orienting ourselves to this diversity, we need to familiarize ourselves with the evolution and classification of organisms.

Origins of the Invertebrates

The first cellular organisms that can be identified in the fossil record are bacteria and algae, which existed over 3 billion years ago. These *prokaryotic* cells (cells without nuclei) constitute the Kingdom Monera, and appear to have been the only cellular organisms on earth for the next 1.5 billion years. There then arose the *unicellular eukaryotes* (cells that contain a nucleus). These are represented by Protozoa, and constitute the Kingdom Protista. Together with a nucleus came a host of other cellular specializations: the formation of chromosomes, the replicative and reproductive mechanisms of mitosis and meiosis, cytoplasmic organelles such as mitochondria and endoplasmic reticulum, cilia containing microtubules, and the capacities for phagocytosis (engulfing of food particles), pinocytosis (pinching off of small vesicles), ameboid movements, and excitability.

These abilities of individual cells to develop specializations of structure and function provided the basis for the next great evolutionary advance, to *multicellular eukaryotic organisms*. This involved several steps. *Cells* first organized themselves into *tissues;* different tissues were then combined to form *organs;* different organs were combined to form an integrated *organism*. The organisms at this level of complexity are termed *Metazoa*, and form the familiar kingdoms of plants, fungi, and animals.

Our definition of neurobiology has emphasized the interactions of nerve cells in forming nervous systems, and we therefore will focus our attention on the metazoa of the *Animal Kingdom*. This kingdom is divided into some 30 major groups, called phyla. A much abbreviated list is shown in Table 2.1. Four of these can be regarded as major phyla: roundworms, arthropods, molluscs and chordates. They qualify as major in terms of their large numbers of species, and also, in ecological terms, on the basis that they utilize the largest shares of the energy that originates in the sun and flows through the green plants into the earth's biomass. Among the other phyla, several command attention because they reflect ancestral forms that were crucial at several stages of evolution. These are also included in Table 2.1.

Each of these major animal groups will be briefly described. The main aim is to become familiar with the general form of

Table 2.1 The principal phyla in the Animal Kingdom

Phylum	Numbers of species	Examples	Key characteristics
Coelenterata (Cnidaria)	11,000	jellyfish, corals	diploblastic (tissue grade)
Porifera	4,200	sponges	
Platyhelminthes	15,000	flatworms	triploblastic (organ grade); bilateral
Nemathelminthes	80,000	roundworms (nematodes)	
Annelida	9,000	segmented worms	metameric (segmented)
Arthropoda	800,000	crustaceans, spiders, insects	well-developed central nervous system
Mollusca	110,000	snails, clams, octopus	well-developed central nervous system
Echinodermata	6,000	starfish, sea urchins	deuterostomic; mesodermal pouches; indeterminate cleavage
Hemichordata	100	acorn worms	gill slits
Chordata			
Invertebrate chordata	2,000	lancelots, sea squirts	larval notochord
Vertebrata	43,000	fish, amphibians, reptiles, birds, mammals	well-developed central nervous system

Adapted in part from Russell-Hunter (1968)

the nervous system in each group. This outward form, as seen by the naked eye, is referred to as the *gross morphology* of the system. It reflects only indirectly the actual composition of the system, in terms of its cells and fibers, but, as with any other organ, it is the logical place to start. In each group only the most important characteristics will be described, and certain species which have been particularly well studied will be given special emphasis.

Phylum Coelenterata

The most primitive metazoans are the coelenterates, which arose in Precambrian times some 700 million years ago. Many of these species have a complicated life cycle. As shown in Fig. 2.1A, a fertilized egg gives rise to a larva called a planula, which swims about by ciliary motion, settles on the sea floor, and gives rise to a stem and eventually a hydroid colony by asexual budding. Polyps bud off from the colony to form flat, bell-shaped medusae which grow and come to float on the surface of the water. Gonadal cells in the medusa release eggs or sperms to complete the cycle. In some species (i.e. jellyfish) the medusa stage is dominant; in others (i.e. sea anemones) the sessile polyps predominate. Polyps may excrete and become encased in a hard exoskeleton, as in the case of corals.

It should be obvious from the foregoing description that there is not one single individual or species that is representative or typical of all coelenterates, and much the same will apply to the other phyla. We can only study examples, and deduce principles by making comparisons with other examples. In that spirit, let us look more closely at the medusa.

The basic cellular organization of the medusa consists of two cell layers, an outer *ectoderm* and an inner *endoderm,* as indicated in Fig. 2.1B. The medusa (and also the hydra) is therefore termed *diploblastic.* As shown in Fig. 2.1C, some cells of the ectoderm may be specialized for sensory reception or contraction or for defense (the nematocysts or sting cells). Sim-

A   HYDRANTHS   MEDUSAE

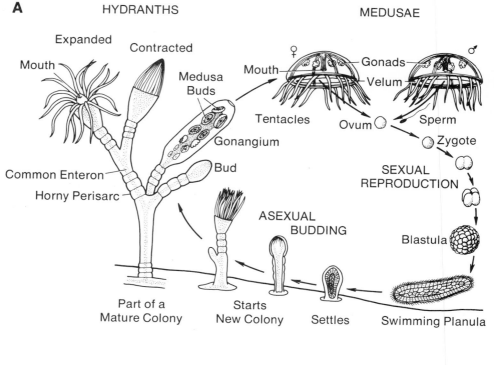

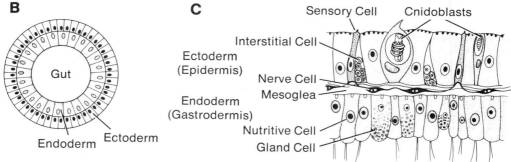

Fig. 2.1. Organization of a coelenterate. **A.** Life cycle of a hydrozoan, *Obelia*. (After Storer, 1943). **B.** Cross section through the wall of a jellyfish (medusa), showing two-layered composition. **C.** Magnified view of cells in body wall. (After Dobzhansky et al., 1977)

ilarly, cells of the endoderm may be differentiated into nutritive or gland cells. The differentiation, however, is not complete; cells typically retain several functions (i.e. a cell may be both epithelial and contractile). Furthermore, the cells are not aggregated into organs. We say, therefore, that coelenterates have reached the tissue, but not the organ, *grade*. The jellyfish (as well as the hydra) is usually regarded as more a colony than an organism.

Between the ectoderm and endoderm is a layer of noncellular substance called *mesoglea*. Within this substance lie nerve cells, derived from the ectoderm (see Fig. 2.1C). These cells give off processes that reach variable distances and make synaptic contacts with each other. In this way are formed two-dimensional nerve nets that extend throughout the medusa. The inputs to these nets are from various sense cells: sensory pits (presumably for chemoreception), an ocellus, or eye-spot, for visual reception; tactile sensory cells; and statocysts, for sensing gravity. The nerve cells themselves have slow spontaneous activity. The nervous outputs go to contractile epithelial cells under the bell which provide for slow swimming movements and righting reflexes; the activity controlling these movements spreads slowly and diffusely through the nerve nets. In some species there are nerve cells grouped in small, loose collections termed marginal bodies; these may be regarded as primitive ganglia, but a central nervous system is lacking.

Phylum Platyhelminthes

The next major stage in evolution was the worm. Although the first such creatures, the flatworms, are primitive indeed, they nonetheless represent several crucial de-

velopments. In addition to ectoderm and endoderm, there is now a true third germ layer, the *mesoderm,* making these organisms *triploblastic* (Fig. 2.2A). This is the condition of all other higher metazoa throughout the Animal Kingdom. Mesoderm appears to have been essential for the development of *organs,* containing two or more types of differentiated cells; examples in flatworms are the organs for excretion (primitive kidneys) and reproduction (gonads). Figure 2.2B shows a diagram of a generalized flatworm; the mouth and anus empty into a common opening, reminiscent of the coelenterate plan.

The flatworms are the first animals to have a definite *longitudinal axis* with head and tail ends, and, associated with that, the first animals to show *bilateral symmetry* with respect to the axis. Sensory cells for chemical and mechanical reception are

Fig. 2.2. Organization of a flatworm (Platyhelminthes). **A.** Cross section of body wall. **B.** Body plan. (After Dobzhansky et al., 1977)

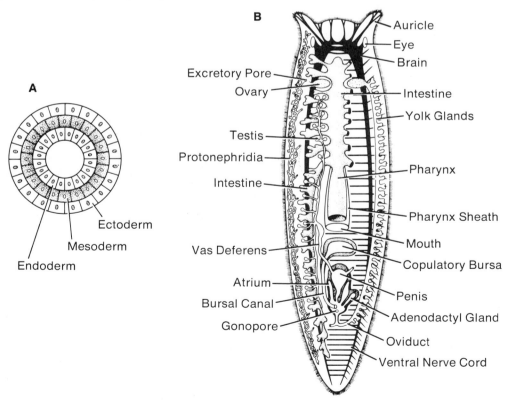

distributed over the body surface; in the head end are groups of taste cells and two "eyes", small cups containing light-sensitive cells. In primitive flatworms the nerve cells form a nerve net not unlike that of coelenterates. In advanced species there is a conglomeration of nerve cells in the head end. This is the crude beginning of a central nervous system; whether or not it qualifies as a "brain" depends on how charitable one is in stretching definitions. Nerve fibers passing to and from this "brain" are coalesced into nerve cords, as shown in Fig. 2.2B. The motor output goes to bands of muscle fibers which run in a longitudinal or circular fashion to provide the means for simple movements such as creeping and swimming. Swimming is also assisted by the ciliated epithelium, as in coelenterate planulae. Flatworms show primitive orienting reflexes, but beyond that their behavior is rather limited (their interest for experiments on memory is mentioned in Chap. 30).

The description above applies to free-living forms, such as triclads and polyclads, of the Class Turbellaria. The other species of this phylum are parasitic, such as the liver flukes and tapeworms which infest humans; they show extremes of adaptation, including reduction or absence of sense organs, nerve cells, and organs of locomotion.

Phylum Annelida

The possibilities of being a worm were not exhausted by the flatworms. We may note the related nematodes such as ribbon worms, and the widespread species of roundworms, hookworms, and pinworms of the Phylum Nemathelminthes. These represent only minor evolutionary changes.

The segmented worms grouped in the Annelida include marine forms such as polychaetes (bristle worms); land and freshwater forms such as oligochaetes (including the common earthworm); and Hirudinae, the medicinal leech used in bloodletting in former times. The annelids demonstrate several important advances toward complex organisms. They have a *tubular gut* running from mouth to anus, so that food passes through a series of stages of digestion and absorption. The body is *segmented* into *metameres;* each metamere may contain a complement of organs, such as sets of muscles and nerve ganglia, or certain internal organs (see Fig. 2.3). Associated with segmentation is the development of a *coelom,* an internal fluid-filled compartment with a peritoneal lining. The significance of the triploblastic condition mentioned earlier is seen in the fact that both segmentation and the coelom are determined by cells differentiating from the mesoderm. All three of these specializations—sequential alimentary system, segmentation, and coelom—are cardinal features of the body plans of higher invertebrates as well as vertebrates.

The tendency that began in the flatworms for nerve cells to be grouped in ganglia continues in the annelids. One can begin to think of these ganglia as forming a true central nervous system, and of those in the head end as a brain. (The leech also has a tail brain!) The ganglia are bilaterally paired within each metamere; they are connected across the midline by commissures, between metameres by longitudinal cords, or connectives, and with the periphery by nerve roots. The ganglia are organized in a way that is typical for most invertebrates: the nerve cell bodies are arranged around the outer surface, while the branches and synaptic connections constitute a neuropil within the ganglionic core. The neurons have a shape that is also characteristic for invertebrates: each cell has a single stout fiber which gives off branches to the neuropil and then enters the connectives or commissures to connect to other ganglia or the nerve roots to innervate the periphery. In leech ganglia (as in many invertebrate species) some cells are large and easily recognized; this has been an aid in electrophysiological studies.

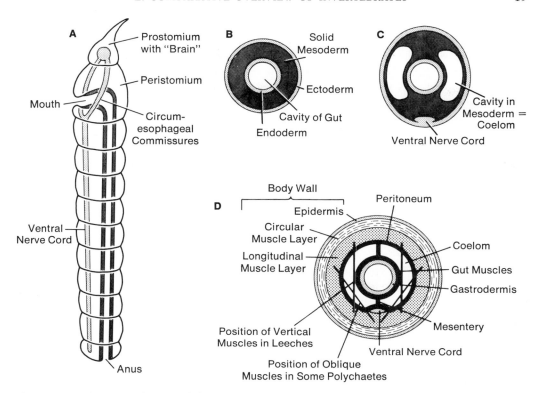

Fig. 2.3. Organization of an annelid worm. **A.** Schematic diagram of a juvenile segmented worm. **B.** Cross section through a segment at an early age. **C.** Later age, showing development of coelom and ventral nerve cord. **D.** Patterns of musculature seen in adult annelid worms. (After Russell-Hunter, 1968)

On the sensory side are various kinds of receptors. Some of these are specialized for touch, pain, and pressure, and thus constitute a primitive somatosensory system for detecting stimulation of the body surface or body wall (see Chap. 13). There are also receptors for sensing balance (statocysts), chemical substances (chemoreceptors), and light (photoreceptors). The latter are arranged in well-defined eyes in some species. On the motor side, the annelids are capable of a variety of movements. These include burrowing, creeping either by peristaltic contractions or by extension of parapodia, "walking" by the use of suckers (as in the leech), and swimming. The movements are more precise and more forceful than in the flatworms because the muscles can contract against the segmental coelom, which forms an in-

ternal hydrostatic skeleton. We will discuss these movements and the neural mechanisms involved in further detail in Chap. 21. Some species (such as earthworms) have a system of *giant nerve fibers* that run longitudinally through the body and mediate rapid reflexes such as startle or escape reactions; these are the fibers so admirably suited to study of the impulse mechanism, as mentioned at the outset of this chapter.

Phylum Arthropoda

Animals with *jointed external skeletons* and *jointed legs,* the arthropods, left their first traces in the fossil record early in the Cambrian period some 580 million years ago. These two adaptations together have

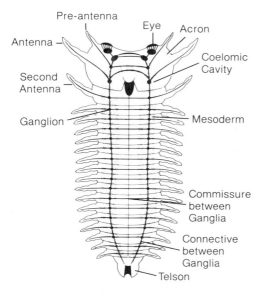

Pre-antenna
Antenna
Eye   Acron
Coelomic Cavity
Second Antenna
Ganglion
Mesoderm
Commissure between Ganglia
Connective between Ganglia
Telson

Fig. 2.4. The body plan of a generalized arthropod. (After Dobzhansky et al., 1977)

been highly successful, as evidenced by the fact that arthropods inhabit nearly every niche of the earth's ecospace and total over 80% of all animal species. Insects account for the majority of these species; other major groups include spiders and crustacea.

Although the arthropods at first glance seem to bear little resemblance to worms, closer examination reveals that they share the same basic body plan (see Fig. 2.4). One speaks therefore of an *annelid-arthropod line* in evolution. In addition to the exoskeleton and the articulated appendages, the arthropods show several important differences from annelids. The metameric segments are merged into distinct body regions: head, thorax, and abdomen (in addition to a segmented tail region); these are, of course, the same terms we use in describing the body plans of higher vertebrates as well. The head region continues to increase in size and importance in this phylum, a tendency referred to as *encephalization*. Finally, the *legs* are specialized for different motor functions. Most of these attributes are indicated in the diagrams of Fig. 2.4.

Because of its relatively large size, the *crayfish* is a convenient species for familiarizing oneself with some of the basic organizational principles of arthropods. Figure 2.5 is a summary view of the main body regions and their internal organs. Most of the attributes mentioned above are seen in the diagrams. Note, in addition, how the sequential alimentary system is elaborated from the annelid plan. Respiration occurs by means of gills. The circulatory system is open; the heart pumps blood through arteries and out into a space called a haemocoel, from whence it returns through veins to the heart. A true coelom is vestigial or absent; it can be reasoned that the hard exoskeleton renders an internal hydrostatic skeleton superfluous.

These and other physiological adaptations should be kept in mind as we turn our attention to the nervous system. In Fig. 2.5 it can be seen that the nervous system conforms rather closely to the annelid plan, with the most anterior ganglion lying dorsal to the mouth and the remaining ganglia lying ventrally, forming the ventral nerve cords. The largest ganglia are the dorsal, called the cerebral (which receives inputs from the antennae and antennules) and the subesophageal, which innervates the mouthparts; together they are considered to constitute the brain.

The trend toward differentiation of sensory receptors is well-exemplified in the crayfish. Chief among the specialized sense organs are the compound eye, mounted on a moveable eyestalk; antennae bearing chemoreceptors; and statocysts. There are also several types of mechanoreceptors involved in the control of the jointed legs: ligament receptors, chordotonal organs, and stretch receptors. The stretch receptor cell of the crayfish is a particularly attractive subject for study of neuronal properties (see Chap. 8) and mechanisms of sensory reception (see Chap. 14). The sensory inputs enter the nerve ganglia to undergo processing and integration with other elements involved in motor control. Control

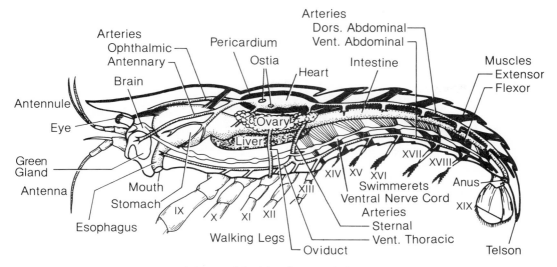

Fig. 2.5. Main organ systems of the crayfish. After Storer, 1943

of the muscles is effected not only through these central interactions, but also by means of interactions between excitatory and inhibitory fibers that end on the muscles themselves. There are thus both peripheral and central mechanisms of motor control in arthropods, as we will discuss in Section IV. Other parts of the motor system include the cardiac ganglion involved in control of the heartbeat (Chap.

19) and the giant fiber system involved in rapid tail flicks for escape maneuvers (Chap. 20).

If we turn now to the insects, we find that the body plan is similar (see Fig. 2.6), but superimposed on this are many modifications in design. In the nervous system the cerebral ganglia are more fused together, and one can identify several distinct regions: a protocerebrum, receiving

Fig. 2.6. Main organ systems of an insect. (After Oldroyd, 1969)

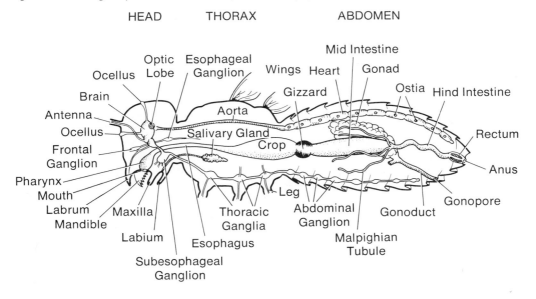

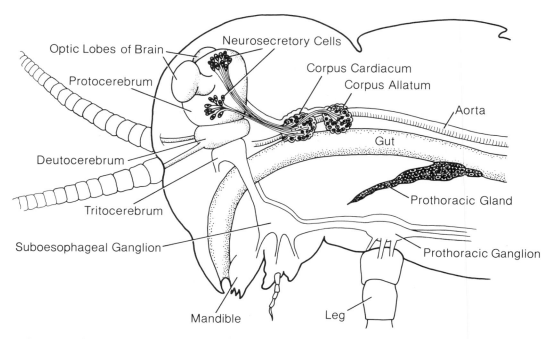

Fig. 2.7. Enlarged view of insect head, brain, and endocrine organs. (After Wells, 1968)

input from the eyes; a deutocerebrum, which receives input from the antennae, and a tritocerebrum, which innervates the anterior alimentary canal and head region (Fig. 2.7). A histological section through the brain (Fig. 2.8) reveals a complicated internal structure, consisting of different groups of cell bodies, neuropil, and fiber tracts. Among the important structures seen are the antennal lobes that receive the olfactory input, and large masses of neuropil, the corpora pedunculata, that serve as complex association areas. The insect eye, and its associated neural pathways in the optic lobe, is particularly highly developed. Insect limbs are specialized for a va-

Fig. 2.8. Cross section of deutocerebrum of the cockroach *Periplaneta americana*. (Photomicrograph by Jurgen Boeckh)

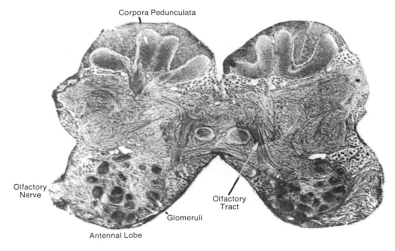

Table 2.2 Phylum Arthropoda

Classification	Examples	Characteristics
Subphylum Trilobita	trilobites (extinct)	three-lobed body
Subphylum Chelicerata	horseshoe crab (Limulus); spiders (Arachnidae)	two-part body; pincers (chelicerae)
Subphylum Mandibulata		mandibles; antennae
Class Crustacea	crayfish (Astacus); lobster (Homarus); crab (Carcinus); shrimp (Daphnia); barnacle (Balanus)	
Class Myriapoda	centipedes, millipedes	
Class Insecta		three-part body
Order Orthoptera	cockroach (Periplanata); grasshopper (Acrididae); locust (Cicadidae); cricket (Gryllus); termites (Macrotermes)	
Order Odonata	dragonflies (Aeschna)	
Order Hemiptera	bugs (Cicada); aphids (Rhodnius)	sucking mouth parts
Order Lepidoptera	butterflies (Danaus); moths (Bombyx)	
Order Coleoptera	beetles (Dytiscus)	
Order Diptera	flies (Musca; Drosophila); mosquitoes (Culicidae)	
Order Hymenoptera	bees (Apis); (Vespa); ants (Monomorium)	social insects

Adapted in part from Storer (1943) and Keaton (1972)

riety of different functions: flying, walking, jumping, manipulation, and even for producing sound. The nerve ganglia of the thorax, where the wings and limbs attach, are correspondingly large and important as centers of sensory integration and motor control.

In addition to nerve centers and fiber connections, the brain of insects, as well as of other arthropods, also uses neuroendocrine organs to control a variety of body processes. Chief among these is the corpus cardiacum. This is situated posterior to the brain (see Fig. 2.7). The paired ganglia (plural, corpora cardiaca) lie near the aorta (hence the name, cardiacum), and are connected to the brain by a nerve trunk. Nerve cells in the brain synthesize hormones which pass through the axons in the nerve trunk to the nerve terminals in the ganglion. Neurohormones are secreted from the nerve terminals, while other hormones are secreted from cells within the ganglion itself. The neurohormones and hormones are discharged into the bloodstream; hence, the corpus cardiacum is referred to as a neurohemal or-

gan. Associated with it is a mixed neuroendocrine and endocrine organ, the corpus allatum. These are often regarded as master organs for neuroendocrine and endocrine control in arthropods, analogous to the pituitary gland of vertebrates. During development, most insects pass through larval stages that bear little or no resemblance to the adult, and require drastic remodeling of the body, including the nervous system, in order to reach the adult form. This is known as *metamorphosis,* and is under control of the neurohemal organs (Chap. 10). We will also discuss the role of these organs in controlling sexual functions in Chaps. 25 and 28.

We should also note that certain insect species have reached the epitome of invertebrate evolution through the formation of colonies in which there is division of labor among different types of specialized individuals. These are the *social insects,* the ants, bees, and wasps. Some of the adaptations and associated nervous mechanisms related to specific social functions in these species will be noted in later chapters.

This provides only the briefest overview of the arthropod nervous system. The diversity of this phylum is expressed in the enormous range of species and corresponding variations in the attributes that have been noted here. Many of the familiar species are summarized for convenient reference in Table 2.2.

Phylum Mollusca

The annelid-arthropod line of evolution seems to point in the same general direction as that of the vertebrates, but before proceeding we must consider another large group of invertebrates, the molluscs (meaning soft bodies). There are several primitive classes, and three major ones: the snails (Class Gastropoda = belly foot), clams (Class Bivalvia = two shells), and the octopus and its relatives (Class Cephalopoda = head-foot). Together these account for more than 80,000 species, making this the second largest phylum in the Animal Kingdom.

The basic plan of the molluscan body can be best appreciated by considering a primitive example, a chiton. The cut-away view in Fig. 2.9 shows the three main body parts: a head-foot, a visceral mass, and a mantle. The *head-foot* can be regarded as a complex muscular organ for locomotion, containing in its head end most of the sense organs and nerve cells. The *visceral mass* contains the organs for digestion, excretion, and reproduction. The *mantle* is the protective covering over the other two. The longitudinal axis of the head-foot and the sequential alimentary system link the molluscs to some common ancestor of the annelid-arthropod line. The mantle secretes a shell that is characteristic of snails and bivalves; within this is a mantle cavity which houses the ctenidia, the featherlike gills that are the characteristic respiratory organs of molluscs.

It is convenient to think of a mollusc as actually two animals, a muscular (head-foot) animal carrying about a visceral animal. Although this arrangement strikes one as somewhat primitive and cumbersome, there are many parts of the ecospace where these creatures are admirably suited, as attested by the large number of species. The particular adaptations take many forms; for instance, the protective mantle shell may completely enclose the two animal halves (e.g. clams), or, at the other extreme, it may be reduced or completely absent, as in slugs and octopuses.

With regard to the nervous system, the molluscs cover almost the entire range of complexity seen in the invertebrates, from primitive forms at the level of flatworms

Fig. 2.9. Organization of a chiton, a primitive mollusc. (After Alexander, 1979)

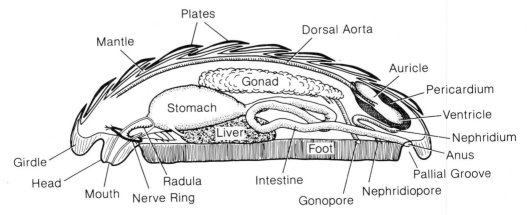

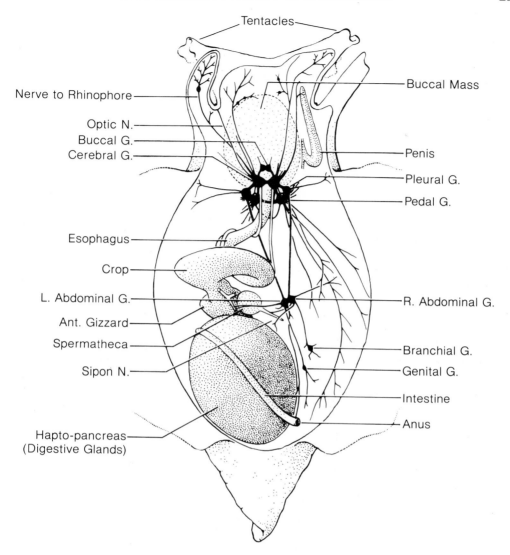

Fig. 2.10. The nervous system of a gastropod, the sea hare *Aplysia,* and its relation to other organs. (From Kandel, 1976)

all the way up to the cephalopods at the level of the most advanced insects. Let us consider first a relatively simple gastropod, the sea-hare, or sea-slug, genus Aplysia. As shown in Fig. 2.10, the nervous system consists of four paired *head ganglia*—buccal, cerebral, pleural, and pedal—that are clustered around the esophagus, and several outlying ganglia. The ganglia are connected by commissures between pairs, and to other ganglia by connectives, as in annelids and arthropods. The *buccal* ganglion innervates the mouth and anterior alimentary canal; the *cerebral* innervates the eyes and feelers (tentacles); the *pleural* and *pedal* innervate the foot. Separate from these is the *abdominal* ganglion, which innervates the organs of the visceral mass. Among sense organs of the head-foot are two small eyes, chemoreceptors on the feelers, and mechanoreceptors. The visceral mass contains a special organ, the osphradium, which senses the osmolarity and chemical composition of the seawater within the mantle cavity. The motor behavior of the head-foot animal is mediated by the head ganglia mentioned above, and consists of simple movements and reflexes involved in locomotion, feeding, and mating. There is also an ink gland at the edge of the mantle which ejects ink during defensive maneuvers.

Other species related to Aplysia include nudibranchs (Tritonia), pleurobranchs (breathing through gills), and pulmonates (breathing through lungs, as in Helix, the common garden snail). They conform to the general plan outlined above, though there are considerable differences in the

size and fusion of the various ganglia. The nervous systems of these species are relatively easy to remove and perform experiments on, and gastropods have therefore been favorite subjects for studies of the neuronal and synaptic mechanisms involved in the behavior of simple systems, as detailed in many later chapters.

We consider finally, as a contrasting example of this phylum, a cephalopod. The characteristic adaptations of the octopus (Fig 2.11) can be seen to include a loss of the mantle shell, the elaboration of long tentacles in the head-foot region, and the development in the mantle region of a siphon with muscles for pumping water. The central nervous system is arranged around

Fig. 2.11. Body plan of cephalopods. **A.** Molluscan archetype. Arrows indicate re-orientation of the head-foot during evolution, bringing it into line with the axis of the visceral mass. **B.** Schematic view of body plan of a modern cephalopod. (After Russell-Hunter, 1968)

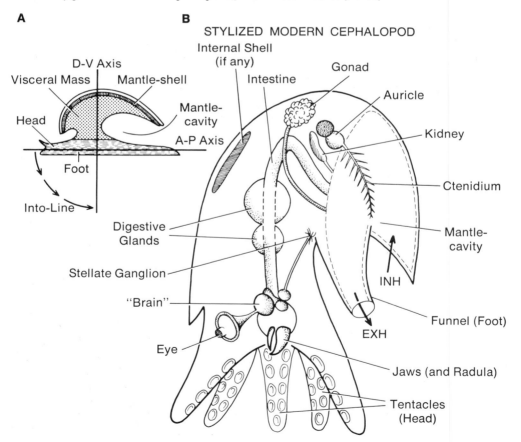

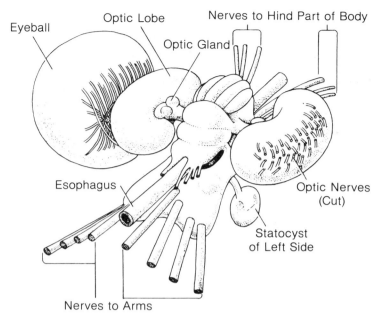

Eyeball

Optic Lobe

Optic Gland

Nerves to Hind Part of Body

Esophagus

Optic Nerves (Cut)

Statocyst of Left Side

Nerves to Arms

Fig. 2.12. The brain of an octopus. (From Wells, 1968)

the esophagus, as in other molluscs. There is considerable growth and fusion of the ganglia, to form a true brain (Fig. 2.12). Among the sensory organs the eyes are extremely well developed, and there is a corresponding eleboration of the optic ganglion into an optic lobe that is the dominant structure of the brain. The neurons within the optic lobe have differentiated into a variety of forms that go far beyond the common unipolar invertebrate type (see Chap. 17). In contrast with gastropods, the octopus and its relatives are active, fast-moving animals; the jet-propulsion of water through the siphon makes these animals among the swiftest in the sea in predation and escape. Escape is aided by giant fiber systems, especially well developed in the squid; this has provided neurophysiologists with the giant axon so important in study of the impulse mechanism.

The octopus has the largest brain among invertebrates, roughly equal in size to the brain of a fish. It has been estimated to contain nearly 170 million nerve cells. It mediates a variety of types of behavior, as we will discuss further in later chapters. The complex brain of the octopus is thus an appropriate point at which to end the survey of invertebrates.

REFERENCES

Alexander, R. A. 1979. *The Invertebrates*. London: Cambridge.

Dobzhansky, T., F. J. Ayala, G. L. Stebbins, and J. W. Valentine. 1977. *Evolution*. San Francisco: Freeman.

Kandel, E. R. 1976. *Cellular Basis of Behavior*. San Francisco: Freeman.

Oldroyd, H. 1962. *Insects and Their World*. Chicago: Chicago.

Russell-Hunter, W. D. 1968. *A Biology of Lower Invertebrates*. New York: Macmillan.

Storer, T. I. 1943. *General Zoology*. New York: McGraw-Hill.

Wells, M. 1968. *Lower Animals*. New York: McGraw-Hill.

Additional Reading

Barrington, E. J. W. 1979. [Chap. 1].

Bullock, T. H. and A. Horridge. 1965. *The*

Structure and Function of the Nervous System in Invertebrates. San Francisco: Freeman.

Hanström, B. 1928. *Vergleichende Anatomie des Nervensystems der Wirbellosen Tiere*. Berlin: Springer.

Keeton, W. T. 1980. *Biological Science*. New York: Norton.

Kuhlenbeck, H. 1967. *The Central Nervous System of Vertebrates*. Vol. 2. Invertebrates and Origin of Vertebrates. New York: Academic.

3
A Comparative Overview
of the Vertebrates

Origins of the Vertebrates

In contrast to the invertebrate forms of body construction, a variety of animals share the common feature of a backbone to which an internal skeleton (endoskeleton) is attached. The backbone is composed of many small bones called vertebrae, and all animals with this construction are therefore called vertebrates. The vertebrae provide anchors for the endoskeleton, and both provide anchors for the muscles as well as a partial casing for the internal organs.

The first traces of vertebrates in the fossil record date from the Ordovician age, some tens of millions of years after the earliest invertebrate fossils (see Fig. 3.1). For this reason, and in view of certain similarities with the higher invertebrates (such as a longitudinal axis, bilateral symmetry, and segmentation of the body, as well as specializations of the nervous system for sensory reception and complex motor behavior) that we have noted in the previous chapter, it might seem that there was a direct line of evolution from the higher invertebrates (the arthropods) to the vertebrates. The origins of the vertebrates are, however, much more complex.

Clues to these origins have been found among another invertebrate phylum, the echinoderms. Although our bodies seem to have little in common with those of adult starfish or other species of this phylum, the embryonic stages are more revealing. As illustrated in Fig. 3.2, there are several aspects of embryogenesis in which the starfish is similar to the vertebrates but differs from the higher invertebrates. These include radial indeterminate cleavage of the fertilized egg, origin of the coelom from mesodermal outpouchings, and the fate of the blastopore. The fate of the blastopore, in fact, is the basis for dividing all higher metazoans into protostomes (blastopore becomes the mouth) and deuterostomes (blastopore becomes the anus). This constitutes a great fork in the road of evolution, as is shown schematically in Fig. 3.1. A further clue to vertebrate origins lies in the fact that the ciliated echinoderm larva is virtually indistinguishable from that of certain species in another phylum, the hemichordates. These species have, among their attributes, pharyngeal gill slits that closely resemble those of vertebrates.

The key step in the evolution of the vertebrates was the development of a *notochord*. This is a flexible, rodlike structure,

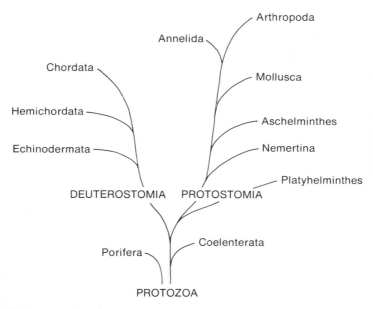

Fig. 3.1. Simplified view of evolutionary relations between invertebrates and vertebrates. (After Keeton, 1980)

neither cartilage nor bone, made up of vacuolated cells. It runs longitudinally through the dorsal part of the body, and is the evolutionary precursor of the vertebral column. It first appears in the larvae of the tunicates (sea-squirts), in which it is associated with a *dorsal hollow nerve cord,* and *pharyngeal gill slits.* These three fundamental specializations are illustrated in Fig. 3.2. The notochord is so important that it provides the basis for the classification of the Phylum Chordata, in which the vertebrates are only a subphylum (see Table 3.1).

The adult tunicate is a rather lowly, sessile creature, in which the pharyngeal gill slits are enlarged for filter-feeding, and the notochord and nervous system are vestigial—not a very exciting candidate for an ancestor! It is believed, instead, that vertebrates evolved from a form resembling the present-day tunicate larva, which not only has the three key specializations mentioned above, but which moves about and hunts for food in an active manner, like most vertebrates. A species which is

partially representative of this form is the lancelet (amphioxus), which, as an adult, exhibits the three specializations, though its lifestyle is pretty much reduced to filter-feeding with its tail buried in shallow water bottoms. Related to the lancelets are the lampreys and hagfish, which lack jaws (hence the designation Agnatha); their filter-feeding larval forms are very similar to those of amphioxus.

With the lampreys and hagfishes we have reached the most primitive representatives of the vertebrates. The different classes of the vertebrates are listed in Table 3.1, and the evolutionary sequence is represented in Fig. 3.3.

It should be stressed that in tracing the course of evolution, we never infer that one living species has evolved from another; as a general rule, lineages trace back to hypothetical common ancestors. It should also be evident that a good deal of speculation is involved, drawing on the evidence provided by careful analysis of features of anatomy, physiology, behavior, ecology, the fossil record, and embryol-

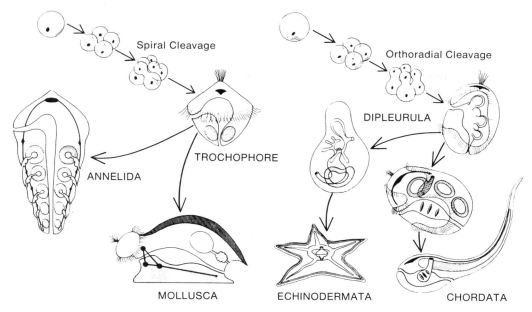

Fig. 3.2. Embryological relations between invertebrates and vertebrates. (From Wells, 1968)

Table 3.1 Major animal groups within the phylum Chordata

Classification	Examples
Subphylum Urochordata	sea squirts (tunicates)
Subphylum Cephalochordata	lancelots (amphioxus)
Subphylum Vertebrata	
Class Agnatha	[mostly extinct] lampreys, hagfish
Class Placodermi	[extinct]
Class Chondrichthyes	cartilaginous fish (sharks, etc.)
Class Osteichthyes	bony fish
Class Amphibia	[many extinct] frogs, salamanders
Class Reptilia	[many extinct] turtles, alligators, lizards, snakes
Class Aves	birds
Class Mammalia	
Order Marsupialia	opossums, kangaroos
Order Insectivora	moles, shrews
Order Chiroptera	bats
Order Edentata	sloths
Order Lagomorpha	rabbits
Order Rodentia	rats, squirrels
Order Cetacea	whales, dolphins
Order Carnivora	dogs, cats, seals
Order Proboscidea	elephants
Order Perissodactyla	horses
Order Artiodactyla	cattle, pigs, sheep
Order Primates	monkeys, apes, humans

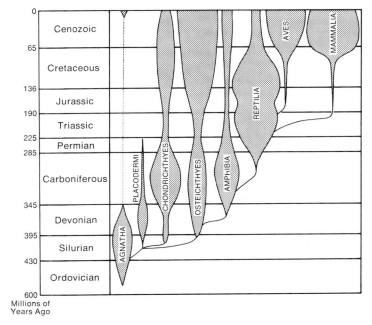

Fig. 3.3. Evolutionary relations of the vertebrate classes. (Adapted from Keeton, 1980)

ogy. Recently, biochemists have added a further source of information, by their powerful tools for analyzing and comparing the structures of complex proteins and enzymes in different organisms. The same or very similar amino acid sequence in a macromolecule implies a close evolutionary relation; differences in the sequences, due to mutations, imply increasing evolutionary distances between two species. A comparison of the molecular structures of the polypeptide neurohormones, oxytocin and vasopressin, that are synthesized in the hypothalamus and secreted from the neural lobe of the pituitary gland (see below), is illustrated in Fig. 3.4. These results have implied a "molecular clock" of ongoing mutations in the DNA of the cell; some of the mutations may be adaptively neutral, and contribute simply to a slow process of "genetic drift", a background for the processes of selective adaptation with respect to particularly favorable or unfavorable mutations. Studies such as these indicate that there is much more to be learned about the nature of evolution-

ary changes at the molecular level. This should provide new insights into the special contribution of the nervous system to the adaptive changes underlying evolution.

With regard to the classification of the vertebrates, we are all familiar with the major types and species. Table 3.1 summarizes them, and reminds us of the tremendous diversity they exhibit. In size, the vertebrates range from larval forms (such as tadpoles) of a few millimeters in length up to the behemoths of land (elephants) and sea (whales). Vertebrates inhabit most of the available ecospace of the earth, and feed on nearly all forms of plant and animal life (including each other!). They reproduce in a variety of ways. Some are cold-blooded, others are warm-blooded. Some live very local lives, within the scope of a few yards of space; others, like eels or birds, migrate to specific locations thousands of miles away. Their life spans range from a few months to a century or more. And one species, *Homo sapiens*, has not only the ability to organize itself socially, but also to exert control over its environment, and pass on those means of social organization and environmental control in the form of culture to succeeding generations.

This diversity is all the more impressive when one takes into account that all these species have the same body plan, the plan that is already established in the cephalochordates. This plan, as already explained, is built around three specializations. All vertebrates have, during embryological development, a *notochord,* which is replaced in the adult by a vertebral column. They all have a dorsal hollow *nerve cord;* as a rule this is enclosed within the vertebral column and, at the head end, is greatly expanded and elaborated into a brain. They all have, during

development, pharyngeal *gill slits;* these are retained in adult aquatic forms but not in adult land forms.

Some essential features of the vertebrate body plan are illustrated in Fig. 3.5. The primitive chordate body, exemplified by the tunicate larvae (A), can be seen to be composed of two main parts, somatic and visceral. The *somatic* part consists of the muscles for swimming; the *visceral* part comprises the pharynx and gut. In a lower vertebrate such as a fish (B) the somatic part has been elaborated for locomotion and, with it, the nervous system has increased in complexity, particularly at the head end. The visceral organs have likewise grown more complex. As Alfred Romer, a great scholar of vertebrate evolution, has observed, the two parts be-

Fig. 3.4. Evolutionary relations at the molecular level. Phylogenetic differences in amino acid composition of neurohypophysial hormones. (After Acher, 1980)

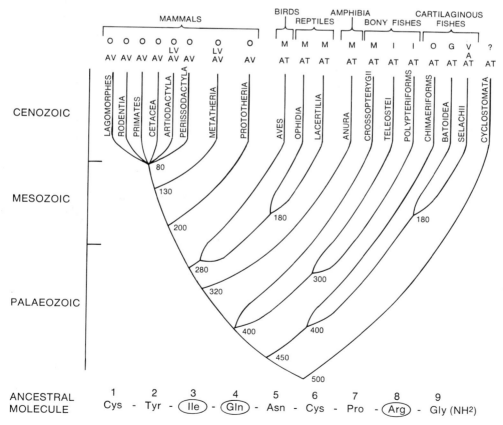

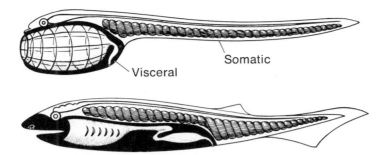

Fig. 3.5. Organization of the vertebrate body. *Above,* Hypothetical primitive chordate. *Below,* Representative lower vertebrate, such as the fish. Note the divisions into somatic and visceral (shaded) body parts. (After Romer and Parsons, 1977)

come more overlapping and coordinated as evolution progresses, but the "weld" between them is an imperfect one, and "in many ways, one can regard a vertebrate as two distinct animals, visceral and somatic". It is interesting to recall that we made a similar observation about the muscular and visceral body parts of the mollusc. The distinction between these parts of the vertebrate body carries over into the nervous system, as we shall see.

Plan of the Nervous System

With this orientation to the vertebrate body and its evolutionary origins, we are in a position to consider the nervous sys-

tem. It has many parts, and in order to understand those parts we need to grasp some principles of organization. To begin with, as shown in Fig. 3.6, there is a central and a peripheral nervous system. The *central* nervous system is composed of the cells and fibers that develop out of the dorsal nerve cord. The *peripheral* nervous system is not really a system; it is merely the fibers that connect the central nervous system to the body, together with outlying groups of cells, called ganglia.

The central nervous system has two main parts. One is the spinal cord, which lies within the vertebral column. The other is the brain, which lies within the cranium (the bones of the head). As shown in Fig.

Fig. 3.6. Basic plan of the vertebrate nervous system.

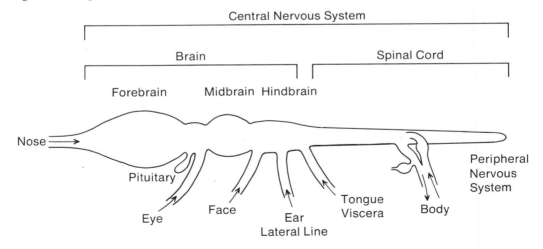

3.6, the brain has three main parts: forebrain, midbrain, and hindbrain. It may be recalled that when we discussed the insect nervous system we noted that each of the three cerebral ganglia has its main type of sensory input, from the antennae, eye, and gut (see Fig. 2.7). Although the comparison is by no means exact, the three parts of the vertebrate brain also have their characteristic types of sensory input. As shown in Fig. 3.6, the *forebrain* receives olfactory input, the *midbrain* receives optic input, and the *hindbrain* receives several inputs, from the ear and the organs of balance, and the viscera. The somatic input to the spinal cord makes its way anteriorly to all three parts of the brain.

Another way of thinking about the plan of the vertebrate nervous system is in terms of the division of the body into somatic and visceral parts that was mentioned in the previous chapter. As shown schematically in Fig. 3.7, this is reflected in the nervous system by a division into those parts concerned with somatic functions and those with visceral functions, the latter

being controlled through the *autonomic nervous system*. As already mentioned, the "weld" between these parts is imperfect and overlapping; in fact, the sites of the weld have been elaborated into a third part, an extensive collection of structures that has come to be termed the *"limbic system"*. In addition, a fourth part of the brain can be characterized as the *neuroendocrine* part, which includes not only the centers concerned with control of the pituitary gland, but also the many types of cells throughout the nervous system which, in recent years, have been found to have receptors for peptide substances and hormones.

Yet another view of nervous organization is illustrated in the diagram of Fig. 3.8. At the spinal level, there are sensory input pathways and motor output pathways. Direct connections between the two provide for reflex arcs that mediate immediate responses to the environment; indirect connections, through interneurons in the spinal cord, provide for more complex types of reflexes and coordinated acts,

Fig. 3.7. Schematic representation of the functional divisions within the brain: somatic, limbic, autonomic (visceral), and neuroendocrine.

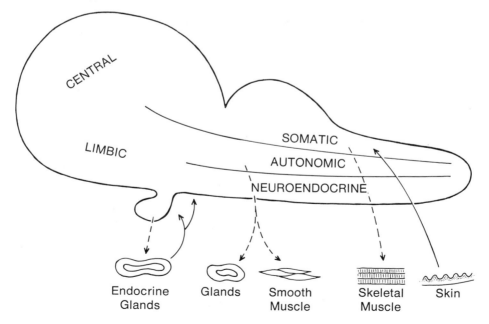

CENTRAL SYSTEMS

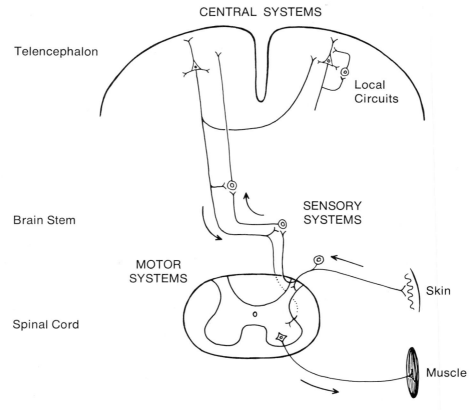

Telencephalon

Local
Circuits

Brain Stem

SENSORY
SYSTEMS

MOTOR
SYSTEMS

Skin

Spinal Cord

Muscle

Fig. 3.8. Some circuits involved in forming sensory, motor, and central systems in the vertebrate brain.

such as those involved in locomotion. This basic type of organization accounts for much of the behavior of invertebrates, as well as that of lower vertebrates and the more automatic acts of higher vertebrates. The brainstem, and even more so the telencephalon, adds internal nervous circuits which greatly amplify the behavior of the animal. As shown in Fig. 3.8, these internal circuits may be involved in further processing of sensory information, in more complex control of motor behavior, or they may constitute central systems, not specifically motor or sensory, which are involved in learning, memory, and the adaptive and cognitive capabilities we regard as "higher mental functions". Although there is increasing overlap of sensory, motor, and central systems as one ascends the neuraxis, these are useful terms

for classifying nervous circuits and nervous functions, and we recognize these divisions in the main sections of this book.

The existence of more than one conceptual framework for studying the vertebrate nervous system should not be a source of confusion. The same would apply in, for example, the study of the organization of a large city; it could be represented in terms of its transportation network, its economic subunits, its political divisions, its neighborhoods, or many other ways. This simply reflects the fact that the nervous system, like the city, is involved in functions that are multiple and overlapping. Each new fact has a place in each of the frameworks that are illustrated in Figs. 3.6–3.8. The better these frameworks are understood, the more each fact will seem not just one more item to be memorized, but a meaningful part of the whole.

Connections between the Nervous System and the Body

Now that the main parts of the nervous system are somewhat familiar, we can study how the parts are connected to the body. For this the student can carry out a dissection of a representative vertebrate animal in the laboratory. Neurobiology is an experimental science, and it is important to get a "feel for the tissue", as the surgeons say. This will also let you see the structures for yourself, and get an idea of how experiments are actually carried out. The dogfish shark is commonly used for dissections, but almost any common species of fish, or a frog, will serve as well. Laboratory study should be supplemented by one of the many textbooks of comparative anatomy that are available. Here, we will note only some of the main structures to look for; further details will be found in later chapters.

Spinal Nerves. Beginning with the spinal cord, we note that there are two main types of nerve: sensory nerves from the body to the spinal cord, which are contained for the most part in the dorsal roots, and motor fibers from the spinal cord to the glands and muscles of the body, which are carried in the ventral roots (see Fig. 3.9). The fibers are referred to as spinal nerves, and there is a pair of roots (dorsal and ventral) for each spinal segment.

Cranial Nerves. Above the spinal cord the nerves all arise within the cranium, and are therefore called cranial nerves. In the brainstem the segments have become fused and elaborated, as part of the process of encephalization, and there are, in addition, nerves for the special sense organs. The same basic pattern of internal organization carries forward from the spinal cord to the brainstem, but it is much modified because of these factors, as illustrated in Fig. 3.10. Altogether, there are ten cranial nerves in lower vertebrates, and two more become incorporated from the spinal

Fig. 3.9. The spinal cord and its relations to the peripheral nerves: motor, sensory, and autonomic.

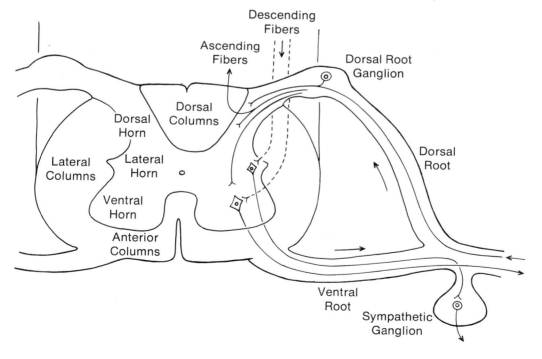

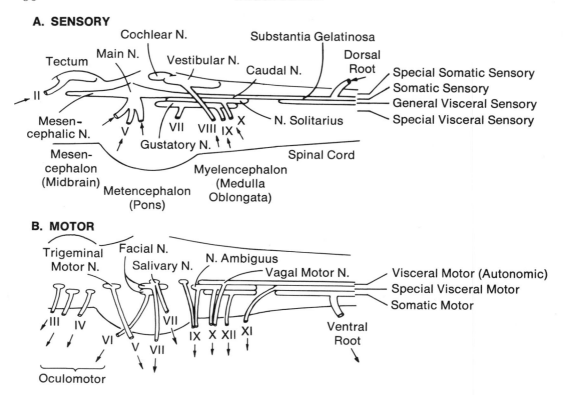

Fig. 3.10. Schematic representation of the nuclei of the cranial nerves. Note the separation into sensory (**A**) and motor (**B**) types, similar to the dorsal and ventral regions of the spinal cord. (Modified from Romer and Parsons, 1977)

cord in higher vertebrates. Figure 3.10 shows in a schematic fashion how most of them are related to the different nuclei in the brainstem, and Table 3.2 gives a summary of how each nerve is classified. Note that the distinction between somatic and visceral nerves is an important one in understanding the organization of the cranial nerves and their nuclei.

Autonomic Nervous System. The motor innervation of the viscera is referred to as the autonomic nervous system. It is characteristic of all vertebrates that there is a relay through a peripheral ganglion. In the most primitive vertebrates the ganglia are all situated in the organs that they innervate. In sharks, some ganglia are found near the vertebral column (Fig. 3.11A). Beginning with bony fish, these vertebral ganglia become interconnected to form a

chain. In the mammal, this part of the autonomic nervous system is clearly differentiated into the *sympathetic* system (Fig. 3.11B). The sympathetic ganglia send fibers diffusely to the viscera, and there is a complementary contribution to the actions of this system through the adrenal medulla. In contrast, the cranial nerves, particularly the vagus nerve, persist in their pattern of innervation throughout the vertebrate series. Together with the sacral innervation of the pelvis, they form the *parasympathetic* system. The sympathetic and parasympathetic systems differ in their neurotransmitter substances, and have complementary or opposing effects in their actions on the glands and visceral muscles, as will be explained in Chap. 19. A differentiated and well-coordinated autonomic nervous system may be a critical element in the development of the moti-

Table 3.2 List of the cranial nerves and their functions

Number	Name	Function
I	Olfactory	sensory input from olfactory receptors
II	Optic	sensory input from retinal ganglion cells
III	Oculomotor	motor output to 4 of 6 extraocular eye muscles
IV	Trochlear	motor output to superior oblique eye muscle
V	Trigeminal	main sensory input from the face
		motor output to the jaw muscles
VI	Abducens	motor output to posterior rectus eye muscle
VII	Facial	main motor output to muscles of the face
		sensory input from some taste buds (chorda tympani nerve)
VIII	Acoustic	sensory input from the inner ear and the vestibular organ
IX	Glossopharyngeal	sensory input from some taste buds and the carotid body
		motor output to muscles of throat, larynx and salivary glands
X	Vagus	main parasympathetic motor output to muscles of heart, lungs, and gut
		motor output to muscles of pharynx
		sensory input from some taste buds
XI	Accessory	motor output to sternocleidomastoid and trapezius muscles
XII	Hypoglossal	motor output to the tongue muscles

Adapted from Romer and Parsons (1977) and Brodal (1981)

vated behavior characteristic of higher vertebrates, as we will discuss in Chap. 29.

Neuroendocrine System. Not all the connections between the nervous system and the body are made by nerve fibers. A part of the nervous system communicates with the body through hormones liberated into the bloodstream. This is the *neuroendocrine* system, as already indicated in Fig. 3.7. The heart of this system, so to speak, is the *pituitary gland.* As shown in Fig. 3.12, part of this gland (the neurohypophysis, or posterior lobe) contains the endings of fibers that come from cells in the hypothalamus; when the cells are stimulated, either by other nerve cells or by circulating substances, they secrete hormones into the bloodstream that control the mammary glands and the kidney. The other main part of the gland (the adenohypophysis, or anterior lobe) contains cells which secrete hormones that control growth, metabolism, and reproductive functions. The secretion of these hormones is under the control of *releasing* or *inhibiting factors;* these factors are liberated by hypothalamic cells and carried to the adenohypophysis by special portal veins of the vascular system.

The ability to bind and respond to circulating hormones was once believed to be limited within the nervous system to these cells of the hypothalamus and pituitary gland. However, as mentioned above, recent work has shown that many cells throughout the nervous system are able to bind peptides and hormones. These cells are concentrated in the limbic parts of the brain, but are also found in the pain pathway and motor regions of the spinal cord. We shall see in later chapters how neuromodulatory and other important behavioral effects may be exerted on such cells by these circulating substances.

The Evolution of the Brain

Despite the modifications that the peripheral nerves and the neurohumoral parts of the nervous system undergo in the course of evolution, they are relatively modest compared with the changes that take place in the connections within the brain. The evolution of more complex behavior in vertebrates is largely due to an increase in

A. SHARK

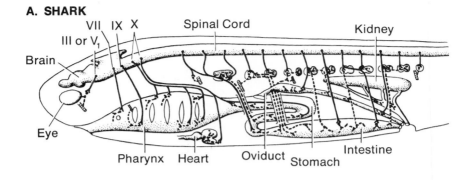

B. MAMMAL

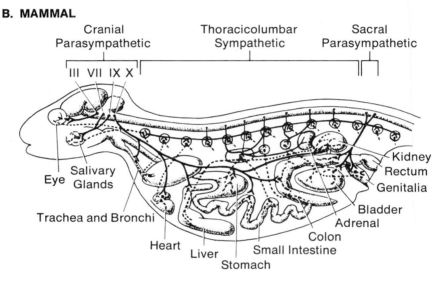

Fig. 3.11. Organization of the autonomic nervous system. **A.** Schematic diagram of the autonomic innervation of a shark. Preganglionic fibers (from motoneurons) shown by continuous lines, postganglionic fibers (from peripheral ganglion cells) shown by dashed lines. **B.** Schematic diagram of the autonomic innervation of a representative mammal. Note the thoracolumbar ganglia connected together in a chain to form the sympathetic system, and the complete overlap in their innervation of the viscera with the fibers and ganglia of the parasympathetic system. (From Romer and Parsons, 1977)

complexity within the brainstem and, most particularly, the telencephalon. Some of these changes are accompanied by complementary changes in the skeleton, muscles, or other tissues and organs (related to the change from water to land forms, or the evolution of an upright posture), but many appear to be largely independent of body structure and seem to reflect the adding of complexity to the brain itself.

We can best appreciate the evolution of

the brains of higher vertebrates by having a thorough understanding of the brains of lower vertebrates. One of the great classical neuroanatomists, C. Judson Herrick, who worked at the University of Chicago during the first half of this century, made a life-long study of the tiger salamander for the reason that

. . . in these small brains we find a simplified arrangement of nerve cells and fibers with a

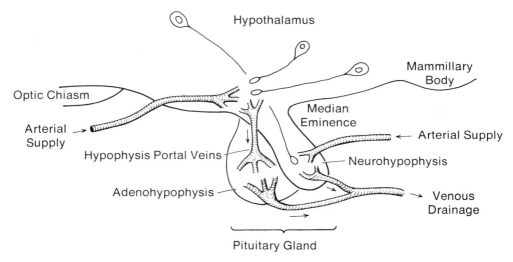

Fig. 3.12. Anatomy of the pituitary, the main neurohemal organ of the vertebrate, showing its two main divisions (the adenohypophysis and the neural hypophysis), its blood supply (note the hypophysial portal system to the adenohypophysis), and its relation to the hypothalamus.

Fig. 3.13. Outline of evolution from simple (A) to complex (B) vertebrate brains. (After Herrick, 1948 and Romer and Parsons, 1977)

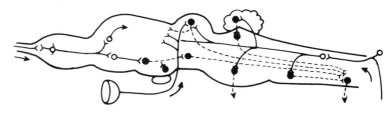

A. LOWER VERTEBRATE BRAIN

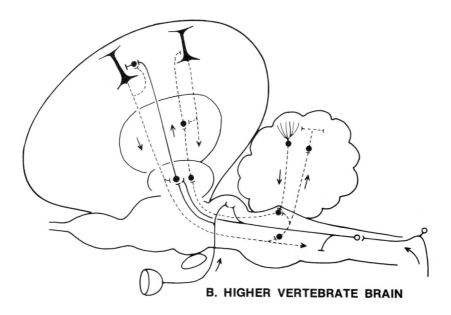

B. HIGHER VERTEBRATE BRAIN

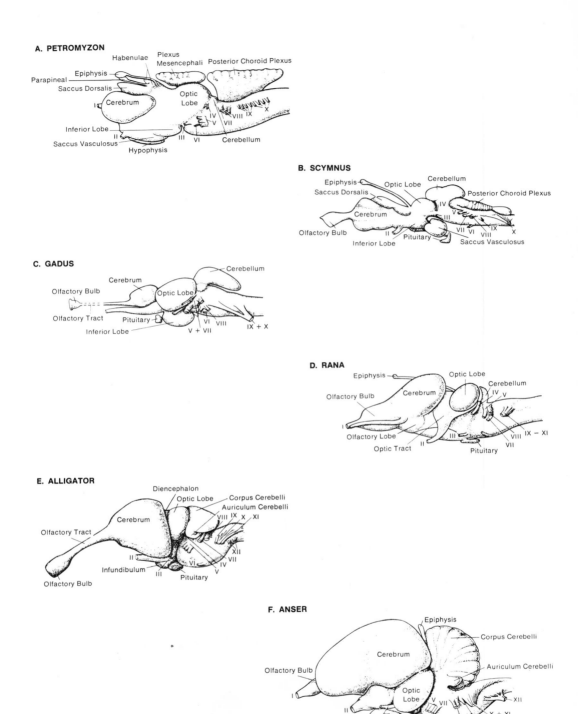

Fig. 3.14. Comparison of representative brains from different classes of vertebrates. **A.** Lamprey. **B.** Shark. **C.** Codfish. **D.** Frog. **E.** Alligator. **F.** Duck. *Opposite page.* **G.** Hedgehog. **H.** Horse. (From Romer and Parsons, 1977)

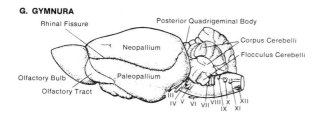

G. GYMNURA

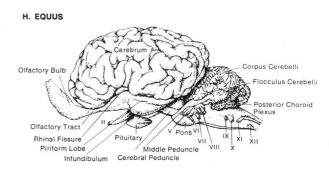

H. EQUUS

pattern of structural organization . . . common to all vertebrates. From this primitive and relatively unspecialized web of tissue it is possible to follow the successive steps in progressive elaboration as the series of animals from salamander to humans is passed in review.

A schematic diagram of a lower vertebrate brain, as exemplified by the tiger salamander, is shown in Fig. 3.13A. The main regions of the brain are evident, as indicated previously in Fig. 3.6. Each region contains various centers, for combining different types of inputs and sending the signals to other centers. The connections are determined by the use of the Golgi stain, combined with other methods for tracing fiber pathways.

Two important points about the ground plan of the vertebrate brain are illustrated by this diagram. First, look at the tectum, the dorsal roof of the midbrain. The tectum receives the input of the optic nerve fibers from the eyes; the cells of the tectum in turn project, through direct or relayed connections, to the spinal cord, to control the muscles. The fibers constitute the tectospinal tract (because they *arise* in the tectum and *end* in the spinal cord), which

is present in one form or another in most vertebrates. Also shown are sensory fibers from the body which enter the spinal cord through the dorsal roots and ascend through one or more relays to reach these same centers in the midbrain. This emphasizes that the midbrain is a key center for integrating sensory inputs and controlling motor outputs.

Next, look at the olfactory bulb to the far left. It receives the input from the sensory receptors in the nose and in turn sends fibers, both directly and through relays, to the entire telencephalon, as far back as the hypothalamus. This emphasizes the point that in vertebrate evolution the telencephalon arises in close association with the olfactory system. In some vertebrates the telencephalon is so much dominated by the olfactory system that it is virtually an olfactory brain.

During evolution, the brain has become modified in the manner illustrated in Fig. 3.13B. Superimposed on the hindbrain is the *cerebellum*, where complex sensorimotor coordination takes place; this divides the hindbrain into a *pons* (the cerebellar part) and a *medulla oblongata*. In

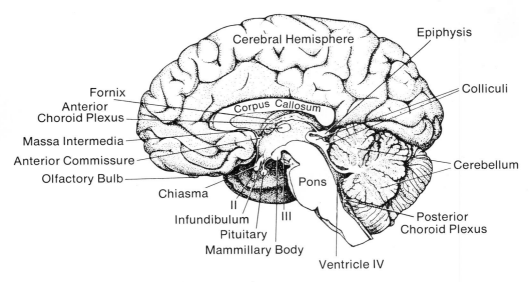

Fig. 3.15. The human brain. (From Romer and Parsons, 1977)

the midbrain, the *tectum* becomes elaborated for processing of the visual input, and also the auditory input. In the forebrain, an enormous development of the outer covering (the pallium, also called the *cortex*) occurs, which, together with associated internal structures termed the *basal ganglia,* forms the *cerebrum.* In birds and mammals, most of this development of the cerebrum is in relation to the visual, auditory, and somatosensory inputs, as well as to complex motor and central processing mechanisms. The *diencephalon* is differentiated to perform two important functions: the relaying of information between the cerebrum and the rest of the brain, and the control of the *pituitary gland,* which in turn controls the endocrine system of the body.

Figure 3.13 shows that despite the modification of each part of the central nervous system during evolution, the primitive chain of structures remains recognizable. The elaboration of the higher parts of the brain for increasing complexity of information processing and behavioral control is an expression of *encephalization,* a principle that applies to the invertebrates, as already noted, and is carried to its most dramatic extent in the vertebrates.

The classical neuroanatomists—Herrick and his contemporaries—believed that brain evolution involved a gradual increase in complexity from lower to higher vertebrates. We now know that the situation is more complicated than this. For example, the cerebellum does not simply grow from a tiny nubbin in lower vertebrates to a large elaborate structure in higher vertebrates. In certain fish the cerebellum undergoes a massive expansion, so much so that it accounts for 90% of the total brain mass in these species (see Chap. 22). Similarly, the classical idea was that the forebrain of lower vertebrates is dominated by the olfactory input, and that in higher vertebrates the other sensory inputs invade the forebrain and come to dominate it. However, recent comparative studies have shown that in lower vertebrates the olfactory input to the forebrain is more circumscribed, and other sensory inputs are also present. Conversely, the olfactory sense does not simply wither away in higher vertebrates, as so many textbooks imply. In fact, in most mammals, olfaction is the dominant sense in the organization of feeding, mating, and social behaviors, as anyone who has a dog for a pet can testify, and as we will discuss in Chaps. 27 and 28.

These facts warn us that we must be cautious in making any generalizations about the specifics of brain evolution. Nonetheless, it is true that there tends to be an overall increase in the size and complexity of the brain as one ascends the vertebrate scale. Figure 3.14 provides examples of the brains of representative species in each of the classes of vertebrates. Note how the main parts of the brainstem and the cranial nerves remain identifiable throughout the series. It is the cerebrum, together with the cerebellum, that change most dramatically. The overgrowth of these structures is expressed in the convolutions that appear in them to further increase their surface areas. This process reaches its greatest extent in humans (Fig. 3.15). The subject of the nature and evolution of the cerebrum is a fascinating one, and we will discuss it in detail in Chap. 31.

REFERENCES

Acher, R. 1980. Molecular evolution of biologically active polypeptides. *Proc. Roy. Soc. B 210:* 21–43.

Dobzhansky et al. 1977. [Chap. 2].

Herrick, C. J. 1948. *The Brain of the Tiger Salamander.* Chicago: Univ. of Chicago.

Keeton, W. T. 1980. [Chap. 2].

Romer, A. S. and T. S. Parsons. 1977. *The Vertebrate Body.* Philadelphia: Saunders.

Sarnat, H. B. and M. G. Netsky. 1981. *Evolution of the Nervous System.* New York: Oxford University Press.

Wells, M. 1968. [Chap. 2.].

Additional Reading

Carpenter, M. B. 1976. *Human Neuroanatomy.* Baltimore: Williams & Wilkins.

Walker, W. F. 1970. *Vertebrate Dissection.* Philadelphia: Saunders.

II
Cellular Mechanisms

4

The Neuron

Despite the diversity that characterizes the many different kinds of nervous systems, the building blocks in each case are nerve cells. That is why in Chap. 1 we emphasized the importance of the cell theory for neurobiology; when we study any nervous system we begin with the fact that it is constructed of nerve cells. Any given system is made up of many different types of nerve cell, but each neuron is a fundamental living unit that sustains all the basic functions that are found in other cells of the body. We therefore, want to have a thorough understanding of what those functions are.

Because most cells are so small, they cannot be seen without the aid of a microscope. There are two basic kinds. In the *light microscope,* rays of light pass through a thin, transparent slice (section) of tissue and are bent by glass lenses to give a magnified image. This is an instrument familiar to every student of biology. It can magnify an image up to about 1000 times. For greater resolution, the *electron microscope* (EM) is used. In this instrument a beam of electrons passes through a specimen and is then bent by electromagnetic lenses to give a magnified image. Magnifications of over 100,000 times can be achieved in this way.

The study of nerve cells with the light microscope began, as we have mentioned, in the 1830's. It flourished over the course of the nineteenth century as better lens systems were made, and better methods for fixing, cutting, and staining thin sections of tissue, were discovered. One line of research led to the Golgi impregnation technique and the visualization of the complicated geometry of entire single neurons, as described in Chap. 1. Another line led to the analysis of the internal structure of the cell body. By the end of the nineteenth century, the main organelles and elements within the cell had been identified. However, the sizes of these structures are near the limits of resolution of the light microscope, and they could only be seen clearly after the electron microscope was perfected in the 1950's.

Today the modern study of cellular structure and function is called *cell biology.* It is based on the use of the electron microscope to reveal the fine structural elements of the cell, and, in combination with special methods of biochemistry and molecular biology, give evidence of their functions. The general theme that has emerged is that the fine structural elements reflect a beautifully orchestrated division of labor within the cell, enabling it to carry out the different functions necessary to sustain its life through specialized interactions with neighboring cells.

The majority of the studies of cellular fine structure have been done in organs other than the brain, such as the liver or pancreas, but most of the results appear to be applicable to nerve cells. A diagram illustrating the main constituents of an animal cell is provided in Fig. 4.1. For comparison, the fine structure of the neuron is summarized in the diagram of Fig. 4.2. We will briefly review the main elements and their functions, with emphasis on those aspects that are special for nerve cells.

Fig. 4.1. Diagram of the fine structure and organelles of a generalized animal cell. Abbreviations: n, *nucleus;* nu, *nuceolus;* ne, *nuclear envelope;* rer, *rough endoplasmic reticulum;* ser, *smooth endoplasmic reticulum;* tre, *transitional element;* gv, *Golgi vesicles;* gs, *Golgi stacked cisternae;* gva, *Golgi vacuoles;* ly, *lysosome;* fp, *free polysome;* ap, *attached polysomes;* ct, *centriole;* mt, *microtubules;* mf, *microfilaments (in bundles);* pl, *plasmalemma;* pv, *plasmalemmal vesicle;* cp, *coated pit;* cv, *coated vesicle;* rf, *ruffle (lamellar pseudopodium);* mv, *microvilli;* cl, *cilium;* bb, *basal body;* m, *mitochondrion;* p, *peroxisome;* ld, *lipid droplet;* gly, *glycogen.* (From Palade and Farquhar, 1981)

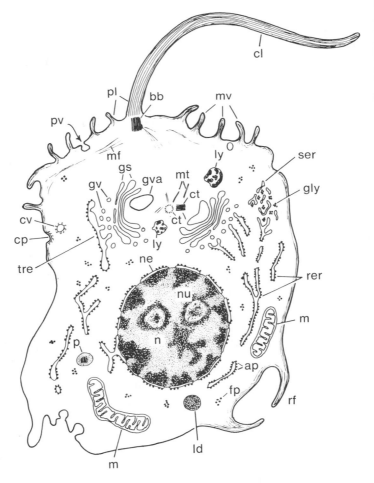

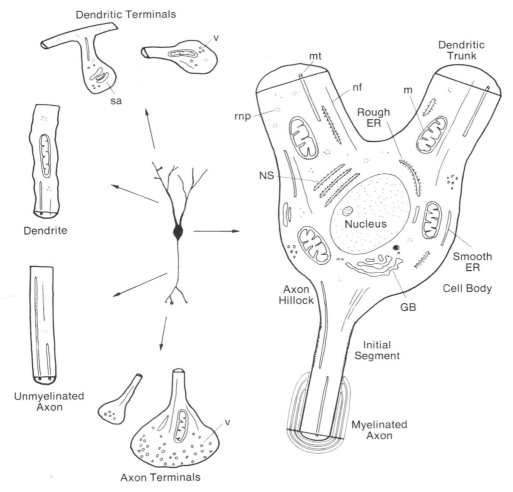

Fig. 4.2. Diagrams of the parts of the neuron. A neuron (as stained by the Golgi method or by intracellular injection of dyes), shown at center, is surrounded by schematic drawings of fine structure (as viewed in the electron microscope) of the different parts. ER, endoplasmic reticulum; GB, Golgi body; NS, Nissl substance; mt, microtubule; nf, neurofilament, rnp, ribonucleic particles; sa, spine apparatus; v, vesicles; m, mitochondria. (From Shepherd, 1979)

The Plasma Membrane

The nerve cell, like all other cells of the body, is bounded by a plasma membrane. In cross sections of electron micrographs at low magnification the membrane appears as a single dark line, about 8 nm thick (just less than one one-hundredth of a micron). At higher magnification it can be seen that there are, in fact, two dark lines with a light space between them. This gives the membrane a three-layered structure, with inner and outer leaflets.

The three-layered structure was originally termed the *unit membrane,* and was thought to consist of oriented lipid and protein complexes. The present conception is that the bilayer is due to oppositely oriented lipids that form a matrix within which proteins may be completely contained, or may be partially embedded,

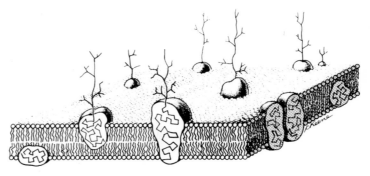

Fig. 4.3. The fluid mosaic model of the plasma membrane, showing polysaccharide chains of glycoproteins protruding into the extracellular space. (From Fawcett, 1981)

sticking out on one side or the other. Both lipid and protein components are in fact in a fluid state, as illustrated by the *fluid mosaic membrane model* in Fig. 4.3. Lateral movements of lipid and protein components are in fact relatively rapid. However, they are constrained by attachments to the immediately underlying cytoplasm; this provides the basis for *regional specializations* of the membrane, which are important in nerve cells, as seen in the differing structures of axons, dendrites, and synapses.

Many of the membrane proteins are glycoproteins, with polysaccharide chains that protrude from the external surface as shown in Fig. 4.3. Together with other carbohydrate molecules they form a thin layer covering the cell surface, called a glycocalyx. Nerve cells are characteristically tightly packed together, with only a space, or cleft, of 20 nm separating them. The glycocalyx fills this extracellular space, and in this position has several important roles to play. The glycoproteins are believed to function as "cell recognition molecules", which help to guide migrating neurons to their targets. They may also serve as "cell adhesion molecules", which help to bind neurons together. The composition of the glycocalyx may be important in regulating the diffusion of molecules in the extracellular space. It has also been speculated that the membrane glycoproteins may be sensitive to weak elec-

tric currents that flow around active neurons (see Chap. 25).

In all cells of the body the plasma membrane controls the interchange of substances between the cell and its environment. In nerve cells it is especially important for several reasons. First, the membrane controls movements of substances that directly affect nerve signaling. Second, the membrane is the site of the *electrical activity* that is the basis of rapid nerve signaling. Third, it is the site of action of peptides and hormones. Finally, it provides the sites for *synapses*, where signals are transferred from one cell to another. Thus, much of the study of neurobiology is actually concerned with the organization and properties of the neuronal plasma membrane, and we will learn much more about those properties in the following chapters.

The Nucleus

Each nerve cell contains a *nucleus*. As in other eukaryotic cells, the nucleus contains the genetic material of the cell in the form of *chromosomes*. The chromosomes are composed of *deoxyribonucleic acid (DNA)* and proteins, which together form the *genes* which are the basic units of heredity. Through the genes the nucleus has two essential functions. First, it controls the *differentiation* of the cell into its final form. The forms of nerve cells are especially complicated, and obviously crucial for the kinds of connections and interactions typical of nerve cells. This role of the nucleus is further considered below and in Chap. 10. The second essential function is the control of *protein synthesis* throughout the cell. This can be seen to be part of its role in controlling cell growth and differentiation, but it also continues after the cell has reached its mature form. For these reasons, the nucleus is regarded as the master control center of the cell.

The nucleus is separated from the cytoplasm by two membranes, one placed against the nucleus and the other against the cytoplasm (see Fig. 4.4). The two membranes meet at intervals to form pores in the nuclear envelope. The ar-

rangement has been likened to bridges over a moat. The pores provide the links for communication and transport of substances between the nucleus and cytoplasm.

In the control of protein synthesis, DNA is acted on by special enzymes to manufacture *ribonucleic acid* (*RNA*), which contains the code for controlling the synthesis of a particular protein or enzyme. This initial process is known as *transcription*, and the RNA produced is known as *messenger RNA*, or *mRNA*. At the same time, the manufacture of ribosomes is proceeding. Ribosomes are macromolecular complexes of RNA (*ribosomal RNA* is termed *rRNA*) and protein, which serve as the actual sites for protein synthe-

Fig. 4.4. Diagram of the relations between the nucleoleus, nucleus, and cytoplasm in a generalized animal cell. Abbreviations: rRNA, ribosomal RNA; mRNA, messenger RNA; tRNA, transfer RNA; s, molecular size in sedimentation units. (From Hopkins, 1978)

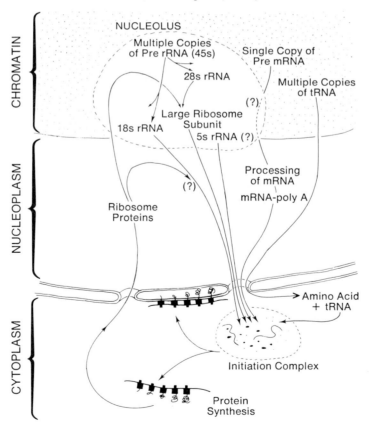

sis. They are assembled in a special part of the nucleus called the *nucleolus*. The mRNA and the ribosomes are transported to the cytoplasm, where protein synthesis takes place by a process known as *translation* (see below). The proteins involved in the assembly operations within the nucleus come from the cytoplasm, so there is a busy two-way traffic through the nuclear pores, as indicated in the diagram of Fig. 4.4. The molecular machinery contained in the nucleus can be affected in several different ways. For example, the nucleus is the prime target of one of the major classes of hormones, the steroid hormones. Estrogen and testosterone bind to cytoplasmic receptors to form a complex which is transported to the nucleus, where it stimulates an increase in mRNA synthesis that leads to synthesis of specific proteins in the cytoplasm. This underlies the actions of these hormones on the reproductive organs and their associated tissues, and also their actions on nerve cells in the hypothalamus and related regions of the limbic brain (Chaps. 25 and 28). Certain chromosomal aberrations lead to deficits or malfunctioning in nerve cells, as in Down's syndrome (mongolism). Finally, the nucleus may be the site of action of environmental toxins; for example, certain mushroom toxins inhibit the nuclear polymerases that produce mRNA. These actions on nuclear mechanisms offer the opportunity to neurobiologists for experimental manipulations that can provide insight into the relations between gene expression, neuronal properties, and behavior.

As in other cells, the position of the nucleus defines the location of the *cell body* (also called soma); the cell body, in other words, is the part of the neuron that contains the nucleus. This might seem pretty obvious, but we will see that the definition is not always easy. The size of the nucleus varies with the size of the cell body. In the largest neurons the cell body may reach 100 μm or more in diameter, and the nucleus may be as large as 20 μm. The smallest nerve cell bodies are around 5 μm in diameter. In these cells the nucleus may almost fill the cell body, leaving only a very thin rim of cytoplasm. The fact that processes may extend for long distances poses a special problem for the nucleus in controlling protein synthesis in all parts of the nerve cell (see below).

Ribosomes and the Rough Endoplasmic Reticulum

When the ribosomes reach the cytoplasm they are sorted into two populations. Some remain "free" within the cytoplasm, either singly or in clusters ("polyribosomes"). In most cells of the body these ribosomes manufacture proteins that remain within the cell. The other population of ribosomes is attached to an extensive internal membrane system called the *endoplasmic reticulum* (ER). As shown in the diagram of Fig. 4.1, the endoplasmic reticulum is continuous with the envelope around the nucleus, and extends throughout the cytoplasm of the cell body as a system of sheets, channels, and membrane-enclosed spaces (large, flat spaces called cysternae, small spaces called vesicles). The part of this system that has attached ribosomes is called the *rough ER*. The membrane-bound ribosomes synthesize proteins that in most cells are destined for export out of the cell.

The functions of the ribosomes are summarized in Fig. 4.5. Synthesis of proteins depends on yet a third type of RNA called *transfer RNA* (*tRNA*). This combines with a given amino acid to "activate" it, so that it is ready to be assembled into place. The assembly is directed by mRNA. The mRNA attaches to the ribosomes and moves across them, bringing its template into position to select (*translate*) the right sequence of activated amino acids to form a given polypeptide. By suitable foldings of the chain, the polypeptide becomes a protein.

The properties of ribosomes described above have been worked out mainly in

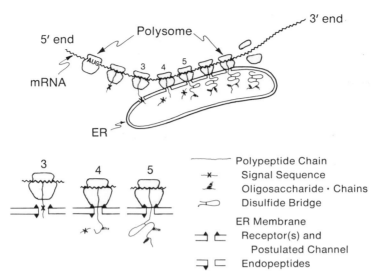

Fig. 4.5. Schematic view of the steps involved in the synthesis of proteins. Above: translation of mRNA into a secretory peptide begins in the cytoplasm. The initial amino acids produced constitute a signal sequence; as this begins to emerge from the ribosome it is recognized by receptors in the endoplasmic reticulum (ER). The ribosome attaches to the membrane (step 3) and the peptide grows into the cisternal space (steps 4 and 5), shedding the signal sequence. Below: Within the cisternal space there is final formation of disulfide bridges and oligosaccharide chains, according to the particular peptide or protein. (From Palade and Farquhar, 1981)

nonnucleated cells (prokaryotes) such as *E. coli* bacteria, and in cells such as those of the pancreas and liver. The general properties appear applicable to nerve cells, but there are also important differences. In nerve cells there is a characteristic accumulation of rough ER near the nucleus that is termed the *Nissl substance*. This is obviously a site of intense protein-synthesizing activity. In large neurons the Nissl substance is large and dense; in small neurons it may consist only of scattered particles. Close examination reveals that many of the ribosomes within the Nissl substance are not attached to the ER membrane, but lie between the membranes as polyribosomes. It has been speculated that these clusters may be involved in synthesizing complex proteins specific for nerve cells, perhaps specific for different types of nerve cells. Some of the protein synthesized in the Nissl substance may be destined for secretion in the form of transmitter substances. However, it has

been speculated that most proteins are probably used for maintenance of the large expanses of branching processes of the neuron.

The ribosomes manufacture the molecular machinery for most of the characteristic functions of cells: enzymes, regulators, carriers, receptors, transducers, contractile and structural elements, and membranes. As in the case of the nucleus, this machinery is susceptible to modification or disruption by various influences. In bacteria, for example, antibiotics exert their effects by interfering at various specific steps in the transcription process. In nerve cells, diphtheria toxin inactivates one of the elongation factors responsible for assembly of polypeptides.

The research on ribosomes and on other cell constituents employs a variety of biochemical methods. One of the most important is based on *cell fractionation*. The main steps in this procedure are outlined in Fig. 4.6. Conceptually it is quite simple:

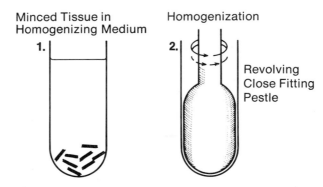

Minced Tissue in
Homogenizing Medium

1.

Homogenization

2.

Revolving
Close Fitting
Pestle

Centrifuge and Decant Supernatant

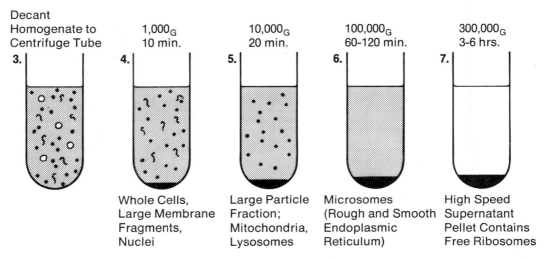

Decant Homogenate to Centrifuge Tube **3.**	1,000$_G$ 10 min. **4.**	10,000$_G$ 20 min. **5.**	100,000$_G$ 60-120 min. **6.**	300,000$_G$ 3-6 hrs. **7.**
	Whole Cells, Large Membrane Fragments, Nuclei	Large Particle Fraction; Mitochondria, Lysosomes	Microsomes (Rough and Smooth Endoplasmic Reticulum)	High Speed Supernatant Pellet Contains Free Ribosomes

Fig. 4.6. Steps involved in the method of cell fractionation by means of differential centrifugation. (From Hopkins, 1978)

cells are ground up and suspended in a medium to make a kind of soup, which is then placed in a test tube and centrifuged at increasing speeds. The different cellular elements come down to form pellets, which are then subjected to biochemical analysis. In nerve cells, in addition to the general cellular constituents, this method yields a subfraction that contains fragments of synaptic terminals called synaptosomes.

Secretion and the Golgi Complex

We have described the rough ER; what about the other part of the endoplasmic reticulum, that lacks attached ribosomes?

This is called the *smooth ER*. It is an extremely versatile structure, which is put in the service of cells in a variety of ways. With regard to other cells of the body we will note only two examples. At one extreme, the smooth ER may form a rigidly defined inner system of sheets and channels, as in the skeletal muscle fiber. In that case it is called the sarcoplasmic reticulum, and appears to have as its primary functions the conduction of the impulse into the interior of fiber, and the regulation of the calcium level there in relation to muscle contraction. This will be discussed further in Chap. 18.

In contrast to the muscle fiber, a secretory cell such as that of the pancreas employs its smooth ER in quite a different manner. As shown in Fig. 4.7, the proteins manufactured by the rough ER are transferred (via shuttle vesicles) to a system of flattened pancakelike sacks, or cysternae, called the *Golgi complex*. The Golgi complex actually has an orientation, there being an internal, *forming* face and an external, *releasing* face. From the latter, vesicles bud off to form secretory granules. The function of the Golgi complex thus is to store, concentrate, and package secretory proteins. The secretory granules remain within the cytoplasm of the cell until the cell is stimulated with the appropriate factors. The granules then move to the apical surface where their membranes fuse with the plasma membrane and discharge their contents. This process is called *exocytosis,* and requires energy and the presence of free calcium ions.

In these examples the role of the smooth ER seems rather clear. In nerve cells, however, the role remains somewhat enigmatic, despite the fact that the Golgi complex was first observed in nerve cells in 1898, by the same man who was responsible for the Golgi neuron stain. In nerve cells, the Golgi complex is represented by smaller accumulations of cysternae that are not clearly polarized and that tend to be dispersed in the cytoplasm and extend out even into the dendrites (but not the axon). In the neighborhood of the Golgi complex are clouds of small vesicles which may well be analogous to the shuttle vesicles in a secretory cell (see Fig. 4.7). However, most neurons do not secrete large granules like those of secretory cells. The relation of the smooth ER and the Golgi complex to the secretion of transmitter and neuromodulatory substances is still being worked out.

Lysosomes

In addition to systems for manufacture and transport of substances, the cell also has an internal digestive system comprised of *lysosomes.* Like the smooth ER, lysosomes are membrane-bound structures.

Fig. 4.7. Organization of the smooth endoplasmic cell in a typical secretory cell. (From Hopkins, 1978)

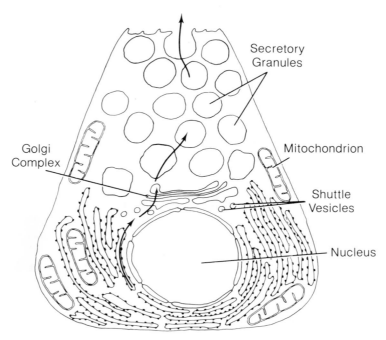

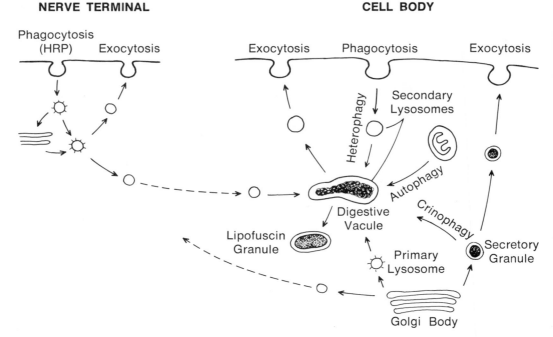

Fig. 4.8. Formation and movements of lysomes. (Adapted from Palade and Farquhar, 1981)

They differ, however, in having no particular shape. They vary in size from small vesicles to large, rounded sacks; and they contain a variety of hydrolytic enzymes that degrade and digest a wide range of substances that originate both inside and outside the cell.

Some of the functions of lysosomes, and the complex interrelations with other cell constituents, are indicated in Fig. 4.8. *Primary lysosomes* are formed from the Golgi complex by the budding off of vesicles which then acquire a dense matrix about them; these are termed *alveolate vesicles.* They contain acid hydrolases specific for different digestive tasks. When these processes begin, the vesicle becomes a *secondary lysosome,* and may assume a variety of forms as a digestive vacuole. The material that is digested may come from within the cell (digestion of these substances is called *autophagy*), or from outside the cell (this is called *heterophagy*). A third type of action occurs in some secretory cells; the number of secretory gran-

ules stored in the cytoplasm may be reduced and regulated by a process of *crinophagy.* The contents of the vacuoles are disposed of by diffusion of the breakdown products into the cytoplasm, or by exocytosis.

This general scheme appears to apply to nerve cells, but with some interesting differences. Because of the long distances between many nerve terminals and their cell body, the terminals must carry out some functions in semiautonomy. Nerve stimulation causes alveolate vesicles to appear in the terminal, and Fig. 4.8 indicates that there seems to be a cycle of pinocytosis and exocytosis within the terminal that shares some common features with the sequence of steps that occurs through the lysosomal system in the cell body. Figure 4.8 also indicates that alveolate vesicles are in communication with a transport system from the terminal to the cell body. This system is believed to provide the structural basis for an important experimental method for tracing nerve connections. An enzyme, *horseradish peroxidase* (HRP), that is injected into a region of terminals will be taken up by the terminals and transported back to the cell bodies. Appropriate staining procedures can visualize the transported HRP, thus establishing the connection between the site of injection and the cell bodies which send fibers to that site (see Fig. 4.9). We will refer to this method often in discussing central nervous system pathways in later chapters.

A distinctive feature of nerve cells is the presence of *lipofucsin granules*. These form during adult life, and gradually increase with age. For this reason they are believed to represent the effects of "wear and tear" on the cell. They also are implicated in certain diseases. As Fig. 4.8 indicates, there is evidence that these granules are derived from lysosomes.

Mitochondria

Most of the cellular functions we have described require energy, and most of this energy comes from *mitochondria*. Apart from the nucleus, this is the most complex organelle within the cell. As indicated in Fig. 4.10, it is cigar-shaped, with a smooth outer membrane and an inner membrane that is thrown into internal folds called cristae. In general, the higher the energy demands in a particular cell, the more tightly packed the cristae. The inner membrane is relatively impermeable, so movement of substances across this membrane requires special transport mechanisms. The outer membrane is freely permeable to ions and water. Recent electron microscopical observations indicate that the outer membrane is continuous with the smooth endoplasmic reticulum.

The mechanisms for production of energy are summarized in Fig. 4.10. One source of energy is *glycolysis,* the chain of reactions that breaks down glucose by *anaerobic metabolism* to yield, for each molecule of glucose, a net of two molecules of *adenosine triphosphate* (ATP) with its high-energy phosphate bonds. All the glycolytic enzymes in the chain are soluble proteins which exist free within the cytoplasm. In contrast, *aerobic metabolism,*

Fig. 4.9. Uptake and transport of the enzyme horseradish peroxidase (HRP) in nerve cells. The HRP was injected into the superior colliculus of the cat; it was taken up by nerve terminals and retrogradely transported to their cell bodies located in layer v (see inset) of area 19 of the visual cortex. Bar indicates 100μm. (From Gilbert and Kelly, 1975)

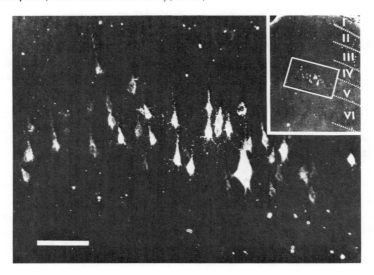

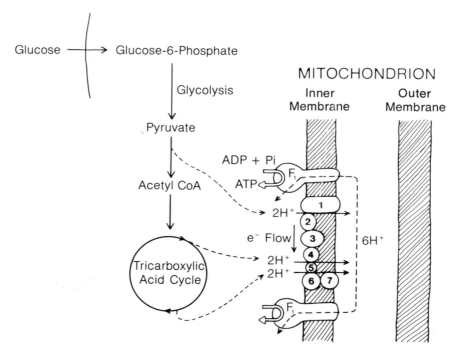

Fig. 4.10. Metabolic pathways for producing energy in the mitochondrion, showing the coupling of oxidative phosphorylation to ion movements across the mitochondrial membrane, according to the chemiosmotic hypothesis. H^+ is produced by oxidation within the tricarboxylic acid cycle. The enzymes of the electron transport chain are components of the inner mitochondrial membrane. The free energy of the electrons is used to transport H^+ outward across the membrane, setting up a H^+ gradient across the impermeable membrane. The potential energy stored in this gradient is used to synthesize ATP. (From Hopkins, 1978)

involving the acetylation of pyruvic acid and the reactions of the *citric acid cycle,* yields a net from each glucose molecule of 36 molecules of ATP, obviously a much more efficient source. All of the citric acid cycle enzymes are contained within the inner matrix of the mitochondria. The enzymes of the associated electron transport chain are components of the inner mitochondrial membrane. It is believed that electron transfer sets up a gradient of H^+ across the inner membrane, and the potential energy in this gradient is used to form ATP from ADP (see Fig. 4.10). The ATP is then available for the various energy-requiring processes of the cell.

In most cells of the body a variety of sugars can be taken up by the cell and metabolized to yield energy, or be stored within the cell as glycogen. However, nerve cells in the vertebrate brain are special, in that they are almost exclusively dependent on glucose. (In invertebrates the corresponding substance for supplying energy is trehalose.) Other substances are excluded by the blood–brain barrier, as described in the next chapter. Most nerve cells also lack the ability to store glycogen, further increasing their dependence for energy on circulating glucose, as well as the oxygen needed for its aerobic metabolism. This is why we lose consciousness if the blood supply to our brains is interrupted for only a few seconds. Among the other functions of mitochondria is the ability to store calcium, which, as we shall see, can be a factor in regulating calcium in nerve terminals.

Mitochondria also contain small ribosomes and even a few strands of DNA. This indicates that the mitochondrion itself has most of the features of a cell, and, indeed, it is believed that mitochondria probably originated from a prokaryotic microbelike ancestor. It is hypothesized that this aerobic microorganism developed a symbiotic relation with the anerobic eukaryotic cell and became incorporated into it, to the mutual benefit of both.

Microtubules and Microfilaments

In addition to the organelles mentioned above, the cytoplasm also contains other formed elements of smaller size and simpler structure. Among these are several types of fibrils; in order of decreasing diameter, they are neurotubules (20–30 nm), neurofilaments (10 nm), and microfilaments (5 nm).

Microtubules, as the name implies, consist of long, unbranched tubes of various lengths with a hollow core (see Fig. 4.11). The walls are composed of subunits of a specific protein with a molecular weight of 120,000, called *tubulin*. Microtubules are employed in various ways. In all cells undergoing mitotic division, the mitotic spindle consists of microtubules. In motile cilia, and in the tails of spermatozoa, they are arranged in a rigid pattern, consisting of a ring of 9 pairs (doublets) around a central pair. This appears to provide an internal skeleton for the cilium, as well as mediating the forces that move it. In contrast, in many cells the microtubules are structural elements which lack any obvious orientation. In nerve cells they are present in the cell body singly or in loose groups that weave their way through the cytoplasm and out into the axon and dendrites. Biochemical studies have shown that guanosine triphosphate appears to provide the energy for assembly of the tubulin subunits. Other studies have shown that certain plant alkaloids, such as *colchicine*, bind with the microtubules to depolymerize them, stopping mitosis in metaphase and also inhibiting the transport of substances in the axon (see below).

Neurofilaments are thinner than microtubules; high-resolution electron microscopy shows that they too appear to be tubular in construction. Biochemical studies of axons have isolated filamentous proteins that are smaller in molecular weight and have different solubilities and amino acid compositions from those of tubulin; these may be the proteins of neurofilaments. Neurofilaments are found only in nerve cells. They are especially prominent in large axons, where they outnumber the microtubules; on the other hand, in small axons and dendrites the proportions are reversed. Neurofilaments, and their relation to microtubules, change during ageing, and extreme changes, such as the development of tangles and placques, appear to be associated with the loss of neuronal function that underlies the progressive senility seen in Alzheimer's disease.

The presence of microtubules and neurofilaments in axons and dendrites has naturally suggested that they might be involved in the transport of substances, and a variety of biochemical studies, including those with colchicine (see above), has supported this notion. Intracellular transport between cell body and outlying processes is vital to the economy of the nerve cell, and we have already noted one example

Fig. 4.11. Different sizes of tubular and filamentous structures in cells.

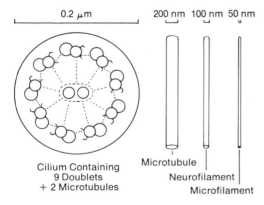

0.2 μm   200 nm 100 nm 50 nm

Cilium Containing
9 Doublets
+ 2 Microtubules

Microtubule
Neurofilament
Microfilament

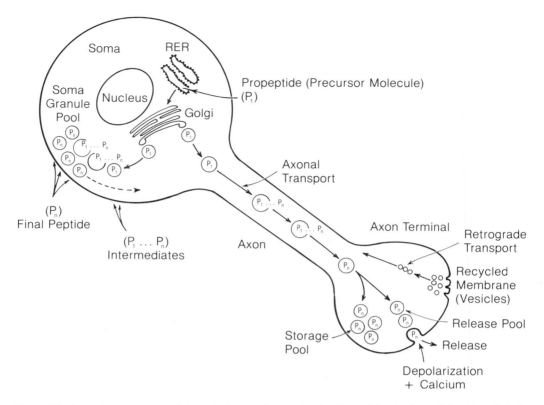

Fig. 4.12. Axonal transport and its relation to the synthesis of peptides in the cell body and their release from terminals. (From Mains et al., in Gainer and Brownstein, 1981)

of this in the transport of substances (including HRP) from nerve terminals to the cell body. This direction is referred to as *retrograde.* Transport from cell body to terminals, on the other hand, is in the *orthograde* direction. This can be demonstrated in several ways, as for example by direct microscopic observation of movements within a large axon such as that of the squid, or by observations of bulging of an axon on the cell body (proximal) side of a site of constriction.

Definitive experiments have shown that, after injection of radioactively labeled amino acids in the vicinity of cell bodies, the amino acids are taken up by the cell bodies and incorporated into protein, which is then transported down the axon to the terminals. These experiments have identified two general types of *axonal transport: slow transport* at a rate of about

one millimeter per day, and *fast* (rapid) *transport* at rates of several hundred millimeter per day. Many of the substances transported are intimately related to functions involved in synaptic transmission, as discussed in Chap. 9. The transport of peptides is illustrated in Fig. 4.12.

Intracellular transport has provided the basis for a valuable method for demonstrating nerve connections in the central nervous system. The location of labeled substances after an injection can be ascertained by making sections of the tissue and exposing them to photographic film, a method known as *autoradiography* (the tissue takes its own photograph, so to speak). An example of this method is shown in Fig. 4.13. In later chapters we will often refer to results obtained in this way.

Equally important is the transport of

substances in dendrites. In 1968 Tony Stretton and Ed Kravitz at Harvard showed that a dye (Procion yellow) injected from a micropipette into the cell body of a neuron is transported into the dendrites and can be visualized by fluorescence microscopy. This was a key discovery for cellular neurobiology, for it en- abled an investigator to see the whole dendritic tree of the cell that was being recorded. It was like having a Golgi stain of the very neuron one wished to study. Since then a host of substances has been used for this purpose, including HRP and most recently lucifer yellow; visualization of radioactively-labelled amino acids in mo-

Fig. 4.13. Intracellular transport of radiolabeled compounds, as demonstrated by autoradiography. **A.** Transport of 3H-proline into visual cortex of monkey. Injection was made into one eye; 3-H-proline was incorporated into protein in retinal ganglion cells, transported to their terminals in the lateral geniculate nucleus, and transferred to cells therein which project to the cortex. The alternating bands demonstrate ocular dominance columns (see Chap. 17). (From Wiesel et al., 1974) **B.** Transport of 3H-fucose into dendrites of a motoneuron after intracellular injection into the cell body, where the amino acid is incorporated into glycoprotein. (From Kreutzberg, et al., 1975)

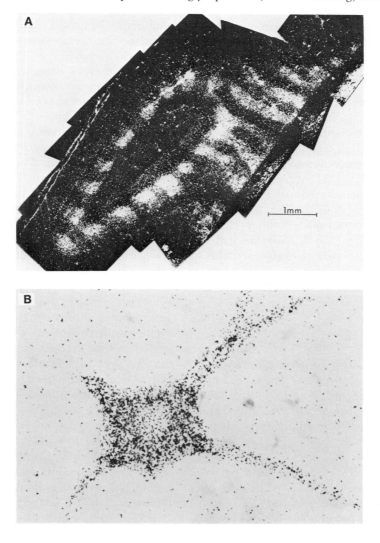

toneuronal dendrites by autoradiography is illustrated in Fig. 4.13B. The ability to correlate physiological properties with the morphology of the cell is the basis of much of our understanding of the integrative functions of neurons.

The third type of fibrillar structure in the cell is the *microfilament*. The best understood of these are in skeletal muscle, where thick filaments (12 nm diameter, composed of myosin) and thin filaments (5 nm diameter, composed of actin) are arranged in a highly geometrical array to provide the mechanism for muscle contraction (Chap. 18). Even in many non-muscular cells, actin surprisingly accounts for up to 10% of the total cell protein, and most or all of this may be in the form of microfilaments. Microfilaments are abundant in growing nerve processes (Chap. 10). They are also abundant in neuroglia, as discussed in the next section, and they are involved in certain kinds of neuronal junctions (next chapter). In many freely moving cells they are present just beneath the plasma membrane, where it is believed they control movement of the membrane and fluidity of the underlying cytoplasm. Evidence for this has been obtained by observing the inhibition of movements of macrophages after treatment with cytochalasin B, a substance obtained from fungi that disrupts microfilaments. Similar experiments are aimed at understanding the role of microfilaments in nerve cell functions.

Neuroglia and Nerve Sheaths

The nervous system contains other types of cells besides nerve cells. These are important, because they help to control the environment of the nerve cells, and they play an essential role in many of their functions.

Neuroglia. At any given site on a nerve cell there may be two kinds of neighbors facing it across the extracellular cleft. One is the process of another nerve cell or fi-ber. The other is a nonnervous cell. These are termed *neuroglia,* or simply *glia.* Their name comes from the famous German neuropathologist, Rudolf Virchow, who, in 1856, observed that there was an amorphous kind of substance that appeared to surround nerve cells, and he bestowed on it a name—neuroglia—meaning "nerve glue". A number of studies with the light microscope in the early part of this century suggested that the neuroglia are composed of specific kinds of cells (see Fig. 4.14). Studies with the electron microscope have proven this, and fully characterized the different types.

Neuroglial cells are very numerous; in some parts of the nervous system they outnumber the nerve cells by 10 to 1. They have been most closely studied and classified in the vertebrate nervous system. One of the main types is the *astrocyte.* These have many processes which radiate out in all directions from the cell body, giving the cell a star-shaped appearance. Within the central nervous system some of the processes terminate as end-feet on the surfaces of blood vessels. Astrocytes located in the white matter of the brain are called *fibrous* astrocytes, by virtue of the large numbers of fibrils present in the cytoplasm of their cell bodies and branches. Those located in the gray matter have fewer fibrils, and are called *protoplasmic* astrocytes. In the electron microscope, astrocytes are seen to have a somewhat dark cytoplasmic matrix and large numbers of neurofilaments (these are the fibrils seen in the light microscope) as well as glycogen granules in the cytoplasm, all characteristics that are different from those of nerve cells. Astrocytes also have certain kinds of junctional connections with each other, and with nerve cells.

The functions of astrocytes are believed to include: (1) providing structural support for nerve cells; (2) proliferation and repair following injury to nerves; (3) isolation and grouping of nerve fibers and terminals; and (4) participating in metabolic pathways which modulate the ions,

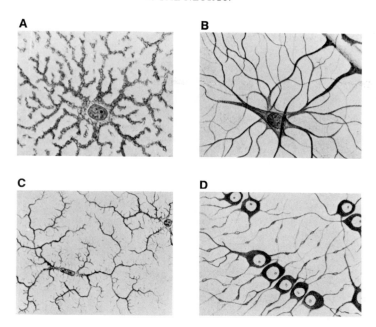

Fig. 4.14. Different types of neuroglia. **A.** Protoplasmic astrocytes. **B.** Fibrous astrocytes. **C.** Microglia. **D.** Oligodendrocytes. (After del Rio-Hortega, in Bloom and Fawcett, 1975)

transmitters, and metabolites involved in functions of nerve cells and their synapses. Earlier speculations, that they form part of the blood–brain barrier, or that they are involved in the transport of nutrients from the blood vessels to the nerve cells, seem now to be largely discounted. In the vertebrate central nervous system, a special kind of cell, called radial glia, appear only during embryonic life, and provide guidelines for migrating neurons to follow (Chaps. 10 and 31).

Some glial cells have distinctly fewer and thinner branches than astrocytes, and these are termed *oligodendrocytes* (oligo-few, dendro-branches). In the electron microscope, they are seen to contain few neurofilaments and glycogen granules, but numerous microtubules. The branches are often hard to distinguish from those of nerve cells, but can be differentiated because they never take part in synaptic connections. The functions of oligodendrocytes are not yet fully established; there is good evidence that they are responsible for the formation of the myelin around axons

in the central nervous system (see below), and it has also been proposed that they have a symbiotic relation with certain nerve cells, involving complex metabolic exchanges.

A third main type of glial cell is termed *microglia*. These are small cells scattered throughout the nervous system. Wherever there is injury or degeneration, these cells proliferate, move to the site, and transform into large macrophages that remove and phagocytize the debris. They thus appear to be the nervous system representatives of the macrophages of the reticuloendothelial system, which defend against inflammation and infection in the body.

Nerve Sheaths. A very important function of neuroglia is to provide special sheaths around the long axons that interconnect different parts of the nervous system. These sheaths not only protect the axons, but are also intimately involved in structural modifications of the axons needed to conduct signals over long distances.

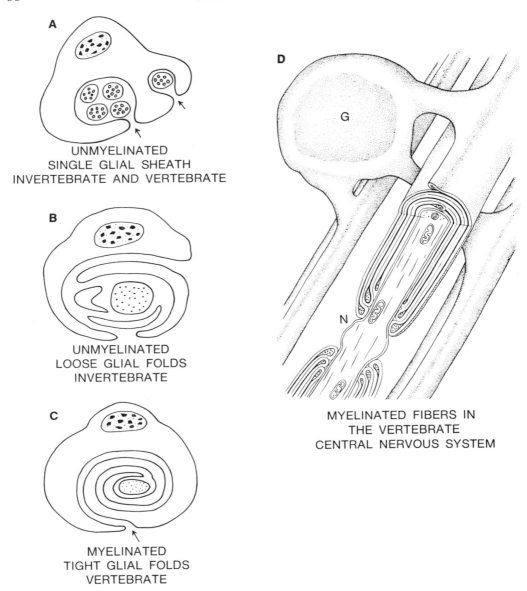

A

UNMYELINATED
SINGLE GLIAL SHEATH
INVERTEBRATE AND VERTEBRATE

B

UNMYELINATED
LOOSE GLIAL FOLDS
INVERTEBRATE

C

MYELINATED
TIGHT GLIAL FOLDS
VERTEBRATE

D

MYELINATED FIBERS IN
THE VERTEBRATE
CENTRAL NERVOUS SYSTEM

Fig. 4.15. Nerve sheaths. **A.** Single glial cell surrounding thin nerve fibers. **B.** Loose glial wrappings. **C.** Tight glial wrapping, forming myelin. **D.** Relation of glial (G) cell to myelin folds around nerve fiber and node (N) of Ranvier. (From Bunge, 1968)

The simplest arrangement is one in which a single axon, or group of axons, is embedded in a glial cell, as shown in Fig. 4.15A. This is the common situation for very small-diameter fibers, in both invertebrates and vertebrates. The cells that provide these sheaths in peripheral nerves are modified glial cells, called *Schwann*

cells. The point at which the Schwann cell membranes come together to enclose the axon or axons is called the *mesaxon* (it is analogous to the mesentery that encloses the intestines in the abdomen). The axons ensheathed in this manner are termed *unmyelinated,* for reasons that will become apparent below.

A somewhat more complicated arrangement is found where there are several loose folds of Schwann cell membrane around a given axon. This is characteristic of many larger invertebrate axons (see Fig. 4.15B).

The most complicated arrangement is one in which there are a number of layers of Schwann cell membranes tightly packed around a single axon. The layers are formed by the wrapping around of the Schwann cell membrane in a spiral manner during development, as indicated in Fig. 4.15C. By virtue of their tight packing and modified composition, these layers form a special tissue called *myelin*. This is such an important structure that all nerve fibers can be generally classified as either *unmyelinated* (see above), or *myelinated*.

Myelinated tissue has a fatty consistency and, to the naked eye, a white appearance (as in the white matter of the brain). The fibers are revealed in the light microscope as *black* structures when treated with the common lipid stains. Biochemical studies have been carried out on myelin isolated by various cell fractionation procedures (see Fig. 4.6). These have shown that myelin is about 80% lipid and 20% protein; cholesterol is one of the major lipids, with various other substances such as cerebrosides and phospholipids present in variable amounts in different tissues and species. X-ray diffraction data show that myelin consists of repeating units with a period of about 18 nm. In the electron microscope, myelin is clearly recognized as repeating light and dark layers with a period of about 18 nm, which, after allowing for shrinkage during preparation of the tissue, corresponds to two thicknesses of compressed plasma membrane.

A single Schwann cell in peripheral nerve supplies myelin for a length of about 1 mm of axon. At the borders of this region the myelin layers overlap progressively in the manner shown in Fig. 4.15D. There is a gap of 1–2 μm between neighboring myelinated regions that is known as the *node of Ranvier*. Here the plasma membrane of the axon is unsheathed and exposed to the surrounding connective tissue of the whole nerve trunk. A myelinated fiber thus consists of *nodes* of naked (unsheathed) nerve membrane alternating with *internodes* of myelinated membrane. The manner in which this imparts special properties for efficient conduction of nerve impulses is explained in Chap. 7.

We may close this account by noting that myelin is found almost exclusively in vertebrates. It would be possible to think of myelin, therefore, as an essential element in the higher nervous functions of which vertebrates are capable. The main contribution of myelin is probably that it permits efficient signal conduction over long distances. This allows precise integration of information from widely separated regions, which may be presumed to be necessary for the evolution of higher nervous functions. The nature of those functions depends, in addition, on the synaptic interactions that take place within the regions themselves.

Neuron Terminology

Neurons are so various in form that students may find the terminology applied to different parts of a neuron and to different types of neuron somewhat confusing. To begin with the parts of a neuron, the cell body is that region of the cell around the nucleus. In nerve cells, as in other cells, the main organelles of the cytoplasm are gathered here in order to interact with the nucleus and with each other. These include the Golgi body and (in nerve cells) the Nissl substance, in addition to large numbers of mitochondria, rough and smooth ER, polysomes, and fibrillar structures.

What then about the branches? One of the cardinal features of neurons is that their branches have widely different patterns. Neurons resemble trees in this respect, and, in both cases, the particular branching pattern allows us to identify different types. However, the branching patterns are so diverse that it is sometimes difficult to make the distinction between what is an axon and what is a dendrite. Let us see if we can take some logical steps toward making these distinctions.

Some nerve cells have long fibers that connect to other regions of the nervous system. These are called *projection neurons, principal neurons,* or *relay cells.* They characteristically have a single, long axon that makes the distant connections. This process can be recognized in Golgi-stained material because the fiber arises from a cone-shaped part (axon hillock) of the cell body or a dendritic trunk. It usually (but not always) maintains the same diameter throughout its length, despite giving off branches. The branches usually arise at right angles. Large axons and their branches may have a myelin covering. Under the electron microscope, the origin of the axon at the hillock can usually be rec-

ognized by a dense undercoating of the plasma membrane, and a funneling of microfilaments (see Fig. 4.2).

Thus, in projection neurons, an axon can nearly always be identified by one or another (often all) of the above criteria. Then, all the other processes of the cell are dendrites. Thus, *dendrites are all those branches of a nerve cell that do not fulfill the criteria for being an axon.* Figure 4.16A shows several examples of projection neurons in which these definitions have been applied. Note that despite the specializations of the dorsal root ganglion cell and the invertebrate neuron, the definition can be applied with ease. The term "neurite" is sometimes applied to the dendritic branches of invertebrate neurons.

The other main type of nerve cell is contained wholly within one region of the nervous system. These are called *intrinsic neurons,* or *interneurons.* Examples of

Fig. 4.16. Types of neurons and their branches. Dendrites are shown with stippling, axons with clear profiles.

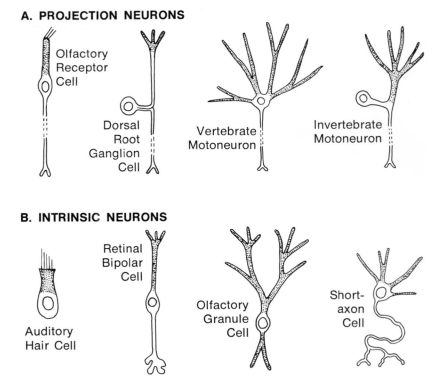

A. PROJECTION NEURONS

Olfactory Receptor Cell

Dorsal Root Ganglion Cell

Vertebrate Motoneuron

Invertebrate Motoneuron

B. INTRINSIC NEURONS

Retinal Bipolar Cell

Auditory Hair Cell

Olfactory Granule Cell

Short-axon Cell

these are shown in Fig. 4.16B. The problem that arises here is that many intrinsic neurons do not require an axon for their functions. Thus, some have almost no processes whatever (the hair cell); others have only short processes (the bipolar cell); some have no process qualifying as an axon (the granule cell). The latter are usually called *anaxonal*, or *amacrine* (a = no, macrine = long process) cells; their processes may thus all be called dendrites. Only in the case of a cell with a short axon (short-axon cell) does one have an interneuron in which one can make the usual distinctions that apply to the projection neuron.

As noted in Chap. 1, dendrites were originally termed "protoplasmic prolongations", and the modern studies with the electron microscope have fully confirmed the correctness of that idea. As indicated in Fig. 4.2, the main organelles of the cell body extend without any sharp boundaries into the trunks of the dendrites. Thus, large dendrites can be clearly distinguished from large axons. However, small axons and small dendrites are not so dissimilar in their fine structure. The terminals of axons are often characterized by a large number of synaptic vesicles (see next chapter), but small axon terminals differ little from small dendritic branches and terminals in their fine structure. The sites of synapses on axons and dendrites will be considered in the next chapter.

REFERENCES

Barondes, S. H. 1981. Biochemical approaches to cell adhesion and recognition. In Siegel et al. (see below).

Bloom, W. and D. W. Fawcett. 1975. *A Textbook of Histology*. Philadelphia: Saunders.

Bunge, R. P. 1968. Glial cells and the central myelin sheath. *Physiol. Rev. 48:* 197–251.

Carpenter, M. B. 1976. [Chap. 3].

Fawcett, D. W. 1981. *The Cell*. Philadephia: Saunders.

Gainer, H. and M. J. Brownstein. 1981. Neuropeptides. In Siegel et al. (see below).

Gilbert, C. D. and J. P. Kelly. 1975. The projections of cells in different layers of the cat's visual cortex. *J. Comp. Neurol. 163:* 81–106.

Hopkins, C. R. 1978. *Structure and Function of Cells*. London: Saunders.

Keeton, W. T. 1980. [Chap. 2].

Kreutzberg, G. W., P. Schubert, and H. D. Lux. 1975. Neuroplasmic transport in axons and dendrites. In *Golgi Centennial Symposium* (ed. by M. Santini). New York: Raven. pp. 161–166.

Palade, G. E. and M. G. Farquhar. 1981. Cell biology. In *Pathophysiology. The Biological Principles of Disease*. (ed. by L. H. Smith and S. O. Thier). Philadelphia: Saunders. pp. 1–56.

Shepherd, G. M. 1979. *The Synaptic Organization of the Brain*. New York: Oxford.

Stretton, A. O. W. and E. A. Kravitz. 1968. Neuronal geometry: determination with a technique of intracellular dye injection. *Science 162:* 132–134.

Wiesel, T. N., D. H. Hubel, and D. M. K. Lam. 1974. Autoradiographic demonstration of ocular-dominance columns in the monkey striate cortex by means of transneuronal transport. *Brain Res. 79:* 273–279.

Additional Reading

Lehninger, A. L. 1975. *Biochemistry*. New York: Worth.

Ochs, S. 1981. Axoplasmic transport. In Siegel et al. (see below).

Peters et al. 1976. [Chap. 1].

Rakic, P. (ed.). 1976. *Local Circuit Neurons*. Cambridge, Mass.: MIT Press.

Siegel, G. J., R. W. Albers, B. W. Agranoff, and R. Katzman. 1981. *Basic Neurochemistry*. Boston: Little Brown.

Watson, J. D. 1978. *The Molecular Biology of the Gene*. Menlo Park: W. A. Benjamin.

5

The Synapse

In Chap. 1 we saw that the main business of neurobiology is to understand how the individual building blocks, the neurons, are organized into functional systems. The principal means of organization is through connections between the neurons. These connections are called *synapses*. As Sanford Palay, a modern scholar of the nervous system, has expressed it: "The concept of the synapse lies at the heart of the neuron doctrine." Let us take a brief excursion into history to see how our knowledge of synapses has come about.

The origin of the idea of the synapse is particularly associated with one man, Charles Sherrington, an English physiologist. Around 1890, when Cajal and his contemporaries were establishing the anatomical evidence for the neuron as a cell, Sherrington was just beginning his study of the reflex functions of the spinal cord. His work involved a painstaking analysis of the anatomy and physiology of the spinal nerves and spinal cord, and the results provided the foundation for all subsequent concepts of the reflex as a basic unit of function in the spinal cord as well as in other parts of the nervous system, as will be discussed in Chap. 20.

Sherrington's results also set him to thinking about how activity conducted in the sensory fibers to the spinal cord is transferred to the motor cells that innervate the muscles. His studies had convinced him that the transfer involved properties that are different from those involved in the conducting of signals in the fibers themselves. If Cajal and his colleagues were right, and the sensory nerves arborize and terminate in free endings, then these different properties must be associated with some kind of special contact between those endings and the motor cells. And so it was, when Michael Foster came in 1897 to revise his standard physiology textbook of the day, and asked Sherrington to contribute the chapters on the spinal cord, that Sherrington advanced the following simple proposal:

> So far as our present knowledge goes, we are lead to think that the tip of a twig of the arborescence is not continuous with but merely in contact with the substance of the dendrite or cell body on which it impinges. Such a special connection of one nerve cell with another might be called a *synapse*.

The term *synapse* is derived from the Greek, meaning to clasp, connect, or join. Sherrington thought of it, anatomically, as

70

a site of "surfaces of separation," but he always emphasized that it was first and foremost a *functional* connection. He conceived of the possible functions very broadly, as shown in a passage from his famous book, *The Integrative Action of the Nervous System,* published in 1906:

> Such a surface might restrain diffusion, bank up osmotic pressure, restrict the movement of ions, accumulate electric charges, support a double electric layer, alter in shape and surface-tension with changes in difference of potential . . . or intervene as a membrane between dilute solutions of electrolytes of different concentration or colloidal suspensions with different sign of charge.

We will see that a broad framework of this kind is very much needed to embrace the varieties of interactions between nerve cells shown by modern studies.

One of the important properties of spinal reflexes is that they always proceed from sensory to motor, never in the reverse direction. Sherrington suggested that this is imparted by a one-way valvelike property of the synapses. This seemed to fit with another idea, that the dendrites and cell body of a neuron are its *receptor* parts, where signals are received, and the axon and its terminals are the *effector* parts, where signals are emitted. This had been deduced around 1890 by Cajal and a Belgian anatomist, Arthur van Gehuchten, who had taken up the Golgi method very soon after Cajal, and it was christened the *Law of Dynamic Polarization.* This "law" was soon accepted as a corollary to the neuron doctrine, and provided an attractive and logical framework for understanding how individual nerve cells could be connected into groups and chains for transmitting nerve signals (A, B in Fig. 5.1). It is only with recent studies of the microanatomy and physiology of synaptic organization that this law has had to be revised, to take account of complex synaptic interactions of dendrites and axonal terminals.

Modern research in neurobiology has focused much of its attention on the synapse and its role in the functioning of the nervous system. This is not by accident, for it is possible to regard the synapse as the essential and defining property of the neuron. Thus, one can suggest that a *neu-*

Fig. 5.1. Diagrams by Cajal, to show the direction of transmission of signals in nerve cells and nerve circuits according to his Law of Dynamic Polarization. **A.** Invertebrate ganglion. **B.** Cerebellum. (From Cajal, 1911)

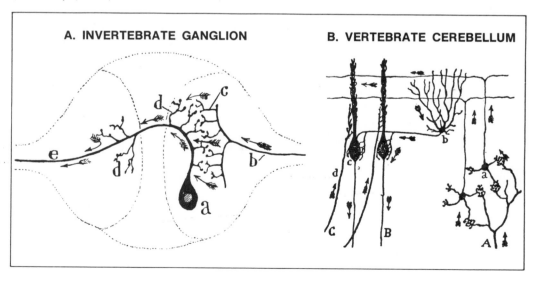

ron is a cell connected to other cells by synapses that mediate specific signals involved in behavior. Note how this parallels rather closely our definition of the subject matter of neurobiology in Chap. 1.

Having stated the importance of the synapse, we also want to recognize that it is not the only means by which nerve cells can interact with each other. Interactions, in fact, take many forms, and the organization of neurons is built on these as well. Our study therefore requires a broad view of the nature of interneuronal relations.

In any relations between two nerve cells there are three components. One is the cell or cell process from which activity is sent. This is called the *presynaptic* process. Another is the cell or cell process which receives the activity; this is the *postsynaptic* process. The third component is whatever *intervenes* between the two processes. This may be just as important in determining the nature of the interaction as the other two components. In fact, on the basis of this intervening component, we can identify three main degrees of relatedness between the other two: the two may be at a *distance* from each other; they may be next to (*juxtaposed* to) each other; and they may be actually in contact or joined to each other to form a morphological *junction*. Let us organize our discussion in terms of these three degrees of relatedness.

Distant Relations Between Neurons

The most distant relation is between two cells that are in two different animal bodies. Specific interactions of this type are those in which a particular substance is secreted into the air or water by one member of a species, and is detected and responded to by another member of that same species (see Fig. 5.2). Such a substance is called a *pheromone,* and is an important factor in the behavior of many species, as will be described in Chaps. 12 and 28. Dietrich Schneider, one of the pioneers in studies of pheromones, has suggested humorously that this situation can

PHEROMONE

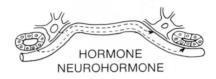

HORMONE
NEUROHORMONE

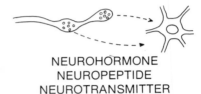

NEUROHORMONE
NEUROPEPTIDE
NEUROTRANSMITTER
NEUROMODULATOR

Fig. 5.2. Types of long-distance chemically mediated interactions between cells.

be thought of as a "giant synapse", and, indeed, not only are the three components present, but the specific molecular receptors and actions share many properties with those in synaptic transmission. However, the emitting component in this case is a gland cell, not a neuron, so this is not an example of interneuronal communication, but rather of specific activation of a *receptor cell* to trigger a specific behavior.

Within the same body, two cells in different organs may interact with each other over long distances. This occurs when one of them secretes a *hormone,* which is carried in the bloodstream to elicit a specific response in cells of another organ. Hormones play essential roles in the economy of the body, as we will note in later chapters. In some cases, hormones are secreted by gland cells and act on other gland cells or on smooth muscle cells of various internal organs. However, some hormones are secreted by nerve cells to act on glands or muscles, and some are secreted by glands to act on nerve cells. Most important, an enormous amount of evidence is accumulating for a variety of hormonelike substances secreted by neurons and acting on other neurons. These are called *neurohormones* or *neuroactive peptides*. The neurons that synthesize and secrete these substances are called *neuroendocrine* cells. It is becoming increasingly difficult to make the distinction between a neuroendocrine cell and a nerve cell that, in addition to the usual types of nerve signaling, also secretes a neuroactive peptide or hormone. Neuroendocrine cells are very common in virtually all the invertebrate phyla as well as in vertebrates. As indicated in Fig. 5.2, in the case of a neurohormone, one has the three components of a synapse, but with the intervening component comprised by interstitial fluid or the bloodstream.

The similarities that may exist between hormonal and synaptic actions are exemplified by adrenaline (epinephrine). Adrenaline has been traditionally regarded a hormone, secreted by the adrenal medulla and preparing the body for "fight or flight". The secretion is stimulated by nerves of the sympathetic nervous system. Adrenaline is derived from noradrenaline (norepinephrine), which has many similar actions and, in addition, is a transmitter substance at some synapses. Furthermore, adrenaline acts on some of the same receptors that noradrenaline acts on, and the receptors in turn activate the "second messenger", cyclic AMP, which is also implicated in the postsynaptic responses at some synapses. Thus, there is a great deal of overlap between some kinds of hormonal and synaptic actions (see Chap. 9).

Within a given part of the nervous system, a terminal or other part of a neuron may release substances which diffuse through the intercellular clefts and affect neurons not actually in contact with it. Cells in the midbrain of vertebrates, for example, project their axons diffusely to many parts of the nervous system, where they ramify and terminate, in many cases, without making definite contacts with specific structures. The branches and terminals nonetheless contain vesicles and neurotransmitter substances, and it is therefore believed that such axons release these substances to act on nearby neuronal processes (see Fig. 5.2). Similar release appears to occur from dendrites in certain areas. The range of action of such substances is limited by diffusion, as well as other factors. These substances may act as *neuromodulators* as well as specific *neurotransmitters*, as discussed in Chap. 9.

Membrane Juxtapositions

Let us now consider the situation in which the membranes of two neurons come close together, separated only by the ubiquitous extracellular space, or cleft, of about 20 nm. We term this a *juxtaposition* (juxta = next to) of the two membranes. This relationship is a very common one in the nervous system; in fact, one can say as a general rule that neurons usually are crowded against each other, with their membranes in juxtaposition to each other, except where glial membranes are intruded in order to keep particular processes apart. As indicated in Fig. 5.3, cer-

Fig. 5.3. Membrane juxtapositions, as exemplified by a bundle of unmyelinated axons, which provide for interactions through ions or electric current.

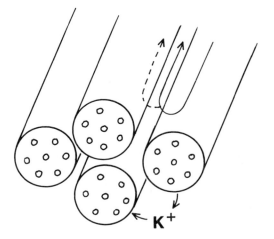

tain types of fine, unmyelinated axons (for example, the axons of the olfactory nerve, or the parallel fibers of the cerebellum) have this membrane-to-membrane relationship with each other. It also occurs throughout the neuropil of the local regions of the nervous system, between the terminals of axons and dendrites. The membranes of neurons and glia are juxtaposed nearly everywhere they occur together.

This juxtaposition of membranes provides for several possible functions. Any movement of substances, such as ions or metabolites, out of one cell into the intervening cleft may have effects on that same cell as well as all the juxtaposed processes of other cells. Uptake of substances may occur by this route, as for example the uptake of K$^+$ or the uptake of the neurotransmitter GABA by glial cells. It is fair to say that our knowledge of all the molecular traffic that may occur across juxtaposed membranes is still at an early stage. Juxtaposed membranes also provide for electrical interactions between neighboring processes under some conditions; the sites at which such interactions occur are called ephapses (see Chap. 8).

Membrane Junctions

The closest stage of relatedness between neurons is a specific contact of their membranes. This occurs at sites where (1) the two membranes come close together or are fused and/or (2) the membranes appear more dense. Such sites are found between cells throughout the body. Depending on details of structure, they are called occluding junctions, desmosomes, tight junctions, gap junctions, septate junctions, or zonulae adherens. They vary widely in size and form, ranging from small spots to long strips or patches. Such junctions provide for several possible functions: simple adhesion; transfer of substances during metabolism or embryological development; restriction of movement of substances in the extracellular compartment. An instance of the latter function is provided by the *tight junctions* between the cells that line the blood vessels and ventricles of the brain. The two outer leaflets of the unit membrane of these junctions, as illustrated in Fig. 5.4, are completely fused, to form a five-layered complex. These tight junctions restrict the movement of substances in the extracellular space and are

Fig. 5.4. Types of junctions between nerve cells. (From Shepherd, 1979)

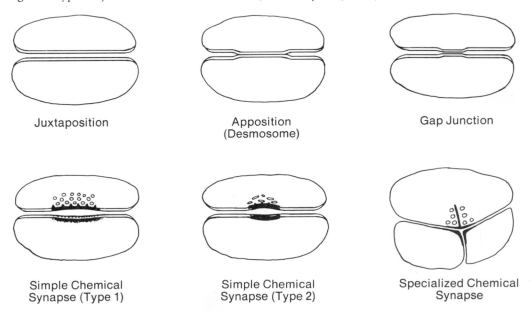

Juxtaposition

Apposition
(Desmosome)

Gap Junction

Simple Chemical
Synapse (Type 1)

Simple Chemical
Synapse (Type 2)

Specialized Chemical
Synapse

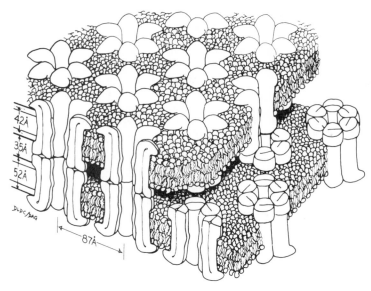

Fig. 5.5. Diagram of a gap junction (electrical synapse). Channels provide for intercellular exchange of low molecular weight substances and electric current. Some gap junctions pass current in only one direction (rectifying junctions). Channel walls are composed of six protein subunits which span the lipid bilayer of each plasma membrane. Because of the gap between the membranes, extracellular substances can percolate between the channels. (From Makowski et al., 1977)

responsible for the so-called *blood–brain barrier.*

An important type of membrane junction in the nervous system is the so-called *gap junction.* Here, the outer leaflets are separated by a gap of 2–4 nm, to form a seven-layered complex (Figs. 5.4 and 5.5). In several cases, the presence of these junctions has been correlated with the physiological finding of a low-resistance electrical pathway between two neurons. On this basis they have been categorized as *electrical synapses.* The junction varies in diameter from 0.1–10 μm. At high resolution, dense material is seen beneath each apposed membrane, and it can be shown that the membranes are part of two systems of channels, the one continuous with the extracellular space, the other connecting the two cells. Electrical synapses are a common form of interneuronal connection in invertebrates, and in lower vertebrates; they have also been found at several sites in the mammalian brain. Gap junctions are found between many types of cells in the body besides neurons. Some functions proposed for gap junctions and related cell-to-cell channels are listed in Table 5.1. Most of these presumably apply to neurons.

Chemical Synapses

The most complicated type of junction in the nervous system, and the type considered to be the most characteristic, is the chemical synapse (see Fig. 5.6). It differs morphologically from other types of membrane appositions in being strongly oriented, or polarized, from one neuron to the other. This polarization is determined mainly by two features: (1) an unequal *densification* of the two apposed membranes and (2) the presence of a group of small *vesicles* near the synaptic site. In certain cases (e.g., the neuromuscular junction), it can be shown unequivocally that transmission is from the vesicle-containing process to the other process, so that one can identify the *presynaptic* and *postsynaptic* process with confidence.

Synapses were first identified in the

Table 5.1   Physiological roles of cell-to-cell channels

A. Tissue homeostasis
   1. Equilibration of individual cell differences in electrical potential
   2. Equilibration and buffering of individual cell differences in small molecules
   3. Transport of nutrient substances from cell to cell
B. Regulating signal transmission
   1. Signals affecting cytoplasmic processes
      a. Chemical signals: cyclic nucleotides, various metabolites
      b. Electrical signals: propagation of electrical activity in heart, smooth muscle, electrical synapses
   2. Signals affecting genetic processes
      a. Cellular differentiation: ubiquity of cell-to-cell channels in embryonic tissue
      b. Cellular growth: channels are necessary for control of growth and prevention of unregulated (cancerous) growth
C. Cellular organization
   1. Amplification of cell responses through diffusable messenger modules (such as cyclic nucleotides) or voltage-sensitive electrical responses
   2. Hierarchical interactions: driving of secondary cells by a primary pacemaker, as in the heart and some neural circuits

Adapted from Loewenstein (1981)

electron microscope in the mid-1950's, as mentioned in Chap. 1. In 1959, E. G. Gray of London, working on the cerebral cortex, obtained evidence for two morphological types. There is a growing consensus that, despite many local variations and gradations between the two, this division has some validity. The two types are illustrated in Figs. 5.4 and 5.6. The distinguishing features may be summarized as follows. Type I: synaptic cleft approximately 30 nm; junctional area relatively large (up to 1–2 μm in extent); prominent accumulation of dense material next to the postsynaptic membrane (i.e., an asymmetric densification of the two apposed membranes). Type II: synaptic cleft approximately 20 nm; junctional area relatively small (less than 1μm in extent); membrane densifications modest and symmetrical.

Following the recognition of these types, evidence was obtained in 1965 by Uchizono of Japan that, in many parts of the

Fig. 5.6. The structure of the chemical synapse. **A.** Diagram of simple contact. (From Akert et al., 1972). **B.** Diagram of bar synapse (in metathoracic ganglion of cockroach). (From Wood et al., 1977)

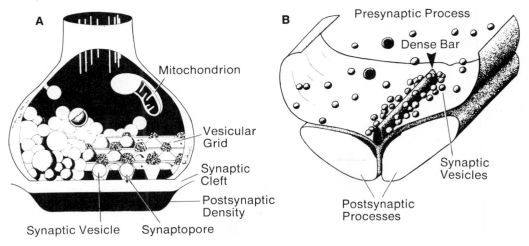

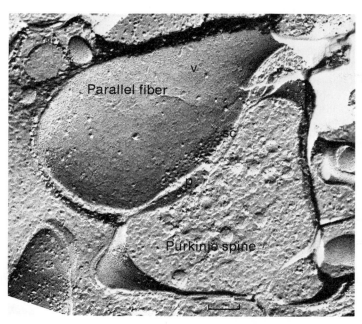

Fig. 5.7. A freeze-fractured specimen of synaptic terminals in the cerebellum. The line of cleavage is such that one sees the inner surface of an outer leaflet of a Purkinje cell dendritic spine; it also cuts across a synaptic terminal of a parallel fiber. Note the vesicles (v) in the presynaptic terminal, the widened synaptic cleft (sc), and the accumulation of small particles (p) in the postsynaptic terminal membrane. Bracket 0.1 μm. (From Landis and Reese, 1974)

brain, type I synapses are associated with large spherical vesicles (diameter approximately 30–60 nm) which are usually present in considerable numbers. Type II synapses, on the other hand, are associated with smaller (10–30 nm diameter) vesicles, which are less numerous and which, significantly, take on various ellipsoidal and flattened shapes. The distinction between round and flat types of vesicles is by no means a sharp one; in many synapses a vesicle simply tends to the one shape or the other.

These two morphological features (symmetry of membrane density and shape of vesicles) have provided a convenient means for characterizing synapses. The differences are vividly revealed by the freeze-fracturing technique, in which a tiny block of tissue is frozen and then fractured by a swift blow with a sharp blade. A micrograph of a specimen prepared in this way is shown in Fig. 5.7. The lines of

cleavage are not between the membranes of the two neighboring neurons, but between the inner and outer leaflets of the same membrane. As can be seen, the fracture line jumps from one membrane to the next, or cuts entirely through a process, in its course through the tissue. In this view, the fracture line has cut through a synapse between a pre- and postsynaptic process. There is a collection of intramembranous particles on the inner surface of the outer leaflet of the postsynaptic membrane. This is characteristic of a type I synapse. Type II synapses, by contrast, lack this concentration of particles.

The recognition of these two types of synapse has provided anatomists with a most useful tool to unravel the synaptic organization of local brain regions. Much of this usefulness has been based on the premise that all the synapses made by a given neuron onto other neurons are either of one type or the other. This is commonly called the *morphological corollary of Dale's Law*, Dale's Law being usually understood as stating that a given neuron has the same physiological action at all its synapses. As we will see in Chap. 9, this is neither what Dale, in fact, put forward nor what electrophysiology reveals. Nor has it been proved that the morphological corollary has universal validity. In most regions of the brain, the premise that all the synapses made by a given neuron are of the same type has been generally assumed.

Many neuroanatomists have been skeptical of the validity of the two types of synapse on the basis of the fact that the flattening of vesicles has been shown to depend on the osmolarity of solutions used in preparing the tissue for electron microscopy. But, in a sense, everything the electron microscopist sees is a distortion of the true dynamic living state. The interpretation of electron micrographs, and of any preparations of anatomical specimens, must be made with this constantly in mind. That the recognition of the two types of synapse has been the basis for remarkable progress in the understanding of the synaptic organization of the brain may be regarded as sufficient reason for using it as the basis for our review of present knowledge.

Vesicles

Synaptic vesicles are a subject in themselves. They come, in the felicitous phraseology of Sanford Palay, like chocolates, in a variety of shapes and sizes, and are stuffed with different kinds of filling. Small vesicles (20–40 nm in diameter) are the most common; they are the ones we have discussed in regard to type I and type II synapses (see Fig. 5.8). At some synapses, there is evidence that acetylcholine is bound to, or contained within, the vesicles; such synapses are, therefore, called cholinergic. At other synapses, the vesicles appear to be associated with certain amino acids. These are the putative transmitter

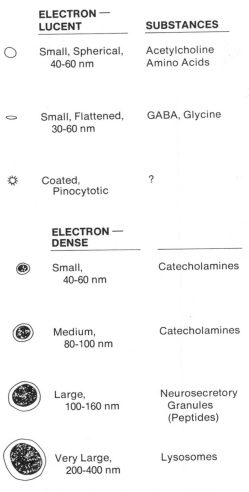

ELECTRON—LUCENT		SUBSTANCES
○	Small, Spherical, 40-60 nm	Acetylcholine Amino Acids
⊖	Small, Flattened, 30-60 nm	GABA, Glycine
✸	Coated, Pinocytotic	?

ELECTRON—DENSE		
◉	Small, 40-60 nm	Catecholamines
◉	Medium, 80-100 nm	Catecholamines
◉	Large, 100-160 nm	Neurosecretory Granules (Peptides)
●	Very Large, 200-400 nm	Lysosomes

Fig. 5.8. Types of vesicles and granules in nerve cells.

substances that are released by the presynaptic terminal when it is activated and that mediate the synaptic action onto the postsynaptic membrane, as will be described in Chaps. 8 and 9.

Another type of vesicle is medium sized (50–90 nm in diameter) and contains a dense granule; these vesicles are associated with monoamines. Large vesicles (120–150 nm in diameter) are characteristically found in neurosecretory cells, for example, in the nerve endings of hypothalamic neurons which send their axons to the pituitary. A large, dense droplet within these vesicles contains a polypeptide hormone, which is released in response to the appropriate behavioral stimulus. A neuron, or indeed a single terminal, may contain more than one type of vesicle, possibly for transport and storage, or for immediate release at the synapse.

This very brief account only scratches the surface of the subject of synaptic vesicles. The main point to be made here is that the vesicles are structural evidence of the fact that chemical synapses constitute a variety of neurosecretory apparatuses. Like other secretory mechanisms, they are activated by specific stimuli, have specific targets, and exert particular actions on those targets. The dynamics of these mechanisms are the subject of Chaps. 8 and 9.

Types of Synapses and Terminals

Types I and II synapses provide relatively small areas of contact between neurons. They may be characterized as *simple* synapses. They are typical of the contacts made by small terminals, both axonal and dendritic, and they are also the type of contact made by most cell bodies and dendrites when those structures occupy presynaptic positions. It is probably fair to say that they make up the majority of synapses in the brain. This, in itself, bespeaks an important principle of brain organization, that the output of a neuron is fractionated, as it were, through many synapses onto many other neurons and, conversely, that synapses from many sources play onto a given neuron. This is an essential aspect of the complexity of information processing in the brain.

In addition, there are, in many regions, much more extensive contacts with more elaborate structure that may be characterized as *specialized synapses.* The neuromuscular junction is an example in the peripheral nervous system. In the central nervous system, we find an example in the retina, where the large terminal of a receptor cell makes contact with several postsynaptic neurons; within the terminal, the synaptic vesicles are grouped around a special small dense bar. This arrangement is shown very schematically in Fig. 5.4 and is described in detail in Chap. 17.

One may also characterize the terminal structures in the geometrical sense. A terminal may be small and have a single synapse onto a single postsynaptic structure, as shown in most of the diagrams of Fig. 5.4. These may be characterized as *simple terminals.* On the other hand, a large terminal, with complicated geometry, may be characterized as a *specialized terminal:* examples are the neuromuscular junction and the basket cell endings around the Purkinje cell (Chap. 22). In many regions of the brain, large terminals have synapses onto more than one postsynaptic structure; the receptor terminal in the retina mentioned above is an example. Another example is the large terminal rosette of the mossy fiber in the cerebellum, which has as many as 300 synaptic contacts onto postsynaptic structures (see below).

Within the brain are all possible combinations of synapses and terminals. Simple synapses may be established by any of the parts of the neuron: terminals, trunks, or the cell body. Simple synapses may also be made by specialized terminals, as in the case of the mossy fiber of the cerebellum. On the other hand, specialized synapses may be made by small terminals, as in the spinule synapses of the hippocampus, and, finally, specialized synapses may arise from specialized terminals, as in the case of the retinal receptor.

Patterns of Synaptic Connections

Synapses are also categorized by the kinds of processes that take part in the synapse. Thus, for example, a contact from an axon onto a cell body is termed an *axosomatic* synapse, whereas that onto a dendrite is termed an *axodendritic* synapse (Fig.

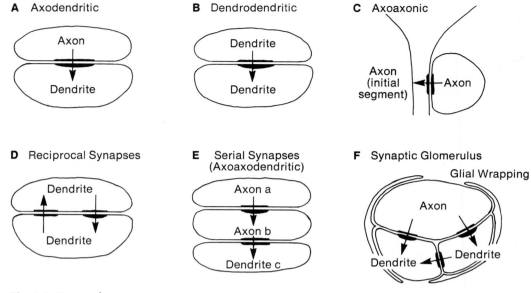

Fig. 5.9. Types of synaptic arrangements.

5.9A). Similarly, a contact between two axons is termed an *axoaxonic* synapse (C, E), and a contact between two dendrites is termed a *dendrodendritic* synapse (B).

A single synapse seldom occurs in isolation in the brain; it is usually one of a number of synapses that together make up a larger pattern of interconnecting synapses. The simplest of these patterns is that formed by two or more synapses situated near each other and oriented in the same direction; they are all axodendritic. A more complicated pattern is one in which there is a synapse from process (a) to process (b), and another from (b) to (c). Such a situation is diagrammed in Fig. 5.9E. These are referred to as *serial* synapses; examples are axoaxodendritic sequences and axodendrodendritic sequences.

Another pattern has a synapse from process (a) to process (b), and a return synapse from (b) to (a). This is diagrammed in Fig. 5.9D. It is referred to as a *reciprocal* synapse. If the two synapses are side by side, they are called a *reciprocal pair.* If the two synapses are far apart, a *reciprocal arrangement* results. Finally,

there are patterns of synaptic connections between tightly grouped clusters of terminals, called *synaptic glomeruli* (Fig. 5.9F).

The first synapses identified by electron microscopists were simple contacts made by simple terminals, of the axosomatic and axodendritic type. Since these simple arrangements were in accord with the idea of a "polarized" neuron, they came to be regarded as "classical" synapses. The axoaxonic and dendrodendritic types were identified later, as were the serial and reciprocal arrangements and the various types of specialized synaptic contacts and terminals. Since these synapses, terminals, and patterns did not fit classical concepts, the practice grew up of referring to the simple synapses as "conventional" and to all the other synapses as "unconventional" or even "nonusual".

In recent years so many examples of complex synaptic arrangements have come to light that we are in danger of believing that most parts of the nervous system, in invertebrates and vertebrates, are organized in unconventional ways! This of course is absurd. It simply shows that nature does not always work according to man's simple preconceptions. Certainly the nervous system does not put these labels on its synapses. We may conceive that, in any given region, it is faced with specific tasks of information processing, and it assembles the necessary circuits from the available neuronal components. Thus, far from being unconventional, the complex synaptic arrangements, in fact, give expression to the extraordinary flexibility of the nerve cell as the fundamental anatomical unit of the nervous system.

Identification of Synaptic Connections

If the synaptic connections between neurons are so complex, how do we identify which neuronal processes contribute to a given synapse or synaptic cluster? Neuroanatomists have developed several

Fig. 5.10. Examples of synaptic arrangements. A. Human retina, showing ribbon synapse (dark arrow) between bipolar terminal (BT) and amacrine (A) and ganglion cell (G). Also shown is a reciprocal synapse from amacrine to bipolar cell (open arrow). r, ribosomes. (From Dowling and Boycott, 1966). B. Olfactory bulb, reconstruction in 3-dimensions from serial EM sections, showing reciprocal synapses between mitral (m) and granule (g) cell dendrites. (From Rall et al., 1966). C. Rat olfactory bulb, treated with antibodies for glutamic acid decarboxylase (GAD), the enzyme that synthesizes GABA. Reaction product is found in granule cell spine (g), pedicle (p), and dendrite (d), but not in mitral cell dendrite (m). Arrow indicates site of granule-to-mitral dendrodendritic synapse. (From Ribak et al., 1977)

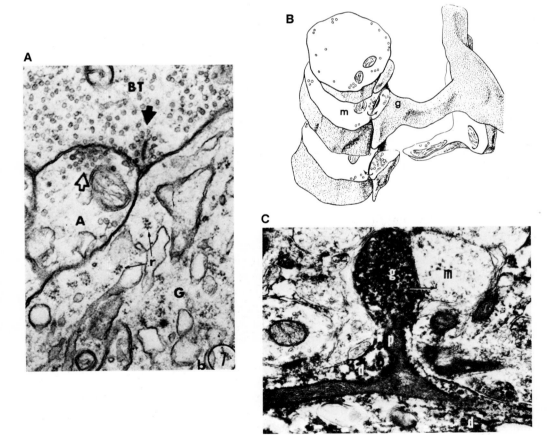

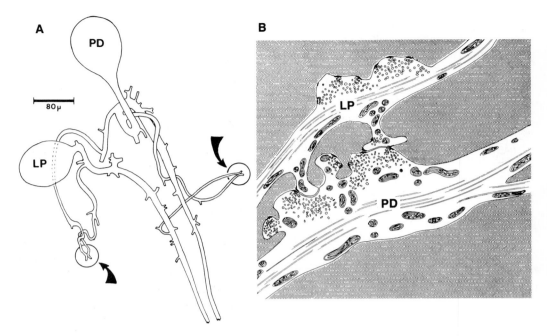

Fig. 5.11. Lobster stomatogastric ganglion. **A.** Two cells (pyloric dilator (PD) and lateral pyloric (LP)) have been reconstructed from serial sections. Circles show sites of synaptic connection between the cells. **B.** Synaptic connections, as reconstructed from serial EM sections. (From Selverston et al., 1976)

methods for doing this. Sometimes the fine structure differs sufficiently enough to identify the processes in single sections, as in the case of the retina shown in Fig. 5.10A. As a general rule, however, three-dimensional reconstructions from serial sections are necessary, as illustrated in the olfactory bulb in Fig. 5.10B. Another method is to treat the tissue with antibodies to an enzyme that is involved in the synthesis of a neurotransmitter. Figure 5.10C shows that, in olfactory bulb tissue treated with antibodies to glutamic acid decarboxylase the enzyme (the enzyme that synthesizes GABA), the granule cell gemmules are positive, whereas the mitral cell dendrites are not. This is consistent with other evidence that the granule cell dendrites inhibit the mitral cell dendrites by the action of GABA at the dendrodendritic synapses. A fourth method is to inject a cell with lucifer yellow or HRP which under EM is electron-dense. A fifth method

is to transect a bundle of input fibers and identify the synapses made by degenerating terminals. A final method is to impregnate tissue by the Golgi method and then partially deimpregnate and examine the synapses made by or onto partially deimpregnated cells and terminals.

The examples above are all taken from vertebrates. An example from invertebrates is shown in Fig. 5.11. Here (5.11A) the cell bodies of two neurons in the stomatogastric ganglion of the lobster were injected with the dye Procion Yellow. The neurons were visualized under light microscopy in whole mounts of the ganglion, and precisely reconstructed from serial sections made through the cells. In the EM, serial reconstructions of ultrathin sections show that the dendritic trees that arise from the axons of these cells have numerous expansions (varicosities) where synapses are present. A typical reconstruction is shown in Fig. 5.11B. The results have been summarized by Allen Selverston, Don Russell, John Miller, and David King of San Diego as follows:

> Each synaptic varicosity is functionally bipolar . . . ; it both projects synapses onto and receives synapses from many other processes. These bifunctional varicosities are found on all of the dendrites of the neuron. Hence input and output are each distributed over the entire dendritic arborization. Although neuronal input and output are traditionally thought of as segregated onto polarized regions of the neuron (onto "dendrites" and "axons"), this does not seem to be the case in stomatogastric ganglion neurons. In this, the stomatogastric ganglion may show functional similarity to those regions of vertebrate central nervous system (such as olfactory bulb and retina) where dendro-dendritic interactions are important.

From Synapses to Circuits

From these considerations it is obvious that the flow of information through a neuron and between neurons is much more complicated than depicted in the diagrams of Cajal in Fig. 5.1. Although this seems perplexing at first, some relatively simple general principles about how synapses are organized into circuits have begun to emerge.

A useful generalization to begin with is that synapses are usually made by one of three types of neuronal element. First are the *inputs* coming from other regions, usually ending as axon terminals. Second are the *relay neurons* of the given region. Third are the *intrinsic neurons* within that region. Then, as shown in Fig. 5.12, a given synapse can be made by any one of these elements, and a complex synaptic arrangement generally involves some specific way in which the three elements are interrelated. We call these three elements the *synaptic triad*. Sometimes the elements are very tightly organized, as in serial or reciprocal synapses. Sometimes they are loosely organized, as in spread-out regions like the ventral horn of the spinal cord or the cerebral cortex. Sometimes the interneuronal elements may be lacking, as in some simple relay structures. Or perhaps the output neuron is lacking, if the output is humoral, or the cell body is situated elsewhere. In the face of all this diversity, it is useful to use the synaptic triad as a general framework for identifying the

Fig. 5.12. Diagram showing how the triad of synaptic elements—input terminals, projection neuron, and intrinsic neuron—provides the basis for synaptic organization of local circuits in vertebrates and invertebrates.

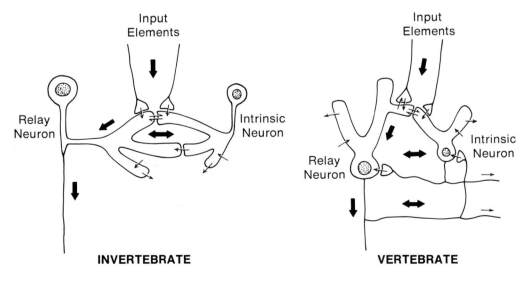

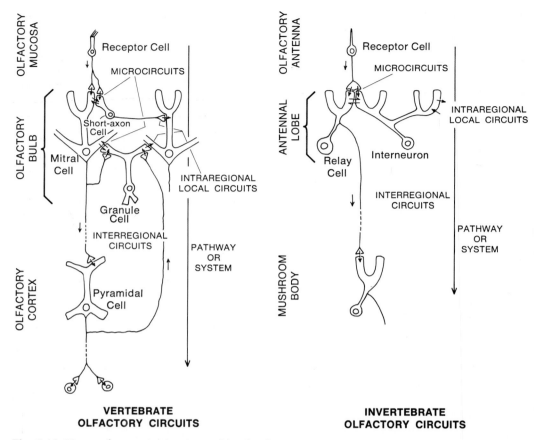

Fig. 5.13. Types of synaptic circuits, and levels of organization, as seen in the vertebrate and invertebrate olfactory pathways.

main kinds of connections present in a region, and comparing them with those of other regions.

With the identification of patterns of synaptic connections, we are in a position to begin to identify circuits at different levels of organization (see Fig. 5.13).

At the finest level of organization is the arrangement of synapses at a local site on a cell body, dendrite, or axon terminal. This may involve simple *convergence* of several inputs onto that site, or simple *divergence* to several output sites. In addition, it may involve *serial* relays of information, or *reciprocal* interactions. In all these cases, a given site acts as a very local *integrative unit.* We can speak of it as the

most local type of *local circuit,* or a *microcircuit.* It is very common for a particular type of microcircuit to be repeated throughout a given layer or on a given cell type, thus acting as a *module* for a specific kind of information processing.

At the next level of organization is the circuit that connects different neurons within a given region over longer distances. This transmission may take place through a dendritic branch or dendritic trunk, or it may take place through the axon of an interneuron, or the axon collateral of an output neuron. These may also be termed local circuits, because they remain within a given region. Their function characteristically appears to be to spread activity from a site, or to provide for antagonistic interactions between neighboring integrative units within a region.

The next highest level of organization involves connections of one region with another. Usually a region receives input from more than one other region, and usually a region projects output to more than one other region. Thus, the same principles of convergence, divergence, and integration of different kinds of information operate at this level, too. It is also common for there to be feedback from one region to another. Note that feedback loops are present at all levels. The more local feedback loops can be regarded as *nested* within the more extensive loops.

At a still higher level are sequences of connections through several regions. These are said to constitute a *pathway* or *system*. The function is usually to transmit information from the periphery into the central nervous system (as in a sensory system), or from central to periphery (as in a motor system). However, in any pathway there are often connections running in the opposite direction to provide for *descending, ascending,* or *centrifugal* control.

Finally, at the highest level (at least the highest thus far identified) are sets of connections between a number of regions, which together mediate a behavior that involves to some extent the whole organism. These are called *distributed systems.* They are characteristic of higher functions of motor and sensory systems, and of many central systems.

REFERENCES

Akert, K., K. Pfenninger, C. Sandri, and H. Moore. 1972. Freeze etching and cytochemistry of vesicles and membrane complexes in synapses of the central nervous system. In *Structure and Function of Synapses* (ed. by G. D. Pappas and D. P. Purpura). New York: Raven. pp. 67–86.

Bloom, W. and D. W. Fawcett. 1975. [Chap. 4].

Cajal, S. Ramon y. 1911. *Histologie du Systeme Nerveux de l'Homme et des Vertebres.* Paris: Maloine.

Dowling, J. E. and B. B. Boycott. 1966. Organization of the primate retina: electron microscopy. *Proc. Roy. Soc. B. 166:* 80–111.

Foster, M. 1897. *A Textbook of Physiology.* London: Macmillan.

Landis, D. M. D. and T. S. Reese. 1974. Differences in membrane structure between excitatory and inhibitory synapses in the cerebellar cortex. *J. Comp. Neurol. 155:* 93–126.

Loewenstein, W. R. 1981. [Chap. 1].

Makowski, L., D. L. D. Caspar, W. C. Phillips, and D. A. Goodenough. 1977. Gap junction structure. II. Analysis of the X-ray diffraction data. *J. Cell Biol. 74:* 629–645.

Rall, W., G. M. Shepherd., T. S. Reese, and M. W. Brightman, 1966. Dendrodendritic synaptic pathway for inhibition in the olfactory bulb. *Exp. Neurol. 14:* 44–56.

Ribak, C. E., J. E. Vaughn, K. Saito, R. Barber, and E. Roberts. 1977. Glutamate decarboxylase localization in neurons of the olfactory bulb. *Brain Res. 126:* 1–18.

Selverston, A. I., D. F. Russell, J. P. Miller, and D. G. King. 1976. The stomatogastric nervous system: structure and function of a small neural network. *Progr. Neurobiol. 7:* 215–289.

Shepherd, G. M. 1979. [Chap. 4].

Sherrington, C. S. 1906. The *Integrative Action of the Nervous System.* New Haven: Yale University Press.

Wood, M. R., K. H. Pfenninger, and M. J. Cohen. 1977. Two types of presynaptic configuration in insect central synapses: an ultrastructural analysis. *Brain Res. 130:* 25–45.

Additional Reading

Bennett, M. V. L. 1977. Electrical transmission: a functional analysis and comparison in chemical transmission. In *Cellular Biology of Neurons.* Vol. 1, Sect. 1, *Handbook of Physiology, The Ner-*

vous System (ed. by E. R. Kandel). Bethesda: Am. Physiol. Soc. pp. 367–416.

Peters et al. 1976. [Chap. 1].

Rakic, P. 1976. [Chap. 4].

Tolbert, L. P. and J. G. Hildebrand. 1981. Organization and synaptic ultrastructure of glomeruli in the antennal lobes of the moth *Manduca sexta:* a study using thin sections and freeze-fracture. *Proc. Roy. Soc. London B 213:* 279–301.

6

The Membrane Potential

We have seen that a nerve cell, like other cells of the body, contains a number of organelles for carrying out different basic functions. In addition, a neuron has unique modifications—synapses—that provide for specific interactions with its neighbors. We now want to consider the types of activity that enable a nerve cell to use its synapses. The activity may be very quick, in which case it is mediated by electrical currents, or it may be slow, in which case it may involve movements of chemical substances as well as slow electrical changes. In this chapter we will begin to consider the mechanisms of the electrical signals. In order to do so, we will first consider some basic aspects of the physicochemical milieu of the neuron.

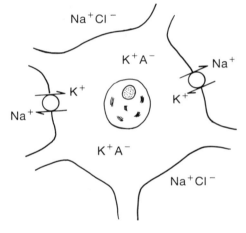

Fig. 6.1. A nerve cell and its ions. (A) organic anions, (Cl) chloride, (K) potassium, (Na) sodium.

Nerve Cells and Their Ions

The organelles of a neuron are embedded in a cytoplasm that is made up mostly of *water, protein,* and *inorganic salts,* as shown schematically in Fig. 6.1. The proteins range from structural macromolecules and enzymes of high molecular weights, down through smaller subunits like polypeptides and peptides, all the way to the various amino acids. Many of these

molecules have terminal groups that are dissociated in the aqueous medium of the cytoplasm, and their net electrical charge makes them *ions.* In the squid giant axon these *organic ions* can be determined simply by squeezing out the axoplasm and assaying it. The main organic ion is isethionate; it has a net negative charge, and is therefore an organic *anion,* represented by the large A^- in Fig. 6.1. Glutamate, aspartate, and organic phosphates have been

87

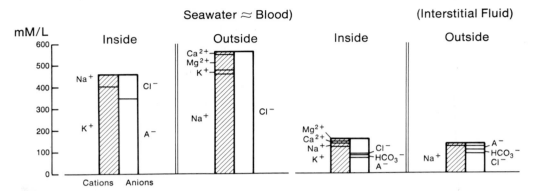

Fig. 6.2. Ionic concentrations for an invertebrate neuron (squid axon) and a mammalian muscle fiber. (Based on from Aidley, 1971)

suggested to be present in other nerves. Whatever their identity, the net charge on these molecules makes them anions.

In addition to organic ions there are *inorganic ions*. These are needed for the operation of many enzymes; for maintaining electrical, chemical, and osmotic equilibrium within the cell and between it and the outside; and for other functions. The main intracellular *cation* is potassium, as shown by the large K$^+$ in Fig. 6.1. Also

present in smaller but significant amounts are calcium and magnesium. The inorganic *anions* include chloride, phosphate, and sulfate. Outside the cell, the main *extracellular cation* is sodium (large Na$^+$)and the main *anion* is chloride (large Cl$^-$)

It can be seen at a glance in Fig. 6.1 that the electrolyte composition inside and outside the cell is quite different. This is summarized more quantitatively in Fig. 6.2 and Table 6.1, for the case of an inverte-

Table 6.1   Ionic concentrations for squid axon and mammalian muscle fiber

Ions	Invertebrate squid axon (seawater ≈ blood) Internal	External	Vertebrate muscle (neurons) (interstitial fluid) Internal	External
Cations				
K$^+$	400	(10)	124	2
Na$^+$	50	460	10	(125)
Ca^{2+}	(.4)	10	5	2
Mg^{2+}	10	54	14	1
other	—	—	—	—
Total	460	534	153	130
Anions				
Cl$^-$	40–150	560	2	77
HCO$_3^-$	—	—	12	27
(A)$^-$	345	—	74	13
other	—	—	(65)	(13)
Total	460	560	153	130

Concentrations in mM/liter. The values for the mammalian muscle fiber are believed to be representative of neurons. ( ) indicates estimates, to give electroneutrality between cations and anions. Note lack of osmotic equilibrium across the membrane (between internal and external medium).

After Aidley (1970)

brate cell (the squid giant axon) and a vertebrate cell. The latter is exemplified by frog muscle fibers, which have been well studied, and are believed to be similar to vertebrate neurons in these respects.

The electrical activity of nerve cells is derived from the unequal distribution of electrolytes across the cell membrane, as depicted in Figs. 6.1 and 6.2. There are two steps we want to understand: first, how the unequal distribution comes about, and second, how it gives rise to an electrical potential.

The Donnan Equilibrium

Our understanding of the first step is based on a classical paper by F. G. Donnan in 1924, entitled *The theory of membrane equilibria*. Many studies in the later nineteenth and early twentieth century had established the physicochemical properties of substances in solution: in particular, the dissociation of salts into ions, and the passive diffusion of ions through a solution from a region of high concentration to a region of low concentration. If two such regions are separated by a membrane, the diffusion will take place at a rate depending on how *permeable* (i.e., permissive) the membrane is in allowing the specific type of ion to pass through it. Eventually, the diffusion results in equal concentrations of all the diffusible and permeable ions on either side of the membrane. However,

Donnan showed that if a large *impermeable organic ion* is present on one side, the permeable ions distribute themselves unequally on either side of the membrane. Donnan, being a physical chemist, used an artificial collodion membrane for his experiments, together with an organic electrolyte like phenol red that could serve as a convenient visual marker.

The application of the Donnan model to the case of the biological cell is illustrated in the diagram of Fig. 6.3. We begin with solutions of the salt KCl, which dissociates into K^+ and Cl^- ions, and a membrane that has a small but significant permeability to both ions. As shown in ①, the concentration of KCl on either side will be equal, in order to preserve *chemical equilibrium* across the membrane, and the concentrations of K^+ and Cl^- will be equal on each side, in order to preserve *electrical neutrality* on each side.

Next (step ②) we add to one side a large concentration of organic anions (A^-), to which the membrane is completely impermeable. The anions are accompanied by an equal charge of cations (K^+). Although the K^+ preserves electroneutrality inside, it upsets the chemical concentration balance across the membrane. Therefore, diffusion of K^+ and Cl^- to the outside occurs, because K^+ moves down its concentration gradient and Cl^- accompanies it to preserve electroneutrality. Donnan showed that this diffusion con-

Fig. 6.3. Steps in the establishment of a Donnan equilibrium. See text.

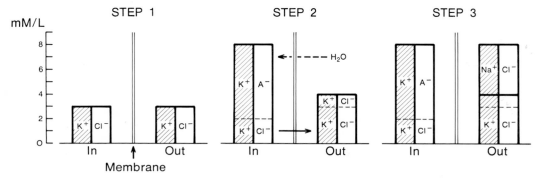

tinues until an equilibrium is reached that is defined by the following relation:

$$\frac{[K^+]_{OUT}}{[K^+]_{IN}} = \frac{[Cl^-]_{IN}}{[Cl^-]_{OUT}} \qquad (6.1)$$

In the example of Fig. 6.2, this occurs when the original concentrations of KCl (3 units on each side) are replaced by 2 units inside and 4 outside. Thus, the equation defining equilibrium changes from

$$\frac{3}{3} = \frac{3}{3}$$

in step ① to

$$\frac{4}{8} = \frac{2}{4}$$

in step ②.

This defines a *Donnan equilibrium*, with electroneutrality on both sides. However, the system is not in *osmotic equilibrium*, because of the excess of total electrolyte inside, which has the effect of drawing water into the cell to dilute the electrolyte. In model systems this excess water builds up a pressure that can be measured as *hydrostatic*, or *osmotic, pressure*. In plant cells, a certain amount of such pressure can be sustained without bursting the cell because the cell wall is reinforced with cellulose. While this is fine for the sedentary lives of plants, it is not well suited to the mobile, active lives of animals. Thus, in animals, osmotic equilibrium across the cell wall is achieved by making up the electrolyte deficit on the outside with NaCl (step ③). In order to ensure the exclusion of Na^+ from within the cell, the membrane is *relatively impermeable* to Na^+. The external Na^+, in effect, balances the osmotic effect of the internal organic anions. This is an economical strategy for a marine invertebrate cell, because of the abundance of NaCl in the surrounding sea. In terrestrial invertebrates and vertebrates, an internal sea has been created by preserving the approximate saline composition of the interstitial fluid (see Fig. 6.2 and Table 6.1).

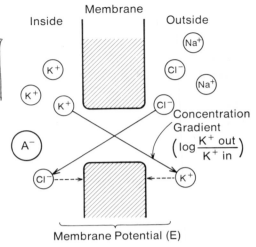

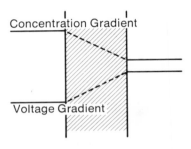

Fig. 6.4. Relations between electrical and chemical gradients across the membrane. (Modified from Woodbury, 1976)

The Nernst Potential

We have seen that ions diffuse through the membrane to achieve a balance of chemical forces, and now we can discuss how this gives rise to an electrical difference. In order to do this, we will delve a bit deeper into the nature of diffusion processes; the diagram of Fig. 6.4 serves as an intuitive guide to the following discussion.

When a substance diffuses in a solution, the force that moves the molecules from a region of high concentration to one of low concentration is a *chemical force*. We say that this force moves the molecules down their *concentration gradient*, like gravity makes marbles roll down an inclined plane. This can be described mathematically in several ways, for example, in terms of how fast the substance moves (called the *flux*), or how much *work* would be necessary to oppose the movement of the substance. If we consider our system of two regions separated by a membrane permeable to K^+, then the unequal concentrations of K^+ on either side mean that there is a force on K^+ that moves it *outward*, down its concentration gradient. In terms of the work (W_C) to oppose this chemical force, we have

$$W_c = 2.3\, RT \log\frac{[K^+]_{OUT}}{[K^+]_{IN}} \quad (6.2)$$

where R = gas constant (a measure of the energy of the substance), T = absolute temperature (a substance is more active as the temperature is raised), and the concentrations of K^+ inside and outside are in moles. For present purposes we will not worry about the units for these parameters, but only concern ourselves with gaining an intuitive grasp of the relations.

Now, as K^+ diffuses outward through the membrane, Cl^- is diffusing *inward*, down *its* concentration gradient (see again Fig. 6.3 as well as Fig. 6.4). This means there is a tendency for K^+ to become separated from its accompanying negative ion. However, since opposite charges attract, there is an *electrical force* tending to pull the K^+ back inside toward the inwardly diffusing Cl^- ions. The work (W_E) required to oppose this electrical force is given simply by

$$W_E = FE \quad (6.3)$$

where F = Faraday's constant (a measure of electrical charge per mole of substance) and E = electrical potential difference, due to the charge separation across the membrane, measured in volts.

When the system is at equilibrium, there will be no net movement of K+ or any other substance, and the chemical force tending to move K^+ out will be just balanced by the electrical force tending to move it in. The two forces are therefore

equal, and that means we can set equation 6.2 equal to equation 6.3, thus

$$W_E = W_C$$

$$FE = RT \log\frac{[K^+]_{OUT}}{[K^+]_{IN}}$$

$$E = 2.3\frac{RT}{F}\log\frac{[K^+]_{OUT}}{[K^+]_{IN}} \quad (6.4)$$

This is the *Nernst equation*, named for its discoverer, W. Nernst. We refer to (E) as the *Nernst potential*, or the *diffusion potential*. For the case of the squid axon at room temperature (18°C) the constant $2.3\, RT/F = 58$, and, for the concentration of K outside and inside, we have

$$E_K = 58 \log\frac{[K^+]_{OUT}}{[K^+]_{IN}}mV$$

$$= 58 \log\frac{10}{400}mV$$

$$= -75 \text{ mV}$$

If you learn only one equation in your study of neurobiology, the Nernst equation is the one to learn, because it is fundamental to the nature of electrical potentials in all cells, as well as the electrical activity in neurons. For any given ion species, E is the potential at which there is no net flux of ions across the membrane; it is therefore referred to as the *equilibrium potential* for that ion. In other words, it is the potential that the membrane tends toward when the membrane is permeable to that particular ion. Since the potential E exists across the cell membrane, it is called the *membrane potential*. When we take up the specific kinds of electrical activity that are associated with synapses and with impulses, we will see that they all take the form of changes in the membrane potential.

The Membrane Potential

Sir Arthur Eddington, the British astronomer, once remarked that "You cannot believe in astronomical observations before they are confirmed by theory." Much the same applies to the experiments we do in biology: we can only begin to believe in results if we have an adequate grasp of the theories that seek to explain the nature of the systems we study. That is why some of the theoretical basis of the membrane potential has been presented. With an understanding of how a membrane potential *might* arise, we are ready to set up an experiment that will tell us what in fact the membrane potential *is,* and how it fits with the theory.

The aim of this experiment will be to measure the electrical potential across a nerve membrane, using the giant axon of the squid as our test subject. All electrical measurements involve recording the difference between some quantities of electricity at two electrodes. In this case, one electrode is outside the axon, and the other is inside. The squid axon is so large (up to 1 mm in diameter) that the internal electrode can be a fine wire inserted longitudinally through a cut end. Generally,

however, a nerve cell is much smaller, and in order to insert the electrode through the membrane, one uses a microelectrode, fabricated especially for this purpose.

The method used for making a microelectrode for *intracellular* recording is to take a length of glass capillary or pipette tubing, heat it in the middle, and quickly pull it apart so that one obtains tips which are very fine but still open; they are called *micropipettes.* The first ones, made around 1950, were pulled by hand over a small Bunsen burner flame (it took a steady hand and eye to do it!), but machines (microelectrode pullers) were soon devised to make them automatically. A salt solution is placed in the tubing at the large end; if the tubing contains a fine glass thread, the solution will fill the pipette to the tip by capillary action (Fig. 6.5). The micropipette is now a microelectrode. When the pipette tip is inserted into the axon, the salt solution serves as an electrical conductor between the axoplasm at the tip and a wire in the large end, connected to a suitable electronic amplifier and recorder.

Fig. 6.5. The micropipette, used for intracellular recording, stimulation, and injection. The diagram on the right shows the arrangement for recording from a squid axon, and observing potentials on a cathode ray oscilloscope (CRO).

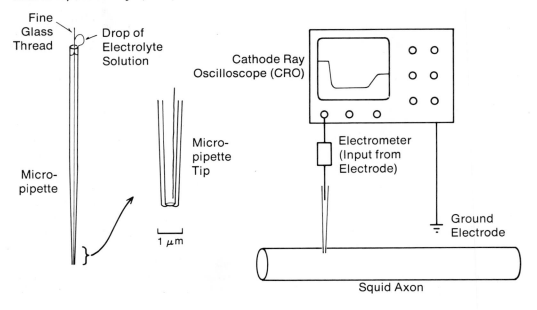

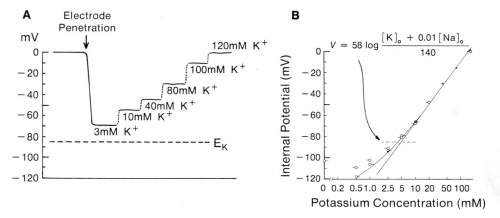

Fig. 6.6. A. The resting membrane potential and its dependence on K$^+$ outside the membrane. **B.** Graph of results (open circles), and comparison with theoretical curves. (From Hodgkin and Horowicz, 1971)

The most convenient recorder is a *cathode ray oscilloscope*. The cathode ray tube is constructed on the same principle as a television tube, except that it has only a single beam that travels across the screen, to register electrical changes at different speeds and at different amplifications (see Fig. 6.5).

When both electrodes are outside the nerve there is naturally no signal registered on the oscilloscope (the beam just keeps moving across and being reset at the same level). However, when the pipette tip is delicately pushed through the axonal membrane (sometimes a gentle tap on the table will help), the oscilloscope beam is abruptly deflected in a direction that indicates that the pipette tip has become electrically *negative* relative to the outside electrode (this occurs at the arrow shown in Fig. 6.6A). If it is a "good" penetration, the membrane seals around the pipette, and, if nobody trips over a cord in the dark or slams a door (!), the recording may be stable for many minutes or even hours.

Under these conditions, the stable negative potential that is recorded is the *resting membrane potential;* we assume that all the potential difference between the two electrodes is due to the potential difference across the membrane. The value of the resting membrane potential in a typi-

cal experiment is in the range of −60 to −70 mV. Because of this internal negativity, we say that the membrane has a negative polarity. If the membrane potential moves toward zero we say that it becomes *depolarized;* if it increases above the resting value we say it becomes *hyperpolarized.* The significance of such changes in polarization will soon become apparent.

The recorded membrane potential is close to the value predicted by the Nernst equation for potassium but it is not exactly the same. To test further the correspondence between theory and experiment, the concentration of [K$^+$]$_{OUT}$ in the bathing medium can be varied and the effects on the membrane potential observed. This is illustrated in Fig. 6.6A. As [K$^+$]$_{OUT}$ increases, the concentration gradient across the membrane decreases, as does the membrane potential; the membrane thus becomes progressively depolarized. The results are plotted in B and compared with those expected from the Nernst equation. It can be seen that there is a good fit for higher potassium concentrations, but the experimental curve deviates from the theoretical one at low concentrations, the prevailing situation under natural conditions.

These experiments suggest that normally the membrane potential reflects the presence of other ions besides K^+, and indeed, in our discussion of the Donnan equilibrium, we assumed that the membrane is also slightly permeable to both Cl^- and Na^+. We can calculate individual Nernst potentials for these ions as well; for Na, we have

$$E_{Na} = 58 \log\frac{[Na^+]_{OUT}}{[Na^+]_{IN}} \qquad (6.5)$$

$$= 58 \log\frac{460}{50}$$

$$= +55 \text{ mV}$$

Thus, the equilibrium potential for Na^+ has a polarity opposite to that for K^+, in accord with their opposing concentration gradients (see Fig. 6.2). If the permeability of the membrane for Na^+ were equal to that for K^+, then the two equilibrium potentials would tend to cancel each other out, and the membrane potential would be near zero. However, the permeability to Na^+ has been shown to be only about 1/25 of that of K^+, so that the effect of Na^+ is to decrease (depolarize) only slightly the membrane potential from the K^+ equilibrium potential.

The combined effects on the membrane potential of more than one ionic species can be expressed in a single large equation as follows

$$V_m =$$

$$58 \log\frac{P_K[K^+]_{OUT} + P_{Na}[Na^+]_{OUT} + P_{Cl}[Cl^-]_{IN}}{P_K[K^+]_{IN} + P_{Na}[Na^+]_{IN} + P_{Cl}[Cl^-]_{OUT}}$$

$$(6.6)$$

in which V_m = membrane potential and P = relative membrane permability. This equation was derived by David Goldman of Bethesda in 1943. One of the premises on which it is based is that the potential gradient, or electrical field, within the membrane is constant; hence it is referred to as the *constant-field equation*. It lets us take account of the contribution of any

ionic gradient to the membrane potential by simply weighting its effect in accord with the permeability.

For present purposes we neglect the contribution of Cl^- (its equilibrium potential is very close to that of K^+) and focus on the effect of Na^+. Using the weighting factor of $1/25 = 0.04$ for P_{Na} (and neglecting Cl^-), Eq. 6.5 yields a value of -60 mV for V_m, and the curve for different values of $(K^+)_{OUT}$ now falls very closely on the curve obtained from the experimental data (Fig. 6.6B).

We thus have a reasonable explanation for the membrane potential, and we would like to have a convenient way to represent it. Representing the various factors with diagrams is cumbersome, and carrying around equations in one's head is too abstract. The most convenient form is an electrical analogue, or model, as shown in Fig. 6.7. This little electrical circuit represents the membrane, or more correctly, a membrane site. Each equilibrium potential is represented by a *battery* across the membrane, which has the appropriate polarity and voltage (E) for that ion. In series with the battery is a *resistance* (R) which is related to the membrane permeability for that ion. The relation is a bit indirect. First, what we are really interested in is the *conductance*, which is the reciprocal of the resistance ($R = 1/G$). Second, electrical conductance (G) is related to membrane permeability (P) as follows (using K^+ as the ion in question):

$$G_K \propto P_K \frac{[K^+]_{OUT}}{[K^+]_{IN}} \qquad (6.7)$$

Thus, theoretically the membrane could be quite permeable to K^+, but if there are no K^+ ions outside, the conductance would be zero (there would be no ions to carry the current through the permeability channels). Under physiological conditions, however, Eq. (6.7) is a reasonable approximation.

The "channels" for each ionic species are separate and independent, as shown in

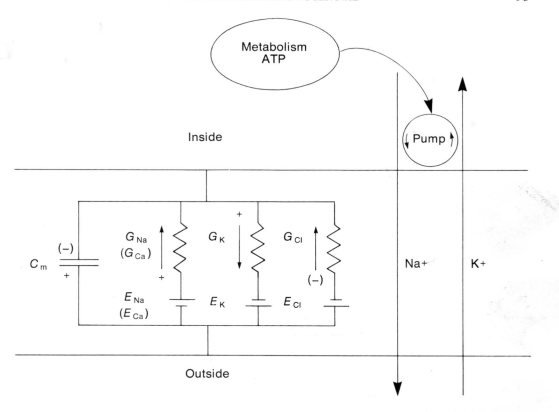

Fig. 6.7. Equivalent electrical circuit for the electrical properties of the nerve membrane.

Fig. 6.7. In addition, the lipids of the membrane impart an electrical *capacitance* (C) to it; that is, they are poor conductors, and are able to store electrical charges on either side of the membrane. In fact, the membrane potential we record, representing the algebraic sum of the ionic batteries, is the potential due to the separation and storage of charge across the membrane capacitance (C), as illustrated in the circuit of Fig. 6.7. When changes in the membrane potential occur slowly, we can neglect the effects of the storage of charge across the capacitance, but when changes are rapid, the time course over which the capacitance charges or discharges is a very important factor in shaping the signals. We will see later how this comes about during synaptic and impulse activity.

The Membrane Potential and Metabolism

The fact that we can account for our experimental recording as a combination of diffusion potentials does not mean the end of our interest in the nature of the membrane potential. In many ways it is only the beginning. In our theoretical discussion we simply assumed a high concentration of K^+ inside the cell to begin with. But during life, the cell is supplied with nutrients and substances through the blood and interstitial fluid, where the K^+ concentration is, as we have seen, very low. How does the cell actually obtain K^+, and replenish the small amounts that are continually lost by leakage due to outward diffusion through the permeability channels? It cannot be by passive diffusion, be-

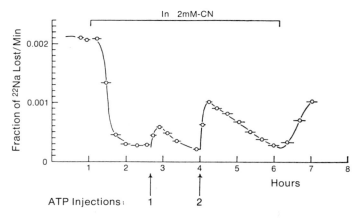

Fig. 6.8. Efflux of radioactively labeled Na$^+$ from a squid axon, its suppression by a metabolic poison (cyanide, CN), and its dependence on ATP. (From Caldwell et al., 1960)

cause the concentration gradient is only in the direction of *outward* diffusion. A similar problem concerns Na$^+$; how does the cell prevent a buildup of Na$^+$ at rest, and particularly as a consequence of impulse activity (see next chapter). And, in the face of these ion movements, how does the cell maintain osmotic equilibrium, so that it does not swell up and burst?

From these considerations it is clear that the cell is more than a mere bag of salt solution. The cell must contain metabolic mechanisms that can maintain and adjust ion concentrations under resting as well as changing conditions, and against ion concentration gradients. More specifically, there must be mechanisms in or at the membrane to pump ions across the membrane against their concentration gradients, and a source of energy in the cell to keep the pumps going. The process of moving substances in this way is called *active transport,* and the mechanism for doing it is called a *metabolic pump.* There is an obvious analogy with the raising of well-water by a good old-fashioned barnyard pump, worked by an energetic farm kid.

The first step in identifying this mechanism was to show that ion transport across the membrane requires energy. This was revealed in experiments on the squid giant axon, in which the rate of efflux of radioactive Na$^+$ was measured. Under resting conditions the rate is relatively low, but it can be raised by stimulating the axon repetitively, which loads the axon because of Na$^+$ influx during the impulse (see next chapter). Following such stimulation, the rate of Na$^+$ efflux is relatively high (see Fig. 6.8). The efflux is blocked when the axon is poisoned with cyanide, a well-known metabolic inhibitor. Injection of ATP partially restores the efflux (see Fig. 6.8), suggesting that the energy supply comes through ATP.

Direct evidence has subsequently been obtained that the membrane pump produces an actual current flow across the membrane. Such currents are called *membrane currents.* In order to demonstrate them, electrophysiologists use a method called a *voltage clamp.* An elegant experiment demonstrating pump currents with the voltage clamp was carried out by Roger Thomas of England in 1968. He used a giant cell of the snail *Helix,* in which four electrodes (one a double-barreled electrode) could be inserted. The arrangement is shown in Fig. 6.9. Electrode ① was used to measure the membrane potential. Electrode ② was used to "clamp" the membrane potential at a preset value and record the current necessary to hold it at that value. Electrode ③ was used to inject Na⁺ into the cell, and electrode ④ was used to complete the circuit, by injecting K⁺, so that this current would not cross the membrane. Electrode ⑤ was an ion-sensitive electrode that monitored the Na⁺ concentration in the cell. The results in Fig. 6.9 showed that when Na⁺ was injected, it was necessary to pass an inward current to hold the membrane potential "clamped". This implied that there was an equal and opposite outward current associated with the raised Na⁺ concentration, due to the action of the pump. The net current flow represented movement of only about one-third of the injected Na ions, implying that the pump ejects three Na ions for every two K ions that enter the cell.

The general conceptual model that has emerged to explain the pumping of ions across the membrane is illustrated in Fig. 6.10. As can be seen, there are three basic steps involved. First, the ion *combines* with a *carrier* molecule to form a *carrier–ion complex.* Next, the complex moves or *transfers* the charge across the membrane.

Finally, the ion is *released* on the other side of the membrane. In parallel are similar steps that move ions in the opposite direction. The most studied system is the one that moves both Na⁺ and K⁺ ions across the membrane against their respective concentration gradients. The energy supply for these movements comes from the splitting of ATP by an ATPase. This enzyme is referred to as *Na⁺, K⁺ activated ATPase.* Studies have shown that this enzyme in fact also acts as the ion carrier. It is a large, membrane-bound enzyme, with two polypeptide components (M. W. 100,000 daltons each), which extend across the membrane, with smaller glycoprotein chains anchored on the outside. There is preferential binding of Na⁺ and ATP on the inside of the membrane, whereas K⁺ and various glycoside inhibitors bind to the outside (see Fig. 6.10). This gives the normal orientation of ion transport, although reverse movements of these ions can take place if the concentration gradients across the membrane are sufficiently reversed.

A metabolic pump, such as the one

Fig. 6.9. Experimental set up for carrying out voltage-clamp experiments in a snail neuron. Recordings to the right show **(A)** "clamped" membrane potential, recorded by (1); **(B)** injected Na⁺, recorded by (5); and **(C)** the current due to the Na⁺ pump, rewarded by (2). See Chap. 7 for further details of voltage-clamp method. (Modified from Thomas, 1972)

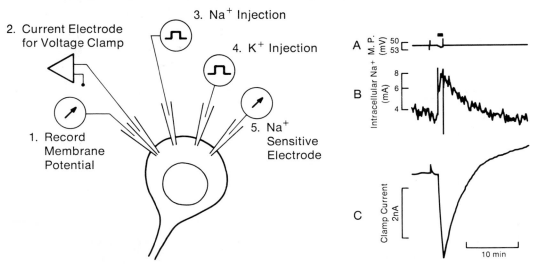

shown in Fig. 6.10, that exchanges one Na for one K, maintains the passive gradients of ions but makes no other contribution to the membrane potential. However, if the ratio of exchange is not 1:1, the pump makes its own additional contribution to the membrane potential. Such pumps are called *electrogenic*. In the cell illustrated in Fig. 6.9, the pump is electrogenic, because the ratio of Na:K movements is 3:2. In this cell, the pump is normally activated only after impulse activity. However, there are by now many examples of cells in which an electrogenic pump contributes to the normal resting potential. Most of these experiments have been carried out in the large cells of invertebrate species, such as molluscs. In addition to pumps for Na^+ and K^+, pumps for moving Ca^{2+} and Cl^- have been identified and characterized. The role of Ca^{2+} in the cell is a very important one, and we will discuss this further in the next chapters.

In this discussion we have focused on one possible mechanism for carrier-mediated transport of ions. It is important to bear in mind that this is only one of the many ways that substances can move across a membrane. Figure 6.11 summarizes some of the main categories of transport mechanisms that have been identified in biological membranes. Beginning at the left are the simplest cases, of ① passive diffusion of ions and ② simple bulk flow. Next is carrier-mediated passive diffusion, in one direction ③ or in both directions ④. A very common passive mechanism is the linking of one substance to another; thus ⑤ sugars and amino acids are co-transported along with Na^+ down its concentration gradient in many cells. Finally, we have the systems requiring energy. These include the active pump just discussed ⑥, driven by high-energy phosphate, and the proton pump ⑦, driven by respiratory enzymes, that is present in the inner membrane of the mitochondrion, as discussed in Chap. 4. While these mechanisms are all present in biological membranes, most of them have also been dem-

Fig. 6.10. Schematic representation of active transport of ions across the cell membrane. (After Stein, 1980)

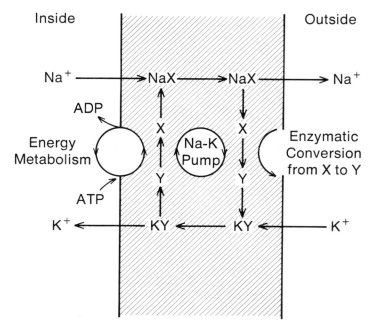

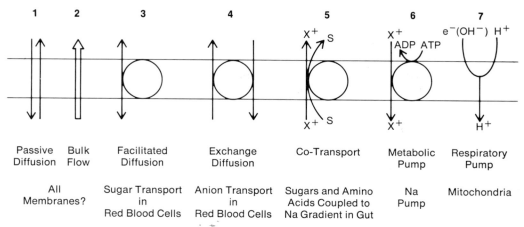

Fig. 6.11. Main categories of transport mechanisms in biological membranes. (Diagram adapted from C. L. Slayman)

onstrated in artificial membranes composed of various organic substances. This has provided a powerful tool for experimental analysis, and has suggested that transport phenomena are to a large extent inherent in the properties of organic molecules and macromolecular complexes, when arranged in monolayers or very thin membranes.

In conclusion, both passive and active properties contribute to the membrane potential. These properties are present in different combinations in different cells. As a reflection of this, it is being recognized that the membrane potential does not have the same value in all neurons, nor do neurons respond in the same ways to changes brought about by activity. In some cells or fibers the membrane potential may have a relatively high value, around −80 mV inside negative. In other cells, the value may be lower, as low as −40 mV. A low value is found, for example, in vertebrate retinal receptor cells, where it is associated with a large resting leak of Na ions (see Chap. 17). The metabolic mechanisms for active transport are *temperature dependent*, which means that their contribution to the membrane potential in poikilothermic animals will vary according to temperature changes during the day, or in different seasons. The amount of pumping will also depend on the *size* of a nerve process. The smaller the process, the higher the surface-to-volume ratio, and the higher the rate of pumping activity required to maintain internal concentrations. Thus, the membrane potential, even at rest, is a very important variable for the different functions of nerve cells.

REFERENCES

Aidley, D. J. 1978. *The Physiology of Excitable Cells.* Cambridge: Cambridge University Press.

Caldwell, P. C., A. L. Hodgkin, R. D. Keynes, and T. I. Shaw. 1960. The effects of injecting "energy-rich" compounds on the active transport of ions in the giant axons of *Loligo. J. Physiol. 152: 561–590.*

Hodgkin, A. L. and P. Horowicz. 1959. The influence of potassium and chloride ions on the membrane potential of single muscle fibers. *J. Physiol. 148: 127–160.*

Stein, R. B. 1980. *Nerve and Muscle. Membranes, Cells and Systems.* New York: Plenum.

Thomas, R. C. 1972. Electrogenic sodium pump in nerve and muscle cells. *Physiol. Rev. 52: 563–594.*

Woodbury, J. W. 1965. The cell membrane: ionic and potential gradients and active transport. In *Physiology and Biophysics* (ed. by T. C. Ruch and H. D. Patton). Philadelphia: Saunders. pp. 1–25.

Additional Reading

Devoe, R. D. and P. C. Maloney. 1980. Principles of cell homeostasis. In *Medical Physiology,* Vol. 1 (ed. by V. B. Mountcastle). St. Louis: C. V. Mosby. pp. 3–45.

Hubbard, J. I., R. Llinas, and D. M. J. Quastel. 1969. *Electrophysiological Analysis of Synaptic Transmission.* Baltimore: William & Wilkins.

Katz, B. 1962. The transmission of impulses from nerve to muscle, and the subcellular unit of synaptic action. *Proc. Roy. Soc. B 1955:* 455–477.

Katz, B. 1966. *Nerve, Muscle and Synapse.* New York: McGraw-Hill.

Siegel, G. L., W. L. Stahl, and P. D. Swanson. 1981. Ion Transport. In Siegel et al. (1981)[Chap. 4].

7

The Action Potential

The earliest ideas about the nature of the signals in the nervous system, going back to the Greeks, involved notions that the brain secretes fluids or "spirits" that flow through the nerves to the muscles. However, a new era opened in 1791 when Luigi Galvani of Bologna showed that frog muscles can be stimulated by electricity. His postulate of the existence of "animal electricity" in nerves and muscles soon led to a focus of attention almost exclusively on electrical mechanisms in nerve signaling.

In the 1840's, Galvani's countryman, Carlo Matteuci, who also had a distinguished career in Italian government, obtained the first evidence for the electrical nature of the nerve impulse. This was soon followed up and put on a sound and systematic basis by the extensive studies of Emil du Bois Reymond of Berlin. In 1850, Reymond's colleague, Herman von Helmholtz, later to be the famous physicist, was able to measure the speed of conduction of the nerve impulse, and showed for the first time that, though fast, it is not all *that* fast. In the large nerves of the frog, it is about 40 meters per second, which is about 40 miles per hour. This was another landmark finding, for it showed that the mechanism of the nerve impulse has to involve something more than merely the physical passage of electricity as through a wire; it has to involve an *active biological process*. The impulse therefore came to be called the *action potential*.

The electrical nature of the nerve impulse and its finite speed of conduction were important discoveries for physiology in general, and indeed for all science, because they constituted the first direct evidence for the kind of activity present in the nervous system. It appeared that, just as the heart pumps blood and the kidney makes urine, so now one could say that the nervous system does its work by producing impulses. In addition, the fact that the impulse moves at a finite speed had tremendous implications for psychology, for it seemed to separate the mind from the actions that the mind wills—in effect, it provided a basis for separating mind from body. It therefore was one of the stepping stones toward development of modern psychology and the study of behavior, as well as contributing to the debate on the nature of the mind and the body.

Excitability as a General Cellular Property

The ability of a nerve to respond to an electrical shock with an impulse is a property referred to as *excitation,* and we say that the nerve is *excitable.* In the early experiments there were no instruments that could record the impulse directly; it could only be detected by the fact that, if a nerve was connected to its muscle, the shock was followed (after a brief period for conduction in the nerve) by a twitch of the muscle. The brief nature of the twitch indicated that an impulse must also occur in the muscle, so that the muscle was also recognized as having the property of excitability.

Ever since these early experiments, the impulse has been regarded as the characteristic functional property of the nerve cell. It has been assumed that this property of peripheral nerves can be generalized to all nerve cells within the brain. This has led to two common beliefs: first, that the nerve cell can be defined as a cell that generates impulses, and second, that impulses are the only means by which nerve cells communicate with each other. These beliefs survive even today.

The idea that nerve cells communicate only through impulses was perhaps natural—after all, it is the only means by which signals can travel rapidly over a long stretch of peripheral nerve. It therefore seems reasonable to suppose that rapid signaling over long pathways within the brain similarly depends on impulses. However, much of the communication within brain regions takes place over short distances, and in these cases the electrotonic spread of synaptic potentials within nerve cells can be sufficient, without need of action potentials. We will describe this type of signaling in the next chapter. For present purposes we simply note that many nerve cells are able to carry out nervous functions without generating action potentials.

A second reason for doubting that the impulse is the one defining property of the neuron is that the neuron is not the only kind of cell that can generate impulses. As mentioned above, skeletal muscle was recognized to have this property, and so was cardiac muscle. As so often happens in science, these were easily regarded as exceptions to the rule. However, it was soon found that they were not the only exceptions; in the 1870's John Burdon-Sanderson, one of the leading British physiologists, showed that, when a venus fly-trap is touched by an insect (or by an experimenter), impulses can be recorded in association with the rapid closing of its leaves around the prey. This experiment showed that the impulse is not exclusive to nerve cells, or even to the Animal Kingdom.

These results have been confirmed and amplified in recent years, particularly since the advent of the microelectrode and the development of techniques to record intracellularly from a variety of organisms. The surprising finding has been that many very different kinds of cells show the ability to generate impulses. Some examples are illustrated in Fig. 7.1. In the giant cells of the fungus *Neurospora* (A), impulses are very slow, lasting over 1 minute. By comparison, a number of higher plants have cells that generate impulses in bursts (B); these cells are found especially in long-stemmed plants like peas and pumpkins, where they appear to be involved in pumping sap through the vasculature. In single-cell organisms like the *Paramecium* (C), impulses are involved in sensory responses as well as in the control of ciliary movement.

Within the Animal Kingdom, a number of studies have shown that oocytes of many species respond to an electric shock with an impulse; the example in (D) is from a primitive chordate (*Tunicata*), and similar findings have been reported in invertebrates (for example, the oocyte of annelid worms) and in higher vertebrates (for example, the rat). Impulses have also been recorded in the skin of tadpoles (E).

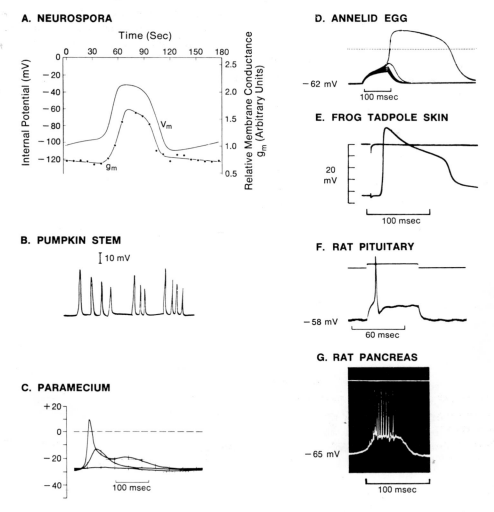

Fig. 7.1. Action potentials in different types of non-nervous cells. (Diagram A from Slayman et al., B from Sinyuhkin and Gorchakov, C from Eckert et al., D from Hagiwara and Miyazaki, E from Roberts and Stirling, F from Douglas and Taraskevich, G from Dean et al.) (From Shepherd, 1981)

In mammals, a number of types of gland cells have been found to generate impulses; two examples are the cells of the pituitary that secrete pituitary hormones (F) and the islet cells of the pancreas that secrete insulin (G).

These examples by no means exhaust the list; one might mention, for instance, the finding of impulses in certain kinds of cancer cells. However, they are sufficient to indicate that impulse generation is a property that is present in a wide variety of cells throughout the plant and animal kingdoms. This is a good illustration of why it is important to take a broad cellular approach to the functions of nerve cells. In line with that approach, we would say that *excitability*—the ability to generate impulses—*is a general cellular property that is expressed to a greater or lesser extent in many different cells, depending on their particular functions.*

In later chapters we will study the function of the impulse in embryonic cells (Chap. 10), in gland cells (Chap. 19), and in muscle cells (Chap. 18). In this chapter

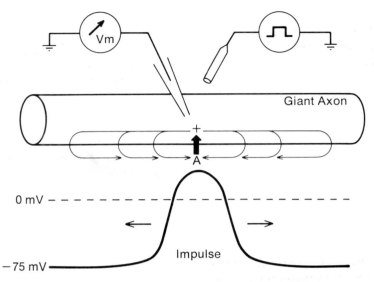

Fig. 7.2. The impulse in the squid axon. The impulse has been triggered by a brief depolarization at (A). Note that the impulse has the ability to spread in both directions when elicited experimentally in the middle of a nerve.

our focus is on the impulse in nerve cells.

From the foregoing considerations an important general concept emerges that sets the stage for our study. If the impulse is a basic cellular property that may be present or absent in different types of cells, the same variation undoubtedly applies to nerve cells; excitability may be present or absent in different nerve cells or different parts of a nerve cell. Our task therefore is to study the basic principles of the impulse mechanism from the perspective of the variety of contributions that excitability may make to the functions of nerve cells and the building of nervous systems.

Analysis of the Excitation Mechanism: the Hodgkin-Huxley Model

There are several essential facts about the impulse in nerve (or in any other cell, for that matter) that we start with in analyzing the underlying mechanism. First, the action potential is a *membrane event;* it consists of a transient change in the *membrane potential.* This was already suspected in the nineteenth century, and it has been elegantly demonstrated recently in

squid axons, which conduct impulses even though all the axoplasm has been squeezed out.

The second important fact about the action potential is that it consists of a transient *depolarization* of the membrane potential. This had also been suggested by the experiments of the nineteenth century, but direct demonstration was only obtained with intracellular recordings from the squid axon. The basic experimental setup for recording the membrane potential in the squid axon has been described in Chap. 6 (see Fig. 6.6), and the similar arrangement for recording the impulse is shown in Fig. 7.2. The earliest results, by K. C. Cole and D. R. Curtis at Rockefeller in 1939, showed that not only does the membrane depolarize (in other words, become less negative inside), but it passes zero and actually becomes almost 50 mV positive inside at the peak of the action potential.

What can account for this finding? It cannot be simply a transient breakdown in permeability to allow all ions to move across the membrane, because that would only depolarize the membrane to zero, not beyond. The clue is provided by a third key fact, that in squid axons the action potential depends on the presence of *sodium ions* in the external medium. If they are removed, the action potential is reduced in amplitude, as illustrated by the recordings and the graph in Fig. 7.3. It may be remembered that changing sodium has very little effect on the resting membrane potential, in accord with its low permeability relative to potassium in the resting membrane (see Fig. 6.6). The results of Fig. 7.3 indicate that, in contrast, the sodium permeability, and hence the sodium conductance, is very high at the peak of the action potential.

These three basic facts thus suggest that the action potential in the squid axon involves a transient increase in the conductance of the membrane for sodium, providing for an inward rush of positively charged Na ions down their concentration gradient. This reduces the charge difference across the membrane and actually reverses it, as the membrane potential tends toward the sodium equilibrium potential of about 55 mV positive inside. We next want to know the time course of the ionic conductance change and current flow

across the membrane, and we want to know also if any other ions might be involved. To do this we must set the membrane potential at different levels and determine how the ionic currents vary. This requires a technique for achieving a *space clamp* of the membrane, so that the impulse is held stationary over a length of the axon, together with a *voltage clamp* of that membrane, which enables the membrane potential to be set and held at a particular value and the response of the membrane measured in terms of the transmembrane current. The basic setup is illustrated in Fig. 7.4A, and the principles of measuring the ionic currents are illustrated and explained in B–D.

This method was applied by Alan Hodgkin and Andrew Huxley of Cambridge University in a famous series of experiments that was published in 1952. The way they went about the analysis is indicated in Fig. 7.5. They set the membrane potential at different levels and recorded the membrane currents during voltage clamping; as shown in a, the currents consisted of an early inward phase and a later outward phase. They then repeated the experiments while replacing the Na in

Fig. 7.3. Dependence of the action potential on Na ions. **A.** Impulse in normal (100%) seawater, and reduction in amplitude of impulse when external Na⁺ is reduced to one-third normal concentration. **B.** Graph of effect of different external [Na⁺] on action potential amplitude. (From Hodgkin and Katz, 1949)

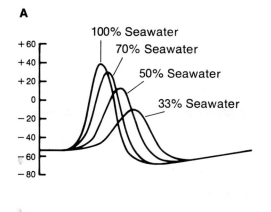

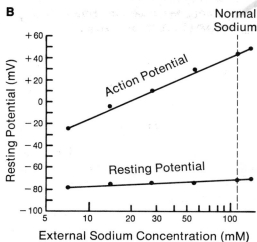

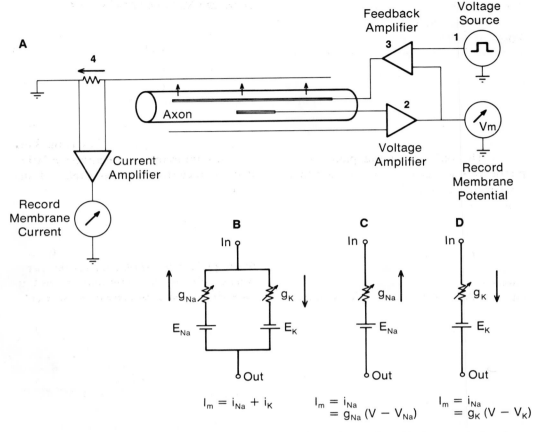

Fig. 7.4. A. Experimental setup for space-clamp and voltage-clamp of squid giant axon. A voltage source ① sets the membrane at a given level, which is recorded by an amplifier ②. This amplifier is connected to a feedback amplifier ③, that feeds back current across the membrane that just balances off the ionic current induced by the imposed voltage. The current is measured across a resistance ④. (After Kandel, 1976) B–D. Simplified equivalent circuits for flow of ionic currents under conditions of space and voltage clamp. (Modified from Hubbard et al., 1969)

the external medium. This produced recordings, as Fig. 7.3b, consisting of only a later outward phase, which increased in amplitude as the membrane was set at more depolarized levels. They postulated and confirmed that this component of the current is carried by K^+; the current is stronger the further the membrane is depolarized away from the K^+ equilibrium potential. When this component was subtracted from the control recording, they obtained an early component, as in Fig. 7.5c; this began to appear with small depolarizations, was largest at around zero

potential, and reversed to an opposite polarity around +55 mV. This is what would be expected if this component was carried by Na^+, driven by the Na^+ equilibrium potential of around +55 mV.

Subsequent experiments using poisons that selectively block Na^+ and K^+ conductances have confirmed these basic results. As shown in Fig. 7.5B, when K^+ conductance is blocked by adding tetraethylammonium (TEA) to the external medium, only the early, Na^+ component remains. When, on the other hand, the Na^+ conductance is blocked, by adding tetrodotoxin (TTX), a poison found in the ovary of the puffer fish, only the late, K^+ component is present.

From measurements of ionic currents, Hodgkin and Huxley were able to obtain the Na^+ and K^+ conductances by the application of Ohm's law to the reduced circuits for the membrane, as illustrated in Fig. 7.4. They then derived equations that describe the turning on of these conductances. The only remaining piece of the puzzle was to account for the fact that, after rising rapidly, the Na^+ conductance quickly falls. This was described by a process of Na inactivation; in subsequent experiments it has been possible to block this selectively by application of the enzyme pronase within the axon.

The interrelations between these three factors—*Na^+ conductance, K^+ conduct-* *ance, and Na^+ inactivation*—are shown in Fig. 7.6. This figure also brings out a crucial property of the Na conductance, which is that it is involved in a positive feedback relation with the membrane depolarization. When the membrane begins to be depolarized, it causes the Na^+ conductance to begin to increase, which depolarizes the membrane further, which increases Na^+ conductance, and so on. This is the kind of self-reinforcing, *regenerative* relation that characterizes various kinds of devices—for example, a similar relation between heat and chemical reaction underlies the explosion of gunpowder. One can say that it is the property that puts the "action" in the action potential! It gives the impulse a *threshold*, makes the nerve briefly *refactory* to restimulation, and allows the impulse to propagate at a *con-*

Fig. 7.5. **A.** Response of the membrane under voltage clamp to a depolarization of 60 mV. a. Response in normal seawater. b. Response due to potassium current (I_K) when extracellular Na^+ is replaced by choline. c. Calculated response due to Na^+ current ($I_{Na} = I_{total} - I_K$). (From Hodgkin and Huxley, 1952). **B.** Separation of ionic currents using nerve poisons. a. Normal response. b. Response due to I_K when I_{Na} is blocked by tetrodotoxin (TTX). c. Response due to I_{Na} when I_K is blocked by tetraethylammonium (TEA). (From Hille, 1976)

A. ION REPLACEMENT

B. PHARMACOLOGICAL BLOCKAGE

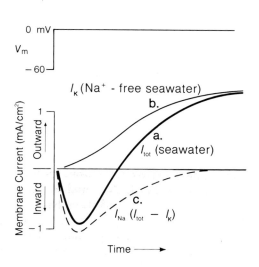

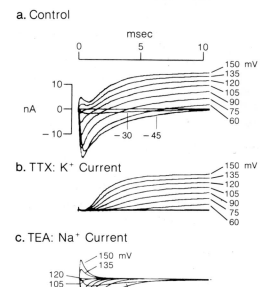

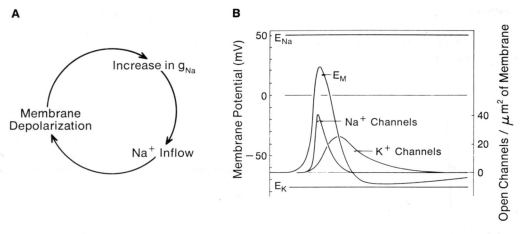

Fig. 7.6. A. Regenerative relation between membrane depolarization, increase in Na⁺ permeability and conductance, and Na⁺ current. **B.** Reconstruction of changes in ionic conductance underlying the action potential according to the Hodgkin-Huxley model. (From Hodgkin and Huxley, in Hille, 1981)

stant amplitude for long distances, properties that we will discuss further in later sections. This nonlinear, regenerative behavior, in which the Na⁺ and K⁺ conductances occur in *sequence,* rather than simultaneously, are the key ways in which the mechanism of the action potential differs from the mechanism of the synaptic potential.

Based on their analysis of the experimental results, Hodgkin and Huxley were able to finish their study by deriving equations for the variables controlling the conductances, and, using these equations, construct a model that reproduced the action potential. As implied in Fig. 7.6B, the fit of experiment and theory is very close. We will not have space to go into details of the model; there are many excellent accounts of it, as noted in the references. It will be sufficient to note that the Hodgkin-Huxley model of the nerve impulse is a consummate matching of experiment and theory, and is one of the great achievements of modern neurobiology and, indeed, of modern science. Its importance for neurobiology in general, and the study of membrane mechanisms in nerve cells in particular, cannot be over-

emphasized; it has been the solid touchstone for all subsequent research.

Molecular Mechanisms of Excitation

One of the attributes of a good theory is that it postulates specific properties that can be tested experimentally, and in this respect the Hodgkin-Huxley model has been very fruitful indeed. We will briefly discuss some of the insights that subsequent work has given into the molecular mechanisms of the membrane.

Channel Properties. A key question raised by the Hodgkin-Huxley model is the nature of the membrane mechanism that controls the changes in ionic conductances. Hodgkin and Huxley conceived of the conductances in terms of hypothetical "channels", which permit free movement of a given ion across the membrane down the concentration gradient for that ion. Most workers in this field believe in these channels as physical realities, actual pores in the membrane. Many indirect lines of evidence support this idea, but the postulated diameter of 3–5 Å puts them at the limit of the resolving power of even the most powerful present-day electron microscope; there is as yet no direct proof of their existence. Nonetheless, it is a rich field for speculation. It is theorized, for example, that the sodium channel opens into a funnel-shaped widening in the membrane, and that there are molecular "gates" which control the opening (activation) and closing (inactivation) of the Na⁺ channel. These properties are indicated in the diagrams of Fig. 7.7A. It is further speculated that the channel itself is lined with six negatively charged oxygen atoms, that remove the water shell from the Na ion to allow it to pass through the channel. The diameter of the channel is critical for the selectivity of the channel for Na⁺; other ions, such as calcium or lithium, may or may not be able to pass through the Na⁺ channel, depending on these factors. Various drugs, poisons, and other substances have their actions at specific sites or components of the channel structure, as indicated in Fig. 7.7B.

Gating Currents. In their model, Hodgkin and Huxley pointed out that the gates that control the sodium channel would most likely have an electrical axis (dipole) associated with them, and that any change in their orientation should produce its own contribution to the potential across the membrane. The changes are so tiny that they remained undetected until the early 1970's, when electronic methods for summing and averaging thousands of repeated tests and responses finally revealed them. The changes are called *"gating currents"*, and are currently under investigation for the information they can give about the properties of the gating molecules and their relation to the conductance channels (see Fig. 7.7A).

Artificial Membranes. One might be tempted to think of excitability as a special property of biological membranes, but recent work has shown that it is also present in artificial membranes. In these stud-

ies, a membrane is formed of lipid bilayers, and is treated with a substance such as amphotericin. When a voltage is applied across the membrane, the potential across it begins to oscillate in an all-or-nothing manner. It is believed that the applied voltage induces channels and gating particles to form in the membrane, as shown in Fig. 7.7C. An interesting aspect of this work is that there may be partial formation of channels, so that the excitability may not be complete (see diagram). This is one way in which nerve cells might also show partially excitable properties during development or in different parts of the neuron.

Channel Densities and Local Excitability. Using the fact that the nerve poison tetrodotoxin (TTX) selectively blocks Na⁺ channels, studies have been carried out to determine the amount of binding of radioactively labeled TTX (and related poisons) to nerve fibers, in order to obtain an estimate of the density of Na⁺ channels per area of membrane. Studies of this type have revealed that the density varies considerably in different neurons, and in different parts of the neuron. Table 7.1 summarizes some results, together with estimates for related properties such as pumping sites and receptors. The extremely high density of Na⁺ channels in the node of Ranvier presumably reflects the specialization of this small patch of membrane for generation of the action potential during saltatory conduction (see below). The differences among the nerves shown may reflect in part their differing sizes; for example, olfactory nerves are among the thinnest fibers in the nervous system (diameter 0.2μm), with correspondingly very high surface-to-volume ratio.

These studies make it clear that the density of voltage-dependent ion channels varies widely, as an expression of the functional specialization of the nerve membrane. Local regions of a neuron may thus have different excitable properties, an

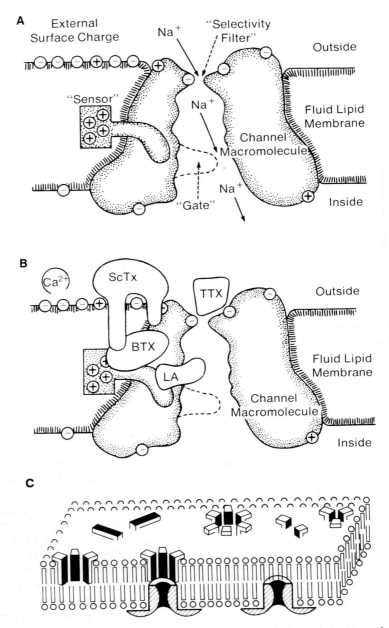

Fig. 7.7. Schematic representation of a Na⁺ channel. **A.** Normal channel. **B.** Sites of action of different agents. TTX: tetrodotoxin; ScTx: scorpion and anemone toxin; BTX: batrachotoxin; LA: local anesthetics; Ca^{2+}: calcium ions screening negative charge on membrane surface. (From Hille, 1981). **C.** Excitable channels in an artificial lipid bilayer. The molecules forming the gating parts of the ionic channel are in the upper half of the bilayer, and link up with the ion-selector molecules of the lower half to permit ions to pass through the channel. The channels of the lower half are formed by treatment with such substances as amphotericin; the gating molecules aggregate and insert through the membrane as shown, under the influence of the membrane potential. (From Mueller, 1979)

Table 7.1 Densities per μm^2 of Na^+ channels and other sites in nerve membranes

Sodium channels	
Garfish olfactory nerves	1–35
Squid giant axon	100–600
Rabbit vagus nerve	100
Rabbit myelinated nodes of Ranvier	12,000
Sodium pumping sites	
Garfish olfactory nerve	300
Rabbit vagus nerve	750
Receptor molecules	
Muscle endplate: acetylcholine receptors	12,000
(fat cells: insulin receptors)	1

For references, see Hille (1981)

important principle underlying the complexity of neuronal organization.

Different Ion Conductances. One of the most active areas of research in recent years has been the study of ionic conductance mechanisms in different kinds of nerve cell. This work has considerably extended the Hodgkin-Huxley model based on a single Na^+ and a single K^+ conductance underlying the impulse. Much of this work has been carried out on molluscan cell bodies, which present invitingly large targets for the intracellular methods required in voltage-clamp analysis. There is the hope that the properties of the cell body membrane revealed in this work may represent to some extent the properties of synaptic terminals, and thus give clues to the membrane properties controlling synaptic outputs, especially as they relate to mechanisms in development and learning (see Chap. 30).

The number of ionic conductances identified has grown rapidly, and it is impossible in an introductory account to describe them adequately. Table 7.2 presents a summary of the main types.

Among the *inward currents*, one of the main achievements has been the recognition that in many neurons, calcium also enters the cell during the action potential, and may in fact carry most of the current in some cells. The Ca^{2+} channel seems to be distinct from the Na^+ channel when

both are present. The Ca^{2+} current has a slower time course than Na^+ current, and Ca^{2+} action potentials are correspondingly relatively prolonged. Regional differentiation of the neuronal membrane is shown by the fact that in some molluscan cells the soma action potential is mainly due to Ca^{2+}, whereas the axon impulse is mainly due to Na^+. In vertebrates, there is evidence for both slow Ca^{2+} potentials and fast Na^+ "spikes", for example in the dendrites of cerebellar Purkinje cells.

Calcium mediation of action potentials may be significant for several reasons. First, calcium has many functional roles within the cell; calcium influx during an impulse is an effective way of raising the intracellular free Ca^{2+} concentration. Second, calcium has been found to modulate the conductance of other ions, particularly K^+. Third, Ca^{2+} plays a critical role in the modulation of electrical synapses, and the release of neurotransmitters at chemical synapses. We shall have more to say about these points below, and in Chap. 8.

In addition to Ca^{2+} current during the impulse, a separate Ca^{2+} current (I_C) has been identified that is very slow. This current provides for a slow depolarization that underlies the generation of bursts of impulses in certain kinds of pacemaker neurons.

Among the *outward currents*, an interesting finding has been that at some sites

Table 7.2 Voltage-dependent ion channels

Symbol	Name	Function	Found in	Blocked by
Inward currents				
I_{Na}	fast sodium (classical Hodgkin-Huxley)	rapid depolarization (1 msec) propagating nerve impulse initial peak of prolonged impulses	squid axon many neuron cell bodies and axons skeletal muscle	tetrodotoxin (TTX) saxitoxin (STX)
I_{Ca}	calcium	moderately fast depolarization (up to 10 msec) prolonged impulses (shoulders, plateaus)	embryonic cells growth cones many neuron cell bodies and dendrites heart gland cells	cobalt (Co^{2+}) nickel (Ni^{3+}) nifedopine (in heart)
I_B	slow inward (Na^+ and/or Ca^{2+}) "bursting"	slow depolarization (up to secs) generates bursts of impulses depolarizing afterpotentials	molluscan bursting neurons vertebrate bursting neurons (Purkinje, hippocampal?)	
I_{TI}	transient inward (Ca^{2+} dependent nonspecific cation current)	tonic (background) depolarization "leak currents" in some cells	heart neuroblastoma	
Outward currents				
I_K	delayed rectifier (classical Hodgkin-Huxley) late outward	repolarizes membrane rapidly from Na^+ peak modulates spike shape regulates high-frequency impulse firing	squid axon many neuron cell bodies and axons	tetraethylammonium (TEA) 4-aminopyridine (4-AMP)
I_C $I_{K(Ca)}$	calcium-activated potassium current	turned on by depolarizations role in intracellular Ca^{2+} signaling role in setting membrane potential (controls low-frequency impulse firing)	ubiquitous (except squid axon)	barium (Ba^{2+}), TEA
I_{IR}	anomalous rectifier (inward rectifier)	promotes impulses spread in T-tubules keeps K conductance low during plateau potential	skeletal muscle heart muscle egg cells	rubidium (R6)
I_A	fast (transient) outward current early K^+	controls low-frequency impulse firing sensitive to Ca^{2+} in some cells (role in learning?)	molluscan cells	4-aminopyridine (4-AMP) tetraethylammonium (TEA)
I_M	muscarinic	resting K^+ conductance (turned off by acetylcholine, to give depolarization of cell)	vertebrate sympathetic ganglion cell	

Based on Stephen Smith and Rich Aldrich; see Adams et al. (1980) Thompson and Aldrich (1980), and Stevens (1980)

the late K$^+$ conductance activated by the impulse in the Hodgkin-Huxley model may be absent. This appears to be the case at the node of Ranvier. At these sites, repolarization of the membrane occurs solely as a consequence of Na$^+$ inactivation.

One of the most important findings has been a slow K$^+$ current that depends on an increase in intracellular free Ca^{2+}. In some neurons evidence has been obtained that the Ca^{2+} that enters during the impulse activates this slow K$^+$ conductance. The slow hyperpolarization is believed to contribute to the control of impulse firing at relatively low rates (relatively long interspike intervals).

Another K$^+$ current (I_A) has been found to be present in some molluscan cells. This is activated by very small depolarizations from the resting level, and therefore is important in controlling excitability and impulse firing rates in this range.

In the electrical analogue of the membrane, these ionic conductances are present as elements in parallel with the others.

Some rather sophisticated computer models of nerve cells have been constructed which incorporate these ionic conductances. An example of a neuron in *Aplysia* is shown in Fig. 7.8. It can be seen that the model provides a relatively close approximation to the firing pattern recorded from the neuron.

Patch Clamps. The physiological studies of ionic mechanisms in the membrane we have discussed have relied almost exclusively on intracellular recordings, that is, with the micropipette tip placed inside a cell. A much more direct approach would be to have the tip placed directly against the membrane. This requires a very smooth, clean tip and a tight seal with the membrane. Recently, several groups of workers around the world have perfected this technical advance. As shown in Fig. 7.9, with the tip placed against the cell membrane, a slight suction is applied to the electrode and the tip is withdrawn,

carrying a patch of membrane stuck tightly to it. This "patch clamp" method permits direct recording of individual membrane channel events, and analysis of effects of different agents applied directly to the membrane. This new method promises considerable increase in precision of our knowledge of ionic channel mechanisms underlying impulses and synaptic actions. Single-channel events at the neuromuscular junction are discussed in Chap. 9, and in the insect olfactory cell in Chap. 12.

Voltage Dependence and Neurotransmitter Sensitivity. Thus far we have considered the ion channel to be formed by a macromolecular complex which permits ions to pass through according to the potential difference across the membrane. This is a purely "voltage-dependent" channel. Traditionally it has been believed that this property makes impulse channels distinct from synaptic channels, which are presumed to be sensitive only to the action of a chemical transmitter substance liberated from another neuron. However, recently it has been found that in some cells the voltage-dependent channels are also sensitive to neurotransmitters. A nice demonstration of this has been provided by the experiments of Kathleen Dunlap and Gerald Fischbach, then at Harvard. They made intracellular recordings from disseminated cell cultures of the chick dorsal root ganglion. These cells have a prolonged action potential, with an early peak that is due to Na$^+$ current, and a later component that is carried by Ca^{2+}. Neurotransmitter substances were ionophoresed onto the cells from extracellular micropipettes. As shown in Fig. 7.10, several of these substances (serotonin, gamma-aminobutyric acid, and noradrenaline) reduced the slow Ca^{2+} component of the impulse. Other substances, such as dopamine or various peptides, had no effect.

These cells lack dendrites and receive no synapses onto their cell bodies. However, their axon terminals in the spinal cord receive synapses from several types of fibers

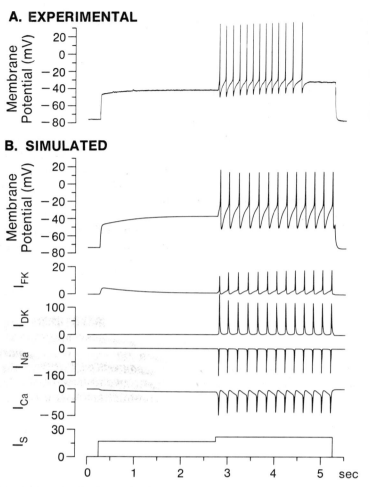

Fig. 7.8. Repetitive impulse firing in ink-gland motoneuron of *Aplysia*. **A.** Experimental recording of intracellular potentials. **B.** Computer model. Simulated intracellular potentials above, time course of different ionic currents below. (From Byrne, 1980)

(these belong to the category of axoaxonic synapses). It has been suggested that these fibers may release one or another of the above transmitters to depress the Ca²⁺ component of the impulse and thereby reduce the amount of transmitter released by the dorsal root fibers onto motoneurons and other spinal cord cells. This mechanism of reducing the input to motoneurons is called presynaptic inhibition. A similar mechanism has been invoked to explain plastic changes of synapses underlying learning in *Aplysia,* as we will discuss in Chap. 30.

These experiments have made it clear that, at specific sites on a neuron, excitable channels may have receptors for neurotransmitters which permit modulation of the excitable properties. Complementing this work are the findings of those working on synapses that, in many cases, the responses to a neurotransmitter may depend on the level of the resting membrane potential. The situation is summarized in Fig. 7.10C. At the far left is the traditional impulse channel, with only a voltage-dependent property, while at the right is the traditional synaptic channel,

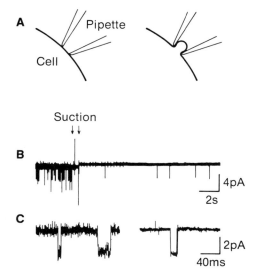

A

Pipette

Cell

Suction

B

4pA

2s

C

2pA

40ms

Fig. 7.9. "Patch clamp" technique for studying single channel events in the end-plate region of frog muscle fibers. **A.** Relation of micropipette to cell membrane, before and after application of slight suction to pipette. The suction increases the sealing resistance from 100×10^6 ohms (100 megohms) to approximately 60×10^9 ohms (60 gigohms). **B.** Continuous recording before and after application of suction. Sharp downward transients signal the opening of single channels activated by acetylcholine in the pipette. **C.** Finer time resolution, before and after suction. (From Hamill et al., 1981)

with only transmitter receptor sites. Between are channels which contain some degree of the other property. These channels obviously provide the nervous system with much greater flexibility in modifying trains of impulses, on the one hand, or integration of synaptic inputs, on the other, depending on the ongoing state of the organism and level of activity in its neural circuits. This should be kept in mind when we discuss the properties of synapses in Chaps. 8 and 9.

Conduction of the Action Potential

We have seen that, during the action potential, positive current carried by Na$^+$ or Ca^{2+} flows into the cell. Where does it go

from there? As shown in Fig. 7.11, the current will have to flow back out through the membrane to complete the circuit. It cannot all return at the point of entry, and it therefore spreads out along the fiber, seeking pathways of least resistance to get outside. How far it extends down the fiber depends on the ratio of the resistance of the cytoplasm to the resistance of the membrane. The higher the membrane resistance (or the lower the cytoplasm resistance) the further the current will tend to flow along the fiber.

This spread of electric current through the constant resistance and capacitance properties of the nerve is called *electrotonus.* It was first studied in the late nineteenth century. At that time, electric cables for long-distance telephone communication were being laid down, and it was recognized that the equations used to describe the spread of electricity in the cables were similar to those that applied to nerve. From that time, the electrotonic properties of nerve cells have been referred to as *cable properties.*

We will consider the spread of electronic potentials, and their crucial role in the integrative functions of dendrites, in the next chapter. Here we simply point out that whenever an impulse is set up, electrotonic currents flow through the neighboring membrane. These currents, also called *local currents,* spread the depolarization of an impulse to neighboring membrane sites where, if threshold is reached, the impulse is also generated. The process continues along the fiber, at a rate determined by the size of the fiber: the larger the fiber, the faster the rate, other things being equal. We say that the local currents spread *passively,* whereas the impulse is *conducted,* or *propagates.*

Continuous propagation of the impulse, as just described, occurs in unmyelinated axons. These may be very large, in certain invertebrate axons like the squid giant axon. In vertebrates, they are the smallest fibers, from several μm diameter down to around 0.2 μm.

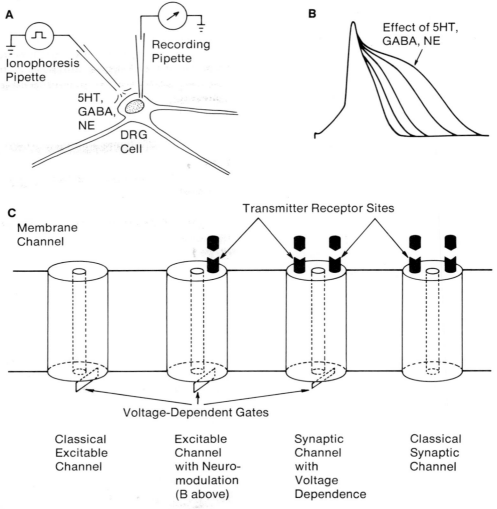

Fig. 7.10. A. Experimental setup for recording intracellularly from a single chick dorsal root ganglion cell in culture while ionophoresing neurotransmitter substances. **B.** Effects of different substances on impulses. Long-duration spikes before, short-duration spikes after, ionophoresis of substances. **C.** Simple models to illustrate different types of voltage-sensitive and ligand (neurotransmitter) sensitive channels. (Diagram B redrawn from Dunlap and Fischbach, 1978)

Myelinated fibers, as we have seen, have a coating of many membranes that is interrupted at intervals by nodes of Ranvier. The nodes are the sites of impulse generation; here, the Na$^+$ channels are packed together at a density of some 12,000/μm^2 (see Table 7.1), the highest density yet known in the nervous system. In contrast, the intervening membrane under the myelin has few voltage-dependent conductance channels, and spread through the in-

ternodal segments is therefore purely electrotonic (see Fig. 7.11B). It is very effective, because the myelin wrapping has a high resistance and low capacitance that makes the current tend to flow down the fiber to the next node rather than leak back across the membrane. The impulse in effect jumps from node to node, and this form of propagation is therefore called *saltatory conduction.* It is an efficient mechanism that achieves maximum conduction speed with a minimum of active membrane, metabolic machinery, and fiber size. It is especially prevalent in vertebrates, where it has been an important factor in making possible high-speed conduction over many channels between many nerve centers.

A variation on this type of conduction is present in the dendrites of some neurons. As shown in Fig. 7.11C, there are patches of active membrane at sites in the dendritic tree. These patches are separated from the site of impulse initiation in the cell body and axon by passive dendritic membrane. The active patches are called "hot spots". They are believed to boost

Fig. 7.11. Mechanisms for spread of the impulse. A. Continuous conduction in an unmyelinated axon. B. Discontinuous conduction from node to node in a myelinated axon. C. Discontinuous spread from "hot spot" to "hot spot" in a dendrite. In all diagrams, the impulses are shown in their spatial extent along the fiber at an instant of time.

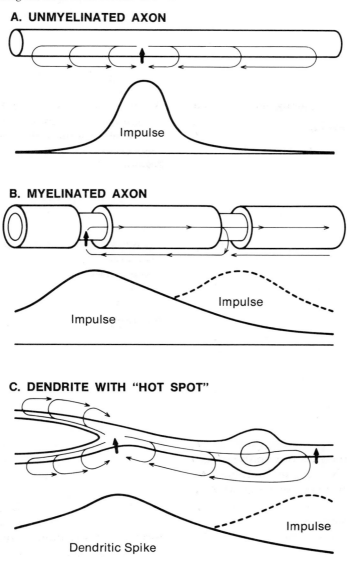

A. UNMYELINATED AXON

Impulse

B. MYELINATED AXON

Impulse

Impulse

C. DENDRITE WITH "HOT SPOT"

Dendritic Spike

Impulse

the response to synaptic inputs in the dendrites, thereby enhancing the effect of distant dendritic inputs in affecting impulse generation at or near the cell body. As already noted, hot spots may generate impulses by Na$^+$ conductance mechanisms, whereas other parts of the dendritic tree may have slower Ca^{2+} conductances. In addition to their role in conduction, dendritic spikes may have significance for other functions of dendrites, especially those concerned with synaptic integration and control of output from presynaptic dendrites, as discussed in the next chapter.

Functions of the Impulse

Until very recently, the only imaginable function of the impulse in nerve cells was to conduct activity in axons at high rates over long distances. The significance of the activity lay in the fact that the frequency of firing constituted the *neural code* for the intensity of stimulation. This impulse code is transmitted to other neurons by synaptic outputs from the nerve terminals, as will be described in the next chapter. Without in any way diminishing the importance of this function, it is now clear that excitability may have many other contributions to make to the life of nerve cells.

In opening this chapter, we took a broad view of excitability as a cellular property. We can now return to that view. Some of the functions of impulses that have been identified in plant and animal cells are summarized in Table 7.3. Some of these, such as bioilluminescence or fertilization, are obviously special for certain types of non-nervous cells. However, some of them have implications for nerve cells as well. These include the possible role of excitability in cell division and morphogenesis; in transfer of ions across membranes; in control of transmembrane movements of various substances; or in motility of nerve processes underlying plasticity.

In addition to these general properties, we have noted certain functions of excit-

Table 7.3 Functions of excitability in cells

Development	Motility
in fertilization	ciliary
in cell division	vascular
in morphogenesis	muscle
Ion transfers across	Nerve signaling
membranes	propagation
Bioluminescence	other functions
Secretion	
hormonal	
glandular	
synaptic	

From Shepherd (1981)

ability already identified in neurons, such as prolonged effects on impulse firing, complex integration in dendrites, and control of output from presynaptic dendrites. Many of these functions are likely to be of increased importance in smaller processes and terminals, where even small conductance changes may have very large effects on membrane potential, internal ion concentrations, and associated metabolic machinery.

Excitability can thus be seen to play many possible roles in nerve cells. Some of these involve general properties common to many other cells. From this perspective, the impulse can be regarded as an expression of the cell biology of the neuron. We will see another aspect of this unity within cell biology when we discuss interactions between neurons that take place without impulses, in the next chapter.

REFERENCES

Adams, D. J., S. J. Smith, and S. H. Thompson. 1980. Ionic currents in molluscan soma. *Ann. Rev. Neurosci. 3:* 141–168.

Byrne, J. H. 1980. Analysis of ionic conductance mechanisms in motor cells mediating inking behavior in *Aplysia californica. J. Neurophysiol. 43:* 630–650.

Dunlap, K. and G. D. Fischbach. 1978. Neurotransmitters decrease the calcium component of sensory neurone action potentials. *Nature 276:* 837–839.

Hamill, O. P., A. Marty, E. Neher, B. Sakmann, and F. J. Sigworth. 1981. Improved patch-clamp techniques for high-resolution current recording from cells and cell-free membrane patches. *Pflug. Arch.* 391: 85–100.

Hille, B. 1977. Ionic basis of resting potentials and action potentials. In *Cellular Biology of Neurons.* Vol. 1, Sect. 1; *Handbook of Physiology, The Nervous System* (ed. by E. R. Kandel). Washington, D.C.: Am. Physiological Soc. p. 111.

Hille, B. 1981. Excitability and ionic channels. In Siegel et al. [Chap. 4] pp. 95–106.

Hodgkin, A. L. and A. F. Huxley. 1952. A quantitative description of membrane current and its application to conduction and excitation in nerve. *J. Physiol.* 117: 500–544.

Hodgkin, A. L. and B. Katz. 1949. The effect of sodium ions on the electrical activity of the giant axons of the squid. *J. Physiol.* 108: 37–77.

Hubbard et al. 1969. [Chap. 6].

Kandel, E. R. 1976. [Chap. 2].

Mueller, P. 1979. The mechanism of electrical excitation in lipid bilayers and cell membranes. In *The Neurosciences: Fourth Study Program* (ed. by F. O. Schmitt and F. G. Worden). Cambridge, Mass: MIT Press. pp. 641–658.

Shepherd, G. M. 1981. The nerve impulse and the nature of nervous function. In *Neurones Without Impulses* (ed. by A. Roberts and B. M. H. Bush). Cambridge: Cambridge University Press. pp. 1–27.

Stevens, C. F. 1980. Ionic channels in neuromembranes: methods for studying their properties. In *Molluscan Nerve Cells: from Biophysics to Behavior* (ed. by J. Koester and J. H. Byrne). Cold Spring Harbor. pp. 11–31.

Thompson, S. H. and R. W. Aldrich. 1980. Membrane potassium channels. In *The Cell Surface and Neuronal Function* (ed. by C. W. Cotman, G. Poste, and G. L. Nicolson). New York: Elsevier/North-Holland. pp. 49–85.

Additional Reading

Hagiwara, S. and L. Byerly. 1981. Calcium channel. *Ann. Rev. Neurosci.* 4: 69–126.

Katz, B. 1966. [Chap. 6].

Liddell, E. G. T. 1960. [Chap. 1].

8
Synaptic Potentials

By the early years of this century the idea of the synapse was firmly established. Cajal had demonstrated that nerve cells are individual entities, requiring that transmission between them takes place, as he phrased it, "by contiguity, not continuity". Sherrington had made contiguity explicit in his concept of the synapse. Sherrington also provided evidence for some of the physiological properties of the synapses in his studies of transmission through reflex arcs in the spinal cord. Thus, reflex discharges were graded in strength, showed summation without refractoriness, displayed inhibition as well as excitation, and often long outlasted the stimulus, all properties which are clearly differentiated from those of impulses in the nerves.

It was implied that these properties were associated with the synapses made on motoneurons and interneurons in the spinal cord. However, physiologists of that time lacked methods for analyzing the synapses directly. The first studies of synaptic activity were not made until around 1940, using extracellular recordings from vertebrate neuromuscular junctions and sympathetic ganglia. Not until the introduction of the microelectrode, and asso-

ciated electronic instrumentation, around 1950, were the means at hand to study synapses directly.

The first synapses studied with intracellular methods were the neuromuscular junction, by Bernard Katz and his colleagues in London, and the motoneuron, by John Eccles and his colleagues in New Zealand and Australia. Since that time many different neurons and their synaptic properties have been analyzed. In general, the synapses conform to the basic plan outlined in Chap. 5, in which activity in a presynaptic process produces a response in a postsynaptic process. The postsynaptic response usually takes the form of a transient change in membrane potential, and this change is referred to as a *postsynaptic potential*, or simply *synaptic potential*.

The study of synaptic actions is therefore largely concerned with the mechanisms for producing synaptic potentials. We will first consider the various mechanisms that have been identified. We will then put this information together with the structure of the nerve cell and its ability to generate impulses, in order to understand how synaptic potentials are involved in the integrative behavior of the neuron.

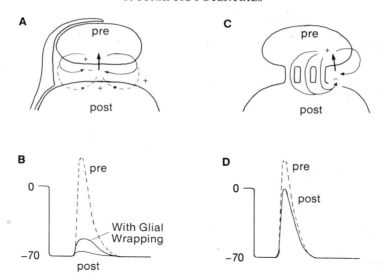

Fig. 8.1. Types of electrical interactions. **A.** Field potential effects through membrane juxtapositions. **B.** Representative recordings from pre- and postsynaptic processes in A. **C.** Current flows through gap junction (electrical synapse). **D.** Representative recordings from C. Note much larger loss in transmission in B than D.

Electric Fields

The simplest mechanism for effecting a change in the membrane potential is through the flow of current from a neighboring cell. Consider the situation diagrammed in Fig. 8.1A. An active site exists in the upper cell which causes current to flow inward at that site (as for example by the inward flow of Na ions). Associated with this is an outward flow of current to complete the circuit through neighboring membrane. For the present we recognize that as the current emerges from the membrane it can flow directly back to the active site through the low-resistance extracellular space (solid arrow), or it can pass through the high-resistance membrane of the neighboring cell (dotted line). Naturally it will prefer the path of low resistance, but a tiny amount will pass through the membrane. If the points of entry and exit are sufficiently separate, there will be a net flow of current at each point, and one can record a corresponding tiny change in the membrane potential.

Representative recordings for this case

are illustrated in Fig. 8.1B. While this seems like a very inefficient mechanism, it can be enhanced in several ways. A large number of tightly packed active processes will heighten the effect, as could occur in the case of unmyelinated axons running together; olfactory nerves and cerebellar parallel fibers are possible sites for this. Large populations of synchronously active cells in the cerebral cortex generate currents sufficient to give rise to the waves of the electroencephalogram (EEG); this might also involve field effects between the cells, particularly between their dendrites. A glial wrapping can restrict the extracellular current flow and increase the amount of current crossing neighboring membrane; this has, in fact, been demonstrated for one of the input terminals onto the Mauthner cell in lower vertebrates (see Chap. 20).

An advantage of this type of interaction is that it requires no extra energy. The disadvantages are that the effects are minimal, diffuse, and nonspecific without structural constraints, and the membrane potential changes are rigidly locked to the original activity.

Electrical Synapses

Effective electrical coupling between cells is achieved through low-resistance connections—the gap junctions described in Chap. 5. The intercellular channels at these junctions have a very low resistance to current passing between the two neurons, and at the same time they prevent loss by leakage to the extracellular space. Thus, a potential change in a presynaptic terminal may be transmitted to a postsynaptic terminal with little attenuation, as shown in Fig. 8.1C,D. Experimentally this is the direct test for the presence of an electrical synapse, and was first reported by Ed Furshpan and David Potter in 1959 at a synapse between two nerve fibers in the crayfish. The synapse they studied is made by the lateral giant fiber onto the giant motor fiber in the abdominal ganglion; it mediates rapid flip movements of the tail that are used for defensive reflexes (see Chap. 20). As shown in Fig. 8.2, an action potential in the presynaptic fiber spreads with little attenuation into the postsynaptic fiber (A), whereas spread in the reverse direction (B) is very limited. This directionality of current flow is called *rectification.*

Electrical synapses (and their morphological substrates, gap junctions) have been found between neurons at many sites in the nervous systems of invertebrates and lower vertebrates.

Three sites have been found in the mammalian brainstem. These are illustrated in Fig. 8.3. In the mesencephalic nucleus of the fifth cranial nerve there are electrical synapses between cell bodies and between cell bodies and initial axonal segments (A). In the vestibular (Deiter's) nucleus the synapses occur between cell bodies and axon terminals. A spike initiated in one cell is transmitted to a neighboring cell as a short-latency depolarization by current flow through the axon terminals and branches, as shown in (B). In the inferior olive, dendritic spines are interconnected by electrical synapses. The spines also received chemical synapses, and it has

Fig. 8.2. Transmission through an electrical synapse in the crayfish. There is effective spread of an impulse from the lateral giant fiber into the giant motor fiber (**A**). The lack of spread in the opposite direction is called *rectification* (**B**). (After Furshpan and Potter, 1959, in Kuffler and Nicholls, 1976)

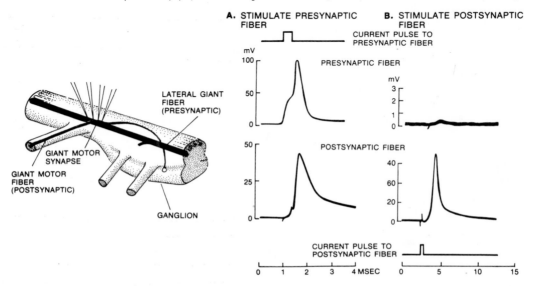

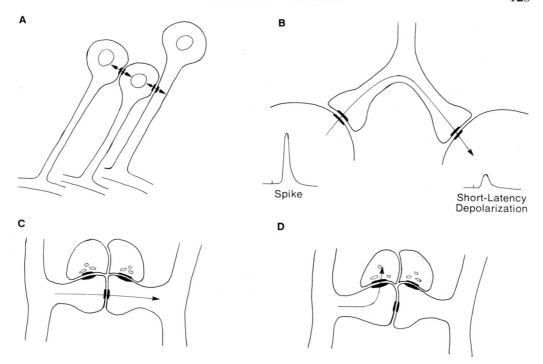

Fig. 8.3. Three examples of electrical synapses in the mammalian brain. **A.** Mesencephalic nucleus of the fifth cranial nerve. (Baker and Llinas, 1971) **B.** Deiter's nucleus, in the vestibular complex of the eighth cranial nerve. (Korn et al., 1973) **C, D.** Inferior olivary nucleus, in the medulla oblongata. (Llinas et al., 1974)

been suggested that when they are active they shunt current away from the electrical synapses, thereby uncoupling the cells. The postulated mechanism is illustrated in Fig. 8.3C,D.

The salient features of electrical synapses derive from the nature of the direct connections. They operate quickly, with little or no delay. They can provide for current flow in both directions, or alternatively they can offer more resistance in one direction than the other (rectification). They provide a means of synchronization of populations of neurons. Their actions can be fixed and stereotyped in the face of repeated use, and less susceptible to metabolic and other effects than chemical synapses. However, this does not mean that electrical synapses cannot be influenced by events within the cytoplasm. Experiments in salivary gland cells have shown that increases in internal Ca^{2+} block

the ability of a small molecule (fluoroscein) to pass through gap junctions. This uncoupling effect may depend on a concomitant fall in intracellular pH. There is evidence from freeze-fracture studies that the uncoupling involves changes in the geometrical arrays of intramembranous particles at the gap junction. Whether this mechanism is operative in the modulation of electrical coupling between nerve cells has not been determined. In addition to mediating electrical transmission, gap junctions are also important in other ways for intercellular communication and the organization of cells into multicellular ensembles as discussed in Chap. 5.

Chemical Synapses

The predominant type of synapse in the mammalian brain is the chemical synapse, operating through the release of a trans-

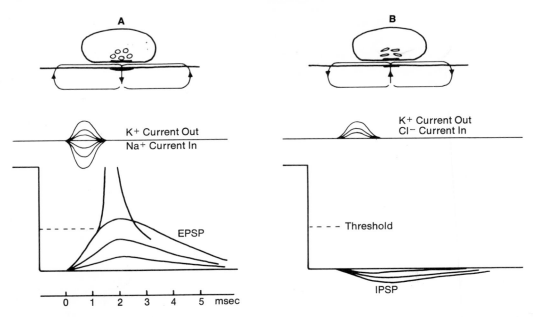

Fig. 8.4. Basic types of action at chemical synapses. *Above,* pre- and postsynaptic terminals, with net positive current flows shown by arrows for depolarizing (A) and polarizing or hyperpolarizing (B) actions. *Middle,* time course of ionic current flows; note that they are simultaneous rather than sequential, as in the case of the action potential. *Below,* recordings of postsynaptic potentials typical for an EPSP (A) and IPSP (B).

mitter substance from the presynaptic to the postsynaptic terminal. As already mentioned, the response of the postsynaptic terminal is called the *synaptic potential.*

Synaptic potentials may be either depolarizing or hyperpolarizing, as illustrated in Fig. 8.4. We consider first the depolarizing synaptic potential. As shown in A, the postsynaptic response consists of a net *inward* movement of positive charge. This can be brought about by a relatively nonspecific increase in conductance to both Na^+ and K^+, and possibly other ions such as Ca^{2+}; it is as if a shunt had momentarily been placed across the membrane. The membrane moves toward an equilibrium potential near zero, the actual value depending on the ions involved and the ratios of their permeabilities.

We shall have more to say about the mechanisms underlying the synaptic potential in the next section and in the next chapter. For the present we note that the ion flows are simultaneous, and vary with the amount of transmitter substance liberated by the presynaptic terminal. The synaptic potential is therefore a graded response, in contrast to the all-or-nothing character of the action potential. Synaptic membrane is thus not "active" in the same sense that impulse-generating membrane is, and the two must not be confused.

Synapses that depolarize the membrane are necessary for bringing about generation of impulses, and these responses were therefore termed *excitatory postsynaptic potentials* (EPSPs) by Eccles and his associates in their pioneering microelectrode studies of the motoneuron. As we will note below, the terminology needs to be qualified somewhat in the light of recent knowledge about synapses onto nonspiking neurons.

The second basic type of synaptic potential is diagrammed in Fig. 8.4B. The action of the transmitter substance is to open conductance channels for a net *outward* movement of positive charge. The equilibrium potential for this ion flow is at a relatively polarized level of -80 to -90 mV; it can be brought about by an increased conductance for outward movement of positive charge (K^+) and/or inward movement of negative charge (Cl^-). These ion flows therefore tend to hold the membrane near its resting potential, or somewhat hyperpolarized. As in the previous case, this synaptic potential is a graded response. Since synapses of this type tend to keep the membrane from depolarizing, and hence work against the initiation of impulses, they are termed *inhibitory postsynaptic potentials* (IPSPs).

We return now to the question of terminology. "Excitatory" and "inhibitory" have classically been defined to relation to impulse initiation, but we shall see that some neurons do not have impulse-generating properties. In these neurons the synaptic response is not converted into impulses; rather, the potential itself is responsible, either directly or through electrotonic spread, for activation or suppression of local synaptic output. How do the terms apply to this situation? Here we note a remarkable consistency; as far as is known, transmitter release only occurs by means of membrane depolarization. To the extent that this generalization

is true, we can therefore extend the definitions as follows: an EPSP is excitatory because it leads to impulse generation and/or synaptic transmitter release; an IPSP is inhibitory because it opposes impulse generation and/or transmitter release.

Synaptic Integration

It is largely through the interaction between excitatory and inhibitory synapses that the competition for control of the membrane potential in different parts of the neuron is carried out. This competition lies at the heart of the study of the dynamics of synaptic organization. The principle goes back to Sherrington; following him, the process by which different synaptic inputs are combined within the neuron is termed *synaptic integration*.

The interaction of a single EPSP and IPSP serves as a paradigm for synaptic integration in neurons, and it will be useful to grasp certain essentials. Let us assume an excitatory synapse and a nearby inhibitory synapse, the activation of which individually produce an EPSP and IPSP, respectively, as shown in Fig. 8.5A. Assume now that the two are activated simultaneously. The effect of the IPSP is to reduce the amplitude of the EPSP, away from the threshold for impulse initiation, as is shown in Fig. 8.5A. The dotted line traces

Fig. 8.5. Integration of EPSP and IPSP at different resting membrane potentials. Illustrates that IPSP conductance change reduces EPSP at all resting levels, but IPSP polarity changes in relation to E_K and E_{Cl}.

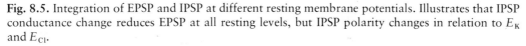
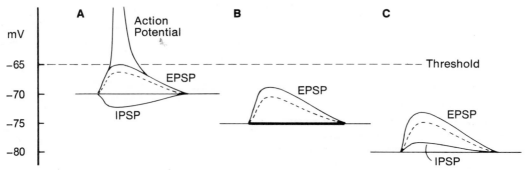

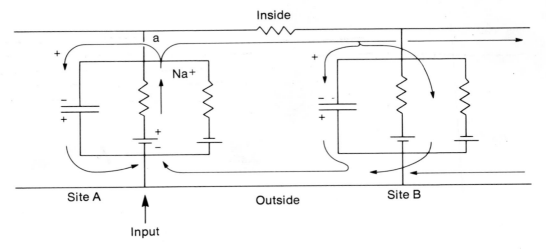

Fig. 8.6. Current flows underlying the depolarization of membrane patches. Initial input (as from an EPSP, applied current, or local potential) causes inward current flow of positively charged Na ions. At (a), current can flow in two directions: outward, to depolarize membrane capacitance, or longitudinally and then outward to depolarize capacitance of neighboring membrane patch. Thus membrane depolarization is brought about by both inward ionic current and outward capacitative current. Note that external current flow completes the circuit.

the resulting transient; it represents the "integrated" result of the two synaptic potentials.

Now it is commonly thought that this process of integration is a matter of simple algebraic addition of the two opposed synaptic potentials; to wit, "depolarization plus hyperpolarization equals membrane potential." However, this simple formula does not have general validity. As shown in Fig. 8.5B, when the resting potential is at the inhibitory equilibrium potential, no IPSP is recorded, but there is still a reduction of a simultaneous EPSP, due to the shunting effect of the increased inhibitory conductance. And when the resting membrane is more polarized (Fig. 8.5C), the IPSP is in fact depolarizing (toward the inhibitory equilibrium potential), yet its effect is still to reduce the EPSP by virtue of the increased conductance. The essential inhibitory action is therefore not a hyperpolarization of the membrane, but rather an increase in ionic conductance that drives the membrane potential toward the equilibrium potential for those ions.

It is thus the opposition of synaptically activated conductances and ionic currents that controls the relative amounts of depolarization and hyperpolarization of the membrane potential. In addition, one must consider the geometrical relations between excitatory and inhibitory synaptic sites in a dendritic tree, and the electrotonic flow of current through the dendrites. Synaptic integration thus involves a complex interplay between ionic conductances and neuronal geometry (see below).

Ionic Currents

It will be useful at this point to consider more closely the relation between an ionic conductance change and the resultant change in membrane potential. For an example we take the case of a brief increase in conductance to Na ions. As shown in Fig. 8.6, Na^+ moves inward through its conductance channel at the active site (A). In the electrical circuit, the current reaches a point on the inside where it can travel in two directions. Some current passes onto the inner surface of the membrane capacitance, where it deposits positive charge that depolarizes the membrane. Some passes along the inside of the nerve cell to the next patch of membrane (site B), where it can follow three paths: onto the membrane capacitance, through the membrane resistance, or further along the fiber. Ultimately all the current must pass out across the membrane and pass back along the outside of the cell to the negative pole of the Na battery.

Careful study of the diagram and current flows will help answer two questions that are often puzzling to the student. The first is, how can inward and outward current both depolarize the membrane? As can be seen, this is because inward current at an active site and outward current at a neighboring site both have the same effect, of putting positive charge on the inside of the membrane capacitance. The same reasoning applies to the relation between oppositely directed current flows and hyperpolarization.

The second question is, what are the time relations between the current flows and the potential changes? When the flow is rapid the potential response is slower, because charge is transiently stored on the membrane capacitance. The amount of slowing depends on the time constant (τ_m) of the membrane, given by the product of the membrane capacitance (C_m) and membrane resistance (R_m): $\tau = RC$. The relation between the rapid synaptic current flows and the slower synaptic potentials is shown in Fig. 8.4. For very slow or constant changes in conductance, a steady state exists in which the capacitance becomes an open circuit and can be ignored, and the spread of current to the neighboring site is determined solely by the resistance along the paths.

These relations between current and potential underlie most of the electrophysiological properties of nerve cells. For instance, the diagram of Fig. 8.6 applies equally to the case of activation of an action potential and its propagation by local currents, as we discussed in Chap. 7. The slowing of potential responses and the decay of potential spread are both governed by electrotonic properties. The diagram also emphasizes that at any site on a nerve cell there can be two pathways for interactions: internally with other parts of the same cell, by means of electrotonic spread or impulse generation, or externally through synapses onto neighboring cells.

Conductance-Decrease Synapses

Transient increases in conductance are the mode of operation at the neuromuscular junction and at many synapses onto central neurons. However, recent studies of sympathetic ganglion cells, retinal receptors, and certain invertebrate neurons have shown that some synapses may operate by an opposite mechanism, a decrease of a conductance. We are now in a position to describe briefly this type of synaptic action.

Let us recall that ion flows across the membrane depend on two factors: the conductance and the electrochemical gradient. Experimentally, if we move the membrane potential toward the equilibrium potential for an ion, the gradient decreases. At the equilibrium potential there is no net flow of the ion, and if the membrane potential moves further, the current through that channel actually reverses in direction. The experiment is illustrated in Fig. 8.7A. The traces represent recordings of synaptic potentials due to Na^+ conductance increases, at different holding potentials. The arrows indicate the directions and relative strengths of Na^+ current flow. Since the synaptic potentials have opposite polarities on either side of it, the equilibrium potential is also referred to as the *reversal potential*.

Now consider the case illustrated in Fig. 8.7B, which differs in two respects. First, the conductance for Na^+ in the resting membrane is increased. The membrane potential is therefore at a lower level (e.g., -40 mV, as indicated by the dashed line),

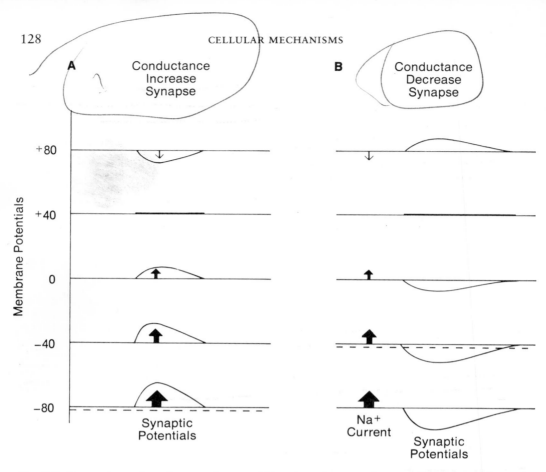

Fig. 8.7. Comparison of conductance-increase (**A**) and conductance-decrease (**B**) synapses. Synaptic potentials shown at different levels of controlled membrane potential. Arrows indicate direction and intensity of Na$^+$ current flow. Dotted lines indicate resting potentials.

due to the depolarizing effect of the inward leak of Na$^+$. Second, the effect of the synapse is to *decrease* the Na$^+$ conductance. This leaves the membrane to move toward the equilibrium potential of the ions to which it is more permeable, i.e., K$^+$ and Cl$^-$. The synaptic potential is therefore *hyperpolarizing*. The potentials decrease and reverse around the Na$^+$ equilibrium potential, but with opposite polarities to those shown in A.

In some cells this hyperpolarizing response functions as an IPSP, as in sympathetic ganglion cells; in other situations, its function is not yet clear, for example, in the retina. In addition to the conductance decrease, we may note other special properties. A hyperpolarization is achieved

by selective control of an ion that depolarizes the membrane. The decreased conductance raises the resistance of the membrane, thereby increasing the membrane time constant and slowing the potential response. Associated with this, these synaptic potentials tend to have slow time courses. With respect to integrative mechanisms, an IPSP produced by this means does not have the current-shunting effect we noted in connection with Fig. 8.5.

It will be appreciated that if a hyperpolarization can be produced by turning off the conductance to Na$^+$, a depolarization could be produced by turning off the conductance to K$^+$. Nature has not missed this opportunity; slow EPSPs produced by this mechanism have been found (Chap. 19).

Integrative Organization of the Nerve cell

We are now in a position to ask: how do the graded potentials set up at the junctions of a cell carry information through the cell and produce a transfer of information to other cells? This function can be best understood by directing our attention to a well-studied nerve cell, the stretch receptor of the crayfish. This preparation was introduced to intracellular electro-physiology by Stephen Kuffler and Carlos Eyzaguirre, working at Johns Hopkins, in a classic series of experiments in the 1950's. We will use this as a model to bring together the different properties we have considered thus far.

A schematic diagram of the stretch receptor cell is shown in Fig. 8.8A. The cell has several large dendritic trunks, which enter the muscle and terminate in fine branches. When stretch is applied to the muscle (Fig. 8.8B), a depolarization is set

Fig. 8.8. A. Stretch receptor cell of the crayfish, showing relation to muscle fibers, inhibitory axon, and motor axons to muscles. B. Excitatory response of receptor cell to stretch of the muscle (arrows), as recorded by intracellular electrode inserted into cell body of sensory neuron (2). Dotted line indicates point in time for display of potentials in Fig. 8.9. C. Inhibition of the excitatory response by stimulation of the inhibitory axon (between arrows). (A from Burkhardt; B from Eyzaguirre and Kuffler, in Aidley, 1978; C from Kuffler and Eyzaguirre, 1955)

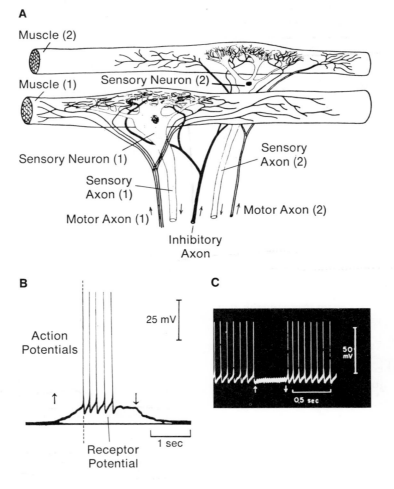

up in the dendritic branches, graded with the amount of stretch. This depolarization is due to an increase in permeability of the membrane to Na ions, and probably also other ions, which moves the membrane potential toward an equilibrium potential around zero. This *receptor potential* is thus similar to an EPSP. We will discuss mechanisms of transduction of the stimulus and other sensory properties in later chapters (Chaps. 11 and 14).

An intracellular electrode inserted into the cell body records the receptor potential together with the discharge of impulses that arise from it (Fig. 8.8B). In this situation, as in all recording experiments, the electrode is in one particular spot in the nerve cell, and we must deduce the sites where the different types of activity are actually initiated. For the receptor potential, the site of generation is in the dendritic terminals, which are 100–300μm away from the cell body. We therefore know that our recording must represent an attenuated version of the true receptor potential, because of the leakage of current across the membrane of the dendritic trunk as the current flows toward the cell body and out into the axon, according to the cable properties of the dendrites. But what about the impulses? Where do they arise—in the dendrites, cell body, or in the axon? An elegant experiment by Charles Edwards and David Ottoson, working in Kuffler's laboratory in 1957, showed that, contrary to expectation, the site of impulse generation is in the axon, at a considerable distance from the cell body. To complete the picture, there are inhibitory nerves which make synapses on the dendrites of these cells. Stimulation of these fibers produces IPSPs, as indicated in Fig. 8.8C. How do these responses interact with the other activity in the cell?

In order to appreciate these relationships we need to think about the nerve cell in its spatial dimension. We need to take a point in time during an impulse response (see dotted line in Fig. 8.8B), and ask: what is the distribution of potentials through-

out the cell at this point in time? We can answer this question in an intuitive way with the help of the diagram in Fig. 8.9. We will follow the methods of Wilfred Rall, of the National Institutes of Health, who has developed most of the methods now used for describing the flow of electrical activity in dendritic systems.

Beginning with the dimensions of the cell in Fig. 8.9A, we construct a model of the cell in which its electrical cable properties are incorporated in a simple equivalent cylinder (B). In (C) we plot the distribution of the different types of potentials in this equivalent cylinder. To begin with, the *receptor potential*, as we have already mentioned, is generated in the fine terminals, and spreads electrotonically through the cell, as indicated in the figure. The action potential, in contrast, is generated in the axon; it propagates in the axon toward the central nervous system and also spreads electrotonically back into the cell body and dendrites. The IPSP is generated in the distal dendrites, and spreads, also by electrotonic means, as indicated in the diagram.

The normal sequence of events is thus: stimulus →set up receptor potential in terminals → electrotonic spread through dendrites and cell body to axon → generation of action potential in axon when depolarization reaches threshold → propagation of action potential forward (orthodromically), and electrotonic spread backward (antidromically) into cell body and dendrites. The IPSP, acting during a response to stretch, opposes the response by making the membrane tend toward the relatively hyperpolarized inhibitory equilibrium potential.

Several questions often arise at this point in students' minds; let's see if we can anticipate and answer them.

Question 1: "It seems to me a funny way to organize a cell; how can the potentials spread so far?" *Answer:* As we noted in Chap. 7, electrotonic spread depends on just three factors: the resistance of the cytoplasm, the resistance of the cell mem-

A. SCHEMATIC REPRESENTATION OF STRETCH RECEPTOR CELL

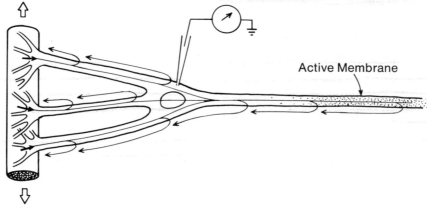

Active Membrane

B. ELECTROTONIC EQUIVALENT CYLINDER OF CELL

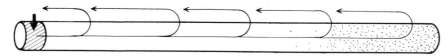

C. SPATIAL DISTRIBUTION OF POTENTIAL IN CELL

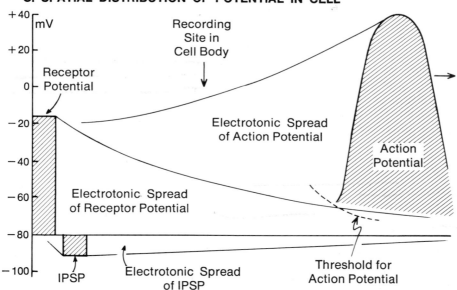

Fig. 8.9. Diagrams illustrating the analysis of spread of electrical activity in the stretch receptor cell. See text.

brane, and the diameter of a dendrite or axon. The two main ways that neurons control the effectiveness of spread is by means of the membrane resistance and the diameter. *The greater the membrane resistance,* the less current leaks out across the membrane, and the more effective is the spread of a receptor potential and synaptic potential (and also, as we saw earlier, the local currents spreading in front of an action potential). *The greater the diameter,* the easier it is for the current to spread through the interior (cytoplasm) of the cell. Thus, stretch receptor neurons have a relatively *high* membrane resistance, and are sufficiently *large,* to provide for effective electrotonic spread of potentials within them.

Different neurons vary greatly in this respect. In many cases, there is effecive spread throughout much of a dendritic tree, and this provides the basis for the integration of many synaptic inputs. In other cases, there is limitation of spread; one sees this, for example, in the thin necks of some spines that arise from dendrites, and in very thin processes that connect parts of cells. In these cases, it appears that there is an isolation of the activity at a given site from the ongoing activity in the rest of the cell, so that different parts of the cell can operate as independent or semiindependent functional units.

Question 2: "Is the electrotonic potential active or passive?" *Answer:* Recall that the electrotonic potential is a *passive* potential. It is the spread that occurs along a process when all of the electrical properties of that process remain constant, at their resting values. Strictly speaking, "active" is used only in reference to the regenerative property of the action potential. Any time there is a change in the membrane potential at some site (due to a receptor potential, synaptic potential, or action potential), current always flows electrotonically through neighboring regions to equalize the distribution of charge. Part of the strategy of the functional organization of a neuron is to restrict syn-

aptic sites and action potential sites to different parts of the neuron, and link them all together with passive electrotonic spread.

Question 3: "I don't understand; is the electrode at the cell body recording directly the receptor potential and the action potential, or isn't it?" *Answer:* Strictly speaking, the electrode is recording the *electrotonically spread* receptor potential and action potential. If we wanted to record the receptor potential directly, we would have to put the electrode tip into the terminals. We would then record a very big depolarization, as indicated in the diagram. Similarly, the action potentials recorded in the cell body are attenuated versions of the action potentials in the axon, as shown by the lower amplitudes in the recordings of Fig. 8.8. This serves as a reminder of the fact that every recording gives a selective view of what is going on in a neuron, being weighted for events happening near at hand.

Question 4: "I thought there was a general rule in the nervous system that inhibition occurs at the cell body. Why does it occur in the dendrites in this cell?" *Answer:* The rule is one of the many that has had to be modified. It is true that many neurons receive inhibitory inputs to their cell bodies, and even initial segments. It is presumed that this provides for very effective control of impulse initiation at these sites. However, the stretch receptor cell shows that another effective placement is near the site of excitatory input. At this site, there is maximum opportunity for shunting of excitatory currents by the increased conductances of the inhibitory channels, thus depressing the receptor potential. Thus, the IPSP at this site tends to gate the receptor potential near its site of origin, rather than gating the impulse near *its* site of origin. The nervous system provides variations on these two themes in different regions, presumably reflecting needs for the interaction of excitation and inhibition in the processing of different kinds of information.

A. VERTEBRATE MOTONEURON

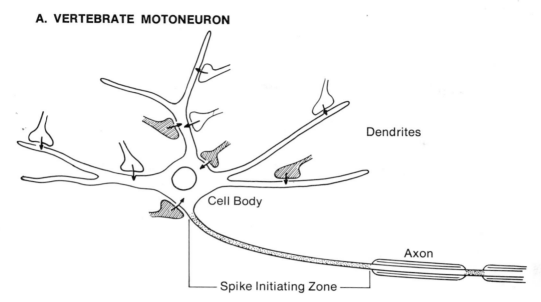

B. INVERTEBRATE MOTONEURON

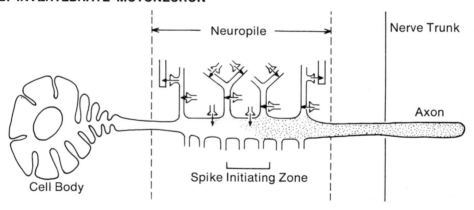

Fig. 8.10. **A.** Diagram of motoneuron in spinal cord of the cat, showing relation of excitatory (open profiles) and inhibitory (shaded profiles) synapses to each other and to the site of impulse output. **B.** Diagram of a motoneuron to a leg extensor muscle in the metathoracic ganglion of a locust. (From Gwilliam and Burrows, 1980)

These questions and answers show how a model cell like the stretch receptor can illustrate basic properties that are involved in integrative actions of nerve cells. Many other cells can be used to demonstrate further these properties. For example, the motoneuron of the mammalian spinal cord shares many properties with the stretch receptor cell, such as the site of impulse initiation in the initial segment, but differs in others, such as the placement of inhibition (see Fig. 8.10A). In comparison, an insect motoneuron has quite a different morphology (Fig. 8.10B). The cell body is to one side, so to speak, and has no significance for transmission

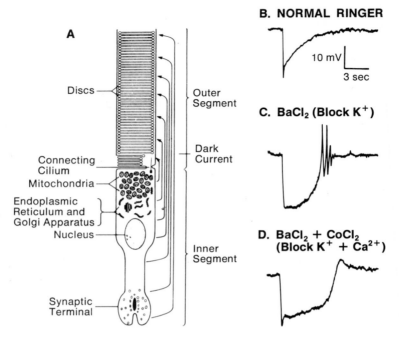

Fig. 8.11. Experiments showing both graded and excitable properties of vertebrate photoreceptors. A. Diagram of a rod receptor of the toad. B. Responses when retina was in normal Ringer solution. C. BaCl₂ was added to bathing medium oᵗ block K⁺ conductance, revealing regenerative spikes. D. CoCl₂ was added to block Ca²⁺ conductance, eliminating spikes. (A from Fain, in Roberts and Bush (1981); B–D from Fain et al., 1978)

of signals. Synaptic responses in the dendrites are integrated in the axon trunk; impulses generated in the spike-initiating zone are conducted into the axon and to the muscles. The synaptic potentials in the dendrites are believed also to activate synaptic outputs from the dendrites to neighboring processes. The diagram indicates the considerable amount of dendrodendritic processing through synaptic potentials (see next section) that is believed to take place in the neuropil, and the differentiation of the membrane of a single neuron into different synaptic, inexcitable and excitable regions.

Nonimpulse Neurons

The stretch receptor and the vertebrate motoneuron are models for nerve cells that have axons, generate impulses, and have dendrites that are postsynaptic only. In the classical view, all neurons are of this type. However, beginning with studies of the vertebrate retina and olfactory bulb in 1966, a number of neurons have been found that do not fit this simple model.

Among the best-studied examples are the cells of the vertebrate retina. The photoreceptors respond to light with a slow potential. The effect of light is to turn off a resting Na⁺ conductance, thereby allowing the membrane potential to move toward the more polarized K⁺ equilibrium potential. Normally, the photoreceptor response consists solely of this slow hyperpolarizing potential (see Fig. 8.11). This slow potential by itself brings about transmission of the light response, presumably by interrupting transmitter release from the photoreceptor terminals onto other retinal neurons. Because of the very short lengths of the photoreceptors, electrotonic spread through the cell is effective, in the absence of impulses. The cells to which the photoreceptors transmit, the bipolar cells and horizontal cells, also operate exclusively by graded potentials. The roles of these cells in visual processing will be discussed in Chap. 17.

An interesting aspect is that although the photoreceptors do not usually generate impulses, their membrane nonetheless has excitable properties. This has been shown in experiments in which the retina is treated with tetraethylammonium, which blocks K^+ currents. Under these conditions, the photoreceptors show spiking activity (see Fig. 8.11). The spikes are blocked by treatment with cobalt, indicating that they are due to a Ca^{2+} current.

The interpretation is that normally the inward Ca^{2+} current is balanced or swamped by outward K^+ current, so that the excitability of the membrane is not expressed. This gives support to the idea that excitability is a widespread property of biological membranes, which is expressed only under specific conditions, as discussed in Chap. 7.

A second example that has contributed to a revision of our concepts of neuronal organization is the vertebrate olfactory bulb. Here, the relay neuron (mitral cell) makes reciprocal dendrodendritic synapses with the interneurons (granule cells) (Fig. 8.12; see also Chap. 5). This synaptic arrangement has implied that input and

Fig. 8.12. Diagram illustrating local interactions between mitral and granule cells in the vertebrate olfactory bulb, by means of synapses between their dendrites. Sequence begins (**A**) with impulse in mitral cell (1); in (**B**) an EPSP has been initiated in the granule cell spine; in (**C**) the spine feeds back an IPSP onto mitral cell (1), and sends inhibition laterally onto mitral cell (2). All interactions are by dendrodendritic synapses. (From Shepherd, 1978)

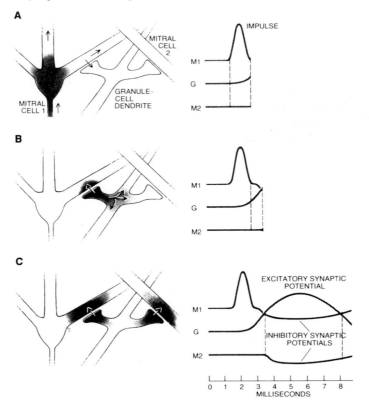

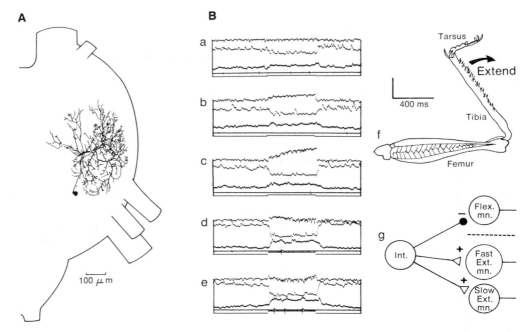

Fig. 8.13. Nonspiking interneurons in the metathoracic ganglion of the locust. **A.** Example of an interneuron filled with cobalt. (From Siegler and Burrows, 1979) **B.** Simultaneous recordings from another type of interneuron (upper trace) and two leg motoneurons: a flexor (middle trace) and an extensor (bottom trace). Current injection in interneuron (increasing intensity from a–e) causes graded depolarization in interneuron, which in turn synaptically hyperpolarized flexor motoneuron and depolarized extensor motoneuron. Resulting movement of leg shown in (f). Synaptic connections shown in (g). (From Burrows, 1978)

output through the granule cells can be mediated solely by the synaptic potentials in the granule cell dendrites, without need of transmission by an impulse. Electrophysiological recordings together with computer models have suggested that the spines act as semiindependent input–output units. The fact that mitral cells take part in these interactions shows that relay neurons that have long axons and generate impulses can also have local synaptic outputs through their dendrites. Thus, the presynaptic dendrites give the mitral cell added capabilities for local processing (see Chaps. 5 and 12).

Among invertebrates, many cells have been identified that show properties similar to those in the retina and olfactory bulb. One of the earliest examples was a stretch receptor cell in the crab, which responds to stretch stimulation with only graded potentials. This is discussed further in Chap. 14. Other examples include several types of interneuron in the central ganglia of insects, which control motoneurons involved in producing coordinated movements of the legs (see Fig. 8.10B above, and Chap. 21). An example of this type of nonspiking interneuron is shown in Fig. 8.13. The neuron in (A) was filled with cobalt, and the $CoCl_2$ precipitate was intensified with silver. Note the cell body on the lower left, the lack of an axon, the extension of the dendritic tree throughout much of the neuropil, and the profuse branching of the dendrites. Nerve cells show their true beauty when stained like this, and we can sense some of the same feelings that Cajal had when he first beheld these sights under the microscope almost a century ago. The dendrites are sites of both input and output synaptic connections with the dendrites of other interneurons and motoneurons. Some interactions mediated through these synapses are shown in (B). Depolarization of an interneuron by prolonged current injection (top trace) gives rise to a graded synaptic excitation of an extensor motoneuron to the leg (bottom trace) and inhibition of a flexor motoneuron (middle trace). The effect of this interneuron is to cause the leg to extend (f), through the connections indicated in (g). Malcolm Burrows and his colleagues at Cambridge have shown that there is an extensive network of interneurons, some nonspiking and some spiking, which control the leg motoneurons.

Isolated Preparations for Studying Synaptic Circuits

How do neurobiologists analyze the actions of synapses that are embedded in complicated local circuits? In the case of invertebrate ganglia, one can excise the intact ganglion, maintain it in a recording chamber, stimulate selected input and output pathways, and record the synaptic responses using intracellular electrodes. This ease of preparation, together with the large sizes of many of the cells, is why invertebrate ganglia are so attractive to electrophysiologists. Studies in the mammalian brain have traditionally been carried out in the intact anesthetized animal, with all its attendant problems of maintaining the proper levels of anesthesia, allowing for the depressant effects of the anesthetic agents, and controlling the respiratory and vascular pulsations that dislodge the electrode from its intracellular position. A big step forward was the discovery of Chosaburo Yamamoto and Henry McIlwain in London in 1966 that slices of the mammalian brain can be prepared and maintained in a recording chamber. Since that time, many parts of the brain have been studied *in vitro,* including even slices of human cortex obtained in neurosurgical operations. Other preparations include the mammalian brainstem perfused through its blood vessels, and the entire brain of the turtle, from medulla to olfactory nerves, simply bathed in Ringer solution.

These *in vitro* preparations allow investigation of individual synapses and synaptic circuits under conditions in which the region is completely stable, and pharmacological manipulations can be carried out with different drugs in the bathing medium. One of the first and best known preparations is the hippocampal slice, which we will describe briefly.

A summary diagram of the synaptic organization of the hippocampus is shown in Fig. 8.14. As can be seen, the cell layers form two C-shaped sheets, facing and overlapping each other. One of these sheets is the hippocampus proper, containing large pyramidal neurons, which are the main output cells. The other sheet is the dentate fascia, whose output neurons are called granule cells. By virtue of the main fiber pathways, there is a natural sequence of activity in these regions. The sequence actually begins in the entorhinal cortex, a region which receives and integrates multisensory inputs from the touch, auditory, olfactory, and visual pathways, as well as inputs from the cingulate gyrus as a part of limbic systems (see Chap. 29). The entorhinal cortical output fibers ① traverse ("perforate") the surrounding cortex and terminate mainly in the dentate fascia. The dentate granule cells have relatively short axons ("mossy fibers") which connect to the nearest part of the hippocampal pyramidal cell population ②. The axons of these pyramidal cells ③ project to the septum through the fornix; in addition, they send a collateral branch ④ to connect to the long apical dendrites of pyramidal cells in another part of the hippocampus. These cells project to a nearby cortical area, the subiculum ⑤, which in turn projects to the septum through the fornix ⑥.

The hippocampus is particularly suitable for preparing in a slice, because it is built in a series of lamellae, each of which

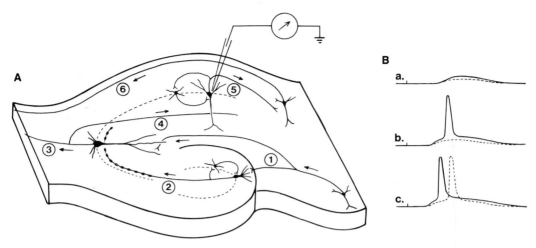

Fig. 8.14. A. Synaptic organization of hippocampus. The circuits are shown as they would be present in a slice of the hippocampus prepared for recording in an isolation chamber. Different parts of the circuits ①–⑥ are described in the text. **B.** Intracellular recordings from pyramidal cell showing plasticity of synaptic actions. a. response to weak volleys in radiation fibers ④ before (dotted trace) and after (solid trace) tetanization of radiation fibers. b and c. Same, stronger volleys. (After Andersen et al., 1977)

contains the whole circuit indicated in Fig. 8.14. In the chamber under the microscope, stimulating electrodes can be placed on each of the layers or pathways and recordings made from each of the types of cell with intracellular microelectrodes. These studies have provided direct confirmation of previous results in the intact animal, and have enabled more precise analyses to be carried out on neuronal properties and synaptic actions. For example, they have shown that the cell bodies of the pyramidal cells generate Na^+ action potentials, whereas their dendrites generate a combination of slow Ca^{2+} and fast Na^+ action potentials. All of the connections shown in Fig. 8.14 are excitatory; the input from the septum is also excitatory. In contrast, the interneurons in the hippocampus and dentate are inhibitory.

The hippocampus has a tendency to generate prolonged, uncontrolled discharges which are the cause of some kinds of epileptic seizures in humans. Analyses of the hippocampal slice are providing evidence for the mechanisms controlling the delicate balance between excitatory and inhibitory synaptic actions, that spell the difference between normal and abnormal function. Glutamate is believed to be the transmitter substance at the perforant pathway synapses, and GABA at the inhibitory interneuronal synapses; the balance between these two is obviously critical for normal function. We will discuss these and other transmitters in the next chapter. The synapses have plastic properties (see Fig. 8.14), which are believed to be involved in memory mechanisms, as will be discussed in Chap. 30.

REFERENCES

Aidley, D. J. 1978. [Chap. 6].

Andersen, P., S. H. Sundberg, O. Sveen, and H. Wigstrom. 1977. Specific long-lasting potentiation of synaptic transmission in hippocampal slices. *Nature 266:* 736–737.

Baker, R. and R. Llinas. 1971. Electrotonic coupling between neurones in the rat mesencephalic nucleus. *J. Physiol 212:* 45–63.

Burrows, M. 1978. Local interneurones and

integration in locust ganglia: *Verh. Dtsch. Zool. Ges.*, Gustav Fischer Verlag. pp. 68–79.

Edwards, C. and D. Ottoson. 1958. The site of impulse initiation in a nerve cell of a crustacean stretch receptor. *J. Physiol. 143:* 138–148.

Fain, G. L., H. M. Gerschenfeld, and F. N. Quandt. 1980. Calcium spike in toad rods. *J. Physiol. 303:* 495–514.

Furshpan, E. J. and D. D. Potter. 1959. Transmission at the giant motor synapses of the crayfish. *J. Physiol. 145:* 289–325.

Gwilliam, G. F. and M. Burrows. 1980. Electrical characteristics of the membrane of an identified insect motor nuerone. *J. Exp. Biol. 86:* 49–61.

Korn, H., C. Sotelo, and F. Crepel. 1973. Electronic coupling between neurons in rat lateral vertibular nucleus. *Exp. Brain. Res. 16:* 255–275.

Kuffler, S. W. and C. Eyzaguirie. 1955. Synoptic inhibition in an isolated nerve cell. *J. Gen. Physiol. 39:* 155–184.

Kuffler, S. W. and J. G. Nicholls. 1976. *From Neuron to Brain.* Sunderland, Mass: Sinauer.

Llinas, R., R. Baker, and C. Sotelo. 1974. Electronic coupling between neurons in the cat inferior olive. *J. Neurophysiol. 37:* 560–571.

Rall, W. 1977. Core conductor theory and cable properties of neurons. In *Handbook of Physiology*, Sect. 1: *The Nervous System*, Vol. 1: *Cellular Biology of Neurons* (ed. by E. R. Kandel). Bethesda: Am. Physiol. Soc. pp. 39–98.

Roberts, A. and B. M. H. Bush (eds.). 1981. *Neurones Without Impulses: Their Significance for Vertebrate and Invertebrate Nervous Systems.* Cambridge: Cambridge University Press.

Shepherd, G. M. 1978. Microcircuits in the nervous system. *Sci. Am. 238:* 92–103.

Siegler, M. V. S. and M. Burrows. 1979. The morphology of local nonspiking interneurones in the metathoracic ganglia of the locust. *J. Comp. Neurol. 183:* 121–148.

Yamamota, C. and H. McIlwain. 1966. Electrical activities in thin sections from the mammalian brain maintained in chemically defined media *in vitro. J. Neurochem. 13:* 1333–1343.

Additional Reading

Bennett, M. V. L. 1977. [Chap. 5].

Kandel, E. R. 1976. [Chap. 2].

9

Neurotransmitters
and Neuromodulators

In the preceding chapter we saw that at chemical synapses the synaptic potential is due to a change of conductance across the postsynaptic membrane. We now ask: what causes this change in conductance? At chemical synapses the change is brought about by means of a chemical substance, a transmitter molecule, that is released by the presynaptic terminal and acts on the postsynaptic membrane. The mechanism is a complicated one, involving elements of ultrastructure, biophysics, and biochemistry. Certain features of the mechanism seem to be common to most synapses, at least those that have short-term actions. However, in other respects there may be many variations; in preceding chapters we have already noted that there may be synaptic actions not associated with morphological junctions, and long-lasting actions that resemble hormonal effects. The uneasy feeling is growing that it will be difficult if not impossible to stretch the definition of synapse to cover all these cases. We will be well-advised to keep in mind the words of Bernard Katz, that "the more one finds out about properties at different synapses, the less grows one's inclination to make general statements about their mode of action!"

Biochemical Background

In contrast to studies of electrical activity in the nervous system, studies of biochemistry had a slower beginning. The apparatus was primitive, and throughout most of the nineteenth century studies were limited to characterizing the presence of fats, proteins, and carbohydrates in ground-up samples of the brain. A decisive step forward was taken around 1900 by a school of English physiologists under John Langley studying the autonomic nerves to the internal organs of the body. They found that electrical stimulation of these nerves produced characteristic bodily changes (increase in heart rate, increased blood pressure), and that these changes were mimicked by the injection of extracts of the adrenal gland. In 1905 T. R. Elliott postulated that impulses in the nerves cause the release of an epinephrine-like substance from the nerve terminals onto the effector cells in the gland. In the same year, Langley, his mentor, further postulated that the cells in the gland have excitatory and inhibitory "receptive substances" which determine what the response and action will be. These were indeed far-reaching suggestions, for in their postulates of a *chemical link* between cells, its dependence on the amount of *electrical impulse activity*, and the presence of specific *molecular receptors*, they presaged most of the essential properties of synaptic transmission that have been analyzed right up to the present day.

The culmination of this line of work was the demonstration in 1921 by Otto Loewi in Germany that the vagus nerve inhibits the heart by liberating the substance acetylcholine. The work of Henry Dale and his collaborators in England in the 1930's provided evidence for acetylcholine as the transmitter substance in autonomic ganglia as well as at the junctions of nerves onto skeletal muscles.

Despite the evidence for chemical transmission at these synapses, the opposite view, that synaptic transmission occurs by means of electrical current passing from one neuron to the next, was held by many neurophysiologists. They objected that many of the biochemical experiments involved collecting substances in perfusates of isolated organs that were stimulated at high rates, so that the results admitted of more than one interpretation. It was also difficult to generalize from these peripheral organs to synapses in the central nervous system where experimental methods, both physiological and biochemical, were at that time almost completely lacking. It was a situation that gave rise to much heated debate, from the 1920's to the early 1950's; some sense of it can be gained from the remarks of Alexander Forbes (one of the few who was able to maintain his good humor) of Harvard, summing up a symposium on the synapse that was held in 1939:

So goes the controversy. Dale in discussing it remarked that it was unreasonable to suppose that nature would provide for the liberation in the ganglion of acetylcholine, the most powerful known stimulant of ganglion cells, for the sole purpose of fooling physiologists. To this Monnier replied that it was likewise unreasonable to suppose action potentials would be delivered at the synapses with voltages apparently adequate for exciting the ganglion cells merely to fool physiologists.

All this confusion was swept away by the advent of the microelectrode and the electron microscope in the 1950's. The old controversy was supplanted as we have seen by the clear evidence that some synapses are chemical and some electrical (and some are mixed).

Molecular Nature of Synaptic Transmission

The chemical synapse that is best understood is the neuromuscular junction, due in large part to the brilliant investigations of Bernard Katz and co-workers in London. The junction, or end-plate, is formed by the axon terminals of a motoneuron on a muscle cell. As a chemical synapse it differs from its counterparts in the brain in several morphological respects: the presynaptic axon terminals are extremely extensive, covering an area of 2000 to 6000 μm^2 (compared with about 1 μm^2 for a simple synaptic terminal in the central nervous system); the synaptic cleft is relatively wide (500–600 Å) and contains a densely staining basal lamina; the postsynaptic membrane (of the muscle cell) forms a trough that receives the axon terminal, the walls of the trough being thrown into numerous folds. Some of these features are shown in Fig. 9.1A. This junctional complex is clearly a synapse, but it just as clearly falls at an extreme end of the morphological spectrum. In line with the comments in Chap. 5, it can be regarded as a specialized synapse of a giant terminal.

An impulse traveling in the motor axon invades the terminals and elicits a relatively large potential response in the muscle, as shown in Fig. 9.2A. This is the end-plate potential (EPP), and is equivalent to an EPSP, being due to the ionic current that flows when the conductances to Na^+ and K^+ are transiently increased. It gives rise to the muscle action potential, which in

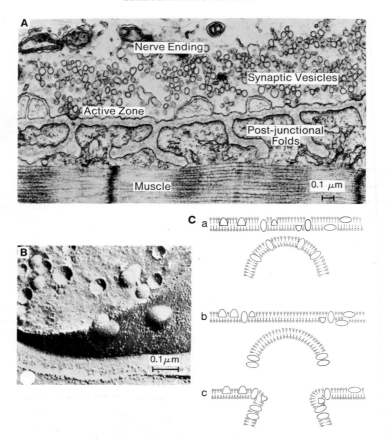

Fig. 9.1. Morphology of the neuromuscular junction of a frog. **A.** Electron micrograph of frog neuromuscular junction. (From Heuser and Reese, 1977) **B.** Freeze-fracture electron micrograph of synaptic vesicles, showing two sites where vesicles are about to fuse with the plasmalemma. Note absence of intramembranous particles at these sites. (From Heuser, 1977) **C.** Diagrams of proposed mechanisms for fusion of vesicle with plasma membrane. Fusion occurs only when fluidity of membrane lipids is raised, allowing lateral displacement (b) of membrane proteins (intramembranous particles) so that fusion can occur (c). (From Maddrell and Nordmann, 1979)

turn activates the contractile machinery of the muscle.

Katz and his colleagues showed that the EPP is built up out of small unitary potentials with similar time courses, which are termed *miniature EPPs* (MEPPs). The summation of three MEPPS is shown in Fig. 9.2B. The unitary nature of the MEPP suggested that it is due to a packet, or *quantum,* of transmitter substance, and it has been calculated that the full EPP is due to the simultaneous release of a total of 100–200 quanta by the impulse in all the terminals. It has also been calculated that

somewhere between 1000 and 10,000 acetylcholine (ACh) molecules are contained in each quantum. Traditionally, it has been tempting to equate one quantum to one vesicle, but recent studies suggest that a quantum may sometimes represent the simultaneous release of several vesicles.

The action of a single ACh molecule has been revealed by slowly passing ACh from a micropipette onto the end-plate, a technique known as microionophoresis. Recordings from the end-plate show the expected slow depolarization, but in addition there are very small fluctuations in the baseline (Fig. 9.2C). Noise analysis has suggested that these are due to the opening and closing of the ionic channels by single ACh molecules as they interact with receptor molecules in the postsynaptic membrane. Patch-clamp recordings have provided evidence for the brief membrane currents through the channels (D) (see also Chap. 8).

Several lines of evidence suggest that the receptor for acetylcholine is a relatively large glycoprotein (M.W. = 200,000). By investigating the effects of toxins that bind to the receptor, it has been estimated that the receptor density is of the order of $10,000/\mu m^2$. This implies that the receptors, and associated channels, are packed into the postsynaptic membrane extremely tightly, with only 10 nm or so between them. It may be recalled from Chap. 7 that this is similar to the density of Na channels in the node of Ranvier, but much higher than the channel densities in axons.

This tight packing of the postsynaptic membrane with chemical receptors appears to be one of the defining characteristics of the synapse at the molecular level.

Graded Release of Transmitter Quanta

The release of transmitter molecules in quanta has been found at several types of synapses, and at present it is believed that such a mechanism may apply to all chemical synapses. We next inquire into the nature of the release. It is essentially controlled by the amount of depolarization of the presynaptic membrane; as shown in Fig. 9.3, the more the applied depolarization in the presynaptic terminal, the more the depolarizing response in the postsynaptic membrane. This is an expression of the generalization linking depolarization with Ca^{2+} entry and transmitter release (see previous chapter). An important point is that the presynaptic depolarization increases the frequency (probability of oc-

Fig. 9.2. Synaptic properties exemplified in different types of recordings from the neuromuscular junction. **A.** Intracellular recording of end-plate potential (EPP) giving rise to an action potential (AP) in the muscle cell: experimental set up shown at left. **B.** High-gain recording, showing summation of miniature end-plate potentials (MEPPs). **C.** Very high gain recording, showing noise induced by ionophoresis of ACh (compare with control trace below). **D.** Extracellular "patch clamp" recording from junctional site, showing currents associated with Na "channels". (A–C from Katz, Miledi, and colleagues (see text); D from Neher and Steinbach, 1977)

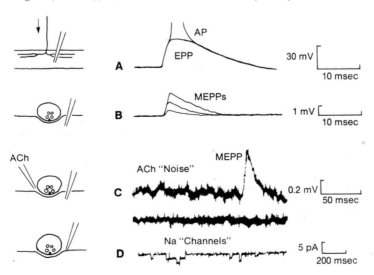

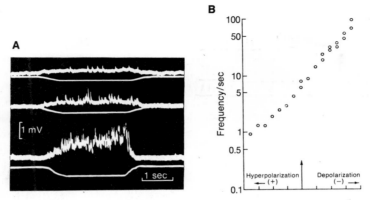

Fig. 9.3. Presynaptic control of the frequency of miniature end-plate potentials (MEPPs). **A.** Recordings at three levels of depolarization of terminals. (From del Castillo and Katz, in Katz, 1962) **B.** Graph showing dependence of MEPP frequency on relative polarization of presynaptic terminals (From Liley, in Katz, 1962)

currence) of the MEPPs; the individual amplitudes remain the same. The postsynaptic depolarization is therefore due to the summation of MEPPs overlapping in time.

The grading of postsynaptic responses with the amount of presynaptic depolarization is a crucial property for synapses in many central regions. A synapse from an incoming axon terminal is normally activated by an impulse invading the terminal, but a synapse from a dendrite may be activated by the graded depolarizations of synaptic potentials within that dendrite. This concept appears to be applicable to the operation of synaptic circuits in a number of regions.

Steps in Synaptic Transmission

The steps in the release process require time. At the neuromuscular junction there is a minimum *synaptic delay*, between the onset of a presynaptic depolarization and the postsynaptic response, of about 0.5 msec. Only about one-tenth of this (50 μsec) can be ascribed to the time for diffusion across the synaptic cleft. We may note in passing that this brief time for diffusion is an expression of an interesting aspect of dimensionality: processes that appear slow on a macroscopic scale are

very fast on a microscopic scale. This is particularly relevant to the mechanisms at work at the microscopic level of synapses; we shall return to this point later.

What accounts for the rest of the synaptic delay? The answer has been sought by examining the junction between two giant nerve fibers which cross each other in the squid. The fibers are large enough to permit microelectrodes to be placed in both pre- and postsynaptic elements, an impossibility at most central synapses (and the reason our understanding leans so heavily on knowledge of peripheral junctions). The junctional area is enormous; 150,000μm^2. Several steps, and the sequence of their timing, have been identified at this giant synapse. It appears that most of the overall synaptic delay is taken up by the opening of Ca^{2+} channels, and that the actual interval between the onset of inward Ca^{2+} current in the presynaptic membrane and the onset of postsynaptic current flow is only some 200 μsec. The amount of postsynaptic response at this junction varies with the amount of presynaptic depolarization, a direct demonstration of the property of graded synaptic action discussed in the previous section.

The synaptic delay is a property that is frequently utilized in the analysis of synaptic circuits. By setting up synchronous volleys in input fibers and noting the times for neuronal responses, the electrophysiologist can determine the pathways for monosynaptic and polysynaptic connections within a local region.

We may summarize the main steps in synaptic transmission thus far identified with the help of the series of diagrams in Fig. 9.4. In A, step 1 is a depolarization of the presynaptic terminal. In B, step 2 is an opening of the gates that permit Ca ions to flow inward (step 3) through their conductance channels. The function of the Ca^{2+} is believed to be promotion of fusion of synaptic vesicles with the plasma membrane (step 4).

The next step is release of transmitter (C, step 5). The nature of this release is keenly debated. Katz and his co-workers noted the possible relation between quanta and vesicles, and suggested that the quantal packets of transmitter are contained in the vesicles and extruded from them at release. Freeze-fracture studies have provided evidence for the attachment of vesicles to the (plasmalemma) (Fig. 9.1B), opening of vesicles into the cleft (Fig. 9.1C), and recycling of membrane to form new vesicles. The elegant experiments of

John Heuser and Tom Reese have provided persuasive evidence for this sequence of events (see also Chap. 4). The process is envisaged as similar to that of exocytosis, which is involved in the release of hormones as shown by W. W. Douglas of Yale in 1970. On the other hand, transmitter is present in the cytoplasm of some terminals, and various lines of evidence have suggested that it may be released directly across the terminal membrane (albeit in quantal packets) with the vesicles playing a storage or otherwise complementary role. The arguments for this view are presented in Cooper, Bloom, and Roth (1982).

After release, diffusion of the transmitter takes place across the cleft (D, step 6), followed by binding to the molecular receptors (step 7). One usually thinks of this as occurring on the postsynaptic terminal, but recent studies have suggested that in some cases a transmitter may also have an action on the presynaptic terminal (autoreceptors).

There then follow events at the molecular level (E, step 8) which range from the simple to the complex. The simplest event is a direct opening of ionic gates (step 9), such as occurs at the neuromuscular junc-

Fig. 9.4. Sequence of events occurring at a synapse.

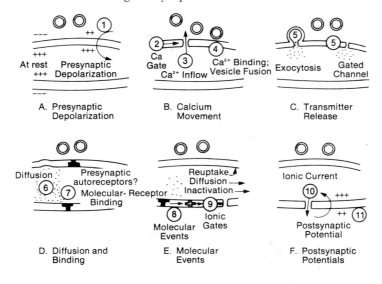

A. Presynaptic Depolarization

B. Calcium Movement

C. Transmitter Release

D. Diffusion and Binding

E. Molecular Events

F. Postsynaptic Potentials

tion and the majority of central synapses that have been studied to date. However, in some cases a series of enzymatic reactions may occur. These have been demonstrated in some hormonal actions on target cells, and similar steps may be involved in some synaptic responses.

While these events are taking place in the postsynaptic membrane, the cleft is being cleared of transmitter by deactivation or hydrolysis, reuptake into the presynaptic terminal, diffusion, or uptake by glial cells.

The final steps, shown in F, are the current flows through ionic conductance channels (step 10) and the resulting synaptic potential (step 11). Of course, any of the steps can be refined to include substeps, or modified to account for other actions (e.g., a conductance decrease instead of increase in step 9).

Calcium and Neuronal Function

At this point it is appropriate to discuss in more detail the role of calcium. Some 30 years ago the cytologist Robert Heilbrun stressed the importance of Ca for many cell functions. Modern research has amply confirmed this view, especially in relation to intracellular free ionized Ca. Several methods are now available for determining these levels. One involves measurements of luminescence of aequorin, a protein isolated from jellyfish, which reacts with Ca^{2+} to emit light. Another method uses metallochromic dyes, such as arsen-

azo III; when this complexes with Ca^{2+} it changes its absorption spectrum, which can be measured by differential spectroscopy. Ion-exchange microelectrodes that are selective for Ca^{2+} have been developed, which give a direct measure of intracellular free Ca^{2+}. Electron microscopy combined with X-ray or proton microprobe spectroscopy has permitted localization of several ion species, including Ca^{2+}, in relation to cell organelles.

All of these methods, together with traditional biochemical methods of measuring radioactive Ca^{2+} fluxes, are in agreement in showing that the levels of free ionized Ca in nerve cells are extremely low. The levels are in the range of 10^{-6} to 10^{-8} M. This may be compared with estimates of about 10^{-4} M of total Ca^{2+}/kg of axoplasm for the case of the squid giant axon (and about 10^{-2} M in seawater). Thus, most of the Ca in a neuron (or any other body cell for that matter) is in the bound form, and only a very small proportion is free and ionized within the cytoplasm. This is one of the keys to the functions of Ca, for it means that the cell can use small changes in local Ca^{2+} levels to promote large or significant effects. This is the basis for the crucial role that Ca^{2+} plays in such diverse functions as secretion, axoplasmic flow, motility, contraction, enzymatic reactions, and membrane permeability. These and other functions are summarized in the diagrams of Fig. 9.5.

With regard to neurotransmitter release, the key event is the influx of Ca^{2+}.

Fig. 9.5. Function of calcium in axons (**A**) and dendrites (**B**). Stimulatory effects indicated by solid thin lines, inhibitory effects by dashed thin lines.

1. voltage-dependent Ca^{2+} conductances, activated by membrane depolarization
2. voltage-insensitive Ca^{2+} conductance, activated by increased levels of cAMP
3. cAmp and cGMP levels modulated by Ca^{2+} through stimulation of phosphodiesterase
4. neurotransmitter activation of adenylate cyclase
5. exocytosis of synaptic and secretory vesicles, dependent on Ca^{2+} influx

7. Ca^{2+} taken up by mitochondria, exchanged for protons
8. sequestration of Ca^{2+} in cisternae
9. neuronal excitability decreased and stabilized by extracellular Ca^{2+}
10. activation of contractile fibrils, either directly by Ca^{2+} or through changes in cAMP levels
11. metabolic pumps for Ca^{2+} efflux and Na:Ca and Ca:Ca exchange

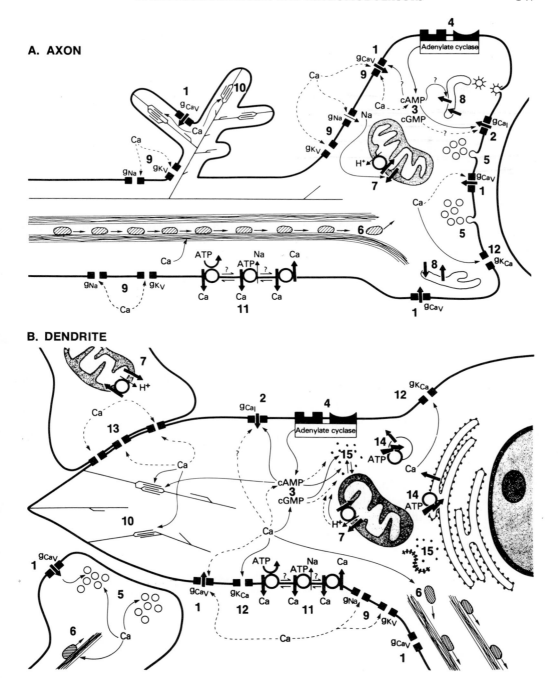

12. Ca^{2+}-dependent K$^+$ conductances, activated by increased Ca^{2+}
13. increased Ca^{2+} causes decrease in conductance of electrical synapses
14. binding of Ca^{2+} to endoplasmic reticulum

and other organelles and macromolecules, including calmodulin
15. Ca effects on neuronal metabolism (lowered pH, effects on enzymes, depression of cAMP and cGMP levels)

(From Erulkar and Fine, 1979)

After the Ca^{2+} has participated in exocytosis of synaptic vesicles and release of neurotransmitter, it must be cleared from the cytoplasm. The most important mechanisms for doing this are binding to calmodulin, and binding to endoplasmic reticulum and other organelles (⑭ in diagram), sequestration in cisternae ⑧, uptake by mitochondria ⑦, and efflux by pumping ⑪. These mechanisms controlling the availability of free Ca are in turn linked in many ways to pathways for transmitter synthesis and the general metabolism of the cell. Through these means, Ca^{2+} plays important roles in longer-term processes underlying synaptic plasticity, development, and memory and learning; these will be discussed in later chapters.

Metabolic Pathways

We have seen that morphologically synapses share certain fine-structural features, and physiologically they share certain steps and actions. This uniformity is remarkable when one considers the diversity of chemical substances that can function as transmitters.

A summary of most of the substances that have been identified as transmitters in the nervous system, and the main metabolic steps and pathways for their synthesis, is shown in the diagrams of Figs. 9.6 and 9.7. The flow in Fig. 9.6 starts at the top, recognizing that metabolism begins with the substances provided from the bloodstream. This is a critical factor for nerve cells, because of the so-called *blood-brain barrier*. The barrier is formed in the vertebrate brain by tight junctions between capillary endothelial cells, which isolate the brain (with the exception of certain regions) from circulating substances in the bloodstream. The only substances to pass the barrier are ions, glucose, and essential amino acids and fatty acids. The central role of glucose in this regard, for energy metabolism and for synthesis of amino acids and proteins, is illustrated in the diagram. We shall recur

to this point below, and later in the chapter.

The diagram indicates at the top the main transmitter categories: acetylcholine, catecholamines, amino acids, and peptides. The closed boxes indicate the different individual types of molecules. A few generalizations may be made at this point. The transmitter compounds are all low molecular weight, water soluble (polar) amines or amino acids and related substances. Acetylcholine and the catecholamines are synthesized from circulating precursors, whereas the amino acids and peptides are ultimately synthesized from circulating glucose. It is a remarkable testimony to nature's conservative ways that, despite differences in circulatory systems and metabolic pathways, invertebrates and vertebrates share most of the same neurotransmitter substances depicted in Fig. 9.6.

The types of synaptic actions (excitatory or inhibitory) that have been correlated with particular compounds are also indicated in the diagram. Although it is commonly believed that a transmitter everywhere has the same specific action, it can be seen that this is not always correct. For example, acetylcholine has an inhibitory action on the heart, but at the neuromuscular junction we have seen that its action is excitatory. Both actions are therefore included beside the box for acetylcholine in the diagram. From this and other examples we recognize an important principle of synaptic organization, that *a specific transmitter substance is not in general identified with only one specific postsynaptic action*. In more general terms, the nervous system can often use the same substance for different purposes; obversely, the same function (i.e., excitation) can be mediated by different substances. This flexible relation between transmitter substance and physiological action may be regarded as a biochemical corollary to the flexible relation that exists between the structure and function of neuronal processes.

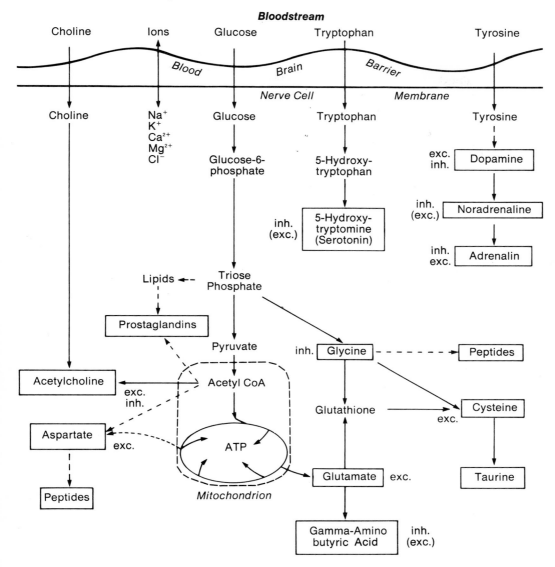

Fig. 9.6. Summary of neurotransmitters and related compounds, and some pathways involved in their transport from the bloodstream and their metabolism within the nerve cell. (Modified from Cooper et al., 1982)

Dale's Principle

Although the nervous system as a whole can use different substances at different synapses, this is not necessarily true for an individual neuron. The metabolic unity of the neuron would seem to require that it release the same transmitter substance at all its synapses. This is *Dale's Principle*

(*Law*) and, since it can be easily misunderstood, it is well to quote the original formulation. In a review of synaptic transmission in the autonomic nervous system many years ago, Dale (1935) wrote

. . . the phenomena of regeneration appear to indicate that the nature of the chemical function, whether cholinergic or adrenergic, is

Compound	Structure	Synthesis	Inactivation
Acetylcholine (ACh)	$H_3C-\overset{O}{\overset{\|}{C}}-O-(CH_2)_2\overset{+}{N}$ (CH_3)	CAT	AChE
Dopamine (DA)	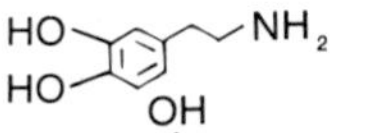 $HO-$⬡$-NH_2$ (with OH)	DDC	Reuptake MAO, COMT
Noradrenaline (NA)	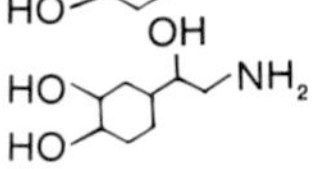 $HO-$⬡$-NH_2$	DBH	Reuptake MAO, COMT
Serotonin (5HT)	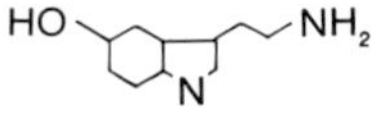 $HO-$⬡$-NH_2$ (indole ring with N)	AADC	Reuptake MAO
Gamma-Amino butyric Acid (GABA)	$H_2\overset{+}{N}-(CH_2)_3-\overset{O}{\overset{\|}{C}}-OH$	GAD	Reuptake GABA-T
Glycine (Gly)	$H_3\overset{+}{N}-CH_2-\overset{O}{\overset{\|}{C}}-OH$	?	?

Fig. 9.7. Summary of molecular structures of principal neurotransmitter substances, together with modes of synthesis and degradation. Synthesis: CAT, choline acetyltransferase; DDC, dopa decarboxylase; DBH; dopamine-B-hydroxylase; AADC, amino acid decarboxylase; GAD, glutamic acid decarboxylase. Inactivation: AChE, acetyl cholinesterase; MAO, monoamine oxidase; COMT, catechol-o-methyl transferase; GABA-T, GABA transaminase. (Modified from Mountcastle, 1980)

characteristic for each particular neurone, and unchangeable. When we are dealing with two different endings of the same sensory neurone, the one peripheral and concerned with vasodilatation and the other at a central synapse, can we suppose that the discovery and identification of a chemical transmitter of axon-reflex dilation would furnish a hint as to the nature of the transmission process at a central synapse? The possibility has at least some value as a stimulus to further experiment.

This is the acorn from which the mighty oak has grown. The principle is profound, for it implies that during development some process of differentiation determines the particular secretory product a given neuron will manufacture, store, and release (see Chap. 10). The usefulness of the principle in the analysis of synaptic circuits is explicit in Dale's statement, for, if a substance can be established as the transmitter at one synapse, it can be inferred to be the transmitter at all other synapses made by that neuron.

A point that is often misunderstood is that Dale's law only applies to the presynaptic unity of the neuron; it does not apply to the postsynaptic actions the transmitter will have at the synapses made by the neuron onto different target neurons.

These actions may be similar, or they may be different. As an example, acetylcholine released at motoneuron nerve terminals has an excitatory action at the neuromuscular junction, whereas acetylcholine released from vagal nerve terminals has an inhibitory action in the heart. Similar possibilities for diversity of action exist for the transmitter released from a single neuron. Such neurons have been termed *multiaction cells*, and have been particularly well studied in invertebrates. Eric Kandel (1976) has summarized the conclusions from this work as follows:

1. The sign of the synaptic action is not determined by the transmitter but by the properties of the receptors on the postsynaptic cell.
2. The receptors in the follower [postsynaptic] cells of a single presynaptic neuron can be pharmacologically distinct and can control different ionic channels.
3. A single follower cell may have more than one kind of receptor for a given transmitter, with each receptor controlling a different ionic conductance mechanism.

As a result of these three features, cells can mediate opposite synaptic actions to different follower cells or to a single follower cell.

These may be regarded as corollaries to Dale's Law. There is as yet limited evidence for multiaction cells in the vertebrate nervous system.

What of the possibility of cells with multiple transmitters? Among invertebrates, four putative transmitters have been reported in single neurons of *Aplysia*. In the vertebrate, there is increasing evidence from the extensive studies of Tomas Hökfelt and his co-workers in Stockholm for the presence of more than one transmitter substance in single nerve terminals in many parts of the nervous system. One common pattern appears to be the presence of a peptide within a monoamine-containing terminal (see below). The fact that some synaptic terminals contain more than one type of synaptic vesicle is also suggestive in this regard.

Identification of Neurotransmitters and Neuropeptides

Thus far we have discussed transmitters as if it were known which substances function at different synapses. The identification of transmitters is in fact one of the most difficult problems in all of neurobiology. Experimentally, certain criteria must be met; each involves a special methodology and, to a degree, indirect evidence, estimates, and inferences. The criteria are summarized in Table 9.1:

There is general agreement that the identification of acetylcholine as the transmitter at the neuromuscular junction comes closest to fulfilling these criteria. The role of GABA at the inhibitory synapses of the crayfish neuromuscular junction was also demonstrated particularly clearly by Ed Kravitz and his colleagues at Harvard. There is also good evidence regarding vertebrate autonomic ganglia and several types of invertebrate neurons. In other cases, all too often our knowledge rests on only one or two, methodological approaches. Thus, the evidence is often fragmentary. As we meet the members of the transmitter family in the various regions of the brain, we must remember that many of them bear the same first name: putative.

One of the most important developments of recent years in neurobiology has been recognition of the widespread distribution of *neuroactive peptides* in the nervous system. Many of these compounds were identified in other organs by biochemists working over the past 50 years or so, and were only recently identified in the

Table 9.1 Steps in identification of neurotransmitters and neuropeptides

Neurotransmitters	Neuropeptides
1. *Anatomical:* presence of the substance in appropriate amounts in presynaptic processes.	1. Development of a quantitative bioassay
2. *Biochemical:* presence and operation of enzymes that synthesize the substance in the presynaptic neuron and processes, and remove or inactivate the substance at the synapse.	2. Evidence that the biologically active material is peptidic in nature
3. *Physiological:* demonstration that physiological stimulation causes the presynaptic terminal to release the substance, and that ionophoretic application of the substance to the synapse in appropriate amounts mimics the natural response.	3. Development of extraction and separation procedures for maximum yields of the purified peptide
4. *Pharmacological:* drugs that affect the different enzymatic or biophysical steps have their expected effects on synthesis, storage, release, action, inactivation, and reuptake of the substance.	4. Chemical and physical characterization of the pure peptide (e.g., molecular weight determination and amino acid composition)
	5. Obtain amino acid sequence of the peptide
	6. Chemical synthesis of the peptide (which is then tested for bioactivity using quantative bioassay)
	7. Produce antibodies to peptide
	8. Characterization of antibodies using synthetic analogs of the peptide (purification of antibodies)
	9. Development of immunological assays and procedures for use on neural tissues (e.g., radioimmunoassay and immunocytochemistry)

From Gainer and Brownstein (1981)

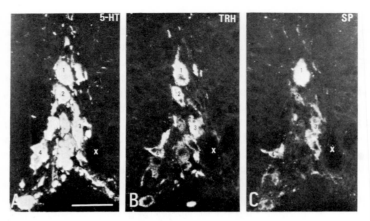

Fig. 9.8. Immunocytochemical demonstration of neuroactive peptides. (A–C) are consecutive thin sections of the raphé nucleus in the medulla oblongata, treated with antisera to serotonin (A), thyroid hormone releasing hormone (B), and substance P (C). Several cells (1–4), identifiable in all three sections, can be seen to be immunoreactive to all three antisera. (X) marks a blood vessel, used to orient the slides. Arrows point to a process emanating from cell 1. (From Johansson et al., 1981)

nervous system. The names of these compounds, such as vasopressin or prostaglandin, reflect the organ in which they were first found or the physiological action that was first studied. Similarly, some have names, like luteinizing hormone releasing hormone (LHRH), reflecting one specific function of the nervous system. A number of peptides previously identified in the gut have turned up in the central nervous system. Thus, the nomenclature for these substances can be somewhat confusing.

Like neurotransmitters, peptides can only be identified as neuroactive substances by meeting certain criteria. Although there is no set number of these, the list in Table 9.1 can serve as a useful guide. It begins with a bioassay, which involves procedures for extraction and testing which are actually quite stringent. Separation and purification of the peptide depend on a number of chromatographic techniques and other standard and advanced biochemical methodologies. The localization of peptides in neural tissue relies on immunological methods, which are especially effective because of their high sensitivity and high specificity. The ability

of a substance to evoke a response when experimentally applied to a neuron is a final, and important, criterion, but only one of many.

One of the biggest advances in recent years is the ability to localize neuroactive substances like peptides within individual neurons using immunological methods. Briefly, the substance of interest (X) is first injected as an antigen into a suitable subject (rabbit) in order to induce circulating antibodies (anti-X). Next, sections are prepared of the nervous tissue in which one wants to study the cellular localization of X. The sections are exposed to a series of agents, beginning with anti-X, which is then reacted with a second antibody to anti-X. This second antibody is then conjugated with an appropriate agent for visualization; this is commonly a fluorescent molecule, or horseradish peroxidase. An example of the result is shown in Fig. 9.8.

Under the procedure just described, the initial antibodies (anti-X) are produced by the entire population of lymphocytes in the immune system of the injected rabbit. These antibodies are thus polyclonal, being produced by lymphocytes with varying degrees of specificity for X. Monoclonal antibodies, specific for X, can be obtained by appropriate screening for the specific lymphocytes. Monoclonal antibodies promise to enhance greatly the specificity of immunocytochemical methods for identifying neuroactive substances in neurons. In addition, the general methodology can be adapted for even greater precision, such as for visualizing specific messenger RNA coded for synthesis of a particular peptide or protein (see Chap. 4).

The best known neuroactive peptides are summarized in Fig. 9.9. This list can be regarded only as provisional; indeed, many things in this fast-moving field are provisional. As one of our colleagues reviewing this field has put it, "We write with pencil in one hand and eraser in the

Fig. 9.9. Neuroactive peptides, arranged in order of increasing number of carbon atoms. (Modified from Iversen, 1979)

Table 9.2   Properties of neurotransmitters and neuropeptides

Properties of neurotransmitters	Properties of neuropeptides
medium to high concentration	extremely low concentration
high affinity binding to receptors	low affinity binding to receptors
low potency	extremely high potency
high specificity	high specificity
moderate rate of synthesis	low rate of synthesis (*in vitro*)
small molecules (2–10 carbons)	small to medium-size molecules (2–100 carbons)

Adapted in part from Reichelt and Edminson (1977)

other"! It can be seen that many of the peptides contain 2–10 amino acids, and thus overlap in size with small amino acid transmitters, on the one hand, and hormones on the other.

The large numbers of peptides, and their idiosyncratic names, give the impression that this is a heterogeneous collection of substances. However, the more that is learned about them, the more it is possible to discern some powerful unifying principles underlying their functions. First, neuroendocrine cells, secreting peptides, were among the first kinds of neurons to appear in the evolution of primitive nervous systems (see Chap. 2). Second, neuropeptides are strongly conserved in phylogeny, so that similar substances or similar amino acid sequences appear in different species, both invertebrate and vertebrate. Third, many peptides of the nervous system are also found in other tissues of the body, such as the gut, as already mentioned. This has suggested that all peptidergic neurons may derive embryologically from a common type of neuroectodermal precursor cell, a cell characterized biochemically by "amine precursor uptake carboxylation: APUD". Finally, neuroactive peptides as a class share certain biochemical and physiological properties. Table 9.2 summarizes some of these, and contrasts them with properties of neurotransmitters.

With this as a general orientation to neuroactive substances, let us consider in more detail the main aspects of their synthesis, molecular receptors, time course of action, and transport within the neuron.

Synthesis. The synthesis of the simpler neurotransmitter substances has been summarized in Fig. 9.6. As a general rule these substances are assembled from simpler precursors. Many steps along the way are susceptible to blocking by pharmacological agents, which is the basis for the action of many drugs that affect the nervous system, as we will note in later chapters.

The synthesis of neuroactive peptides, in contrast, is more complicated. It follows the plan for peptide hormones (Fig. 9.10) in which amino acids and other precursors are first assembled by the rough ER into a large polypeptide *prehormone*. This is then reduced in the Golgi body to a somewhat smaller *prohormone*, which in turn is cleaved into fragments that are the active peptides, and secreted in vesicles. This general sequence has been shown to apply to the manufacture of several neuroactive peptides, including the enkephalins. In fact, it was the fortuitous recognition that the prohormone lipotropin contains the amino acid sequence of enkephalin that led to our knowledge of the steps in manufacture of peptides with morphinelike actions.

In the classical exocrine secretory cell, one cell secretes multiple peptides, whereas in endocrine secretory cells, one cell secretes one peptide hormone (see Fig. 9.10). It has been supposed that, as expressed in Dale's law, neurons resemble endocrine cells. However, as we have already mentioned, there is increasing evidence for the ability of neurons to synthesize and se-

A

Amino Acids and Other Precursors

Prehormone

18-30 amino acids (signal peptide for attachment to ribosomes of RER)

Prohormone

Hormone + Carrier Protein

Hormone

secretion

B

Exocrine Secretory Cell (Exocrine Pancreas; Parotid Gland)

P_1 $P_2 \ldots P_n$

one cell = multiple active peptides (20-40)

Endocrine and Neuroendocrine Secretory Cells

one cell = one hormone (or several hormones?)

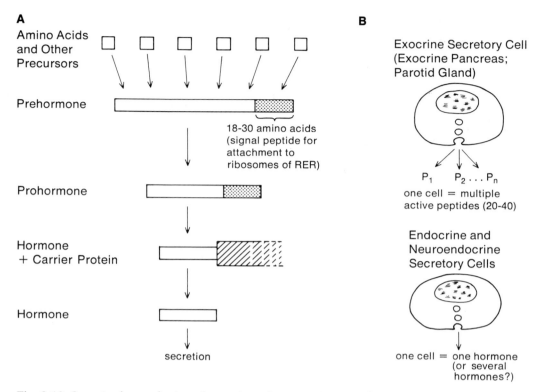

Fig. 9.10. Steps in the synthesis and secretion of neuroactive peptides. **A.** Steps in synthesis at the molecular level. **B.** Differences between an endocrine and an exocrine type of secretory cell.

crete more than one neuroactive substance.

Reception. Let us now consider the mechanisms of reception. Given the wide range of substances with neuroactive properties, it is not surprising to learn that there is a variety of mechanisms of reception at the molecular level. Figure 9.11 provides a summary of some of the main types that have been identified thus far, arranged in order from those associated with simple molecules to more complex types.

At the first level (A) is acetylcholine (ACh), which acts directly on a receptor protein in the postsynaptic membrane. One says that the acetylcholine acts as a *ligand,* which is bound to specific sites in the protein. This produces, in turn, the change in membrane permeability (Fig. 9.4). The membrane response may be rapid or slow (see below). The action of

the ACh is terminated by hydrolysis by the enzyme acetylcholinesterase, with reuptake of the choline into the presynaptic terminal.

In comparison, the action of gamma aminobutyric acid (GABA) is shown in Fig. 9.11B. GABA is believed to be bound to two types of membrane receptors, with high or low affinity. These in turn control the *ionophore* (conductance channel) for Cl^-, the ion that moves during a GABAergic IPSP. The GABA blockers, picrotoxin and bicuilline, act at specific sites on the receptor protein complex to block control of the Cl^- ionophore by GABA. The benzodiazepine drugs act at different sites to produce depression of GABAergic synapses; this is useful clinically in controlling anxiety and depression. The diagram also shows that GABA is cleared from the cleft by uptake into the presynaptic terminal as well as into glia. Glia, in

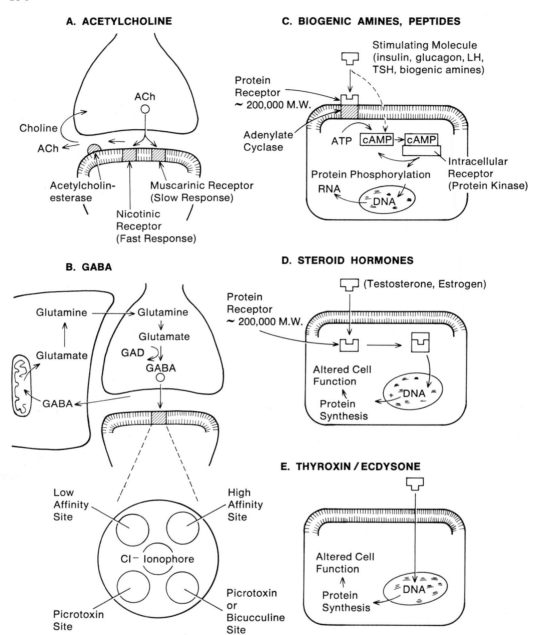

Fig. 9.11. Molecular mechanisms for reception of different neuroactive substances. (Diagrams from many sources)

fact, play an important role in both up-take and metabolism of GABA.

A third prevalent type of mechanism is shown in Fig. 9.11C. Here the transmitter molecule is bound to a membrane protein, as in the previous examples, and there are mechanisms for clearing the cleft and for reuptake. The subsequent response in the postsynaptic terminal is more compli-cated, however (step 9 in Fig. 9.4). The receptor protein is an adenylate cyclase, which in turn activates an internal recep-tor, a protein kinase that brings about protein phosphorylation. This eventuates in a change in the ionic conductance of the membrane. This is the "second messen-ger" system, first worked out for the ac-tion of the hormone insulin by Earl Suth-erland and his colleagues at Vanderbilt in the 1950's, and extended to the nervous system by Paul Greengard at Yale. The mechanism is believed to be involved in the mediation of responses to such diverse substances as the biogenic amines, LHRH, and TRH. In addition to the membrane and subjacent cytoplasm, the response may also involve the genome of the cell, through actions on DNA, and thus pro-duce long-term effects on cell metabolism, growth, and differentiation.

For comparison, the mechanism of ac-tion of a steroid hormone is shown in Fig. 9.11D. Here the receptor protein is en-tirely within the cell cytoplasm; the hor-mone–receptor complex then produces its specific effects on nuclear DNA. There are two types of effect: *organizational,* which operates during development, such as the control of expression of male and female characteristics by sex hormones; and *activational,* which brings about more immediate responses in cell function. We will discuss these actions further in Chap. 28.

A related type of hormonal action is shown in E. Here the hormone enters the cell and acts directly on the nuclear DNA. This applies to the hormone thyroxine, and also to the invertebrate hormone ecdy-sone. Ecdysone controls molting during development of the insect from larval to adult forms (next chapter).

In summary, there are several different types of mechanisms for bringing about binding of a released molecule to a recep-tor molecule, and producing a subsequent change in the postsynaptic neuron. When this change occurs in the membrane to produce a synaptic potential, we say that the released molecule acts as a neuro-transmitter. Changes that occur in other parts of the cell (cytoplasm or nucleus) produce more complicated effects, and we generally say that the released molecules that bring these about are neuromodula-tors. This term can also be applied to cases in which a substance influences the re-lease, binding, or other action of a neuro-transmitter.

Time Course. Associated with the increas-ing number of neuroactive substances being recognized is the fact that their time courses of action vary over a wide range. This is summarized schematically in Fig. 9.12. The time courses of action of the classical neurotransmitters, such as ace-tylcholine, represent the briefest types. The slower actions of neurotransmitters over-lap with the periods of facilitation and depression that occur in the aftermath of activity, and with the effects mediated by peptides and hormones. These in turn overlap with trophic effects, and with the neuronal interactions that underlie such processes as development and plasticity.

Figure 9.12 illustrates further the prob-lem that can arise in defining a neuro-transmitter. Thus, to the traditional crite-ria mentioned previously, one must now add another dimension: the time course of action. At present, substances with brief actions appear to be characteristic of neu-rotransmitters, while those with long-term effects are more representative of neuro-modulators. For substances, such as the monoamines, whose actions generally fall between these two extremes, the term neurotransmodulator has even been sug-gested!

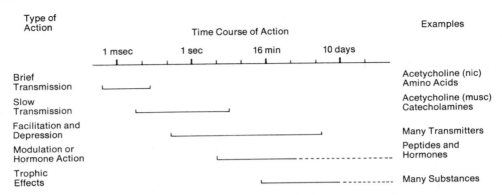

Fig. 9.12. Time courses of action of neurotransmitters and related compounds.

Although this profusion of time courses of action thus complicates our terminology, it is nonetheless telling us something very important about how the nervous system works. Animal behavior involves a wide range of time courses of action. Sensory systems are organized to receive and process information extremely quickly, often within milliseconds. Motor systems similarly provide for very rapid movements, also in the millisecond range such as those made in typewriting or playing a piano. On the other hand, some movements are very slow; examples are the maintenance of a standing posture, or the prolonged contraction of muscles of a clam that close the shell. The same applies to central systems, from the quick initiation of a voluntary movement, to the slow modulation of states of sleep or arousal during the day and night, to the gradual changes that occur during development, maturation, and ageing. One of the most profound questions about the nervous system is how it coordinates all these activities taking place simultaneously within the same neurons and neural circuits. At least part of the answer appears to be that it utilizes different substances with actions on different receptors with different time courses, as we have discussed above.

Transport of Substances

Closely related to synaptic transmission and its associated metabolic processes is the transport of substances within the nerve cell. Far from being the static structure visualized in microscopic sections, the neuron at the molecular level is in constant motion. As noted in the discussion of cell organelles in Chap. 4, there is ongoing synthesis of transmitter molecules, macromolecules, and vesicle membranes in the cell body, and movement out into the axon and dendrites (see Fig. 9.13). Some of these substances pass out of axon terminals and are taken up by postsynaptic cells, as shown by transneuronal transport of labeled amino acids incorporated into protein. Proteins and small enzymes also are taken up by axon terminals and move in the axon toward the cell body; this is the basis of the mapping of axonal projections by the horseradish peroxidase technique. A similar movement of substances takes place in dendrites, involving transmitters, enzymes, and even such large molecules as nucleoside derivatives. Some of these substances are those taken up from neighboring terminals by transneuronal transport. Ions and small molecules move directly between cells through the channels of gap junctions. Thus, there is constant biochemical transport and communication between all parts of the neuron and between neighboring neurons.

These movements take place at different rates. Axoplasmic transport, in mammals, as noted in Chap. 4, ranges from slow (about 1 mm/day) to fast (100–400 mm/day). It is of interest to relate these rates to different levels of dimensionality. This can be done if we plot distance against time on logarithmic scales, as in Fig. 9.14. The fastest transport in axons thus translates to a rate of about 5 μm/sec. Surprisingly, this is similar to the rate that has been estimated for diffusion of the phospholipids in the cell membrane, as shown in the graph. Slow transport is at a rate of 0.01 μm (10 nm)/sec; this is even slower than the estimated rate of diffusion of proteins in the cell membrane. These values serve to emphasize that the membrane, as well as the internal cell substance, is in dynamic flux.

With regard to transport of synaptic transmitters and vesicular membrane, this would take many minutes even by fast transport in the shortest axons (that are a millimeter or less in length), and would be

a matter of hours in the longest axons. This helps to explain why axonal terminals contain some of their own metabolic machinery for transmitter synthesis and reuptake. In the case of output synapses from dendrites, however, the distances from the cell body are characteristically less than one millimeter, and the synapses would seem to be able to draw more directly on the metabolic resources of the cell body for sustaining their activity. For output synapses from the cell body itself, this of course becomes obvious.

Other rates are also shown in Fig. 9.14, for comparison. Note that the slowest rate of nerve conduction is more than five orders of magnitude faster than the fastest axonal transport; even the slowest impulses travel a micron in less than a microsecond. Synaptic transmitter diffusion

Fig. 9.13. Transport of substances within and between nerve cells.

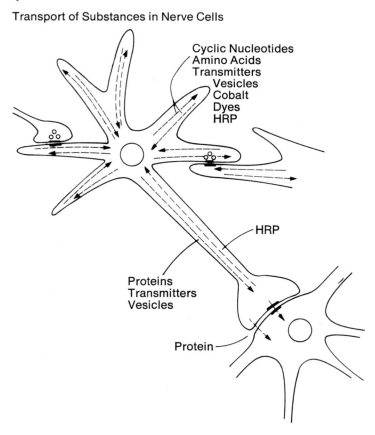

Transport of Substances in Nerve Cells

Cyclic Nucleotides
Amino Acids
Transmitters
Vesicles
Cobalt
Dyes
HRP

HRP

Proteins
Transmitters
Vesicles

Protein

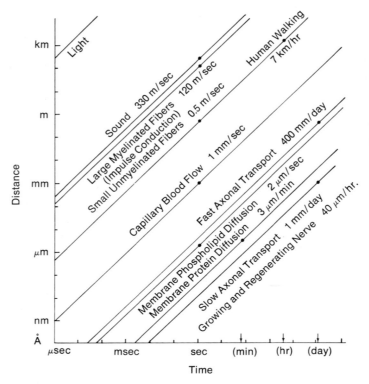

Fig. 9.14. Graph showing rates of movement of substances and conduction of activity for different dimensions of time and space. Small dots indicate values used for common expressions for rates.

through the cleft (see earlier in this chapter) works out to a rate about one micron per millisecond, similar to the rate of capillary blood flow. The reader can insert other rates and relations as well. The general principle, that physiological processes at microscopic levels take place in incredibly short times, is readily apparent. It is also the reason why the time domain for microelectrode analysis of synaptic functions commonly falls into the range of milliseconds.

Energy Metabolism and 2-Deoxyglucose Mapping

In discussing metabolic pathways we noted that the vertebrate brain is virtually completely dependent on glucose for energy metabolism. Glucose is taken up by neurons and phosphorylated by hexokinase to

glucose-6-phosphate. As in other cells of the body, it is then metabolized in the cytosol through the glycolytic chain to pyruvate, which enters the mitochondria and undergoes oxidative metabolism by the Krebs cycle to yield high-energy phosphates. The sequence is indicated in Fig. 9.6, and the initial steps in more detail in Fig. 9.15. The high-energy phosphate is incorporated into adenosine triphosphate (ATP) and made available for the on-going metabolism of the neuron and for the immediate demands related to nervous activity.

What types of activity require energy? We have seen that ions move passively through their conductance channels in the membrane; however, the concentration gradients are maintained by the metabolic pump, which requires energy. The squid giant axon can continue to generate action potentials for hours after metabolic poisoning, because the passive ion flows are small compared with the large amounts of available ions. However, the proportions increase in smaller fibers, with their larger surface-to-volume ratios; in the finest unmyelinated fibers, impulse activity places immediate demands on the metabolic pump. Similar factors are involved at synapses; the ion flows themselves are passive, but the restoration and maintenance of ion concentrations require energy, as does the synthesis of transmitters and the recycling of membrane. Also, higher rates of ion pumping may be expected at sites where the resting membrane potential is relatively low because of an increased permeability to Na (as at nodes of Ranvier, and in retinal receptors). The high density of mitochondria in the small processes of axons and dendrites reflects to a large extent the energy demands of synapses at those sites.

These types of activity thus have immediate energy demands, and there are now methods which use this property to map the distribution of activity in the brain during different functional states. The method was introduced by Louis Sokoloff and his colleagues at the National Institutes of Health, and makes use of an analogue of glucose, 2-deoxyglucose (2DG), which simply lacks an oxygen on the second carbon atom. As shown in Fig. 9.15, 2DG is taken up and phosphorylated by hexokinase like glucose. However, the resulting 2DG-6-P is not a substrate for phosphoglucose isomerase and cannot be metabolized further; it is trapped in the tissue. Sokoloff and his colleagues reasoned that if 2DG was labeled with radioactive carbon (^{14}C) and injected in tracer amounts into an animal, the sites of increased ^{14}C-2DG-6-P could be marked by exposing sections of the brain tissue to X-ray film. As many sections can be made as desired, so that the activity pattern associated with a particular functional state can be mapped throughout the entire brain.

Fig. 9.15. Pathways involved in uptake and initial metabolism in nerve cells of glucose and the analogue, 2-deoxyglucose.

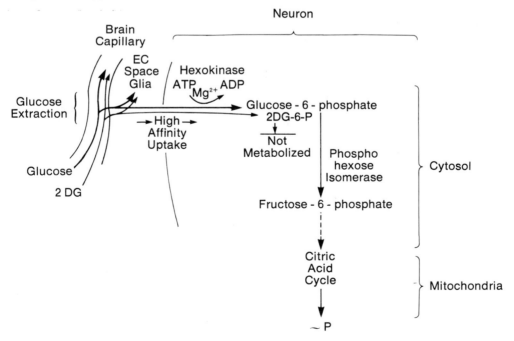

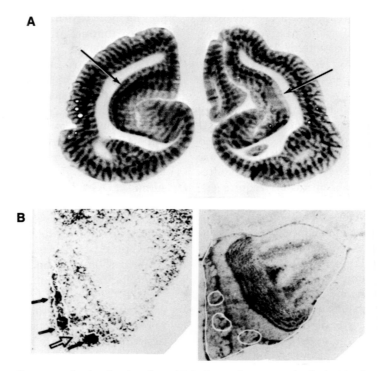

Fig. 9.16. Autoradiograms obtained using the 14C-2-deoxyglucose method. **A.** Monkey visual cortex after removal of one eye. Arrows indicate blind spots. (From Sokoloff, 1977) **B.** Rat olfactory bulb after exposure to odor of amyl acetate. *Left*, autoradiogram showing three small dense foci (arrows) and intervening light region (open arrow). *Right*, outlines of dense foci fall precisely on small groups of glomeruli when superimposed on Nissl-stained section of bulb. (From Stewart et al., 1979)

The method has been applied to many systems. Among the most dramatic results are those that have been obtained in the visual system. A monkey is injected a day after one eye has been removed. The autoradiograms of the visual cortex show alternating dark and light stripes, which represent the ocular dominance columns that had previously been demonstrated by electrophysiology and anatomical methods (see Chap. 17). These results are shown in Fig. 9.16A. For comparison, the method has also been successfully applied to the olfactory system, where relatively little was known about spatial activity patterns. Surprisingly, after an injection into a rat breathing an odor, small intense foci of activity are found in the olfactory bulb over the glomerular layer, where the axons from the olfactory receptor cells terminate. These results are shown in Fig. 9.16B (see Chap. 12 for further discussion of olfactory bulb function).

These results indicate the power of this method for confirming and extending our previous knowledge about particular systems, and for providing new insights into systems in which information about spatial activity patterns has not been obtainable by other methods. The applications of this and related methods range from the analysis of local circuit organization to the identification of activity patterns underlying cognition, as we shall see in Chap. 31.

REFERENCES

Cooper, J. R., F. E. Bloom, and R. H. Roth. 1982. *The Biochemical Basis of Neuropharmacology.* New York: Oxford.

Dale, H. H. 1935. Pharmacology and nerve endings. *Proc. Roy. Soc. Med. 28:* 319–332.

Erulkar, S. D. and A. Fine. 1979. Calcium in the nervous system. *Rev. Neurosci. 4:* 179–232.

Forbes, A. 1939. Problems of synaptic functions. *J. Neurophysiol. 2:* 465–472.

Gainer, H. and M. J. Brownstein. 1981. [Chap. 4].

Heuser, J. E. 1977. Synaptic vesicle exocytosis revealed in quick-frozen frog neuromuscular junctions treated with 4-aminopyridine and given a single electrical shock. In *Soc. for Neurosci. Symp.* Vol. 2 (ed. by W. M. Cowan and J. A. Ferrendelli). Bethesda, Md.: Soc. for Neurosci. pp. 215–239.

Heuser, J. E. and T. S. Reese. 1977. Structure of the synapse. In *Handbook of Physiology*, Vol. 1. *The Nervous System* (ed. by E. R. Kandel). Bethesda, Md.: Am. Physiol. Soc. pp. 261–294.

Iversen, L. 1979. Chemistry of the Brain. *Sci. Am.* 241: 118–129.

Johansson, O., T. Hökfelt, B. Pernow, S. L. Jeffcoate, N. White, H. W. M. Steinbusch, A. A. J. Verhofstad, P. C. Emson, and E. Spindel. 1981. Immunohistochemical support for three putative transmitters in one neuron: coexistence of 5-hydroxytryptamine, substance P-and thyrotropin releasing hormone-like immunoreactivity in medullary neurons projecting to the spinal cord. *Neurosci.* 6: 1857–1881.

Kandel, E. R. 1976. [Chap. 2].

Katz, B. 1962. [Chap. 6].

Maddrell, S. H. P. and J. J. Nordmann. 1979. *Neurosecretion.* New York: Wiley.

Mountcastle, V. B. (ed.) 1980. *Medical Physiology.* St. Louis: Mosby.

Neher, E. and J. H. Steinbach. 1978. Local anaesthetics transiently block currents through single acetylcholine-receptor channels. *J. Physiol.* 227: 153–176.

Reichelt, K. L. and P. D. Edminson. 1977. Peptides containing probable transmitter candidates in the central nervous system. In *Peptides in Neurobiology* (ed. by H. Gainer). New York: Plenum. pp. 171–181.

Sokoloff, L. 1977. Relation between physiological function and energy metabolism in the central nervous system. *J. Neurochem.* 27: 13–26.

Stewart, W. B., J. S. Kauer, and G. M. Shepherd. 1979. Functional organization of rat olfactory bulb analysed by the 2-deoxyglucose method. *J. Comp. Neurol. 185:* 715–734.

Additional Reading

Goodman, L. S. and A. Gilman. 1975. *The Pharmacological Basis of Therapeutics.* London: Macmillan.

Greengard, P. 1978. *Cyclic Nucleotides, Phosphorylated Proteins and Neuronal Function.* New York: Raven.

Kehoe, J. S. and A. Marty. 1980. Certain slow synaptic responses: Their properties and possible underlying mechanisms. *Ann. Rev. Biophys. Bioengin. 9:* 437–465.

Potter, D. D., E. J. Furshpan and S. C. Landis. 1981. Multiple-transmitter status and "Dale's principle". *Neurosci. Comment. 1:* 1–9.

Werman, R. A. 1966. Criteria for identification of a central nervous system transmitter. *Comp. Biochem. Physiol. 18:* 745–766.

10
Development

The ways that neural structures provide for neural functions are one of the main concerns of neurobiology, and of this book. How those structures and functions develop, from conception through the life of the organism, is part and parcel of this concern. In fact, some of the best insights into how a system functions are gained through study of how that system gets put together.

The study of the developing nervous system began with the first microscopic investigations of the nineteenth century. One of the greatest of the early pioneers was Wilhelm His, a Swiss who worked in Leipzig. Much of the work, with many young colleagues, was carried out in his home. It is said that His's microscopic material was of inferior quality, but his ideas were clear and profound. In the 1880's, his description of the axon as an outgrowth from the developing nerve cell was an important step toward the concept of the neuron as a cell and the formulation of the neuron theory. To him also we owe such terms as dendrite, for the branches from the cell body, and neuropil, cell-free regions containing connections between axons and dendrites.

In his abundant investigations of the nervous system, Cajal was fascinated by the development of nerve cells and their connections. He combined study of Golgi-impregnated neurons in the adult with studies of their forms and movements in embryonic tissue, and thus laid the basis for the modern approach to the subject at the cellular level. Figure 10.1 is from his study in the 1890's of the development of granule cells in the vertebrate cerebellum. The diagrams summarize the way in which the granule cells first form near the surface

Fig. 10.1. Cajal's diagrams showing the development of granule cells in the mammalian cerebellum. (From Cajal, 1911)

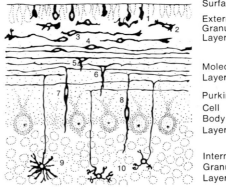

(1,2) and send out processes which become parallel fibers (3,4,5), after which the cell body migrates to the granule layer (6,7,8) to elaborate dendrites and assume its final form (9,10).

These and other early studies were carried out within the field of histology (the light-microscopic study of tissues), and the early events in the formation of different tissues were called *histogenesis*. Today, our focus is on the molecular and cellular mechanisms that are involved, and the study of *neurogenesis* is therefore becoming a branch of cell biology. In a similar vein, neurogenesis was originally thought to occur primarily during embryonic life, and was therefore regarded as a part of *embryology*. Today, we realize that events related to neurogenesis and the laying down of neural circuits continue into early life; moreover, many of the properties underlying the development of neurons and their functional capacities continue to be expressed throughout life, under either normal conditions or in response to injury or aging. We therefore gather all these aspects under the term *developmental neurobiology*, and regard development as a process that extends throughout most of the life of the animal.

A term defined too broadly loses precision, but in the case of development, there is a succession of stages that can be identified. These are summarized in Table 10.1. We will discuss each of these stages in turn.

Cell Birth

The first step is the proliferation of precursor cells (neuroblasts) up to a final cell division that gives rise to a specific type of neuron. The date of birth of the neuron

Table 10.1   Steps in development

1. Cell birth
2. Cell migration
3. Cell differentiation
4. Cell maturation
5. Cell death

can be determined by injections of radioactively labeled thymidine, which is taken up and incorporated into neurons about to undergo mitosis. Cells which have undergone their final mitosis are therefore heavily labeled in autoradiographic sections, and their "birthdates" accurately determined. Thus, despite later displacements of cells, their time of origin can be established. This technique has been very useful, especially in analyzing the way that layers of cells are generated to form a cortex. We will discuss this further below, and in Chap. 31.

Cell Migration

A general rule in the nervous system is that neurons do not remain at their site of origin, but rather migrate to their final position. This is a necessary consequence of the fact that the nervous system starts as a thin tube of ectoderm within the embryo (the neural tube), and the final product is a much larger structure (the nervous system). Also, the initial relation between the sites of origin of neurons may be very different from their final relations, as already indicated in the diagrams from Cajal (Fig. 10.1).

An overview of the way that cells differentiate and migrate from their sites of origin is shown in Fig. 10.2. Cells derived from the *neural tube* may be either neuronal precursors, destined to be neurons, or glial precursors destined to be glial cells. Also associated with the neural tube is a collection of cells called the *neural crest*. The neuroblasts of the neural crest migrate through peripheral tissue and give rise to several types of neurons in the peripheral nervous system, as shown in the figure.

How do cells migrate? The considerable displacements that occur during development imply that the cells actively move. There was keen interest in this question among early investigators. Cajal, with his genius for preparing the right material and drawing the right conclusions, studied

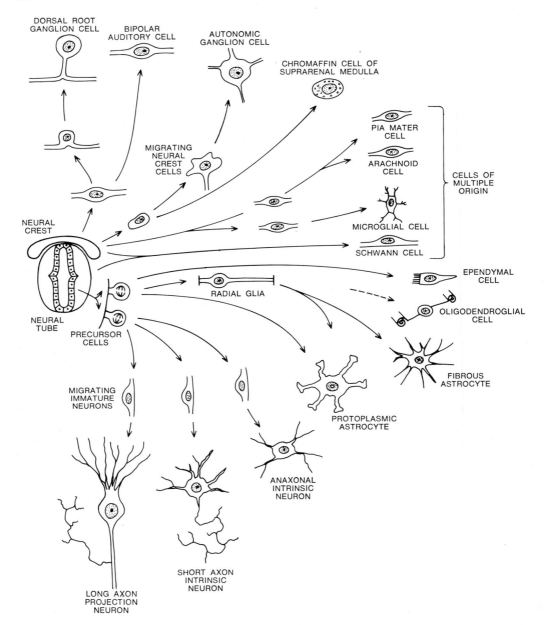

Fig. 10.2. Origin, differentiation, and migration of different types of neurons and glia. (Modified from Crelin, 1974)

single growing fibers in Golgi-impregnated specimens. He saw enlargements at the ends of the fibers, and called them "growth cones". He imagined that the growth cone is endowed with ameboid movements, which enable it to push aside obstacles in its way until it reaches its destination. The evidence that this in fact is true soon came

from the experiments of Ross Harrison at Yale in 1910. Harrison introduced the technique of tissue culture to biology. In pieces of neural tissue excised from the developing nervous system and maintained in artificial media in a dish, he observed the growth cones and the movements that Cajal had hypothesized. The

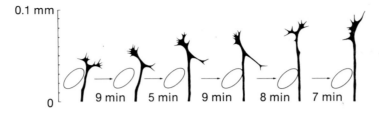

Fig. 10.3. The growth of a nerve fiber of a frog embryo in tissue culture, as observed under a microscope at intervals of time indicated. Ellipse indicates red blood cell, which did not move. (From Harrison, 1910)

results illustrated in Fig. 10.3 have been repeated and confirmed many times since.

It may be noted that tissue culture methods have become one of the most powerful tools for analysis of neuronal properties. There is always a problem of interpreting the results, because a cell grown under artificial conditions has a form much simpler than its normal counterpart, and its properties may be significantly altered. This problem was discussed at a recent meeting of the Society for Neuroscience, and drew the cheerful comment from Richard Bunge, one of the leaders in this field, that "There are no artefacts in the culture dish!" This seemingly outrageous claim was made only partly in fun, for it carried the reminder that what one sees in the culture dish is indeed a property of the neuron, perhaps only accessible or expressed under culture conditions.

Recent studies have begun to reveal the special properties of the growth cone. Movement occurs by means of *microspikes*, thin processes that extend out from larger protrusions (*filopodia*); these attach to surrounding structures, and pull the growth cone along. The growth cones and their processes contain a network of *microfilaments*. It is believed that these contain actin, and are involved in contractile processes underlying the movement of the growth cone and the rest of the cell. Recent studies have suggested that the growth cone membrane generates Ca^{2+} mediated action potentials. A nice demonstration of this has been provided by treating cells in culture with voltage-sensitive dyes, and

measuring the voltage changes in specific portions of the cell using a laser microbeam. The results in Fig. 10.4 show that the optical recordings and electrical recordings of presumed Ca^{2+} action potentials are very similar. It is believed that the Ca^{2+} that flows into the cell during the action potential controls the contractility of the actin filaments and the shape and movement of the growth cone and other parts of the neuron. This function of Ca^{2+} is similar to its critical role in mediating plastic changes of synaptic terminals revealed in experiments on learning (see Chap. 30).

Growth cones also contain mitochondria, microtubules, vesicles, and ribosomes. Freeze-fracture studies have shown that there are fewer intramembranous particles in growth cones than in mature axons and axon terminals. The growth cone is the site of high-energy metabolism and constant synthesis of new membrane and other constituents, and there is active transport of materials between the cell body and growing tip over the intervening axon or dendrite. The growth cones of axons and dendrites have similar properties, and the growth cones of glia are said to be similar to those of neurons. As noted in Chap. 4, within the vertebrate central nervous system, long axons migrate along the processes of radial glia, which will be discussed below and in Chap. 31.

The growth of nerve processes can be influenced by many of the chemical agents that affect nerve membranes or organelles. There are also specific factors that promote growth of certain types of neu-

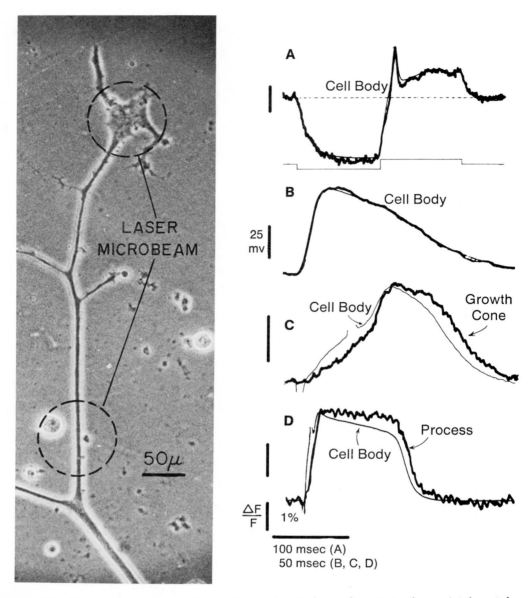

Fig. 10.4. Comparison of electrical recordings and optical recordings (using laser microbeam) from different parts of a neuroblastoma cell growing in culture. Intracellular recordings shown by thin line, optical recordings of fluorescence changes using oxonal dye in the bathing medium shown by thick traces. (From Grinvald and Farber, 1981)

rons. The best-known of these is *nerve-growth factor* (NGF). This is a protein with a molecular weight of 130,000. Its main neuroactive subunit is a polypeptide whose amino acid sequence is similar to that of insulin. This suggests that the two substances may have a common evolutionary precursor. NGF is normally secreted by the target organs of neural crest cells, and stimulates sprouting and growth of the axons of the cells. It plays an essential role in the growth and maturation of the neurons of the dorsal root ganglia of the spinal cord, and of the sympathetic ganglia (see Fig. 10.2). It also has given the experimenter a useful tool in studying the growth of these processes in cell and tissue cultures.

Cell Differentiation

The third step in neuronal development is the differentiation of specific structures, properties, and connections. This overlaps greatly with other steps; in some cases differentiation is well underway before migration starts. The term is also used by some workers to refer to the whole process of generation of the sequence of neuroblast precursors as well as the events that bring about the final neuronal form. Let us consider several examples that illustrate principles underlying neuronal differentiation.

Invertebrate Sensory Hairs. A particularly clear example of the differentiation of cells into final specific types is seen in the development of the sensory hair in insects. The sensory hair (sensillum) is a versatile organ that is used to sense several types of signals. We take as our example the taste hair. The basic structure of a taste hair is shown in Fig. 10.5B, and the development of the individual cells that make up the hair is summarized in Fig. 10.5A.

Fig. 10.5. **A.** Development of the different cells that contribute to the formation of the sensory taste hair from a single precursor "mother cell" (M) in the insect. (After Hansen, 1978) **B.** The structure of the sensory taste hair in the adult. (After Dethier, 1976)

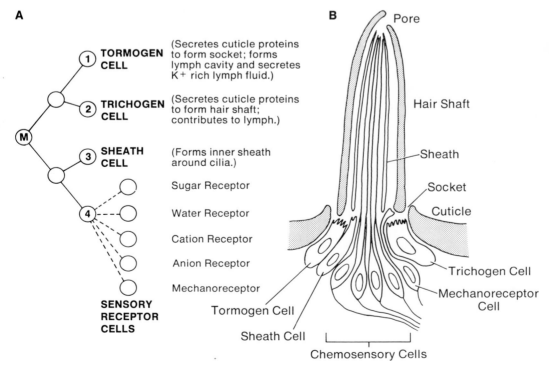

As indicated in Fig. 10.5A, each hair arises from a single precursor "mother cell". After only two cell divisions, the four resulting cells have each become targeted for distinctive functions. *Cell 1* (tormogen cell) forms the junction (socket) between the hair and the surrounding integument. After accomplishing this, the same cell modifies itself into a kind of gland cell, which forms the main lymph cavity of the hair, and may also secrete a K^+-rich lymph fluid that bathes the receptor cell dendrites. *Cell 2* (trichogen cell) secretes specific cuticular proteins that form the hair-shaft and the distal pore opening. This cell then modifies itself like Cell 1 to contribute to the formation of the lymph cavity. *Cell 3* forms a sheath around the receptor dendrites within the hair shaft. *Cell 4* undergoes several further divisions that give rise to the sensory receptor cells.

It can be seen that the individual hair is in reality a multicellular and multifunctional organ. The individual cells provide for structural support and compartmentalization, glandular secretion, and sensory reception. The specializations of cell structure and function are obtained by as few as two cell divisions. In the case of the tormogen and trichogen cells, there are apparently sequential specializations after the final cell division. In contrast, differentiation of the five specific receptor cells requires additional cell divisions. Each cell is specialized for a different sensory stimulus, as will be explained further in Chap. 12.

On a larger scale, the development of the central nervous system of the grasshopper has been the subject of recent collaborative studies by Michael Bates, Corey Goodman, and Nicholas Spitzer. The embryonic nerve cord is relatively thin and translucent, which has allowed individual cells and even their growth cones to be visualized under the microscope in the living animal, and intracellular electrodes have been introduced for recording and dye injection. The entire sequence of steps, from precursor cell to mature form,

has been analyzed for several types of neuron. As illustrated in Fig. 10.6A,B, a ganglion, such as the third thoracic ganglion, contains a specific set of precursor cells. There is a lateral group of 30 neuroblasts (NB), and a midline group of medial precursors (MP) plus a single medial neuroblast (MNB). To the right in the figure, the pattern of cell divisions is indicated. Each MP divides only once. Each NB divides several times to give rise to a chain of ganglion mother cells (GMC); each of these divides into a ganglion cell (GC), which then differentiates to reach its final form as a mature neuron (N). Each NB generates from 10 to 100 progeny according to this fixed pattern, after which it degenerates and dies.

By making intracellular injections of fluorescent dyes at different stages, it has been possible to study the development of axons and dendrites of individual identified neurons. The earliest axonal pathways, connecting neighboring ganglia, are made by "pioneer" cells. One of these is the MP 2 cell, as illustrated in Fig. 10.6C. Similarly, sensory neurons in the periphery (PN 1) send pioneer fibers to the ganglion. Within the ganglion, later differentiating cells send their axons along the paths laid down by the pioneer axon. As an example, the MP 3 cell, which initially lacks any processes, first differentiates an axon at day 6 (see Fig. 10.6D). From day 6 to day 12, there follows an elaboration of the dendritic branches, to reach the final form characteristic of the mature neuron, called an H neuron.

Excitable Properties. Correlated with the differentiation of neuronal form is the acquisition of specific physiological properties. This has been studied in a variety of systems, including muscle cells, neuroblastoma cells in tissue culture, large identified neurons such as Rohon-Beard cells in the frog, and several types of cell in the grasshopper.

A common finding in many studies has been that cells are excitable at early stages

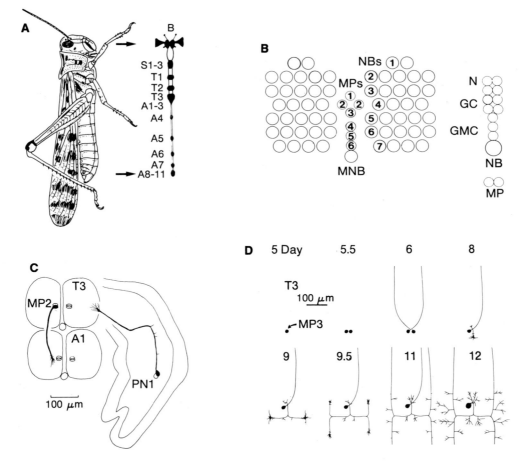

Fig. 10.6. Differentiation of neurons in the grasshopper central nervous system.
A. Lateral view of grasshopper. Central nervous system, showing brain (B) and associated anterior segmental (S), thoracic (T), and abdominal (A) ganglia. **B.** Identified precursor cells in T3 ganglion, including lateral neuroblasts (NB), medial neuroblast (MNB), and midline precursors (MP). *To the right:* Sequence of cell divisions: MP cells give rise to neurons by a single division; NB cells give rise to sequence of cells, from ganglion mother cells (GMC) to ganglion cells (GC), which differentiate into neurons (N). **C.** "Pioneer" axons laid down by the MP2 cell and a peripheral pioneer neuron (PN1). **D.** Differentiation of MP3 cell into an H neuron from 5–12 days of age; drawn from cells injected with Lucifer Yellow.
(A–C from Goodman and Bate, 1981. D from Goodman et al., 1981)

of development, and that the inward (depolarizing) current is carried by Ca^{2+}. This has already been pointed out in Chap. 7. At these early stages the cells are characteristically coupled by gap junctions. The Ca^{2+} spike may be localized in the cell body, or in the growth cone, as discussed above. In some cells the Ca^{2+} spike persists into maturity (for example, in muscle cells). In many systems there is a change to a spike with both a Na^+ and a Ca^{2+} component, and finally one with only a Na^+ component. This particularly applies to projection neurons with long axons. In contrast, many nonspiking cells have inexcitable membranes at all stages of development; alternatively, some pass through earlier stages of excitability.

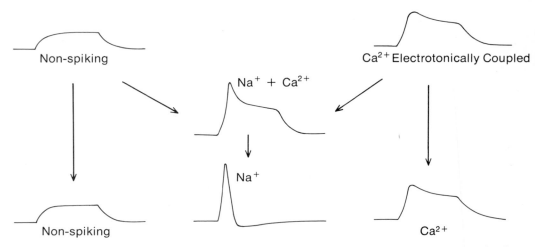

Fig. 10.7. Diagram illustrating some sequences of excitable and nonexcitable properties that have been identified in developing neurons. (Based on Spitzer, 1979)

Some of these relationships are indicated in Fig. 10.7. It should be emphasized that any of these properties may be localized to a particular site in a neuron, a particular stage of development, or in relation to a particular birth date. Thus, there is a population of dorsal unpaired median (DUM) neurons in grasshoppers, which contain subpopulations of cells depending on their dates of birth from the median neuroblast. The earliest cells to be born have both soma and axon spikes, followed by cells with spikes in the dendrites and axon, cells with only axon spikes, and finally nonspiking neurons. This last cell type is a local-circuit neuron. This is consistent with the pattern, found in many vertebrates, that small interneurons are the last to differentiate, and are thus most susceptible to shaping by environmental and other factors (see below).

The presence of Ca^{2+} spikes at early stages of development may be important for the control of the motility of growth cones, as already noted above. In addition, Ca^{2+} must be important in relation to the neurosecretory activity of the developing neuron, and it could also play a role in controlling the insertion of neurotransmitter receptor proteins into the surface membrane. These and other possible

functions of Ca^{2+} in the developing neuron may be reviewed in relation to the diagrams of Fig. 9.4.

Sympathetic Ganglion Cells. We have previously discussed the fact that a neuron has traditionally been regarded as releasing a single neurotransmitter at all its terminals, as expressed in Dale's law. When and how does a neuron become committed to the neurotransmitter it will use?

Experiments on sympathetic ganglion cells grown in cell cultures have thrown light on this question. The background for these studies was the demonstration that when "trunk" regions of the neural crest, that normally give rise to sympathetic ganglion cells, were transplanted to anterior regions that normally give rise to vagal cells, the normal adrenergic character of the trunk cells was lost. In the cell cultures it was found that if the sympathetic ganglion neurons are maintained in the absence of any other cell type, they develop adrenergic properties; that is, they take up, store, synthesize, and release noradrenaline from their terminals. Furthermore, they form morphological synapses that contain small granular vesicles, like normal adult adrenergic synapses.

In contrast, when the neurons are maintained together with (cocultured) other kinds of cells such as cardiac cells, they develop cholinergic properties. They synthesize up to 1000 times as much acetylcholine as the tiny amounts in isolated cultured neurons; they make cholinergic synapses onto other neurons or onto muscle cells; and the amount of NA and the number of granular vesicles is greatly reduced. This can occur solely in the presence of medium that contained the cardiac cells or other non-neuronal cells. The medium is thus called *conditioned medium,* and is believed to contain a substance or substances that mediate the effect. By varying the amount of exposure to other cells or conditioned medium, a balance between adrenergic and cholinergic properties in the same cell can be achieved (see Fig. 10.8).

These results show that neural crest cells are potentially "dual function" neurons. Very early in development, these cells may actually synthesize and release both types of transmitter simultaneously. They retain this ability to be adrenergic or cholinergic past the last mitosis, and the expression of one trait or the other is determined by chemical factors in the environment of the cell. These experiments therefore provide evidence at the single-cell level for the ways in which the cell genotype interacts with the environment to produce the cell phenotype.

Fig. 10.8. Dual transmitter function of developing sympathetic ganglion cells of the rat. **A.** Schematic diagram showing ganglion cell and cardiac muscle cell. **B.** Normal bathing medium; stimulation of neuron causes inhibition of muscle cell impulse discharge. **C.** Addition of atropine to medium; this blocks inhibition (showing its cholinergic nature), leaving excitation. This was blocked by addition of propanolol to medium (not shown), showing its adrenergic nature. (After Potter et al., 1981)

Establishment of Synaptic Connections

As will be emphasized more than once in this book, the essence of nervous organization is the establishment of synaptic circuits. A great deal of precision is demanded in constructing these circuits, and many of the disorders of behavior that occur in humans and other animals are due to abnormalities in the development of the circuit connections (see Chap. 31). In development, as in politics, timing is all. From the experimental evidence it is possible to begin to identify the intricate sequence of steps that is involved in establishing specific connections. Table 10.2 provides a summary of the main steps that have been identified so far. As can be seen, the entire process spans the time from the birth of a neuron, through migration and differentiation, to the final maturation of each part of the cell.

Retinotectal Pathway. The ways in which neuronal populations interact in forming circuits has been studied in many systems, under many experimental conditions. Present thinking has been much influenced by the pioneering experiments of Roger Sperry of the California Institute of Technology. This work was carried out in

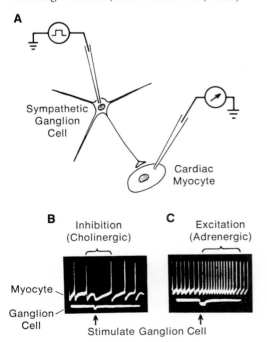

Table 10.2   Steps in establishing specific synaptic connections

1. The neuron must leave the cell cycle at a set time.
2. It must migrate to the appropriate region.
3. It may develop a spatial identity with respect to its neighbors.
4. Dendrites must develop in a characteristic shape and orientation.
5. The axon must leave the cell body and grow in the right direction toward its region of termination.
6. The axon must direct its branches to the appropriate side of the brain.
7. The axon must direct branches to the right region or regions.
8. Within a region, the axon must ramify in the right subdivision or layer.
9. The terminal field of the axon must be ordered in a particular topographic relationship with the cell bodies in the regions of its origin and termination.
10. The axon terminals may end only on certain cell types within the terminal distribution area.
11. The axon terminals may end only on certain parts of these cells (parts of the dendritic surface, for example).

After Lund (1978)

amphibians, in the retinotectal pathway, which is composed of the axons of retinal ganglion cells that project to the optic tectum, the main relay center for visual information in the lower vertebrate brain (see Fig. 3.6). Sperry cut one optic nerve and rotated the eye through 180°. When regeneration of the optic nerve was complete, he found that the axons grew back to their previous target sites; the map of the retina onto the tectum was preserved, despite the rotation of the eye and the disorganization and regrowth produced by the transection (Fig. 10.9). He therefore postulated that there is a *chemical affinity* between the axons and their target neurons. He suggested that this affinity is responsible not only for the reestablishment of connections during regeneration, but also for the establishment of connections during normal development.

Because of the precision with which the retina is mapped onto the tectum, this system has been the object of considerable study. Subsequent work has confirmed and greatly extended Sperry's original finding. It has also somewhat qualified the interpretation. The original hypothesis stressed genetic mechanisms in laying down the patterns of synaptic connections in the nervous system, whereas in most systems it appears that additional factors operate during development (*epigenetic* factors, such as conditioning by experience) and

Fig. 10.9. Visual projection of image of a fly onto the retina of a normal frog (**A**) and a frog in which the eyes have been rotated through 180°. (**B**) Note retinal points A–D and their projections onto the optic tectum. (From Lund, 1978)

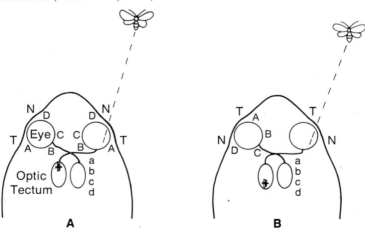

are essential to the final connection patterns.

Genetic Mutations. The formation of synaptic circuits has also been studied under abnormal conditions induced by genetic mutations. In invertebrates, the most studied species from this point of view are the nematode roundworm *C. elegans,* and the fruit fly *Drosophila melanogaster.* The strategy of these experiments is to produce a single mutation by X-irradiation, characterize the behavioral abnormality produced, and then identify the underlying abnormality in synaptic connection.

In vertebrates, mutant species have been particularly useful in studying the ways that cortical structures are formed. The earliest and most complete studies have been carried out in mutant strains of mice by Richard Sidman, Pasko Rakic, and their colleagues at Harvard. Most of these strains have been identified by the effects of the mutation on locomotion, and the cellular mechanisms have been analyzed especially in the cerebellum. Depending on the kind of locomotor disorder, the mutant strains have acquired names of reeler, staggerer, weaver, nervous, jumpy and so on. Each type of disorder is associated with a particular way in which the cerebellar cortex is disorganized.

The results are summarized in Fig. 10.10 for three mutant strains—weaver, reeler, and staggerer—and compared with the normal. In brief, the normal cerebellar cortex (A) consists of an orderly layering of the main neuronal types, and sets of specific connections between them (we will examine these in more detail in Chap. 22). In the homozygous weaver, (B) most of the granule cells degenerate prior to the time of their migration from the surface layer to the deeper position they occupy in the normal adult. Also affected is a type of radial glial cell called a *Bergmann glia,* which normally serves as a guide for the migration of the granule cell bodies during development. There is also evidence that serum cholesterol and related lipids are abnormally high in weavers, which may have deleterious effects on the granule and glial cells.

In the reeler mutant (C), the main abnormality is a lack of granule cells, which remain in a layer at the surface, so that the normal relations between the layers in the adult are reversed. As a consequence, there are few parallel fibers, and the Purkinje cells lack their characteristic branching pattern. The effects on the Purkinje cell are taken to indicate that the maturation of dendritic branches and dendritic spines into their final form is under control of the granule cell axons in their normal arrangement as parallel fibers.

As a final example, in the staggerer mutant (D), the main site of gene action appears to be the Purkinje cells, which fail to develop their mature dendritic tree, and retain several embryonic characteristics. The granule cells migrate, leaving behind their axons as parallel fibers in the normal manner. However, in the absence of their normal Purkinje cell dendritic targets, the granule cells degenerate. This occurs despite the fact that postsynaptic specializations (submembranous densities) are present in the malformed Purkinje cell dendrites.

These studies thus give evidence of the multiple factors involved in the establishment of neuronal circuits. A problem in interpretation is that there is never an isolated site of gene action; on the contrary, each mutant exhibits a mixture of effects. The effects are not confined to the cerebellum, but involve a variety of abnormalities throughout the nervous system. Despite these complications, some of the gene actions are surprisingly specific, as already discussed. In addition, electrophysiological recordings from the Purkinje cells in weaver and reeler indicate that these cells, despite their grossly abnormal morphology, have relatively normal excitable membrane properties. The picture one obtains clearly shows the profound effects of genetic abnormalities on development, and the resourcefulness of

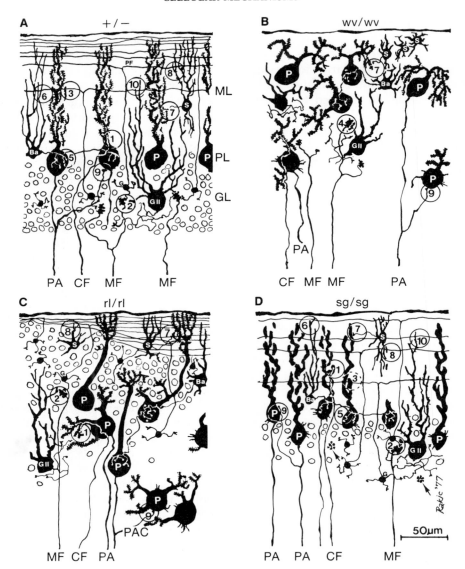

Fig. 10.10. The cell tyes in the normal mouse cerebellum (**A**) and in the cerebellum of several mutant strains (**B–D**). Abbreviations: Ba, basket cell; CF, climbing fiber; G, granule cell; GII, Golgi type II cell; MF, mossy fiber; P, Purkinje cell; PA, Purkinje cell axon; PF, parallel fiber; S, stellate cell. Circled numbers indicate corresponding types of synapses. See text for explanations. (From Caviness and Rakic, 1978)

the developmental process in attempting to assemble its circuits despite the abnormalities which may occur.

Maturation

Maturation refers to the process by which a neuron and its circuits achieve their final form. It cannot be specified precisely, because it is continuous with the preceding steps of differentiation, and involves the finalization of many of the processes listed in Table 10.2. Of these various steps, we will discuss two of special interest.

The first point is that the neurons in a given region do not all differentiate, migrate, and achieve maturation at the same time. We have seen in the cerebellar cortex, for example, that the granule cells migrate to their final positions and take on their final form long after the Purkinje cells have been in place. Studies in other regions have indicated that small interneurons similarly reach their final positions and shapes after the projection neurons. It has been postulated that this may be a general rule in the nervous system, and that the small neurons and the local synaptic circuits are more open to influence by the experience of the animal.

An important step in maturation is the acquisition of myelin. The ability to stain for myelin led the early histologists to focus their studies of development on the onset of myelination, and to use this as a criterion of maturation. However, most axons in the brain are thin, and are unmyelinated or only thinly myelinated, and it is now recognized that the myelination of larger axons is only one among many steps in maturation. Nonetheless, it is true that different regions vary considerably in their times of myelination. It is one of the last stages of maturation, beginning usually late in embryonic life or early in postnatal life after the projection neurons are well in place, and continuing for considerable periods of time (into childhood, in the case of humans).

Cell Death

We tend to think of death as the end point of old age, but that is not the view from the perspective of development. From this perspective, degeneration and death of specific cells, fibers, and synaptic terminals are an integral part of the process of development. This was first shown in the vertebrate nervous system in 1949 by two modern pioneers in the field of developmental studies, Viktor Hamburger and Rita Levi-Montalcini, at Washington University. They found that in dorsal root ganglia and in the spinal cord motor regions, a large amount of cell degeneration occurs during brief and specific time periods early in embryonic life. It was observed that this occurs approximately at the time when the peripheral fibers establish their connections in the periphery.

Like many important discoveries, this lay dormant for a time, but after a decade or so the question was taken up and pursued in a number of other regions. The results have shown that cell death is a common phenomenon in many regions. The amount of loss is considerable, ranging as high as 75% in some cases (see Fig. 10.11). In many cases there is a coincidence of cell death with the time at which the cells of that region are innervating their targets. From this it has been hypothesized that there is a competition for innervation of neuronal targets, and the cells that die are the ones that lose out in the competition. This, in turn, implies that the cells that survive receive some signal or sustaining trophic factor from the cells they innervate. Thus, the establishment of synaptic connections appears, at least in some cases, to involve competition for targets, validation of successful connections, and elimination of unsuccessful or redundant connections.

These properties relating to cell death are seen at the level of individual terminals and synapses, too. For example, in spinal motoneurons there are synapses on the initial segment of the axon that disappear later in embryonic life. In the cerebellum, there is a time during early development when the Purkinje cell bodies bristle with small spines which receive climbing fiber synapses; later, these spines, and their synapses, completely disappear. Perhaps the early connections help to guide other synapses to their sites, or perhaps they provide for some control of excitability that is necessary at a particular stage of development.

Molting. Probably the clearest evidence for mechanisms governing the remodeling that takes place during development comes from studies of metamorphosis in insects. The fact that passage of an insect through successive larval stages to final adulthood

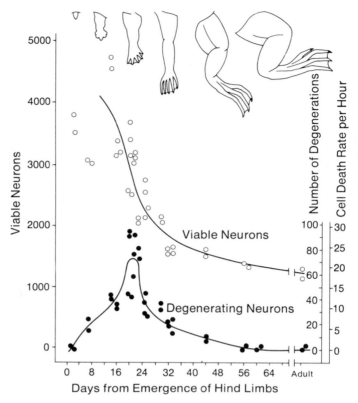

Fig. 10.11. Numbers of viable neurons and degenerating neurons in the ventral horn of the lumbar spinal cord of the frog at different times in relation to development of the hirdlimbs. (Modified from Hughes, in Jacobson, 1978)

depends on control by the brain was established in a classic series of studies by Victor Wigglesworth in England in the 1930's and 40's. The story is well-known and is summarized only briefly here. Wigglesworth studied a blood-sucking bug called *Rhodnius*. During each of its five nymphal stages (instars) this bug must ingest a single enormous meal of blood. The stretching of the alimentary canal stimulates receptors which set up impulses in fibers to the brain. Although the precise pathways are not yet known, connections are eventually made to neurosecretory cells in the protocerebrum that manufacture *thoracotropic hormone* (see Fig. 10.12). When stimulated, these cells release this hormone from their nerve endings in the corpora cardiaca into the bloodstream. Thoracotropin stimulates the thoracic

gland, an endocrine organ in the thorax, to secrete the hormone *ecdysone*, which acts on body cells to bring about molting. Ecdysone is a steroid hormone, closely related in chemical structure to the steroid hormones in vertebrates.

Ecdysone thus stimulates growth and development. Balanced against it is another hormone that acts to inhibit development. This is named *juvenile hormone*. It is secreted by cells in another endocrine organ called the corpora allata (see Chap. 2). The corpora allata contain secretory cells of an epithelial type (lacking the fine-structural characteristics of neurons such as Golgi bodies or axons), which are believed to secrete the juvenile hormone. In addition, they receive innervation from the neurosecretory cells in the brain, some of whose axons pass through the corpora

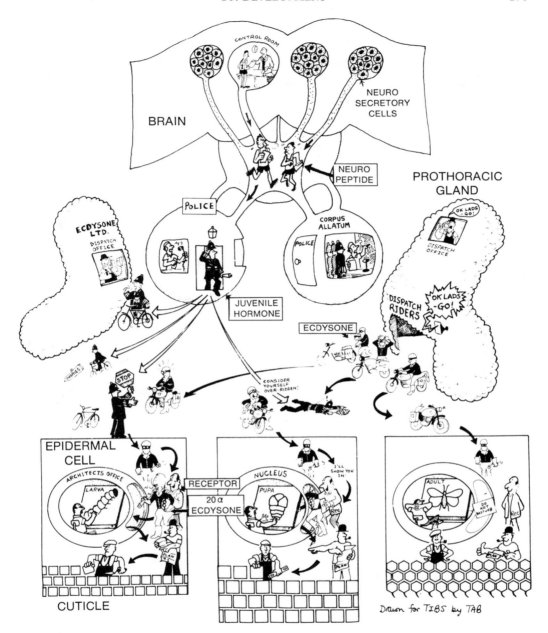

Fig. 10.12. An artist's view of the neuroendocrine system of the insect and its role in the control of development. (From Coudron et al., 1981)

cardiaca and terminate in the corpora allata. As long as juvenile hormone is secreted, the animal continues to molt through its nymphal stages (it remains in a juvenile state). However, the secretion of this hormone decreases drastically by the last instar stage, thus permitting met-amorphosis to proceed to the adult form.

Emergence from the last larval stage is called *eclosion*, and it is under control of yet another hormone, manufactured in the brain and secreted from the corpora cardiaca. This is called, appropriately, *eclosion hormone*, a peptide with a molecular

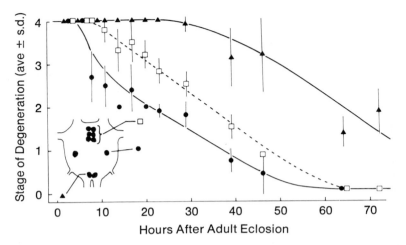

Fig. 10.13. Cell death occurring with different time course in three types of motoneuron in the abdominal ganglion during development of the sphinx moth *Manduca sexta*. (From Truman and Schwartz, 1980)

weight of approximately 8500 daltons. In addition to triggering eclosion, this hormone also appears to coordinate the timing of many developmental processes.

Certain of the neurons and muscles in the larva have functions that are specific only for the larva, and after eclosion they no longer are needed. James Truman, who has provided much of our basic knowledge about eclosion mechanisms, and his colleagues in Seattle have shown that these neurons and muscles degenerate according to a sequence that is under control of eclosion hormone. Figure 10.13 shows the time course of reduction and disappearance of motoneurons in the abdominal ganglion (the muscles they innervate show similar reductions). As in most invertebrate ganglia, many neurons have characteristic shapes and positions within the ganglion, so that the sequence of disappearance of cell types could be clearly demonstrated.

This type of cell loss is called *programmed cell death,* and serves as a model for this general phenomenon, including the examples we have previously discussed. It is presumed to be due in the insect to a direct action of the peptide hormone on the specific muscles and neurons. The pro-

cess can be delayed by artificially stimulating the motoneurons. Truman has obtained evidence that the action of the hormone is associated with an elevation in intracellular levels of cyclic GMP, and therefore appears to be mediated by this "second messenger" mechanism.

Metamorphosis in insects is thus controlled by a complex series of hormonal actions, which are in turn under control of the central nervous system. Similar principles apply to metamorphosis in lower vertebrates like the frog, and also the more continuous, less drastic changes during development of higher vertebrates. We will discuss the actions of sex hormones on vertebrate development in Chaps. 24 and 28.

Regeneration and Plasticity

Some tissues of the body retain the ability to form new cells from existing precursors during the life of the animal. For example, the cells in the skin are constantly turning over, and the liver can regenerate much of its substance. The nervous system is severely limited in this respect. A few instances are known, such as the olfactory receptor cells in vertebrates (Chap. 13), in which there is continued turnover in the adult. However, it appears to be a general rule, applicable to both invertebrates and vertebrates, that once the processes of development are complete there is little or no further generation of new nerve cells. This, of course, is the main reason why injuries to the nervous system have such devastating effects.

This inability to generate new neurons might imply that the adult nervous system is a static, "hard-wired" machine. This is far from the truth. Although new neurons cannot be generated, each neuron retains the ability to form new processes and new synaptic connections. Thus, although the nerve cell body is a relatively fixed component within each center of the adult nervous system, the synaptic circuits it forms with the processes of other neurons are subject to ongoing modification. The behavioral evidence that we learn new skills and new facts, remember them, and use them in different ways, in itself argues strongly that our neural circuits are modifiable. Research at the cellular level has provided considerable evidence for changes of cellular properties that are dependent on use, and even some glimpses of these mechanisms at the molecular level. These mechanisms will be discussed in several chapters, particularly in regard to cellular and molecular properties underlying memory and learning in Chap. 30, and functions of the cerebral cortex in Chap. 31.

What then of the ability of nerve cells to respond to injury? Here again, although the nervous system cannot generate new neurons to replace lost ones, each cell can proliferate new processes to replace those that have been lost or damaged. The experiments cited above on regeneration of the optic nerve demonstrate this capacity, as well as the ability to reestablish specific synaptic connections.

Within the central nervous system, a vivid demonstration of regeneration has been provided by the experiments of Patricia Goldman-Rakic and her colleagues.

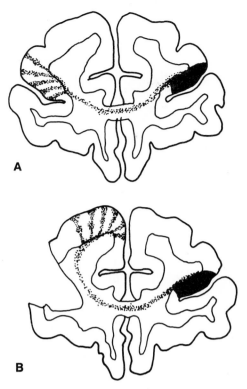

Fig. 10.14. Diagram of frontal sections of the prefrontal lobes of the rhesus monkey. **A.** Injections of tritiated amino acids in the right hemisphere, showing pattern of projection through the corpus callosum to the left hemisphere. **B.** In this animal, the contralateral region of the prefrontal cortex was ablated two months previously. The regenerating fibers revealed by the injected amino acids innervate a new region of cortex. Note columnar patterns of innervation in both cases. (From Goldman-Rakic, 1981)

They made injections of tritiated amino acids into the frontal association cortex of monkeys on one side, and found transport through fibers of the corpus callosum to the same region of the frontal cortex of the contralateral side (Fig. 10.14A). The experiment was then repeated in animals in which the contralateral site was ablated. The callosal fibers regenerated; when they reached the contralateral side and found their normal target absent, they swerved and terminated in a neighboring region of cortex (Fig. 10.14B). Although it is not known whether these connections are functional or not, the results attest to the tremendous "force" operating within each neuron to grow out new axons and make new connections even when the normal targets for the axon are not available. A further point of interest in these experiments is the arrangement of the fiber terminations in columns, in both the normal and experimental situations. The column is one of the organizing principles of cortical synaptic circuits, as we shall discuss in later chapters.

Associated with this innate tendency to generate new connections when injured, nerve cells are also primed to make new connections when other cells are lost. A key experiment was the study of William Chambers and John Liu, of the University of Pennsylvania, in 1958. They transected the pyramidal tract in the spinal cord, and several years later examined the fields of termination of dorsal root fibers within both sides of the cord. They found that the field of termination was larger on the side of the tract lesion, suggesting that the dorsal root fibers give off collateral sprouts that take over the vacated synaptic sites.

An elegant demonstration of this process at the synaptic level was provided by Geoffrey Raisman at Oxford in 1969. He studied the septal nucleus, a region in the forebrain that receives two well-defined inputs: one from the hippocampus, the other from the median forebrain bundle (MFB). Each makes characteristic synaptic connections onto septal neurons, as shown in Fig. 10.15. When the hippocampal input is cut, there is an increase in incidence of large terminals making double synaptic contacts, presumably from MFB fibers. On the other hand, when the MFB is cut, the synaptic sites on the soma are taken over by hippocampal terminals.

These results reflect the same kind of competition for synaptic sites that occurs during normal development. Loss of a particular type of synaptic terminal stimulates the production of axonal *sprouts,* which have the *mobility* to move to the vacated sites, and the necessary *chemoaf-*

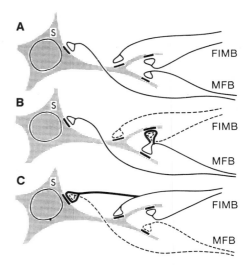

Fig. 10.15. Remodeling of synaptic connections in the septal nuclei of the rat. **A.** Normal inputs to septal (S) cell. Fimbria (FIMB) fiber terminate on dendrites, whereas medial forebrain bundle fibers (MFB) terminate on both dendrites and soma. **B.** Lesion of FIMB (degenerating fibers shown by dashed lines); MFB terminals occupy vacated synaptic sites on dendrites. **C.** Lesion of MFB; FIMB terminals occupy vacated sites on cell body. (From Raisman, 1969)

finity to establish new synaptic connections. In many respects the process involves reactivation of mechanisms that operated during development.

Similar experiments have now been carried out in a number of regions, demonstrating that when one input is transected another input expands its terminal field into the vacated sites on cell bodies or dendrites. These include such regions as the hippocampus, red nucleus, olfactory cortex, and superior colliculus in the vertebrate. In addition to specific pathways, nonspecific pathways also exhibit these properties. Thus, when the cerebellum is ablated, the amount of histofluorescence for noradrenaline increases in the forebrain. Cells in the locus ceruleus send noradrenergic fibers to both cerebellum and forebrain (see Chap. 25), so it appears that loss of the cerebellar branches induces sprouting of the forebrain branches.

This kind of *compensatory sprouting* has been seen in a number of cells, and suggests that a cell is programmed to make a certain number of synapses, and reacts to injury in a way to compensate for the loss and try to restore its appropriate number of connections, even though those connections may be in uncharacteristic or inappropriate places.

These experiments give evidence of the ongoing competition to make synaptic connections that each neuron engages in during development and throughout adult life. This competition is the basis of much of the plasticity that is inherent in neural circuits. Neurobiologists are only beginning to understand the potentials of this plasticity. For example, recent studies show that a given region of the mammalian brain can be excised and grafted onto the brain of another animal, where it will send out processes that establish connections with the host brain. These kinds of experiments carry the hope that we can not only reveal more of the plastic capabilities of nerve cells that are normally at work, but also eventually use them to compensate for the effects of injuries to the human brain.

REFERENCES

Cajal, S. Ramón y. 1911. [Chap. 5].

Caviness, V. S. Jr. and P. Rakic. 1978. Mechanisms of cortical development: a view from mutations in mice. *Ann. Rev. Neurosci.* 1: 297–326.

Coudron, T. A., J. H. Law, and J. K. Koeppe. 1981. Insect hormones. *Trends Biochem. Sci.* 6: 248–251.

Crelin, F. S. 1974. Development of the nervous system. *CIBA Clinical Symposia.* 26: 1–32.

Dethier, V. G. 1976. *The Hungry Fly.* Cambridge, Mass: Harvard University Press.

Goldman-Rakic, P. S. 1981. Development and plasticity of primate frontal association cortex. In *The Organization of the Cerebral Cortex* (ed. by F. O. Schmitt, F. G. Worden, G. Adelman, and S. G. Dennis). Cambridge, Mass.: MIT Press. pp. 69–97.

Goodman, C. S. and M. Bate. 1981. Neuronal development in the grasshopper. *Trends in Neurosci. 4:* 163–169.

Goodman, C. S., M. Bate, and N. C. Spitzer. 1981. Embryonic development of identified neurons: origin and transformation of the H cell. *J. Neurosci. 1:* 94–102.

Grinvald, A. and I. C. Farber. 1981. Optical recording of calcium action potentials from growth cones of cultured neurons with a laser microbeam. *Science 212:* 1164–1167.

Hansen, K. 1978. Insect chemoreception. In *Taxis and Behavior. Receptors and Recognition,* Series B, Vol. 5. (ed. by G. I. Hazelbauer). London: Chapman and Hall. pp. 231–292.

Harrison, R. G. 1907. Observations on the living developing nerve fiber. *Anat. Rec. 1:* 116–118.

Jacobson, M. 1978. *Developmental Neurobiology.* New York: Plenum.

Lund, R. D. 1978. *Development and Plasticity of the Brain.* New York: Oxford.

Potter, D. D., S. C. Landis, and E. J. Furshpan. 1980. Dual function during development of rat sympathetic neurones in culture. *J. Exp. Biol. 89:* 57–71.

Raisman, G. 1969. Neuronal plasticity in the septal nuclei of the adult rat. *Brain Res. 14:* 25–48.

Spitzer, N. C. 1979. Ion channels in development. *Ann. Rev. Neurosci. 2:* 363–397.

Truman, J. W. and L. M. Schwartz. 1980. Peptide hormone regulation of programmed death of neurons and muscle in an insect. In *Peptides: Integrators of Cell and Tissue Function.* Soc. Gen. Physiol. Series, Vol. 35 (ed. by F. E. Bloom). New York: Raven. pp. 55–68.

Additional Reading

Landmesser, L. and G. Pilar. 1974. Synaptic transmission and cell death during normal ganglionic development. *J. Physiol. 241:* 737–749.

Lund, R. D. 1980. Tissue transplantation: a useful tool in mammalian neuroembryology. *Trends in Neurosci. 3:* XII–XIII.

Thomas, J. B. and R. J. Wyman. 1982. A single gene mutation alters the morphology of the giant fiber in *Drosophila.*

III
Sensory Systems

11

Introduction:
from Receptors to Perceptions

Sensory systems are good starting points for the study of the organization of nerve cells. From early childhood we are aware of the multitude of sensations and perceptions that occur as a part of the business of living. Those that are particularly painful or pleasurable become powerful factors in molding the way we develop, the kinds of personalities we acquire, and the goals we work toward. Since sensory experience is so immediate, it is much more readily understandable than many other aspects of nervous function. We all agree, more or less, on what different kinds of senses there are. We know that our senses not only inform us, but may often fool us; they constantly test our abilities to make judgments about things.

The fact that sensory perceptions are so accessible to our introspection means that when humans first acquired the ability to think and speculate about their own nature, they were very much aware of the importance of sensory experience. The early Greek philosophers of the sixth century B.C. were able to make the distinction between reason on the one hand, and the senses on the other. This is exemplified in the statement of Heraclitus, that "knowledge comes to man through the door of the senses." It was realized that different senses are mediated by different sense organs, but also that the different sensory impressions are united in our minds. Some of these philosophers even suspected that the site of this integration is in the brain. In these ideas lay the origins of physiology and psychology.

Sensory Modalities

It would be fascinating to trace the development of concepts about the senses since then, but to understand the foundation of modern concepts we need go back only to the nineteenth century. In the 1830's, Johannes Muller of Berlin published a monumental *Handbook of Human Physiology*, which served as the definitive textbook of physiology in Europe and America for many years. In it he summarized the work on sensory physiology, and promulgated the *"law of specific nerve energies"*. This states that we are aware, not of objects themselves, but of signals about them transmitted through our nerves, and that there are different kinds of nerves, each nerve having its own "specific nerve energy". The kinds of nerves considered by Muller corresponded to the

187

five primary senses that Aristotle had recognized: seeing, hearing, touch, smell, and taste. The specific nerve energy represented the *sensory modality* that each type of nerve transmitted. The key point is that the nerve transmits this modality no matter how it is stimulated. Thus, an electric shock or a blow on the head may both stimulate the nerves of hearing, and elicit sounds in our ears.

The doctrine was applied in a famous law case in which Muller was called in for expert testimony. A man had been assaulted at night, and had accused someone. When asked how he could identify the assailant since it was pitch dark, he replied that he caught a glimpse of him in the light caused by the blow to his head!

Muller pointed out that pressure on the eye does indeed cause a light sensation—a phosphene—but this is an expression of the fact that the eye responds to any stimulation with a light sensation, and that this is an entirely internal phenomenon.

In modern terms, we recognize that there are specific *receptor cells* tuned to be sensitive to different forms of *energy* in the environment. The forms of energy serve as *stimuli* for the receptor cells. A summary of the main types of receptor cells in the human body, the organs in which they are located, and the forms of energy to which each is sensitive, is provided in Table 11.1. Note that there are many more modalities than the five senses that we think of in everyday life. Among the conscious

Table 11.1 Main types of sensory modalities

Sensory modality	Form of energy	Receptor organ	Receptor cell
Chemical			
common chemical	molecules	various	free nerve endings
arterial oxygen	O_2 tension	carotid body	cells and nerve endings
toxins (vomiting)	molecular	medulla	chemoreceptor cells
osmotic pressure	osmotic pressure	hypothalamus	osmoreceptors
glucose	glucose	hypothalamus	glucoreceptors
pH (cerebrospinal fluid)	ions	medulla	ventricle cells
Taste	ions and molecules	tongue and pharynx	taste bud cells
Smell	molecules	nose	olfactory receptors
Somatosensory			
touch	mechanical	skin	nerve terminals
pressure	mechanical	skin and deep tissue	encapsulated nerve endings
temperature	temperature	skin, hypothalamus	nerve terminals and central neurons
pain	various	skin and various organs	nerve terminals
Muscle			
vascular pressure	mechanical	blood vessels	nerve terminals
muscle stretch	mechanical	muscle spindle	nerve terminals
muscle tension	mechanical	tendon organs	nerve terminals
joint position	mechanical	joint capsule and ligaments	nerve terminals
Balance			
linear acceleration (gravity)	mechanical	vestibular organ	hair cells
angular acceleration	mechanical	vestibular organ	hair cells
Hearing	mechanical	inner ear (cochlea)	hair cells
Vision	electromagnetic (photons)	eye (retina)	photoreceptors

Modified from Ganong (1978)

senses, we must include pressure, temperature, and pain under "touch", and also joint position and the sense of balance. It is also evident from the list that we have specialized cells that are sensitive to many stimuli within our bodies that never reach consciousness. Particularly important in this group are stretch receptors in the vasculature and muscles, and a variety of receptors sensitive to different kinds of chemical factors. The receptors in the viscera and other internal organs are often called *interoceptors* or visceroceptors, to distinguish them from the olfactory, auditory, and visual *exteroceptors* that receive signals from outside the body (also called teleceptors: tel-distant). Taken as a whole, our array of receptors provides information that ranges from the minutest changes in the internal milieu of our bodies to the faintest signals that waft our way from the furthest reaches of our external world.

Within a modality there may be different submodalities, or *qualities*. Thus, we perceive different tastes and smells; we describe temperature sensations in terms of warmth and cold; we see different wavelengths of light as different colors. In general, just as a modality is determined mainly by a type of receptor, so is a sensory quality based on a differentiation of receptors into subtypes. Each receptor cell subtype is tuned to a more narrow spectrum of the stimulus band. Thus, odor qualities depend on receptor cells in the nose being differentially sensitive to different airborne molecules, and different colors depend on photoreceptors in the eye with different sensitivities to wavelengths of light.

The sense organs and modalities listed in Table 11.1 are those that are found in the human. If we look back over the course of evolution, we see that in general the main categories of modalities are present in most of the main animal groups. Perhaps the most basic are the chemical and touch modalities which are necessary aspects of the mere existence of an animal, together with some capacity for light sensitivity, which permits a sense of the cycles of night and day.

At the level of molecules and cell membranes, the basic receptor mechanisms within a given modality share many common features across different phyla and species. However, the receptor cells and sense organs show diversity of forms, as is evident from the survey of the diversity of body plans and nervous systems throughout the Animal Kingdom in Chaps. 2 and 3. Thus, it is not surprising that the eye of a flatworm or an insect should be different from our own. We could expect that some species should have sense organs that we lack, such as electric fish with their organs for sensing electric currents, or the mollusc with its osphradial organ for sensing water entering the mantle cavity. Nor is it surprising that many sense organs may be absent, as with the extreme adaptations of the tapeworm to a parasitic existence in the gut of its host. Finally, despite this diversity, we should not be surprised to learn that some sensory cells and organs are such successful adaptations that, like the vertebrate receptor cells for smell, or the vertebrate eye, they are present relatively unchanged across many different species.

In the six remaining chapters in this section we will learn about the six main classes of sensory modalities and their respective sense organs and sensory systems. For each modality we will discuss examples from invertebrate and vertebrate species, and finish by considering the human.

It will be useful to recognize at the beginning that there are some *basic mechanisms* that are common to all the sensory modalities. These mechanisms operate at three main levels: the sensory receptors themselves, the pathways that transmit the information, and the circuits and properties that underlie sensory perception. These are summarized in Table 11.2. Let us consider briefly the main aspects of these common mechanisms before proceeding to the individual sensory systems.

Table 11.2 Some common mechanisms of sensory processing at levels of receptors, circuits, and perception

Receptor level	Circuit level	Perceptual level
Mechanisms		
transduction	divergence–convergence	cell assemblies
receptor potential	receptive fields	intensity coding
electrotonic potential	contrast enhancement	feature abstraction
impulse coding	centrifugal control	
Properties		
detection	detection	threshold
specificity	specificity	quality discrimination
intensity	intensity	magnitude estimation
adaptation	adaptation	adaptation
amplification	amplification	spatial discrimination and acuity

Sensory Receptors

In order to detect and discriminate different stimuli in the environment or within the body, the stimuli have to be converted from their different forms of energy into the common currency of nervous signals. This conversion is termed *transduction*, and the cells in which it takes place are, by definition, *sensory receptor cells*.

One of the most fascinating aspects of sensory systems is the variety of receptor cells. Figure 11.1 represents schematically some of the main types in the vertebrate. The sites at which transduction occurs are indicated in shading. An entire cell may transduce a stimulus, as in some chemical receptor cells such as those sensitive to oxygen tension in the blood (to the far left in the figure). In most cases, however, transduction takes place at a specialized site in the sensory cell. The specializations may have many different forms. In some cases they may be microvilli (as in taste), in others they may be cilia (smell or vision). In most receptors of the skin, viscera, and muscles, the sites of transduction are in the terminals of nerve fibers. The terminals may be free (naked nerve endings), as in the skin, or embedded in special structures, as in corpuscles or muscle spindles. Finally, the sites may be in special intracellular membranes or organelles, as in visual receptors.

Let us consider briefly the basic steps at the receptor level in getting from the applied stimulus to an impulse message in the sensory nerves. With regard to the first step, *transduction* of the sensory stimulus, the nature of the molecular mechanisms in the membranes of receptor cells is a subject of considerable interest. Unfortunately, the interaction between the stimulus and its specific molecular receptors is still little understood in most cases. This is because the receptor sites have very small dimensions, they are often rather inaccessible, and the transduction events take place quickly. Whatever the mechanism, receptor membranes are extremely sensitive to detection of their appropriate stimulus; we will see that in most cases they appear to be at the theoretical limit of sensitivity (for example, the hair cells of the ear are able to detect a movement approximately as small as the diameter of a hydrogen atom).

About the next step in transduction, the conversion of the change in the molecular receptor to a change of the membrane potential of the receptor cell, there are at least some conceptual models. Figure 11.2 illustrates some postulated mechanisms for three receptor types. It can be seen that in each case there is a channel or some equivalent structure to permit the flow of ions across the membrane. The channel is

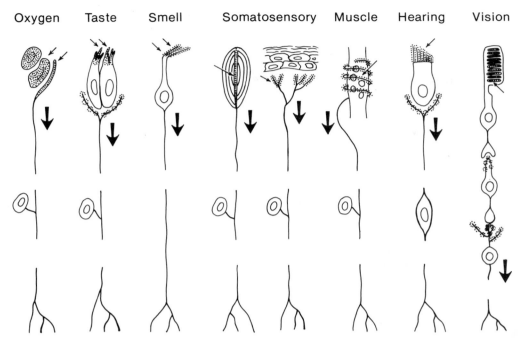

Fig. 11.1. Different types of sensory receptor cells in vertebrates. Small arrows indicate sites where sensory stimuli act. Stippling indicates sites for transduction of the sensory stimuli, and also for synaptic transmission; both of these sites mediate graded signal transmission. Large arrows indicate sites of impulse initiation. (Adapted from Bodian, 1962)

controlled by a gating molecule(s). In the chemoreceptor, a specific molecule stimulates a receptor molecule to retract the gating molecule, thus allowing ionic flow through the channel. In the mechanoreceptor, it is envisaged that distention of the membrane may increase the channel size, permitting ionic flow to occur. In the vertebrate photoreceptor, ion flow occurs mainly in the dark, and is blocked as a consequence of light acting on the disc membranes within the receptor.

These and other mechanisms at the molecular level will be discussed further in the remaining chapters of this section (Chaps. 12–17). For now we note that they all have in common the property of ultimately affecting the movement of ions that depolarize the membrane, as indicated by the arrows in Fig. 11.2. This changes the charge across the membrane, and the resulting change in the membrane potential is called the *receptor potential*. The mech-

anism is similar in principle to that of a synaptic potential (see Chap. 8).

The next step in the receptor cell is to get from the receptor potential to the impulse. In general, this does not occur directly. As can be seen in Fig. 11.1, the sites of sensory transduction and impulse initiation (thick arrows) are usually separated. In some cases, the separation is some distance within a cell body or nerve fiber; in others a synapse intervenes. In the case of the retina, two synapses intervene between the sites of transduction and impulse initiation (see Fig. 11.1).

As we have already discussed in Chap. 8, the spread of a receptor potential, like that of a synaptic potential, is accomplished by means of *electrotonic potentials*. The diagrams in Fig. 8.9 remind us of this fact. In the case of the stretch receptor cell, stretch increases the inward positive current across the nerve terminal membrane (as in B of Fig. 11.2), setting up

TRANSDUCER MECHANISMS

AT REST   **DURING STIMULATION**

A. CHEMORECEPTOR

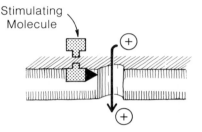

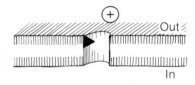

B. MECHANORECEPTOR

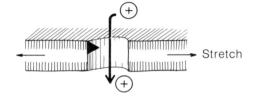

C. VERTEBRATE PHOTORECEPTOR

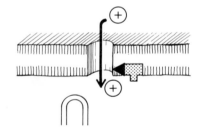

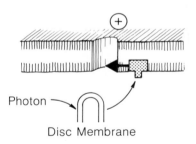

Fig. 11.2 Conceptual models of transducer mechanisms in three types of receptors.

the receptor potential in the terminals. This spreads by electrotonic currents through the cell to the site of impulse initiation in the axon. In the case of the vertebrate photoreceptor, the action of the photon on the disc membrane leads to blockade of the dark current, and the resulting membrane potential change spreads through the cell to the site of synaptic output at the receptor terminal. For further details on these mechanisms, the reader may refer to Chap. 8, and the Chaps. 12–18 that follow.

The final step at the receptor level is the encoding of the electrotonically transmitted receptor response into an *impulse discharge* in the afferent nerve fiber that carries the information to the rest of the nervous system. This process, as exemplified by a vertebrate stretch receptor cell, is illustrated in Fig. 11.3. The stimulus in this case is a stretch applied to the muscle. An important distinction is between the *dynamic* (phasic) period of the stimulation, when the stretch is increasing, and the *static* (tonic) period, when it is maintained constant. If impulses are blocked artificially (as by tetrodotoxin) in order to observe the receptor events, it is seen that the receptor potential rises to a peak at the end of dynamic stretch, and then falls to a lower, slowly declining level during static stretch. When the impulse discharge is recorded, the impulse frequency also rises sharply during dynamic stretch, and declines to a lower level during static stretch. The close correlation between receptor potential and impulse frequency can be seen in the graph at the top of Fig. 11.3.

An important point is that the receptor potential is graded smoothly and continuously in amplitude in relation to the intensity of the stimulus. Sensory reception thus involves the transformation, or mapping, from a continuously varying domain of sensory stimuli into a neural domain of all-or-nothing impulses. One can view it as converting from analogue signals to digital signals. As we noted in Chap. 8, this is also what takes place during transmission at many types of synapses. The impulse discharge can function in this way, because the intervals between impulses (hence the impulse frequency) vary continuously in relation to the underlying depolarization level of the receptor potential and its rate of change.

From results such as these it is concluded that the impulse discharge faithfully encodes the parameters of the ap-

Fig. 11.3. Stimulus encoding in the frog muscle spindle. Diagrams show the relations between an applied stretch (containing dynamic and static phases), the graded receptor potential, the impulse discharge, and the impulse frequency. (After Ottoson and Shepherd, 1971)

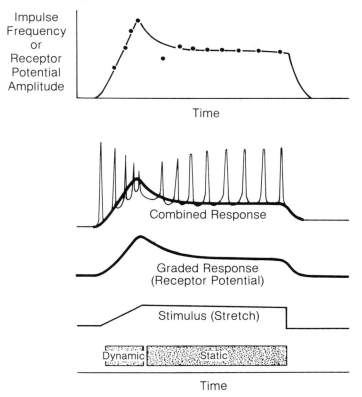

plied stimulus. However, we can see that it does more than this; in the case of the stretch receptor, it tends to heighten the response when the stimulus is increasing. This property is termed *dynamic sensitivity*. In addition, receptors vary in how rapidly the response declines during static stimulation. The decline is termed *adaptation*. Receptors that must signal slow and prolonged changes are *slowly adapting,* or *tonic* receptors; those that signal brief changes are termed *rapidly adapting* or *phasic* receptors. Our ability to maintain positions of our muscles over long periods of time depends on the slowly adapting properties of our muscle receptors, whereas the rapid fading of our appreciation of a pressure stimulus is due to the rapid adaptation of pressure receptors (Pacinian corpuscles). Adaptation may also be a property of the transmission of signals through sensory pathways (see below).

We may summarize our overview of events at the receptor level in terms of the steps and properties listed in Table 11.2. We have seen that there are four main steps (transduction, receptor potential generation, electrotonic spread, impulse generation) in the transfer of information from the domain of the sensory stimulus to the domain of the impulse discharge. We have also seen how the receptor determines the basic properties of the sensory response. Thus, *specificity* resides in the molecular mechanisms of the sensitive membrane. *Intensity* is mapped from graded receptor potentials into an impulse frequency code. *Adaptation* determines the profile of the response in relation to the dimension of time; there is often a tendency to heighten the sensitivity to stimulus change. The distribution of the whole population of receptors determines the *spatial organization* of the incoming information, as we shall soon discuss.

Sensory Circuits

The stimulus has been converted into a frequency code and the impulses are on their way to the central nervous system. Within the central nervous system, sensory information characteristically is relayed through a series of centers. In each center there is opportunity for processing of the signals and integration with other types of information. A *sensory pathway* thus consists of a series of modality-specific neurons connected by synapses. All the circuits within and related to this pathway constitute a *sensory system*.

The circuits of different sensory systems share some common properties, as illustrated in Fig. 11.4. The axons of primary sensory nerves divide to supply more than one neuron; this is referred to as *divergence*. A neuron in turn is contacted by more than one axon; this is termed *convergence*. These features apply to connections both within and between different centers; thus, incoming axons diverge to more than one center, and different sources converge onto a given center. The chains of connections mean that a pathway consists of connections in *series*, in which there is obviously a temporal *sequence* of events. However, because of the divergence and convergence of connections at successive levels, there are connections in *parallel*, so that different forms of information can be transferred and combined at the same time.

Some central pathways are primarily concerned with transmitting the input from one type of receptor; these are termed *specific sensory pathways*. Other pathways, by divergence of their fibers and convergence with other inputs, become increasingly *multimodal,* or *nonspecific*. Finally, *centrifugal* connections provide for *feedback* of information from one level to the next. In general, specific sensory pathways provide for precise transmission of sensory information, while nonspecific pathways provide for sensory integration and adjustments in behavioral status of the whole organism. Both can be seen to be necessary for the analytic and synthetic functions of the organism.

An important concept in sensory physiology is the *receptive field*. For any neuron in a sensory pathway, the receptive

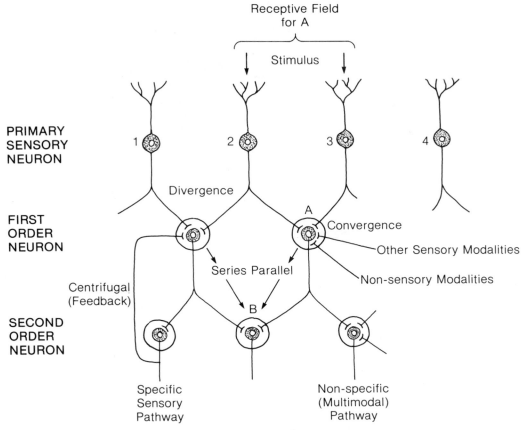

Fig. 11.4. Some common aspects of the organization of sensory circuits.

field consists of *all the sensory receptors that can influence its activity.* Thus, cell A in Fig. 11.4 has a receptive field consisting of the two receptors (2 and 3) which connect to it. Cell B, at the second level in this system, has a receptive field consisting of receptors 1, 2, and 3. The connections to a cell may be excitatory or inhibitory, and they may be mediated by interneurons at a given level as well as relay neurons connecting levels. As we will see in following chapters, the properties of receptive fields generally reflect the increasing degree of information processing and feature extraction that occurs in neurons at successively higher levels in sensory pathways.

Within any center in the nervous system, the types of neurons and synaptic connections have many forms. However, as noted in Chap. 4, the organization of a center is usually built up within a frame-

work of three elements: input fibers, output cells, and intrinsic neurons. These principles of organization are demonstrated very clearly in the centers of many sensory pathways.

Two examples are illustrated in Fig. 11.5. Part A is a schematic diagram of the neurons in the vertebrate retina, and their main patterns of synaptic interconnection. There are input elements (the receptors) and output neurons (the ganglion cells). There are interneurons for straight-through transmission (the bipolar cells), and there are interneurons for horizontal interactions. The horizontal connections are organized at two levels, the first (horizontal cells) at the level of receptor input, and the second (amacrine cells) at the level of ganglion cell output. The amacrine cells take part in a variety of reciprocal and serial synaptic connections, that correspond

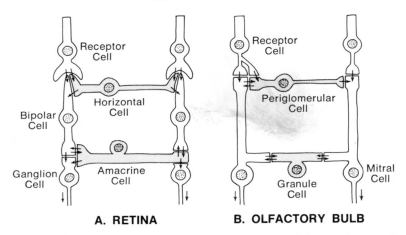

A. RETINA   **B. OLFACTORY BULB**

Fig. 11.5. Comparison between simplified basic circuit diagrams of the vertebrate retina and olfactory bulb. (After Shepherd, 1978)

to the complexity of processing that occurs at this level (see Chap. 17).

Figure 11.5B is a similar diagram of the neurons and connections in the vertebrate olfactory bulb. Here, too, are input elements (the olfactory receptors) and output neurons (the mitral cells). In this case the straight-through pathway is provided by the primary dendrite of the mitral cell. Horizontal connections are organized at two levels. The first, through periglomerular short-axon cells, is at the level of receptor input; the second, through granule cells, is at the level of mitral cell output. The granule and mitral cells interact through reciprocal synapses.

From this comparison it can be seen that, although the retina and olfactory bulb process two very different types of sensory information, their basic organization has many points in common. In both cases there is provision for straight-through transfer of signals to the output neuron, and local processing of signals through the interneurons and local circuits.

We have mentioned that in addition to transmitting faithfully certain aspects of the stimulus, receptors also enhance some aspects. This appears also to be a function of the intrinsic synaptic circuits at successive levels in a sensory pathway. Perhaps

the best known example of this is the lateral inhibition that enhances spatial contrast in the visual system. This was first revealed by Keffer Hartline and his colleagues at Rockefeller University in their studies of the eye of the horseshoe crab, *Limulus.* The essence of their findings, illustrated in Fig. 11.6, was that at edges of light, the activity in the optic pathway is modified so that it signals a peak of higher intensity on the side which is lighter and a trough of lower intensity on the side that is darker. This modification is mediated by lateral inhibitory connections within the eye, hence, the term *lateral* inhibition.

The classical studies of *Limulus* emphasized the importance of lateral inhibition for contrast enhancement and feature extraction, but recent work suggests that it also has other functions. In invertebrates, lateral inhibition appears to aid in image reconstruction by contributing to compensation for blurring of the image due to dispersion of light as it passes through the lens. Another function is as a gain control. *Limulus,* for example, responds to intensities over 11 log units. In order to cover this enormously wide range, and still have mechanisms that enhance sensitivity at low levels near threshold, there must be a reduction of sensitivity as the intensity of stimulation increases. One mechanism for achieving this kind of gain compression is through feedback inhibition (see Chap. 17).

Sensory Perception

The end effect of stimulating a sensory system is to produce a behavioral response of the organism. In studies of animals, the only end effect we can measure is an observable reflex response. In human experience, however, we know that a reflex response may or may not be obligatory; in most cases, what is produced is an internal representation, a conscious image, of the stimulus, and we then proceed to act on that. This process of producing an internal image we call *perception*. It involves our recognition that stimulation has occurred, and our ability to discriminate various aspects of the stimulus.

The study of the quantitative relations between stimulus and perception constitutes the field of *psychophysics*. One of the aims of sensory neurobiology is to understand the neural mechanisms underlying these relations. The ultimate aim is to identify the *building blocks of perception*—the functional mechanisms used to construct our perceptual representation of the world about us.

The main aspects of a stimulus that contribute to sensory perception were listed in Table 11.1. Let us briefly review them here as an introduction to the following chapters.

Detection. The simplest aspect of a perception is the ability to detect whether a stimulus has occurred. This level of intensity is called the *behavioral threshold*. We have seen previously that each receptor has its characteristic threshold for responding to some minimum amount of its specific stimulus. As a general rule, several receptor responses must summate in order for transmission to occur in the sensory pathway. This was first shown in a classic study of the visual system by S. Hecht, S. Shlaer, and M. H. Pirenne in 1942. They calculated that a single photon is adequate for stimulating a single photoreceptor in the human retina, but the simultaneous activation of about seven receptors is neces-

Fig. 11.6. Enhancement of spatial contrast in *Limulus* eye. **A.** Surface of *Limulus* eye, with superimposed rectangular stimulus pattern; pattern is divided into lighter (left) and darker (right) regions. Pattern is centered on test ommatidium (⊗). Arrows show directions in which the test pattern was displaced, to produce lower curve in graph in (B). **B.** Recordings of spike frequency in axon from test ommatidium in (A). Lower curve: responses to rectangular test pattern in (A). Upper curve: responses to small spot of light, at high and low intensities corresponding to those of test pattern (see inset). The differences between the two curves illustrate that lateral inhibition enhances the response on the light side of an edge (because there is less inhibition from the more darkly lit neighbors to the right), and depresses the response on the dark side of an edge (because there is more inhibition from the brightly lit neighbors to the left). (From Ratliff, 1965)

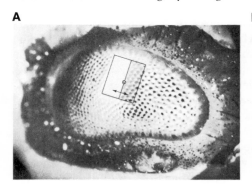
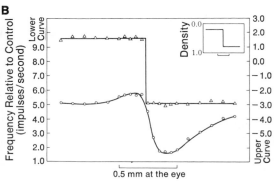

sary to perceive that stimulation has occurred. The behavioral threshold is therefore somewhat higher than the individual receptor threshold, a general finding in most sensory systems.

Magnitude Estimation. The next important property of a stimulus is how much of it there is. Primitive visual receptors (occeli) of invertebrates, and the eyes of primitive vertebrates, are examples of receptors that are concerned mostly with this property. More advanced sensory systems are exquisitely tuned to registering stimulus magnitude over a wide range of intensities, in addition to other sensory qualities.

The study of magnitude estimations involves varying the stimulus in a quantitative manner and determining the physiological, behavioral, or perceptual response along some quantitative scale. This was first attempted and formalized by Ernst Weber (1834) and Gustav Fechner (1860) in Germany, and was the foundation stone of psychophysics as a science.

As is well known, these studies suggested that the response varies with the stimulus according to an exponential relation. This "law" was widely believed until around 1960, when S. S. Stevens at Harvard obtained evidence that in many systems the relation can better be described by a power law. The beginning student does not have to be concerned about the relative merits of these laws. Over limited magnitude ranges, both are reasonable approximations, as illustrated by the graphs in Fig. 11.7. What is important is that in most sensory systems the psychological perception varies in strength with the intensity of stimulation in a quantitative manner.

In an attempt to get physiological evidence for this relation, neurobiologists have made recordings at various levels in several of the sensory pathways. Thus, as shown in Fig. 11.8, the concentration of a taste substance on the tongue was varied while recordings were made from the nerves from the tongue. The results showed that the magnitude of stimulation, of nerve response, and of perceptual estimation were all closely correlated. This experiment could be carried out in humans because of the accessibility of the nerve from the tongue for recording as it passes through the chamber of the middle ear. Another approach has been to study the behavioral responses and physiological recordings in primates, as a model for humans. In the somatosensory system, behavioral responses are closely correlated with the impulse discharges of neurons at successive levels, as we shall see in Chap. 13.

Spatial Discrimination. In several sensory systems, natural stimulation of the receptors occurs in some spatial pattern. The ability to identify the site or pattern of stimulation is termed *spatial discrimination.* This applies to the visual and somatosensory system, and also to the auditory system, in which different sounds affect different parts of the receptor population. A common way to study the somatosensory system for this quality is to test for *two-point discrimination,* to see how close together two points on the skin can be stimulated and still be perceived as two points rather than one. The comparable tests in the visual system are with two points of light (a measure of *visual acuity*), and with two tones in the auditory system.

The general finding is that at low intensities of stimulation, discrimination is poor, and is not much in evidence until some level of intensity above threshold. This is taken to indicate that weak stimulation mainly activates straight-through pathways in sensory systems, to enhance detection, and that only with increased intensities do horizontal interactions, such as those indicated in the diagrams of Figs. 11.4 and 11.5 come into play, to enhance spatial discrimination. This region, between threshold and discrimination, is called the *atonal area* in the auditory sys-

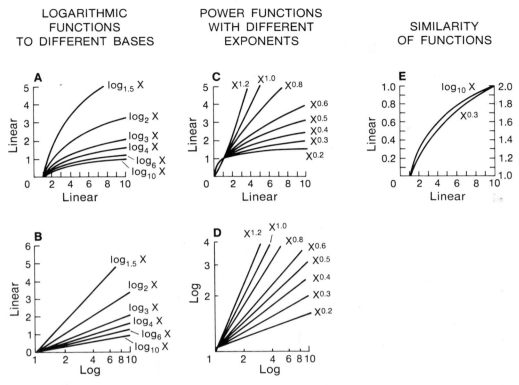

Fig. 11.7. Hypothetical relations between stimulus and response. Stimulus intensity is plotted on the abscissa, response intensity on the ordinate. Logarithmic relation (according to Fechner) is plotted on linear (**A**) and logarithmic (**B**) scales. Exponential relation (according to Stevens) is plotted on linear (**C**) and logarithmic (**D**) scales. The curves may be very similar, as shown in **E**. (From Somjen, 1972)

Fig. 11.8. Stimulus–response relations in a sensory system. Graph plots subjective intensity of taste sensation and frequency of impulse discharge in chorda tympanic nerve in response to stimulation of the tongue with citric acid and glucose. Recordings were made in humans undergoing middle ear surgery, which exposes the chorda tympani nerve. (Modified from Borg et al., 1967)

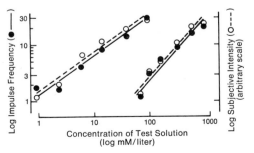

tem; it is the region between the point at which we say "yes, I hear something" and "yes, I hear a different tone." The student can verify the phenomenon by weak and strong stimulation with two pencil points on his skin. That will also demonstrate that two-point discrimination varies widely in different parts of the body surface, as will be described further in Chap. 13.

Feature Abstraction. Natural stimulation does not usually consist of spots of light or points jabbing into the skin. Rather, it involves complex interplays of several stimulus properties. The strategy in studying the components that contribute to perception of a natural stimulus is to begin with spots of light, or a simple grating, in the case of the visual system, for example, and then change to increasingly more complex stimuli, such as moving spots and edges with different orientations, as we reach higher levels in the cerebral cortex. The results imply that a unit of perception involves a set of neurons and their connections that is tuned to a coordinated set of several stimulus properties, such as, in this case, light, movement, shape, orientation, and size. The set of properties may be said to constitute a feature, and the mechanisms whereby a neuron or circuit is tuned to this feature in preference to others is called *feature abstraction* or feature extraction. In the somatosensory system, the comparable process relates to the way we feel the texture of a surface by moving our hands over it ("active touch"), or the way we feel the texture of food with our tongues, which makes important contributions to the overall perception of palatability of food.

Both two-point discrimination and feature extraction, as it relates to spatial features, involve mechanisms of lateral inhibition and other types of interactions within sensory pathways organized to enhance contrast between stimulated and unstimulated regions, and to enhance changing stimuli over stationary ones. Analysis of these mechanisms has been one of the main achievements of sensory neurobiologists, as we will see in succeeding chapters.

Quality Discrimination. As pointed out previously, a given sensory modality characteristically contains several submodalities or qualities, and the discrimination of these as distinctly different is one of the main attributes of sensory systems. In general, the discrimination of qualities is regarded as being of two types, either analytic or synthetic. Consider a stimulus containing a mixture of two submodalities. In *analytic* discrimination, each submodality retains its individual character. Thus, in the taste modality, there are four basic qualities—sweet, salt, sour, and bit-

ter. When we taste a mixture of, say, sugar and salt, the individual qualities can still be discerned; they do not merge to form a new sensation. The perception is analytic; it can be analyzed into its components. In contrast, in the perception of color, there are primary colors—red, yellow, green—which when mixed together yield most other colors. The other colors are in effect *synthesized* from the primary colors, and have their own qualities, distinct from those of the primaries.

Pattern Recognition. In studying sensory mechanisms, we do experiments to analyze the system into its components, and then infer the process whereby the system uses those mechanisms to build up its behavioral response or conscious perception. In some cases sensory systems may actually operate in that way, building up a perception from individual discriminations. However, one of the most vivid of mental experiences is the ability to take in a scene around us and instantly recognize a familiar pattern, or an unfamiliar one, or one that has some special significance. This is a capability that is prevalent throughout the animal kingdom. The actions of specific visual objects in releasing innate behavior patterns in many lower animals are vivid examples of this capability, as we shall discuss in Section IV.

This property of sensory perceptions was first recognized by the Gestalt psychologists in the early part of this century. Gestalt means form, or shape, but as used by these workers it means the patterns we perceive and recognize as unitary wholes. As Edwin Boring put it:

In perceiving a melody you get the melodic form, not a string of notes, a unitary whole that is something more than the total list of its parts or even the serial pattern of them. This is the way experience comes to man, put up in significant structured forms . . .

This idea is sometimes thought to be opposed to the concept that perceptions are built up out of neural units, such as we have been discussing, but in fact there is no inconsistency. They are different aspects of the same problem, much as a table is made up of atoms, yet looks like a table. The important point is that many of our sensory experiences consist of complex patterns, either in space or in time, and we tend to perceive them as wholes more than in terms of their individual parts. This implies that such perceptions involve very large populations of neurons and very extensive sets of circuits. A related point is that although two patterns may be very similar, we can perceive them as distinctly different. The traditional example of this is the ability we all have to recognize our own grandmother in a crowd. Thus, although patterns may be similar, or may grade into each other, our perceptions are separate, distinct, discontinuous entities. This is illustrated in Fig. 11.9, just one of the many examples of this property in the visual system.

These considerations indicate that perceptions involve extensive sets of neurons and circuits, and that these sets, though overlapping, nonetheless mediate distinct responses. The analysis of individual neural components is the starting point, but we will obviously need information from many approaches, both experimental and theoretical, before a final understanding is reached.

REFERENCES

Bodian, D. 1967. Neurons, circuits, and neuroglia. In *The Neurosciences: A Study Program* (ed. by G. C. Quarton, T. Melnechuk, and F. O. Schmitt). New York: Rockefeller. pp. 6–24.

Borg, G., H. Diamant, L. Strom, and Y. Zotterman. 1967. The relation between neural and perceptual intensity: a comparative study on the neural and psychophysical response to taste stimuli. *J. Physiol.* 192: 13–20.

Boring, E. 1950. [Chap. 1].

Ganong, W. F. 1977. *The Nervous System.* Los Altos, Calif: Lange.

Gregory, R. L. 1966. *Eye and Brain. The Psychology of Seeing.* London: Weidenfeld and Nicolson.

Ottoson, D. and G. M. Shepherd. 1972. Transducer properties and integrative mechanisms in the frog's muscle spindle. In *Principles of Receptor Physiology* (ed. by W. R. Lowenstein). *Handbook of Sensory Physiology*, Vol. 1. New York: Springer. pp. 442–499.

Ratliff, F. 1965. *Mach Bands: Quantitative Studies on Neural Networks in the Retina.* San Francisco: Holden-Day.

Schmidt, R. F. (ed.). 1978. *Fundamentals of Sensory Physiology.* New York: Springer.

Shepherd, G. M. 1978. Microcircuits in the brain. *Sci. Am.* 238: 92–103.

Somjen, G. 1972. *Sensory Coding in the Mammalian Nervous System.* New York: Appleton-Century-Crofts.

Fig. 11.9. In this figure, the black areas appear as faces, the white area as the outline of an urn. Our perception alternates between these two interpretations. This illustrates that we perceive patterns as consistent wholes, each distinct from the other. It also illustrates that perception involves making a "decision" about what is the figure ("signal") and what is the background ("noise"). Finally, it shows that perception is not just a passive reception of individual sensory signals, but rather involves an active interpretation by the brain of the meaning of the stimulus patterns it receives. (Legend and figure from Gregory, 1966)

Stevens, S. S. 1975. *Psychophysics*. New York: Wiley.

Additional Reading

Groves, P. and K. Schlesinger. 1979. *Introduction to Biological Psychology*. Dubuque, Iowa: Wm. C. Brown.

Wasserman, G. S., G. Felstein, and G. S. Easland. 1979. The psychophysical function: harmonizing Fechner and Stevens. *Science 204:* 85–87.

12
Chemical Senses

One can begin almost anywhere in studying different sensory systems; each system has a claim to being functionally important and exhibiting properties of general interest. From an evolutionary point of view it is convenient to start with the chemical senses. The first organisms to emerge from the primordial brine defined themselves as organisms by the degree to which they could sustain their own metabolism, and this required the ability to sense the appropriate nutritive constituents in their environment. The chemical senses are thus among our most primitive; on the other hand, they provide us (as well as our animal cousins) with some of our most powerful experiences. If you think about it, the ability of cells to "sense", or respond, to specific chemicals runs as a thread though much of our study of neurobiology: the responses to chemical neurotransmitters and hormones, the development of neural connections, and the sensory responses of chemoreceptors, depend on properties that at the molecular level are on the same continuum. In this respect, no other class of sensory receptors better illustrates the study of nerve cells as a part of cell biology.

Having decided that this is where we

want to begin, we need to define our subject. The chemical senses may be divided into four categories: common chemical, internal receptors, taste, and smell. The *common chemical sense* includes all those cells that are sensitive to specific molecules or other chemical substances and which respond in ways that are communicated as signals to the nervous system. *Internal receptors* are a subclass of those receptors, which are specialized for monitoring various aspects of the chemical composition of the body that are vital for life. *Taste* and *smell* are familiar to everyone as distinct chemical modalities, taste for sensing substances within our mouths, smell for sensing airborne substances originating both in the outside environment and also from ingested foodstuffs.

Common Chemical Sense

Similar in many respects to those primordial inhabitants of Precambrian time are the present-day prokaryotes, the bacteria. Although at first glance they seem far removed from the subject of sensory receptors, they in fact express a number of properties of interest for our study. We can take as an example the gram-negative bacteria, *Escherichia coli,* a normal resident of our intestines, and the organism that has become the basis for much of our understanding of molecular genetics.

E. coli, like many bacteria, shows the property of *chemotaxis* (*chemo*-chemical, *taxis*-orientation). They have tiny flagella by which they move about, swimming toward favorable environments and away from unfavorable ones. They do this by a process known as "tumbling", as illustrated in Fig. 12.1. A favorable environment is one containing nutrients such as sugars and amino acids that are needed for metabolism so that the organism can survive; an unfavorable environment is one bereft of nutriment, or containing toxic or other harmful substances. The organism

Fig. 12.1. Chemoreception in bacteria. Series 1–4 demonstrates chemotaxis. Bacterium swims with flagella together up a favorable nutrient gradient (**1**), "tumbles" when sensing an unfavorable environment (**2**), moves randomly (**3**), and finally senses a favorable gradient and swims up it (**4**). The molecular mechanism of chemical sensing is illustrated below. (After Koshland, 1980)

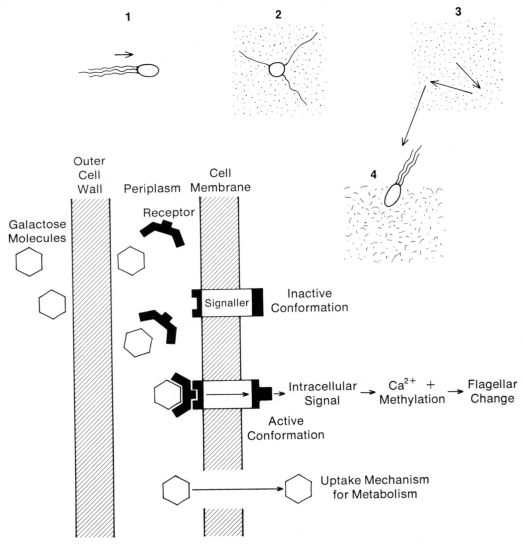

senses the favorable nutrient molecules by means of receptor molecules located just outside the cell membrane, or incorporated within it. The sensing mechanism is illustrated schematically in Fig. 12.1. The binding of the molecule (i.e. galactose) to a receptor molecule creates a molecule–receptor complex, which then activates a specific protein signaler that spans the cell membrane. This activation is believed to induce a conformational change in the protein which acts as a signal to initiate a chain of intracellular responses that leads to appropriate motor control of the flagella.

Although some of the details of this sensory mechanism are special for the bacteria, the principle of a sequence of specific molecular interactions is common to many chemosensory responses. The stimulating molecules serve only as triggers; the molecules that are actually used by the cell for its metabolism are taken up by other mechanisms. The response shows *graded specificity* (galactose acts best on galactose receptors); it shows *summation* (the responses to two or more different types of molecules are additive); and it shows *adaptation* (a brisk response to a new type or amount of stimulation, a declining response to a maintained level of stimulation). Some of the receptor molecules have been characterized (proteins with M.W. = 8,000–76,000 daltons). The genetic control of the receptor molecules and of some of the molecules involved in intracellular processing of the signals has been studied with the use of mutants, and evaluated against the background of all that is known about *E. coli* genetics. Thus, bacteria provide interesting insights into the nature of chemical receptor mechanisms and their genetic control.

Internal Chemoreceptors

As already mentioned (see Table 11.1 in Chap. 11), the responsibility for sensing specific substances essential to the internal economy of the body is delegated to various types of cells. It is usually the case that specific receptor mechanisms are located in one cell type, and these cells are grouped together to form a sensory organ.

Internal receptors for chemical substances in invertebrates have been studied relatively little. One example is the osphradial organ of molluscs. As described in Chap. 2, this is located under the mantle, and is believed to be involved in sensing the composition of water that circulates through the mantle cavity. Since the water enters directly from the outside, the osphradial organ is not really an internal organ, but its function is apparently important for maintaining the composition of the internal fluids of the animal.

Internal receptors for a variety of substances have been identified in vertebrates (see Table 11.1, Chap. 11). We will have more to say about the common chemical sense when we discuss pain receptors (Chap. 13), and we will later study glucose receptors, and receptors for circulating toxins (Chap. 27). Here, we take as an example the *carotid body,* a sensory organ found in most vertebrate animals, which senses the level of oxygenation of the circulating blood, and whose responses contribute to the reflexes which maintain blood oxygen at proper levels.

As shown in Fig. 12.2A, the carotid body is a small organ located between the internal and external carotid arteries which carry the blood supply to the head. Recordings from the fibers of cranial nerve IX (the glossopharyngeal) that connect the carotid body to the brainstem show a resting level of impulse discharge, as in Fig. 12.2, when the animal is breathing normal atmospheric air and the blood is normally oxygenated. When the oxygen tension decreases, under conditions of anoxia, the impulse discharge increases in frequency, as shown in the diagram.

The cellular organization of the carotid body is summarized in Fig. 12.2C. The IX nerve fibers, which arise from cells in the petrosal ganglion (a homologue of dorsal root ganglia), end within the carotid body

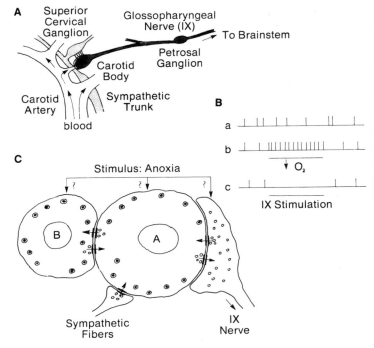

Fig. 12.2. The carotid body in the rat. **A.** Relation to carotid artery. **B.** Recordings from IX nerve, at rest (a), and when O_2 tension in blood is lowered (b). **C.** Basic circuit diagram of synaptic organization of carotid body. (From Shepherd, 1979; (C) modified from MacDonald and Mitchell, 1975)

in large terminals. Also within the carotid body are many *glomus cells.* These have few dendrites, and no axons. However, they have most of the fine structural characteristics of neurons, and they take part in synaptic connections with the large nerve terminals, and with each other. Most of these connections are arranged in pairs so that two synapses with opposite orientations are side-by-side, a type known as *reciprocal synapses,* discussed in Chap. 5.

It has been speculated that the carotid body may function in the following manner: lowering oxygen tension depolarizes the nerve terminal and makes it more excitable. This increases synaptic input to the glomus cells. The glomus cells feed back inhibition onto the nerve terminals, to control and modify the rate of impulse discharge. The glomus cells may be sensitive themselves to changing oxygen tension. They contain dopamine, stored in large dense-core vesicles (see diagram),

which may also contribute to modulation of the afferent signals generated in the nerve terminals. Within the brainstem, the sensory input activates neurons in respiratory centers, to increase the rate of respiration and restore the normal level of oxygenation of the blood.

Invertebrates

The Taste System. Cells that are preferentially sensitive to molecules in food materials may be designated as *taste receptor cells,* and the sensory modality is called taste, or *gustation.* Cells specialized for this purpose may be found almost anywhere on the body surface, for example, an antennae (in snails), tentacles (octopus), or legs (arthropods). A common location is near the mouth, where they can function to test for acceptance of nutritous food or rejection of toxic substances. A common arrangement consists of a group of cells, each with a long distal process that reaches out to a pore opening in a pit at the body surface. Such an arrangement is seen in nematode worms, in a chemical sense organ called an *amphid*. These are paired organs near the mouth; there is often a similar pair of organs at the tail end of the worm. As seen in Fig. 12.3A, the distal processes of the cells are modified cilia. Substances enter the surface pore and stimulate the cilia at their tips.

There must be something effective about this arrangement because chemoreceptors in insects are organized along similar, though more specialized, lines. The characteristic structure housing the receptors in these species is called a *sensillum*. This consists of a modification of the cuticle

into the form of peg, pit, plate, socket, or hair. The hair has been most studied; we discussed its cellular development in Chap. 10. As shown in Fig. 12.3B, the receptor cell bodies are at the base of the hair, and their distal processes enter the hair and extend to its tip. The processes are regarded as dendrites, though they are actually cilia (like those of the nematode), containing a 9 + 2 array of microtubules. At the tip there is a pore opening, which is covered with a tiny drop of a viscous fluid (see inset in Fig. 12.3). Stimulus molecules diffuse in this fluid through the pore and contact the dendritic tips. Here the molecules are believed to bind to receptor proteins, which then bring about a change in membrane conductivity—this is the step of *sensory transduction*. Unfortunately,

Fig. 12.3. A. The chemoreceptor organ (amphid) of a nematode worm. Note sensory neurons terminating in cilia. (From Ward, 1977) **B.** A labellar taste hair (sensillum) of a blowfly (from Fig. 10.5). **C.** Tip of hair at high magnification. Dashed lines: paths for electric current flow induced by chemical stimulation of tips of cilia. (After Hansen, 1978)

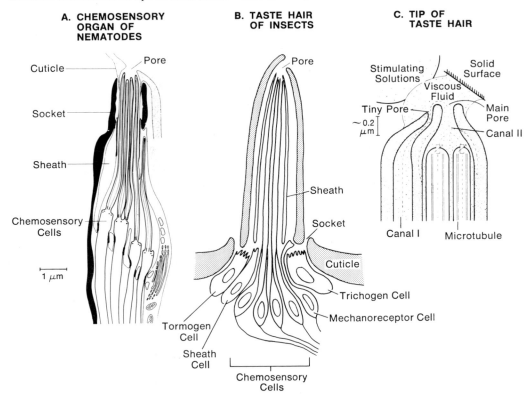

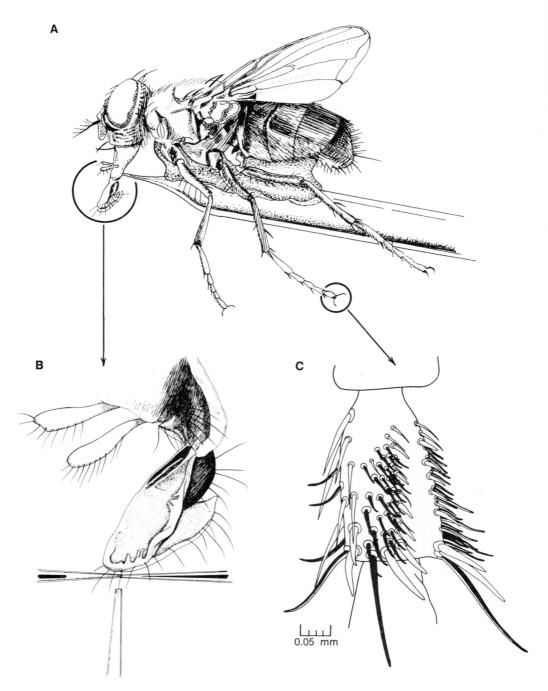

Fig. 12.4.A. Blowfly mounted for chronic recordings from nerves in the proboscis. **B.** Close-up view of labellum, with electrode arrangement for recording from single hair. **C.** Close-up view of chemosensory hairs on one tarsal segment. (From Dethier, 1976)

little is known as yet about these mechanisms.

The physiology of taste receptors has been studied most intensively in the blowfly (*Phormia regina*). Vincent Dethier of the University of Massachusetts has summarized a lifetime of work on this animal in his book *The Hungry Fly*. Figure 12.4A shows a blowfly mounted on the shaft of a capillary micropipette, with the tip inserted into the proboscis for recording from receptor cell axons over long periods of time. Figures 12.4B and C are enlarged diagrams of the two most common locations of taste sensory hairs, the tip (labellum) of the proboscis, and the distal segments (tarsi) of the legs. For short-term recordings, a microelectrode can be inserted into the base of the hair, to record directly from the receptor cells; alternatively, a micropipette containing solutions of substances can be placed with its tip enclosing a hair, for both stimulation and recording.

With these methods it has been found that each of four sensory cells in the hair is preferentially sensitive to a particular type of stimulating molecule. The four taste receptor cell types are water, sugar, and two types of salt receptor, based on sensitivity to the cation or the anion. The final cell type is a mechanoreceptor. Sample recordings from a hair are shown in Fig. 12.5, using a set-up similar to that depicted in Fig. 12.4B.

When we say that a cell is preferentially sensitive to a given compound, we mean that it responds with the lowest threshold and the most vigorous activity in comparison with other compounds. However, there is usually, in addition, some responsiveness to other compounds. Also, there may be inhibitory interactions between the responses to two compounds; these interactions may occur at the receptor membrane sites, or they may occur between the cilia or cell bodies within the hair. These properties are seen in the responses to pure stimuli such as sugar or salt. When the stimuli are natural food substances, the

Fig. 12.5. Receptor responses of a single labellar hair to different substances. (From Dethier, 1976)

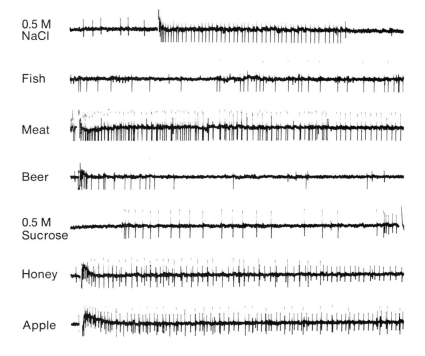

cells within a single hair show even more complicated combinations of responsiveness. Thus, results such as those in Fig. 12.5 have shown that sometimes the response of a hair is dominated by one cell (for example, a salt receptor response to beer), but more often more than one cell contributes significantly to the response. These different response patterns occur, Dethier has concluded,

> because each (natural) substance . . . is chemically complex, and because each receptor cell of the hair has a characteristic action spectrum rather than a unitary specificity. If the central nervous system is capable of analysing these patterns, there is contained within them sufficient information to characterize each substance as different.

We will have more to say about the neural code for different substances when we discuss vertebrate taste receptors later in this chapter.

The physiological evidence for different sensory receptors and for the encoding of taste information has its counterpart in studies of the behavioral responses of the fly. In these studies, the investigator determines the degree of acceptance or rejection of a substance, as judged by the amount of extension (acceptance) or retraction (rejection) of the proboscis. This is a very sensitive method for determining behavioral threshold; stimulation of only a single hair with a highly concentrated sugar solution will elicit the behavioral response of proboscis extension. Feeding behavior can be studied quantitatively with this method, and in Chap. 27 we will learn how the effectiveness of food stimuli is dependent on the state of hunger of the animal.

The Olfactory System. Many molecules of biological importance arise from sources at a distance from the organism. The sources may be plants, predators, prey, or other members of the same species (conspecifics). As we discussed in Chap. 5, molecules that transmit signals between conspecifics are called *pheromones.* Edward Wilson, in his book *Sociobiology,* notes that

> pheromones . . . were probably the first signals put to use in the evolution of life . . . With the emergence of . . . (higher) metazoan phyla, it was possible to create more sophisticated auditory and visual systems equipped to handle as much information as the chemoreceptors of single-celled organisms. Occasionally these new forms of communication have overridden the original chemical systems, but pheromones remain the fundamental signals for most kinds of organisms.

The receptors for pheromones and other distant stimulating molecules are called *olfactory receptors,* and the sensory modality is called smell, or *olfaction.* It is probably safe to say that all organisms have olfactory receptors. In marine animals the stimulating molecules are transmitted through water, whereas in terrestrial animals the transmitting medium is the air. The transmitting medium places certain requirements on the types of molecules that can be transmitted. Thus for aquatic organisms the molecules are generally soluble in water, such as acids and proteins, whereas in terrestrial organisms the molecules may be either lipid soluble or water soluble. Pheromone molecules range from 5–20 carbon atoms, and from 100–300 daltons in molecular weight. The increasing complexity of larger molecules imparts higher information-carrying capacity, but the molecules cannot be too large or they will not be adequately volatile in the air.

The olfactory sense reaches its highest development, among the invertebrates, in the social insects. On the output side, these animals are, in Wilson's phrase, "walking batteries of exocrine glands." Figure 12.6 shows a schematic diagram of a honeybee and locations of these glands, including those that emit pheromones. On the receptor side, most olfactory receptors are located in the *antennae,* which are paired, branching appendages arising from the head of the insect. The antennae of the

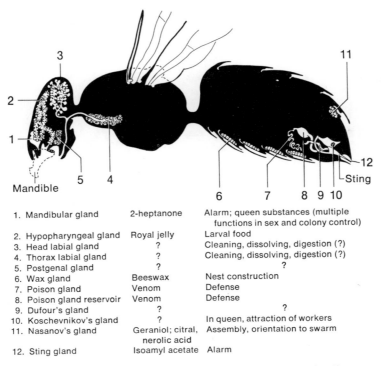

1. Mandibular gland	2-heptanone	Alarm; queen substances (multiple functions in sex and colony control)
2. Hypopharyngeal gland	Royal jelly	Larval food
3. Head labial gland	?	Cleaning, dissolving, digestion (?)
4. Thorax labial gland	?	Cleaning, dissolving, digestion (?)
5. Postgenal gland	?	?
6. Wax gland	Beeswax	Nest construction
7. Poison gland	Venom	Defense
8. Poison gland reservoir	Venom	Defense
9. Dufour's gland	?	?
10. Koschevnikov's gland	?	In queen, attraction of workers
11. Nasanov's gland	Geraniol; citral, nerolic acid	Assembly, orientation to swarm
12. Sting gland	Isoamyl acetate	Alarm

Fig. 12.6. Diagram of the body of a honeybee, showing the locations of different exocrine glands whose secretions are involved in social organization. The glands and their secretions and functions are listed. (From Wilson, 1975)

gypsy moth are shown in the photograph of Fig. 12.7. The total number of receptors in both antennae ranges from 40,000 to 200,000 in different insects.

Like the insect taste receptors, the olfactory receptor cells are organized within *sensilla,* or hairs (see Fig. 12.7). The basic structure is similar to that of the taste hair. However, the sensory cells within a hair may be one or several, and each cell characteristically has several peripheral dendrites (cilia). Olfactory hairs differ also in their surface pore systems. In some cases, there are many tiny pores (up to 15,000 per hair). Each pore opens inward into an enlargement (called a kettle) from which arise several tubules which communicate with the inner sheath space and receptor cell dendrites (see Fig. 12.7). There is evidence that odorous molecules are first absorbed onto an outer cuticle layer and diffuse through it to the pore, where they diffuse inward through the kettle-tubule system to reach receptor dendrites.

The best-studied of the olfactory stimulating molecules are the sex attractants that female moths emit to attract males. The first one, identified in 1959, was that of the silk moth *Bombyx mori,* and was named *bombykol* (a bit easier to remember than the chemical name, *trans-*10,*cis-*hexadecadien-1-ol!). This is a 16 carbon, double unsaturated alcohol (see Fig. 12.8). A number of sex attractants of other insect species have since been isolated and synthesized, and most of them are of a similar order of complexity.

The sex pheromones are legendary for their extremely high potency. It has been estimated that a single molecule is sufficient to elicit a detectable response in a receptor cell (see below), and 200 molecules, eliciting a discharge of 200 impulses per sec, are sufficient to elicit the behav-

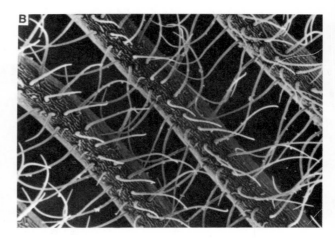

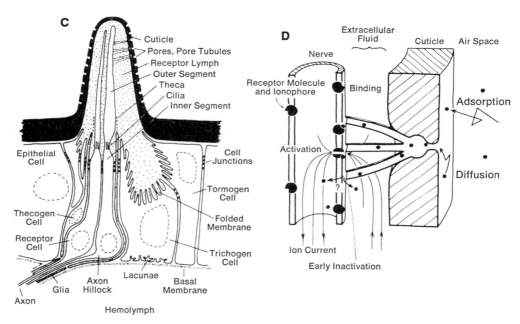

Fig. 12.7. A. Male gypsy moth, showing the two large antennae. The length of the antennae is about 8 mm. **B.** Scanning electron micrograph showing main branches (diameter 50 μm) giving rise to many sensory hairs. Spacing of branches and hairs has been shown to be critical for optimal capture of odorant molecules. (From Schneider et al., 1977) **C.** Schematic diagram of an olfactory sensillum. (From Kaissling and Thorson, 1979) **D.** Schematic representation of transduction processes in a pheromone receptor cell of the silkmoth. (Courtesy of K.-E. Kaissling and J. Boeckh)

ioral response of the male. Thus, olfactory stimulation by pheromones occurs near the theoretical limit of resolution, a situation that we will see also applies to auditory and visual reception; taste stimulation, in contrast, requires much higher stimulus concentrations.

The mechanism of transduction of the molecular stimulus into a receptor response has been studied with high-gain electrophysiological recordings from single olfactory hairs. With very weak stimulation (Fig. 12.8B), small, step-like negative deflections of the baseline can be seen preceding large spike responses. Karl-Ernst Kaissling and John Thorson in Germany have suggested that these deflections are *unitary receptor potentials* that represent the opening of single ion channels. There may be a close analogy with the channel-opening conductance steps at the frog neuromuscular junction, caused by the action of acetylcholine (see Chap. 9). With stronger stimulation (Fig. 12.8C), the unitary potentials of the several cells in the hair summate to give a graded receptor potential, called an *electro-antennogram.* It is presumed that the receptor potentials

Fig. 12.8. Transduction of a pheromone-stimulating molecule. **A.** Molecular structure of bombykol and bombykal. Bombykol elicits fluttering in male moths, which initiates their search for females. Bombykal, acting through different receptors, suppresses fluttering. **B.** Receptor events in a single hair of a male gypsy moth antenna elicited by weak stimulation with bombykol. **C.** Receptor events elicited by strong stimulation with bombykol. (from Kaissling and Thorson, 1979)

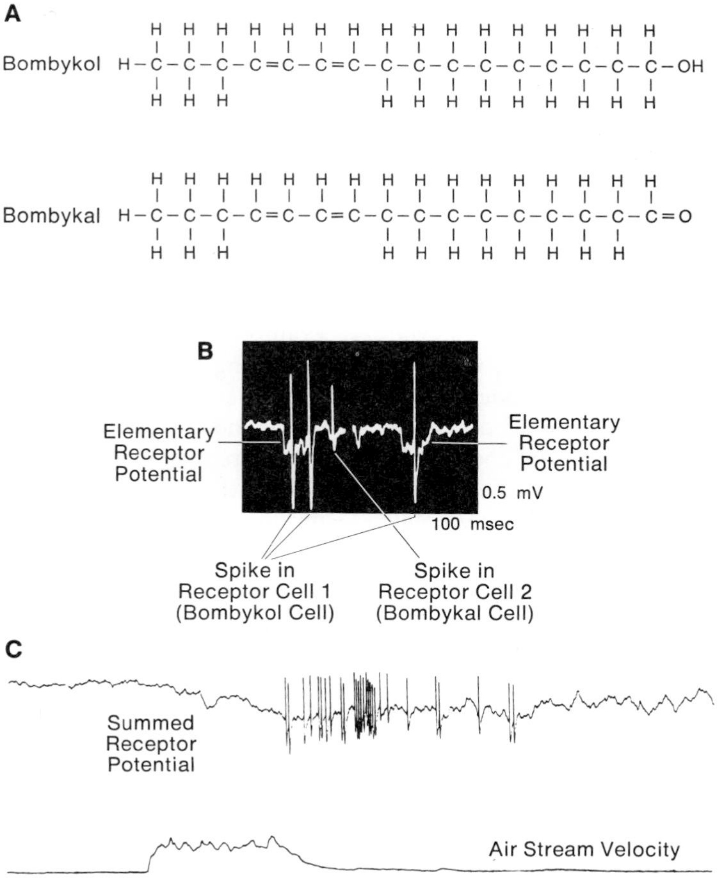

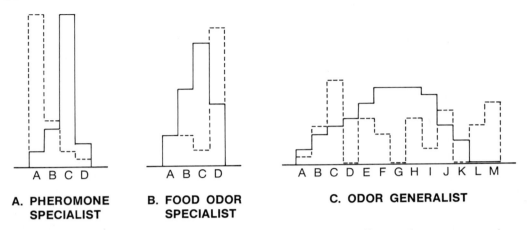

A. PHEROMONE SPECIALIST **B. FOOD ODOR SPECIALIST** **C. ODOR GENERALIST**

Fig. 12.9. Response spectra of different insect olfactory receptors. Different odorous compounds or substances are indicated on the abscissa; intensity of receptor response on ordinate. Two different receptors of same class are indicated by continuous and dotted lines. (After Boeckh, 1980)

are coupled to action potentials by electrotonic spread of current through the dendrites, as we have discussed previously (Chaps. 8 and 11).

When tested with different odors, a given insect olfactory receptor will respond to a certain number, which constitutes its *response spectrum*. When the responses to a wide range of olfactory stimuli are analyzed, it is found that the receptors tend to fall into groups with similar response spectra. According to Jürgen Boeckh of Germany, these may be summarized as follows (see Fig. 12.9). The first cell type is the *pheromone odor specialist*, which is narrowly tuned to a given pheromone molecule. This may be thought of as the receptor end of a "labeled line". Second is a *food odor specialist*. Cells of this type all have similar response spectra for different alcohols, esters, and other compounds that make up the odors of natural foods, such as meats or fruits. It appears that a particular foodstuff is recognized by its stimulation of different receptor types in different combinations. Third is the *odor generalist*. These respond to a wide variety of compounds, and the spectrum of each cell seems to be a unique combination, different from that of other cells. Combinations of these cells may con-

tribute to the ability of an animal to make fine discriminations between different foodstuffs.

The information encoded in the receptor cells is transmitted to the antennal lobe of the deutocerebrum of the insect brain. The interesting finding here is that the receptor axons terminate in small round regions known as *glomeruli* (see Fig. 12.10.). We noted in Chap. 5 the importance of modularization as a basis for the organization of neurons into functional circuits, and the glomerulus is one of the clearest examples of this principle. We are only just beginning to learn about the significance of glomeruli for olfactory processing. One of the most important leads is the finding that there is a distinctive glomerulus, found only in the male, that is involved in transmitting information about the female sex attractant pheromone. We will discuss this further in Chap. 28. Another interesting fact is that olfactory transmission also takes place through glomeruli in the vertebrate olfactory system. Thus, there appears to be something in the nature of encoding information about odor molecules that requires segregating and combining the information in modules. We will return to this question later in the chapter in discussing the vertebrates.

Vertebrates

The Taste System. In lower vertebrates, as in many invertebrates, taste receptors are not always limited to the mouth. For example, in some species of fish that are bottom-dwellers, there are fingerlike projections from the anterior (pectoral) fins that point downward, and carry taste receptors at their tips. This arrangement seems well designed to detect foodstuffs in the muddy bottom where these species live.

In higher vertebrates, taste receptors are characteristically found on the tongue, and to some extent at the back of the mouth and pharynx. At the cellular level, taste receptor cells are grouped together in *taste buds*. Taste buds are found in *papillae,* which are blunt pegs on the surface of the tongue. There are several types of papillae, and these have different distribu-

tions on the tongue surface, as shown in Fig. 12.11A,B.

The cell types within the taste bud are as follows. Types 1 and 2 are believed to be *supporting cells;* they have microvilli at their tips, and appear to secrete substances into the lumen of the taste bud. Type 3 is believed to be the *sensory receptor cell;* it has peglike extensions into the lumen that are probably the sites of sensory transduction. The fourth type of cell is the *basal cell.* Radioactive labeling studies indicate that basal cells arise by inward migration of surrounding epithelial cells. The basal cells, in turn, differentiate into new sensory receptor cells. This process continues throughout adult life, because the receptor cells have lifetimes of only about 10 days. Thus, there is continual turnover of sensory cells in the taste buds. We will see that a similar process occurs

Fig. 12.10. The central olfactory pathway in the insect (cockroach). At the left are indicated the numbers of olfactory and other receptors that project from the antenna to the antennal lobe, where the axons terminate in glomeruli. The numbers of glomeruli, relay and intrinsic neurons, and output axons are indicated in parentheses. The output axons form the central olfactory tract, which projects to the highest centers in the brain, the mushroom bodies and the lateral lobe. This diagram may be compared with the stained section of the insect brain in Fig. 2.7. (From Boeckh et al., 1975)

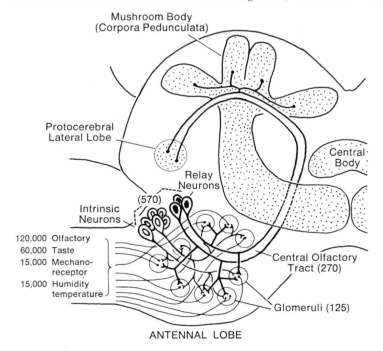

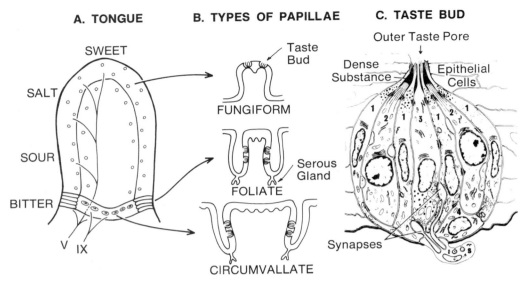

A. TONGUE   **B. TYPES OF PAPILLAE**   **C. TASTE BUD**

Fig. 12.11. **A.** Distribution of taste buds, innervation pattern, and lowest threshold regions for different tastes in the human tongue. **B.** Main types of taste papillae, containing taste buds. **C.** Fine structure of a taste bud. (From Murray, 1973)

in vertebrate olfactory receptors (next section). It is not known how the sensory specificity of a taste bud is maintained in the face of this continual replacement of the sensory elements.

When we eat natural foods, our taste sensations are complicated mixtures of qualities. However, when humans are tested with pure chemical compounds, the taste sensations can all be grouped into four distinct qualities. These are *sweet, salt, sour,* and *bitter*. These qualities were first recognized in a systematic way early in this century, and have dominated thinking about taste mechanisms ever since. When small droplets of different solutions are placed on the tongue, it is found that the taste qualities are preferentially (though not exclusively) elicited from different areas, as indicated in Fig. 12.11.

Many studies have been directed at elucidating the molecular basis of the interaction between the taste molecule and the receptor cell membrane. Most of these studies have been in *psychophysics*. As discussed in the previous chapter, this is

the field in which the quantitative relations between sensory stimuli and sensory perceptions are analyzed, in order to gain insight into the physical nature of the stimulus and the psychological nature of the sensation. These studies may be summarized as follows, in relation to Fig. 12.12C. The *salt* taste is produced in its purest form by NaCl, and also to varying degrees by other inorganic salts and mixtures of various compounds. It has been postulated that the action of the cation (+) on the receptor membranes is excitatory, whereas the anion (−) is inhibitory. The *sour* taste is produced by acids. The sourness may be due to the action of the hydrogen ion in the case of inorganic acids, but it may also depend on the action of the anion of organic acids. The *sweet* taste is believed to depend on the stereochemical configuration of glucose and related organic molecules, and the closeness of their fit to a membrane receptor molecule. The *bitter* taste is characteristically elicited by poisonous or toxic plant substances like quinine. The mechanism of action is unknown; it may occur at the surface membrane, or within the cell (see Fig. 12.12C).

The taste sensory cells have no axons; information is transmitted from them through synapses onto the terminals of sensory fibers within the taste bud (see Fig. 12.11). The fibers arise from ganglion cells of cranial nerves VII (facial nerve) and IX (glosso-pharyngeal nerve) (see Fig. 12.11). Most of the fibers from the anterior part of the tongue run in the chorda tympani, a branch of VII.

The fact that we distinguish four basic tastes and that they can be preferentially elicited from different areas of the tongue,

Fig. 12.12. Intracellular analysis of taste cells, showing recording set-up (**A**) and typical responses (**B**). (From Kimura and Beidler, in Bartoshuk, 1978) **C.** Simplified models of hypothetical transducer mechanisms in the membranes of taste bud cells for reception of the four taste modalities. (Based on Beidler, 1980 and Bartoshuk, 1978)

A. RECORDING SET-UP

B. INTRACELLULAR RESPONSES

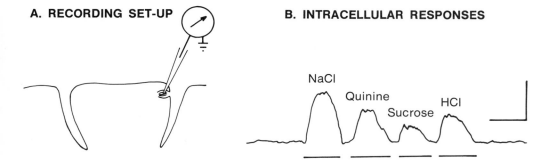

C. HYPOTHETICAL TRANSDUCTION MECHANISMS

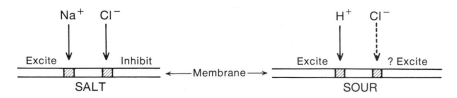

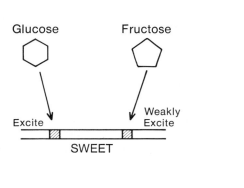

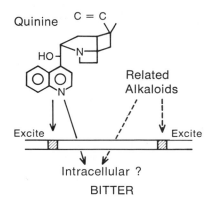

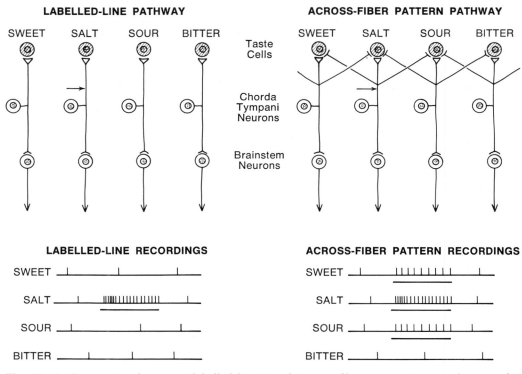

Fig. 12.13. Comparison between "labelled lines" and "across-fiber patterns" as mechanisms for processing information about taste. (Based on Pfaffman et al., 1976)

suggests that each area might be the basis for a *"labeled line"* carrying information about its specific submodality to the brain. This situation is depicted in Fig. 12.13A. However, the first unit recordings from single fibers in the chorda tympani by Carl Pfaffman, then at Brown University, in 1941, showed that this could not be the case. A single fiber might respond best to one stimulation, but it also characteristically showed varying degrees of response to other types of stimuli. This implies that a given fiber receives synapses within the taste bud from several receptor cells with differing response specificities. Pfaffman suggested that "in such a system, sensory quality does not depend simply on . . . activation of some particular fiber group alone, but on the pattern of others active." This became known as the *"across-fiber pattern"* theory of taste quality; it is depicted in Fig. 12.13B.

In recent years there has been much debate among workers in the field of taste as to the relative merits of the labeled line vs. the across-fiber pattern theory. As usual in such cases, there appears, at least to the innocent bystander, elements of the truth in both theories. As Linda Bartoshuk, of the Pierce Foundation, has argued, the four basic tastes still provide the simplest framework for explaining most physiological and psychological results. Within that framework, it is possible to conceive that specific receptor cells, taste buds, and chorda tympani fibers will each have their "best" stimulus, but at each level there may be graded responsiveness to other stimulus types.

The fibers carrying taste information make their synapses centrally in the medulla, in a thin line of cells called the *nucleus of the solitary tract* (see Fig. 12.14). The cells to which they connect give rise to ascending pathways which appear to differ in different species. The best known examples are the rat and the monkey, which are summarized in the diagrams of Fig. 12.14. Note, in the rat, the relay in the pons, the bifurcating connections from there to the basal forebrain and the thalamocortical projections. In contrast, in the monkey, the specific taste pathway connects only to the thalamocortical system. The pathways to somatosensory cortex presumably mediate the conscious perceptions of taste quality, while the pathways to hypothalamus, amygdala and insula are carrying taste information to the limbic system. These pathways may be important for the affective qualities of taste stimulation, and they might also play a role in affective and memory processes that underlie learned taste aversions in feeding behavior, as we will discuss further in Chap 30.

The Olfactory System. Although we think that we smell with our noses, this is a little like saying that we hear with our ear lobes.

In fact, the part of the nose we can see from the outside serves only to take in and channel the air containing odorous molecules; the actual sensing is done by receptors lying deep within the nasal cavity. In a lower vertebrate like a fish or frog, the nasal cavity may be a relatively simple sac, and the stream of water or air passes directly over the receptor sheet (see Fig. 12.15A).

In mammals, the situation is somewhat more complicated. The keenest sniffers, like opossums, rabbits, or dogs, have wondrously complex nasal cavities (Fig. 12.15B). In these species, the inhaled air first passes through a kind of "air conditioner", that consists of many folds of mucus membrane that warm and humidify it. The air then passes into the pharynx, but it also gives rise to eddy currents that circulate through a complex system of turbinates, at the back of the nasal cavity, which are lined with the olfactory receptors. There is as yet no idea of precisely how the air is drawn through these turbinates to reach all the receptors. In the hu-

Fig. 12.14. Taste pathways in the central nervous system of the rat and monkey. VA: visceral afferents; VPM: ventral posterior medial nucleus of the thalamus. (Based on R. Norgren (personal communication) and Norgren, 1978)

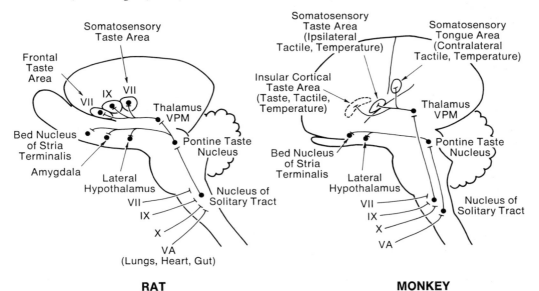

RAT   MONKEY

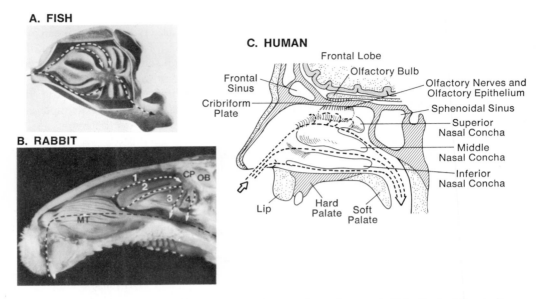

Fig. 12.15. Comparison of the olfactory organs in several vertebrates. **A.** Fish. Dashed line indicates pathway for flow of water over the folds of the receptor sheet. **B.** Rabbit. Dashed lines indicate air flow. MT, maxillary turbinates, where the incoming air is warmed and humidified; (1–4), nasal turbinates, containing the receptor sheet; CP, cribriform plate, the bone through which the olfactory nerves pass; OB, olfactory bulb, where the olfactory axons terminate. (Photograph courtesy of L. B. Haberly) **C.** Human. Dashed lines indicate air flow.

man (C), the turbinates are relatively simple, and the olfactory receptors are confined to a patch of membrane in the most dorsal recess of the nasal cavity.

The olfactory receptor cells lie in a thin sheet. The mature cell has a long thin dendrite that terminates in a small knob at the surface (see Fig. 12.16). This knob gives rise to several cilia, which may be up to 200 μm in length, but are only 0.1–0.2 μm in diameter. The cilia contain microtubules arranged in the 9 pairs + 2 pattern typical of cilia elsewhere in the body. When observed under the microscope at high power, the cilia can be seen to be waving, slowly but asynchronously, in contrast to the coordinated, rapid beating of respiratory cilia. The cilia lie in a thin layer of mucus which is secreted by supporting cells and by Bowman's glands (see diagram, Fig. 12.16).

A fascinating aspect of the olfactory receptor cells is that they are not a static population of neurons. They differentiate during fetal life from precursor basal cells, and this process continues during adult life. As shown in the diagram, the developing cell sends its primitive dendrite toward the surface and its axon deep to join bundles of other axons. After a lifespan of about 60 days, they degenerate and are phagocytized. This turnover of cells resembles that of taste bud cells (see above), but with the difference that the olfactory receptors are true neurons, with an axon. As mentioned in Chap. 10, generation of new neurons is generally thought to cease shortly after birth. The olfactory receptor cell is the only neuron known to undergo continual turnover throughout adult life. Further study is needed to understand the basis of this remarkable property.

Olfactory molecules presumably stimulate the receptors by first being absorbed into the mucus, diffusing to the cilia (and perhaps olfactory knob), and binding to receptor molecules in the membrane. This is believed to open ionic channels, so that electric current flows across the membrane, as was illustrated in Fig. 11.3. This sets up a receptor potential, that spreads from the cilia through the dendrite to the cell body by essentially the same process of electrotonic spread that we discussed in the crustacean stretch receptor cell (Chap. 8). In the cell body the depolarization triggers action potentials, which are conducted in the axon to the first relay station, the olfactory bulb.

Olfactory receptor cells are very small and difficult to penetrate with an intracellular electrode, and the receptor events described above have therefore had to be inferred from extracellular recordings. Such recordings have shown that, in response to stimulation with a battery of odors, a given receptor cell characteristically shows a broad spectrum of sensitivity. As shown in Fig. 12.17, it may respond briskly to odor A, weakly to odor B, and not at all to odor C. A cell may be sensitive in this way to varying degrees to up to 10 or 12 different odors. These responses thus fall into the category of "odor generalist" previously described for insect olfactory receptors.

Several studies have shown that olfactory receptors respond to prolonged or repeated stimulation with a slowly adapting, prolonged discharge of impulses (see Fig. 12.17). This is in contrast of course to our behavioral experience that odor sensations fade rapidly. Thus, when entering a closed, stifled room with an unpleasant odor, we are initially disgusted, but after a minute or two may cease to be aware of the odor unless we inhale more deeply. It appears that this adaptation is not due to fading of the receptor response, but rather is a property of inhibitory interactions in central neural circuits in the olfactory pathway.

In the olfactory bulb, the olfactory axons terminate in rounded regions of neuropil called glomeruli. These are a constant feature of the bulb throughout the vertebrates, and are similar to the glomeruli in the insect olfactory pathway. As

Fig. 12.16. The cellular organization of the vertebrate olfactory epithelium. (From Warwick and Williams, 1973)

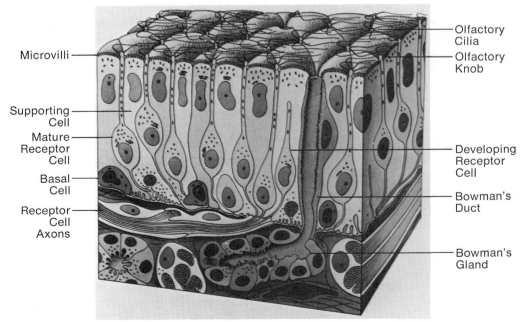

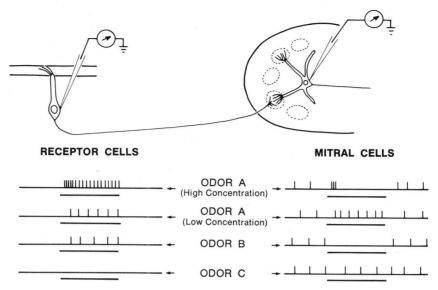

Fig. 12.17. Extracellular single unit recordings of responses to odors of receptor cells (left) and mitral cells (right) in the salamander, showing different types of responses and different temporal patterns of activity. (After Kauer, 1974 and Getchell and Shepherd, 1978)

mentioned previously, this suggests that a recombination and segregation of receptor inputs in glomerular clusters is essential to the neural encoding of odor information.

The synaptic organization of the olfactory bulb has been discussed previously (Chaps. 5, 8, and 11). The olfactory axons make synapses within the glomeruli onto the dendrites of mitral and tufted cells, which are the output neurons of the olfactory bulb. In single-unit recordings, mitral cells show a range of responsiveness to different odors; in some studies it appears that the range is narrower than in the receptors, implying a higher specificity of response. In response to the same battery of odors, the mitral cells have been found to display a greater variety of response patterns. As shown in Fig. 12.17B, a cell may respond with excitation: a slow, prolonged discharge at threshold, changing to a brief burst followed by suppression at higher concentrations. Or a cell may respond with suppression throughout the stimulation period, and at all concentra-

tions. Or a cell may not be affected at all by a given odor. One interpretation has been that the suppression is due to inhibition mediated by the dendrodendritic synapses of granule cells onto mitral cells. These extensive connections in effect lay down a curtain of inhibition throughout the bulb, which the excitatory responses punch through, as it were, carrying specific information about a given odor and its concentration.

In addition to these temporal patterns of activity, odor processing also involves spatial patterns. As already discussed in Chap. 9, the 2-deoxyglucose (2DG) method of Sokoloff has revealed that odor stimulation elicits different degrees of activity in different glomeruli. This is presumably due to different degrees of activity in the receptors converging onto the glomeruli. Stimulation with one odor, such as amyl acetate (which has a fruity smell) activates glomeruli in certain regions of the olfactory bulb of a rat. Stimulation with a different odor, such as camphor, activates glomeruli in regions which overlap those of amyl acetate, but nonetheless have a different distribution. The maps for these two odors are illustrated in Fig. 12.18. These results, together with those from studies using electrophysiological recordings and anatomical tracing, have suggested that the spatial distribution of activity in the olfactory bulb may carry part of the neural code for different odors. Since we do not locate odors in our environment the way we locate visual or tactile stimuli, it appears that space can be used for encoding other aspects of the stimulus, such as the stereochemical configurations of the odor molecules or specific binding properties, in this nonspatial system.

Further studies of the localization of ol-

factory bulb activity, elicited by a pheromone that mediates suckling in infant mammals, will be discussed in relation to feeding mechanisms in Chap. 27.

From the olfactory bulb the mitral and tufted cells send their axons to the olfactory cortex. Although not illustrated, there is a parallel pathway, from the vomeronasal organ to the accessory olfactory bulb, and from there to a specific cortical site in the amygdala. The vomeronasal organ is a narrow tube lined with olfactory receptors, that is well developed in certain reptiles and mammals. It appears that the receptors are tuned to specific kinds of substances in these species. For example, in snakes, scents of prey are detected by

Fig. 12.18. Spatial patterns of activity in the rat olfactory bulb. **A.** Map of the glomerular sheet, showing distribution of 2-deoxyglucose foci in 21 animals exposed to amly acetate odor (open circles) and 6 animals exposed to camphor odor. **B.** In 12 control animals exposed only to pure air, few foci were observed. A.A., amyl acetate; AOB, accessory olfactory bulb; LOT, lateral olfactory tract. **C.** High-resolution study of the cellular uptake of 2DG in the olfactory bulb of the salamander exposed to the odor of amyl acetate. Autoradiograph shows dense concentration of uptake in the olfactory nerve (N) and glomerular (G) layers, and uptake in scattered cells in the external plexiform (E), mitral (M), and granule (GR) layers. The methods included preparation of the tissue by freeze-substitution, 14C-2DG autogradiography, and 2 μm thick sections. Bar is 125 μm. **D.** Higher magnification, showing a labeled mitral cell body. **E.** Same, several labeled granule cell bodies [from the area marked by the asterisk in (C)]. Bar is 25 μm. These results show that it is possible to obtain 2DG labeling of both the projection neurons (mitral cells) and interneurons (granule cells) in a central region of the brain. (A,B from Stewart et al., 1979; C–E from Lancet et al., 1982)

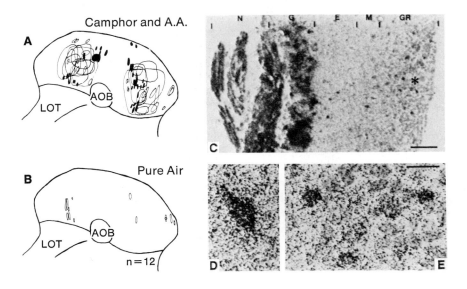

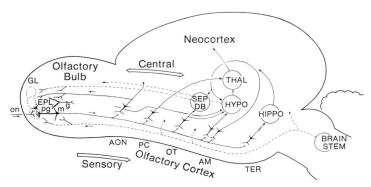

Fig. 12.19. The central olfactory pathway in the rodent, showing connections to central limbic structures. Abbreviations for olfactory bulb: on, olfactory nerves; pg, periglomerular cell; m, mitral cell; g, granule cell; GL, glomerular layer; EPL, external plexiform layer. Abbreviations for olfactory cortical areas: AON, anterior olfactory cortex; PC, pyriform cortex; OT olfactory tubercle; AM, amygdala; TER, transitional entorhinal cortex. Abbreviations for limbic regions: SEP-DB, region of septum and diagonal band; HYPO, hypothalamus; THAL, thalamus; HIPPO, hippocampus. (From Shepherd et al., 1981)

flicking the tongue into the air and drawing it back over the inlet of the organ at the base of the nose. In hamsters, it mediates part of the response of a male to the vaginal odor emanating from a receptive female, and is thus an important link in reproductive behavior (see Chap. 28).

The olfactory cortex is divided into five main areas. Each has distinct connections and different functions, which we will briefly describe. The *anterior olfactory nucleus* is an integrative center connecting the two bulbs through the anterior commissure. The *piriform cortex* is the main area involved in olfactory discrimination. The *olfactory tubercle* is also the recipient of ascending dopaminergic fibers from the midbrain (Chap. 25); it has been implicated in various functions of the limbic system (Chap. 29). It has been hypothesized that malfunction of the olfactory tubercle may contribute to certain kinds of schizophrenia. The *corticomedial* parts of the *amygdala* receive inputs from both the main and accessory olfactory bulbs. Finally, a part of *entorhinal cortex* receives olfactory input, and projects to the hippocampus.

Some of the central projections of the cortical areas are indicated in the diagram. The piriform cortex projects to the mediodorsal thalamus, which in turn projects to the frontal lobe. This presumably is the circuit for conscious olfactory perception and discrimination. The amygdala, in contrast, projects mainly to the hypothalamus. Through these connections the amygdala is more concerned with the emotional and motivational aspects of odor stimuli (see Chap. 29).

It remains to note that the olfactory bulb is the recipient of many centrifugal fibers from the brain. These arise from the olfactory cortical areas, the basal forebrain (horizontal limb of the diagonal band), and the midbrain (locus ceruleus and raphé). Through these fibers the olfactory bulb is modulated by central limbic centers, so that a given odorous substance has a different meaning depending on the behavioral state of the animal. Thus, the aromas of food are perceived quite differently, depending on whether we are hungry or sated. Through these centrifugal connections, the bulbar microcircuits are probably an integral part of central limbic circuits as they mediate nonolfactory functions as well. The olfactory bulb is also a rich repository of neuroactive substances. It has among the highest levels of taurine (an amino acid), carnosine (a dipeptide), thyroid hormone releasing hormone (a tripeptide), and opiate receptors in the entire brain. These multiple controls of olfactory bulb synapses and circuits presumably reflect the sensitiveness of olfactory functions to different developmental and behavioral states, and, in return, the pervasive influence of olfactory inputs on the life of the animal. This appears to be as true for the lives of most vertebrate species as for invertebrates, and we shall see ample evidence of this when we discuss feeding (Chap. 27) and mating (Chap. 28).

REFERENCES

Altner, H., H. Sass, and I. Altner. 1977. Relationship between structure and function of antennal chemo-, hygro-, and thermoreceptive sensilla in *Periplaneta americana*. *Cell Tiss. Res. 176:* 389–405.

Bartoshuk, L. M. 1978. Gustatory system. In *Handbook of Behavioral Neurobiology*. Vol. 1, *Sensory Integration* (ed. by R. B. Masterton). New York: Plenum. pp. 503–567.

Beidler, L. M. 1980. The chemical senses: gustation and olfaction. In *Medical Physiology*, Vol. 1 (ed. by V. B. Mountcastle). St. Louis: C. V. Mosby. pp. 586–602.

Boeckh, J., K.-D. Ernst, H. Sass, and U. Waldow. 1975. Coding of olfactory quality in the insect olfactory pathway. In *Olfaction and Taste V* (ed. by D. Denton). New York: Academic. pp. 239–245.

Boeckh, J. 1980. Ways of nervous coding of chemosensory quality at the input level. In *Olfaction and Taste VII* (ed. by H. van der Starre). London: IRL Press. pp. 113–122.

Dethier, V. G. 1976. [Chap. 10].

Getchell, T. V. and G. M. Shepherd. 1978. Responses of olfactory receptor cells to step pulses of odour at different concentrations in the salamander. *J. Physiol. 282:* 521–540.

Hansen, K. 1978. [Chap. 10].

Kaissling, K. E. 1974. Sensory transduction in insect olfactory receptors. 25. Mosbacher Colloquium Ges. Biol. Chem. (ed. by Jaenicke). pp. 243–273.

Kaissling, E. E. and J. Thorson. 1979. Insect olfactory sensilla: structural, chemical and electrical aspects of the functional organization. In *Receptors for Neurotransmitters, Hormones, and Pheromones in Insects* (ed. by D. B. Satelle, L. M. Hall, and J. G. Hildebrand). Amsterdam: Elsevier. pp. 261–282.

Kauer, J. S. 1974. Response patterns of amphibian olfactory bulb to odour stimulation. *J. Physiol. 243:* 675–715.

Koshland, D. E. Jr. 1980. Bacterial chemotaxis in relation to neurobiology. *Ann. Rev. Neurosci. 3:* 43–76.

Lancet, D., C. A. Greer, J. S. Kauer, and G. M. Shepherd. 1982. Mapping of odor-related activity in the olfactory bulb by high resolution 2-deoxyglucose autoradiography. *Proc. Natl. Acad. Sci. 79:* 670–674.

McDonald, D. M. and R. A. Mitchell. 1975. The innervation of glomus cells, ganglion cells and blood vessels in the rat carotid body: a quantitative ultrastructural analysis. *J. Neuroctyol. 4:* 1770–220.

Murray, R. G. 1973. The ultrastructure of taste buds. In *The Ultrastructure of Sensory Organs* (ed. by I. Friedmann). New York: Elsevier. pp. 1–81.

Norgren, R. 1980. Neuroanatomy of gustatory and visceral afferents systems in rat and monkey. In *Olfaction and Taste VII* (ed. by H. van der Starre). London: IRL Press. p. 288.

Pfaffman, C., M. Frank, L. M. Bartoshuk, and T. C. Snell. 1976. Coding gustatory information in the squirrel monkey chorda typmani. In *Progress in Psychobiology and Physiological Psychology* (ed. by J. M. Sprague and A. N. Epstein). New York: Academic. pp. 1–27.

Schneider, D. W. A. Kafka, M. Beroza, and B. A. Bierl. 1977. Odor receptor responses of male gypsy and nun moths (Lepidoptera, Lymantriidae) to disparlure and its analogues. *J. Comp. Physiol. 113:* 1–15.

Shepherd, G. M. 1979. [Chap. 4].

Shepherd, G. M., M. C. Nowycky, C. A. Greer, and K. Mori. 1981. Multiple overlapping circuits within olfactory and basal forebrain systems. In *Adv. Physiol. Sci., Vol. 30. Neural Communication and Control* (ed. by G. Szekely, F. Labos, and S. Damjanovich). Budapest: Pergamon. pp. 263–278.

Stewart, W. B., J. S. Kauer, and G. M. Shepherd. 1979. Functional organization of rat olfactory bulb analysed by the 2-deoxyglucose method. *J. Comp. Neurol. 185:* 715–734.

Ward, S. 1977. Use of nematode behavioral mutants for analysis of neural function and development. In *Society for Neuroscience Symposia.* Vol. II, Approaches to the Cell Biology of Neurons* (ed. by W. M. Cowan and J. A. Ferrendelli). Bethesda, Md.: Society for Neuroscience. pp. 1–26.

Warwick, R. and P. L. Williams. 1973. *Gray's Anatomy.* Philadelphia: Saunders.

Wilson, E. O. 1975. *Sociobiology.* Cambridge, Mass: Harvard.

Additional Reading

Graziadei, P. P. C. and G. A. Monti-Graziadei. 1978. Continuous nerve cell renewal in the olfactory system. In *Handbook of Sensory Physiology,* Vol. 9 (ed. by M. Jacobson). New York: Springer. pp. 55–83.

13

The Somatic Senses

Every organism has an external skin or other covering that encloses its body and separates it from the environment. Through this covering, the animal receives information about the presence of objects, other organisms, or physical changes in its environment. The Greek word for body is *soma*, and the sensory modalities that are signaled by receptors in and near the body surface are referred to collectively as the *somatic senses*.

Before identifying the different components of the somatic senses, it is well to be reminded that the body covering in which receptors are embedded is not a simple structure. Table 13.1 lists some of the functions of the covering (integument) in different animals. It can be seen that the integument has a complex structure which provides for multiple functions. Sensory reception is only one among many special functions. Thus, the sensory receptors in any given animal have structures which reflect the particular functional adaptations of the integument in that species.

Because of the enormous variations in the structure and function of the integument in different species, it is not always easy to assign particular receptor cells to distinct categories. By the same token, it

Table 13.1 Functions of the integument

Protection against:
  physical harm
  chemical damage
  infection
  water gain or loss
  excessive sunlight
  heat gain or loss
Camouflage (pigmentation)
Structures for:
  locomotion (cilia, feathers)
  aggression and defense (claws, horns, antlers)
  social displays
Exchange of substances:
  respiration of O_2 and CO_2
  excretion of metabolites
Glandular excretions
Special sensory structures

Table 13.2 The somatic senses

Noxious (pain)
Temperature
Diffuse touch (light touch, pressure)
Tactile (spatial discrimination, vibration)

is hazardous to assume too readily that a particular sensory modality is exactly equivalent in widely separated species. Despite such misgivings, however, it is common to consider that the somatic senses are comprised of four main modalities. These are summarized in Table 13.2. Perhaps the most basic and primitive is the noxious sense, the reception of stimuli that are harmful or signal potential harm to the organism. A second modality is the ability to sense the ambient *temperature.* A third category may be referred to as *crude touch;* this includes *light touch* and *pressure,* which are distinct in some organisms and mixed in others. Finally, there is the fine *tactile* sense, the ability to make precise discriminations in space and time.

It will be realized that these sensory modalities can also be grouped according to the nature of the stimulus energy. Thus, stimuli that affect the body may be classed as chemical (some kinds of noxious stimuli), radiant (temperature, sometimes noxious), and mechanical (some noxious stimuli, crude touch, and tactile). Chemical stimuli require chemical transduction by *chemoreceptor* mechanisms in the sensory membrane; temperature is transduced by *temperature receptors;* and the various kinds of mechanical stimuli are transduced by *mechanoreceptors.* The molecular bases of the transduction mechanisms have already been discussed in Chap. 11.

It doesn't matter too much which method we use to classify the sensory modalities; in any case the receptors share some basic properties, even across different phyla. We will consider examples of each type among the invertebrates and vertebrates. Our focus will be on the properties of the receptor cells, and the main outlines of the organization of the sensory pathways.

INVERTEBRATES

Our remarks about the complexity of the integument apply with special force to the invertebrates. Because of the small size of many invertebrate species, respiratory and excretory functions can take place through the integument, rather than requiring special internal organ systems. Also, because of their small size, the ratio of external surface area to internal volume is relatively high. While this helps in the exchange of substances, it also magnifies other problems, such as maintaining constant water balance in a changing environment. Small terrestrial organisms, for example, are at great risk of desiccation during periods of hot weather and drought. Special properties of the integument are therefore crucial for the survival of many organisms.

These considerations help us to understand the nature of the integument in which we find the sensory receptors. For the reasons mentioned above, invertebrates (above the sponges) characteristically have a tough outer covering, called a *cuticle.* In worms and molluscs, the cuticle is soft; in arthropods it forms a hard exoskeleton. We will consider briefly some receptors found within these two types of cuticle.

Leech Sensory Neurons

A very useful preparation for studying the physiology of sensory neurons is the medicinal leech, *Hirudo medicinalis.* This was the organism used by medieval doctors for bloodletting, to rid the body of excess or unhealthy blood, a practice which continued through the eighteenth century, much to the detriment of George Washington and many others. (This is also the little creature that caused Humphrey Bogart and Katharine Hepburn such distress in the film *The African Queen!*)

The central nervous system of the leech consists of a central chain of 21 segmental ganglia, plus a head "brain" and a smaller tail ganglion. The nerve fibers that join the ganglia to each other form *connectives,* and those that run between the ganglia and the periphery form *roots.* The connectives are analogous to the spinal tracts of the vertebrate spinal cord, and the roots are analogous to the dorsal and ventral roots, though not separated into sensory and motor divisions, as in the vertebrate.

The leech exhibits most of the characteristics that make invertebrate nervous

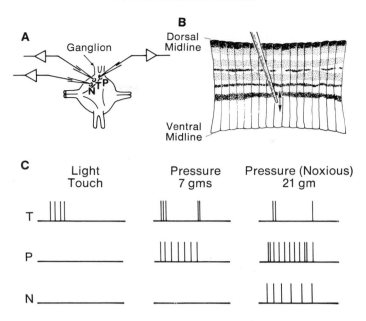

Fig. 13.1. Somatosensory neurons of the leech. **A.** A single segmental ganglion, showing location of noxious (N), touch (T), and pressure (P) neuron cell bodies. **B.** Piece of skin with nerves attached to the ganglion. The probe was used to stimulate the sensory endings by touch or pressure. **C.** Characteristic responses of T,P, and N cells to different types and intensities of stimuli applied to the skin. (Modified from Kuffler and Nicholls, 1976)

systems so attractive for neurobiological research. The ganglion is less than 1 mm thick, and is transparent, so that its cells can be observed under the microscope during an experiment. One can carry out intracellular recording and stimulating experiments in the intact animal, or in the isolated ganglion. Each ganglion contains about 350 cells. Under the microscope, individual cell bodies can be observed, and many of the larger ones can be identified by their distinctive size, shape, and position in the ganglion (see Fig. 13.1A). Using this preparation, John Nicholls and his collaborators at Harvard and Stanford have been able to investigate many basic properties involved in nervous signaling, such as the correlation of neuronal branching patterns with synaptic properties, the effects of prolonged activity on ionic conductances and electrogenic membrane pumps, and the roles of neuroglial cells during nervous activity. These results have contributed, together with those ob-

tained in other invertebrate species, to the growing synthesis of concepts about the cell biology of the neuron, as discussed in Section II. Here, we wish to concentrate on the studies of properties of sensory neurons.

In contrast to the situation in the vertebrate, in which the primary sensory cell bodies are located in peripheral ganglia (the dorsal root ganglia), the sensory cell bodies in most invertebrates (including the leech) are found within the main segmental ganglia (the equivalent of the vertebrate spinal cord). By probing the skin with different types of natural stimuli while recording from cells in the ganglia it has been possible to identify specific cells for three cutaneous sensory modalities: touch, pressure, and noxious. The results of these experiments are summarized in Fig. 13.1C. The *touch* (T) cells are extremely sensitive (have a *low threshold*) to light touch, whether by a small probe, such as a whisker, or eddy currents in the bathing medium. The response to a simple maintained stimulus is a brief burst of impulses; this is, in other words, a *rapidly adapting* response. A prolonged discharge can be sustained by a stimulus continually *moving* within the receptive field.

With a stronger maintained stimulus such as a pressure indentation of the skin (Pressure 7 g in Fig. 13.1C) the T cell fires faster, and there may be an off discharge as well. In addition, the *pressure* (P) cell begins to respond; we say, therefore, that it has a *higher threshold* of stimulation than the T cell. The P cell in the leech gives a maintained, slowly adapting discharge, that is *graded* in *frequency* with the strength of stimulation (see Pressure 21 g). At the highest stimulation intensities, a third type of cell begins to respond. This cell responds best to noxious stimuli, like crushing or stabbing, that cause tissue damage, and is therefore termed a *nociceptor* (N) cell.

It can be seen that these responses display many of the basic properties of sensory receptors we discussed in Chap. 11. It is particularly interesting that the three modalities of touch, pressure, and nociception are closely comparable to the somatosensory modalities in the vertebrate. Each type of sensory cell makes specific connections onto motoneurons, to establish pathways for reflex responses, as we will discuss in Chap. 20.

Arthropod Sensory Receptors

The importance of the body covering is beautifully exemplified by the insects, as attested to in the following quotation from David Smith:

> The development of a cuticle resisting desiccation and the acquisition of a tracheal system for respiration of atmospheric oxygen opened up the terrestrial environment to the insects, an evolutionary opportunity that they exploited to the full.

Biochemically, the key constituent of the cuticle of the insect (and other arthropods) is *chitin*. This is a polysaccharide containing acetyl-glucosamine residues bonded together to form long, unbranched molecules of high molecular weight. It shares some structural properties with cellulose. Although found in the integuments of many species, it is absent from the cuticle of annelids; apparently, this represented a significant step in the evolution of the annelid–arthropod line. It is also absent from the deuterostome line, leading from echinoderms to chordates. Chitin is thus an important biochemical marker in the study of evolution.

Chitin is bound together with protein and lipids to form the *endocuticle*, as shown in Fig. 13.2. In most insects the protein component is sclerotinized to impart the rigidity necessary for the exoskeleton. As we discussed earlier, this requires suitable adaptations of sensory receptors, so that they can detect mechanical and other forms of stimuli through the hard outer coating. The simplest and most common type of structure for achieving this is the sensillum trichodeum, or *sensory hair*. We have traced the development of the sensory hair in Chap. 11. The tactile hair is a simplified version of the sensory hairs that we studied in the insect taste and olfactory systems (Chap. 12). As shown in Fig. 13.2, each mechanoreceptive sensillum consists of a hair (seta) set in a flexible socket. The whole sensillum comprises four cells. The trichogen cell secretes the material for forming the hair during development. The tormogen cell forms the socket. A single sensory cell innervates the sensillum; its distal terminals contact the junction of the base of the hair and the socket. A fourth cell encloses the other three.

Sensory hairs are scattered widely over the body surface. Any force that displaces the hair, such as *touch, air movement,* or *changes in pressure,* causes stimulation of the sensory cell. The sensory cells in the cuticle of the body surface send their fibers to their corresponding segmental ganglion in the nerve cord. The further

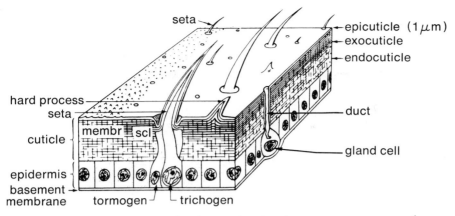

Fig. 13.2. Diagram of the integument of an insect, showing the most common type of sensory hair (seta). (From Richards, in Barrington, 1979)

sensory connections have not yet been worked out.

It will be recalled that each sensory hair in the taste sensilla of the insect has a mechanoreceptor as one of its five sensory cells. There are also mechanoreceptor cells and hairs among the olfactory hairs on the insect antennae. These cells send their axons to the glomeruli of the antennal lobe, along with the other sensory axons. Thus, the glomeruli may function as relay stations for more than one kind of sensory modality (see Fig. 12.10). From the antennal lobe, the mechanoreceptor inputs make connections with motor centers, for mediating immediate motor reflexes, or with higher integrative centers, such as the mushroom bodies (see Chaps. 12 and 25). Unfortunately, little is known as yet about these central circuits of the insect somatosensory system.

VERTEBRATES

Vertebrates differ from invertebrates in that they do not have cuticles and most do not molt, but in other respects their integument is similar in that it can take on a variety of structures and perform many different functions. The adaptations of structure include a toughening of the surface to form scales, as in fish, or plates, as in turtles. The integument also may give rise to auxilliary structures such as feathers, as in birds, and hair, as in mammals—structures that are crucial for the motor abilities of a species, or its ability to withstand extremes of climate and temperature. There are also special adaptations, such as hoofs and claws, for particular kinds of locomotion or manipulation.

There are many fascinating adaptations of the skin senses to these specialized integumentary organs. However, our concern here will be with the reception of stimuli over the whole body surface. By far the greatest amount of information about the general somatosensory system in vertebrates has been obtained in the mammal, much of it in primates and humans. This is partly because the mammalian skin is a relatively general, unspecialized covering. Being soft, it is easy to dissect and experiment upon. An important advantage is that in humans one can stimulate different receptors selectively and test the sensory perception that is aroused. Let us therefore focus our attention on the mammalian skin in general, and the special properties of the human skin where information is available.

Even when we disregard its special structures, the human skin is a complex and fascinating structure. As we all recognize, there are two main types of skin. One type, found on our palms and finger-

GLABROUS (HAIRLESS) SKIN

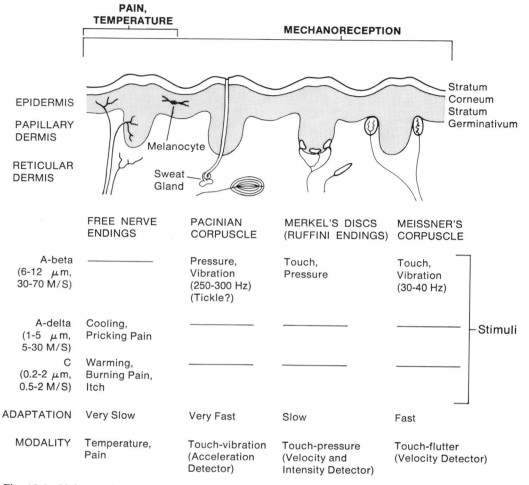

Fig. 13.3. Glabrous (hairless) skin of the human.

tips, is called *glabrous*, or hairless, skin. The other type, found over most of the rest of our body, is called *hairy* skin. Of course, hair on humans varies widely in amount, from a little to a lot, and in the kind of hair, from peach fuzz to coarse. These variations do not affect the division of skin into these two general classes.

The structures of glabrous and hairy skin are shown in the diagrams of Figs. 13.3 and 13.4. First, we see that both types of skin are divided into two main layers, the epidermis and the dermis. The *epider-*

mis is the true outer skin, being derived from the ectodermal germ layer of the embryo. It also gives rise to the various specialized structures (hair, feathers, claws, and glands) that become especially prominent in higher vertebrates. The epidermis is composed of a *stratum germinativum*, where cells undergo continual mitosis and migrate toward the surface. As they reach the surface, they undergo degenerative changes, so that at the surface they form a layer of dead, flattened cells, the *stratum corneum*. This is rich in *keratin*, a very

HAIRY SKIN

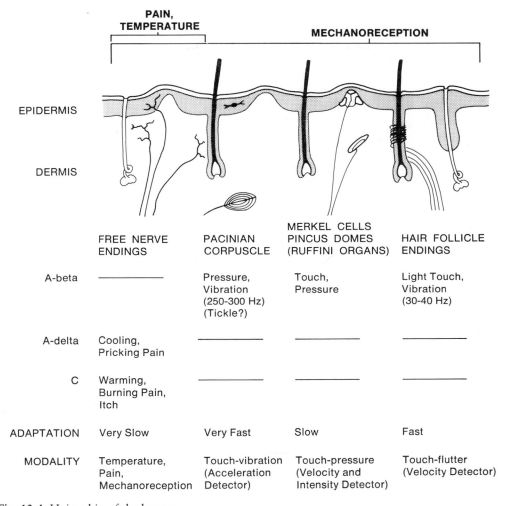

Fig. 13.4. Hairy skin of the human.

stable fibrous protein, resistant to water, most chemicals, and enzymatic digestion. Keratin is to the vertebrates what chitin is to the invertebrates. Also present in the epidermis are *melanocytes,* which contain melanin, derived metabolically from tyrosine. Melanin is responsible for the pigmentation of the skin, and protects the skin and deeper layers from ultraviolet light.

Beneath the epidermis is the *dermis.* This is actually derived from the mesoderm, and becomes connected to the epidermis dur-

ing embryonic development. The dermis is the layer that provides for the thick, bony scales that are so characteristic of lower vertebrates like fish. It is only in higher vertebrates that the dermis has evolved a soft, flexible structure, due to a thick, tightly interwoven layer of *connective tissue.* The layer is rich in collagen fibers, and also contains elastic fibers and, in deeper parts, fat cells. These components not only permit the freedom of movement so characteristic of mammals, but are also important for other functions such as protection, insulation, and temperature regulation.

Sensory Receptors

We are now in a position to identify the sensory elements within the skin. By way of brief history, this work began with the earliest microscopic studies of the skin in the middle of the nineteenth century. By around 1900 a number of specific, small end organs, each attached to a sensory nerve fiber, had been identified. The main interest of the physiologists of the time was in correlating each end organ with a specific sensation. To do this, the skin was stimulated with very small probes: a fine hair or bristle; a pin; a thin wire, heated or cooled. The results seemed to show that sensitivity is not uniform over the skin surface; instead, there appeared to be a mosaic of sensitive "spots". There were "touch spots", "warm spots", "pain spots", and so forth. Furthermore, a given spot seemed to be sensitive to only one modality. These results implied that a sensitive spot is the site of a specific sensory end organ for that modality. A number of correlations between sensory modality and sensory end organ were suggested; thus, free nerve endings for pain, Ruffini organs for warmth, Krause's end bulbs for cold, Pacinian corpuscles for pressure, Meissner's corpuscles and hair follicle endings for touch. These correlations seemed to be a logical realization of the doctrine of specific nerve energies set forth by Muller in the 1830's, as we discussed in Chap. 11.

Our modern correlations differ in certain details, and are not as strict as originally envisioned. Nonetheless, the idea that nerve endings, especially the specialized end organs, have a *preferential* sensitivity for certain types of stimuli, is widely accepted, and is a useful framework for our beginning study. Let us therefore consider each of the main types of sensory ending. We will start with free nerve endings, and move toward the more differentiated or-

gans. Although this reverses the sequence in which they are usually described, it is more in line with the evolutionary development from simple to complex, and leads naturally to the description of central pathways later in the chapter.

Free Nerve Endings. The simplest type of sensory receptor in the skin is the free nerve ending. This is just what its name implies; a nerve fiber divides into branches and terminates in naked, unmyelinated endings in the dermis and deeper layers of the epidermis. The modes of termination are similar in glabrous and hairy skin, as indicated in Figs. 13.3 and 13.4.

Free nerve endings respond to mechanical stimuli, heating, cooling, or noxious stimuli. Some endings respond to only one modality; others respond to two or three modalities—these are called *polymodal* receptors. The endings arise from thin fibers, either thinly myelinated axons (*A-delta fibers*) or unmyelinated axons (*C fibers*). The sensations evoked in these two types of fiber are distinctive. When we touch a hot stove, the immediate sharp pain (*sticking pain*) is mediated by the A-delta fibers; the subsequent constant aching (*burning pain*) is mediated by the C fibers. A correlation of pain fiber discharges with pain perception is shown in Fig. 13.5.

Temperature reception is also apportioned to different fibers in primates, cooling being sensed mainly by the A-delta fibers and warming being sensed by the C fibers. Cooling and warming receptors are actually defined by the fact that they have peak sensitivities that are cooler and warmer, respectively, than the body temperature. As shown in Fig. 13.6, each may fire faster or slower with increases or decreases in temperature, depending on where in the whole temperature range the change is taking place. Presumably, the overlapping ranges of warming and cooling receptors are part of the mechanism for enhancing the ability to discriminate small changes in temperature near body

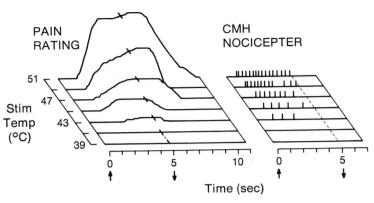

Fig. 13.5. Magnitude ratings of pain by a human subject (left) and evoked activity in a nociceptor fiber in the monkey (right) during heat stimulation of the skin. *Left,* Intensity of pain as judged by a subject during the heat stimulations of 39 to 51°C delivered in steps of 2°C to the volar forearm. Each horizontal line represents the passage of time during one trial. The base temperature was 38°C. Stimulus on and off are indicated by arrows. The vertical axis represents the magnitude of pain as rated continuously throughout testing. Pain threshold, in this case, was 43°C, the minimal stimulus temperature that elicited a rating of pain. *Right,* Responses of a C-fiber mechanoheat nociceptor to the same heat stimuli delivered to the hairy skin of an anesthetized monkey. Each vertical mark represents a single nerve impulse. Response threshold, in this case, was 43°C, the minimal stimulus temperature that evoked a response. (From LaMotte et al., 1982)

temperature; in this range, an increased response in one type is accompanied by a decreased response in the other.

At very high temperatures many thermoreceptors also signal sticking pain. Some C fibers respond to release of substances, such as bradykinin, from the capillary circulation, and mediate the sensation of *itching*. This may be regarded as part of the common chemical sense. Some

Fig. 13.6. Graphs of impulse firing frequencies in relation to applied temperature for "cold" and "warm" receptors. (Modified from Kenshalo, 1976, in Schmidt et al., 1978)

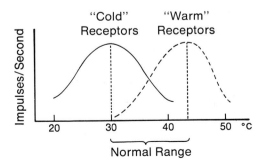

fibers are responsive to various kinds of mechanical stimulation; among these, some A-delta fibers mediate tickling sensations. The free nerve endings thus provide for a rich variety of polymodal sensory reception. All of these fibers are slowly adapting; they continue to discharge impulses as long as the stimulus is present. This seems a necessary property for signaling the relatively slow changes that take place in the modalities of pain and temperature, and for signaling the organism to remove the noxious stimulus or adjust itself to the ambient temperature.

Pacinian Corpuscle. All of the other sensory receptors in the skin are associated with special end organs, and all are endings of medium-sized myelinated fibers, the A-beta type (6–12 μm in diameter). It doesn't matter too much in what sequence we study them. For convenience we start with the Pacinian corpuscle, one of the largest of the end organs, situated deepest in the dermis. In fact, the Pacinian corpuscle has a widespread distribution, in the

connective tissue of muscles, the periosteum of bones, and the mesentery of the
abdomen. It is relatively easy to isolate
single corpuscles from the mesentery, and
much of our information about Pacinian
corpuscles, and indeed about many basic
properties of sensory receptors in general,
has come from these studies.

The Pacinian corpuscle is composed, like
an onion, of concentric layers of cellular
membranes alternating with fluid-filled
spaces. The picture that has emerged from
electron microscopic studies is shown in
Fig. 13.7. In the central core is the naked
ending of the nerve fiber, with a number
of short processes like filopodia emerging
from its bulbous terminal. Surrounding
this is an inner core of incomplete shells
of cell processes and collagen fibers. Making up the bulk of the corpuscle are the
outer complete lamellae.

The Pacinian corpuscle is studied physiologically by pressing on it with a carefully controlled probe while recording the
response from the nerve where it exits from

the corpuscle. If impulse activity is blocked
selectively with such agents as local anesthetics or tetrodotoxin, we can record the
receptor potential as it spreads into the
nerve fiber. As shown in Fig. 13.8A, the
receptor response takes the form of a very
brief potential wave at the onset of the
pressure pulse, and a similar brief wave at
the termination. There is no response during the stationary plateau of the applied
stimulus. This is therefore an extremely
rapidly adapting receptor response. Each
wave gives rise to a single impulse in the
nerve fiber.

How does this type of response arise?
In the isolated Pacinian corpuscle preparation, it was possible for Werner Loewenstein and his colleagues, then at Columbia University, to dissect away very
carefully the onion-skin lamellae, so that
the stimulus could be applied directly to
the naked nerve ending. When this was
done, the receptor potential produced by
a step pulse was a slowly adapting response (see Fig. 13.8B). This showed that

Fig. 13.7. Diagram of a Pacinian corpuscle. (From Spencer and Schaumberg, in Dykes, 1977)

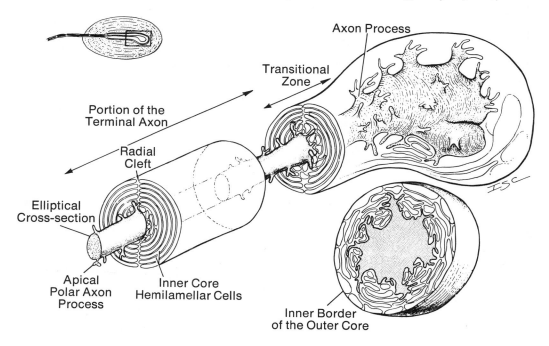

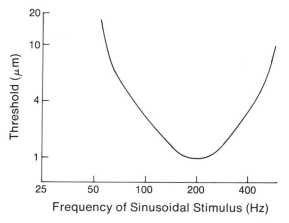

A. NORMAL CORPUSCLE

B. DESHEATHED CORPUSCLE

Recordings:

a   Receptor Potential

a′

b   Impulse Response

b′

c   Stimulus Monitor

c′

C. THRESHOLDS FOR VIBRATORY STIMULUS

Threshold (μm)

20
10
4
1

25   50   100   200   400

Frequency of Sinusoidal Stimulus (Hz)

Fig. 13.8. Experimental analysis of transduction in the Pacinian corpuscle. **A.** Diagram showing probe for stimulating the intact corpuscle, and recording from the nerve. Below, recordings of the receptor potential and impulse discharge. **B.** Repeat of experiment after removal of lamellae. **C.** Sensitivity of Pacinian corpuscle to vibratory stimulation at different frequencies. (A,B based on Loewenstein, 1971; C modified from Schmidt, 1978)

the lamellae act as a filter, to absorb slow changes impressed upon them, while still passing on rapid changes to the nerve endings. Interestingly, the nerve fiber, at the first node of Ranvier, still responds with a single impulse despite the maintained receptor potential, a very nice matching of receptor and nerve properties.

The Pacinian corpuscle is thus constructed to signal rapid changes in *touch-pressure;* this is presumably why our sensation of a steady pressure applied to the skin soon fades away. This organ is well suited for signaling rapid vibratory stimuli; as indicated in Fig. 13.8C, the maximum sensitivity is in the range of 200–300 Hz. This form of stimulation may be important in our tactile perception of objects and textures. Note the extremely high sensitivity of the corpuscle; less than 1 μm displacement at its surface is sufficient to give a threshold response. We have previously discussed the molecular nature of the transduction mechanism in the membrane in Chap. 11.

Superficial End Organs. Most of the other end organs are located superficially in the skin, near the junction between the dermis and epidermis. These are specialized to be sensitive to different aspects of tactile stimuli. One type may be classified as *slowly adapting.* In glabrous skin, these are *Merkel's discs,* located in the deep margins of the dermal papillae. It is believed that these receptors signal the static intensity of touch-pressure stimuli. In hairy skin, there are similar structures, called *Merckel's cells,* grouped within raised sites in the skin called *Pinkus domes.* Within the dermis are *Ruffini organs.* The precise functions of these receptors are not yet known.

The other main type of superficial end organ may be classified as *moderately rapidly adapting.* In glabrous skin, these are represented by *Meissner's corpuscles.* As shown in Fig. 13.3, these are tucked into the base of the dermal papillae. They are sensitive to light touch, and to vibra-

tion in the range of 30–40 Hz. In hairy skin, the *hair shafts* and *follicles* are enclosed by the endings of five to ten sensory nerve fibers. Electron microscopy shows that the nerve fibers lose their Schwann cell coverings near their endings, which are inserted into the basal lamina of the hair shaft. The terminals respond to minute displacements of the hair. These responses also have their lowest thresholds to vibratory movements in the range of 30–40 Hz.

All of the superficial sensory end organs are innervated by medium-to-large myelinated fibers of the A-beta group (5–12 μm diameter). In the next chapter (Chap. 14) we will compare these and other somatosensory afferents (A-delta and C) with the other types of sensory fibers from the muscles.

This group of receptors provides the skin with its ability to mediate two general tactile modalities, *light touch* and *tactile discrimination.* Light touch is what its name implies, as in the light brushing of the skin surface or its hairs. Tactile discrimination may be characterized as either spatial or temporal. *Spatial tactile discrimination* is usually measured by the ability to make *two-point discriminations.* As indicated in the diagram of Fig. 13.9A, the minimum distance that can be perceived between two points varies widely, from about 2 mm on the fingertips, to 30 mm on the arm, to 70 mm on the back. This is correlated with the sizes of receptive fields for single afferent fibers supplying these regions (see Fig. 13.10). It is also correlated with the size of representation of these regions in the cerebral cortex (see below). Two-point discrimination is a standard method used by neurologists to test for the effects of strokes or other cerebral injuries on cortical function.

Temporal tactile discrimination is the ability to perceive vibratory stimuli. A vibrating probe is a very effective stimulus for the Meissner's corpuscles, at 30–50 Hz, as illustrated in Fib. 13.9B. In life, this kind of receptor is probably most often activated by our fingers moving over rough or

A. SPATIAL DISCRIMINATION   **B. TEMPORAL DISCRIMINATION**

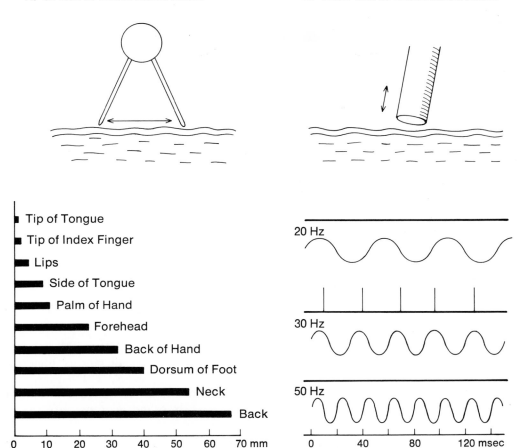

Fig. 13.9. Tactile discrimination in the human. **A.** Spatial (two-point) discrimination: variations in the ability to discriminate the minimum distance between two points placed in different parts of the body. (After Schmidt, 1978) **B.** Temporal discrimination: responses of nerve fiber from a Meissner's corpuscle to vibration at different frequencies. Note driving at about 30 Hz.

irregular objects. If two points on an object are 2 mm apart, and our finger moves past them at a rate of 80 mm per sec, the second point will excite a given site on the finger at a frequency of 40 per sec—just right for a Meissner's corpuscle. Although as physiologists and neurologists we tend to apply a given stimulus at a single site to study receptor responses or sensations, in natural behavior the fingers and hand take an active part by moving over and exploring surfaces in order to give rise to our sensory perceptions. This is called *active touch*. The tactile sense in the distal ex-

tremities thus illustrates vividly the close interrelationship that exists between sensory and motor systems.

Spinal Cord Circuits

The information transduced by the sensory receptors is transmitted in impulse codes in the sensory nerves to the spinal cord. Within the spinal cord the information has two destinations. First, it is involved in local reflexes at the *spinal cord* level. Especially important in this regard are the circuits for withdrawing a limb

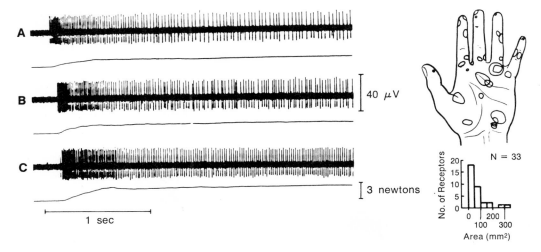

Fig. 13.10. Sensory responses in the ulnar nerve of a human elicited by tactile stimulation of the hand. *Left,* impulse discharges recorded by a microelectrode from a single sensory fiber in an awake subject. **A–C.** increasing intensity stimulation. *Right,* receptive fields of single fibers innervating the hand. (From Knibestol and Vallbo, 1970, in Mountcastle, 1980)

from a painful stimulus, the so-called *flexor reflex.* We will study these circuits in Chap. 20. For its second destination, the information is passed on to *ascending pathways* that relay it to higher brain centers.

The circuits within a segment of the spinal cord are actually very complicated and we are only beginning to understand the principles of organization, thanks to recent studies of fine structure, neurochemistry, and intracellular staining and recording. Some of the basic aspects of organization are summarized in Fig. 13.11. The sensory fibers terminate within the dorsal horn, which is the sensory region of the spinal cord (recall Chap. 3). The dorsal horn is arranged in layers (I–V), as indicated in the figure. The fine, unmyelinated fibers (C fibers) terminate mostly in the superficial layers (substantia gelatinosa) of the dorsal horn. The A-delta fibers terminate in the most superficial layer, called the *marginal zone.* The large myelinated fibers (A-beta) sweep around the dorsal horn, giving off collaterals which ascend in the posterior columns, and then

terminate as climbing fibers on the dendrites of cells in *layers III and IV.*

Each of the types of sensory fiber appears to have specific types of neurons with which it makes connection, as indicated in Fig. 13.11B. Some neurons also receive converging inputs from several types of fibers. This convergence is believed to underlie the interactions between different modalities that can take place at the spinal level.

The most interesting of these interactions, and the one with very important applications to humans, is that between tactile sensations and pain. It is a common observation that pain often can be relieved by gently stimulating around the hurt area, such as light brushing, massage, or tickling. It seems therefore as if the tactile pathway can have an inhibitory action on the pain pathway.

In a celebrated theory published in 1965, Melzack and Patrick Wall, of M.I.T., suggested a specific circuit within the dorsal horn that could account for this action. As shown in Fig. 13.11C, they began with the experimental finding that pain fibers excite relay cells. In addition, they postulated that pain fibers inhibit an interneuron in the substantia gelatinosa that normally inhibits the terminals of the pain fibers onto the relay cells. This *decrease* in presynaptic inhibition (which is called disinhibition) further enhances the transmission of pain inputs to the relay cells. Thus, the more active the pain fibers are, the more the excitability of the relay cells is

enhanced, a kind of positive feedback effect that might underlie the powerful nature of pain sensations. When large mechanoreceptive tactile fibers are stimulated, they excite the relay cells, but they also *excite* the interneurons, bringing about an *increase* in presynaptic inhibition. This not only causes the excitatory effect of a given tactile input to be brief, but it also provides a general dampening

Fig. 13.11. Somatosensory circuits in the mammalian spinal cord. **A.** Diagram of cross-section of spinal cord. **B.** Some of the main neuron types and synaptic connections that have been identified in the dorsal horn. I–V, laminae of the dorsal horn; MC, marginal cell; SC, stalked cell; IC, islet cell; INT, interneuron; PC, projection cell. The large myelinated fibers are believed to be glutaminergic; pain fibers contain substance P, somatostatin, vasoactive intestinal peptide, or possibly cholecystokinin; descending fibers contain noradrenaline or serotonin. (Based in part on discussions with Carole LaMotte) **C.** Simplified diagram illustrating "gate-control theory" of Melzack and Wall (1965). Postulated excitatory terminals shown by open profiles, inhibitory by shaded profiles.

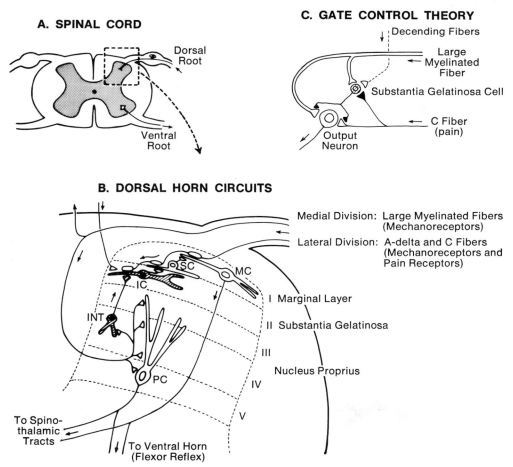

of transmission of pain inputs. Transmission through the dorsal horn is thus seen to depend on the activity of the dorsal horn interneurons, which is the outcome of their own intrinsic resting activity, the tactile and pain inputs, and control by descending fibers from the brain. The interneurons thus can act as "switches" or "gates," to enhance or depress pain transmission, and the theory thus was called the *gate control theory of pain.*

This theory has had an invigorating effect on the whole field of pain research. Some points seem doubtful (for example, the presence of both excitatory and inhibitory terminals arising from the same C fiber). Some points have been modified or expanded; in fact, new information is accumulating so rapidly that the actual status of the theory is unclear; it is undoubtedly incorrect in certain details. But the idea of proposing a specific neuronal circuit for pain mechanisms was a significant step forward, and this goal continues to be a stimulus for many experiments on neuronal mechanisms in the dorsal horn and its equivalent, the caudal nucleus of the trigeminal nerve, in the brainstem.

Two of the most active areas are the search for neurotransmitters, and the identification of synaptic connections. Recent results in both these areas are illustrated in Fig. 13.12. Studies such as these have suggested that substance P is a transmitter in the sensory fiber terminals, that met-enkephalins and opiate receptors are localized in the superficial layers (see Fig. 13.12A,B), and that descending noradrenergic fibers control dorsal horn neurons. Other studies have begun to reveal the complexity of the patterns of connections at the synaptic level (see Fig. 13.12C). Out of these studies a more accurate picture of circuits for pain transmission should soon emerge.

Ascending Pathways

Sensory information reaches the rest of the brain by two main pathways. Since these rise from lower centers to higher centers, they are called ascending pathways. The oldest, phylogenetically, is made up of fibers that arise from dorsal horn cells, cross the midline, and form a tract in the anterolateral part of the white matter of the spinal cord. These fibers ascend all the way through the spinal cord and brainstem, and terminate in the thalamus (see Fig. 13.13). They are thus referred to as the *spinothalamic* tract. These fibers mediate mainly *pain* and *temperature* sensations, but they also include fibers that convey some *tactile* and joint information. Along the way in the brainstem they give off numerous collaterals to the reticular formation. The reticular neurons, in turn, form a system of polysynaptic ascending connections, which eventually also feeds into the thalamus. These neurons are part of the *ascending reticular system,* which is involved in *arousal* and *consciousness* (see Chap. 26).

The phylogenetically newer ascending pathway is made up of collaterals of large, myelinated sensory axons. As shown in Figs. 13.11 and 13.13, these collaterals gather in the posterior, or dorsal, part of the white matter of the cord, and thereby form the *posterior columns,* or *dorsal columns.* As part of the somatosensory pathway, this system first can be delineated along the phylogenetic scale in reptiles. These fibers ascend only as far as the lower margin of the brainstem, where they terminate and make synapses in the *dorsal column nuclei.* From there, fibers sweep across the midline to form the *medial lemniscus,* and ascend to terminate in the thalamus. This whole pathway is often referred to as the *lemniscal system;* as might be expected, it is mainly concerned with conveying the most precise and complex information about touch and pressure, Lemniscal fibers give off collaterals to the reticular formation, and thus also contribute to arousal mechanisms.

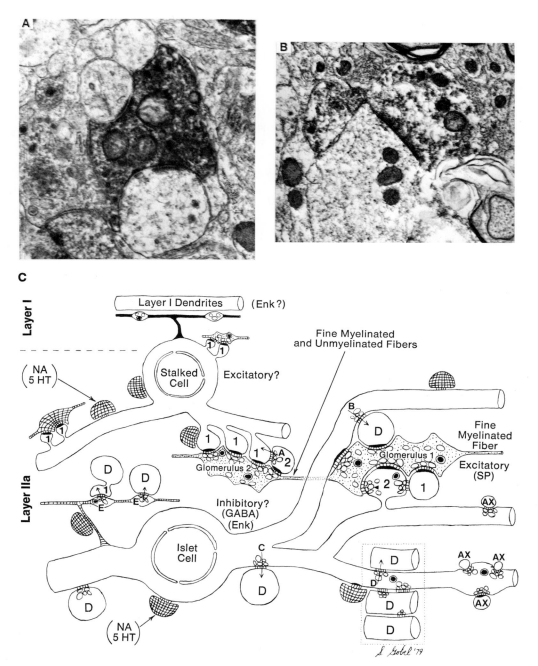

Fig. 13.12. A. Localization of substance P by immunocytochemical method in synaptic terminal of the dorsal horn of the monkey spinal cord. **B.** Localization of met-enkephalin in synaptic terminals of monkey dorsal horn. (Photographs courtesy of Nihal de Lanerolle and Carol LaMotte) **C.** Synaptic organization of the marginal layers of the dorsal horn in the cat. Note complex synaptic arrangements, such as reciprocal synapses (glomerulus 1) and serial synapses (D-D in lower right). (From Gobel et al., 1981)

A. SPINOTHALAMIC PATHWAY   ## B. LEMNISCAL PATHWAY

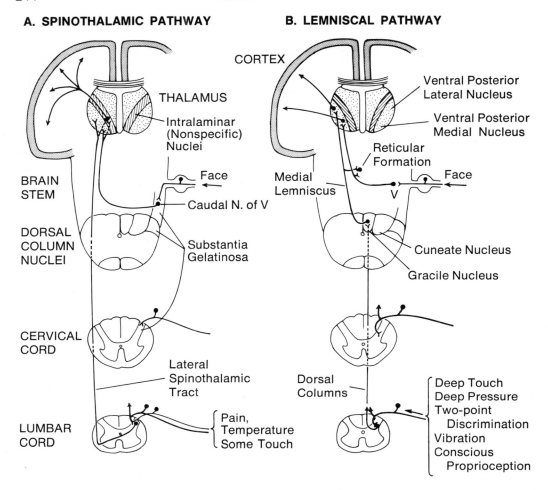

Fig. 13.13. Ascending pathways of the somatosensory system. (Modified from Carpenter, 1976 and Brodal, 1981)

Somatosensory Cortex

The ascending fibers in the somatosensory pathways terminate in the thalamus, and make synapses there with relay cells that project to the cerebral cortex. The thalamus is thus the gateway to the cortex, and it serves this function for all pathways ascending from the spinal cord and brainstem. The somatosensory fibers terminate in the group of cells called the *ventral posterior nucleus* (VP), the lemniscal and spinothalamic fibers in the lateral part (VPL), and the fibers from the trigeminal nucleus, relaying inputs from the face, in the me-

dial part (VPM). In subprimate mammals, like cats, the whole group of cells is referred to as the ventrobasal complex (VBC).

Much of the work on the somatosensory cortex has been concerned with three main questions. First, what is the topographical representation of the body surface? Second, how many cortical areas are there, and how specific are they? Third, what is the intrinsic organization within an area of cortex; what are the basic functional units? These questions are also relevant to the other parts of the cerebral cortex that we will study.

Topographical Representation. Within the ventroposterior nucleus, the fibers terminate in an orderly geometrical arrangement that preserves the relations of the body surface. This arrangement is called *somatotopy,* or *topographical representation;* it is as if the body surface were projected onto the nucleus. This arrangement, in turn, is preserved in the projection of the relay cells onto the cortex. The area within which these fibers terminate defines the somatosensory cortex. Within this cortex, the relations of the body surface are preserved, but the relative areas are modified. This was established by Wilder Penfield and his colleagues at Montreal in their studies, from the 1930's to the 1950's, of patients undergoing neurosurgical operations. With punctate electrical stimulation, Penfield elicited descriptions from the patients of the tactile sensations (numbness, tingling, pressure) and their apparent sites on the body surface. From this emerged the well-known drawing called a "homunculus" depicted in Fig. 13.14, with its characteristic distortions, particularly the large areas given over to the the lips, face, and hands. It is believed that the area of cortex varies with the acuity of perception, and the large cortical areas reflect the high sensitivity and fine discrimination possible in these parts of the body (a direct measure of this is provided by the two-point discriminations in Fig. 13.10).

Two particularly striking examples of the precision of cortical representation deserve mention. In the raccoon, the part of the somatosensory cortex representing the forepaw ("hand") is greatly developed. It has been possible to identify five individual, small gyri (folds), one for each finger,

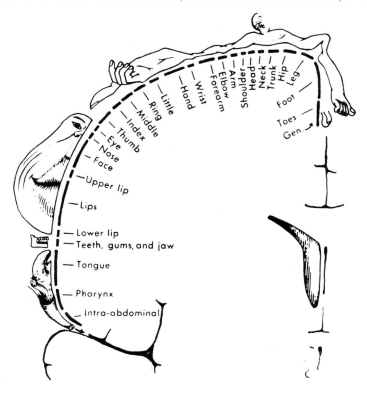

Fig. 13.14. The somatosensory "homunculus", representing the body surface as projected onto the postcentral gyrus of the human cerebral cortex. (From Penfield and Rasmussen, 1950)

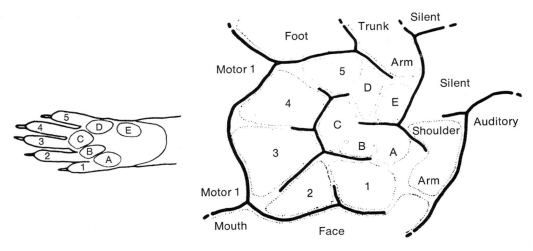

Fig. 13.15. Somatosensory cortex of the racoon. There is a fold (gyrus) for each finger (1–5) and each palm area (volar pad: A–E) of the paw. (From Welker and Seidenstein, 1959)

and another five gyri for each of the volar pads of the paw. A summary of the maps obtained is shown in Fig. 13.15. The elaborate nature of this representation is taken to reflect the acute tactile sensitivity of the racoon hand. This sensitivity is expressed both by passive stimulation, and by "active touch" during the dextrous movements of the hand (see Chap. 23).

A second example is the facial area of the rodent somatosensory cortex. In this area, Henrik van der Loos and Thomas Woolsey at Johns Hopkins discovered in 1969 a regular series of five rows of cell groups with hollow interiors, looking much like the cell clusters surrounding olfactory glomeruli in the olfactory bulb. They called each cluster a *"barrel"*, and showed that each barrel represents a vibrissa (whisker) on the animal's snout (Fig. 13.16) When a vibrissa is removed early in life, the corresponding barrel disappears from the row. When a vibrissa is stimulated continuously, a single, dense focus of 2-deoxyglucose uptake can be demonstrated in the corresponding barrel. The fibers that innervate a vibrissa are tuned to several different submodalities, and these are transmitted to the barrel for that vibrissa. A barrel is thus a *morphol-*

ogical unit, and it is also a *functional unit* within which *multisensory integration* takes place.

Cortical Areas. The maps described above were soon shown to apply in their general outline to many species of mammals. In addition, these studies showed that there is a second, smaller area where the body surface is represented. The main area was called S I, and the second area S II. With the methods available, it appeared that S I was the only region that receives the thalamic input. The belief therefore arose that *serial processing* takes place at the cortical level, beginning with analytical mechanisms in the primary cortex (S I), and proceeding to more integrative mechanisms in secondary cortex (S II). The final step was believed to occur in neighboring regions called *association cortex,* which appeared to lack topographical representations of the body surface, and therefore could be concerned with the synthetic mechanisms that seem to be necessary for perception to occur. This traditional view is depicted in Fig. 13.17A.

This tidy sequence has not been borne out by recent experiments. Instead, it has been found that there are not one but several subdivisions of the thalamus that relay somatosensory information, and these each have their specific inputs to one or more of several somatosensory areas. Furthermore, with more refined microelectrode recording techniques, it has been found that each cortical area is selective in

Fig. 13.16. A. Snout of a mouse; the vibrissae (whiskers) are marked by dots. **B.** Section across the somatosensory cortex receiving input from the snout. Note the rings of cells ("barrels", or glomeruli), each corresponding to a vibrissa (summarized in **C**). (From Woolsey and van der Loos, 1970)

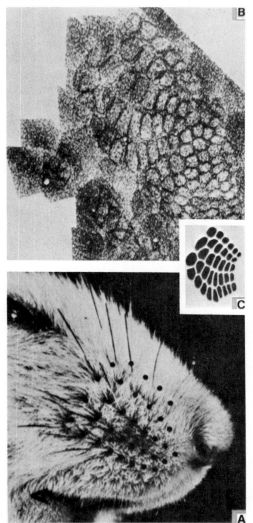

the submodalities it processes. This new evidence is summarized in Fig. 13.17B.

These results have emphasized the importance of *parallel processing* of different aspects of somatosensory stimuli at the cortical level. They have indicated that there is much more detailed mapping present in the cortex, particularly in parts believed to be "associational", than previously suspected. This has required rethinking the question of where and how our unified perceptions are formed. We will examine similar evidence as it relates to other sensory systems in the following chapters, and return to this question in our final discussion of the cortex in Chap. 31.

Cortical Columns. In the early years of studying the cortex with the new microelectrode recording methods that had become available during the 1950's, Vernon Mountcastle at Johns Hopkins University carried out an analysis of cell responses in somatosensory cortex of the cat to various types of stimuli. He found that when his electrode penetrated the cortex perpendicular to the surface, all the units he encountered tended to respond to the same sensory submodality (for example, light touch, or joint movement), but when he made an oblique electrode track, he encountered a series of units with different submodalities. From this he deduced that the cortex contains columns of cells with similar functional properties. Figure 13.18 illustrates some typical results from one of these early experiments, performed in collaboration with T. P. S. Powell of Oxford, in which functionally characterized units were localized anatomically.

The concept of the column as a basic functional unit has turned out to be widely applicable in the cortex. The characterization of columnar organization has been one of the dominating forces in studies of sensory areas, of motor areas, and even of association areas, as we shall see in subsequent chapters. From this and related work it is beginning to appear that the cortical column expresses a fundamental tendency

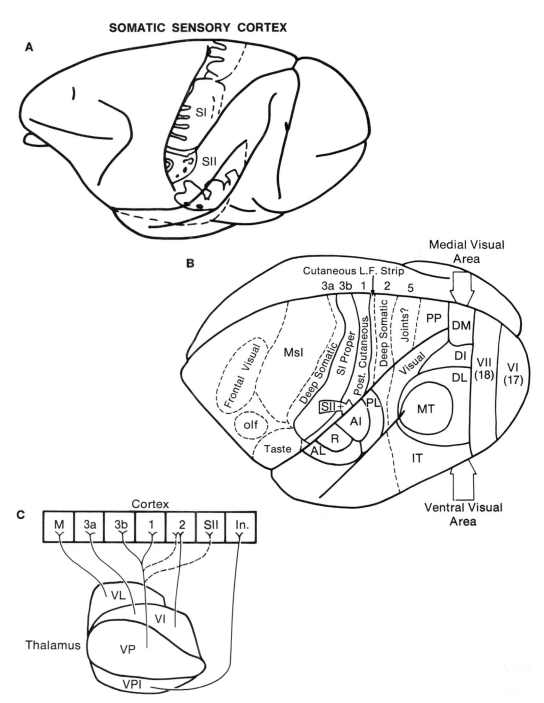

SOMATIC SENSORY CORTEX

Fig. 13.17. A. Traditional view of the monkey somatosensory cortex. **B.** Current view of subdivisions of monkey somatosensory cortex, together with cortical areas for other sensory modalities. **C.** The main thalamocortical connections of the somatosensory system. AL, anterior lateral auditory field; DI, dorsointermediate visual area; DL, dorsolateral visual area; DM, dorsomedial visual area; MsI, motor-sensory area I; MT, middle termporal visual area; PL, posterior lateral auditory field; PP, posterior parietal visual area; R, rostral auditory field; VI, ventralis intermedius nucleus; VL, ventralis lateralis nucleus; VP, ventroposterior nucleus; VPI, ventroposteroinferior nucleus. (From Merzenich and Kaas, 1980)

248

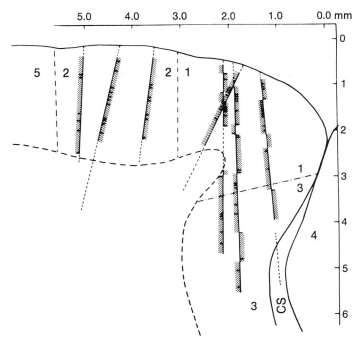

Fig. 13.18. Columnar organization of somatosensory cortex. Cross-section containing electrode tracks, showing sites of unit recordings (short horizontal bars) and modality of units (shading on left for units activated by stimulation of the skin, on right for units activated by stimulation of joint, periosteum, or deep tissue). (From Powell and Mountcastle, 1959)

of nerve cells and circuits to be organized in more or less discontinuous groups, or modules. We have already seen a clear example of this in the olfactory glomeruli, as well as in the somatosensory barrels. A point of some interest is that olfactory glomeruli and somatosensory barrels have dimensions of 100–300 μm, which is similar to the widths of several hundred micrometers for columns in the rest of the somatosensory cortex. Thus the smallest unit of anatomical representation yet identified—the barrel—appears to be equivalent in size to the basic functional unit, the column. Other work has similarly revealed fine-grained representations that approach the dimensions of single columns.

Is the cortical column a building block of perception? This was an obvious possibility from the moment of its discovery. Mountcastle early stressed that events

within the column probably are involved in only the initial steps in cortical processing of sensory information. This view has been supported by studies of other areas, too, such as visual cortex. Thus, the discoveries of columns, of fine details in somatotopy, and the multiple representations of the body surface are steps along the way to perception, but there is still a way to go, as we will discuss in Chap. 31.

REFERENCES

Barrington, E. J. W. 1979. [Chap. 1].

Brodal, A. 1981. [Chap. 13].

Carpenter, M. B. 1976. *Human Neuroanatomy.* Baltimore: Williams & Wilkins.

Dykes, R. W. 1977. Sensory receptors. In *Reconstructive Microsurgery* (ed. by R. K. Daniel and J. K. Terzis). Boston: Little, Brown. pp. 320–330.

Gobel, S., W. M. Falls, G. J. Bennett, M. Abdelmoumene, H. Hayashi, and E. Humphrey. 1980. An EM analysis of the synaptic connections of horseradish peroxidase-filled stalked cells and islet cells in the substantia gelatinosa of adult cat spinal cord. *J. Comp. Neurol. 194:* 781–807.

Kenshalo, D. R. 1976. In *Sensory Functions of the Skin in Primates* (ed. by Y. Zotterman). Oxford: Pergamon. pp. 305–330.

Knibestol, M. and A. B. Vallbo. 1970. Single unit analysis of mechano-receptor activity in the human glabrous skin. *Acta Physiol. Scand. 80:* 178-

Kuffler, S. W. and J. G. Nicholls. 1976. [Chap. 8].

LaMotte, R. H., J. G. Thalhammer, H. E. Torebjork, and C. G. Robinson. 1982. Peripheral nerval mechanisms of cutaneous hyperalgesia following mild injury by heat. *J. Neurosci.*

Loewenstein, W. R. 1971. Mechano-electric transduction in the Pacinian corpuscle. Initiation of sensory impulses in mechano-receptors. In *Handbook of Sensory Physiology.* Vol.1, *Principles of Receptor Physiology* (ed. by W. R. Loewenstein). New York: Springer. pp. 269–290.

Melzack, R. and P. D. Wall. 1965. Pain mechanisms: a new theory. *Science 150:* 971–979.

Merzenich, M. M. and J. H. Kaas. 1980. Principles of organization of sensory-perceptual systems in mammals. In *Progress in Psychobiology and Psysiological Psychology* (ed. by J. M. Sprague and A. N. Epstein). New York: Academic. pp. 2–43.

Mountcastle, V. B. (ed). [Chap. 9].

Penfield, W. and T. Rasmussen. 1952. *The Cerebral Cortex of Man.* New York: Macmillan.

Powell, T. P. S. and V. B. Mountcastle. 1959. Some aspects of the functional organization of the cortex of the postcentral gyrus of the monkey: a correlation of findings obtained in a single unit analysis with cytoarchitecture. *Bull. J. Hopkins Hosp. 105:* 133–162.

Schmidt, R. F. (ed.) 1978. [Chap. 11].

Smith, D. S. 1968. *Insect Cells. Their Structure and Function.* Edinburgh: Oliver and Boyd.

Spencer, P. S. and H. H. Schaumburg. 1975. An ultrastructural study of the inner core of the Pacinian corpuscle. *J. Neurocytol. 2:* 217-

Welker, W. I. and S. Seidenstein. 1959. Somatic sensory representation in the cerebral cortex of the raccoon (Procyon loter). *J. Comp. Neurol. 111:* 469–501.

Woolsey, T. A. and H. van der Loos. 1970. The structural organization of layer IV in the somatosensory region (SI) of mouse cerebral cortex. The description of a cortical field composed of discrete cytoarchitectonic units. *Brain Res. 17:* 205–242.

14

Muscle Sense and Kinesthesia

The tactile systems we studied in the previous chapter tell us about the world around us. What about the world within? How do we know *when* we move our muscles; how do we know *how much* to move our muscles, limbs, and joints? The precise control of movements has a high priority in the behavior of most organisms, and increasingly so in higher animals. Different kinds of motor behavior will be discussed in later chapters; the two examples in Fig. 14.1 illustrate that motor control is the outcome of a complex interplay between genetics, motivation, training (especially in humans), and sensory factors. Sensory information is needed to help control posture and sequences of movements, and make adjustments to changes in the environment.

Information about movement is signaled by several different types of receptors. The receptors are located at almost every possible site in the musculoskeletal system at which movement can take place. As indicated in Fig. 14.2, the main sites are in the muscles, tendons, and joints. In addition, tactile receptors are also involved when movements are associated with movement of the skin.

It should be obvious that the central nervous system wants as much information as possible about ongoing movements. As is so often the case, it doesn't entrust that task to just one information channel, but spreads the task among as many complementary kinds of channels as it can. As usual, this makes the subject more interesting, but makes definitions of terms more difficult. Table 14.1 lists some of the common terms and classifications.

Table 14.1 Different sensory modalities related to movement, and their respective sensory receptors

Muscle sense	Proprioception	Kinesthesia	(Functions)
muscle receptors	muscle receptors	muscle receptors	Sensations of position and movement
tendon receptors	tendon receptors	tendon receptors	
	joint receptors	joint receptors	
		skin receptors	Sensation of force and weight
		central efferents	Sense of effort

251

Fig. 14.1. Examples of motor behavior requiring precise sensorimotor coordination. *Left,* A male three-spined stickleback fish assumes a threat posture toward its own reflection in a mirror. According to Tinbergen, "this activity is innate, dependent on internal (motivational) and external (sensory) factors. It has an intimidating effect on other males. . . . Historically, it is displacement sand-digging, changed by ritualization". (From Tinbergen, 1951) *Right,* A ballerina, Jane Brayton, executing an arabesque. Ballet is a typical higher human activity, in which sensory factors, motivation, and innate capacities are molded by instruction, practice, and individual expression. (Photograph by Curt Meinel, courtesy of Ruth and Robert Brayton)

Muscle sense usually means the sensory information arising in the muscles and tendons. *Proprioception* is a term introduced by Sherrington to refer to all sensory inputs from the musculoskeletal system, which therefore includes inputs from joint receptors. Neither muscle sense nor proprioception necessarily implies conscious perception, and both can therefore be applied to invertebrates as well as all levels of vertebrates. *Kinesthesia* is the sense of the position and movement of the limbs. Contributing to this are skin receptors as well as proprioceptors. This sense includes conscious sensations—what Charles Bell, in the early nineteenth century, referred to as our "sixth sense"—and therefore applies primarily to higher vertebrates, especially humans. Kinesthesia also includes our sensations of effort, of force, and of weight; contributing to these sensations are signals in descending pathways within the central nervous system.

In this chapter we will focus on the proprioceptors in the musculoskeletal system. We will discuss briefly their central pathways and, in humans, their possible contributions to conscious sensations.

INVERTEBRATES

Proprioceptors are present in many invertebrate species, and are especially important in arthropods. In concert with the development of specialized muscle groups to control the body segments and long, articulated appendages were various kinds of specialized sensory receptors. Among the simplest of these is the stretch receptor cell of the crayfish. We have discussed the spread of electrotonic potentials in this cell in Chap. 8, and the basic properties of the sensory response in Chap. 11. Here we will further use this cell as a model for the control of excitability of muscle receptors.

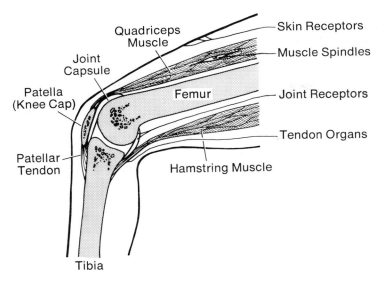

Fig. 14.2. Sites of sensory receptors for muscle sense and kinesthesia, as illustrated by the knee joint.

The long abdomen of the crayfish is composed of a number of segments (see Fig. 14.3). The dorsal cuticular plates of each segment are hinged on each other, so that when the segmental muscles contract the abdomen is flexed. The abdomen can thus be flipped like a tail, which is the method a crayfish uses for a quick retreat from danger. The muscles contain two types of fibers, the regular muscle fibers, that move the plates when they contract, and modified muscle fibers that contain the terminals of the sensory cells. The modified fibers contribute little to the movement of the plates, but indicate to the sensory cells the state of tension or

Fig. 14.3. The stretch receptor cell of the lobster, showing relation to muscles and segments of the abdomen. MRO, muscle receptor organ; RM 1, 2, receptor muscles (compare with Fig. 8.8). (A, B from Florey, in Bullock, 1976; C, D from Alexandrowicz, 1951)

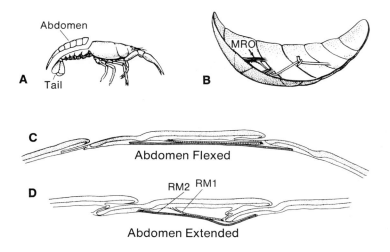

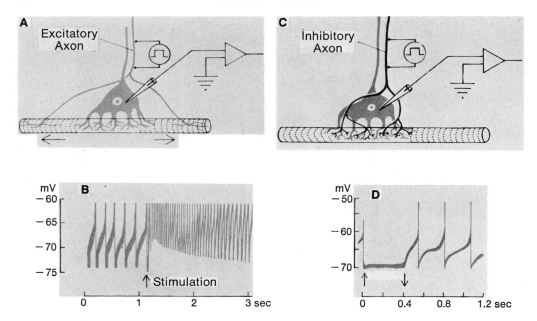

Fig. 14.4. Centrifugal control of sensory responses. **A.** Set up for stimulating the excitatory motor axon to the receptor muscle. **B.** During the receptor response to a maintained stretch, stimulation (at arrow) of the motor nerve produces contraction of the receptor muscle, further stretching the receptor cell membrane and increasing the receptor response. **C.** Set up for stimulating the inhibitory motor axon to the receptor cell dendrites. **D.** High-frequency electrical shock (150/sec) to the inhibitory axon (between arrows) inhibits the ongoing receptor response to a maintained stretch. (Adapted from Kuffler and Eyzaguirre, in Kuffler and Nicholls, 1976)

lengthening of the muscle. The modified muscle fibers occur in two types of bundles, depending on whether they are slow fibers (slow summation of contraction) or rapid fibers (individual contractions). There are correspondingly slowly adapting and rapidly adapting types of receptor cells (see Figs. 8.8 and 14.3).

Each muscle bundle receives a motor innervation in the form of collaterals from the motoneuron axons to the main muscle fibers. Thus, whenever the motoneurons send impulses in their axons to signal the main muscles to contract, they also produce contractions of the sensory muscle fibers. Now, the question arises: what is the reason for having the sensory muscle fibers contract at the same time as the main muscle fiber? The answer is that if the sensory fibers did not contract, they would fall slack as the rest of the muscle con-

tracted and shortened. By contracting at the same time, they, in effect, adjust themselves to the new length of the main muscle, and can therefore signal any departure from that length, such as if an obstacle is encountered. The increase in sensitivity produced by motor stimulation is shown in Fig. 14.4B.

Each sensory cell also receives an inhibitory axon. Stimulation of this axon produces an IPSP in the sensory cell, as we saw in Chap. 8, and the effect of the IPSP in depressing and interrupting an impulse discharge in the receptor cell is shown in Fig. 14.4D. The inhibitory axons arise from cells in the segmental ganglion. Because of their orientation *away from* the central nervous system and its higher centers, they are referred to as *centrifugal fibers.*

It can now be seen that the stretch receptor cell, even though it is located in the periphery, among the muscles it inner-vates, is under exquisite control by the central nervous system. The nervous sys-tem can either increase or decrease the sensitivity of this receptor. It is interesting that the output in the motoneurons them-selves, in fact, functions as part of the cen-trifugal control, through the collaterals to the sensory muscle fibers. This control over the *reception* of stimuli in the body is a common feature in the organization of the invertebrates. In the vertebrates, in con-trast, centrifugal control of sensory input reaches only to the site of the first synaptic relay in the spinal cord. This is taken to reflect the *encephalization* of nervous con-trol, and the shifting of nervous integra-tion to higher centers, that is an important feature in the evolution of higher or-ganisms, a point we introduced in our overview of the brain in Chap. 3. A

similar progression can be seen in motor systems (Chap. 18).

A stretch receptor that fulfills the same sensory function as the abdominal recep-tor, but achieves it by different properties, is the stretch receptor at the base of each leg, called the *thoracicocoxal receptor*. As shown in Fig. 14.5, the cell body of this receptor is located in the segmental gan-glion; it sends a long process to the pe-riphery, to terminate among the muscles that control the joint between the limb and the thorax. As shown in Fig. 14.5, a brief stretch to the muscle sets up a receptor potential that resembles that seen in the abdominal receptors. The remarkable dif-ference between the two cases is that the receptor potential is the entire signal in the thoracic receptor; there are no impulses. This was described in 1968 by S. H. Ripley, Brian Bush, and Alan Roberts at

Fig. 14.5. A. Reflex circuit comprising the thoracic-coxal muscle receptor and the promotor neuron of the crab. **B.** Intracellular recordings from sensory neuron. When stretch is applied to muscle, the receptor cell responds with graded potentials (b–d, different amplitude of graded response), which are sufficient for synaptic transmission and impulse response of the promotor neuron (a) (recorded extracellularly from the motor nerve). Under some conditions a small graded "spike" may be pres-ent (e), which appears to be due to a small number of voltage-sensitive sodium channels in the receptor cell membrane. This spike may aid in signaling very rapid muscle stretches. (Based on Bush, 1981)

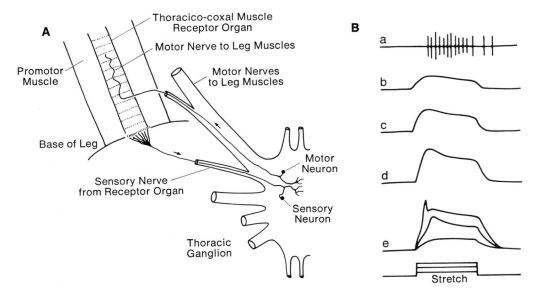

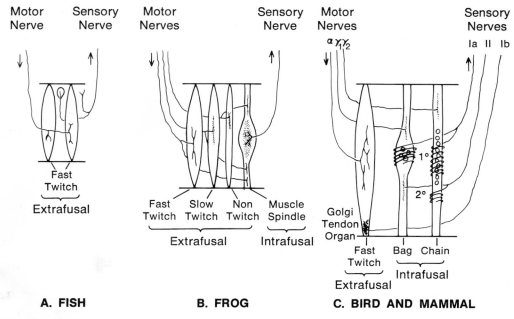

Fig. 14.6. Evolution of vertebrate muscle and tendon receptors. (Based on Barker, 1978)

Bristol, and was one of the first demonstrations of nonimpulse transmission in neurons (see Chap. 8). The effectiveness of transmission was shown by recording the motor response in the motoneuron axons (see Fig. 14.5); presumably this is mediated through the central branches of the axon within the ganglion onto the motoneurons. The receptor potential spreads passively through the axon by electrotonic means, and synaptic output is caused by graded depolarization of the presynaptic branches, as we have previously discussed (Chap. 8).

We see here a very nice demonstration of how the same function (signaling of stretch) can be mediated by two cells that have very different structures, and use two different properties—graded electrotonic spread and all-or-nothing impulses—to transmit the signals. Thus, although transmission takes place in the analog and digital modes, respectively, in the two cases, the overall functions are nonetheless similar. The fact that nerve cells with different structures and different proper-

ties may carry out similar functions is an important principle in the organization of nervous systems.

VERTEBRATES

Specialized muscle receptors are rather late to appear in vertebrate evolution. There are apparently no sensory nerve endings in the body musculature of fish. In some species, however, there are sensory fibers, including free nerve endings and corpusclelike organs, within the connective tissue surrounding the muscles to the fins (Fig. 14.6). These fibers signal extension and compression produced in the connective tissue by lengthening and contraction of the muscles that control the bending of the fins.

Fins, of course, were the evolutionary forerunner of the limbs of terrestrial animals. The amphibians are the first animals in the phylogenetic scale to possess muscle spindles; it is believed that they evolved to provide the sensory input required for the limb muscles to oppose the force of gravity and maintain posture. Within the muscles are modified muscle fibers, gathered in small bundles and surrounded by a capsule. Their widened midregions reminded early histologists of the spindle used in spinning wool, and they were therefore named *muscle spindles*. There is a single sensory fiber which innervates each muscle spindle (Fig. 14.6). Each spindle also receives a motor innervation via collaterals from motor axons to the muscles. In the frog, the limb muscles characteristically are composed of different types of muscle fibers with different speeds of contraction. There are, accordingly, fast-twitch, slow-twitch, and non-twitch fibers, and there are corresponding motor nerve fibers to each type of fiber, and corresponding collaterals to the muscle spindles (see Fig. 14.6). The fibers that make up the main mass of the muscle and do all the work are called *extrafusal fibers,* and the modified muscle fibers within the spindle are called *intrafusal fibers* (these names being derived from the fusiform appearance of the spindle). The basic similarities in the arrangements of motor and sensory innervation of the frog spindle and the crayfish stretch receptor may be seen by comparing Fig. 14.6 with Fig. 14.4.

Further steps in evolution are seen in birds and mammals. In these species, several differences are evident, as illustrated in Fig. 14.6. The first difference is that there are two types of intrafusal fibers. One type has a collection of nuclei within a saclike central portion, and is called a *nuclear-bag fiber*. The other type contains a chain of nuclei, and is called a *nuclear chain fiber*. In the central portion each type receives the spiral ending of a large sensory nerve fiber. The ending is called a *primary ending*. It arises from a group Ia axon, the largest of all the peripheral nerve fibers (see Table 14.2). Near its central portion, the nuclear chain fiber receives smaller spiral endings. This is called a *secondary ending*. It arises from a group II axon. There may also be a small twig from a group II axon that supplies secondary endings to the nuclear chain fibers.

A second difference is that, rather than the motor innervation being derived from the motor nerves to the extrafusal muscles, the intrafusal muscles receive their own motor axons. These have small diameters, and are called *gamma fibers* to distinguish them from the large *alpha fibers* to the extrafusal muscles. Another name for them is *fusimotor fiber*. The gamma fibers to bag and chain fibers are distinct from each other.

A third difference is that a new type of sensory organ makes its appearance. This was first described by Golgi in the late nineteenth century, and is therefore named the *Golgi tendon organ*. As indicated in the diagram of Fig. 14.6, this organ is embedded in the tendon at the end of the muscle. It is innervated by a group Ib axon, only slightly smaller in diameter than the Ia axons.

Nearly all muscles in the mammalian body contain muscle receptors organized along the lines just described. This is rather remarkable, considering how radically such muscles as those in the legs, fingers, tongue, esophagus, and eye differ from each other. Acording to David Barker of England, who has carried out many detailed studies of muscle receptor anatomy, muscle spindles are present in highest densities in the hand, foot, and neck, where they are believed to be important in controlling *fine movements*, and also in certain leg muscles (such as the soleus) which are important for *maintaining posture*. In contrast, spindles are fewest in shoulder and thigh muscles, and in muscles (such as gastrocnemius) involved in initiating gross movements. Spindles are also present in high density in the *extraocular muscles* of the eye in most mammals (such as primates, horses, pigs, etc.). In these muscles, the muscle fibers are divided into subclasses, and the spindles receive some of their motor innervation from motoneuron axon collaterals. The situation thus appears intermediate between the frog and the common mammalian pattern. Muscle spindles have been reported absent from

Table 14.2   The fiber spectrum of the peripheral nerves in the mammal

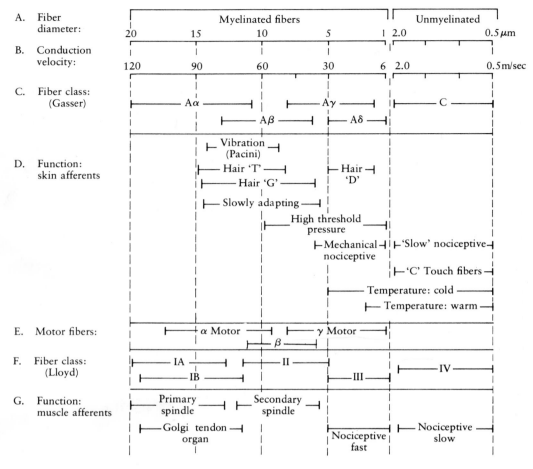

After Somjen (1972)

the extraocular muscles in several species (such as rat, cat, and dog). There is as yet no explanation for this puzzling difference.

With this background, let us consider more closely the properties of muscle receptors, as exemplified by the frog and the mammal.

Frog Muscle Spindle

The frog muscle spindle, like the Pacinian corpuscle, has played an important part in the development of our knowledge about sensory receptor mechanisms. It was the

first receptor from which single unit recordings, from the sensory axons, were made; this was accomplished by Yngve Zotterman and Edgar Adrian at Cambridge University in 1926. Its response properties were analyzed in a quantitative manner by Brian Matthews in Cambridge in the 1930's. It was the first receptor from which a receptor potential was recorded; this was carried out by Bernard Katz in London in 1951.

A careful analysis of the frog spindle has been carried out by David Ottoson and his colleagues in Stockholm. With fine forceps Ottoson dissected out a single spindle with its single afferent axon and mounted it between two thin rods in a recording chamber. The setup is shown in Fig. 14.7. Below the setup are schematic diagrams of the ultrastructure of different regions of the spindle: the muscle, a transition zone, and the central, main sensory zone. In the central zone the regular striations of the muscle are partially replaced by connective and reticular tissue, within which are embedded the sensory terminals. The terminals consist of bulbous varicosities, several microns in diameter, alternating with thin, linking processes, only a few tenths of a micron in diameter. It is believed that

sensory transduction occurs in the bulbs.

With the setup shown in Fig. 14.7 stretch is applied very close to the sensory endings, and the receptor properties can be studied with great accuracy. Examples of typical recordings are shown in Fig. 14.8. Note the extremely regular nature of the impulse discharge shown in A, even when the stretch is applied very slowly. The receptor potential shown in B is finely graded in rate of rise and in amplitude in correlation with the applied stretch. The greater sensitivity of the spindle during the dynamic phase of the applied stretch is seen in the recordings in A and B, and is

Fig. 14.7. The muscle spindle of the frog. A. Darkfield photomicrograph of a spindle mounted between two nylon rods (thickness, 300 μm). The two thin lines indicate the central sensory region. B. Diagram of a spindle mounted as in (A), showing the recording set up. C. Diagram of the fine structure of the spindle, showing the relation of motor and sensory terminals to the intrafusal muscle fiber. (A,B from Ottoson and Shepherd; C from Karlsson et al.; for references, see Ottoson and Shepherd, 1971)

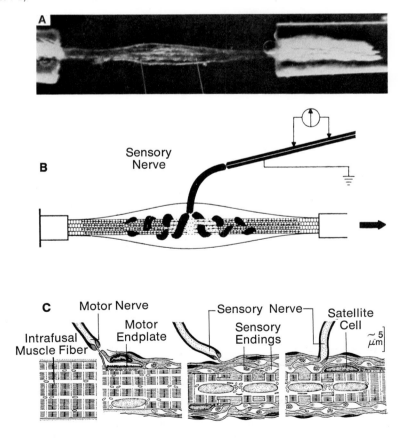

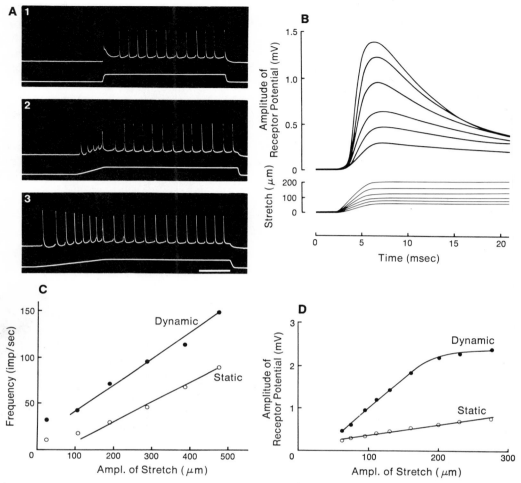

Fig. 14.8. Responses of the frog muscle spindle to different amounts and rates of stretch. **A.** Impulse response to stretches of decreasing rate of extension (1–3), to the same steady extension. 1, 130 mm/sec; 2, 13 mm/sec; 3, 5 mm/sec. Time bar, 50 msec. **B.** Receptor potential recorded from the sensory nerve after blocking impulses with local anesthetic in the bathing medium. **C.** Comparison between impulse firing frequencies at the dynamic peak and the static plateau of the response. Dynamic stretch rate was 2.6 mm/sec; static plateau frequencies were measured 200 msec after the dynamic peak. **D.** Comparison between amplitudes of the dynamic and static receptor potentials for rapidly applied stretches to different static levels. (From Ottoson and Shepherd, 1971)

plotted in the graphs of C and D. These studies leave little doubt of the ability of the spindle to signal the rate of change and the steady amplitude of an applied stretch with exquisite precision.

Mammalian Muscle Receptors

As we have seen, mammalian muscle receptors are characterized by differentia-

tion into spindles and tendon organs, and the spindle fibers are further differentiated into bag and chain fibers, each with primary and secondary sensory endings, and separate gamma motor supply. This makes for a rather complicated situation, which permits a number of combinations of sensory signaling under different states of muscle activity. Many of these combinations have been studied, mostly using the muscles of the hindlimb of the cat (for example, the soleus). Many workers have contributed to this study, and the diagrams in Fig. 14.9 summarize much of this work. Since there are so many permutations of sensory and motor activity, the student should examine this figure slowly—one diagram at a time!

The simplest situation is stretch applied to a passive muscle. As shown in Fig. 14.9A, the primary spindle endings give a brisk response, especially to dynamic stretch, while the secondary endings give a slowly adapting response with little dynamic sensitivity. From this it has been concluded that the primary endings are the

Fig. 14.9. Responses of mammalian muscle spindles and tendon organs under different conditions of muscle stretch, muscle contraction, and centrifugal (gamma) control. α, axon of alpha motoneuron; γ, axon of gamma motoneuron [dynamic (D) and static (S)]. (Based on Pi-Suñer and Fulton, Leksell, Hunt and Kuffler, Matthews, Gordon and others; references in Kuffler and Nicholls, 1976)

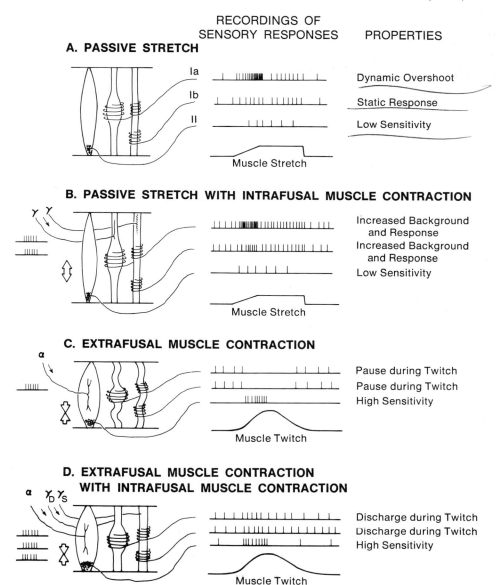

RECORDINGS OF
SENSORY RESPONSES   PROPERTIES

A. PASSIVE STRETCH

Ia   Dynamic Overshoot
Ib   Static Response
II   Low Sensitivity

Muscle Stretch

B. PASSIVE STRETCH WITH INTRAFUSAL MUSCLE CONTRACTION

Increased Background
   and Response
Increased Background
   and Response
Low Sensitivity

Muscle Stretch

C. EXTRAFUSAL MUSCLE CONTRACTION

Pause during Twitch
Pause during Twitch
High Sensitivity

Muscle Twitch

D. EXTRAFUSAL MUSCLE CONTRACTION WITH INTRAFUSAL MUSCLE CONTRACTION

Discharge during Twitch
Discharge during Twitch
High Sensitivity

Muscle Twitch

main channel through which information about changing stretch of a muscle is communicated, and secondary endings are more specialized for transmitting information about position. Tendon organs show a high threshold and low sensitivity to passive stretch, and thus contribute little information under these conditions.

In the normal animal there is ongoing activity in the gamma motor fibers, and the effects of this activity on responses to passive stretch are shown in Fig. 14.9B. In general, there is increased background firing of the sensory fibers, due to the background contractions of the intrafusal muscle fibers, and an increased sensitivity to an applied stretch. There is no effect of the intrafusal contractions on tendon organs, however.

The activity of the muscle receptors during active contraction of a muscle is shown in Fig. 14.9 C and D. During a brief muscle twitch (C), both primary and sensory endings of muscle spindles show a "pause"—an interruption in their ongoing discharge. Tendon organs, in contrast, give a high-frequency burst of impulses during the contraction. In a brief paper in 1928, Pi-Suñer and John Fulton, then at Harvard, speculated that this difference arises because the tendon organ is in series with the contracting muscle, whereas the spindles are in parallel. Because of this arrangement, the tendon organ is subjected to increased tension, while the spindle tends to fall slack. Note the high sensitivity of the tendon organ to active contraction, which stands in contrast to its low sensitivity to passive stretch.

Finally, we consider the case of active contraction with gamma innervation intact, as in the normal cat (Fig. 14.9D). As in part B of the figure, the background discharge is increased, but, in addition, the sensory endings continue to give rise to impulses during the twitch, so that there is no pause. This role of the gamma fibers was first indicated by the work of Lars Leksell in Stockholm in 1945, and was established in a classical series of papers by

Carlton Hunt and Stephen Kuffler at Johns Hopkins in the 1950's. By this means, the muscle spindle remains under tension during a muscle contraction, and can thus signal changes in load when they occur. The separate gamma innervation of the bag and chain fibers (see D) allows the dynamic and static responsiveness of the sensory endings to be controlled independently, thereby adding to the precision of the sensory signals.

Joint Receptors

Joints are typically encased in tough connective tissue capsules and the endings of ligaments of muscles. Embedded in the joint capsules are several kinds of sensory receptor. Each appears to be a modified version of a corresponding receptor in the skin. They have been classified as follows (see Fig. 14.10). Type I consists of small corpuscles around the branches of thin, myelinated fibers. These resemble Ruffini end organs in the skin. They respond to stretch with slowly adapting discharges. Type II is a large corpuscle supplied by a medium-thick myelinated fiber. These resemble Pacinian corpuscles, and like them, are rapidly adapting. Type III consists of a large, dense arborization of a large, myelinated fiber. This is found in ligaments near the capsule, and resembles a Golgi tendon organ. They have high thresholds and are slowly adapting. Type IV are free nerve endings of fine, unmyelinated fibers, resembling those in the skin.

This rich innervation suggests that sensory information from the joints might contribute to position sense. The early experiments provided evidence that type I receptors are tuned to respond over narrow angles within the range of joint movement (Figure 14.10). It was proposed that these slowly adapting discharges signal joint position, whereas the rapidly adapting type II receptors are acceleration detectors. This provided a beautifully tuned system for signaling joint position, and seemed all the more persua-

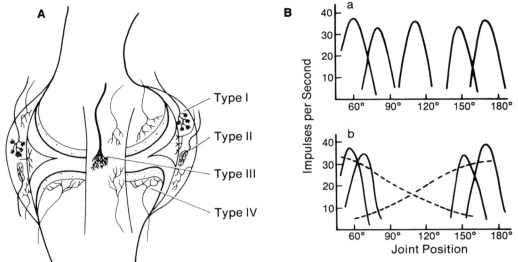

Fig. 14.10. A. Sensory receptors innervating the knee joint. Type I receptors resemble Ruffini endings in the skin. Type II receptors have the form of flattened Pacinian corpuscles. Type III receptors resemble Golgi tendon organs. Type IV receptors are unmyelinated nerve endings, resembling pain fiber terminals. (From Brodal, 1981) B. Tuning curves of joint receptor nerves for different joint positions in the cat. a. Population of fibers covering most of the range of joint position. (From Skoglund, 1973) b. Population of fibers covering only extremes of the range of joint position. Dashed lines show recordings from primary endings of muscle spindles in antagonistic muscles around the ankle joint. Muscle receptors may contribute to sensation of joint position through this activity, which Burgess et al. have termed an opponent frequency code. (Based on Burgess et al., 1982)

sive in view of other behavioral evidence that muscle receptors did not seem to contribute to position sense.

In recent years, however, the relative significance of the roles played by joint and by muscle afferents has been reversed. Reinvestigation of the slowly adapting fibers indicates that most of these fire impulses only at the extremes of joint movement, but rarely over the middle range, where signals in the normal physiological range of joint position and movement are needed (see Fig. 14.10). On the other hand, there has been increasing evidence for the contribution of muscle receptors to kinesthesia. We will return to these questions when we discuss cortical mechanisms below.

Ascending Pathways

As we have seen, information from muscles and joints is carried to the spinal cord in an array of different axons, ranging from the largest myelinated axons (type I and II from muscle receptors) to the several types of fibers from joint receptors. The array of fibers is similar from both the hindlimb and forelimb, but in the spinal cord, the connections and ascending pathways are different.

The fibers from the _hindlimb_ bifurcate within the cord. One branch terminates within the cord, to take part in segmental reflex circuits (Chap. 20) or to connect to cells of a nucleus called Clarke's column, which projects to the cerebellum via the spinocerebellar pathway (Chap. 22). These fibers also give off collaterals to a nucleus with the somewhat mysterious monicker of "nucleus Z", which in turn relays through the medial lemniscus to the thalamus. These connections are summarized in Fig. 14.11.

The fibers from the _forelimb_ also bifur-

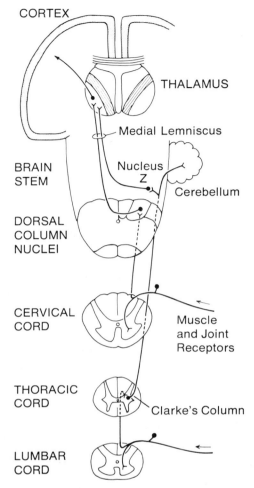

Fig. 14.11. Ascending pathways carrying sensory information from muscles and joints. Compare with somatosensory pathways shown in Fig. 13.13. (Adapted from Carpenter, 1976 and Brodal, 1981)

cate on entering the cord, but their destinations are simpler. One branch takes part in local reflex circuits, while the other ascends to the dorsal column nuclei, at the anterior end of the cord. This ascending pathway, through the medial lemniscus to the thalamus, is thus similar to that for cutaneous afferents, as discussed in the previous chapter.

The different central connections presumably reflect the different functions of hindlimbs and forelimbs. The spinocere-

bellar pathway, for example, provides for integration of muscle and joint information with cerebellar mechanisms that are essential for sensorimotor coordination and maintenance of muscle tone and posture. This is particularly relevant to the functions of the hindlimbs in standing posture and in locomotion. In contrast, the forelimbs are closely related to the neck and head; their direct connections to lemniscal pathways presumably reflect the more discriminative functions, including manipulation by the paw or hand, of the forelimb. The separation of these two pathways may therefore reflect functional specialization that was important in the evolution of primates.

The Cortex and Kinesthesia

The ascending pathways carrying muscle and joint information enter the medial lemniscus and terminate in the VP nucleus of the thalamus, as indicated in Fig. 14.11. The fibers terminate topographically, similar to the cutaneous fiber terminations. From here, muscle and joint information is relayed to the cortex. These submodalities have their own specific areas in the cortex, which are closely related to the multiple representations of the somatosensory system. As we noted in connection with Fig. 13.17B, the main cortical representation for muscles is area 3a, which receives input relayed especially from Ia fibers from muscle spindles. There is a representation of some muscle afferents in area 5 of the parietal lobe, and of various deep tissues in area 2 (see Fig. 13.17B).

These cortical representations are all recent findings, made possible by application of modern techniques such as HRP tracing and unit recordings in unrestrained animals. They have brought about a revision in our thinking about perception of movement. As mentioned above, the traditional view had been that muscle afferent pathways do not reach the cortex, and that our perceptions of joint position

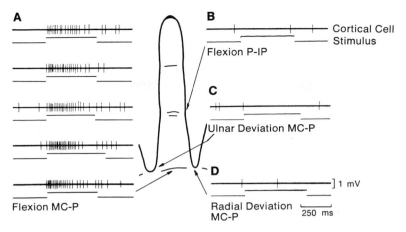

Fig. 14.12. Response of a neuron in the motor cortex of an awake monkey to flexion of the joint at the base of the middle finger (metacarpophalangeal (MC-P) joint), as shown in (**A**). The neuron did not respond to other types of movement: (**B**) flexion of proximal interphalangeal joint (P-IP), (**C**) ulnar (lateral) deviation of MC-P joint, and (**D**) radial (medial) deviation of MC-P joint. (From Lemon and Porter, 1976)

and the movements of our joints and muscles are mediated only by joint receptors. Proprioceptors were supposed to take part only in subcortical and subconscious muscle reflexes. This seemed to receive support from behavioral studies in humans, in which finger joints were infiltrated with local anesthetic, producing loss of position sense.

This conception began to topple with the finding that relatively few joint receptors are tuned to the physiological range of mid-joint ankle position, as mentioned above. Then, in 1972, Peter Matthews, Ian McCloskey, and G. M. Goodwin at Oxford carried out careful behavioral studies which showed that, with local anesthesia of all cutaneous afferents from the arm, position sense of the figures still persisted. This showed that muscle afferents have access to mechanisms of perception, and it implied that there must be projections of the muscle afferent pathways to the cortex for this to occur. Recent work, as we have seen, has confirmed the presence of these connections.

Muscle and joint afferents not only have access to somatosensory cortex, they also are relayed to the motor cortex. This is illustrated in Fig. 14.12, which shows results from an experiment in an unanesthetized monkey by Robert Porter and R. N. Lemon in Australia in 1976. The recording is from an identified projection neuron (a pyramid cell) in motor cortex, which, as can been seen, responds briskly to movement at a single joint of the finger. Results such as this extend the concept of parallel and serial processing mechanisms underlying perception to include sensory mechanisms within motor areas as well. We shall discuss how this may relate to kinesthesia and "sense of effort" in Chap. 22.

REFERENCES

Adrian, E. D. and Y. Zotterman. 1926. The impulses produced by sensory nerve endings. Part 2. The response of a single end-organ. *J. Physiol.* 61: 151–171.

Alexandrowicz, J. S. 1951. Muscle receptor organs in the abdomen of *Homarus vulgaris* and *Palinarus vulgaris*. *Q. J. microsc. Sci.* 92: 163–199.

Barker, D. 1974. The morphology of muscle receptors. In *Handbook of Sensory Physiology*. Vol III/2, *Muscle Receptors* (ed. by C. C. Hunt). New York: Springer. pp. 1–190.

Brodal, A. 1981. [Chap. 13].

Bullock, T. H. 1976. *Introduction to Neural Systems*. San Francisco: Freeman.

Bush, B. M. H. 1981. Non-impulsive stretch receptors in crustaceans. In *Neurones Without Impulses* (ed. by A. Roberts and B. M. H. Bush). Cambridge: Cambridge University Press. pp. 147–176.

Carpenter, M. B. 1976. [Chap. 13].

Goodwin, G. M., D. I. McCloskey, and P. B. C. Matthews. 1972. The contribution of muscle afferents to kinesthesia shown by vibration induced illusions of movement and by the effects of paralysing joint afferents. *Brain 95:* 705–748.

Katz, B. 1950. Depolarization of sensory terminals and the initiation of impulses in the muscle spindle. *J. Physiol. 111:* 261–282.

Kuffler, S. W. and J. G. Nicholls. 1976. [Chap. 8].

Lemon, R. N. and R. Porter. 1976. Afferent input to movement-related precentral neurones in conscious monkeys. *Proc. Roy. Soc. B 194:* 313–339.

Matthews, B. H. C. 1931. The response of a single end organ. *J. Physiol. 71:* 64–110.

Matthews, P. B. C. 1972. *Mammalian Muscle Receptors and their Central Actions*. London: Arnold.

McCloskey, D. I. 1978. Kinesthestic sensibility. *Physiol. Rev. 58.*

Ottoson, D. and G. M. Shepherd. 1971. Transducer properties and integrative mechanisms in the frog's muscle spindle. In *Handbook of Sensory Physiology. Vol I, Principles of Receptor Physiology* (ed. by W. R. Loewenstein). New York: Springer. pp. 443–499.

Ripley, S. H., B. M. H. Bush, and A. Roberts. 1968. Crab muscle receptor which responds without impulses. *Nature 218:* 1170–1171.

Skoglund, S. 1973. Joint receptors and kinaesthesis. In *Handbook of Sensory Physiology. Vol II, Somatosensory System* (ed. by A. Iggo). New York: Springer. pp. 111–136.

Somjen, G. 1972. [Chap. 11].

Tinbergen, N. 1951. *The Study of Instinct*. Oxford: Oxford University Press.

Additional Reading

Burgess, P. R., J. Y. Wei, F. J. Clark, and J. Simon. 1982. Signalling of kinesthetic information by peripheral sensory receptors. *Ann. Rev. Neurosci. 5:* 171–187.

Matthews, P. B. C. 1982. Where does Sherrington's "muscular sense" originate? Muscles, joints, corollary discharge? *Ann. Rev. Neurosci. 5:* 189–218.

15

The Sense of Balance

All animals exist in a physical environment, and must therefore be able to orient appropriately within it in order to carry out their functions. In a few species, simple contact with the environment is sufficient. This is true, for example, for a sessile animal like the tapeworm that lives its life attached to the gut wall. However, active organisms are always changing in their relations to the environment, and therefore require constant monitoring of those relations. In general, the more active they are, the more important it is to obtain precise information about different aspects of position and movement. This information is the basis for maintaining the *balance,* or *equilibrium,* of the animal, either in anticipation of motor tasks that involve changes in body position or movement, or through reflexes induced by disturbances from the environment.

The different kinds of sensory information that are used in maintaining balance are indicated in Fig. 15.1. Proprioceptive inputs are a constant source of information about the relative positions and movements of different parts of the body. Cutaneous inputs also contribute. Visual information is important, as anyone can discover by seeing how long it is possible

to stand on one foot with eyes closed! Generally, however, these inputs from other sensory systems are not enough, and most organisms have therefore evolved sense organs that are specially adapted for this function.

In general, these special organs fall into two categories. One is the *statocyst.* This characteristically takes the form of a fluid-filled pocket that has, in its wall, a patch (called a *macula*) of sensory cells (see Fig. 15.2). The cells have fine hairs which support, at their tips, some dense crystals glued together with a jellylike material. When the statocyst is tilted, the heavy crystals weigh on the hairs, making them

Fig. 15.1. Sensory modalities that contribute to maintaining balance.

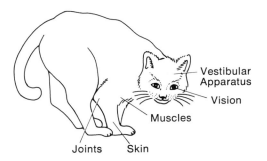

267

A. STATOCYST - MACULA

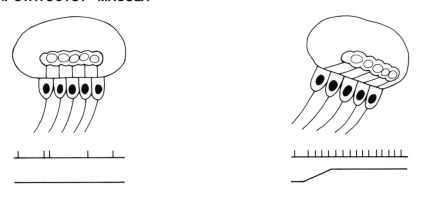

B. CANAL - CRISTA

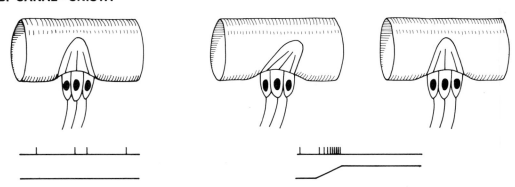

Fig. 15.2. The main types of organs specialized for sensing balance. **A.** The statocyst, or macula, for sensing the force of gravity and linear acceleration. **B.** The canal, with crista, for sensing angular acceleration of movement.

bend (see figure), which leads to an increased discharge of impulses in the sensory fibers. This arrangement is sensitive to velocity and to linear acceleration. Since the mechanism is sensitive to the force of gravity, the statocyst is a *gravireceptor*. Gravity is a universal force on all organisms, and it is not surprising that nearly all active organisms should have gravireceptors. The statocyst must be an effective organ for this purpose, because, with the conspicuous exception of the insects, most animals have gravireceptors constructed along the general lines shown in Fig. 15.2.

The other type of organ contributing to the sense of balance is the *canal*. As shown in Fig. 15.2, it is a fluid-filled canal with a patch of sensory cells in the wall. These cells also have hairs, which project into the lumen, and are embedded in a jellylike substance. The patch of cells forms a raised protuberance which is called a *crista*. When the body moves, the fluid in the canal is displaced, which causes bending of the hairs of the crista, and this is converted into a burst of impulses. As long as the body movement is changing (either accelerating or decelerating) the crista will be bent, but when constant velocity or acceleration is attained, the fluid of the canal moves at the same rate as the body, and the crista returns to its upright position.

Thus, the canal type of organ is specially adapted to detect angular *acceleration*. There are a few examples of this type of organ in invertebrates, but they are a constant feature of the vertebrates, where they are called the *semicircular canals*.

Although the principles expressed in Fig. 15.2 are intuitively clear, the details of the functioning of the organs of balance are exceedingly complicated. This is partly because we are not accustomed to thinking in terms of the properties of movement; thus, although it is relatively easy to think about *static* responses of statocysts to the force of gravity, the relations of mechanical forces to constant *velocity* are more difficult to grasp. Properties related to *acceleration* are even more difficult, involving as they do concepts of mathematical differentiation, phase lag, and the like. This study is becoming increasingly sophisticated, and interested students will

find appropriate references at the end of the chapter. For the remainder of the chapter, however, we will concentrate on the peripheral receptors and their functional circuits within the central nervous system.

Invertebrates

Statocysts were identified in invertebrates by morphologists during the nineteenth century, but they were first mistaken as organs of hearing. Their function as gravity receptors was demonstrated in a classic and oft-told study of Kreidl in Austria in 1893. Kreidl kept an aquarium of shrimp in his laboratory, and was studying their statocysts, which by good fortune (for biologists) open to the outside. Each statocyst contains, as its *statoliths,* grains of sand. Now it happens that each time the shrimp molts, it sheds its statoliths and

Fig. 15.3. Statocyst in a medusa, shown in a horizontal (**A**) and a tilted (**B**) position. (From Singla, in Alexander, 1979)

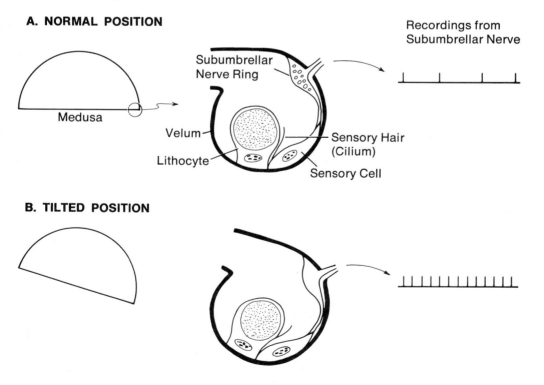

takes in new grains of sand. Kreidl replaced the sand of the aquarium with iron filings, and showed that with a strong magnet he could make the shrimp assume different orientations that were the result of the magnetic and gravitational fields. It could therefore be concluded that the normal stimulus for the statocyst is gravity.

Since that time the statocyst and its gravireceptive function have been demonstrated throughout the invertebrate classes (except for insects). As a matter of fact, the first multicellular sense organs to appear along the phylogenetic scale are the statocyst (for balance) and the ocellus (for vision). Statocysts are found in coelenterates, as in the medusa, where they are located in the rim of the bell. As shown in Fig. 15.3, the *statolith* is contained within the *lithocyte* that secretes it. Next to it is a sensory cell with a cilium that, in the normal resting position of the medusa, does not touch the lithocyte. When the medusa tilts, the weight of the lithocyte presses the lithocyte against the cilium, causing it to bend. This is believed to cause distortion of the sensory cell membrane, setting up a receptor potential and impulses, which are conducted into the subumbrellar nerve ring and induce reflexes that tend to right the organism. It is somewhat sobering to realize that all the basic elements of the sensory and motor systems for sensing and maintaining balance are present so near the lowest rung on the evolutionary ladder!

The nature of the transduction process has been analyzed in the statocyst of the mollusc *Hermissenda*. In this slug, the statocysts are located near the eyes and optic ganglia. A view of the inside of a statocyst, with its group of *statoconia,* is shown in the scanning electron micrograph of Fig. 15.4. Some of the hairs arising from the sensory cells lining the wall can also be seen. Intracellular recordings from single receptor cells during rotation of the experimental preparation have been performed by Daniel Alkon and his colleagues at Woods Hole. With increasing

amounts of centrifugal force, there is an increase in the noise level in the recordings (see Fig. 15.4). These voltage fluctuations are believed to be produced by a shot-noise process of random conductance increases in the hair cell membrane. These fluctua-

Fig. 15.4. **A.** Scanning electron micrograph of the statocyst of the mollusc *Hermissenda*, showing statoconia contacting cilia. **B–D.** Model of statoconia in different relations with cilia. *Right,* Recordings from hair cells, showing increasing depolarization and voltage noise with increasing force of statoconia against cilia, produced by rotating the animal at faster rates. (From Grossman et al., 1979)

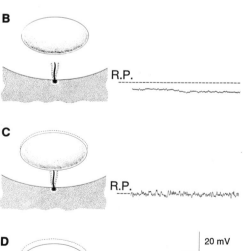

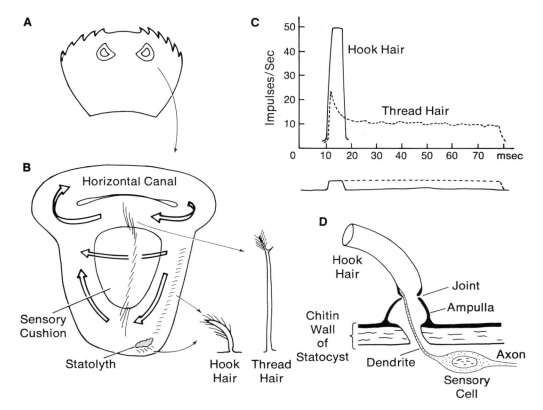

Fig. 15.5. Statocyst of the lobster. **A.** Positions of the statocysts in the body. **B.** Structure of the statocyst, showing difference between hook and thread hairs. **C.** Differing response properties of hook and thread hairs to bending. **D.** Details of base of hook hair and its relation to sensory cell. (Adapted from Cohen, in Markl, 1974)

tions sum to produce the slow depolarizing receptor potential, from which arise impulses at increasing frequencies as the centrifugal force increases. A model of the interactions between statoconium and hair cell that could produce these properties is illustrated in Fig. 15.4B–D.

A more complex type of statocyst is found in crustaceans. In the crab, for example, there is a large statocyst which lies against the antennal nerve that runs from the antenna to the supraesophageal ganglion. The statolith consists of a mass of sand grains stuck together. The hairs that project from the sensory cells into the cavity are of several distinct types (see Fig. 15.5). Depending on their appearance, they are referred to as *hook* hairs and

thread hairs. Some of these hook hairs are in contact with the statoconia, while others end freely. The thread hairs end freely in one part of the statocyst. In general the hairs are quite long, up to 800 μm in length.

Recordings have been made from the axons of the sensory cells under different conditions of movement. Beginning with the studies of Melvin Cohen in Oregon in the 1950's, it has been possible to construct a rather detailed picture of the contributions of the different types of cell. Receptor cells with hook hairs that contact the statolith show slowly adapting responses to bending of the hair (see Fig. 15.5). Since the statolith and the cyst wall are three-dimensional structures, the spa-

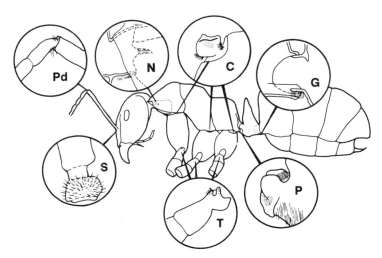

Fig. 15.6. Hair plates at different joints in a worker ant. Pd, joint between first and second antennal segments; N, neck joint; C, coxal joint; G, gaster joint; P, petiole joint; T, joint between trochanter and coxa; S, joint between head and antenna. (From Markl, 1974)

tial pattern of responses from all the sensory cells in contact with the statolith provides a three-dimensional representation to the animal of its position in space relative to gravity. In contrast to the hook hairs, the thread hairs give a phasic-tonic response to an imposed bending (see Fig. 15.5). Since these hairs end freely, they are normally stimulated by movement of the fluid within the cavity caused by rotation of the animal; that is, they are responsive to angular acceleration. Thus, the differing properties of the hairs, and their relations to the statolith and the movement of fluid, enable the statocyst to signal both position of the body relative to gravity and amount of angular acceleration (rotation) of the body.

Among invertebrates, the octopus also has statocysts with these information capacities, which are necessary in animals that move quickly. In both cases, the information is used to bring about reflexes of body musculature to maintain equilibrium. Included in these reflexes are compensatory eye movements that enable the animal to maintain a constant orientation of its eyes despite changes in the position of the body. These properties all have

counterparts, developed to an even higher degree, in the vertebrates.

Before leaving the invertebrates, we should briefly discuss the insects. As already mentioned, insects lack statocysts; one can imagine that these animals need to travel light, and statoliths are too much baggage to carry around. However, the sense of balance is of extreme importance to insects, and this information is provided by an elaborate system of proprioceptors. This system is based on the same fundamental mechanism of the hair cell. As shown in Fig. 15.6, these specialized hair sensilla form *hair plates,* which are present at a number of joints. The hair cells have been found to be extremely sensitive to very small, applied mechanical displacements. It appears, therefore, that the downward pull of gravity on the appendages sets up a differentiated pattern of tonic inputs from the whole set of hair plates, and that this provides the gravitational reference for orienting the muscular activities of the animal. In a sense, the whole exoskeleton of the insect performs the function of the statolith in other arthropods and in molluscs, in providing the hard material that stimulates the hairs; in both cases, gravity is signaled by the entire spatial pattern of tonically firing receptor cells.

Insects also have a mechanism for detecting rotation. In flying insects such as *Diptera,* this is provided by the *halteres.* These are two dumbbell-shaped appendages that are modified hind wings. When the insect is flying, they oscillate rapidly up and down. Changes in direction of flight involve rotation about the axes of the animal, and this is communicated as torques and strains which stimulate certain hair sensilla in the base of the haltere. The haltere thus provides information about angular acceleration in a fashion that in some respects resembles the way that a gyroscope is used for stabilization in aircraft and submarines.

Vertebrates

The fundamental nature of the statocyst as a gravity detector is reflected in the fact that a comparable structure, called an *otolith organ,* is present in all vertebrates. In addition, there are attached to it one or more canals for detecting rotation, which, because of their form, are called *semicircular canals.* Together, the otolith organ and semicircular canals form the *vestibular organ.* In the course of evolution the otolith organ gives rise to an outpocketing which becomes the organ of hearing, the *cochlea.* Together this makes for a very complicated geometry, which the early morphologists (perhaps in bewilderment) dubbed a labyrinth; since it is all enclosed in membranes, the whole structure is called the *membranous labyrinth.*

The key steps in the evolution of the labyrinth are illustrated in Fig. 15.7. These diagrams also indicate the sites of the sensory receptor cells. The otolith organ is divided into two sacs, utricle and saccule, and the receptor cells are grouped in a macula in each sac. Similarly, each semicircular canal has an enlargement (*ampulla*), within which the sensory cells are grouped in a crista.

Structure of the Receptors. The sensory elements of the vestibular organ were diagrammed in Fig. 15.1, and are illustrated in greater detail in Fig. 15.8. Here, again, one finds testimony to the mighty power of the tiny hair as a sensory structure. Each hair cell gives rise to a simple cilium, called a *kinocilium.* This is a true cilium, containing a ring of 9 pairs of tubules. In addition, each cell gives rise to a number of *stereocilia.* These are thin extensions of the

Fig. 15.7. Evolution of the labyrinth in vertebrates. C. ant., anterior crista; C. lat., lateral crista; C. post., posterior crista; M. comm., macula communis; M. lag., macula lagenae; M. negl., macula neglecta; M. sacc., macula sacculi; M. utr., macula utriculi; Pap. bas., papilla basilaris. (From Wersäll and Bagger-Sjöbäck, 1974)

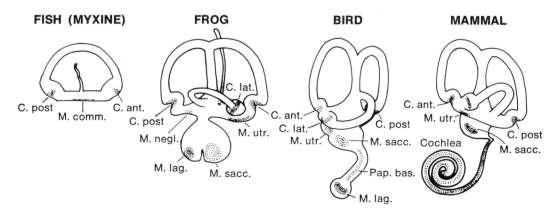

FISH (MYXINE)   FROG   BIRD   MAMMAL

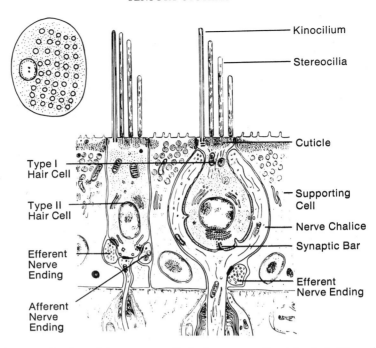

Fig. 15.8. Cellular organization of the sensory cells in the mammalian labyrinth. Note the two types of cell, depending on the size of the afferent terminal. Inset shows relation of single kinocilium to rows of stereocilia. (From Wersäll and Bagger-Sjöbäck, 1974)

cell cytoplasm, enclosed in a three-layered plasma membrane; they are a form of microvillus, rather than a true cilium. These are always shorter than the kinocilium, and grade down in height with distance from it (see Fig. 15.8).

The features thus far described are common to hair cells of both the maculae of the otolith organ and the cristae of the semicircular canals. The accessory structures of the hairs, of course, are quite different. In the maculae, there is a covering of *otoliths*. These are largely composed of calcium carbonate crystals, called *otoconia,* which are glued together by a jellylike matrix to form a thick *otoconial membrane* (see Fig. 15.9). In the cristae, on the other hand, the hairs project into a kind of dome of jelly that reaches across to the other side of the ampulla (see Fig. 15.9).

Because of the placement of the kinocilium to one side of the group of stereoci-

lia, the whole group of hairs has an orientation in the direction of the kinocilium. Each collection of receptors has a characteristic orientation. As shown in Fig. 15.9, in the maculi sacculi the hair cells point away from each other on either side of the midline. In the maculi utriculi the hair cells radiate outward toward a perimeter, where the polarization changes in the opposite direction. As a consequence, movements of the head which cause movements of the otolithic membrane and cupula of the cristae do not simply produce a massive and similar discharge in all the sensory receptors. The situation is nicely summarized in the following quotation from Otto Loewenstein:

In his theoretical exposition of labyrinth function, Mygind . . . compared a macula to the curved palm of a hand holding an irregularly shaped heavy object . . . We are aware of a changing pattern of contact with the complex contours of the object and localize these accurately as the object rolls in the palm . . . In this situation the tactile sense, depending chiefly on an apparently random network of . . . nerve endings, performs a feat of pattern recognition which the orderly arrangement of polarized sensors in a macula is bound to surpass. The difference is that we become aware of tactile sensation but remain ignorant of labyrinthine afference.

Transduction Mechanisms. The hair cells are excited by bending of the hairs in the direction from stereocilia to kinocilia, and inhibited by movement in the opposite direction. The site of transduction of the mechanical stimulus of hair bending into the electrical change in the membrane potential of the cell membrane has been the subject of much speculation. One possibility is that it occurs in the membrane of the kinocilium, or in the basal body at the base of the kinocilium (see Fig. 15.8). Alternatively, it has been suggested that the sterocilia are the site of the response.

This question has been studied directly in recent experiments by Albert Hudspeth

and Richard Jacobs at the California Institute of Technology. They isolated the sacculus of bullfrogs and stimulated the hairs with small probes while recording intracellularly from the hair cell. A typical recording is shown in Fig. 15.10. Then, with very fine microdissection needles, they removed the kinocilium (see Fig. 15.10), and found that the response was unaffected. Stimulation of the kinocilium alone produced no response. They concluded that sterocilia are the structures responsible for transduction in the hair cell. They speculate that the function of the kinocilium is to aid in transmitting mechanical stimuli to the stereocilia, and perhaps to give the hair cell its orientation (as explained above).

Unlike the invertebrate hair cell, which itself gives rise to an axon, the vertebrate hair cell has no axon. The graded receptor response is transmitted by means of chemical synapses to the terminals of sensory fibers. Recent studies have shown that transmission is blocked by the usual

Fig. 15.9. Functional organization of the labyrinth. **A.** Macula, showing covering layer of otolithic membrane. **B.** Different orientations of hairs within the macula. **C.** Crista ampullaris, showing projection of the hairs into a jelly-like tonae. (A from Spoendlin; B from Lindeman, in Wilson and Melvill-Jones, 1979; C from Wersäll and Bagger-Sjöbäck, 1974)

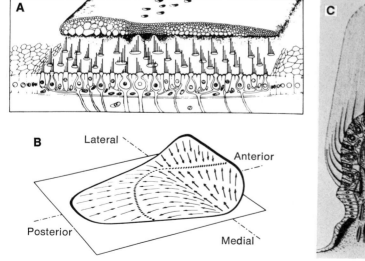

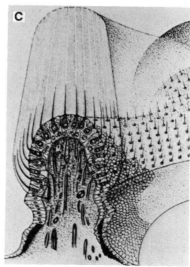

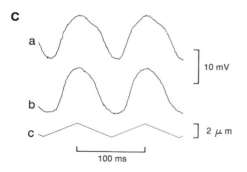

Fig. 15.10. Experiments showing that stereocilia generate the receptor potentials in hair cells. **A.** Scanning electron micrograph showing a group of sterocilia on a single hair cell after removal of the single kinocilium. **B.** View from above, showing how the kinocilium (to the left) was deflected and removed. **C.** Similar receptor potentials obtained from a normal hair cell (a) and from a hair cell with kinocilium deflected as in B. Recordings were by an intracellular electrode. Stimulation was a series of deflections applied to the hair bundle by a vibrating probe (c). (From Hudspeth and Jacobs, 1979)

method of increasing Mg^{2+} and decreasing Ca^{2+}. As indicated in Fig. 15.8, some hair cells (type II) contact small sensory terminals, whereas others (type I) are embraced by large terminals. The significance of this difference is not understood.

Sensory Signaling. Electrophysiological studies have elucidated the relation between head movements and the neural responses transmitted in the nerves. This has required elaborate rotating animal holders, complete with recording instruments. Typical results obtained by Cesar Fernandez and Jay Goldberg at Chicago are illustrated in Fig. 15.11. Note first the high resting rate of impulse activity in these fibers; this high "set point" means that inhibition as well as excitation can be accurately signaled. During slow, constant, angular acceleration (sloped part of monitor trace), the impulse frequency rises to a relatively steady level. This is believed to reflect the press of the displaced endolymph against the cupula of the crista, the amplitude being determined by the balance between the inertial force of the fluid and the elastic restoring force of the cupula. When constant velocity is reached, the discharge returns (with an undershoot) to the resting level. Mathematically, one says that this response represents an integration of the angular acceleration to give a signal proportional to the angular velocity of the head. In doing this, the vestibular mechanism is precisely performing a mathematical operation using mechanical and electrical components, as would an analog computer. When deceleration occurs, this is signaled in the opposite direction, by reduction of the impulse frequency below resting level.

Central Vestibular Pathways

The axons that transmit the hair cell responses to the central nervous system form part of the eighth cranial nerve. There are surprisingly few of these fibers, only about

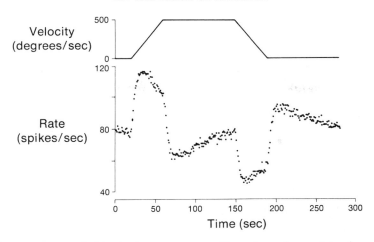

Fig. 15.11. Responses recorded in single sensory nerve fibers from the semicircular canals to stimulation by rotation (angular acceleration) of the whole animal (squirrel monkey). (From Fernandez and Goldberg, 1976)

Fig. 15.12. Divisions of the vestibular nucleus, and their output connections to different parts of the brain. (Modified from Carpenter, 1976)

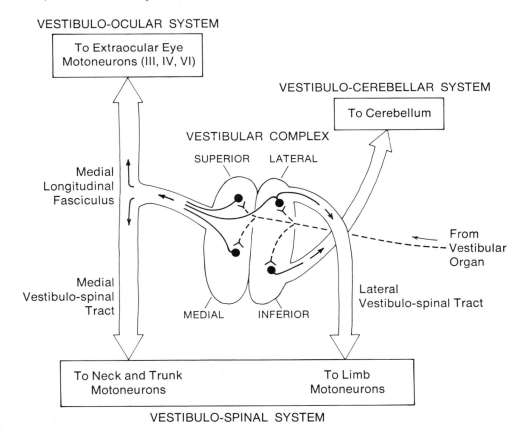

20,000 on each side in most mammalian species, including humans. They enter the brainstem and terminate in several large cell groups, which are called the *vestibular nuclei*. From here there are three main projection systems, as indicated in Fig. 15.12. We will discuss each of these.

Vestibulo-spinal System. Fibers that project to the spinal cord form the vestibulo-spinal pathway. There are two divisions, medial and lateral. The medial tract consists of fibers that arise from cells in most of the vestibular nuclei, and gather in the midline to form the *medial longitudinal fasciculus*. The descending fibers terminate in anterior segments of the spinal cord, where they connect to motoneurons that control the muscles of the neck and trunk. In contrast, fibers to motoneurons that control limb muscles arise from the lateral vestibular nucleus, and descend in the lateral tract. Although these vestibular pathways mediate reflex mechanisms that belong in Section IV, we will discuss them here because they are essential for understanding the sensory functions of the central vestibular pathways.

A basic approach to analyzing vestibular control of body muscles has been to deliver single electrical shocks to the vestibular nerve or vestibular nuclei and record from single spinal neurons. This tells the neurophysiologist whether a synaptic action is excitatory or inhibitory, and whether the action is monosynaptic or mediated through interneurons. Much of this work has been carried out by Victor Wilson and his colleagues at Rockefeller University. A summary of recent studies using these methods is shown in Fig. 15.13. The important conclusions to take away from this diagram are as follows: (1) The macula projects mainly, but not exclusively, to the lateral tract, and the cristae of the canals to the medial tract. (2) The lateral tract is mainly concerned with controlling limb motoneurons, while the medial tract is exclusively concerned with controlling neck and trunk muscles. (3)

Lateral tract fibers are exclusively excitatory, while the medial tract contains both excitatory and inhibitory fibers. (4) Within the spinal cord, lateral tract fibers control motoneurons to the limbs through excitatory or inhibitory interneurons; in other words, the pathway is disynaptic. Medial tract fibers, by contrast, make direct monosynaptic excitatory or inhibitory connections onto neck and trunk motoneurons.

The pathways indicated in Fig. 15.13 provide an extensive system through which the vestibular input can make precise adjustments in body musculature to maintain orientation in space. If we recall the analogy between the vestibular receptor sheet and the palm of the hand, the central system depicted in Fig. 15.13 can be thought of as the internal neural representation of the palm, allowing the body muscles to "feel" the changes occurring in the receptors and adjust their states of contraction accordingly.

Figure 15.13 makes a distinction between the muscles of the head and the body, and this is important in understanding vestibular reflexes. The main point is that the head, which contains the vestibular apparatus, is connected to the neck, the neck to the trunk, and the trunk to the limbs. Neck reflexes are thus the link between movements of the head and the body and limbs. These reflexes were first studied in a systematic way by Rudolf Magnus of the Netherlands in the early part of this century. Modern studies have led to the concept of these reflexes as servosystems for stabilizing the head in space. The neck reflexes act as a closed-loop, negative feedback system; since the neck muscles are attached to the head, their responses to labyrinth stimulation tend to restore the head to its normal position and reduce the stimulation. These reflexes are generally obligatory, and unconscious, which is consistent with the direct synaptic pathways shown in Fig. 15.13. In contrast, body and limb muscles have variable relations to head position, through the linkage of the neck. This may be why the

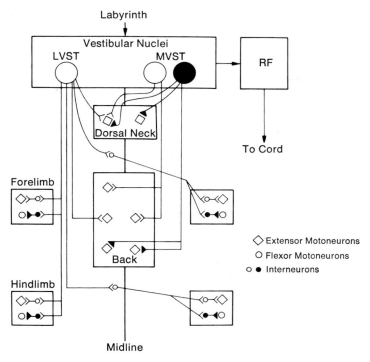

Fig. 15.13. Circuits formed by the medial and lateral vestibulospinal tracts. Open profiles indicate excitatory neurons, closed profiles indicate inhibitory neurons. (From Wilson and Melvill-Jones, 1979)

vestibulospinal system has both excitatory and inhibitory fibers, and the synaptic linkages are through both excitatory and inhibitory interneurons (see Fig. 15.13). A summary of the interacting effects of labyrinthine and neck reflexes on the limbs is shown in Fig. 15.14.

Vestibulo-ocular System. The vestibular system plays a central role in control of the eyes. This is necessary in order to maintain a stable image of the visual field on the retina despite movements of the body. The importance of a stable image is vividly exhibited in the way a bird walks with its head appearing to move with exaggerated jerks. In fact, film analysis of these movements has shown that the head is actually held almost perfectly still relative to the surrounding space, while the body moves along smoothly beneath it! This enables the animal to maintain max-

imal visual sensitivity to movement in its visual field while moving about itself. The stabilization is believed to be brought about by the neck reflexes mentioned above. Presumably, similar though less obvious mechanisms are present in mammals.

Movements of the eyes are controlled by a set of six extraocular muscles; their arrangement is indicated in the diagram of Fig. 15.15. Coordinated movements of both eyes together are called *conjugate movements;* it is obvious that this requires fine coordination of both sets of extraocular muscles.

We can obtain a grasp of the principles involved in this coordination by considering, in a simplified fashion, movements only in the horizontal plane. Consider that we fix our gaze on a point, and then shift our gaze to another point to the left, without moving our head. A recording of this

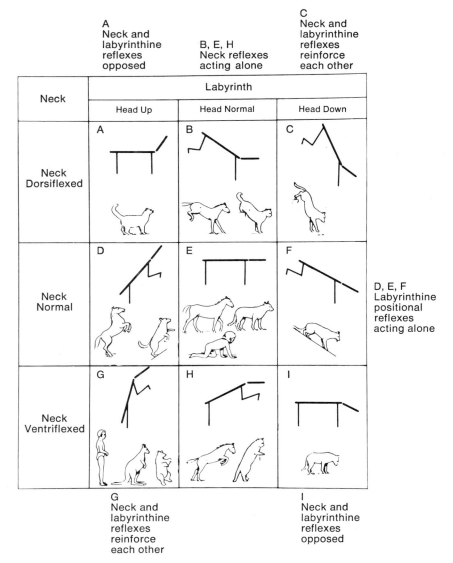

Fig. 15.14. Diagrams showing how the static labyrinthine reflexes and neck reflexes interact in the control of the limbs under different conditions of body posture. (From Roberts, in Wilson and Melvill-Jones, 1979)

mechanical shift of our eyes would look like the trace in Fig. 15.15. In the horizontal plane, this movement is brought about by contraction of the lateral rectus muscle and relaxation of the medial rectus muscle of the left eye, and the opposite activation of muscles in the right eye. This situation, of jumping (*saccadic*) eye movements with the head held still, is characteristic of ac-

tivities like reading or examination of near objects. These movements are controlled by fibers descending from the frontal eye fields of the cerebral cortex to the extra-ocular motoneurons, and do not involve the vestibular system.

Now consider the case in which the gaze of the eyes is directed to a new point in the visual field and the head moves in order to maintain the point at the center of the visual field, with the eyes in their normal centered positions. In this case, the gaze can only remain fixed in the new position by means of compensatory eye movements which are in the opposite direction to the rotation of the head. The relative movements of eye and head are indicated in the traces of Fig. 15.15. The compensatory eye movements are brought about by the *vestibulo-ocular reflex.* For movements in the horizontal plane, the circuit that connects the input from the horizontal canals to the motoneurons controlling the medial and lateral rectus motoneurons muscles is shown in Fig. 15.16. This circuit operates without benefit of visual or other sensory feedback; in systems terminology, one says it is an *open-loop reflex,* in contrast to the closed-loop neck reflexes described previously.

The circuit shown in Fig. 15.16 constitutes a disynaptic pathway from vestibular afferents to extraocular motoneurons. This pathway is supplemented by polysnaptic connections through the *reticular formation,* as is also true for the vestibulospinal system. The disynaptic pathway is consistent with the rapid transmission necessary in controlling eye movements.

One might suppose that a pathway of this kind would be "hard-wired" and immutable. However, much evidence indicates that the connections in this system have an extraordinary degree of plasticity. For example, after removal of one labyrinth, the ability of monkeys to perform a complicated locomotor task falls to zero and then slowly recovers; the recovery presumably depends on the establishment of new or more effective synaptic connections. More dramatically, when people wear spectacles with prisms that invert the visual field, they are initially disoriented and helpless, but gradually learn to move about in a near-normal fashion. This has implied a considerable rearrangement of the synaptic circuits involved in vestibular reflexes. Recent microelectrode studies of single neurons carried out in several laboratories have documented plastic changes in the synaptic connections of the central vestibular pathways after ablations of different components of the system.

Vestibulo-cerebellar System. The importance of the vestibular system for sensorimotor coordination is further shown by

Fig. 15.15. Organization of the extraocular muscles. **A.** Arrangement of the six muscles around the right eyeball. **B.** Jumping saccadic movement, brought about through activity of the descending motor system. **C.** Compensatory eye movements, to maintain visual fixation after movement of the head; this is brought about by the vestibulo-ocular reflex. (Based in part on Morasso et al., in Wilson and Melvill-Jones, 1974)

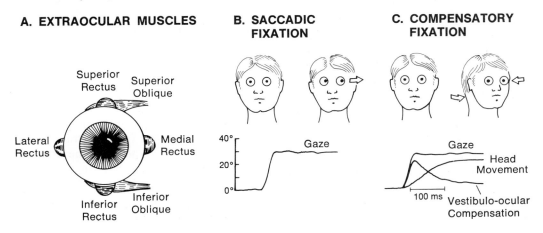

A. EXTRAOCULAR MUSCLES

Superior Rectus   Superior Oblique

Lateral Rectus   Medial Rectus

Inferior Rectus   Inferior Oblique

B. SACCADIC FIXATION

40°
20°
0°

Gaze

C. COMPENSATORY FIXATION

Gaze

Head Movement

100 ms   Vestibulo-ocular Compensation

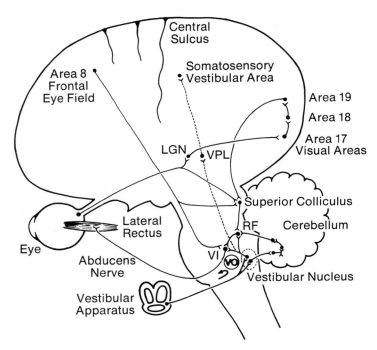

Fig. 15.16. Circuits involved in control of eye movements. For simplicity, only the control of the lateral rectus muscle is illustrated. Similar connections are involved in control of the other extraocular muscles. VI, trochlear nucleus giving rise to the abducens nerve; RF, reticular formation; LGN, lateral geniculate nucleus; VPL, ventroposterior lateral nucleus of thalamus; VO, vestibulo-ocular reflex. (Adapted from Robinson, Gouras, Schmidt, Brodal, and other sources)

the close relations of vestibular pathways to the cerebellum (see Fig. 15.16). We will discuss these relations and functions further in Chap. 22.

Vestibular Cortex. A small number of fibers ascend from the vestibular nuclei to terminate in a small part of the ventral posterior nucleus of the thalamus. From here there is a projection to a small region of cortex within the face area of somatosensory cortex (see Fig. 15.16; also 13.17). It is attractive to suppose that this vestibular cortex is involved in conscious perceptions of balance and movement arising from vestibular inputs. Other studies have suggested that other areas of cortex receive vestibular thalamic inputs, including the somatosensory arm area and the temporal lobe, depending on the species of animal investigated. In addition to these

sensory areas, we should also note that there is a specific and well-known area of the frontal lobe which contains cells that control the voluntary eye movements mentioned above. This is called the frontal eye field; electrical stimulation of this area causes conjugate eye movements to the opposite side. Figure 15.16 summarizes these cortical sensory and motor areas in the human.

The Vestibular System and Weightlessness

We live in the space age. The most dramatic sensory effect of space travel is the effect of weightlessness on the sense of balance. Dr. Joseph Kerwin, who was aboard Skylab 2 in 1973 as the first U.S. physician astronaut in space, describes the experience in the following words,

. . . I would say there was no vestibular sense of the upright whatsoever. I certainly had no idea of where the Earth was at any time unless I happened to be looking at it. I had no idea of the relationship between one compartment of the spacecraft or another in terms of a feeling for "up or down" . . . What one thinks is up, is up. After a few days of getting used to this, one plays with it all the time . . . It's a marvellous feeling of power over space—over the space around one. Closing one's eyes made everything go away. And now one's body is like a planet all to itself, and one really doesn't know where the outside world is.

As the above quotation indicates, the astronauts adapted quickly, over the course of a few days, to the condition of weightlessness, and found the experience (apart from occasional episodes of motion sickness) rather pleasant and intriguing. This adaptability is remarkable if one considers that the vestibular system and the other systems contributing to balance evolved over millions of years without ever having been exposed to these conditions.

Some indication of the neural processes of adaptation that take place during flight is seen in the behavior of the astronauts after return to earth. In a simple experiment carried out by J. L. Hornick and his colleagues, the astronauts were tested on their ability to stand, one foot in front of the other, on narrow rails of different widths, from ¾ in. to 2¼ in. (1.9–5.7 cm), as well as on the floor. The Skylab 3 pilot was typical in showing a deficit on the day after splashdown in his ability to stand on relatively narrow rails with eyes open, with recovery to normal on subsequent testing days. Even with the thickest rail, there was a long-lasting deficit in the ability to maintain standing balance with the eyes closed; in fact, on the day after splashdown, he could barely stand on the floor with eyes closed, but improved to normal on the subsequent test.

These data give clear evidence that postural mechanisms are affected by prolonged periods (8–10 weeks) of weightlessness. Probably several systems contribute to these results. First, the leg muscles undergo a degree of disuse atrophy during flight, which probably affects the ability to stand in the immediate recovery period. Second, muscle tendon reflexes are hyperactive; this could cause incoordination of the muscles used in standing. Finally, it has been postulated that a "pattern center" in the central nervous system undergoes a process of habituation during flight, and that this process must be reversed on return to earth. This pattern center integrates inputs from the vestibular organ, the muscle and tendon receptors, and the tactile receptors in the skin and deep tissues. It represents the distributed system for the maintenance of standing posture. The ability of this entire system to adapt between the conditions of normal gravity and zero gravity is in accord with the remarkable degrees of plasticity that are present in nervous circuits in general, and have already been demonstrated in parts of the vestibular system, as mentioned above in connection with the vestibulo-ocular system. It may be hoped that there will be opportunities to test this hypothesis, through experiments on animals as well as humans, in further space flights in the near future.

REFERENCES

Alexander, R. McN. 1979. *The Invertebrates.* Cambridge: Cambridge University Press.

Carpenter, M. B. 1976. *Human Neuroanatomy.* Baltimore: Williams & Wilkins.

Fernandez, C. and J. M. Goldberg. 1976. Physiology of peripheral neurons innervating otolith organs of the squirrel monkey. III. Response dynamics. *J. Neurophysiol. 39:* 996–1008.

Grossman, Y., D. L. Alkon, and E. Heldman. 1979. A common origin of voltage noise and generator potentials in statocyst hair cells. *J. Gen. Physiol. 73:* 23–48.

Homick, J. L., M. F. Reschke, and E. F. Miller II. 1977. The effects of prolonged exposure to weightlessness on postural equilibrium. In *Biomedical Results from Skylab* (ed. by R. S. Johnston and L. F.

Dietlein). Washington, D. C.: National Aeronautics and Space Administration. pp. 104–112.

Hudspeth, A. J. and R. Jacobs. 1979. Stereocilia mediate transduction in vertebrate hair cells. *Proc. Natl. Acad. Sci. 76:* 1506–1509.

Kerwin, J. P. 1977. Skylab 2 crew observations and summary. In Johnston and Dietlein (eds.), op. cit., pp. 27–29.

Loewenstein, O. E. 1974. Comparative morphology and physiology. In *Handbook of Sensory Physiology.* Vol VI/I, *Vestibular System Part 1: Basic Mechanisms* (ed. by H. H. Kornhuber). New York: Springer. pp. 75–123.

Markl, H. 1974. The perception of gravity and of angular acceleration in invertebrates. In Kornhuber (op. cit.), pp. 17–74.

Wersäll, J. and D. Bagger-Sjöbäck. 1974. Morphology of the vestibular sense organ. In Kornhuber (op. cit.), pp. 123–170.

Wilson, V. J. and G. Melvill-Jones. 1979. *Mammalian Vestibular Physiology.* New York: Plenum.

Additional Reading

Precht, W. 1979. Vestibular mechanisms. *Ann. Rev. Neurosci. 2:* 265–289.

16
Hearing

The senses we have considered thus far are widespread throughout the animal kingdom. Information about molecules and chemicals, the physical environment, muscular states, and spatial orientation may be considered obligatory for any multicellular organism that carries on an active life. We now consider a type of information that is less widespread. Audition—the sense of hearing—is largely limited to the insects and the vertebrates. This, of course, does not mean it is any less important; on the contrary, those species that have this sense use it with great effectiveness in various ways, e.g., to escape predators, find mates, and communicate socially. And in humans, there can be little doubt that hearing has been the key to development of language and, through it, much of our culture.

A good approach to our discussion of this modality is to begin with some definitions. Audition in its broadest interpretation is the sense of sound. Generally speaking, sound consists of waves of compression of air or water. Sound waves are produced by a wide variety of natural phenomena, including many kinds of animal movements—the beating of wings, for example, or the clatter of hooves. These sounds are important; indeed, they may be matters of life or death, e.g., a warning of an approaching predator. However, audition is commonly treated more specifically as the reception of sounds made explicitly by one member of a species to communicate to another; it is here that the full potentialities of the auditory sense are realized.

The mechanisms that animals have developed for producing sounds for communication will be considered in Chap. 24. Here we will note that the sounds vary in their frequency over a wide range; the ranges for a number of different animals are shown in Fig. 16.1. Some species have relatively narrow ranges (some crickets, frogs, birds). Some ranges extend to extremely low frequencies (fish, whales and dolphins, man). The lowest frequencies, in fact, involve vibrations that act as stimuli for various kinds of mechanoreceptors in the body, as well as auditory receptors. Some species are able to sense extremely high frequencies, as high as 100 kHz (various mammals and insects). It is interesting to compare the wavelength at this frequency (a few millimeters) with that at the extremely low frequencies (almost 20 feet). Finally, some species have very broad

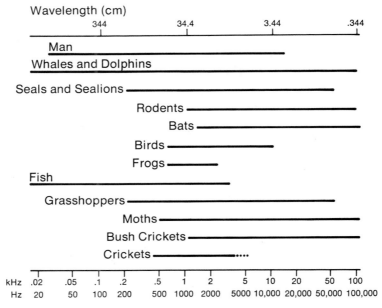

Fig. 16.1. Hearing ranges of different animals. Scales: kHz, 1000 cycles per seconds; wavelength, centimeters. (After Lewis and Gower, 1980)

ranges (especially whales and dolphins, and man). Within these different ranges, many species are tuned to certain frequencies of special importance for their behavior, as we shall see.

Modern studies of audition employ sophisticated instruments and rigorous mathematical methodologies, and many of the results are expressed in terms of decibels, power spectra, Bode plots, and other concepts that are difficult for the beginning student to grasp. We will therefore limit our attention to the structures and properties of different kinds of auditory receptors, and the central nervous circuits for processing auditory information.

INVERTEBRATES

Most invertebrates are sensitive to low-frequency vibrations emanating from their environment. In general, these vibrations are due to sounds, like a clap of thunder, or the tread of an animal, which signal danger, and produce generalized startle or escape reactions. Such vibrations produce

physical displacements which are sensed in most animals by mechanoreceptors of the somatosensory and proprioceptive systems, without further specializations.

Auditory Receptors

Insects have developed special receptors for low-frequency sounds. One type of such a receptor is the *thread hair*. This is a kind of hair sensillum located on small appendages called *cerci*. Another type of receptor is called *Johnston's organ*. This is located at the base of an antenna, and consists of a cavity spanned by one or more elongated sensory cells called a *chordotonal sensillum*. Thread hairs and Johnstone's organs are sensitive to sounds up to about 2 kHz (in other words up to a medium-pitched hum).

Reception of high-pitched, true "auditory" sounds is found only in certain insects. The receptors are the *tympanic organs*. These function like the ears of vertebrates, except that they are markedly different in structure and functional properties. Also, insect ears may be located in many different places on the body: on the antennae (flies), thorax (moths), abdomen (beetles), or legs (locusts). The tympanal organ is actually a modification of an inlet of the tracheal system used for respiration. It consists of a thin membrane of cuticle, called a *tympanum*, drawn over an air cavity to make a kind of drum head. Sound waves produce vibrations of the membrane, and these are sensed by chordotonal sensilla attached at one end to the drum (see Fig. 16.2). There may be only one chordotonal sensillum, or there may be as many as 1000 sensilla. Regardless of how many there are, each contains a bipolar sensory neuron with a cilium at one end; the cilium attaches to the underside of the tympanum through a complicated joint. Variations in the structure of this joint and in the resonant properties of the tympanic membrane confer different frequency-tuning characteristics on the tympanal organs of different species.

A standard way of analyzing auditory receptors is to record from single cells and determine the stimulus intensity necessary to give a threshold response at different frequencies of pure tones. This yields what is called a *tuning curve*. Figure 16.3 shows typical results obtained in recordings from single fibers of receptor cells in crickets. Two classes of response are found in this animal. One class has a low threshold at a

Fig. 16.2. Cross section through tympanal organ of a noctuid moth. (From Treat and Roeder, in Gordon, 1970)

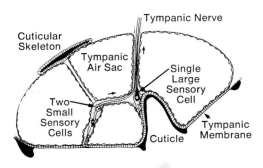

medium frequency around 5 kHz, but the threshold rises rapidly when tested with surrounding frequencies. Such cells are said to have a *best frequency* or *characteristic frequency* around 5 kHz, and to be *sharply tuned*, or have *narrow bands*. The frequency of the song that crickets use to call to each other has a frequency of about 5 kHz, so these receptors appear to be adapted for the purpose of hearing this song.

The nature of this song, and the motor mechanisms for producing it, will be discussed in Chap. 24. Here we note simply that the song consists of sound bursts (*chirps*) repeated at different intervals. Thus, the main variable in information transmission is the amplitude modulation of the signal. The tympanal receptors are slowly adapting, which ensures accurate reception and encoding of the changes in signal amplitude and duration. Several other properties of the receptors are also important. One is that the receptor response varies with the logarithm of the stimulus intensity. Another is that different receptors have different thresholds at their best frequencies. These two properties provide the basis for *intensity discrimination*, and with it, the ability to determine the distance of a calling cricket. Finally, the construction of the tympanal organ (see Fig. 16.2) imparts a directionality to signal reception, so that the cricket has the means for *sound localization*. Thus, the properties of the tympanal organ and its receptors provide the mechanisms for discriminating most of the characteristics of the auditory signal from a conspecific individual: frequency, amplitude, intensity, and localization.

The second main class of tympanal auditory receptors is broadly tuned over a wide band that covers high frequencies (see Fig. 16.3). In crickets the frequencies reach beyond the human range, up to 30 kHz, and in other insects they may go even higher (see Fig. 16.1). These high frequencies are part of the courtship call between crickets (see below). In addition, they cover

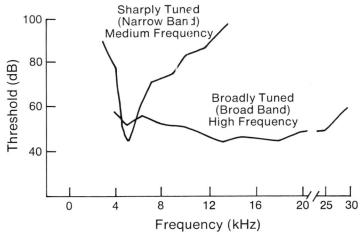

Fig. 16.3. Tuning curves for single auditory nerve fibers in the cricket. (After Markovich, in Elsner and Popov, 1978)

the range of sounds emitted by various predators (for example, bats). The receptors do not have to be sharply tuned for these information purposes; hence, their broad band and relatively low threshold (high sensitivity). It appears that these receptors are specially adapted for detecting the sounds of natural predators and alerting the organism so that it can perform appropriate escape maneuvers.

Central Auditory Pathways

The auditory receptor cells in insects give rise to axons which connect directly to the central nervous system. Recent studies of these connections, and the central auditory pathways arising from them, illustrate in a beautiful way the effective use of single-neuron recording and staining techniques. The results may be illustrated in relation to the diagrams of Figs. 16.4 and 16.5.

The axons of relatively low-frequency (LF) receptors (those tuned to 5 kHz) enter their segmental ganglion and terminate in a circumscribed region called the *auditory neuropil*. Some neurons in the ganglion receive and integrate these inputs

from both sides of the body, and therefore play a role in sound localization. Other neurons receive the inputs and, through ascending axons, transmit the signals to other ganglia and to the brain. These neurons have similar LF tuning properties to those of LF hair cells; these *LF relay cells* therefore mediate specific information about the conspecific calling sound. Appropriate to this task, the responses of these neurons reflect very accurately the characteristics of the "chirps" as transmitted by the LF hair cells. The ascending axons of these cells make monosynaptic connections onto motoneurons, to bring about immediate motor orientation to the right calling song. In the brain, the axons distribute terminals in the vicinity of the mushroom bodies, the highest integrative centers in the insect nervous system.

The axons of high-frequency (HF) hair cells also terminate, but more widely, in the segmental auditory neuropil (see Fig. 16.4B). There they make connections onto *HF relay neurons*. These neurons receive bilateral inputs, and their ascending axons make more widespread connections in the neuropil of other ganglia and of the brain. The HF neurons have broad tuning curves

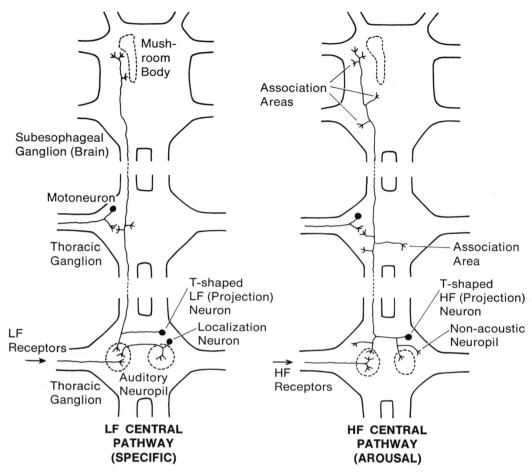

Fig. 16.4. Central auditory pathways in the cricket. Single neurons are shown, as stained by intracellular dye injection and identified physiologically as low-frequency (LF) cells for specific auditory discrimination (on the left), and high-frequency (HF) cells for arousal (on the right). (After Rehbein, in Elsner and Popov, 1978)

over the higher frequency range, similar to HF hair cells, and are therefore tuned to mediate information about sounds of predators. They also are tuned to the high-frequency sounds that are part of the courtship call of the cricket. The widespread connections of the HF relay neurons provide for generalized arousal and escape reactions of the animal in response to the high-pitched sounds of predators. The courtship call, in contrast, consists of alternating low-frequency "chirps" and high-frequency "ticks"; this specific se-

quence causes arousal of the female without eliciting the escape reactions (see Fig. 16.4), and leads to mating (see Chap. 28).

The central auditory pathways thus illustrate a division between specific pathways for sensory discrimination and more widespread pathways for arousal, a division that is also present in vertebrates. Also, the temporal sequence of sensory signals in these pathways is critical in calling forth different behavioral responses, another important principle in the organization of central nervous systems.

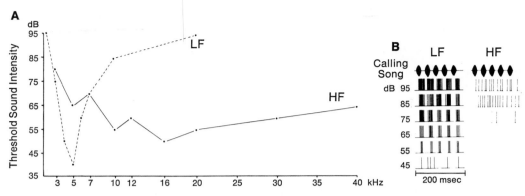

Fig. 16.5. A. Tuning curves for single low-frequency (LF) and high-frequency (HF) auditory cells in the central nervous system of the cricket. **B.** Different response properties of LF and HF cells in response to the conspecific calling song. (From Rheinlander et al. in Elsner and Popov, 1978)

VERTEBRATES

Lateral Line Organs and Electroreception

The sense of hearing in the vertebrates has an interesting and rather complicated phylogenetic history (see Table 16.1). It is very closely related to the development of the vestibular apparatus. Both senses are commonly regarded as adaptations of the *lateral line organ.* Lateral line organs are found in all aquatic vertebrates, from primitive cyclostomes like the lamprey up through the amphibia. They consist of either pits (*ampullae*) or tubes along the sides of the body, head, or snout of the animal. At the base of the pit, or at intervals along the tubes, are tight clusters of cells, called *neuromasts.* The cells are a type of hair cell, with the hairs embedded in a gelatinous mass that projects into the fluid-filled pit or tube.

The specific stimulus for the hair cells varies in different species. In some it is *mechanical vibrations* set up by the turbulence of the water around the fish. In others it may be changes in *hydrostatic pressure.* The receptors in some species are also very sensitive to *temperature,* or to the *salinity* (saltiness) of the water. Finally, in certain species of fish, these receptors are sensitive to *electrical signals.*

Although electroreception is not found in higher vertebrates, it is a fascinating sensory capability that deserves mention here. The most sensitive electroreceptors are in pits called *ampullae of Lorenzini,* which are distributed on the head and snout of certain species of fish. The threshold for eliciting a response in an in-

Table 16.1 Evolution of organs for electroreception and hearing in the vertebrates

	Lateral line	Electro-location	Hearing	Echo-location	Hearing for communication
Cyclostomes					
Cartilaginous fish					
Bony fish					
Amphibians					
Reptiles					
Birds					
Mammals					

dividual receptor can be as low as 1 μV/cm (that is, an electric field with a gradient of 1 μV for each centimeter of distance). The threshold for a behavioral response is 10–100 times higher. The electric fields may be set up by discharge of an electric organ in the same fish; nearby objects produce distortions of the field, which are sensed by the electroreceptors. Alternatively, the electroreceptors may sense the fields set up by the electric organ discharges of other fish.

The mechanism of electroreception is summarized in Fig. 16.6. The stimuli applied by the experimenter are steps of voltage. Within the ampulla these become rounded, because the walls have a high capacitance. In this way the ampulla acts as a low-pass filter (it reduces the high-frequency step while letting the steady voltage pass through; this is just the opposite of the action of a Pacinian corpuscle on a pressure step). The stimulus is transduced into a receptor potential in the hair cell. This alters the release of neurotransmitter at synapses onto nerve terminals. The postsynaptic potentials in the terminal encode the receptor response as modulations in the ongoing spontaneous activity of the nerve.

Note that the hair cell has no axon and transmits only graded potentials; this is a basic characteristic of the vertebrate hair cell, whether vestibular or auditory. The synaptic linkage provides for more complex processing at this peripheral level than is the case for invertebrate hair cells. Note also the high rate of resting impulse discharge in the nerve; this means that inhibitory as well as excitatory changes are faithfully encoded. This high set point is a common property of many cells in the vestibular and auditory pathways and the associated cerebellar system. In some species the resting frequency is incredibly constant, which enhances the ability of the nerve to transmit extremely small signals and have them detected by centers in the central nervous system.

The sequence of events illustrated in Fig. 16.6 applies to ampullary electroreceptors in teleost (bony) fish. The details of the sequence vary in other species, and in other types of receptor organs. Thus, in the am-

Fig. 16.6. Organization and physiological properties of cells in the ampullary electroreceptor organ of the marine catfish. (After Obara, in Viancour, 1979)

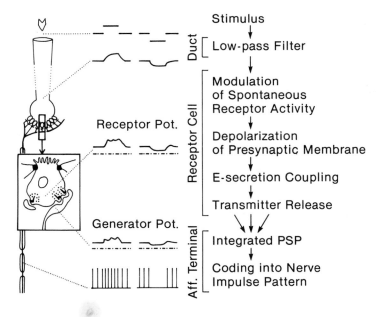

pullary electroreceptors of elasmobranch (cartilaginous) fish, the polarities of electric signals giving depolarizing and hyperpolarizing receptor potentials are the opposite of those shown in the figure. Tuberous electroreceptor organs, found in some electric fish, are generally less sensitive than ampullary receptors, and show lower resting discharge rates and differences in the way electric signals are encoded into impulse discharges.

The Ear of Mammals

Hearing reaches its highest development in birds and mammals; in fact, the organ of hearing in these animals is one of the most complex of all sensory organs. We will describe this organ and the central auditory pathways in the mammal, with brief mention of lower forms.

The organ of hearing—the ear—has three main parts (see Fig. 16.7). The *outer ear* aids in the collection of sound and funnels it through the external ear canal to the tympanic membrane. The *middle ear* contains a system of small bones—hammer, anvil, and stirrup—that conveys the vibrations of the tympanic membrane to the inner ear. The *inner ear* consists of a fluid-filled bag, the *cochlea*, which developed as an outpouching from the vestibular labyrinth (see Fig. 15.7). The fluid of the cochlea is continuous with the perilymph of the vestibular labyrinth. Through the middle of the cochlea stretches the *basilar membrane*, containing the hair cells which are the auditory sensory receptors.

In order for sound to stimulate the hair cells, it must first be transmitted mechanically to the inner ear, and then stimulate the hair cells in an appropriate manner. The first step requires changing the sound waves from vibrations in air to vibrations of the perilymph. This is achieved through the intermediary movements of the middle ear bones. Since air is highly compressible but perilymph is incompressible, the bones must provide for a matching of the forces

in the two media, a process called *impedance matching*. They do this by absorbing energy from the large area of the tympanic membrane and concentrating it in the small area of stirrup where it fits against an opening (the *oval window*) in the bone onto the membrane surrounding the cochlea.   round

The next step is to induce appropriate vibrations in the basilar membrane that contains the hair cells. The cochlea in humans is a coiled structure; we can understand its function best if we imagine it straightened out, as in Fig. 16.7C. We then see that the overall size of the cochlea tapers like a cone toward a tip, so that there is a *base*, at the oval window, and an *apex*, at the tip. In contrast, the basilar membrane is *narrower* at the base, and *widens* at the apex. The student has to remember, therefore, that the basilar membrane gets wider while the cochlea gets narrower.

When the early anatomists first examined the basilar membrane under the microscope, they observed cross-striations that reminded them of the strings of a piano. They imagined that the short strings would resonate in response to high notes, and the long strings to low notes. Helmholtz, the great physiologist and physicist of the late nineteenth century, formulated these ideas as the *resonance theory of hearing*, which states that different frequencies are encoded by their precise position along the basilar membrane. This attractive theory fell victim, however, at least in part, to a stubborn fact. A string will not vibrate unless it is under tension; when George von Bekesy tested this by making tiny slits in the basilar membrane of cochleas obtained from cadavers, he found that the edges of the slit did not pull apart, as they would if the membrane were under tension.

By direct observation, von Bekesy found that vibratory movement is transmitted as a *traveling wave* along the basilar membrane from the round window to the apex. As shown in Fig. 16.7D, the wave has its largest amplitude at a specific site along

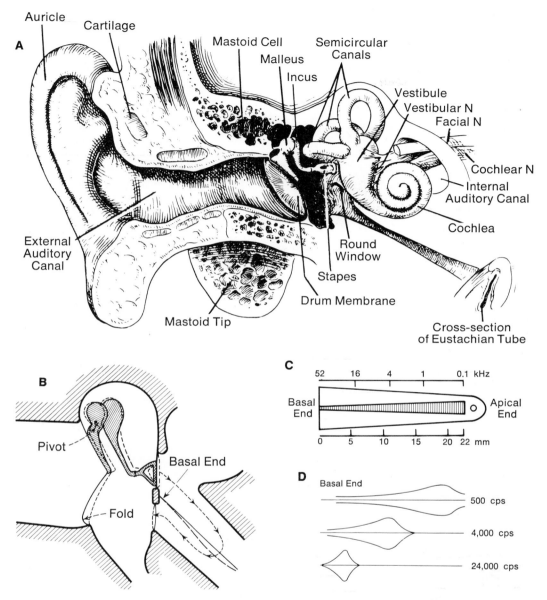

Fig. 16.7. The human ear. **A.** The main structures of the outer, middle, and inner ear. **B.** Transmission of sound vibrations through the middle ear to the inner ear (cochlea). **C.** Diagram of the cochlear partition and the basilar membrane (above), and the travelling waves and their external envelopes induced by sound at different frequencies. (A,B from Davis and Silverman, 1970. C, D based on von Bekesy, 1960)

the membrane, depending on the frequency. Thus, although the wave itself travels, the envelope of the wave is stationary for a given frequency. The peak displacements for high frequencies are toward the base (where the basilar membrane is narrowest) and for low frequencies are toward the apex, just as Helmholtz postulated, but the envelope of the traveling wave is broader than he envisaged.

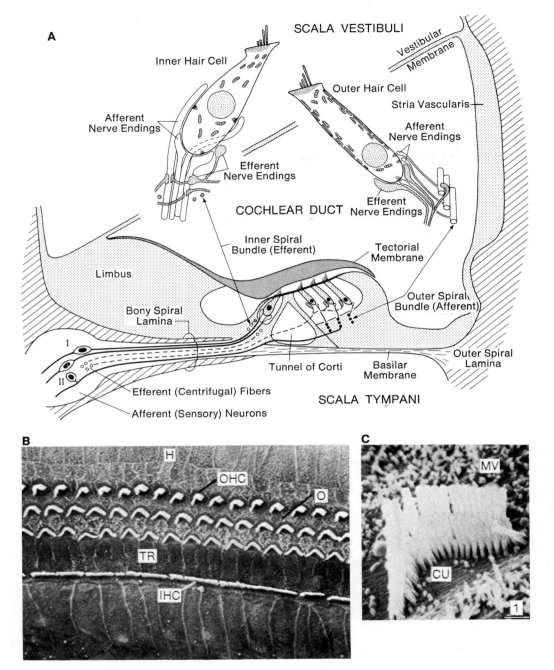

Fig. 16.8. A. Cellular organization of the cochlea (organ of Corti) of the guinea pig. Enlarged diagrams (see arr[o]
summarize the fine structure of the inner and outer hair cells. **B.** Scanning electron micrograph, looking down on
cells, showing differences in arrangements of the inner (IHC) and outer (OHC) hair cells and their stereocilia
Henson's cell; TR, tunnel rod. **C.** Scanning electron micrograph of stereocilia of an outer hair cell. MV, micro
(stereocilia); CU, cuticular plate. (From Smith, in Eagles, 1975; A redrawn from Smith in Brodal, 1981)

It is sharpened at higher frequencies by the fact that the fibrous matrix of the basilar membrane is more elastic and freer to move (less loaded) toward the base.

Hair Cell Receptor Mechanisms. How do these movements of the basilar membrane cause stimulation of the hair cells? As shown in Fig. 16.8, the hair cells rest on the basilar membrane, with their raised tips covered by a thin flap of tissue called the *tectorial membrane.* There are two types of hair cell, depending on their relation to the tunnel of Corti (see Fig. 16.8). *Outer hair cells* number about 20,000, and are arranged in three rows. Their hairs are organized in a characteristic V-shape, as seen from above (Fig. 16.8). *Inner hair cells* number about 3500 (in humans), and are arranged in a single row. The hairs of hair cells are actually microvilli, equivalent in structure to the stereocilia of vestibular hair cells; there are no kinocilia in mature auditory hair cells. The auditory

stereocilia vary in height (particularly those of outer hair cells), and the tallest have their tips actually embedded in the tectorial membrane (Fig. 16.8). It is believed that movements of the basilar membrane relative to the tectorial membrane produce a shearing movement in the hairs, and that this constitutes the stimulus of the hair cell, but the membrane mechanisms are still unknown. The mechanisms probably are similar to those in vestibular hair cells; this conclusion is supported by the similar structure of the stereocilia, the fact that in the vestibular cells the stereocilia (not the kinocilia) are the site of the transduction (see Chap. 15), and the similar large gradients of electric potential between perilymph and hair cells in the two cases.

Intracellular recordings have been very difficult to obtain because of the small size and relative inaccessibility of the hair cells, but recently these experiments have been accomplished. A typical recording is shown in Fig. 16.9a. When tested with

Fig. 16.9. Intracellular recordings from single inner hair cells in the guinea pig cochlea. Graph shows tuning curves for the receptor potential, as obtained from two-tone suppression. Excitatory iso-response curve for DC response component shown by (●); inhibitory iso-response curve for AC response component shown by (○). Insets: a, DC receptor potential at best frequency (17kHz); b, tone burst monitor; stimulus duration, 80 msec; c, DC responses to series of tone bursts at frequencies from 1 to 23 kHz, showing best frequency response around 17 kHz; d, example of recordings showing two-tone suppression. During repeated responses to test tone at 17 kHz, the suppressing tone was swept from 1 to 23 kHz. Note suppression in upper (AC) trace, and response to suppressing tone at 17 kHz in lower (DC) trace. e, same, louder suppressing tone. These data were used to plot graph. (From Russell and Sellick, 1978, and Sellick and Russell, 1979)

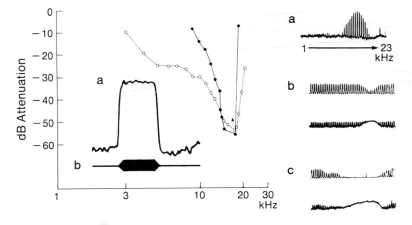

different tones, hair cells show a *best,* or *characteristic* frequency, with much lower responsiveness to other frequencies; in other words, they are *sharply tuned.* This came as something of a surprise, because the sharpness of the tuning curve is in contrast to the broad envelope of the traveling wave. This has implied that there is a sharpening mechanism between the movement of the basilar membrane and the displacement of the hairs. It has been suggested that this mechanism may involve some special properties of the tectorial membrane, and of the relation of the membrane to the tips of the hairs.

Another interesting result of the intracellular studies has been the finding of *two-tone suppression* in the hair cells. The experiment works like this. One records the response of a hair cell to a tone at its best frequency. A second tone is then added at different frequencies above and below the best frequency. One finds that the effect is to reduce the responsiveness of the cell in the region around the best frequency. This effect is shown in insets *d* and *e* of Fig. 16.9, and plotted in the graph. This reduction in responsiveness is a form of *contrast enhancement,* one of the fundamental properties of sensory systems, as we discussed in Chap. 11. It is also seen at higher levels in the auditory pathway, and was thought for a long time to arise by synaptic mechanisms, such as those involved in lateral inhibition in other systems. The experiments in hair cells, however, show that to some extent this property is present already at the level of transmission of the mechanical stimulus to the hairs, or in the process of sensory transduction. From these studies has arisen the notion that cochlear transmission of sound involves a *first filter,* the traveling wave, and a *second filter,* the sharpening mechanisms discussed above.

Further insight into the mechanisms for frequency analysis at the receptor level can be gained by considering the ears of lower vertebrates. In *amphibians,* the hair cells are contained in an elongated patch called

a *papilla* (see Fig. 15.7). These cells have relatively sharp tuning curves, and also display two-tone suppression, despite the absence of a basilar membrane (and its traveling wave). In *reptiles,* such as lizards, a tectorial membrane covers only the low-frequency region of the papilla, and it has been suggested that high-frequency selectivity may depend on graded differences in lengths of the cilia of the hair cells. In *birds,* mechanical transmission in the middle ear is mediated by only one middle ear bone, and there are a number of differences in the cellular components of the cochlea. Thus, comparative studies indicate that some properties, such as the traveling wave, are adaptations for certain species, and that the basic mechanism of frequency selectivity and frequency response interactions may depend on special properties of the hair cells themselves. In mammals, there is speculation at present that the generally linear properties of the basilar and tectorial membranes, that have been observed to date, may be significantly modified by nonlinear properties not seen in preparations from cadavers, or which may be obscured by present experimental techniques.

Auditory Nerve Fibers. Since vertebrate hair cells lack axons, the auditory signals are transmitted to the central nervous system by a second-order neuron. This is a bipolar ganglion cell, with its cell body in the cochlea. The peripheral fiber of this cell receives synapses of the hair cells. The innervation pattern of the hair cells is quite complex, and puzzling in many respects. We have previously remarked on the relatively small number of hair cells. Similarly, there are only about 25,000 auditory nerve fibers in mammals, including humans. It is sobering to think that human language, and so much of our society and culture, depends on these fibers. It recalls the words of Winston Churchill: "Seldom has so much been owed by so many to so few."

The puzzling aspect of the hair cell innervation is that 95% of the sensory auditory fibers connect only to the inner hair cells, which, it will be recalled, number only a few thousand, and account for only about 20% of the total hair cell population. In contrast, the more numerous outer hair cells connect to only a few sensory fibers. There is thus multiple innervation (convergence) of inner hair cells, which presumably gives great security of transmission, in contrast to the ramifying innervation of many outer hair cells by a single fiber (divergence), which would make activation of the fiber by a single hair cell contingent on simultaneous activity in its neighbors (see Fig. 16.10). The functional significance of these differences is not yet understood. The fact that it is only the hairs of outer cells that make firm contact with the tectorial membrane adds to the possible functional contrasts. At present it is thought that the major flow of au-

Fig. 16.10. **A.** Patterns of innervation of the hair cells. Afferent (sensory) nerves shown on left, efferent (centrifugal) fibers shown on right. SG, spiral ganglion (sensory) cells. **B.** Tuning curves for single auditory nerve fibers. (A from Spoendlin, in Patton et al., 1976; B from Galambos and Davis, 1943)

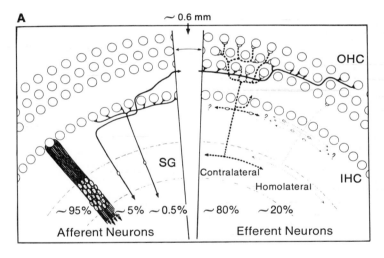

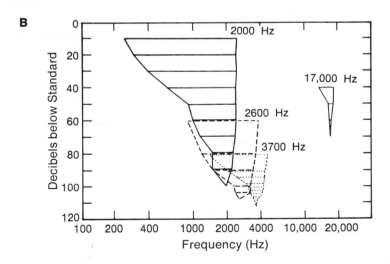

ditory responses is through the inner hair cells, with critical contributions to signal properties made by the outer hair cells.

Single-unit recordings from individual auditory nerve fibers provided some of the earliest and most essential information about the encoding of auditory signals. This work, by Hallowell Davis and David Galambos in the 1940's, showed that each fiber has a characteristic tuning curve (see Fig. 16.10). As already mentioned, it is now known that the hair cells themselves have similar tuning curves, so the synaptic coupling between hair cells and nerve fibers provides for faithful transmission of this crucial property. An important result of the single-fiber recordings was also the finding that the nerve impulses fired in synchrony with low-frequency vibrations, but only up to about 1 kHz, or about 1000 per sec. The fibers cannot fire above this frequency because the refractory period associated with each impulse lasts about 1 msec. These results proved that auditory frequency could not be encoded solely by the frequency of impulse firing. Rather, frequency is encoded primarily by position along the basilar membrane, referred to as *tonotopic organization*. Impulse frequency may contribute to coding at low frequencies, but in general it is primarily involved in coding stimulus *intensity*. It may be noted that in the absence of stimulation, the auditory fibers show considerable spontaneous activity. This means that hair cells, synapses, and auditory fibers are primed to respond to threshold stimuli and small changes in stimulation, just as in most other sensory systems.

In addition to the afferent fibers carrying sensory inputs, there are also efferent fibers to the hair cells. These arise from cells in the olivary nucleus of the brainstem, and make synaptic connections to the hair cells (see Fig. 16.10). Stimulation of these fibers causes suppression of the responses of the hair cells. Centrifugal, or descending, control is common in sensory systems. These fibers might in some way protect the hair cells from overstimula-

tion, but beyond this their function is unknown.

Central Auditory Pathways

Since the auditory nerve contains so few fibers, it might be wondered if the auditory input would simply get submerged when it enters the central nervous system. Our acute sense of hearing tells us that this is not so, and a consideration of the synaptic organization at the first central relay shows how this comes about.

There are two specializations that ensure that auditory acuity is preserved despite the small number of input channels. The first is that each auditory nerve fiber, on entering the brainstem and reaching the collection of cells known as the *cochlear nucleus*, divides into a large number of terminal branches. Within the nucleus, the branches form a rigid geometrical array. In this way, each fiber projects to several terminal regions in an orderly fashion. In addition, the tonotopic sequence along the basilar membrane is projected by the array of auditory fibers onto the separate regions of the cochlear nucleus. Thus, the single cochlea is mapped into *multiple representations* within the cochlear nucleus.

The second specialization is seen in the types of synapses and cells in the different parts of the nucleus. The main parts have large and distinctive relay neurons, each of which receives a distinctive type of synaptic terminal. Two examples are shown in Fig. 16.11. The significance of these specializations is twofold: they provide for a very secure coupling of input to output, and they provide the morphological basis for different kinds of input–output processing of the auditory signals.

The nature of the processing that takes place at these different relay sites has been revealed by single-cell recordings. A useful scheme of classification was introduced in 1966 by Ross Pfeiffer, on the basis of the type of response to a pure-tone stimulus. Figure 16.12 shows the main response

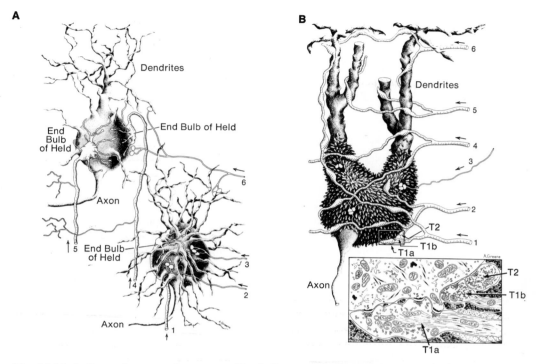

Fig. 16.11. A. Synaptic connections onto a "bushy" neuron in the anterior ventral cochlear nucleus. **B.** Synaptic connections onto an octopus cell in the posterior ventral cochlear nucleus of the cat. (From D. K. Morest, in Eagles, 1975)

types, together with diagrams of the cells and simplified circuits which may account for the response properties. The legend of this figure may be consulted for details. The important general conclusion from these data is that the bifurcations of the primary axons and their synaptic connections with different types of relay cell provide the basis for the conversion of the single response envelope in the primary axons into different output patterns. The different synaptic circuits, in effect, create new classes of responses, each class representing an abstraction of one particular feature of the input. For example, the simple ON response is ideally suited to transmitting high-frequency stimulation. The "primary-like" response obviously preserves the envelope of the auditory input signal. The "pauser" and "build-up" types provide for a differentiation of the onset

and ensuing phases of a tone, similar to the dynamic and static phases of responses we have noted in other sensory systems.

The organization depicted in Fig. 16.12 provides a means by which different properties of the auditory stimulus are given their own private (or semiprivate) channels. This is an expression of the same general principle found operating in other sensory systems: different functional properties are processed and transmitted in parallel pathways. Each channel has its own unique set of connections, mediating a special function.

There are extraordinarily rich and complex relations between each part of the cochlear nucleus and various brainstem centers (see Fig. 16.13). However, if we keep in mind the principle of parallel pathways, some of the relations can be

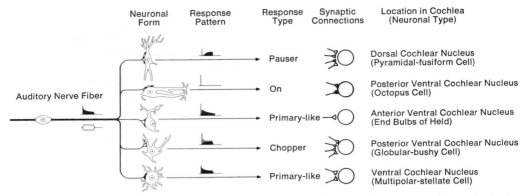

Fig. 16.12. Correlation of synaptic connections and neuron types with response properties in the cochlear nucleus. Responses to a tone burst (50 msec duration) are displayed as poststimulus time histograms. Some postulated circuit connections are indicated to the right (open terminals are excitatory, filled terminals are inhibitory). (Adapted from Kiang, in Eagles, 1975)

seen to be logical. For example, the spherical and globular cells make ipsilateral and contralateral connections to a cell group known as the *olivary nuclear complex,* a center that is essential for the binaural localization of sounds in space. As another example, the octopus cells project to cells within the same complex which, in turn, project through the olivocochlear bundle back to the cochlea, to provide for centrifugal control of the hair cells, as previously mentioned. Cells of the dorsal cochlear nucleus do not share these close relations with lower brainstem centers; instead, their outputs are destined for higher centers, in the midbrain (inferior colliculus) and thalamus. It may be noted that the general organization of these pathways, with some information processed at lower levels and some at higher levels, is similar to that in the insect auditory system discussed previously.

Auditory Cortex

Cortical Areas. The main thalamic relay nucleus for auditory information is the medial geniculate nucleus (MGN). As in the somatosensory and visual systems, the projection area of the relay cells onto the cortex defines the primary auditory cortex. Traditionally, it has been thought that there is a single area of primary cortex,

but here, as in the other systems, recent work has provided evidence for multiple divisions within both thalamic relay nucleus and cortex, and parallel pathways connecting them. For example, HRP injections were made by Irving Diamond and his colleagues at Duke University into different areas, and the labeled cells in the thalamus were identified. As summarized in Fig. 16.14, these studies showed that, in the cat, the most specific thalamic projection is from a ventral subdivision of the MGN to primary auditory cortex. In contrast, the magnocellular subdivision projects not only to the primary cortex, but to a number of surrounding cortical areas as well. Several other subdivisions have multiple, but more specific, projections. Diamond has suggested that the multiple and diffuse projections are phylogenetically older and the single specific system projection is more recent, in analogy with the presumed phylogeny of the two ascending pathways in the somatosensory system.

Multiple auditory areas are also found in primates (Fig. 13.17). The auditory areas in humans are localized on the dorsal aspect of the temporal lobe (see Fig. 31.1). We will discuss their relations to other cortical regions, including the language and speech areas, in Chap. 31.

Tonotopic Representation. The topographical representation within the primary somatosensory cortex suggested that there might be a corresponding representation in auditory cortex of the cochlea (*cochleotopy*) or of the localization of tones along the cochlea (*tonototopy*). The first evidence for tonotopic representation was obtained in experiments on dogs by Archie Tunturi in Oregon in 1940. This fit very well with other evidence showing precise tonotopy in lower centers like the inferior colliculus and medial geniculate nucleus. However, subsequent workers had difficulty in replicating the results in the cortex, and for many years the matter was unresolved. One of the problems appears to have been that tonotopic organization is more evident in anesthetized than in unanesthetized animals. In 1975, Mi-

Fig. 16.13. Organization of the central auditory pathways in the cat. AVCN, anterior ventral cochlear nucleus; Cent. Nuc. Inf. Coll., central nucleus of inferior colliculus; Dors. Ac. Str., dorsal accessory stria; DCN, dorsal cochlear nucleus; End Bulb of H., end bulb of Held; Interm. Ac. Str., intermediate accessory stria; Lat. Lemn., lateral lemniscus; LSO, lateral superior olive; MSO, medial superior olive; NTB, nucleus of trapezoid body; OCB, olivo-cochlear bundle; Perioliv. Nuc., periolivary nucleus; PVCN, posterior ventral cochlear nucleus. (From Moore and Osen, 1979)

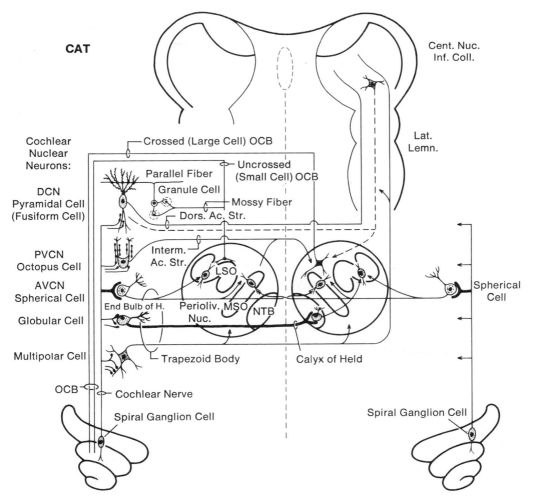

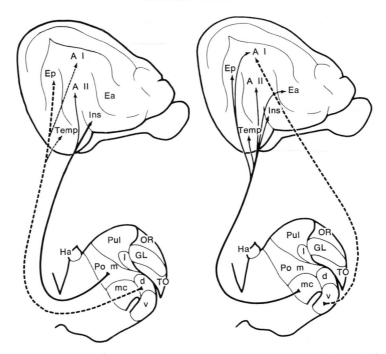

Fig. 16.14. Projections of different parts of the auditory thalamus (medial geniculate nucleus) to the cerebral cortex. A I, auditory area I; A II, auditory area II; Ea, anterior ectosylvian gyrus; Ep, posterior ectosylvian gyrus; GL, dorsal lateral geniculate body; d, dorsal division of the medial geniculate body; mc, magnocellular division of the medial geniculate body; v, ventral division of the medial geniculate body; Ha, habenula; I, inferior division of the pulvinar complex; Ins., insular area; OR, optic radiations; Po m, medial division of the posterior nuclear group; Pul. pulvinar complex; Temp, temporal field; TO, optic tract. (From Diamond, 1979)

Fig. 16.15. Tonotopic organization of the auditory cortex in the cat and the mustache bat. EP, posterior ectosylvian gyrus; I, insula; T, temporal field. Frequency bands in cortical maps are indicated in kHz. (Based on data from Woolsey, Merzenich, et al., and Suga; in Suga, 1978)

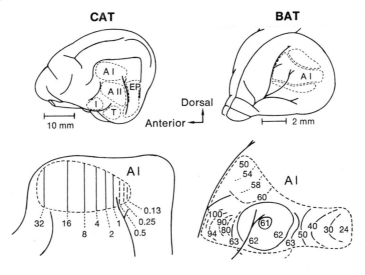

chael Merzenich and his colleagues in San Francisco clearly demonstrated tonotopic organization in the auditory cortex of anesthetized cats. A typical map is shown in Fig. 16.15.

These results have been followed up and confirmed in other species. In most mammals there is an area in primary auditory cortex that has a large and detailed map; this is called A I. There are additional representations in several other areas. There are also some areas receiving thalamic input, as discussed above, which are not organized tonotopically; for example, A II in the figure.

The regular progression of frequency bands in the tonotopic representation of animals like cats and humans reflects the broad spectrum of sounds to which we are responsive. What then of an animal like the bat, which uses special vocal signals as a kind of radar for echolocation? Let us discuss one example, the mustache bat. The echolocating sound emitted by this animal is an almost pure tone of 61 kHz (far above the hearing range of humans). The specializations of the bat for sensing this signal begin in the periphery, where auditory nerve fibers with relatively broad tuning curves may be found across the whole frequency spectrum, but those with best frequencies of 61 kHz have extremely narrow tuning curves. In the cortex, there is a tonotopic organization within A I, but it is distorted by an extremely large representation for 61 kHz (see Fig. 16.15). One can consider this as analogous to the large thumb area in somatosensory cortex, or the large area for the fovea in visual cortex, all places where the highest acuity occurs. The acuity in this auditory area is used to detect Doppler shifts between the emitted sound and the echo, to tell the bat whether a moth or other prey is approaching or receding.

Functional Units. In view of the difficulty in demonstrating the tonotopic organization of auditory cortex, it is perhaps not surprising that there has been less clear

evidence for columnar functional organization than in the somatosensory or visual systems. However, in penetrations perpendicular to the surface, an electrode characteristically records units in different layers that respond to the same frequency,

Fig. 16.16. Relation of tonotopic bands to binaural bands in cat auditory cortex. In this schematized view, isofrequency bands are at right angles to binaural bands (EE: neurons excited by both ears; EI: neurons excited by stimulation in contralateral ear and inhibited by ipsilateral ear). The combination of a binaural band and an isofrequency band forms a hyperband, or hypercolumn. A 1, primary auditory area; AAF, anterior auditory field. Frequencies indicated in kHz. (Based on Middlebrooks et al., in Merzenich and Kaas, 1980)

A. COCHLEAR REP. in TWO CAT AUDITORY FIELDS (AAF and AI)

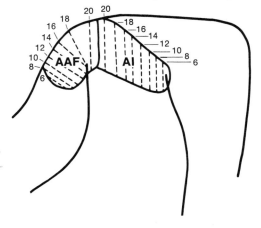

B. BINAURAL BANDS within AI

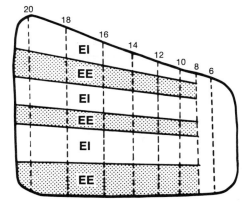

which would appear to represent the same principle of functional organization as in the other systems. The isofrequency bands, of course, are in the form of slabs, not columns. In addition, recent experiments indicate that, when tested with tones in either ear, cortical cells show either summation of excitation from both ears (EE), or excitation by the contralateral ear and inhibition by the ipsilateral ear (EI). The EE and EI responsive cells are organized into slabs which cut across the isofrequency bands at right angles, as shown in Fig. 16.16. This overlay of slabs with different functional properties is also present in the visual cortex, as we shall see.

REFERENCES

Davis, H. and S. R. Silverman. 1970. *Hearing and Deafness.* New York: Holt, Rhinehart and Winston.

Diamond, J. T. 1979. The subdivisions of neocortex: a proposal to revise the traditional view of sensory, motor, and association areas. In *Progress in Psychobiology and Physiological Psychology* (ed. by J. M. Sprague and A. N. Epstein). New York: Academic. pp. 2–44.

Eagles, E. L. (ed.). 1975. *The Nervous System, Human Communication and its Disorders.* New York: Raven.

Elsner, N. and A. V. Popov. 1978. Neuroethology of acoustic communication. In *Advances in Insect Physiology,* Vol 13 (ed. by J. E. Treherne, M. J. Berridge, and V. B. Wigglesworth). New York: Academic. pp. 229–355.

Galambos, R. and H. Davis. 1943. The response of single auditory-nerve fibers to acoustic stimulation. *J. Neurophysiol. 6:* 39–57.

Gordon, M. S. 1972. *Animal Physiology: Principles and Adaptations.* New York: Macmillan.

Lewis, D. B. and D. M. Gower. 1980. *Biology of Communication.* New York: John Wiley.

Lorente de No, R. 1933. Anatomy of the eighth nerve. III General plan of structure of the primary cochlea nuclei. *Laryngoscope 43:* 327–350.

Merzenich, M. M. and J. Kaas. 1980. Principles of organization of sensory-perceptual systems in mammals. *Prog. Psychobiol. and Psychol.,* Vol. 9 (ed. by J. M. Sprague and A. N. Epstein). New York: Academic. pp. 2–43.

Moore, J. K. and K. K. Osen. 1979. The human cochlear nuclei. *Exptl. Brain Res. (Suppl. II): Hearing Mechanisms and Speech* (ed. by O. Creutzfeld, H. Scheich, and C. Schreiner). New York: Springer. pp. 36–44.

Patton, H. D., J. W. Sundsten, W. E. Crill, and P. D. Swanson (eds.). 1976. *Introduction to Basic Neurology.* Philadelphia: W. B. Saunders.

Pfeiffer, R. R. 1966. Classification of response patterns of spike discharges for units in the cochlear nucleus: tone burst stimulation. *Exp. Brain Res. 1:* 220–235.

Russell, I. J. and P. M. Sellick. 1978. Intracellular studies of hair cells in the guinea pig retina. *J. Physiol. 284:* 261–290.

Sellick, P. M. and I. J. Russell. 1979. Two-tone suppression in cochlear hair cells. *Hearing Res. 1:* 227.

Suga, N. 1978. Specialization of the auditory system for reception and processing of species-specific sounds. *Fed. Proc. 37:* 2342–2354.

Tunturi, A. 1944. Audio frequency localization in the acoustic cortex of the dog. *Am J. Physiol. 141:* 397–403.

Viancour, T. A. 1979. Peripheral electrosense physiology: a review of recent findings. *J. Physiol. (Paris). 75:* 321–333.

von Bekesy, G. 1960. *Experiments in Hearing.* New York: McGraw-Hill.

17

Vision

The earth is bathed in a constant flow of energy from the sun and the rest of the universe. This energy is in the form of electromagnetic radiation that has both the properties of waves and also of particles, called photons. The radiation all travels at the speed of light (300,000 km per sec), but it has different wavelengths, as indicated in Fig. 17.1. Radiation with short wavelengths (and correspondingly high frequencies) has high energies that are deleterious to life because they disrupt molecular bonds; fortunately, these waves are absorbed by the protective blanket of ozone in the atmosphere, or else life as we know it would not be possible. Radiation with long wavelengths has very low energy, for which there are few known receptors in living organisms. However, there is a narrow band of wavelengths with not too much energy nor too little, and this we call *light*. Given the crucial role that this radiation plays in sustaining life on this planet, it is not surprising that plants and animals have developed special mechanisms for sensing it, and for using these signals to control a variety of behavioral actions.

The simplest kind of sensitivity to light is the ability to perceive different *intensi-*ties of diffuse illumination. This ability is present in many plants and most animals. We can refer to it as the basic property of *photosensitivity*. We will discuss the mechanism of photosensitivity below, but for now it may be noted that this property is found in single-cell animals, in the skin of many simple organisms, as well as in specialized visual organs. Sensitivity to different levels of light underlies the daily rhythms of activity that govern the lives of most animals (see Chap. 26).

Most complex organisms have evolved mechanisms for sensing changes in illumination that are more rapid in time and more localized in space. These abilities constitute what we call the sense of *vision*. A remarkable feature of light is the large number of submodalities, and there are correspondingly a number of functions that vision may subserve. As shown in Table 17.1, the simplest function, beyond the sensing of intensity, is the ability to detect *motion* in the visual field; this capacity is widespread among animals, attesting to its usefulness in detecting both predators and prey. This function requires that the receptors be arranged in a sheet in order to portray the movement across the visual field. Discrimination of the *form* of ob-

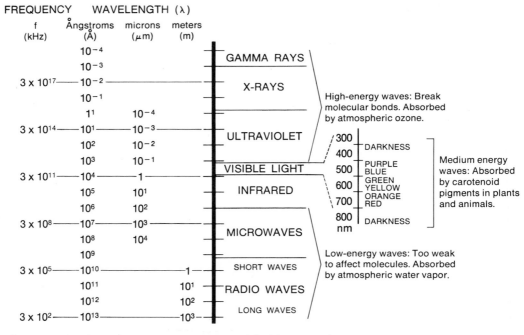

Fig. 17.1. The electromagnetic spectrum. (Modified from Gordon, 1970)

jects, so they can be recognized and manipulated, requires focussing of the visual image, and the development of a number of accessory structures for accomplishing this. Many animals can discriminate the *polarization* of diffuse light, and use it for orientation and navigation. Since most animals are organized bilaterally, the two images from the eyes need to be combined, and this is used in some animals for *depth perception.* Finally, a few species have mechanisms for discriminating dif-

ferent wavelengths within the visible spectrum, and thus can perceive *colors.*

The neuronal mechanisms underlying these functions have received a great deal of attention from neurobiologists, for several reasons. First, although other senses, such as the olfactory, play the dominant role in providing the cues that initiate feeding and mating behavior in most animals, vision is often crucial in carrying out the behavior. Second, vision becomes increasingly important in the higher inver-

Table 17.1 Submodalities of light

Function	Mediated by
Photosensitivity (diffuse light)	Photosensitive molecule (rhodopsin) plus microvilli/cilia
Form discrimination (spatial localization)	Sheet of photoreceptors (continuous or cartridges) plus focusing mechanism
Movement discrimination	Sheet of photoreceptors
Binocular vision and depth perception	Fusion of images (extraocular muscles, etc.)
Polarized light	Cellular organization and orientation
Color vision	Different photopigments

tebrates and vertebrates, particularly insects and mammals. Third, vision is overwhelmingly important in the life of humans; the more we learn about vision, the more we learn about ourselves, and also, hopefully, the more we learn about ways to prevent or cure the diseases that can cause blindness. Finally, light is a stimulus that can be controlled easily and accurately, which gives the experimenter a great advantage in analyzing neural mechanisms. The work in the visual system has thus not only given us insight into vision, but has also provided some of the best models for the functional organization of nervous systems.

It is obvious from the list in Table 17.1 that, once again, we are confronted with more diversity than can be covered adequately in a single chapter. We will begin by noting some basic properties of photoreception, and then discuss examples of visual systems among invertebrates and vertebrates that have been particularly well studied.

Mechanisms of Photoreception

In a number of places in this book we learn about a particular mechanism that is so effective that it has been adapted for use across a wide range of different cells and organisms. Such, for example, is the nature of the Krebs cycle for energy metabolism, the actin–myosin complex for muscle contraction, and the synapse for neuronal communication. The same applies to photoreception. We have noted that radiation in the narrow band of visible light has energy just sufficient to be absorbed by molecules but not so much that it disrupts them. What is needed is a molecule that will convert light energy into a maximum possible amount of chemical free energy. The molecules that do this most efficiently belong to the class called *carotenoids,* of which vitamin A is a member.

As explained by George Wald, who received a Nobel Prize for his studies of photopigments, these molecules include parts with straight chains that can readily undergo geometrical isomerization. One particular molecule is 11-*cis*-retinal, which has its long-chain part bent up and twisted in a very unstable configuration. When a photon of light is absorbed, there is a change, through several intermediate forms, to the more stable 11-*trans* isomer, with a release of free energy (see Fig. 17.2A). This energy can then be used within the cell as the signal for photoreception.

The 11-*cis*-retinal is normally bound to a colorless protein called opsin, to make a molecule called *rhodopsin;* this, in one variation or another, is the nearly universal molecular mediator of photoreception in animals. The effect of light, in addition to isomerization, leads to splitting of the retinal and opsin. This causes loss of color of the molecule, an effect called *bleaching.* Reconstitution of rhodopsin occurs by enzymatic resynthesis, requiring biochemical energy in the form of high-energy phosphate bonds (ATP).

The whole rhodopsin molecule has a molecular weight of 28,000 daltons. It is associated with the plasmalemma of the photoreceptor cell. A schematic representation of the molecule, and the way it spans the membrane and projects beyond both inner and outer surfaces of the membrane, is shown in Fig. 17.2B. In the disc membranes of vertebrate photoreceptors it has been estimated that the rhodopsin molecules constitute up to 80% of the protein of the membrane, which indicates how specialized photoreceptors are for capturing photons.

In the cells specialized for photoreception, we find a second expression of a universal mechanism; in most species, the photoreceptor part of the cell consists of fine hairlike processes. In some cases these are cilia, or modifications of cilia; in other cases they are microvilli, or modifications thereof. Richard Eakin of the University of California at Berkeley has reviewed the varieties of these structures in different

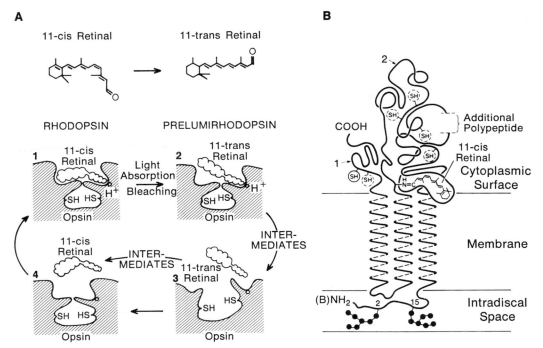

Fig. 17.2. A. Changes in rhodopsin that occur when it absorbs a photon of light. (Adapted from Wald, in Gordon, 1972) **B.** Postulated organization of the rhodopsin polypeptide in the disc membrane of the photoreceptor. (From Hubbell and Fung, in Hubbell and Bownds, 1979)

species, and has suggested that there are two main lines in the evolution of photoreceptors. As summarized in Fig. 17.3, there is a line through flatworms-annelids-arthropods which uses the microvillus, arranged in a rhabdome, as the site of rhodopsin and photoreception, and a line through coelenterates-echinoderms-chordates which uses modified cilia at these sites. Although there are exceptions in these lines (as always in biology), the schema is a useful way of summarizing the diversity across species, and it also serves to highlight the importance of hairlike processes as sites of sensory transduction. Eakin has suggested that membranes of cilia or microvilli "provide a plano-arrangement of the molecules of photopigment for the most effective absorption of photons of light."

INVERTEBRATES

Types of Eyes

The simplest organ specialized for sensing light is a group of cells in a shallow surface pit. This is called an *ocellus* (see Fig. 17.4A). It is present in the coelenterates, and is thus, together with the neuromast, one of the first special sense organs to appear in phylogeny. Its main function is sensing light intensity. It must do this quite effectively, for ocelli are present in many invertebrate organisms, including the social insects.

In order for an eye to mediate true vision, it must have a way of forming an image. There are three main ways to do this, and the invertebrates have tried all of them. The simplest uses the principle of the pinhole camera, in which the image is formed by narrow rays passing from the object through the pinhole. The eye of the mollusc *Nautilus* is constructed on this principle (see Fig. 17.4B). Because of the small pinhole, the eye can work effectively only in bright light.

A much more efficient way to form an image is to funnel the light through multiple channels. If the channels are arranged so that they point out at different angles, a large visual field will be projected onto a small sheet of receptors, thus producing a magnification effect. By virtue of many separate channels, called *ommatidia,* this is referred to as a *compound eye* (see Fig. 17.4C). It is the characteristic eye of arthropods. As noted by A. Knowles and J. A. Dartnall, the great advantages of this type of eye are that:

(1) its great depth of focus makes it sensitive to movement at any distance; (2) the relatively short path length for light entering the ommatidium minimizes the loss of UV radiation, and this, coupled with freedom from the chromatic

Fig. 17.3. Postulated lines of evolution of light-sensitive cellular structures. There are two main lines, one utilizing modified cilia, the other the elaboration of the rhabdome. (From Eakin, 1968)

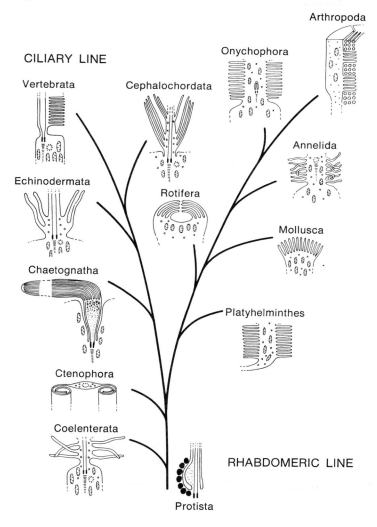

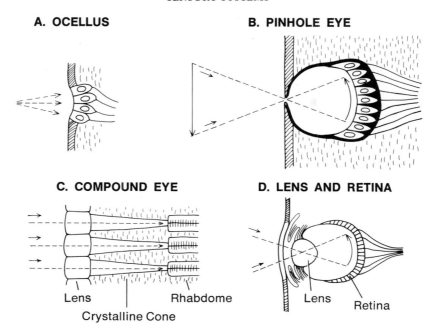

Fig. 17.4. Different types of eyes in invertebrates. (Adapted from Knowles and Dartnall, 1977)

aberration of lens systems, allows it to operate over a very wide range of wavelengths, and (3) the receptor cells can be arranged to make the eye sensitive to the plane of polarization of light.

In order to achieve its advantages, the compound eye sacrifices resolving power, which, by contrast, is maximized in the *refracting eye*. In the refracting eye, the image is formed by refraction through lenses. The image formed is brought into focus on a receptor sheet, called the *retina*. This, of course, is similar to the lens system and film of a modern camera. The refracting eye is found in certain molluscs, such as the octopus, and is characteristic of all vertebrates (see Fig. 17.4D).

The ocellus and the compound eye have been studied intensively by neurobiologists; let us briefly consider examples of these two types.

The Ocellus

The ocelli of the barnacle have most of the advantages that neurobiologists seek in a simple invertebrate system: few cells (3–5), large cell bodies (30–100μm diameter), and easy accessibility. Their only known function is to sense the shadow of a passing object and mediate a protective "shadow reflex." Stimulation of one of these photoreceptors with a step of light produces a receptor potential that is graded with the light intensity, as shown in Fig. 17.5. The response is depolarizing, and the inward current that brings about this change in the membrane potential is carried by both Na^+ and Ca^{2+}. As can be seen in Fig. 17.5, the response has a complicated time course, with an early phasic overshoot followed by adaptation to a slowly declining static phase. This adaptation is due to several factors, including reduction of the inward Na^+ current by the rise in intracellular Ca^{2+}, and changes in the membrane properties due to a voltage-dependent K^+ conductance. Thus, although the response is "non-spiking," it is nonetheless shaped by several mechanisms that include voltage-dependent processes. Thus, studies of this simple receptor permit the conclusion that, as expressed by Simon Laughlin of Canberra, "the neural membrane is a multicomponent system capable of great functional plasticity", This is in line with comments in Chap. 8, and we will see further evidence of the generality of this statement in Chap. 30.

The ocellar cell has an axon, with a diameter of 10–20 μm and a length of up to 10 mm or so, that connects to the supraesophageal ganglion. The axon does not conduct action potentials: the receptor potential spreads passively through the axon to the axon terminals, as indicated in Fig. 17.5. Because of the large diameter of the axon, there is only moderate decrement of the passively spreading potential. There appears to be partial compensation for this decrement by virtue of voltage-dependent Ca^{2+} channels in the terminals. In the presence of TEA, which blocks outward current through K^+ chan-

nels, the terminals generate a Ca^{2+} action potential. By this means, even a small signal can give rise to a significant increase in intracellular Ca^{2+} in the terminal, which in turn can enhance release of neurotransmitter from the terminal. This may serve as a model for gain control and amplification at other synapses in the nervous system.

The Compound Eye

Limulus. The horseshoe crab, *Limulus*, has several eyes, including a pair of dorsal ocelli and a ventral eye. Like other arthropods, of which it is an ancient member, it has a pair of compound eyes. Their simple structure and accessibility made them the first simple system for studying visual mechanisms, and the use of this preparation by Hartline and his colleagues for elucidating the basic principle of lateral inhibition has been discussed in Chap. 11.

Fig. 17.5. *Left,* diagram of medial photoreceptor of the barnacle *Balamus. Middle,* intracellular receptor potentials at 4 different light intensities, recorded in the soma (above) and axon terminals (below). *Right,* intensity–response relations plotted from recordings such as those shown, for the dynamic peak (pk.) of the response, the static plateau (pl.), and the afterhyperpolarization (h.a.p.). (From Hudspeth, Poo, and Stuart, in Laughlin, 1981)

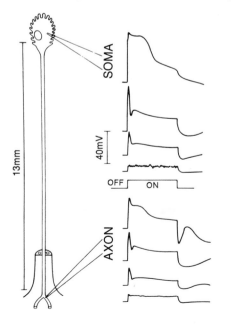
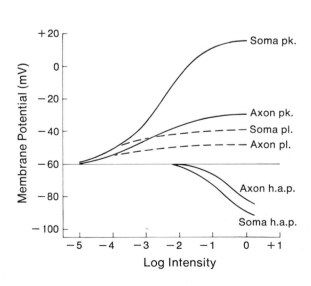

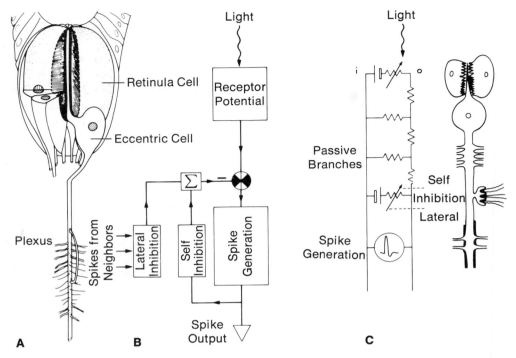

Fig. 17.6. Some approaches to understanding the lateral eye of the horseshoe crab *Limulus*. **A.** Diagram of structure of the ommatidium. **B.** Systems model of functional organization of the eccentric cell. **C.** Electrical model of the eccentric cell and its relation to other cells. (A from Ratliff, Hartline, and Miller; B from Knight et al.; C from Purple and Dodge in Laughlin, 1981)

Here we want to discuss further the properties of the photoreceptors.

The compound eye of *Limulus* consists of some 800 ommatidia. Each *ommatidium* has at its surface a corneal lens. Behind it are 10–15 receptor (*retinula*) cells arranged in a circle (Fig. 17.6). As in other arthropods (see Fig. 17.3), the sites of photoreception are microvilli, whose interdigitations form a structure called a *rhabdome*. At the center of the receptor group is the dendrite of a cell whose cell body is deeper and placed to one side, which has given it the name *eccentric cell*. This is a modified receptor cell: it has few microvilli, but a long thick axon, and is the principal projection neuron from the ommatidium (see Fig. 17.6).

Intracellular recordings have shown that the photoreceptors are electrically coupled to the eccentric cell dendrite. By this means, the output from the eccentric cell represents the summation of inputs to all the photoreceptors. The electrical synapses are rectifying; they pass current from the receptors to the eccentric cell dendrites, but not in the opposite direction. This prevents the electrical activity of the eccentric cell from interfering with the responses of the photoreceptor.

At rest, the eccentric cell shows background activity consisting of occasional, small depolarizing waves, first called "Yeandle bumps" after their discoverer. These represent photoreceptor responses to single photons, transmitted to the eccentric cell through the electrical synapses. With light stimulation, these quantal events fuse into a graded receptor potential which depolarizes the membrane (see also Fig. 17.12 below). There is evidence that the ionic membrane properties discussed above for the barnacle photoreceptor also apply, to a greater or lesser extent, to the generation of the receptor potential in *Limulus*.

The receptor potential gives rise to action potentials, which encode the intensity and time course of the stimulation, and transmit this information to the central nervous system. The impulses arise in the axon at a distance from the cell body. The mechanism of electrotonic spread of receptor potential into the axon is similar to that discussed for the crayfish stretch receptor in Chap. 8. The axon gives rise to a number of collaterals which form a plexus beneath the ommatidia. Within this plexus, the collaterals are interconnected by reciprocal and serial synapses. These form the circuits which mediate the lateral inhibitory interactions.

The great amount of work on this eye has resulted in a complete description of the system by the methods of systems analysis. A brief summary of a systems model of the eccentric cell is shown in Fig. 17.6. A nonlinear model such as this can completely describe the input–output functions of the eccentric cell. Unfortunately, the description is in mathematical terms which are beyond the ken of most biologists. As Laughlin has ruefully observed:

> . . . this analysis is a considerable achievement, (but) until the dry Weiner kernels can be given the flesh and sap of biological processes, they will remain in the domains of instrumentation and mathematical abstraction.

Insects. The most highly developed compound eyes are found in arthropods, particularly the fast-moving animals such as the insects. The insect eye has been intensively studied, and we will draw on several examples for our discussion.

The large eyes of an insect like the common housefly are familiar to anyone who has taken a close look after swinging a flyswatter (see Fig. 17.7). Each eye consists of a mosaic of some 10,000 individual ommatidia. The ommatidium is more highly developed than in the case of *Limulus*. An ommatidium comprises eight re-

Fig. 17.7. A. Anterior view of head of a fly, showing large, compound eyes. **B.** Dorsal view; on the right, the cut-away shows the relations between the retina (R) of the compound eye and the next stages in the visual pathway: the lamina (L) and medulla (M). Stippling indicates one ommatidium and its projection to lamina and medulla. **C.** Relatively poor resolving power of compound eye is shown by this representation of a man with compound eyes which have a resolving power equivalent to that of the human eye. Each facet pictured on the man actually represents 10,000 facets. (A, B from Meinertzhagen, 1977, C from Kirshfeld, in Land, 1981)

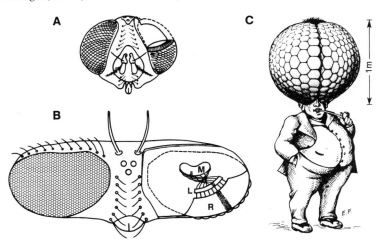

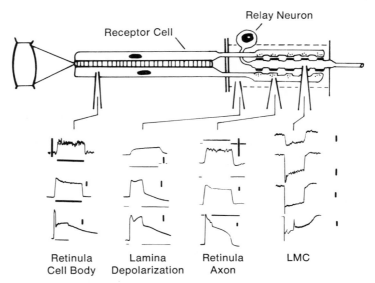

Fig. 17.8. Graded receptor potentials in response to light, recorded from different locations in the eye of the dragonfly. Stimuli last 500 msec; voltage calibrations (vertical bars) are 10 mV. (From Laughlin, 1981)

ceptor cells, each an identifiable cell with a characteristic morphology and placement. Each cell gives rise along its length to thousands of microvilli that form a *rhabdomere.* The corneal lens focuses incoming light such that it is funneled through the rhabdomere, where photoreception takes place. Unlike the case in *Limulus,* the insect photoreceptors themselves have long axons, which project to the first site of synaptic transmission and integration in the optic lamina just beneath the eye.

Intracellular recordings have been made from the photoreceptors, from their terminals in the lamina, and from the relay cells in the lamina; Fig. 17.8 summarizes these findings. It can be seen that the receptor potential consists of a graded depolarization, as in other invertebrate photoreceptors. The response to weak stimulation (upper trace) is "noisy." The small deflections are believed to reflect both photon quantum bumps, and transducer noise due to molecular fluctuations in conductance channels. Note at high intensities (bottom trace) the complicated

response envelope, presumably reflecting complex membrane conductances, as discussed above. There are numerous electrical synapses between the photoreceptors, which presumably function to enhance the signal-to-noise ratio and increase photon capture.

Transmission of the receptor potential through the axon to the axon terminals is by passive electrotonic spread; as in the other examples we have considered, there is little evidence for spike activity in these axons under normal conditions (see Fig. 17.8). In the optic lamina, the terminals make multiple synapses onto the relay neurons, called large monopolar cells (LMC). As can be seen in the figure, these cells respond to input from the photoreceptors with a hyperpolarization. The response is mediated by a neurotransmitter, possibly acetylcholine. There are several factors in the presynaptic terminal which work together to enhance transmitter release at low signal intensities. These include the fact that the synapses are continually active in the dark; that they have no threshold for transmitter release; that at background illumination they are in the most sensitive part of their operating range; and that there are multiple synapses from individual terminals. These properties have already been discussed in relation to other invertebrate photoreceptors, and we will see that they are shared by vertebrate receptors as well.

Central Visual Pathways. Figure 17.8 shows the essential synaptic connections for straight-through transmission of visual information, but it does not indicate the circuit connections through which the information from all the ommatidia interact to provide for movement discrimination and pattern recognition.

Fig. 17.9. A summary diagram of the neuronal organization of the optic lobe, illustrating the sequence of processing and the output to the lateral protocerebrum. (From Strausfeld and Nässel, 1981)

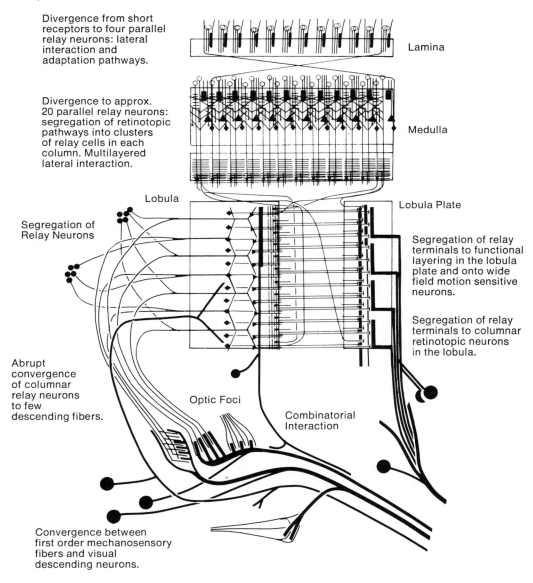

Divergence from short receptors to four parallel relay neurons: lateral interaction and adaptation pathways.

Divergence to approx. 20 parallel relay neurons: segregation of retinotopic pathways into clusters of relay cells in each column. Multilayered lateral interaction.

Lamina

Medulla

Lobula

Segregation of Relay Neurons

Lobula Plate

Segregation of relay terminals to functional layering in the lobula plate and onto wide field motion sensitive neurons.

Segregation of relay terminals to columnar retinotopic neurons in the lobula.

Abrupt convergence of columnar relay neurons to few descending fibers.

Optic Foci

Combinatorial Interaction

Convergence between first order mechanosensory fibers and visual descending neurons.

The main centers in the visual pathway are indicated in Fig. 17.9. As can be seen, there is a sequence from the *lamina* through the *medulla* to a bipartite structure, *lobula* and *lobula plate,* and from these to the *protocerebrum* of the brain. Studies of the neurons within and connecting these centers began with the first use of the Golgi method in the late nineteenth century, and have culminated in the exhaustive analysis by Nicholas Strausfeld in Heidelberg in the 1970's. Figure 17.9 gives a summary of some of the circuits and organizational units identified in this analysis. We do not have space to follow through these circuits in detail; suffice it to say that they provide for most of the principles of sensory processing we discussed in Chapter. 11: divergence, convergence, lateral interactions, functional segregation, topographical ordering.

This overall scheme has been extended in several more specific directions by recent work. For example, the synaptic connections within the lamina have been analyzed under the electron microscope, aided by single-cell staining and identification. From this work the simple relay connections depicted in Fig. 17.8 have been fleshed out with circuits for local processing through a variety of interneurons, much as in the vertebrate retina. As another example, physiologists have pieced together circuits that mediate specific types of visual behavior. Perhaps the best understood at present is the *movement detector system* in the locust. This circuit is tuned to respond optimally to rapid movements of small objects in the visual field, and elicit an escape jumping reaction. The elements of this circuit have been identified all the way from the peripheral visual system through the brain down to the thoracic motoneurons that elicit the jumping. The part of the circuit that feeds into the giant movement detector in the lobula is shown in Fig. 17.10. One sees here the way that the properties of sensory processing, mentioned previously, are utilized in a circuit for a specific behavioral

function. The heirarchical nature of such a circuit, and its relation to motor control, will be discussed in Chap. 22.

VERTEBRATES

The importance of vision in vertebrate life is paralleled by the attention given by neurobiologists to this subject. It is probably true that studies of vertebrate visual systems, in all their aspects, exceed those for any other part of the nervous system. Some of these aspects, such as the optics of the eye, are subjects for special study. From a cellular point of view we wish to concentrate on cellular properties and synaptic circuits, in order to understand some of the principles that underlie visual processing. We will compare these principles with those in invertebrates, and also assess the insights they may give us into the neural basis of visual perception.

The Retina

The vertebrate eye works on the principle of the refracted image, as already mentioned. The photoreceptors, together with the neurons involved in the first two levels of synaptic processing, are arranged in a thin sheet called the *retina* at the back of the eye, where the image is formed (see Fig. 17.4).

Photoreceptors. The receptors are arranged along the outer (posterior) surface of the retina. This is different from the situation in the compound eyes of invertebrates, where the light has direct access to the photoreceptor membranes, and it is also different from the squid eye, which, though also working on refractive principles, has the photoreceptors arranged on the inner surface. The explanation offered is that this peculiar arrangement is due to the embryological origins of the retina as an outpouching from the brain. There is in any case little loss of light, because the retina is transparent.

The receptors are of two types, *rods* and

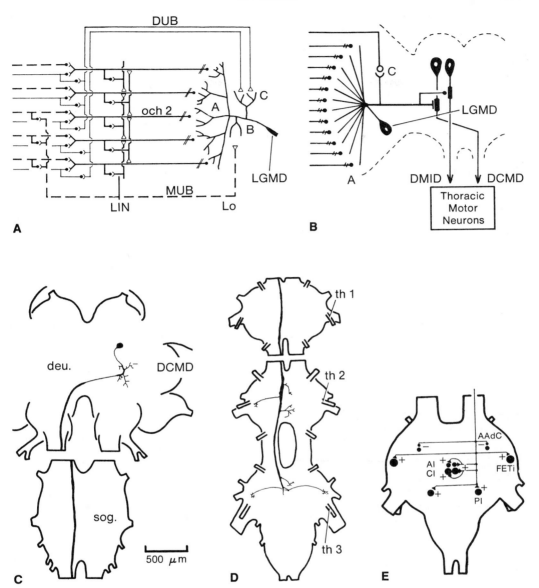

Fig. 17.10. The central visual pathway in the locust mediating movement detection. A–C. Receptor sites on dendritic tree of LGMD cell; AAdC, anterior coxal adductor motoneuron; AI, anterior inhibitory flexor tibiae motoneuron; CI, common inhibitory motoneuron; DCMD, descending contralateral movement detector neuron; deu., deutocerebrum; DMID, descending ipsilateral movement detector neuron; DUB, dorsal uncrossed bundle; FETi, fast extensor tibiae motoneuron; LGMD, lobula giant movement detector; LIN, lateral inhibitory network; Lo, lobula; MUB, medial uncrossed bundle; och 2, second optic chiasm; PI, posterior inhibitory flexor tibiae motoneuron; sog., subesophageal ganglion; th 1–3, thoracic ganglia. (Based on Rowell et al. and others, in Strausfeld and Nassel, 1981)

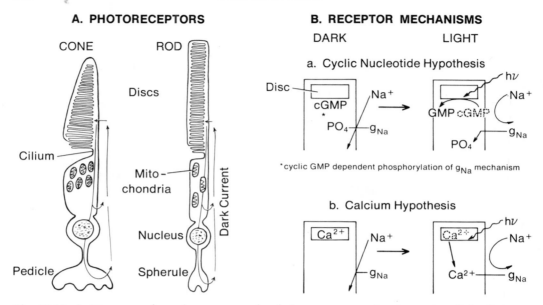

Fig. 17.11. **A.** Diagrams of vertebrate cone and rod photoreceptors, showing main cellular features and pathways for flow of dark current. **B.** Possible receptor mechanisms. Above: role of cGMP as an internal messenger linking photoreception in disc membrane with closing of Na channels in plasma membrane. Below: Possible role of Ca^{2+} as internal messenger. (B from Hubbell and Bownds, 1980)

cones (Fig. 17.11). In both types the *outer segments* are modified cilia. They contain stacks of *disc membranes,* which are formed by inpouchings of the plasma membrane. The disc membranes contain the photopigment molecules: rhodopsin in rods, and related molecules sensitive to red, green, and blue wavelengths in cones. The receptors continually shed disc membranes from their distal tips and synthesize new membranes proximally. The location of the receptors against the outer surface of the retina would appear to facilitate the removal of the discarded membranes. The cones of reptiles and birds contain oil droplets of different colors in their inner segments, a filtering mechanism that contributes to color vision; this is an additional use of the outward placement of the receptors.

With regard to color vision, this is limited in most mammals, reflecting the fact that the early mammals were probably nocturnal animals. Color vision reemerged mainly in the line leading to primates, in

association with the adoption of diurnal habits. As Timothy Goldsmith of Yale has pointed out, our color vision system has been reconstructed, in an evolutionary sense, from a less capable retina. It therefore lacks the specializations, such as oil droplets and sensitivity to ultraviolet light, that make the avian retina the supreme instrument for both day and night vision.

In Chap. 8 we discussed the fact that the receptor response is a slow, graded potential, and in Chap. 11 we indicated the problem for the receptor in generating this potential from the initial action of photons on rhodopsin. Figure 17.11 summarizes the situation. Under low illumination there is a continual dark current, due to a relatively high conductance to Na^+. The effect of light is to turn off the Na^+ conductance, and make the membrane hyperpolarized. There are at present two main explanations for the linkage, as indicated in Fig. 17.11. One explanation assumes that in the dark, the Na^+ channel is kept open by a cyclic GMP-dependent phosphorylation of the channel protein; isomerized rhodopsin activates a sequence of reactions leading to enzymatic degradation of cyclic GMP, which causes dephosphorylation of the channel protein and closing of the channels. The second mechanism presumes that the isomerized rhodopsin releases Ca^{2+} that has been sequestered in the disc membranes, and that the rise in intracellular Ca^{2+} leads to closing of the Na^+ channels. In both cases there is an amplification, from a few molecules of isomerized rhodopsin to many conductance sites in the membrane. Current work is directed toward discriminating between these two "second messenger" mechanisms. The high metabolic activity of the receptors and the large resting conductances make these experiments difficult.

A direct measure of the quantal responses to single photons in single receptors has been obtained by Denis Baylor and his colleagues at Stanford University using an elegant recording technique. They prepared small pieces of toad retina, teased out single rod receptors, and gently sucked them into the tip of a micropipette (see Fig. 17.12, A,B). They could then shine a thin bar of light across the outer segment. The resulting response of the rod, due to the closing of Na^+ channels, changes the amount of current flowing across the membrane, as discussed previously. This

Fig. 17.12. Recordings of responses from single isolated rod photoreceptors of the toad. **A.** Suction electrode approaching the outer segment of a receptor protruding from a piece of retina. **B.** Outer segment is sucked up into electrode. Light bar is shone on small parts of the outer segment, while membrane currents, proportional to longitudinal current flowing along the outer segment, is recorded by the electrode. **C.** Receptor responses, showing quantal events at low illumination (bottom), merging to a smooth graded response at higher illumination (upper traces). Note that these are recordings of membrane current (in pA: 10^{-12} A); the upward deflections signal the current flows associated with the membrane hyperpolarization that is characteristic of vertebrate photoreceptors. Intensity of light stimulation in photons μm^{-2} sec^{-1}. (From Baylor et al., 1979)

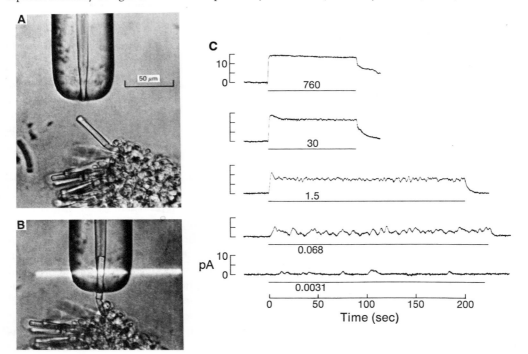

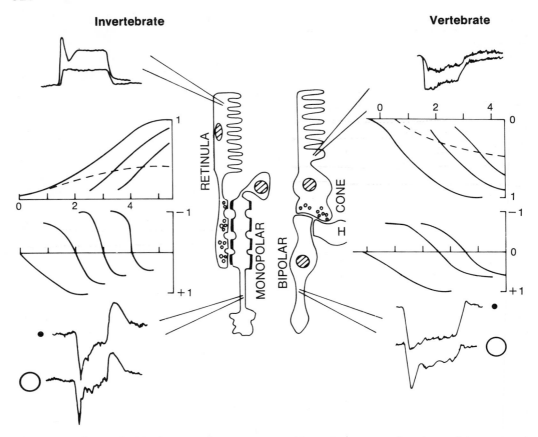

Fig. 17.13. The similarities between the responses and intensity/response functions of the receptors and first-order interneurons of invertebrate and vertebrate retinas. Despite the difference in response polarity, the graded potentials of the receptors (insect retinula cells and vertebrate cones) both exhibit a broad dynamic range, a relatively small range shift with light adaptation, and a standing background signal (---). The relay neurons (monopolar and bipolar cells) also respond with graded potentials, but have a narrow dynamic range that is shifted in step with background intensity so that there is little representation of the standing background intensity level. Comparisons between the responses to a point source (•) and a broad stimulus (○) show that both interneurons are subject to lateral inhibition. (Figure and legend from Laughlin (1981), based on data from Laughlin and Hardie, and Normann and Werblin)

current has to flow electrotonically along the rod to complete the electrical circuit. The tight seal of the electrode tip against the rod places a high resistance in this longitudinal current path, which generates voltages that can be recorded by the electrode.

Using this method, Baylor and coworkers found that with very weak illumination it was possible to record small voltage fluctuations, as shown in Fig. 17.12C (bottom trace). They concluded that each fluctuation is a quantal event,

due to the photoisomerization of a single rhodopsin molecule by a single photon. They calculated a quantal current of 1pA (10^{-12} amperes), and a corresponding conductance change very similar to that of a single acetylcholine-sensitive channel in the neuromuscular junction. The quantal event at the neuromuscular junction represents abrupt transitions of the channel between closed and open states, which last only about 1 msec (see Chap. 9). In contrast, the photoreceptor quantal response has a rounded shape and a duration of a few seconds. It is believed that this represents the action of the internal messenger at a number of sites on the plasma membrane of the photoreceptor.

With stronger illumination, the quantal events merge, and the response becomes a smoothly graded waveform (Fig. 17.12C). Note the similarities of these responses to those of the invertebrate receptors discussed previously.

The fact that vertebrate receptors normally respond to light only with graded potentials, added to the evidence in invertebrates, indicates that this is a near-universal property of animal photoreceptors. This similarity is all the more striking in view of the fact that the response to illumination in the invertebrates is depolarization, and in the vertebrates is hyperpolarization. Given the similar graded nature of the responses, it is perhaps not surprising that many of the properties we discussed in invertebrate receptors also appear to apply to vertebrates. These include voltage-sensitive channels for Na^+ and K^+, normally masked by other conductances; high sensitivity to small signals in the presynaptic terminal, enhanced by voltage-dependent conductances; and multiple synaptic contacts onto second-order neurons. These and other properties are summarized and compared in Fig. 17.13.

Retinal Circuits. The basic organization of the retina has already been discussed in Chap. 11. It may be recalled that there are five main cell types—receptors, bipolar cells, horizontal cells, amacrine cells, and ganglion cells—and that these are arranged in a kind of lattice-array that provides for straight-through transmission as well as lateral interactions. The synaptic connections between the cells include some of the specialized types that were discussed in Chap. 5.

The first systematic intracellular recordings from all the cell types were obtained by Frank Werblin and John Dowling, then at Johns Hopkins, in 1968. These experiments were carried out in the retina

of *Necturus,* the mudpuppy. The cell bodies in this retina are large, making inviting targets for the probing microelectrode. A summary of the results is shown in Fig. 17.14. The diagram is arranged to show, on the left, the responses of each cell to a spot of light and, on the right, to a surround.

There are three main points to take away from this diagram. First, in addition to the receptors, the horizontal cells and bipolar cells show only graded responses to stimulation. These have thus far provided the clearest examples of nonspiking neurons in the vertebrate nervous system. Amacrine cells show mostly graded po-

Fig. 17.14. Synaptic actions in the vertebrate retina, as recorded intracellularly from neurons in *Necturus* (mudpuppy). *Left,* responses recorded at the center of a spot of light (bar above). *Right,* responses in the surround. R, receptor; B, bipolar cell; H, horizontal cell; A, amacrine cell; $G_{1,2}$, ganglion cells. (From Dowling, 1979)

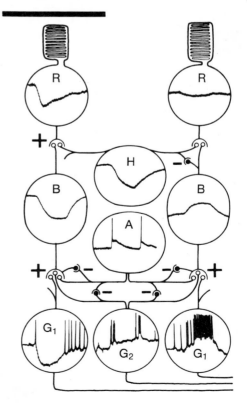

tentials also, though they do generate a few small spikes, which may help to boost transmission through their long dendritic processes. Only the ganglion cells generate large action potentials, which is consistent with their role as the output neurons of the retina.

Second, there are marked differences between the responses in the center and the surround. The bipolar cell potentials are of opposite polarities, and ganglion cell (G_1) shows excitation at the center and inhibition in the surround. This expresses the fundamental property of center–surround antagonism in the organization of receptive fields of ganglion cells. Since the receptors show only a grading down of their responses in the surround, these results demonstrate that the center-surround antagonism is the result of processing by the synaptic circuits in the retina, principally those through the laterally oriented elements, the horizontal and amacrine cells.

Third, the ganglion cell (G_2) depicted in Fig. 17.14 shows transient responses at ON and OFF of the stimulus. This type of response is especially tuned to transmitting information about moving stimuli. This property also is due to synaptic circuits, principally through complex interactions of the amacrine cells.

Different species differ in the amount of synaptic processing that takes place in their retinas. One of the most complex retinas in this respect is that of the frog or toad. As shown in the pioneering studies of H. R. Maturana, Jerome Lettvin, and their colleagues at M.I.T. in 1960, frog ganglion cells may be tuned to one of several features of a visual stimulus, including a stationary edge, a convex edge, a moving edge, or a dimming or brightening of illumination. Some cells are so narrowly tuned that they seem to function virtually as "bug detectors"! An interesting note is that complex retinas are found in some mammals (such as rabbits) as well as in lower vertebrates, so there is not a consistent phylogenetic progression. However, the fact that higher mammals, like cats and primates, have relatively simple retinas is taken as an expression of encephalization of nervous control; that is, the tendency for complex processing to be shifted from peripheral to central sites, where interactions with other circuits can take place. We will return to this theme when we discuss the visual cortex.

In the mammal, the ganglion cells are differentiated into several distinct morphological types, each with special functional properties. These are summarized in Table 17.2. We will see that these properties continue to be transmitted in separate channels as far as the visual cortex.

Table 17.2 Summary of different morphological types of retinal ganglion cells and their functional properties, in the cat

	X	Y	W
Morphology			
ganglion cell size	medium	large	varied
number	many; most near fovea	few; most in periphery	few
axons	medium conduction rate	fast conduction rate	varied conduction rate
projection sites	lateral geniculate nucleus	lateral geniculate nucleus and superior colliculus (and medial interlaminar nucleus)	lateral geniculate nucleus and superior colliculus
Function			
spatial summation	linear	nonlinear	mixed
movement sensitivity	+	+++	±
directional selectivity	no	no	yes (a few cells)
center-surround antagonism	yes	yes	±
color coded	yes (in primates)	no	?

Central Visual Pathways

The ganglion cell axons run along the inner surface of the retina and gather together to form the optic nerve. This is the second cranial nerve. By embryonic origin it is a part of the central nervous system. The position and relations of the optic nerve may be reviewed in Chap. 3. In lower vertebrates, the main projection of the optic nerve is to the optic tectum of the midbrain (see Fig. 3.6). The retina is mapped in an orderly, *retinotopic* manner onto the optic tectum, as discussed in Chap. 10. Single-unit studies have shown that in the frog or toad, tectal cells are exquisitely tuned to detect particular types of movements and spatial patterns that allow them to discriminate prey (such as a worm or fly), which elicits prey-catching behavior, or predator, which elicits escape reactions.

In mammals, the optic nerve also projects to the lateral geniculate nucleus (LGN) in the thalamus (Fig. 17.15). The input to the superior colliculus, the hom-

Fig. 17.15. Schematic diagram of the central visual pathway in the human. Note the projections of the visual fields onto the retinae, the partial decussation of the optic tracts, and the orderly projection from the lateral geniculate body in the thalamus to the primary visual cortex in the occipital lobe. (From Popper and Eccles, 1977)

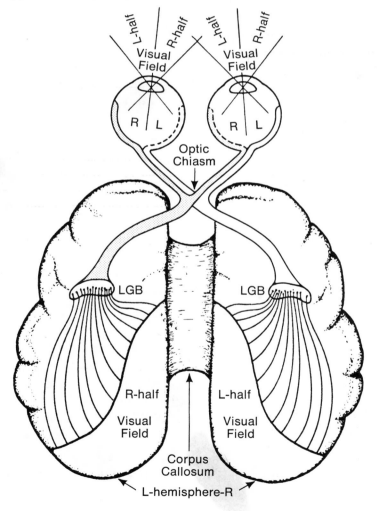

ologue of the optic tectum, still mediates midbrain reflexes important in prey and predator behavior. Most of this input is carried by the Y axons, which arise from ganglion cells in the peripheral parts of the retina, and are tuned to detecting movements in the peripheral visual field. In contrast, the input to the LGN is carried in both X and Y axons. The X axons arise mostly from ganglion cells in the *fovea*, the center of the visual field, where visual acuity is highest.

In lower vertebrates, the two optic nerves cross (decussate) and supply the tectum and thalamus on the opposite side. In most of these animals the eyes are set on the side of the head, and there is little overlap of the two visual fields. In most mammals, however, the eyes are set forward in the head, and the two visual fields partially overlap. Associated with this is usually only a partial decussation of the optic nerve fibers. The situation in the primate is depicted in Fig. 17.15. As can be seen, the ipsilateral fibers are those that arise from the outer (temporal) half of the retina, which receives stimuli from the inner (nasal) half of the visual field. In the LGN, the inputs from the two eyes are kept separated from each other in a series of layers before being relayed to the visual cortex.

In addition to the visual projections to the midbrain and thalamus, a projection to the hypothalamus has recently been identified. This is important in the control of circadian rhythms, as will be discussed in Chap. 26.

Visual Cortex

Cortical Representation. Figure 17.15 indicates that in humans the LGN projects to the occipital lobe of the cerebral cortex. This projection defines the primary visual cortex, called V I by physiologists and area 17 by anatomists. As in other sensory systems, the visual pathway retains a precise topographical order, in which the map of the retina, and hence of the visual field, is projected onto the cortex. The fovea, where acuity is highest, occupies a large part of the cortical representation, similar to the way that regions of highest acuity dominate the maps in other sensory cortical areas.

In the traditional view, the only precise retinotopic map was contained in area 17, and the surrounding bands of cortex (areas 18 and 19) were given over to nontopographical "association" functions. As in the auditory and somatosensory systems, recent studies indicate that there are more representations of the peripheral fields than previously suspected. The situation in the relatively simple cortex of a lower mammal, the hedgehog, is depicted in Fig. 17.16A, where it can be seen that there are just two mappings of the retina, areas V I and V II. In contrast, in the monkey there are a number of additional representations: two are indicated in the figure (DM and MT) and there may be as many as half a dozen more. Most of these additional maps occur within areas previously regarded as "associational".

Where do these cortical areas obtain their retinal input? Recent studies suggest that they receive it through the pathway that projects first to the superior colliculus, and then relays in a part of the thalamus called the *pulvinar*. These connections are shown in Fig. 17.16B. The pulvinar is a part of the thalamus which becomes especially prominent in primates. There are thus a number of parallel pathways from the periphery, through separate relays in the thalamus, to separate areas in the cortex. In these respects the similarities to the somatosensory and auditory systems are indeed striking.

What are the functions of these different parallel pathways? As summarized recently by David van Essen at the California Institute of Technology, the direct pathway, through the lateral geniculate nucleus to primary (striate) cortex, appears to mediate fine-grained pattern analysis. The indirect pathways, through superior colliculus and pulvinar to non-

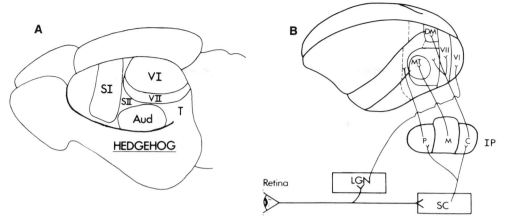

Fig. 17.16. Comparison between the visual cortical areas in a primitive mammal and a monkey. **A.** Brain of the hedgehog, showing visual areas (VI and VII) and other cortical areas: somatosensory (SI and SII); auditory (Aud); temporal cortex (T). **B.** Pathways to different visual cortical areas in the monkey. The pathways are all topographically organized; between thalamus and cortex the connections are also reciprocal. Parallel pathways for X, Y, and W retinal ganglion cells are not shown. Abbreviations: DM, dorsomedial visual area; IP, inferior pulvinar complex, consisting of central (C), medial (M), and posterior (P) divisions; LGN, lateral geniculate nucleus; MT, middle temporal visual area; SC, superior colliculi; V I and V II, primary and secondary visual areas. (From Merzenich and Kass, 1980)

striate cortical areas, appear related to such functions as visual attention, movement detection, and control of eye movements. The many connections between the different centers provide for rich interactions at all levels of visual processing.

Functional Units. The discovery by Stephen Kuffler in 1953 of the center–surround organization of ganglion cells not only was the basis for our understanding of the retina, but also provided the key to unlocking the mysteries of the cortex, which until then had seemed too complex to yield to single-unit analysis. Armed with this tool, David Hubel and Torsten Wiesel, in Kuffler's laboratory, took the first step centrally by recording from single cells in the LGN. They found little difference from the properties of ganglion cells. Emboldened, they tackled the visual cortex. By careful control of the visual stimuli, they were able to elucidate a logical sequence of processing of visual signals, and suggest some simple ways the cortex could

be organized to accomplish this. Their work called forth an enormous outpouring of papers, which have extended and modified the original findings and concepts in many ways. However, for a generation the Hubel and Wiesel approach has been the touchstone for virtually all other work in the field. It has not only focused speculations on the visual mechanisms underlying perception, but it has been an inspiration to those working in other parts of the nervous system as well, in showing that a complicated system can be made to be understandable. This was recognized by the awarding of the Nobel prize in 1981.

The basic findings of Hubel and Wiesel begin with the fact that, in the primary visual cortex, the terminals of LGN input fibers are the only elements with center–surround antagonism. The simplest properties of cortical cells are responsiveness to a bar or edge of light, with a particular orientation, in a particular position in the visual field. Cells with these properties are called *simple cells*. More complicated are

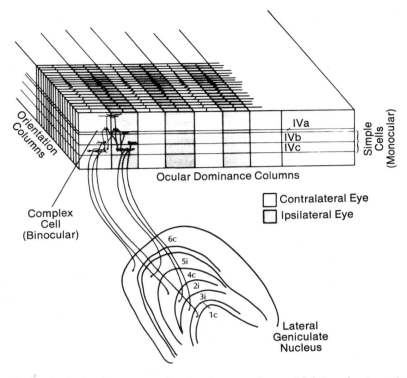

Fig. 17.17. Idealized relation between ocular dominance columns (slabs) and orientation columns (slabs) in visual cortex. Also shown are connections from lateral geniculate nucleus to simple cells, and from latter to complex cells, as proposed in hierarchical scheme. The columns in reality are less rigidly orthogonal to each other than shown here. (From Hubel and Wiesel, 1974)

responses to a bar or edge, with a specific orientation, but placed anywhere in the visual field. Cells with this property, of signaling orientation independently of position, are called *complex cells.* Responses to bars of specific length and width are another type, initially called *hypercomplex;* some workers consider these to be variations of the other two types. In addition to these properties, cells can be classified as to whether they are driven by one eye or the other (*ocular dominance*) and by their sensitivity to movement.

With the same technique of making vertical electrode penetrations used by Mountcastle in somatosensory cortex, Hubel and Wiesel found that cells encountered in a single microelectrode penetration all tend to be driven by one eye or the other. This suggested that cells are

organized in alternating *ocular dominance* columns. Similarly, it was found that all the cells in a penetration tend to be tuned to the same orientation of an edge or bar. These are called *orientation columns.* A schematic diagram showing how, in an idealized manner, the two types of columns combine to form a *hypercolumn,* is depicted in Fig. 17.17.

The ocular dominance columns have been demonstrated by a variety of anatomical techniques, such as transport of labeled amino acids from one eye (see Chap. 4). The most dramatic demonstration of both types of columns has come from the combined application of amino acid transport and the 2DG method (see Fig. 17.18). Note that, in both Figs. 17.17 and 17.18, the organization is in terms of slabs or rows of columns, rather than individual columns. Note also that the ocular dominance and orientation columns intersect much more variably in the experimental results than they do in the idealized model—a common failing of the real world!

There has been much interest in the neural organization within a column. The original suggestion of Hubel and Wiesel was that the sequence of response properties from simple to complex could be explained by a simple model in which LGN terminals converge onto simple cells, which then converge onto complex cells.

Fig. 17.18. Demonstration of cortical columns, as rows or slabs. **A.** Monkey injected with 3H-proline in one eye and brain processed for autoradiography after 2 weeks. Figure is a montage of sections cut tangentially through Layer IVc of the visual cortex. Light stripes are ocular dominance bands of radioactive label as seen under dark-field microscopy. **B.** Same monkey, stimulated with vertical stripe pattern to remaining eye after systemic injection of 14C–2DG. Stripes indicate bands of orientation columns as seen in X-ray autoradiograph. (From Hubel et al., 1978)

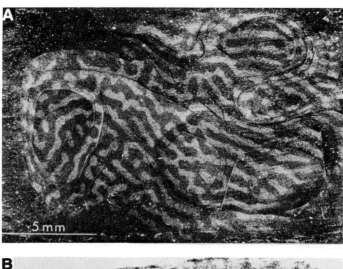

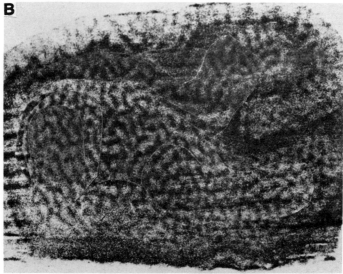

A. COLUMN FOR SERIAL PROCESSING

B. COLUMN FOR SERIAL AND PARALLEL PROCESSING

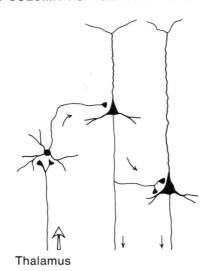

Thalamus

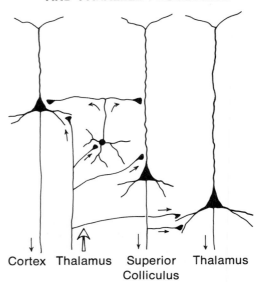

Cortex Thalamus Superior Thalamus
                  Colliculus

Fig. 17.19. Circuit diagrams of synaptic organization of visual cortex, showing serial and parallel connections of inputs from thalamus, and multiple output pathways originating from cells in different layers.

This became known as the *serial* or *hierarchical model*. However, in recent years anatomists have found that LGN axons make connections onto both simple and complex types of cells. Physiologists have found that LGN cells relaying X inputs connect to simple cells, whereas Y inputs connect to complex cells. Thus, there appear to be parallel connections to simple and complex cells, and this has given rise to a *parallel model*. The two models are depicted in Fig. 17.19. The two conceptions are by no means mutually exclusive; rather than parallel vs. serial, the processing of information within a cortical functional unit probably involves both types of connections. How they interact to give rise to the functional properties of cortical neurons is under active study at present.

REFERENCES

Baylor, D. A., T. D. Lamb, and K. -W. Yau. 1979. The membrane current of single rod outer segments. *J. Physiol. 288:* 589–611. ibid., Responses of retinal rods to single photons, pp. 613–634.

Dowling, J. E. 1979. Information processing by local circuits: the vertebrate retina as a model system. In *The Neurosciences: Fourth Study Program* (ed. by F. O. Schmitt and F. G. Worden). Cambridge, Mass.: MIT Press. pp. 163–182.

Eakin, R. M. 1965. Evolution of photoreceptors. *Cold Spring Harbor Symp. Quant. Biol. 30:* 363–370.

Goldsmith, T. H. 1980. Hummingbirds see near ultraviolet light. *Science 207:* 786–788.

Gordon, M. S. 1972. [Chap. 16].

Hubbell, W. L. and M. D. Bownds. 1979. Visual transduction in vertebrate photoreceptors. *Ann. Rev. Neurosci. 2:* 17–34.

Hubel, D. H. and T. N. Wiesel. 1974. Sequence regularity and geometry of orientation columns in the monkey striate cortex. *J. Comp. Neurol. 158:* 267–294.

Hubel, D. H., T. N. Wiesel, and M. P. Stryker. 1978. Anatomical demonstration of orientation columns in macaque monkey. *J. Comp. Neurol. 177:* 361–380.

Knowles, A. and H. J. A. Dartnall. 1977. The photobiology of vision. In *The Eye*, Vol. 2B. (ed. by H. Dawson). New York: Academic.

Land, M. F. 1981. Optics and vision in invertebrates. In *Handbook of Sensory Physiology*. Vol. VII/6B, *Comparative Physiology and Evolution of Vision in Invertebrates. B: Invertebrate Visual Centers and Behavior I* (ed. by H. Autrum). New York: Springer. pp. 471–594.

Laughlin, S. 1981. Neural principles in the visual system. In *Handbook of Sensory Physiology*. Vol. VII/6B, ibid., pp. 133–280.

Maturana, H. R., J. Y. Letvin, W. S. McCulloch, and W. H. Pitts. 1960. Anatomy and physiology of vision in the frog. (*Rana pipiens*). *J. Gen. Physiol. 43:* 129–175.

Meinertzhagen, J. A. 1977. Development of neuronal circuitry in the insect optic lobe. In *Soc. for Neurosci. Symp. II* (ed. by W. H. Cowan and J. A. Ferrendelli). Bethesda, Md.: Soc. for Neurosci. pp. 92–119.

Merzenich, M. M. and J. H. Kaas. 1980. [Chap. 13].

Popper, K. R. and J. C. Eccles. 1977. *The Self and Its Brain*. New York: Springer.

Shaw, S. 1981. Anatomy and physiology of identified non-spiking cells in the photoreceptor-lamina complex of the compound eye of insects, especially Diptera. In *Neurones Without Impulses* (ed. by A. Roberts and B. M. H. Bush). Cambridge: Cambridge University Press. pp. 61–116.

Strausfeld, N. J. and P. R. Nässel. 1981. Neuroarchitecture of brain regions that subserve the compound eyes of crustacea and insects. In *Handbook of Sensory Physiology*. Vol. VII/6B, ibid., pp. 1–132.

van Essen, D. C. 1979. Visual areas of the mammalian cerebral cortex. *Ann. Rev. Neurosci. 2:* 227–263.

Wald, G. 1968. Molecular basis of visual excitation. *Science 162:* 230–239.

Additional Reading

Stone, J., B. Dreher, and A. Levinthal. 1979. Hierarchical and parallel mechanisms in the organization of visual cortex. *Brain Res. Rev. 1:* 345–394.

Werblin, F. S. and J. E. Dowling. 1969. Organization of the retina of the mudpuppy, *Necturus maculosus*. II. Intracellular recording. *J. Neurophysiol. 32:* 339–355.

IV
Motor Systems

18
Introduction:
the Nature of Motor Function

Animal experience begins with information about the world that flows in through sensory organs and sensory pathways, as discussed in the previous section. However, the behavior of an animal depends on how it combines that information with its internal states and drives in order to do something. Doing something requires motor organs and the nervous circuits to control them, which together form what is called *motor systems*.

Motor systems bring about movement, and the importance of movement has always been apparent to students of animal life. The early Greek philosophers recognized that the ability to move is the essence of being alive. Furthermore, the ability of an organism to move itself about and perform actions on its environment, under control of a nervous system, is one of the crucial features that distinguishes animals from plants. In the evolution of animal life, it seems safe to say that different motor abilities have been among the chief agents for the diversity of adaptations that characterize different species. Motor abilities have been no less important in human evolution. The making of fire, development of tools, invention of the wheel, and the use of weapons for hunting

and implements for farming, all involved the elaboration and extension of man's motor apparatus. Finally, the capacities for speech, writing, and artistic expression are all motor activites.

The study of this amazing array of activities is a fascinating one for neurobiologists. In one respect, the study is easy, because motor actions are observable and can be measured. To get much farther than this, however, is very difficult. One of the main problems is that has been difficult to identify basic units of nervous organization relative to motor function. When reflexes were recognized in the course of the nineteenth century, it was hoped that the reflex arc might serve as a basic functional unit. This has been true to some extent, as we shall see in Chap. 20. However, modern studies are leading toward a wider view in which motor organization shares many of the basic principles that characterize the general organization of nerve circuits throughout the nervous system.

As we now extend our study to motor systems, it may seem that they are quite different from the sensory systems discussed in the preceding section. After all, information flows *into* the organism (through *afferent* pathways) in sensory systems, whereas it flows *out of the organism* (through *efferent* pathways) in motor systems. Furthermore, the peripheral motor organs—glands and muscles—appear to be radically different from the receptors that receive sensory stimuli. However, at the *cellular* level, glands and muscles represent logical variations on the basic cellular plan discussed in Chap. 4. The *junctions* between these motor organs and the nerve fibers that innervate them are similar in principle to synapses between neurons, and between neurons and receptors (Chap. 5 and Section III). Finally, motor pathways are organized into *circuits* along many of the same general principles as are sensory pathways.

These similarities mean that we can approach the study of motor systems using the same logical approach to basic mechanisms that was applied to sensory systems. These basic mechanisms operate at the same three main levels: the peripheral *motor organs*, the *neural circuits*, and the *behavior* of the whole organism (see Table 18.1). In this chapter we will become familiar with the basic properties of the motor organs and their motor nerves. Later chapters in this section will examine the neural circuits of different motor systems.

Effector Organs

In sensory systems, we saw that we could identify different types of sensory receptors. Similarly, there are different types of motor organs. Because their actions have effects, we also refer to them as *effectors* or *effector organs*.

In very primitive animals, effectors may be present in rather special forms. Thus, the motor activity of the single-cell *Paramecium* involves the beating of *cilia*, which propels it in the manner shown in Fig. 18.1). Motile cilia are, of course, present on many types of cells throughout the invertebrates, but in general they are not under nervous control. In the coelenterate *Hydra*, one of the main effector organs is the *nematocyst* (arising from the cnidoblast; hence, the class name, *Cnidaria*). The nematocyst is released on contact by an appropriate foreign organism. The local sensory stimulus is sufficient to trigger discharge (see Fig. 18.1), without intervention of the nerve net of the *Hydra*. This has the advantage of an immediate response, but the disadvantage is that the discharge cannot be incorporated by nervous control into integrated and purposive acts of the whole organism.

Among higher metazoans the two main types of effector organs are *glands* and *muscles*. Corresponding to these are the two main types of effector (motor) actions, *glandular secretion* and *muscle contraction*. It has been said (somewhat irreverently) that the only things an animal can do are squirt a juice and squeeze a muscle! It is true that glands and muscles are the characteristic effector organs of most invertebrates and vertebrates. However, as Table 18.2 shows, this simple statement hides a wealth of diversity. To begin with, glands are divided into two main classes (endocrine and exocrine). Within these two classes is an enormous variety of specialized types; Table 18.2 lists only a few examples. Similarly, muscles are divided into two main types, smooth and striated, and these are deployed in many different ways. Finally, there are other types of effectors;

Table 18.1 Comparison of levels of organization in sensory and motor systems

Organizational level	Sensory systems	Motor systems
peripheral organs	sensory receptors	glands and muscles
circuits	afferent pathways	efferent pathways
behavior	perception	motor patterns

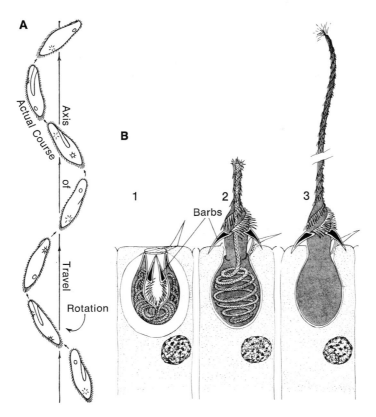

Fig. 18.1. Specialized motor structures of primitive animals. **A.** Locomotion of paramecium by ciliary beating. The animal progresses in a spiral manner because of the asymmetry of the body. **B.** The nematocyst of Hydra. This single-cell organelle is discharged in the manner shown. Different nematocysts are specialized for attachment and for stinging (killing or defense). (A from Storer, 1943; B from Wells, 1968)

these include, for example, the electroplaque organ, which is composed of modified muscle cells. Thus, as Table 18.2 illustrates, animals can send shocks, spin silk, change color, and do a number of things not adequately accounted for by the traditional functions of simple glandular secretion or muscular contraction.

With this perspective on effector organs, let us consider briefly the cellular structure and functional properties of glands and muscles.

Glands

The cellular basis for the secretory activity of gland cells has been described in Chap.

4. It will be recalled that in secretory cells the smooth endoplasmic reticulum of the cytoplasm is grouped in stacks, called the Golgi complex, where the specific proteins are stored, and packaged into secretory granules. The granules are released when the cell receives its appropriate stimulus. The features do vary considerably, depending on the particular type of secretory activity. For example, secretory granules may not be demonstrable in the electron microscope in some cells, particularly those that secrete small amounts rather continuously. On the other hand, granules tend to be more prominent in cells that store the secretions and release them intermittently in massive amounts. Secre-

Table 18.2   Types of motor organs

	Examples	
	Invertebrate	Vertebrate
Glands		
Endocrine	neuroendocrine cells	neuroendocrine cells
		hypothalamus
	neurohemal organs	pituitary gland
	endocrine organs	endocrine organs
Exocrine		
internal	goblet cells (mucus)	goblet cells (mucus)
	digestive glands	digestive glands
	salivary glands	–
	(enzymes, silk, jelly)	
external (integument)	slime-secreting cells	sweat, sebaceous glands
	adhesive-secreting cells	–
	pheromone-secreting cells	pheromone-secreting cells
	toxin-secreting cells	toxin-secreting cells
	ink glands	–
	chromatophores	chromatophores
Muscles		
Smooth muscle	(rare)	visceral (involuntary)
Striated muscle	–	heart
cardiac, skeletal	gut, trunk, appendages	trunk and appendages
Modified muscle	–	electroplaque organ
Cilia	numerous small organisms	lining of various organs
Self-contained organs	nematocysts	–

tory cells exhibit appropriate variations in fine structure, reflecting these differences in function.

Types of Glands. As previously noted, there are two main classes of glands. *Endocrine* glands manufacture hormones which are secreted into the bloodstream and act on distant cells and organs within the body. Some of these glands consist of nerve cells and their processes that, in addition to their "neuronal" properties, such as synaptic actions or impulse generation, are also modified to secrete hormones. Such cells are termed variously *neurosecretory* or *neuroendocrine* cells. They appear to have arisen very early in animal evolution. For example, some cells in the nerve net of *Hydra* contain large neurosecretory granules. It is believed that these granules contain hormones that are secreted during growth, budding, and regeneration of branches, and are involved in activating or controlling those processes. An example of an invertebrate

neurosecretory cell is shown in Fig. 18.2A.

Neurosecretion is a good mechanism for mediating hormonal effects, particularly in small animals, because fibers can extend from the central nervous system to make close contacts with target organs. In large animals, however, this process becomes unwieldy. Some neuroendocrine cells are therefore grouped in peripheral ganglia, and act on their target organs by discharging their hormones into the bloodstream or other body fluid. These ganglia, in invertebrates, are referred to as *neurohemal* organs (see Chaps. 2 and 10). This mode of action, to be most effective, requires a well-developed circulatory system, which seems to be why neurohemal cells and organs have arisen later in evolution. They are prominent mainly in annelids and arthropods. In vertebrates, counterparts of the neurohemal organ are found in the hypothalamus, posterior pituitary, and adrenal medulla (see Chap. 3). An example of a neurosecretory cell of the hypothalamus is shown in Fig. 18.2B.

In higher metazoans there are, throughout the body, many types of cells grouped in glands that do not depend on direct innervation for their control. Secretions of these cells are controlled by blood-borne factors, which may arise from distant nerve cells, from other glands, or from target organs. Such cells may be grouped in special endocrine organs, like the thyroid or adrenal cortex, or be found within other organs, such as the kidney or gonads. Although a full account of the endocrine system falls outside the scope of this book, we will often refer to the various endocrine organs in the context of their ultimate neural control through the hypothalamus and pituitary gland.

In contrast to endocrine cells is the *exocrine* type of secretory cell. Characteristically these cells are grouped together to form a gland, and the substance is carried away in a duct. Glands of this type perform a variety of functions in the body. Some are involved in nonnervous functions, such as the digestive glands of the gastrointestinal system. Most, however, are under some degree of nervous control. This control is exerted through the autonomic nervous system, which we will consider in the next chapter.

We generally think of the glands of the body as involved mostly in housekeeping chores, helping to maintain the constancy of the internal environment (*milieu interieur*) and enabling it to respond to stress. These are indeed important functions. However, as indicated in Table 18.2, many glands are parts of the motor apparatus through which the animal operates on the external world. The neural control of these glands characteristically involves sensory recognition of the appropriate releasing stimuli and precise timing of secretion in relation to a sequence of behavioral acts.

Excitation-Secretion Coupling. In glands under neural control, stimulation occurs by means of a neurotransmitter liberated

Fig. 18.2. Neurosecretory cells. **A.** Neurosecretory cell of a worm (Planaria). Note variety of vesicle sizes and contents, including large neurosecretory granules. R, ribosomes. For other organelles, consult Fig. 4.1. **B.** Neurohyphophysis (posterior lobe) of the rat pituitary gland. Note nerve terminals containing large dense-core neurosecretory granules and small clear vesicles; note also fenestrated capillary wall, permitting passage of secreted materials into bloodstream. (A from Lentz, 1968; B from P. Orkand and S. L. Palay, in Bloom and Fawcett, 1975)

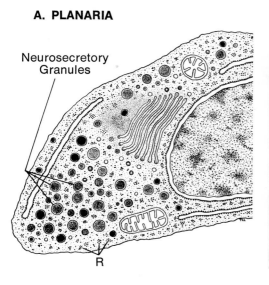

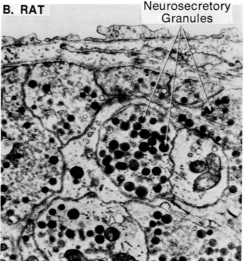

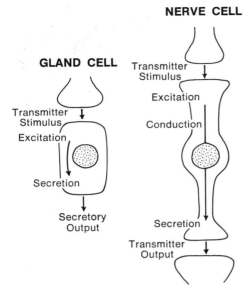

Fig. 18.3. Diagrams showing similarities between excitation-secretion coupling in gland cells and nerve cells.

from the terminals of the motor axon. The neurotransmitter generally brings about a depolarization of the gland cell, similar to the end-plate potential in a muscle. The depolarization gives rise to an action potential in some gland cells, as was pointed out in Chap. 7; in others the electrical response consists only of the graded postsynaptic potential. What is the linkage between this depolarization and the release of secretory substances? This linkage has been termed *excitation-secretion coupling* as mentioned previously, in analogy with excitation-contraction coupling in muscle. In the gland cell, the coupling usually involves the following sequence: depolarization of the membrane; influx of Ca^{2+}; rise in intracellular free Ca^{2+}; movement of superficial granules to plasmalemma; fusion of vesicle membrane and plasmalemma and release of secretory substances. The sequence is similar to the steps controlling release of neurotransmitter at a chemical synapse. In fact, it has been suggested that the basic mechanism of excitation-secretion coupling became adapted in evolution for synaptic trans-

mission. A representation of the relations between the two processes is shown in Fig. 18.3.

Skeletal Muscle

Like gland cells, muscle cells owe their properties to specializations of their cytostructure. Also like gland cells, these structures are part of the basic equipment of all cells, but developed to a higher degree. In the case of muscle, the properties reside in two filamentous proteins, *actin* and *myosin*. These proteins are widely distributed in body cells, and subserve a variety of functions related to cell movements, such as formation of pseudopodia and the cell movements that occur during development (Chap. 10). In muscle, these proteins and their mechanism of interaction have become specialized for the specific tasks of producing movement, not just of individual cells, but of whole organs.

We know most about these proteins and their mechanisms in *skeletal muscles*, those that move bones and joints. Skeletal muscle is also called *striated*, or *striped*, muscle, because under the light microscope the individual muscle fibers have a banded appearance. The bands reflect the division of each fiber into a series of *sarcomeres*, which are the contractile units of the fiber. Each sarcomere is composed of a set of myofilaments; the myofilaments are actin or myosin, organized in a precise overlapping array. These features are depicted in Fig. 18.4.

The explanation for how the overlapping actin and myosin molecules bring about contraction is embodied in the *sliding-filament model*. This was first conceived in 1954 by two independent groups of workers, Hugh Huxley and Jean Hanson in London, and Andrew Huxley and Robert Niedergerke in Cambridge, England. Their work was initially based on observations in the light microscope, and has since been confirmed and greatly elaborated by many studies with the electron microscope.

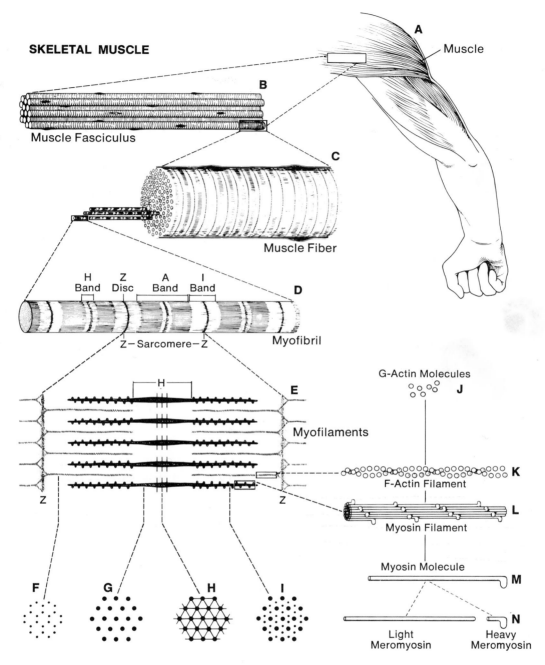

SKELETAL MUSCLE

A — Muscle

B — Muscle Fasciculus

C — Muscle Fiber

D — Myofibril
H Band   Z Disc   A Band   I Band
Z — Sarcomere — Z

E — Myofilaments
H
Z   Z
F   G   H   I

J — G-Actin Molecules

K — F-Actin Filament

L — Myosin Filament

M — Myosin Molecule

N — Light Meromyosin   Heavy Meromyosin

Fig. 18.4. Levels of organization of skeletal muscle, from the whole muscle to its cellular and molecular constituents. (From Bloom and Fawcett, 1975)

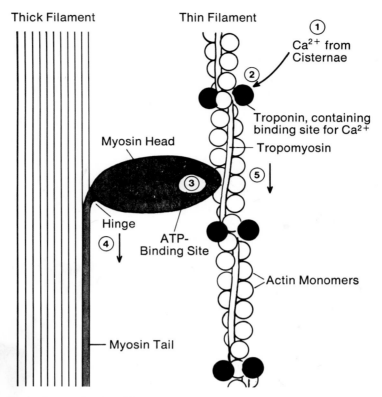

Fig. 18.5. Molecular basis of sliding filament mechanism. See text. (Adapted from Huxley, in Lehninger, 1975)

The essence of the model is illustrated in Fig. 18.4. It had previously been speculated that contraction might come about by a shortening or crumpling of the individual filaments, but this was replaced by the idea that the filaments slide along between each other. This sliding brings about changes in the widths of some of the bands, without changing the lengths of the filaments themselves.

The molecular mechanism which brings about the sliding of the actin filaments past the myosin filaments is illustrated in Fig. 18.5. Actin filaments contain tropomyosin and troponin, in addition to actin. In the relaxed state, tropomyosin inhibits the myosin attachment sites on the G-actin filaments. Also, in the relaxed state, free Ca^{2+} is very low around the filaments. Muscle activation begins with release of Ca^{2+} ①, which binds to the troponin. This induces a conformational change in the troponin ②, which exposes the myosin binding sites of the G-actin subunits. The attachment of myosin ③ forms a *force-generating complex*. This induces a conformation change in the heavy meromyosin head, and a consequent rotation at the hinge between the head and the rest of the myosin molecule ④. The rotation generates the *power stroke* that causes the actin to be displaced ⑤.

The energy for these movements is supplied by ATP. The myosin heads have binding sites for ATP. It is believed that the ATP may be bound in the form of ADP + P with the energy of the phosphate bond transferred in some way to the myosin head to hold it in the *energized* conformation (Fig. 18.5). At the end of the power stroke, the myosin head assumes its *deenergized* form; the ADP + P are released, to be replaced by new ATP, which causes the myosin head to return to its energized conformation.

There remains to account for the initial release of Ca^{2+} that sets this molecular machinery in motion. The full sequence of these events is depicted in Fig. 18.6. It starts with the end-plate potential (EPP) that we discussed in Chap. 8. In some muscles, usually smaller and more slowly contracting fibers, the graded EPP may be the only electrical response. In large and rapidly contracting muscles, an action potential is set up by the EPP. The action potential propagates along the muscle membrane in essentially the same manner as the action potential in a nerve. The depolarization spreads rapidly into the interior of the muscle fiber through a special membrane system called the *t-tubule system*. The t-tubules are in close apposition (30 nm) to the membrane of the sarcoplasmic reticulum. Depolarization of the tubules brings about depolarization of the cisternae, which causes release of free calcium into the sarcoplasm surrounding the muscle myofilaments. The Ca^{2+} binds to troponin and initiates the events depicted in Fig. 18.5. The Ca^{2+} is restored to the cisternae by a very active *Ca pump*.

The whole sequence of events shown in Fig. 18.6 brings about a transformation from the electrical signal in the muscle membrane to a mechanical change in the myofilaments. This sequence is referred to as *excitation-contraction coupling*. It is analogous to the sequence of *excitation-secretion coupling* that takes place in gland cells.

The events just described are understood best in vertebrate skeletal muscle, where the myofilaments are packed together at very high density in very regular arrays. In vertebrate *cardiac muscle* the sarcomere structure is similar, and the sliding filament mechanism is believed to be basically the same.

Smooth Muscle

Smooth muscle also contains actin and, in smaller amounts, myosin, but they are not organized into repeating sarcomere units. Contraction also depends on Ca^{2+}, although the ion appears to bind directly to

Fig. 18.6. Sequence of events (1–6) in "excitation-contraction" coupling. Diagram emphasizes relations between T-tubule system, sarcoplasmic reticulum, and the sliding filaments. (Adapted from Guyton, 1976)

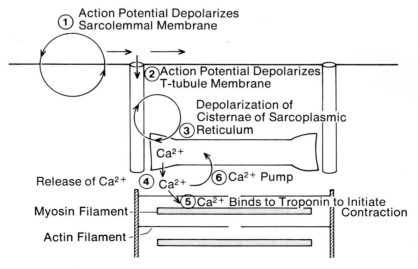

myosin (rather than troponin), where it activates the myosin ATPase and brings about attachment of the myosin head to the actin. The contractile mechanism itself is believed to involve sliding of the actin past the myosin, essentially as in the sliding-filament model. Other types of filaments are also present in smooth muscle, which may provide for additional force generation, as well as attachment to the cell wall. A t-tubule system is usually absent; rapid spread of depolarization into the interior of the fiber seems not to be needed for the slower time course of contraction of smooth muscle. The mechanism of excitation-contraction coupling thus differs in certain respects from that in skeletal muscle. In addition, the electrical activity underlying the excitation varies considerably. Some smooth muscles, such as those in the gut, undergo spontaneous contractions. These are due to periodic slow depolarizing waves which generate action potentials in the fibers. The effect of nerve stimulation is to modify and coordinate this spontaneous rhythm. Other smooth muscles are active only when stimulated by their autonomic nerve supply.

Invertebrate Muscle

In invertebrates, most muscles, whether skeletal or visceral, are of the striated type. The organization of the sarcomeres is similar to that in vertebrates, and the sliding-filament model seems to apply in general. There are a number of variations on this basic plan, however, reflecting the diverse ways that muscle is employed. This extends from the extremely rapidly contracting flight muscles of insects to the very slowly contracting "catch" muscles of molluscs. The adaptations to this range of functions involve such differences as the ratios of actin to myosin filaments, details of molecular composition of the actin and myosin, and the distribution of t-tubules and mitochondria (see below).

Diversity of Muscles, Junctions, and Nerves

From the foregoing discussion it can be appreciated that muscle fibers vary considerably in their structure and their functional properties. The same may be said of the junctions between the muscle fibers and their motor nerves. The neuromuscular junctions of skeletal muscles have a specialized structure, as we discussed in Chap. 8; in contrast, the motor nerves to smooth muscles terminate in free nerve endings among the fibers, with little evidence of special contacts.

All these differences mean that there is actually a rich variety of combinations of properties that the peripheral motor apparatus can have. The variety is largest in invertebrates, consistent with the fact that invertebrates have more complexity of neural control in the periphery, in contrast to vertebrates with their tendency toward central control. A particularly good preparation for demonstrating these properties is found in the limb muscles of crustaceans. Work on the neural control of these muscles began with the pioneering experiments of Kees Wiersma and Graham Hoyle, and has been carried forward by many workers in different disciplines. We will summarize some of the principles that have emerged, drawing on the recent studies of Harold Atwood and his colleagues in Toronto.

A single muscle may contain fibers with different structures and properties. As shown in Fig. 18.7, the opener muscle of the crab *Chionoecetes* contains fibers that vary in the lengths of their sarcomeres, the lengths of their myofilaments, and the distribution of the t-tubule system. Associated with this structural diversity are differences in the electrical properties of the muscle membrane. The fibers with long sarcomeres show mostly graded responses to electrical stimulation. Fibers with intermediate-length sarcomeres respond with partially regenerative depolarizations. Only the fibers with short sarcomeres gen-

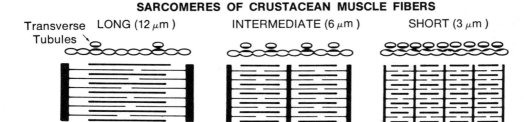

SARCOMERES OF CRUSTACEAN MUSCLE FIBERS

Transverse LONG (12 μm)   INTERMEDIATE (6 μm)   SHORT (3 μm)
Tubules

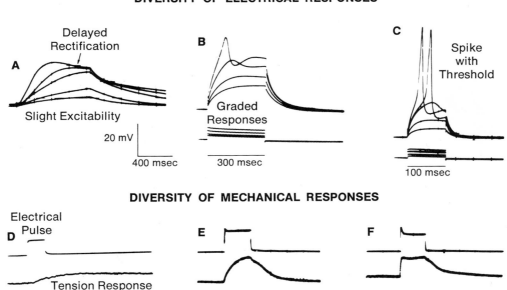

DIVERSITY OF ELECTRICAL RESPONSES

A
Delayed
Rectification

Slight Excitability

20 mV

400 msec

B
Graded
Responses

300 msec

C
Spike
with
Threshold

100 msec

DIVERSITY OF MECHANICAL RESPONSES

D
Electrical
Pulse

Tension Response

E

F

Fig. 18.7. Diversity of muscle fibers and their functional properties, in the opener muscle of the crab, *Chionoecetes,* and lobster muscle fibers (E,F). (From Atwood, 1977)

erate large, brief action potentials. Also illustrated are three types of mechanical properties, varying from slow to rapid development of tension when the muscle contracts. In these muscles, therefore, there is a close correlation of structural, electrical, and mechanical properties. In other muscles, however, there may be diversity of function without apparent structural differences. These studies indicate that the muscles themselves provide the basis for considerable diversity of functional properties.

The neuromuscular junction is the second site of functional diversity. The ver-

tebrate muscle fiber receives its excitatory input from the branch of a single motoneuron, but invertebrate fibers may be innervated by more than one nerve fiber (*polyneuronal innervation*). The innervation pattern of the opener muscle of the crab is outlined in Fig. 18.8. There is a large-diameter, fast-conducting axon, and a small diameter, slowly conducting axon. The former mainly innervates the fast-acting, more excitable muscle fibers, whereas the latter tends to innervate the more slowly acting, less excitable fibers.

Repetitive nerve stimulation of the fast axon sets up, initially, a large EPP that

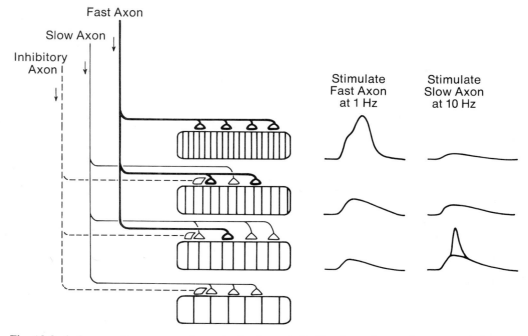

Fig. 18.8. A. Innervation pattern of muscles in the crab. **B.** Use-dependence of neuromuscular junctions at fast and slow muscles. (After Atwood, 1973)

gives rise to an action potential. As stimulation continues, the EPP decreases in amplitude, and the action potential fails. The repetitive stimulation is called *tetanization*, and the decrease of the response is called *depression*. In contrast, repetitive stimulation of the slow axon first elicits only a small, slow, graded potential response. However, as tetanization proceeds, the response begins to increase in size, and may even give rise to an action potential (see Fig. 18.8). This increase in response is called *facilitation*. These results are mainly due to differences in the mobilization and release of the neurotransmitter glutamate at the neuromuscular junction. They demonstrate that the functions of these synapses are exquisitely dependent on the duration and pattern of nerve stimulation. This property of "*use dependence*" is an expression of synaptic plasticity, one that is important in the synaptic mechanisms underlying memory and learning (Chap. 30).

In addition to these excitatory axons,

there is also an inhibitory axon that supplies all the muscle fibers in the opener muscle. The terminals of this axon have been shown to make two kinds of inhibitory synapses (Fig. 18.9). One is onto the muscle itself; by this means, the axon produces an inhibitory *post* synaptic potential (IPSP) in the muscle fiber. The other is onto an excitatory terminal; by this means, an IPSP is produced in the terminal. We say that this causes *pre* synaptic inhibition of the muscle fiber. The inhibitory transmitter is GABA, which causes an increase in Cl^- conductance of the post synaptic membrane.

We thus can see that the excitatory and inhibitory nerve terminals actually form, together with the muscle, a kind of local circuit, which is organized along principles very similar to those that we outlined for synaptic circuits in neural centers in Chap. 5. This peripheral microcircuit provides for local control of input–output transmission at the final relay from the nerves to the muscle. It is as if the organism wants to fine-tune its motor output, out to the last possible step of neural control.

Development of the Vertebrate Neuromuscular Junction

Because of its accessibility and the ease with which it can be experimentally manipulated, we know more about the vertebrate neuromuscular junction than any other synapse. Studies of the developing junction have been particularly important in this regard. The hope in much of this work is that it will be possible to identify the molecular mechanisms that guide the nerve to its target and control the differentiation of the junctional complex. Thus far, it has been possible to specify four main types of interaction that take place between nerve and muscle, and these are summarized in Fig. 18.10.

The most obvious factor is the activity of the presynaptic nerve. As indicated in (A), this may have several effects on the postsynaptic target. It may contribute to the differentiation of the myotube and development into a mature muscle cell, either by release of transmitter or through electrical junctions; it may also help to shape other membrane properties of the muscle.

At the junction, the release of transmitter (acetylcholine) by presynaptic activity affects the distribution of extrajunctional ACh receptor molecules, and encourages stable deposition of the degrading enzyme acetylcholinesterase.

The dense clustering of ACh receptor molecules that occurs in the postsynaptic membrane depends on the presence of the presynaptic terminal. Although it is attractive to think that the clustering might be induced by presynaptic motoneuron activity, in fact it has been shown to be independent of this. It appears instead that clustering is induced by release of one or more substances, probably polypeptides, which also may have other actions on the developing myotube (Fig. 18.10A, B).

If the presynaptic axon is crucial for the development of the postsynaptic muscle, the opposite is also true. When the motor axon terminal first arrives at the muscle it has a very primitive form, and most of the morphological differentiation of the terminal occurs after a synaptic contact has been established, under the influence of the postsynaptic muscle. This appears to be mediated by several factors, which include specific molecules from three possible areas: (1) contained within the extracellular matrix around the terminal, (2) pro-

Fig. 18.9. Synaptic organization of nerve terminals at the neuromuscular junction. (Based on Atwood, 1977)

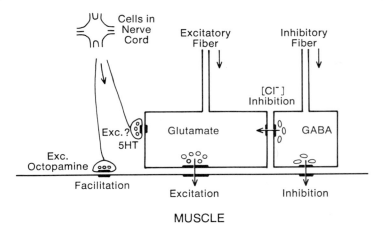

MUSCLE

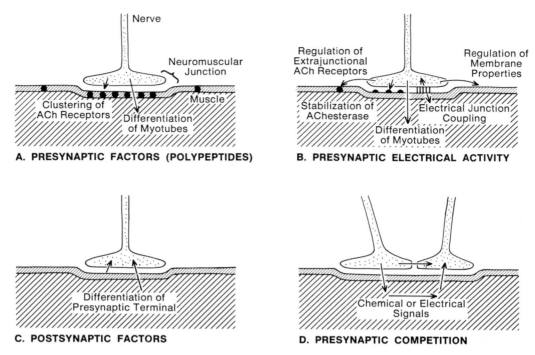

Fig. 18.10. Summary of main types of interactions between nerve and muscle involved in the development of the vertebrate neuromuscular junction. (Based on Lømo and Rosenthal, 1973; Thompson et al., 1979; Frank and Fischbach, 1979; Landmesser, 1980; Dennis, 1981; and many others)

jecting from the postsynaptic membrane, or (3) released from the muscle cytoplasm (see Fig. 18.10C).

Finally, the axons interact among themselves. A given muscle first receives axons from several motoneurons (polyneuronal innervation); in the course of development, all the synapses except those from one motoneuron are eliminated. This appears to reflect competition between the axons. The signals mediating this competition may be either chemical or electrical. They may pass directly between the axons, or indirectly by first affecting the muscle, as shown in Fig. 18.10D.

Although the picture is far from complete, it seems clear at this stage of our understanding that the development of specific synaptic sites, as exemplified by the neuromuscular junction, depends not on one factor, but on multiple factors. The presynaptic process, extracellular matrix, and postsynaptic process each contribute,

in a carefully programmed sequence of mutual interactions. Both chemical and electrical factors are involved. Axons from several presynaptic cells compete for input to one postsynaptic cell. In these basic mechanisms, the neuromuscular junction exemplifies many of the properties of development discussed Chap. 10, and many of the plastic properties involved in regeneration and learning that we encounter in different neural circuits.

REFERENCES

Atwood, H. L. 1973. An attempt to account for the diversity of crustacean muscle. *Am. Zool. 13:* 357–378.

Atwood, H. L. 1977. Crustacean neuromuscular systems: past, present, and future. In *Identified Neurons and Behavior of Arthropods* (ed. by G. Hoyle). New York: Plenum. pp. 9–29.

Bloom, W. and D. W. Fawcett. 1975. *A Textbook of Histology*. Philadelphia: Saunders.

Dennis, M. J. 1981. Development of the neuromuscular junction: inductive interactions between cells. *Am. Rev. Neurosci. 4:* 43–68.

Frank, E. and G. D. Fischbach. 1979. Early events in neuromuscular junction formation in vitro. Induction of acetylcholine receptor clusters in the post synaptic membrane and morphology of newly formed synapses. *J. Cell Biol. 83:* 143–158.

Guyton, A. C. 1976. *Textbook of Medical Physiology*. Philadelphia: Saunders.

Hopkins, C. R. 1978. [Chap. 4].

Hoyle, G. 1982. *Muscles and their Nervous Control*. New York: Wiley.

Huxley, H. E. 1973. Muscular contraction and cell mobility. *Nature 243:* 445–449.

Landmesser, L. T. 1980. The generation of neuromuscular specificity. *Ann. Rev. Neurosci. 3:* 279–302.

Lehninger, A. L. 1975. [Chap. 4].

Lentz, T. 1968. *Primitive Nervous Systems*. New Haven: Yale University Press.

Lømo, T. and J. Rosenthal. 1972. Control of ACH sensitivity by muscle activity in the rat. *J. Physiol. 221:* 453–513.

Storer, T. I. 1943. [Chap. 2].

Thompson, W., D. P. Kuffler, and J. K. S. Jansen. 1979. The effect of prolonged, reversible block of nerve impulses on the elimination of polyneuronal innervation of new-born rat skeletal muscle fibers. *Neurosci. 4:* 271–281.

Wells, M. 1968. [Chap. 2].

19

Autonomic Functions

The survey of the invertebrates in Chap. 2 reminded us of the fact that, despite all the variations in body form, one can usually divide the animal body into two parts: a *visceral* part containing the internal organs, and a *somatic* part consisting of the musculoskeletal apparatus and skin. The first is concerned with maintaining the internal evironment and functions within the body, the second with moving the animal about and mediating interactions with the external environment. In animals like molluscs, the division between the two is so clear that it seems almost as if there are two animals, the muscular animal moving about with a visceral animal on its back. In the vertebrates we saw a similar principle at work, with visceral and somatic body parts distinguishable, from the most primitive chordates up through mammals and primates.

The nervous system coordinates the activity of both these parts of the body. This chapter is concerned with the visceral part.

The discovery that the nerves to the viscera constitute a distinct system was made by anatomists from observations in humans. Thomas Willis in 1664 first described the two chains of ganglia running on either side of the vertebral column.

Willis also made the important distinction between nerves that subserve voluntary (somatic) and involuntary (visceral) functions.

In 1732 (how slow progress can be!) Winslow, in France, described the many nerves that connect the chain to the internal organs, and speculated that these nerves bring the organs into "sympathetic" relation with each other. Modern studies of these nerves began with Gaskell and Langley in England, around 1900; the contributions made by their early work toward laying the foundation for our concepts of the chemical nature of synaptic transmission were noted in Chap. 9.

The terms that are now generally used date from that time. All the nerves to the internal organs constitute the *autonomic nervous system* ("autonomous" indicates the involuntary, automatic nature of most of the functions). The system has two main divisions: the *sympathetic* nervous system (originally termed the orthosympathetic by Langley) and the *parasympathetic*. The sympathetic nerves arise from the thoracolumbar segments of the spinal cord, whereas the parasympathetic nerves arise from the brainstem and form the sacral part of the spinal cord. These relations were shown in Fig. 3.11, which the reader should consult for review.

It may be noted that, as commonly defined, the autonomic nervous system consists only of the nerves carrying motor impulses to the internal organs; by this definition, it is exclusively peripheral and motor. While it is useful to be able to define this component, a larger view of the nervous mechanisms involved in regulating the body requires a much broader perspective. Thus, we must take account of the sensory information from the internal organs. We must also understand the effects of a great many peptides and hormones. Finally, we must be able to trace the circuits in the central nervous system that control the peripheral ganglia and nerves. These points have already been touched on in the overview of organization in Chap. 3.

This chapter will deal mainly with the motor ganglia of the autonomic system, comparing the organization of ganglia in the invertebrates and vertebrates. There are many types of ganglia; our focus will be on the nerves that control the heart. In both invertebrates and vertebrates, these nerves have provided particularly clear examples of the principles involved in the functional organization of the autonomic nervous system. We will also note other nerves and ganglia which are covered in other chapters. We will briefly note some central circuits involved in autonomic controls, in anticipation of further treatments in Chaps. 28 and 29.

Basic Plans

Schematic representations of the basic types of organization which characterize the peripheral autonomic nervous system have been shown in Chaps. 2 and 3. The plan for invertebrates is relatively simple; it consists of a ganglion containing output cells that innervate a particular visceral organ or organs. The ganglion, in turn, receives input fibers from other ganglia, which in many cases are part of the central nervous system, or "brain". Actual systems, of course, include more complicated networks of fibers and ganglia, building on this simple scheme.

Among the vertebrates, there is a rather stereotyped organization found from amphibians through higher species. We have already noted the division into parasympathetic and sympathetic parts. As depicted in Fig. 3.11, in the *parasympathetic* division, the peripheral ganglia are located in the organs that their cells innervate. The ganglia, in turn, receive their neural inputs by way of fibers arising from cells in certain nuclei of the brainstem (and sacral spinal cord). By virtue of their positions relative to the ganglia, fibers innervating a ganglion are called *preganglionic*, and those arising from it are *postganglionic*. *Sympathetic* ganglia, in contrast, are arranged in a cord along the vertebral column (see Fig. 3.11) or in the mesentery of the gut. Their cells have long, postganglionic fibers which branch and innervate the internal organs. The cells, in turn, are innervated by preganglionic fibers of cells located in the intermediolateral column of the thoracolumbar portions of the spinal cord. Therefore, in both divisions of the autonomic nervous system, there is, in addition to the centrally located motoneuron within the spinal cord, a peripherally located motoneuron within a ganglion.

It remains to note that a special subdivision of the sympathetic system is located in the interior (medulla) of the adrenal gland. Here cells known as *chromaffin* cells are packed together. These cells contain vesicles filled with catecholamines (mostly epinephrine). Like sympathetic ganglia, the adrenal receives its innervation from motor cells of the intermediolateral column of the spinal cord. The chromaffin cells themselves lack axons; upon stimulation, they discharge their epinephrine into the bloodstream. Through this mechanism, the sympathetic nervous system can mediate hormonal-type actions on various organs throughout the body.

The main types of transmitters found in

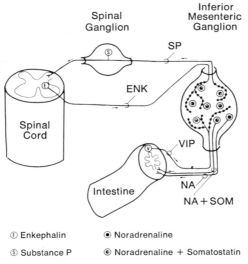

Ⓔ Enkephalin   ◉ Noradrenaline

Ⓢ Substance P   ◉ Noradrenaline + Somatostatin

Ⓥ Vasoactive Intestinal Polypeptide (VIP)

Fig. 19.1. Schematic diagram of the motor and sensory innervation of the gut of the guinea pig. Note the localization of neuropeptides in different neuronal elements: enkephalin in preganglionic motor neurons, somatostatin in postganglionic motor neurons, VIP in neurons of the gut itself, and substance P in sensory neurons. Note also the coexistence of somatostatin and noradrenaline in the same neuron. Some neurons of the gut are also believed to contain gastrin and cholecystokinin. (From Hökfelt et al., 1980)

nomic control of visceral glands and muscles in invertebrates.

Visceral Glands. A good example of this type is found in the salivary gland of various gastropods. The cells of this organ secrete a fluid containing enzymes which aid in digestion. As shown in Fig. 19.2, the gland cells receive their innervation through fibers of an identified neuron (no. 4) in the buccal ganglion. Intracellular electrodes can be introduced into both a 4 neuron and a gland cell to study the response properties of the gland cells. As shown in Fig. 19.2, depolarizing current injected into the 4 neuron elicits single action potentials. In the acinar gland cells, the response, after a delay for impulse conduction and synaptic transmission, consists of

Fig. 19.2. A. Diagram of the innervation of the salivary gland in the snail *Helisoma*. Chemical synapses shown by open terminals, electrical synapses by sawtooth lines. **B.** Electrophysiological recordings in the slug *Ariolimax*. a, Monitor of depolarizing current injected into neuron; b, intracellular response of salivary gland acinar cell; c, response of buccal ganglion neuron into which current was injected. (From Kater, 1977)

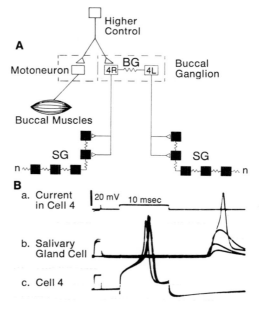

the autonomic nervous systems of invertebrates and vertebrates have been discussed in Chap. 9. As indicated in Fig. 19.1, preganglionic fibers throughout the vertebrate autonomic nervous system use ACh as their transmitter. Postganglionic parasympathetic fibers are also cholinergic; postganglionic sympathetic fibers are adrenergic. To these classical transmitters must now be added the neuropeptides that have been revealed by recent studies. Fig. 19.1 indicates how four of these peptides are localized in different parts of the sympathetic innervation of the gut.

Invertebrates

Let us now consider several types of systems which are representative of auto-

single, discrete EPSPs which, if large enough, give rise to an action potential. The action potential is presumably responsible for an influx of Ca^{2+} that is involved in "excitation–secretion coupling". We have previously noted (Chap. 6) that many types of gland cells are excitable, and the *Helisoma* salivary cell nicely demonstrates this property.

Another interesting property of these cells is that they are electrically coupled to each other. Intracellular experiments show that there may be coupling coefficients between neighboring cells as high as 0.8 (i.e., 8/10 of a signal set up in one cell can be recorded in another cell). By this means, action potentials set up in one part of the acinar cell population rapidly propagate to other cells. This provides for both rapid spread and synchronization of the activities of all cells. The outputs to the right and left halves of the gland are synchronized by means of electrical coupling between the 4 cells.

Figure 19.2 also indicates that the activity of the acinar cells is coordinated with the ingestion of food. This takes place through coordination of 4 neurons with motoneurons of the buccal ganglion during the feeding cycle.

Visceral Muscles. When microelectrode techniques first became available in the 1950's, neurobiologists realized that the simpler ganglia of invertebrates were attractive for the study of neuronal organization; the smaller the ganglion, it was reasoned, the more hope of completely describing its properties and circuits. In this respect, the cardiac ganglion of crustacea, containing only nine cells, all identifiable, seemed ideally suited. This humble structure thus came to play an important role in the early studies of neuronal organization, which adds to its interest as a representative ganglion subserving visceral motor functions.

Muscle activity characteristically involves rhythmic contractions, and these rhythms can be generated by two general types of mechanisms. The rhythmic nature can reflect properties of the muscles themselves (*myogenic rhythm*), or it can be imposed by nervous activity (*neurogenic rhythm*). These two types of mechanisms are basic to rhythmical behavior in most animals, and we will often refer to them in later chapters.

The rhythmic contractions of heart muscle may have either a myogenic or neurogenic basis. In the lobster, the rhythm is neurogenic; if the cardiac nerves are cut, the heart ceases to beat.

The cardiac nerves arise from the cardiac ganglion. This ganglion is actually not a tight cluster of cells, as most ganglia are, but rather a linear chain of cells on the dorsal surface of the heart (see Fig. 19.3).

Fig. 19.3. Functional organization of the cardiac ganglion of the lobster. (Based on Hartline, 1979)

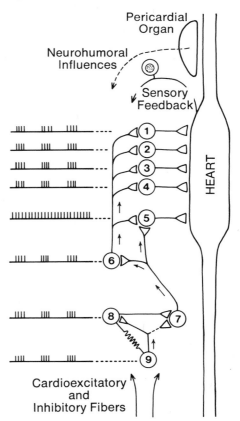

The five most anterior cells are relatively large, and have axons which innervate the heart through excitatory chemical synapses. One can therefore designate these as autonomic *motorneurons*, or *ganglion cells*. The four posterior cells in the chain are small in size. Their axons connect to each other and to the ganglion cells, but they do not leave the ganglion; they are thus designated *interneurons*.

All of the cells in the cardiac ganglion show rhythmic activity, which, under normal conditions, occurs in a coordinated sequence. Cell 9 fires first, and therefore appears to act as a *pacemaker*. The interneurons 6–8 fire their bursts of impulses in close correlation, followed by the motoneurons 1–5. Coordination and sequencing of the activity takes place through the primarily excitatory synaptic interconnections, as indicated in the diagram of Fig. 19.3. Thus, although each cell has the intrinsic ability to be rhythmically active, a rather complicated network is necessary for achieving the appropriate *burst durations, burst intervals, firing frequencies*, and long-term *stability* of heart rate.

The heart rate in the lobster is thus generated by a neurogenic mechanism. However, it is subjected to several other types of influence. As shown in Fig. 19.3, these include *sensory feedback* from stretch receptors in the heart, *neurohormonal effects* mediated via the pericardial organ, and *central nervous control* mediated by cardioaccelleratory and cardioinhibitory fibers. These serve to modulate the heart rate in relation to changes in the internal environment (especially those brought about by feeding and metabolism) or the external environment (such as changes in ambient illumination or presence of prey or predators).

All other crustacea that have been studied so far have heart rates generated by mechanisms similar to those in the lobster. Among other invertebrates, the leech has also been found to have a neurogenic heart rate. In this case, the activities of ganglion cells innervating the heart are coordinated by inhibitory connections of interneurons.

Aplysia provides, by way of contrast, an example of an invertebrate that has a myogenic heartbeat. The heart continues its rhythmic contractions despite severance of all innervation. The rhythms are due to endogenous waves of membrane depolarization in the cardiac cells. Despite the fact that the heart is thus independent of the nervous system for generating its basic rhythm, the rhythm is nonetheless modulated by neural circuits every bit as elaborate as those discussed above. As shown in Fig. 19.4A, there are two identified neurons that excite the heart and two that inhibit it. There are two main types of interneuron: L 10 and INT II. Their actions may be excitatory or inhibitory, depending on the postsynaptic receptors of different cells (cf. Chap. 9); in general, their actions on the heart are antagonistic. The inhibitory action of INT II is illustrated by the recordings in Fig. 19.4B.

The synaptic connections that regulate the heart are integral parts of larger systems controlling related structures. Thus, there are three identified neurons which innervate the great vessels of the heart. These are also under control of L 10 and INT II. L 10 has connections to several other visceral motor organs, including the gill, mantle shelf, and siphon. In general, L 10 activity appears to be mainly responsible for increasing cardiac output, by increasing the heart rate while decreasing vasoconstriction of the aorta. On the other hand, INT II activity decreases cardiac output in synchrony with pumping actions of the gills. Several other interneurons have been found, each controlling a different combination of motoneurons in the abdominal ganglion.

The circuit diagram in Fig. 19.4 illustrates several important principles. It can be seen that there is a *hierarchy of control*, through successive sets of neurons and their connections. The connections of each motoneuron are directed to a specific target organ. The connections of interneurons, however, may go to motoneurons of

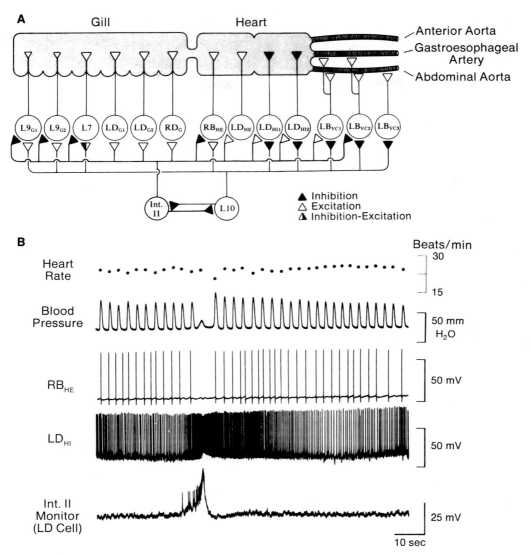

Fig. 19.4. A. Synaptic organization of the cardiorespiratory system in *Aplysia*. Two interneurons (Int. II and L10) make synaptic connections to many motoneurons, identified as indicated by labels. **B.** Intracellular recordings showing that activity in Int II causes synaptic excitation of LD_{HI} and inhibition of RB_{HE}, resulting in decrease in heart rate and blood pressure. (A from Kandel; B from Koester et al., in Kandel, 1976)

different organs; the motoneurons may be excited or inhibited, depending on their postsynaptic receptors for the transmitter substances. In this way, the action of a single neuron may bring about a coordinated sequence of motor activity involving one or several organs. One refers to a cell with this property as a *command neuron*, and the motor sequence elicited is felt by some investigators to constitute a *fixed-action pattern*. We shall have much more to say about these principles of motor control in succeeding chapters.

Vertebrates

As noted in the introduction of this chapter, the autonomic nervous system in ver-

Table 19.1 Effects of autonomic nervous activity on different body organs

Organ	Effect of sympathetic stimulation	Effect of parasympathetic stimulation
Eye: Pupil	dilated	contracted
Ciliary muscle	none	excited
Glands: Nasal	vasoconstriction	stimulation of thin, copious
Lacrimal		secretion containing many enzymes
Parotid		
Submaxillary		
Gastric		
Pancreatic		
Sweat glands	copious sweating (cholinergic)	none
Apocrine glands	thick, odoriferous secretion	none
Heart: Muscle	increased rate	slowed rate
	increased force of contraction	decreased force of atrial contraction
Coronaries	vasodilated	constricted
Lungs: Bronchi	dilated	constricted
Blood vessels	mildly constricted	none
Gut: Lumen	decreased peristalsis and tone	increased peristalsis and tone
Sphincter	increased tone	decreased tone
Liver	glucose released	none
Gallbladder and bile ducts	inhibited	excited
Kidney	decreased output	none
Ureter	inhibited	excited
Bladder: Detrusor	inhibited	excited
Trigone	excited	inhibited
Penis	ejaculation	erection
Systemic blood vessels:		
Abdominal	constricted	none
Muscle	constricted (adrenergic)	none
	dilated (cholinergic)	
Skin	constricted (adrenergic)	dilated
	dilated (cholinergic)	
Blood: Coagulation	increased	none
Glucose	increased	none
Basal metabolism	increased up to 100%	none
Adrenal cortical secretion	increased	none
Mental activity	increased	none
Piloerector muscles	excited	none
Skeletal muscle	increased glycogenolysis	none
	increased strength	

From Guyton (1976)

tebrates falls into two divisions, the parasympathetic and the sympathetic. Table 19.1 summarizes some of the main actions of the two divisions.

Several general conclusions about the relations between the two divisions can be drawn from the table. First, either system may be stimulatory or inhibitory to a given organ. Second, when an organ is innervated by both systems, they are usually (but not always) opposed to each other in their actions. Third, many organs are predominantly controlled by one system or the other. Fourth, some organs are exclu-

sively controlled by one or the other system.

The different patterns of innervation of the two divisions depicted in Fig. 3.11, are the basis for some essential differences in the effects of the two divisions on the behavior of the organism. The ganglion cells in the sympathetic system have wide fields of peripheral innervation, and this means that their activity tends to have widespread effects and evoke mass responses. Traditionally, it has been believed that the overall effect of the sympathetic system is to decrease activity in the visceral organs and stimulate the heart and somatic muscles, and that these effects prepare the whole organism for "fight-or-flight" behavior. In contrast, the ganglion cells of the parasympathetic system, being located in their target organs, have narrow fields of innervation. It has been generally thought that their effects are thereby local, and related to facilitating the activities of their respective organs. While the patterns of innervation in the two systems are indeed clearly different, and while it is true that sympathetic activity has more global effects, Table 19.1 makes it clear that there are many exceptions to the traditional generalizations about the functions of the systems.

We will take up the question of the relation of autonomic activity to behavior in greater detail in Chaps. 25–29. For the remainder of this chapter we will consider examples of mechanisms involved in the control of the three types of vertebrate autonomic effector cells: glands, smooth muscle, and cardiac muscle.

Glands. As indicated in Table 19.1, a number of glands are under autonomic control. Glands in the walls of the intestinal tract are the *tubular* type, which take the form of pits or tubules. They contain cells that secrete either mucus, to lubricate the gut wall, or enzymes, to aid in digestion.

The other main type of gland is the *acinar* type, which consists of collections of cells which discharge their contents into central ducts. This characterizes more complex glands, such as the salivary glands, pancreas, and liver.

Secretion may be stimulated in several ways: by local chemical cues from the ingested food; by nervous reflexes elicited by local chemical, tactile, or mechanical cues; by central nervous activity; or by circulating hormones. The relative importance of these mechanisms varies for different glands.

The cellular mechanisms of glandular secretion in vertebrates are similar to those in invertebrates. The same sequence of basic steps in excitation-secretion coupling has been found in many cells. These steps include: activation of specific molecular receptors; influx of Ca^{2+}; depolarization of the cell membrane by increased conductance and ionic flows of Na^+ and other ions; exocytosis and release of secretory granules. As in the invertebrate (see Fig. 19.2), there is considerable electrical coupling between the cells.

One of the earliest and best studied examples in vertebrates is the salivary gland. Intracellular recordings from salivary gland cells are shown in Fig. 19.5. The salivary gland is of interest because it can be activated by both parasympathetic and sympathetic nerve stimulation, by local application of their respective neurotransmitters, ACh and NE, and by substance P. A surprising, and puzzling, finding has been that, with these routes of stimulation, the secretory activity is accompanied by a *hyperpolarization* of the cell membrane. Recent experiments using intracellular recordings have helped to clear up this mystery. As shown in Fig. 19.5A, there is (following an influx of Ca^{2+}), an initial depolarization, due to an increase in conductance for Na^+ and K^+. This is followed by a slow hyperpolarization, due to the action of a Na/K pump (see Chap. 6). Some of the molecular mechanisms involved in these responses are illustrated in Fig. 19.5B. Note the membrane receptors for NA, ACh, and substance P; the linkage of noradrenergic β receptors to cytoplasmic cAMP; the movements of Ca, Na, and K; and the secretory activity at the lumenal surface of the cell. Note also how closely this cell conforms to the model of excitation—secretion coupling of gland cells discussed in the previous chapter (Fig. 18.2).

Smooth Muscle. As mentioned earlier, motor nerves do not connect to smooth muscle cells by means of distinct neuromuscular junctions. Instead, the nerve fibers ramify and terminate within the muscle in free nerve endings. The effect of the

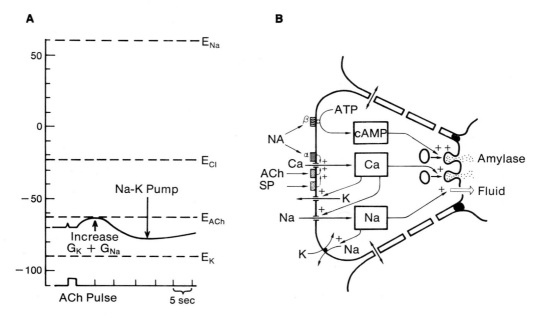

Fig. 19.5. Salivary gland acinar cells. Excitation-secretion coupling in the mammalian salivary gland cell. **A.** Intracellular response to an ionophoretically applied pulse of acetylcholine (ACh). Equilibrium potentials (E) for different ions and for the ACh response (due to both Na and K) are indicated. **B.** Schematic diagram of gland cell, summarizing molecular mechanisms of excitation-secretion coupling. Note the polarity of the cell: excitation occurs at the outer surface, secretion at the inner, lumenal, surface. (From Petersen, 1980)

nerve on the muscles depends on their physical proximity. The muscle fibers that receive nerve contacts respond to release of transmitter by graded postsynaptic potentials; in many cases, the fibers do not generate action potentials. Neighboring fibers are depolarized by spread of these responses through electrical synapses. Activation of more distant fibers is believed to require spread of action potentials through electrical synapses; in addition, there may be activation or modulation by transmitter diffusing from distant terminals. This grading of the response of muscle fibers to nerve stimulation resembles the spread of electrotonic currents in gland cells of *Helisoma*, mentioned above.

The smooth muscle of the gut undergoes *myogenic* spontaneous contractions, which are modulated by two ganglia within the gut wall, named Meissner's and Auerbach's plexuses. From a combination of morphological, neurochemical, and

electrophysiological studies, a picture of the organization of Auerbach's plexus has emerged, which is summarized in Fig. 19.6. As can be seen, the circuit has its own source of *neurogenic* rhythm, in the "burst-type oscillators" that fire periodic bursts of impulses. These drive bursting follower cells that have inhibitory noradrenergic synapses on the muscles. Tonically discharging interneurons, activated by stretch of the muscles, have inhibitory synapses on the follower cells; through these connections, they can release the circular muscles of the gut from inhibition. By sequential activation of mechanoreceptors and interneurons, a peristaltic contractile wave moves along the gut wall, as from left-to-right in the figure. The slow and smoothly graded nature of the contractions arises from the diffuse spread of neurotransmitter to the muscle, the modulatory action of neuropeptides present in the gut wall, and the electrical synapses that couple the muscles together in a functional syncytium. J. D. Wood of the University of Kansas has characterized this neural circuit as "a simple integrative system analogous to ganglia . . . of invertebrate animals", that functions to coordinate and program the various patterns of mobility of the gut. He has suggested that it shares common integrative properties with many centers in the central nervous system.

Sympathetic Ganglia. Diagrams of the autonomic nervous system such as those of Figs. 3.11 and 19.1 usually give the impression that a sympathetic ganglion is the site of a simple relay of information from a preganglionic fiber to a postganglionic cell. However, both physiological and anatomical studies have shown that the sympathetic ganglion is considerably more complicated than this.

As shown in Fig. 19.7, stimulation of the preganglionic fibers gives rise to a sequence of synaptic effects in a ganglion cell. The briefest action (A, in Fig. 19.7) is a *fast EPSP,* lasting 10–20 msec. It is mediated by ACh, liberated from the nerve endings and acting on nicotinic receptors (receptors that are blocked by the substance nicotine).

The next component of the response (B in Fig. 19.7) is a *slow IPSP,* lasting several hundred msec. This appears to be mediated by a conductance-decrease synapse, which hyperpolarizes the membrane by turning off Na^+ conductance (see Chap. 8). A number of studies have been carried out to identify the transmitter for this synaptic action. A most attractive model has been that the nerves excite an interneuron, and that this interneuron inhibits the ganglion cells by releasing a catecholamine, either dopamine or noradrenaline. Anatomical studies have shown that many ganglia contain small cells, packed with large dense-core vesicles. Since these cells fluoresce when treated with the paraformaldehyde technique, they are called *small intensely fluorescing* cells, or SIF cells. It has been proposed that the response of the ganglion cell involves activation of an adenylate cyclase and a second messenger system, as described in Chap. 9, though other mechanisms are also possible.

The third response component is a *slow EPSP,* lasting several seconds (C in the figure). This is mediated by ACh acting on muscarinic receptors (receptors sensitive to blocking by the substance muscarine). The mechanism for this action is also believed to involve a conductance decrease, the de-

Fig. 19.6. Neuronal circuit that mediates inhibitory control of intestinal circular muscles. Nerve cells have excitatory (+) or inhibitory (−) connections. Muscle cells are interconnected by electrical synapses. (From Wood, 1975)

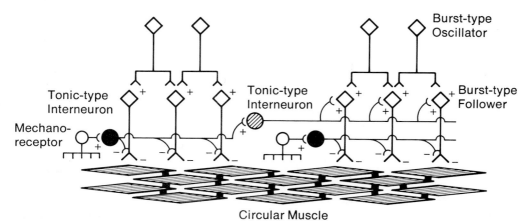

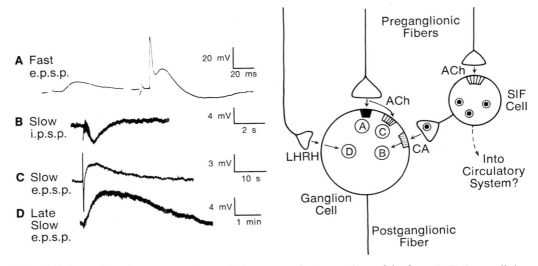

Fig. 19.7. Synaptic actions on ganglion cells in a sympathetic ganglion of the frog. **A–D.** Intracellular recordings from a ganglion cell show responses to electrical stimulation of preganglionic fibers; note increasingly slower time bases from A to D. (From Jan et al., 1979) *Right,* Summary of synaptic organization of sympathetic ganglion. Sites for generation of response components are indicated by A–D. (Modified from Libet, and Shepherd, 1979)

polarization being due to a turning off of K+ conductance.

The final response component (D) is a *very slow EPSP,* lasting several minutes. An elegant analysis by Lily Yeh Jan, Yuh Nung Jan, and Stephen Kuffler of Harvard implicated the polypeptide LHRH (see Chap. 9) in mediating this response. This study is particularly instructive because several procedures could be carried out, such as microionophoresis of LHRH and its analogues, and radioimmunoassay for presence of LHRH in the ganglion, which thus satisfied several of the criteria deemed necessary for positive identification of a neurotransmitter or neuro-modulator in Chap. 9. Even with this compelling evidence under near-ideal experimental conditions, the authors went no further than suggesting that "the action appears to be mediated by a LHRH-like substance"—exemplary caution that is all too rare.

The sympathetic ganglion is thus not a simple relay, but rather a local circuit system in its own right (see diagram in Fig. 19.7). This system is controlled by both

nervous and hormonal inputs, and it integrates this activity by distinct transmitter and modulator mechanisms, acting over a considerable range in time, from milliseconds through several minutes. These facts are likely to be important in the contribution of the sympathetic system to the control of the behavior of the organism.

Heart. The vertebrate heart is *myogenic,* that is, it continues to contract in the absence of innervation. In this it resembles the molluscan heart, but differs from the arthropod heart (see earlier). Although the heart thus can beat in isolation, it nonetheless has extensive innervation, from both parasympathetic and sympathetic nerves. This is part of the nervous control of the cardiovascular system that is essential for providing the flexibility that is necessary to adapt the organism's motor performance to ongoing needs.

Rhythmic activity arises in the heart in the sinus node (see Fig. 19.8 A,B). Since activity here leads the activity in other parts of the heart, it is called the "pacemaker". The impulses spread through the cardiac muscles of the atrium to a second pacemaker site, in the A-V node. From here arise *Purkinje fibers,* which course together in a bundle and then distribute themselves throughout the ventricular walls. The Purkinje fibers are large, contain few myofibrils, and are closely coupled electrically. By these specializations, they conduct impulses at 2–4 meters per second, some six times faster than normal cardiac fibers.

The action potential takes on characteristic forms in the different types of cardiac fiber, and these forms reflect the differing ionic conductances involved. In general, there is a sequence of Ca^{2+} and Na^+ influx, followed by K^+ efflux, similar to that in skeletal muscle cells or nerve fibers. In the pacemaker cells, there are, in addition, slow conductance components which control the slow depolarization and repolarization of the membrane. In the Purkinje fibers and muscle fibers, there is a prolonged plateau of depolarization, which is due to a continued Na^+ inactivation and continued slow inward movement of Ca^{2+} which offsets a persistent K^+ efflux. The fiber is refractory during this plateau, which helps to prevent hyperexcitability and too fast firing in the conducting system. These ionic mechanisms are indicated in the diagram of Fig. 19.8 C (see also Chap. 8).

The nervous pathways that provide for modulation of the heart are shown in Fig. 19.9. The sympathetic innervation comes from postganglionic fibers of the sympathetic chain. When stimulated, these fibers release NE from their terminals; the NE acts on β_1 receptors on the cardiac cells. The receptor, in turn, activates an adenylate cyclase, and a subsequent series of steps similar to that discussed above and in re-

Fig. 19.8. **A.** The conducting system of the human heart. The electrical impulses begin in the sinus node, and are conducted to the A–V node, through the bundle of His, to the branches and finally the Purkinje fibers which connect to the cardiac muscle fibers. Conduction velocities (meters per second) are indicated by numbers in parenthesis. **B.** Intracellular recordings of action potentials at different sites. **C.** The action potential in a cardiac muscle fiber, showing the time courses of different ionic conductances. (From Shephard and Vanhoutte, 1979)

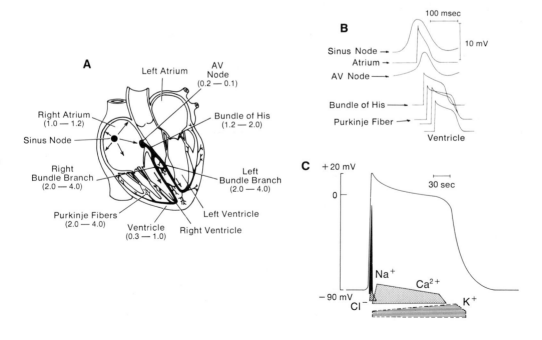

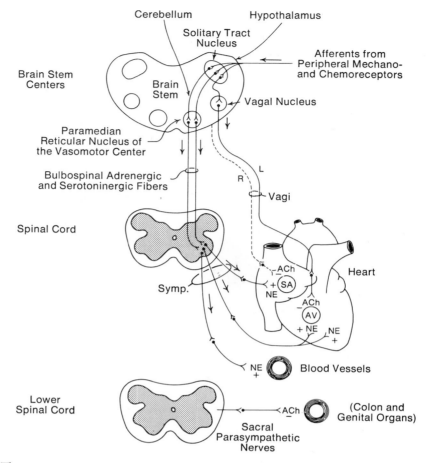

Fig. 19.9. The autonomic innervation of the heart. The right (R) and left (L) vagi mediate parasympathetic control; sympathetic control is mediated through the sympathetic (Symp.) nerves. SA, sinoatrial node; AV, atrioventricular node; ACh, acetylcholine; NE, norepinephrine (noradrenaline). (Adapted from Shepherd and Vanhoutte, 1979)

lation to Fig. 9.9. This brings about an increase in ionic permeability of the cardiac cell membrane, mainly to Ca^{2+}, which results in increases in heart rate, impulse conduction, and contractility. The increase in permeability to Ca^{2+} resembles the modulatory effects of neurotransmitters on excitable Ca^{2+} channels that have been demonstrated in some neurons (see Chap. 9).

The parasympathetic innervation of the heart comes from *pre*ganglionic fibers arising in the motor nucleus of the vagus, situated in the brainstem. The vagus is the

source of most parasympathetic fibers to the viscera. The cardiac fibers, being preganglionic, do not innervate the heart cells directly, but instead terminate on ganglia located in the heart. The ganglia contain interneurons, and there are interactions between interneurons and ganglion cells. The ganglia thus appear to be complex integrative centers, like sympathetic ganglia. The studies of Kuffler and his colleagues have shown that the vagal fibers have *excitatory* cholinergic synapses on the cells of the ganglion. The ganglion cells, in turn, have *inhibitory* cholinergic synapses on the cells of the heart. Acetylcholine inhibits the heart by decreasing Ca^{2+} permeability, thereby prolonging the action potential and slowing the heart rate.

These details of synaptic organization are of interest for two reasons. First, they illustrate rather nicely how a transmitter (ACh) can have an excitatory action at one synapse and an inhibitory action at another. Second, they should be kept in mind when one encounters the common statement that "the vagus inhibits the heart". The vagus, as we have just seen, actually *excites* the cardiac ganglion, which then inhibits the heart. Furthermore, under natural conditions the ganglion is likely to mediate more subtle modulations of cardiac activity, through its local circuit interactions, than the simple inhibition revealed by strong electrical stimulation of the vagus. Thus, knowledge of synaptic organization gives us a much richer understanding of the peripheral neural mechanisms involved in controlling visceral functions.

Brainstem Centers. The sympathetic motoneurons of the spinal cord are under control of descending catecholaminergic and serotonergic fibers originating in the vasomotor center of the brain stem. The "vasomotor center" is, in fact, a collection of different nuclei, that include the motor nucleus of the vagus and the nucleus of the solitary tract, which receives sensory inputs from mechanoreceptors and chemoreceptors that are relevant to control of the cardiovascular system (see Fig. 19.9). This level of organization, in the brainstem, is probably analogous to the central ganglia controlling the cardiac ganglia in invertebrates. The brainstem nuclei, in turn, are affected by higher nervous centers, especially the cerebellum, hypothalamus, and the limbic system (see Fig. 19.9).

REFERENCES

Guyton, A. C. 1976. [Chap. 18].

Hartline, D. K. 1979. Integrative neurophysiology of the lobster cardiac ganglion. *Am. Zool.*

Hökfelt, T., O. Johansson, Å. Llungdahl, J. M. Lundberg, and M. Schultzberg. Peptidergic neurones. *Nature 284:* 515–521.

Jan, L. Y., Y. N. Jan, and S. W. Kuffler. 1979. A peptide as a possible transmitter in sympathetic ganglia of the frog. *Proc. Natl. Acad. Sci. 76:* 1501–1505.

Kandel, E. R. 1976. [Chap. 2].

Kater, S. B. 1977. Calcium electroresponsiveness and its relationship to secretion in molluscan exocrine gland cells. In *Soc. for Neurosci. Symp.*, Vol. II (ed. by W. M. Cowan and J. A. Ferrendelli.). Bethesda, Md: Soc. for Neurosci. pp. 195–214.

Petersen, O. H. 1980. *The Electrophysiology of Gland Cells.* London: Academic.

Shepherd, J. T. and P. M. Vanhoutte. 1979. *The Human Cardiovascular System.* New York: Raven.

Shepherd. G. M. 1979. [Chap. 4].

Wood, J. D. 1975. Neurophysiology of Auerbach's plexus and control of intestinal motility. *Physiol. Rev. 55:* 307–324.

Additional Reading

Gershon, M. D. 1981. The enteric nervous system. *Ann. Rev. Neurosci. 4:* 227–272.

Goodman, L. S. and A. Gilman. [Chap. 9].

Hagiwara, S. and L. Byerly. 1981. [Chap. 9].

Kehoe, J. S. and Marty. 1979. [Chap. 9].

Stent, G. S., W. J. Thompson, and R. L. Calabrese, 1979. Neural control of heartbeat in the leech and in some other invertebrates. *Physiol. Rev. 59:* 101–136.

Tsien, R. W. 1977. Cyclic AMP and contractile activity in heart. In *Adv. Cyclic Nucl. Res.*, vol. 8 (ed. by P. Greengard and G. A. Robison). New York: Raven. pp. 363–420.

Tazaki, K. and I. M. Cooke. 1979. Spontaneous electrical activity and interaction of large and small cells in cardiac ganglion of the crab, *Portunus sanguinolentus. J. Neurophysiol. 42:* 975–999.

20
Reflexes and Fixed Action Patterns

One of the primary objectives in the study of motor systems is to identify the *elementary units of motor behavior*. There are two main concepts that have dominated thinking about this problem. One is the idea that the simplest unit of behavior is the *reflex*, and that complex behavior is built up by a compounding of reflexes. The other idea is that much of behavior (particularly in invertebrates and lower vertebrates) involves stereotyped sequences of actions that are either generated within the organism or triggered by appropriate environmental stimuli. These are usually referred to as *fixed action patterns*. Figure 20.1 and Table 20.1 summarize the main features of these types of behavioral units.

This chapter first gives a brief historical background of these two concepts and then presents examples of both types in the invertebrates. Finally, in the vertebrates, we will consider some basic reflexes and reflex circuits. The relevance of the fixed action pattern concept for more complex types of behavior, in both invertebrates and vertebrates, will be discussed in later chapters.

Reflexes

Although the fact that there are immediate motor responses to sensory stimulation was apparent through the ages, and implicit in the writings of many scholars, the term "reflex" actually did not appear in the language until the eighteenth century. It comes as a surprise, for example, to realize that Shakespeare could dramatize so much of the human condition without using the word. Georg Prochaska of Vienna was one of the first to use the

Table 20.1

Reflex	Fixed action pattern
1. A simple motor action, stereotyped and repeatable.	1. A complex motor act, involving a specific temporal sequence of component acts.
2. Elicited by a sensory stimulus, the strength of the motor action being graded with the intensity of the stimulus.	2. Generated internally, or elicited by a sensory stimulus. The stimulus acts as a trigger, causing release of the motor act in all-or-nothing form.

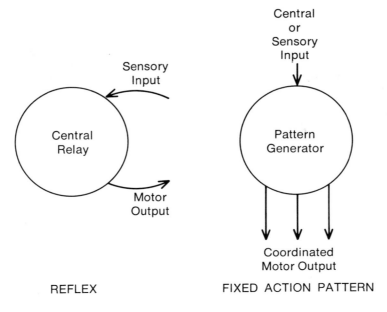

Fig. 20.1. Comparison between a reflex and a fixed action pattern.

term in 1784 when he wrote: "The reflexion of sensorial into motor impressions . . . takes place in the sensorium commune (common sensory center) . . . This reflexion may take place either with consciousness or without . . ."

The present meaning of the term dates from the earliest experimental investigations of the role of the spinal cord in mediating muscle responses to sensory stimuli. Among the important studies were those of Charles Bell in England and Francois Magendie in France, who first established in the 1820's that sensory fibers are contained in the dorsal roots, and motor fibers in the ventral roots, of the spinal cord. Bell stated it clearly: "Between the brain and the muscle there is a circle of nerves; one nerve conveys the influence of the brain to the muscle, another gives the sense of the condition of the muscle to the brain." Like so many other classical laws, this, too, has had to be modified; recent studies by Richard Coggeshall, William Willis, and their colleagues in Texas have shown that in many mammalian species a number of fine unmyelinated sensory fibers enter the spinal cord through the ventral roots.

Marshall Hall (1790–1857) vigorously advocated the notion that spinal reflex movements are distinct from voluntary movement, dependent on the spinal cord but unconscious and independent of the rest of the brain. Hall and many other workers in the course of the nineteenth century identified and categorized a number of types of reflexes. Much of this work, however, was clouded by wrangling about whether reflexes were conscious or not, and the prevailing reticular theory misled many people in thinking about the nervous pathways involved.

It was at this stage, around 1890, that Charles Sherrington came onto the scene. We have already seen (Chap. 5) how his work led to the concept of the synapse. With regard to reflexes, his work was built on two essential foundations: he carried out a careful anatomical analysis of the nerves to different muscles, and he then used this knowledge to analyze quantitatively the reflex properties of specific nerves and muscle groups. It was painstaking work, rather dull at first, but it was the means for obtaining the first clear view of the reflex as a combined structural and functional entity. This established the reflex arc as a subject for further anatomical and physiological analysis by many twentieth-century workers. In addition, Sherrington emphasized the importance of the reflex as an elementary *unit of behavior*, and thus laid one of the cornerstones for the modern studies of animal behavior.

Fixed-Action Patterns

There are, in general, two ways to study the behavior of an organism. One is to bring the animal into the laboratory and devise various kinds of instruments and procedures to test its abilities. This type of approach began around 1900, and gave rise to the fields of *behaviorism* and *animal psychology*. We shall discuss these fields and their methods further in Section V.

The other approach is for the investigator to go out in the field and observe the animal in its daily life. This, of course, is as old as mankind itself, but it only became a science in the late nineteenth century. Charles Darwin's other great book, *The Expression of Emotions in Man and Animals* (1873), in which he attempted to demonstrate similarities in instinctual behavior between animals and man, is often regarded as the starting point for the systematic study of naturally observed behavior. This led to the modern field of *ethology*.

We will have much more to say about ethology and behavior in later chapters. Our concern at present is to determine how the observations of natural behavior can provide evidence for basic units of behavior. A number of workers in the early part of this century contributed to this study by their careful observations of animals in the field. This culminated in 1950 with the suggestion of Konrad Lorenz that much of the repertoire of individual motor actions and motor responses of animals can be described as *fixed-action patterns*. These are acts that are instinctual, stereotyped, and characteristic of a given species. Table 20.1 summarizes some of their attributes.

In the time since 1950, there has been much debate about whether fixed-action patterns are really fixed, and have all the other attributes that have been used to define them. We will take up these questions in later chapters. For the present it is sufficient to say that the fixed-action pattern has seemed to many scholars to provide a second example, besides the reflex, of an elementary unit of behavior.

Invertebrates

Apart from their importance for behaviorists and ethologists, the reflex and the fixed-action pattern have been useful tools in guiding the experiments of neurobiologists on the cellular mechanisms of motor systems. This has been particularly true in invertebrates, where it has been possible to isolate and study relatively simple nervous components that correspond rather closely to the circuits for specific reflexes and even simple fixed-action patterns. Let us discuss several of the best-understood of these circuits.

The Leech: Skin Reflexes. The neurons involved in receiving stimuli in the skin of the leech and transmitting the information to the central nervous ganglia were described in Chap. 13. It will be recalled that touch, pressure, and noxious modalities are transmitted by T, P, and N type cells, respectively. Each has an identifiable cell body located in a given part of the segmental ganglion. Among the other cells in the ganglion are motoneurons that innervate the segmental muscles. These also have identifiable cell bodies and given locations (see Fig. 20.2). One main type of motoneuron is the L-type, which innervates the longitudinal muscles. When these contract, they shorten the segment. The other main type is the AE motoneuron,

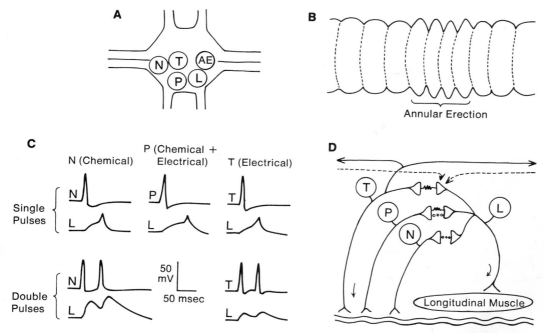

Fig. 20.2. Skin reflexes in the leech. **A.** Segmental ganglion, showing positions of touch (T), pressure (P), and noxious (N) sensory neuron cell bodies, and two motoneurons, the longitudinal (L) and annulus erector (AE). **B.** Stimulating the L motoneuron shortens the segment. **C.** Intracellular recordings from different combinations of sensory and motor neurons, to show chemical and electrical transmission, and summation of responses. **D.** Circuit diagram summarizing the pathways for the skin reflexes. (Based on studies of Nicholls and collaborators, in Kuffler and Nicholls, 1976)

which innervates the annulus erector muscles. When these contract, they pucker the segment into a sharp ridge.

When touch, pressure, or noxious stimuli are applied to the skin of the intact animal, contractions are elicited in the segmental muscles. One therefore has a simple reflex pathway, and we can deduce right away that it has the three components of a classical reflex arc: a sensory inflow pathway, a central relay site, and a motor outflow pathway. The key questions for the neurobiologist are: what kinds of connections are made between the sensory and motor cells, and what are their functional properties?

The work of John Nicholls and his collaborators at Stanford has provided answers to these questions. Let us consider the case of the L cell. Intracellular electrodes were introduced into a sensory cell

body and a motoneuron cell body in the same ganglion. When the sensory cell was directly stimulated by an electrical pulse through the intracellular electrode, an impulse was elicited in that cell, and also a response in the L cell. The L cell response consisted of a synaptic depolarization leading up to a small spike (see Fig. 20.2). When the latencies and other properties of the responses were analyzed for the responses elicited by the three types of sensory cell, it was found that the T cell is coupled to the L cell by an electrical synapse, the N cell by a chemical synapse, and the P cell by a combination of electrical and chemical synapses. It was further found that the chemical synapses are readily modifiable, giving a much facilitated response to a second pulse, whereas the electrical synaptic response was relatively invariant (see Fig. 20.2).

In addition to these short-term effects, there are long-term changes in the reflex pathways brought about by sustained or repeated natural stimulation of the skin. This is seen as a hyperpolarization of the sensory cells that may last for seconds or minutes after stimulation has ceased. Nicholls and his colleagues have shown that the hyperpolarization may be due either to an electrogenic sodium pump, activated by the influx of Na^+ during the impulse discharge, or by a prolonged Ca^{2+}-dependent increase in K^+ permeability (see Chaps. 7 and 8 for discussion of these mechanisms). The pump mechanism predominates in T cells, the K^+ permeability mechanism in N cells, and both are present in P cells. The hyperpolarizations induced in these cells raise the thresholds for impulse generation and affect synaptic integration, but the significance of these effects for the reflex behavior of the organism is not yet understood.

The diagram in this figure summarizes the circuits for the reflex arcs from T, P, and N cells through L cells. Since the connections are direct, without intervention of an interneuron, we say that these are monosynaptic pathways, and monosynaptic reflexes. Note that the cells in these pathways make connections with other central neurons, and in turn receive connections from other neurons; these are the means for coordinating the reflexes with other nervous activity. It is of interest that the pathway for reflex withdrawal from a noxious stimulus is monosynaptic; some withdrawal reflex pathways in invertebrates are polysynaptic, and the corresponding pathway in vertebrates is polysynaptic (see below).

The Crayfish Stretch Reflex. As our second example, let us consider a muscle reflex. In Chaps. 8 and 14 we discussed the stretch receptor cell of the crayfish, and saw how it is exquisitely tuned to signal the rate and amount of stretch that takes place in the abdominal muscles. Where

does this information go, and how is it used in the control of the muscles?

As we saw in Chap. 14, when the muscles are stretched, as by flexion of the abdomen, the stretch receptor cell is depolarized, and an impulse discharge is set up in the axon. Our present understanding is that the axon makes synapses directly on a special type of motoneuron to the muscle. Thus, impulses in the receptor cell axon bring about a monosynaptic excitation of these motoneurons. The effect of this is to cause a contraction in the muscles that originally were stretched, thus counteracting the effect of the imposed passive stretch and tending to restore the muscle to its original resting length.

Figure 20.3 diagrams the circuit for this reflex. Since it is elicited by muscle stretch, it is referred to as a *stretch reflex*. Because the reflex is directed to the muscle within which the sensory signals arise, it is also referred to as a *myotatic reflex* (*myo* = muscle, *tatic* = attracted to). The special property of this reflex—the tendency to maintain a muscle at a given constant length—makes it particularly suited to the maintenance of posture and the mediation of postural adjustments (see below and next Chap.).

In addition to mediating reactions to imposed stretch, the myotatic reflex also has an important function to play during centrally generated or voluntary movements. When the main motoneurons to the muscle are activated by central commands, they excite muscle fibers to contract. At the same time they excite the muscle in which the receptor cell is located; the resulting contraction *stretches* and excites the receptor cell terminals. As was described in Chap. 14 the stretch receptor muscle is thus maintained under some tension, and the stretch receptor excitability is maintained, even though the main muscle is contracting. Under these conditions, the stretch receptor cell is able to signal changes in load or resistance to movement when these occur.

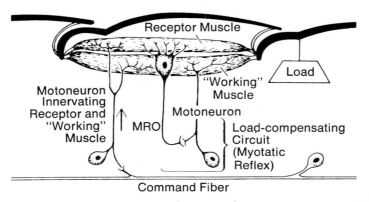

Fig. 20.3. Neuronal circuits mediating the stretch reflex in the abdomen of the crayfish. Impulses in the command fiber lead to activation of both the "working" muscle and the specialized muscle to which the stretch receptor cell is connected. If the shortening of the contracting muscle is opposed by a load, the resulting tension in the muscle will excite the receptor cell dendrite terminals. This will activate the myotatic reflex pathway, adding reflex excitation to the "working" muscle to oppose the load. (From Kennedy, 1976)

From these considerations we can see how the stretch reflex operates as a unit of behavior, as part of the animal's response to its environment, and also a part of centrally generated motor performance.

Crayfish Escape Response. For our third example we will consider a motor response that shares some of the features of both reflexes and fixed-action patterns.

A common type of behavior in many invertebrates is a quick escape movement. This is elicited by a sensory stimulus, and consists of a sudden synchronous contraction of special fast muscles that moves the animal away from the site of danger. Animals as diverse as the earthworm, crayfish, and squid all show this type of behavior (and also some vertebrates; see below). In all cases it has been found that a giant axon is an essential part of the nervous pathway. This is logical, because, as we learned in Chap. 7, the larger a fiber the faster the conduction rate of the impulses, and the essence of an escape movement is speed. The reader may review the physiology of the giant axon of the squid in Chap. 7.

The neural circuit mediating the escape response has been worked out in most detail in the crayfish, and the components and the sequence of events can be summarized in relation to the diagram of Fig. 20.4A. Abrupt mechanical stimulation of the integument excites the hair cells to discharge an impulse, which activates electrical synapses on a giant fiber and chemical synapses on an interneuron; the interneuron, in turn, also has electrical synapses on the giant fiber. Although the hair cell thus has a direct connection to the giant fiber, the route through the interneuron is actually much more powerful. The impulse set up in the giant fiber excites segmental motoneurons in rapid sequence as it passes through successive segmental ganglia; this occurs by means of electrical synapses. These, in fact, were the first electrical synapses to be identified, and their mechanism has been described in Chap. 8. The excited motoneurons then activate their respective muscles to contract.

This response is similar to the reflexes of the leech that were discussed above, in that a sensory stimulation activates a ner-

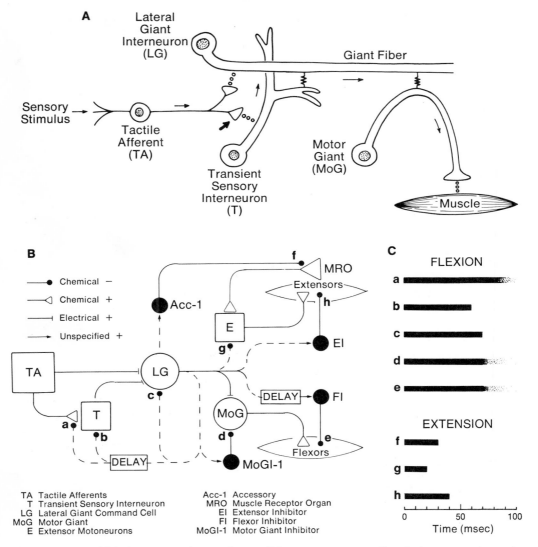

Fig. 20.4. A. Simplified circuit mediating the crayfish escape response. Chemical synapses shown by dots, electrical synapses by zig-zag lines. Short thick arrow indicates site of habituation. **B.** Expanded circuit, including additional polysynaptic reflex pathways and pathways for command-derived inhibition. Connections (a–e) cause inhibition at five different sites in the command circuit that mediates flexion. Connections (f–h) cause inhibition at three different sites in the extension circuit. **C.** Durations of unitary IPSPs set up in each of the connections of the circuits in (B) are indicated by the lengths of the black bars. Note that inhibition in the flexor circuit lasts longer than inhibition in the extension circuit. (From Wine and Krasne, 1981)

vous pathway which leads to an immediate motor act. It differs, however, in several important respects. Instead of one synaptic relay, it involves at least three synaptic links; we say, therefore, that it is

a *polysynaptic* reflex. It has a relatively high threshold for sensory activation; this is because it is a specialized movement which is only appropriate under specific environmental conditions. It therefore has the character of an *all-or-nothing re-sponse,* in contrast to the reflexes we discussed above in the leech, whose magnitude is *graded* with the intensity of the stimulation. This difference in stimulus–response relation is illustrated by the two curves in the graph of Fig. 20.5.

The escape response is produced by the discharge of only a single impulse in the successive components of the nervous pathway. In the case of the leech reflexes, the motor responses are small pieces of larger behavioral patterns. In the case of the escape response, the motor action is an entire purposeful behavioral act in itself. There are, in fact, two giant fibers in the crayfish, medial and lateral. The medial giant fiber connects to all segments, and the resulting muscle contractions propel the animal backwards. The lateral giant fiber lacks connections in the most posterior ganglia; this tends to produce an upward movement of the animal. The giant fiber connections and correlated behaviors are shown in Fig. 20.6.

The escape response happens so quickly that there is not time for feedback information to guide or adjust the movement. Thus, there is no role for feedback information from muscle receptors, for example. Thus it is a movement that, once triggered by peripheral stimuli, is completely under *central control.*

The ability of a single neuron or fiber, such as the giant fiber, to trigger an entire behavioral act implies that it occupies some special position in the hierarchy of motor control. From this has emerged the concept of the *command* neuron or fiber, and the idea that such a neuron or fiber has some kind of executive power to initiate or control a specific coordinated motor act. We shall discuss this concept further in Chap. 22.

This by no means exhausts our present knowledge of the principles underlying escape responses, or the details of their mechanism. The simple circuit in Fig. 20.4A represents only a rudimentary beginning. For example, the reflex *habitu-*

ates with repeated stimulation. If a crayfish is tapped at intervals of one minute, the escape response disappears within 10 minutes. Most of this is accounted for by decreased release of neurotransmitter from the sensory afferent terminals onto the sensory interneurons (arrow in Fig. 20.4A). We will discuss mechanisms of habituation more fully in Chap. 30.

The simple circuit of Fig. 20.4A is a part of much *more extensive circuits* mediating control of the escape response and related motor behavior; some of these additional neurons and connections are indicated in Fig. 20.4B. Also shown in B are pathways by which the command neuron (LG) not only excites the motoneurons that cause the tail flip, but also mediates feedback inhibition. This inhibition is massive and widespread, and affects synaptic sites at virtually every level in the hierarchy of motor control (a–h in diagram). This *command-derived inhibition* has several functions; for example, it can set the threshold for subsequent elicitation of the response, and protect against the onset of habituation. Finally, recent work gives testimony to the pervasive effects of diffuse *arousal systems,* that set and modulate the level of activity in specific neural circuits. Thus, a hungry crayfish is highly aroused; its escape threshold is high, and it will fight for food until it acquires it, at

Fig. 20.5. Comparison between the stimulus–response relations for a reflex and a fixed action pattern. (After Kandel, 1976)

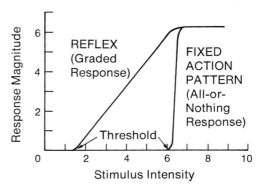

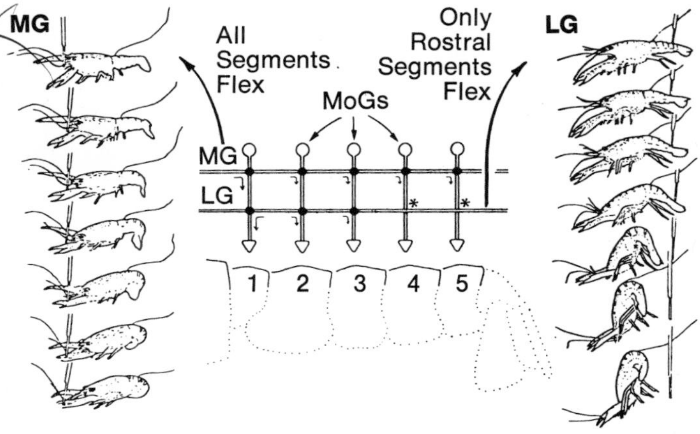

Fig. 20.6. Flexion responses of the crayfish. *On the left,* an electrical shock delivered to the medial giant fiber elicits postsynaptic responses in motoneurons (MoG) in all segmental ganglia (G_1-G_5). *On the right,* a shock to the lateral giant fiber elicits responses in motoneurons only in segmental ganglia G_1-G_3. The differences in behavioral responses are shown in the sketches of frames from high-speed cinematography; the tail flip mediated by the medial giants moves the animal backward, that by the lateral giants moves the animal upward. Large dots indicate sites of electrical synapses from giant fibers onto motor giants. These synapses are lacking at sites marked by asterisks. (From Wine and Krasne, 1981)

which time the escape threshold abruptly lowers.

The escape response is thus not the simple reflex it first appears to be. It possesses many of the defining properties of a fixed-action pattern. It exhibits many of the functional properties that are characteristic of more complex motor and central systems. Finally, it illustrates the very important principle that each synapse within a neural circuit is not just a simple relay, but rather is a site at which *multiple controls* are present. These controls enable the circuit to operate in different modes, depending on the history of use of the circuit, and the behavioral state of the organism. This has only recently become evident, but it appears to be one of the general operating principles of neural circuits in both invertebrates and vertebrates.

Vertebrates

Mauthner Cells. The studies of invertebrates illustrate the advantages of being able to work on systems composed of large, identifiable cells and fibers. In the vertebrates, similar advantages are offered by Mauthner cells. These cells are present in the medulla oblongata of many species of fish and amphibians. When the fish is exposed to a sudden vibratory stimulus (such as a tap on the aquarium), it responds with a quick flip of the tail that displaces the animal sideways (see Fig. 20.7). It is thus essentially similar to an escape response; another term is a *startle response.*

The Mauthner cell is the key element in the startle response. Because of its large size, it has been possible to study it carefully. As indicated in Fig. 20.8, there is a single Mauthner cell on each side, situated at the level where the eighth nerve enters, carrying input from the auditory and vestibular nerves. The eighth nerve fibers make direct electrical synapses on the distal parts of the lateral Mauthner cell dendrites by means of large club endings. Other eighth nerve fibers make synapses on vestibular nucleus neurons, which then make excitatory chemical synapses on the lateral dendrite. There is thus both a monosynaptic and disynaptic pathway from the eighth nerve fibers to the Mauthner cell. The student may note the close similarity of this arrangement to that in the afferent connections to the giant fiber in the crayfish escape response circuit (see Fig. 20.5 above).

Another set of connections mediates feedback control of the Mauthner cell. After the Mauthner fires its impulse, the impulse not only travels down the axon to excite the tail motoneurons, but also invades axon collaterals to excite interneurons. Through polysynaptic pathways, two kinds of interneurons are ultimately excited that feed back onto the Mauthner cell. One type has chemical inhibitory synapses on the lateral dendrite. The other has axon terminals which wind around the axon hillock and initial segment of the Mauthner cell. This region is encased in a thick wrapping of glial membranes, which form an *axon cap*. The terminals make electrical synapses on the initial segment, and the axon cap increases the effectiveness of their inhibitory action by limiting the spread of extracellular current. (This mechanism was explained more fully in Chap. 8.)

At a *cellular* level, the Mauthner cell illustrates the importance of dendrites in integrating different types of synaptic inputs. It also exemplifies the strategic siting of a specific type of synapse to control the axonal output of the cell at the initial segment. At a *behavioral* level, the startle response resembles the crayfish escape response in showing many of the properties of a fixed-action pattern. In both systems, the giant nerve fibers are admirably adapted for mediating this special motor act.

Motoneurons and Spinal Reflexes. The best known examples of reflexes, and the ones most characteristic of vertebrates, are those mediated by the spinal cord. Our knowledge about them has progressed in several stages over the past 100 years or so, being dependent on the experimental techniques available.

Sherrington's first studies, as we have mentioned, involved a correlation of anatomical tracing of sensory and muscle nerves with meticulous observations of

Fig. 20.7. Moving picture analysis of startle responses in different kinds of fish. Frames were taken at 5 msec intervals. Stimulus was a tap of a mallet on the aquarium, delivered at time indicated by arrow. (From Eaton et al., 1977)

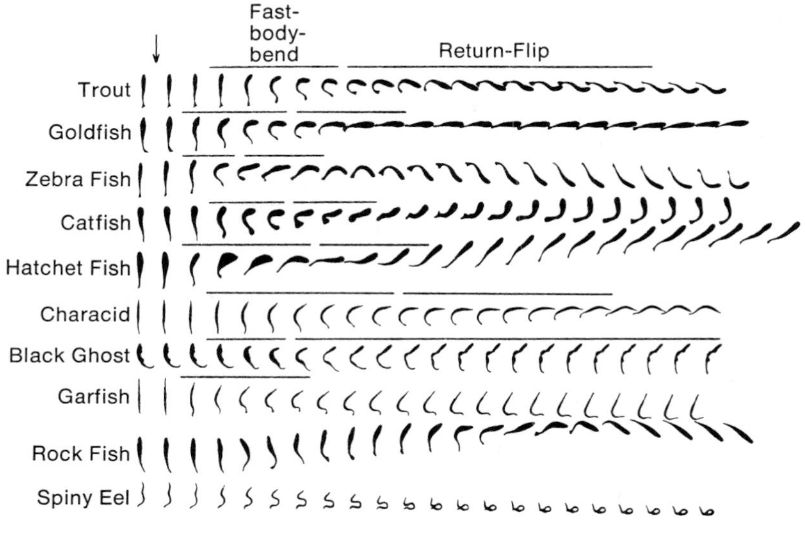

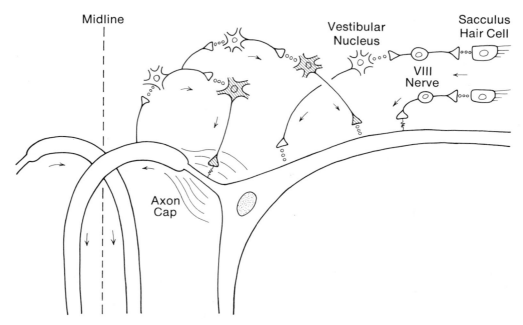

Fig. 20.8. Synaptic organization of the Mauthner cell. (After Furakawa, in Kuffler and Nicholls, 1976)

different reflex behaviors. He introduced methods for cutting across the brainstem of a cat at the level of the midbrain (between the superior and inferior colliculi), which produced a great enhancement of tone in the extensor muscles of the limbs. This was termed *decerebrate rigidity*. The extensor muscles are the ones responsible for maintaining the animal in a standing position. In order to study the reflex basis of this activity, Sherrington and his collaborators in 1924 began to analyze the responses to passive stretch of an extensor muscle (for example, the quadriceps femoris of the thigh, which attaches to the knee cap).

Figure 20.9 illustrates the experimental set-up and results. Stretch of the muscle by only a few millimeters gives rise to a large increase in tension, as measured by a strain gauge. If the muscle nerve is cut, the tension developed is small, because it results only from the passive elastic properties inherent in the muscle and its tendon. This shows that the large tension depends on a reflex pathway that passes

through the spinal cord. The reflex activity produces contractions of the muscle that was stretched. Because the reflex feeds back specifically to the stretched muscle, it is a *myotatic reflex;* because it is elicited by stretch, it is also called a *stretch reflex*. This is the familiar "knee-jerk" reflex elicited by a tap on the tendon of the knee. All muscles show this type of reflex, though extensor muscles that work against gravity show it the best. Although the feedback to the muscle stretched is excitatory, there is, in addition, an inhibitory effect on muscles with antagonistic actions at a joint; thus, when a knee-flexor is stretched, some of the tension in the knee-extensor melts away (see Fig. 20.9). This illustrates the principle of *reciprocal innervation* of the muscles to a joint.

The next step was to analyze the nervous pathways involved in these and other types of reflex activity. David Lloyd at Rockefeller University began these studies around 1940. The experiments required laborious dissection of individual peripheral nerves combined with removal of the laminae of the vertebral bones (laminectomy) to expose the spinal cord so that electrodes could be placed on the dorsal and ventral roots. A single volley can then be set up in a peripheral nerve, and the response of motoneurons can be recorded in terms of the compound action potential of their axons in the ventral root. Representative results are shown in Fig. 20.10. Stimulation of a muscle nerve produces a short-latency, brief volley in the ventral root. This shows that the input from muscles is carried over large, rapidly conduct-

ing axons, and that there is only one, or at most two or three synaptic relays in the spinal cord. In contrast, the ventral root response to a volley in a skin nerve has a long latency, and lasts a long time. This suggests the involvement, in skin reflexes, of slower-conducting fibers, polysynaptic pathways, and prolonged activity in the neurons in these pathways.

The most definitive analysis has been with the use of intracellular recordings. We have already discussed the properties of synaptic excitation and inhibition in mo-

Fig. 20.9. **A.** Testing for the stretch reflex by tapping the patellar tendon of the quadricips muscle. **B.** Different conditions of a muscle. **C.** Experimental set up for analyzing the stretch reflex in the cat. **D.** Tension of quadriceps muscle in response to stretch, before (active) and after (passive) cutting the motor nerve. Arrow indicates onset of reciprocal inhibition of quadriceps motoneurons produced by stretch of the semitendinosus muscle, an antagonist. (Based on Liddell and Sherrington, in Henneman, 1980)

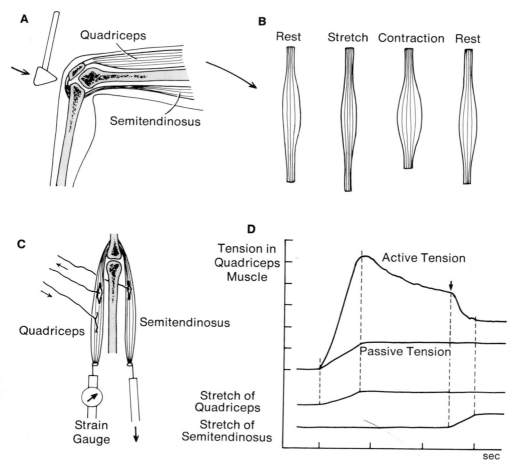

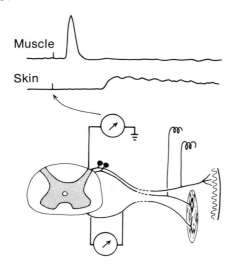

Fig. 20.10. Comparison of reflex responses of motoneurons to electrical stimulation of a muscle nerve (gastrochemius) and a skin nerve (sural) in the cat. (after Lloyd, in Henneman, 1980)

toneurons, and the mechanisms of integration (see Chap. 8). A key question has been what are the number and type of synaptic connections within the spinal cord for each of the main types of reflex pathways. The first evidence from intracellular recordings was obtained by John Eccles and his collaborators in the 1950's, and this has been largely confirmed and much

extended by subsequent studies. As shown in Fig. 20.11, inputs over the different types of muscle nerves are set up by either brief muscle stretch or a shock to a nerve. Motoneuron responses are recorded and synaptic relays estimated from delay times. From such measurements it has been concluded that group Ia afferents make monosynaptic excitatory synapses onto their own motoneurons and disynaptic inhibitory synapses onto antagonist motoneurons. Group II afferents, by comparison, make mostly disynaptic excitatory synapses onto their own motoneurons (see Fig. 20.11). (The terminology of peripheral nerve groups was covered in Chap. 13.)

The study of these and other spinal reflexes is a vast field of inquiry, and we can briefly summarize the main types of reflexes at the segmental level using the simplified circuit diagrams in Fig. 20.12. The circuits are categorized in terms of their main type of sensory input. The top three are muscle reflexes, and the bottom one is a skin reflex. The reader may review the main types of sensory fibers in Chaps. 13 and 14. Let us briefly review each circuit here; the role of each in relation to locomotion and larger patterns of motor behavior will be discussed in subsequent chapters.

Fig. 20.11. Experimental demonstration of monosynaptic and disynaptic connections onto motoneurons of the cat. (Based on Eccles, 1957, and Watt et al., 1976)

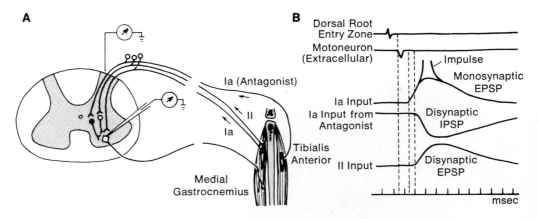

MEMORIZE

A. STRETCH (MYOTATIC) REFLEX

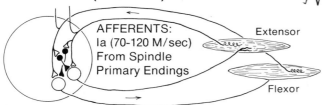

AFFERENTS:
Ia (70-120 M/sec)
From Spindle
Primary Endings

Extensor

Flexor

DETECTS: Phasic Stretch
of Muscle
FUNCTIONS:
Control of Movement
? Anti-gravity

B. INVERSE MYOTATIC REFLEX

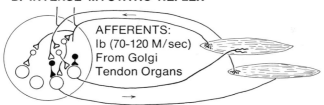

AFFERENTS:
Ib (70-120 M/sec)
From Golgi
Tendon Organs

DETECTS: Active Stretch
of Tendon
FUNCTIONS:
Control of Muscle Force
Control of Muscle
Stiffness
? Prevents Overstretch

C.

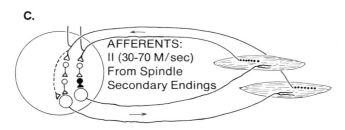

AFFERENTS:
II (30-70 M/sec)
From Spindle
Secondary Endings

DETECTS: Steady Stretch
of Muscle
FUNCTIONS:
Posture
Extensors: Contributes
to Myotatic Reflex
Flexors: Contributes
to Flexor Reflex

D. FLEXOR REFLEX

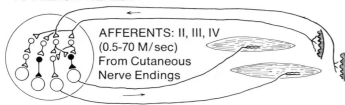

AFFERENTS: II, III, IV
(0.5-70 M/sec)
From Cutaneous
Nerve Endings

DETECTS: Harmful Stimuli
FUNCTIONS:
Withdraw Limb from Harm

Fig. 20.12. Neural circuits for the main types of spinal reflexes. (Based in part on Matthews, 1972, 1982) See text.

The largest-diameter sensory nerves, the Ia fibers from muscle spindles, make, as we discussed above, monosynaptic excitatory synapses on their own motoneurons, and disynaptic inhibitory synapses onto antagonist motoneurons. This is the main pathway for the stretch reflex. Figure 20.12 shows that this reflex is present for both extensors and flexors. Primary endings are believed to contribute especially to control of fine movements. Classically, the prominence of the stretch reflex in anti-gravity extensor muscles was presumed to provide the reflex basis for maintenance of upright posture.

The second circuit shown in Fig. 20.12 is that established by the large-diameter group Ib fibers from Golgi tendon organs.

The connections onto motoneurons are all disynaptic. The effects on the motoneurons from a given muscle are exactly the reverse of those in the stretch reflex pathway, giving rise to the term *inverse myotatic reflex*. As we discussed in Chap. 13, Golgi tendon organs are particularly sensitive to muscle contraction. Recent studies suggest that tendon organ discharges contribute to the reflex control of muscle force. Tendon organs respond to passive stretch of muscles only at high levels of stretch, where their inhibitory action is believed to have a protective function against overstretch.

The third circuit in Fig. 20.12 is that involving the medium-size group II fibers from muscle spindles. These make mono- and polysynaptic connections onto motoneurons. The excitatory connections contribute to the stretch reflexes, particularly those involved in maintaining posture and postions of joints. In addition, there are inhibitory connections to extensors which may contribute to the flexor reflex.

Stimulation of the skin or muscles by a noxious stimulus characteristically produces withdrawal of the affected limb. This is termed the *flexor reflex*. It can be mediated by a wide range of receptors and fibers, which are often referred to collectively as *flexor reflex afferents (FRA)*. The bottom diagram in Fig. 20.12 indicates that these fibers make polysynaptic connections which are excitatory to flexors and inhibitory to extensors. In addition, these fibers make widespread connections throughout the spinal cord which have the opposite effect: excitation of extensors and inhibition of flexors. Thus, while the hindlimb is being withdrawn, the other limbs are being extended, for maintaining posture and participating in locomotion. Or, in more picturesque terms, the hindlimb is removed from danger, while the other three legs run away! This is another demonstration of the fact that reflexes do not take place in isolation. Here, as in the other examples in Fig. 20.12, the reflex circuit not only plays back upon the stim-

ulated limb, but also calls forth appropriate and coordinated actions of the other limbs.

REFERENCES

Eaton, R. C., R. A. Bombardieri, and D. L. Meyer. 1977. The Mauthner-initiated startle response in teleost fish. *J. Exp. Biol.* 66: 65–81.

Eccles, J. C. 1957. *The Physiology of Nerve Cells*. Baltimore: Johns Hopkins.

Henneman, E. 1980. Organization of the spinal cord and its reflexes. In *Medical Physiology* (ed. by V. B. Mountcastle). St. Louis: Mosby. pp. 762–786.

Kandel, E. R. 1976. [Chap. 2].

Kennedy, D. 1976. Neural elements in relation to network function. In *Simple Networks and Behavior* (ed. by J. C. Fentress). Sunderland, Mass: Sinauer. pp. 65–81.

Krasne, F. B. and J. J. Wine. 1976. Control of crayfish escape behavior. In *Identified Neurons and Behavior of Arthropods* (ed. by G. Hoyle). New York: Plenum. pp. 275–292.

Kuffler, S. W. and J. G. Nicholls. 1976. [Chap. 18].

Lorenz, K. 1950. The comparative method in studying innate behavior patterns. *Symp. Soc. Exp. Biol.* 4: 221–268.

Matthews, P. B. C. 1972. [Chap. 14].

Matthews, P. B. C. 1982. [Chap. 14].

Watt, D. G. D., E. K. Stauffer, A. Taylor, R. M. Reinking, and D. G. Stuart. 1976. Analysis of muscle receptor connections by spike-triggered averaging. 1. Spindle primary and tendon organ afferents. *J. Neurophysiol.* 39: 1375–1392.

Wine, J. J. and T. B. Krasne. 1981. The cellular organization of crayfish excape behavior. I, *The Biology of Crustacea*. Vol. III *Neural Integration* (ed. by H. Atwood and D. Sandeman). New York: Academic.

Additional Reading
Boring, E. G. 1950. [Chap. 1.]
    See sections on history of reflexes.
Brooks, V. B. (ed.). 1981. *Motor Control*. Vol. II of *Handbook of Physiology*, Sect. 1: The Nervous System. Bethesda, Md.: American Physiological Society. See es-

pecially the articles by Matthews, Rack, and Houk and Rymer.

Burgess et al., 1982. [Chap. 14].

Faber, D. S. and H. Korn. 1978. *Neurobiology of the Mauthner Cell.* New York, Raven.

Lewis, B. D. and D. M. Gower. 1979. [Chap. 16].
Discussion of reflexes and fixed-action patterns as units of behavior.

Liddell, E. G. T. 1960. [Chap. 1]. Historical background for Sherrington's work on reflexes.

McIntyre, A. K. 1974. The central actions of impulses in muscle afferent fibers. In *Handbook of Sensory Physiology.* Vol. III/2, *Muscle Receptors* (ed. by C. C. Hunt). New York: Springer. pp. 235–288.

21

Locomotion

The ability to move about can be regarded as the most important characteristic of animal life. We generally refer to this overall ability as locomotion. Locomotion can be defined, in precise terms, _as the ability of an organism to move in space in purposeful ways under its own power, by efficient mechanisms suitable for the purposes of the movement._ In this chapter we will be concerned with the main types of locomotor activity in invertebrates and vertebrates, and the types of nervous organization that control these activities.

Down through the ages people have made careful observations of the movements of their fellow humans and of the animals about them, but naked-eye observations of rapid movements could be little more than fleeting impressions, and of the most rapid movements, such as the wing movements of a hummingbird, there was only ignorance. Of course, ignorance is the fertilizer for the flowers of debate, and by the nineteenth century there were heated controversies about such matters as the exact positions of a horse's legs during trotting or galloping, or how a cat held upside down can right itself as it falls. (Some scholars were able to prove that the latter is theoretically impossible!)

Accurate knowledge of locomotor activity thus awaited the application of photographic techniques in the late nineteenth century. The pioneers in this were Emil Marey in Paris and Eadweard Muybridge in the United States. Muybridge set up a battery of 24 still cameras side-by-side along a track, and triggered them in sequence while an animal walked or ran by. Examples of his results are shown in Fig. 21.1. These studies cleared up the old controversies about galloping horses and the like, and provided a wealth of information about the locomotor patterns of a wide variety of animals, including humans.

Evolution of Locomotor Structures and Functions

In order to understand the neural systems that control a locomotor pattern like that shown in Fig. 21.1, we need to backtrack briefly at this point and recall the phylogeny of invertebrates and vertebrates, as outlined in Chaps. 2 and 3. As we discussed there, much of the basis for the evolution of different body forms is to be found in the adaptations for different types of locomotor activity.

Fig. 21.1. Sequences of still photographs of a galloping horse and, for contrast, a slowly walking pig. (Obtained by Eadweard Muybridge in 1878 republished in 1957)

The simplest types of locomotion are found in unicellular or small multicellular organisms, which move about mainly by means of *pseudopodia* or *cilia,* aided often by *secretions* of slime. These mechanisms are in fact, exploited in higher organisms in many cellular functions, as we saw in Chap. 4. However, as mechanisms for moving the body through the environment they are effective only for very small organisms. Several additional specializations accompanied the development of larger and more complex organisms. A key one was the ability to develop significant amounts of *force* through muscular contractions. This depended on the development of a *skeleton,* of a hydrostatic type in worms and molluscs, and a rigid type in arthropods and vertebrates. A second adaptation was the ability to carry out different *specialized functions* (for example, walking, grasping, feeding, etc.); this is greatly enhanced by the *metameric* body form, with its potential for specialization of different segments. A third specialization was the development of *appendages,* adapted for locomotion, and for many different types of locomotion. These specializations of body structure and func-

tion, and their significance for the main types of locomotor activity, are summarized in Table 21.1.

Some Common Principles in Nervous Control of Locomotion

The modern study of locomotion depends on a variety of methods. In addition to cinematographic recording of movement patterns, measurements are made of joint positions and angles, and the forces generated. The activity in individual muscles can be recorded by means of fine electrodes inserted into the muscles; the recordings are made on an *electromyograph* (EMG). Underlying any study, of course, is a thorough knowledge of the anatomy of the bones and muscles involved in the movements of interest.

Whatever the pattern of locomotor activity, it is ultimately due to a pattern of nervous activity. In the analysis of nervous mechanisms there have been several areas of interest. The first efforts, directed at *muscle reflexes,* originated in the studies of Sherrington and co-workers. One of the main concepts that came out of these studies is the idea that locomotion in-

Table 21.1   Relations of structural specializations to modes of locomotion

Modes of locomotion	Adaptations of body structure	Significance for locomotion
swimming, creeping	hydrostatic skeleton (coelenterates)	transmission of pressure into force
swimming, creeping	coelom (annelid worms, molluscs)	more efficient transmission of pressure into force
swimming, creeping, burrowing	metamerism (annelid worms, arthropods)	1. more effective deployment of force 2. opportunity for specialization of segments 3. coordination of segments by specialized nervous system
swimming, walking, running, flying	jointed skeleton with appendages (arthropods, vertebrates)	1. extreme localization of force 2. amplification of force through limbs acting as levers 3. reduction and specialization of appendages, sometimes for multiple functions 4. more complex nervous controls

volves a modulation of postural reflexes. A second area, to which Sherrington also contributed, concerns the ability of the spinal cord to generate *intrinsic rhythms*. This concept owes its origin particularly to Graham Brown in England, who studied cats with transected spinal cords, in the early part of this century. A third area of research is concerned with the control of the spinal cord by *higher motor centers*. Many workers have contributed to this area, as we shall see in the next chapter.

At one time or another there have been claims for the predominant influence of each of these main types of mechanisms for the control of movement. One of the important developments in motor studies in recent years has been the synthesis of all these mechanisms into a general framework for nervous control. This synthesis is summarized in Fig. 21.2. The key element in this framework is the *central pattern generator* in the spinal cord (or the relevant ganglia in the case of invertebrates). This contains the essential neural mechanisms for generating coordinated rhythmic outputs of the motoneurons which innervate the *effector organs* (glands or muscles). The central pattern generator is activated and controlled by descending fibers from *higher motor centers*. There is

commonly a succession of higher centers, which form a hierarchy of motor control. Third, there are *sensory inputs* which can activate directly either the spinal cord or higher centers. Finally, there are *feedback circuits*, which feed back information from the *muscles* (proprioceptor reflexes); from the internal or external *environment* through other sensory pathways; and, within the nervous system itself, from lower to higher *centers* (central feedback; also called corollary discharge or efference copy).

Despite the variety of body forms and types of locomotive activity in different species, these main components are present to some extent in the nervous systems of most higher organisms. It is useful to begin the study of locomotor mechanisms with this common framework in mind, and use it as a basis for assessing the relative importance of the different components, and their particular properties, in any given case.

Before considering examples of different motor systems, it will be helpful to discuss a bit further the nature of central pattern generators. As indicated in Fig. 21.2, the pattern generator occupies a key position in any system for locomotive control. The view emerging from recent

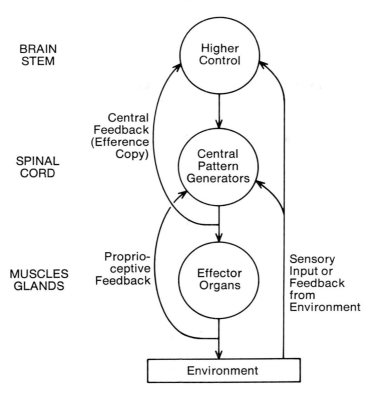

Fig. 21.2. The main neural components common to most motor systems.

studies is that, despite the diversity of body structure and locomotion patterning in the animal world, the basic types of neural circuits for generating rhythmic motor output are actually quite limited. Three main types have been proposed, and they are illustrated in Fig. 21.3.

The first model (A) was proposed by Graham Brown to account for the alternating activation of flexor and extensor muscles of the limb of the cat during walking. Each pool of motoneurons for flexor (F) or extensor (E) muscles is activated by a corresponding "half-center," or pool, of interneurons. Another set of neurons (D) provides for a steady excitatory drive to these interneurons. Between each pool of interneurons are inhibitory connections which ensure that, when one pool is active, the other is suppressed. Graham Brown hypothesized that, as activity in the first pool progressed, a process of fatigue

would build up, soon shutting off the activity and allowing the other pool to become active, and so on. In more modern terms, the process of fatigue can be replaced by any process bringing about self-inhibition of the active cells. The application of this model to the cat has received support from the more recent studies of Anders Lundberg and his colleagues in Sweden, and it has also been applied to wing beat control in the locust by Donald Wilson of the University of California at Berkeley.

A second, and related, type of model (B) conceives of the interneurons as organized in a "closed-loop" of inhibitory connections. There are corresponding pools of motoneurons activated, or inhibited, in sequence. Because of the fractionation of the pools of interneurons and motoneurons, there can be a finer differentiation in the activation of different muscles. This

A. HALF-CENTER MODEL   **B. CLOSED-LOOP MODEL**   **C. PACEMAKER MODEL**

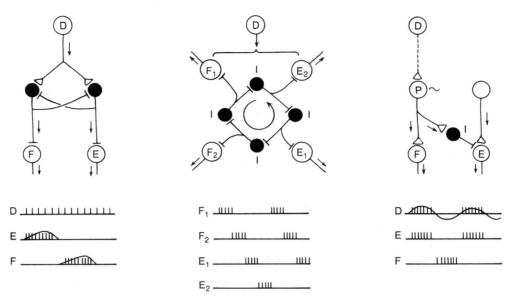

Fig. 21.3. Basic types of rhythm generators. A–C. Simplified diagram of minimum number of neurons and connections. Abbreviations for types of neurons: D, driver; E, extensor motoneuron; F, flexor motoneuron; P, pacemaker; I, interneuron. Neurons with excitatory actions shown by open profiles, inhibitory by filled profiles. Sequences of spike firing or graded potentials shown in idealized recordings below. (For sources, see text)

seems to be a more accurate description of the slightly different activation patterns of individual muscles during many locomotor acts. George Szeckely of Hungary proposed this model for the salamander in 1967, and it has been applied also by the Russian school of Shik and Orlovsky in the cat.

In the models of Fig. 21.3A and B, rhythms result from neuronal circuit organization. In contrast, in the model of C a rhythm arises as a membrane property of a *pacemaker* cell or group of cells. This cell undergoes rhythmic excitation by intrinsic membrane mechanisms, most likely involving the interplay of ionic currents, as discussed in Chap. 7. The pacemaker cell may be a nonspiking neuron that undergoes its rhythmic depolarization and hyperpolarization without generation of action potentials; the graded depolarizations, in turn, bring about release of synaptic transmitters without mediation of

action potentials, by the mechanisms described in Chap. 8. This involvement of nonspiking neurons was first suggested by Martin Mendelson in Oregon for the generation of respiratory rhythms in crustacea, and has been elaborated in detail by Keir Pearson in Alberta and Malcolm Burrows in England for insect locomotor systems. The diagram in C depicts Pearson's suggestion that the pacemaker cell drives flexor motoneurons directly, and brings about concurrent inhibition of extensor motoneurons through inhibitory interneurons (see below).

Invertebrates

With these principles in mind, let us examine some locomotor systems in invertebrates. We will take as examples three species that illustrate the nervous organization involved in control of swimming, walking, and flying.

Swimming. Swimming generally takes place by means of undulatory (wavelike) movements of the whole body. This type of mechanism is very widespread in the animal world, and characterizes, for example, the whiplike movements of the tail of a sperm, and the locomotion of animals as diverse as worms, molluscs, fish, and snakes. Swimming is closely related to *creeping* and *burrowing*. They all involve coordinated sequences of muscle contractions, and their effectiveness (in terms of increased *speed* or *force* of movement) is enhanced by the development of a hydrostatic coelom, metameres, and a more complex organization of muscles and nervous system.

The *leech* is an interesting example because it can move by both creeping and swimming. When *creeping*, it alternately places its anterior and posterior suckers while contracting and extending its body. When *swimming*, it moves by undulations of its body in an up-and-down direction. The efficiency of these movements is enhanced by a flattening of the body, due to steady contractions of a set of muscles that run in the *dorsal-ventral* direction. *Circular* muscles, on the other hand, which are important in creeping movements, remain relaxed during swimming, and forward propulsion through the water is brought about by waves of contractions in the *longitudinal* muscles, the contractile waves alternating between dorsal and ventral muscle groups.

The neural circuit controlling these movements has been studied intensively by Gunther Stent and his colleagues at Berkeley and some of the main results are summarized in Fig. 21.4. The key elements in the circuit are the *motoneurons* to the

Fig. 21.4. Swimming generator circuit in the leech. A. Activity patterns in different types of neuron, showing sequence of activity in relation to phases of movement. Bars indicate periods of impulse firing. B. Neural network generating swimming rhythm. Symbols: small bar, excitatory synapse; filled circle, inhibitory synapse; arrow and bar, rectifying electrical synapses; dotted lines, connections not included in model of (C). C. Activity in electronic models ("neuromimes") of 8 swimming neurons (shaded neurons in (B)). (From Friesen et al., 1976)

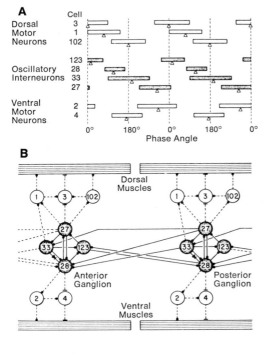

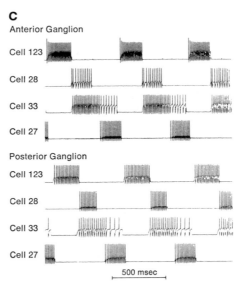

dorsal and ventral muscles, and the *inter-neurons* in the segmental ganglion that control them. As shown in A, each cell fires a burst of impulses that has a strict relation to the phase of the movement oscillation, and is in sequence with the firing of the other cells. The types of synaptic connections between the cells have been analyzed in intracellular recordings, and the network that has been reconstructed is shown in Fig. 21.4B. The interneuronal network has been modeled on a computer, and the firing of the "cells" (called "neuromimes" in the model) in the network is shown in C. The burst discharges and their temporal sequencing are very similar to those observed in the experimental recordings.

The network within one ganglion, as portrayed in Fig. 21.4B, can be seen to be similar in principle to the circuit of 21.3B, based on sequences of inhibitory interactions. In addition, the interganglionic connections are essential to the proper sequencing and frequency of the contractile wave as it spreads longitudinally through the body.

Walking. An essential aspect of the mechanism of swimming is that it involves the whole body. Terrestrial animals, moving through the less resistive medium of the air, can achieve greater efficiency by developing appendages (legs) that are specialized for the purpose. As summarized in Table 21.1, appendages evolved in conjunction with the advantages of a rigid, jointed skeleton and associated musculature. The problem for the body is thus changed, from alternating contractions of the axial musculature in the case of swimming, to alternating contractions of appendage musculature and coordination between the different appendages. The coordinated movements of the appendages are referred to as *stepping* or *striding*. Depending on the rate of movement, locomotion by this means is called *walking* or *running*.

Walking is a very effective and adaptable means of locomotion, as shown by the many forms it takes among the thousands of species in the phylum Arthropoda. In general, the fewer the legs, the more efficient the locomotion, at least as far as speed is concerned. Part of the reason for this is illustrated in Fig. 21.5, which compares an animal with many legs (a centipede) with one with few legs (a crayfish). The centipede can actually move rather

Fig. 21.5. Comparison of locomotor appendages (legs) of the fastest centipede (*Scutigera*) and a crayfish (*Leander*). Heavy lines indicate the movement of the "foot" relative to the body during one step forward. (From Manton, in Barrington, 1979)

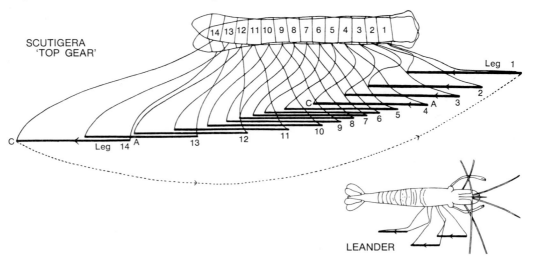

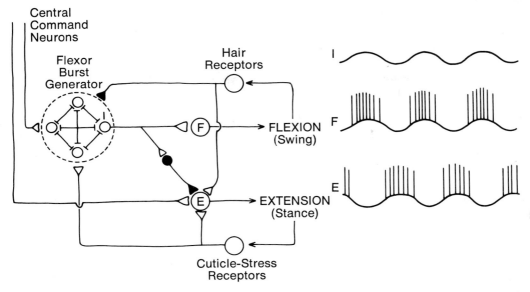

Fig. 21.6. Rhythm generator for stepping in the cockroach. Diagram shows neural circuit controlling one leg. Characteristic activity patterns recorded from burst-generator interneuron and from flexor and extensor motoneurons are shown at right. (Modified from Pearson, 1976)

quickly (about 0.4 m per sec, or better than one ft per sec), and does so by means of relatively long legs, with slightly differing lengths. However, with so many legs, there is a tremendous problem of coordination, and there are severe restrictions on individual leg movements, in order that the poor centipede doesn't continually trip over itself. In contrast, rapid locomotion is achieved in the crayfish (and many other arthropods) by means of only a few pairs of legs. In those animals with only three pairs, it is often the case that the front legs are specialized for *traction* or *attachment,* the middle ones for *support,* and the rear ones for *propulsion.* An additional advantage of fewer legs is that it permits other appendages to be specialized for other functions, such as grasping prey (claws) or rapid escape maneuvers (tail).

Among the species that have been studied, the *cockroach* provides some particularly interesting examples of the neural mechanisms that are involved (see Fig. 21.6). The central rhythm generator is composed of a group of cells which undergo oscillations of their membrane

potential. Keir Pearson and Charles Fourtner in Alberta showed that some of these are nonspiking cells, which synaptically drive the motoneurons that innervate flexor muscles of the leg. At the same time, the extensor motoneurons are inhibited through an inhibitory interneuron. Both the flexor-burst generator cells and the extensor motoneuron pool are under tonic excitatory drive from higher command fibers, and the result is that extensor excitation can only occur "out-of-phase" with flexor excitation. This assures an orderly alternation of contractions in the flexor and extensor muscles of the leg, and is the basis of stepping. This network thus is similar to the basic model of Fig. 21.3C, with the addition that the oscillating element driving the flexors is actually a group of cells, organized along lines similar to those of the model of Fig. 21.3B.

Flying. The extraordinary utility of the articulated appendage is well-illustrated in the ability of many insects to fly. A characteristic of invertebrates is that the appendages for this purpose—the wings—

have developed independently of the legs for walking. This means that flying insects retain their mobility and other motor capabilities on surfaces. Also it means that the wing is not a modified walking leg, but rather is designed solely for the purpose of flying. This is believed to account for the great variety of wing structures and flight mechanisms of insects, as compared with birds (see below).

Flight involves the generation of *lift* (to counteract gravity) and *thrust* (to move forward against the resistance of the air). Both of these depend on the aerodynamics of the wing structure, and the *orientation, force,* and *frequency* of the wing beat. These three factors, in turn, are the out-

come of the properties of the peripheral muscles and skeleton, and the signals that come from the nervous system.

In assessing the relative importance of all these factors, a basic distinction is first made between *synchronous* and *asynchronous* flight mechanisms (see Fig. 21.7). In the synchronous type, each impulse in a motoneuron gives rise to a contraction of a muscle and a beat of the wing. The muscles attach to the wing itself (*direct muscles*). The wing beat frequency is commonly in the range of 10–30 per sec. This type is characteristic of most flying insects.

The asynchronous mechanism is found only in a few insect orders: Hemiptera

Fig. 21.7. Comparison between two types of flight muscle in insects. *Left,* synchronous flight muscle, with direct connection of muscles to wing, as in the damselfly. *Right,* asynchronous flight muscle, with indirect relation to wing, as in the wasp. *Below,* characteristic activity in motor nerves (impulses), flight muscles (mechanical tension), and wing (movements). (After Smith, 1965, in part)

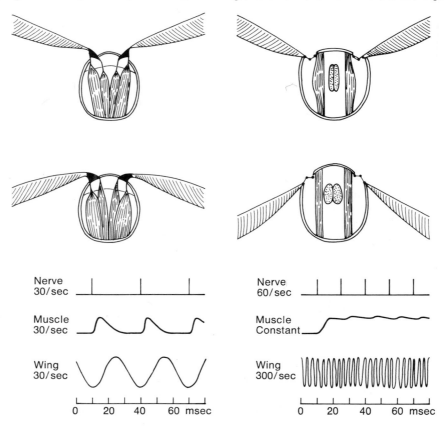

(bugs), Coleoptera (beetles), Hymenoptera (bees and wasps), and Diptera (flies and mosquitoes). As indicated in Fig. 21.7, in this mechanism there is not a one-to-one relation between nerve impulse firing and the wing beat. Instead, the nerve impulses set up a tonic contraction state in thoracic (*indirect*) muscles. The contractions of these muscles put tension on the articulation of the base of the wing with the thorax, and a special property of this joint allows it to snap back and forth ("click" mechanism) at a high frequency. Thus, any unpatterned nerve discharge with sufficiently high frequency to set up the tonic state will generate the wing beats. This mechanism is well-suited for generating very high wing-beat frequencies. The frequencies for the housefly and honey bee, for example, are in the range of 200 beats per sec, and those for the mosquito are as high as 1000 beats per sec (only 1 msec between beats)!

The asynchronous mechanism thus depends on special properties of the thoracic muscles and wing joints. This is economical for the nervous system, which is freed of the burden of providing precise timing at high frequencies, with the attendant demands on nervous controls and energy metabolism. The spike intervals are so brief, in fact, that the nerve fibers could not fire fast enough to drive the muscles one-for-one, because of the duration of the refractory period (it may be recalled that a similar problem arises with the encoding of information about high-frequency tones in the auditory nerve, in Chap. 16). For the synchronous mechanism, on the other hand, there is close coupling between nerve firing and muscle contractions. For this mechanism, similar principles for the generation of rhythmic activity apply as in the other forms of locomotion we have considered.

Vertebrates

Despite the differences in body structure, vertebrates engage in the same basic types of locomotion as invertebrates (see Table 21.1). Let us briefly consider some of the principles involved, with particular emphasis on walking in the mammal.

Swimming. As already mentioned, the undulatory motions of swimming in fish or slithering in snakes are similar to those of worms. Higher speeds are achieved by increasing the frequency of the alternating contractions of muscle groups that underlie the body undulations. The waves persist after deafferentation of the spinal cord when most of the dorsal roots are cut. After a high spinal transection, interrupting all descending fibers, most fish show no spontaneous movements, but during tonic sensory stimulation (such as a pinch of the tail), wavelike contractions of the body appear. From such experiments it has been concluded that a central rhythm generator is present in the spinal cord, which in many species requires tonic input for its expression.

Walking. Apart from the snakes, terrestrial vertebrates have particularly exploited the locomotory abilities of the leg in their invasion of the land. The evolution of legs from fins follows a logical sequence. In lower fish the function of the fins is mainly to provide *stabilization*, but in higher (bony) fish the fins are more specialized and contribute to *propulsion*. In the transitional forms (Crossopterygia) the pectoral and pelvic fins are more elaborate, and have the appearance of being the basis for the fore- and hindlimbs of tetrapods.

The primitive walking movements of amphibians reflect rather strongly the basic swimming movements of fish. This is illustrated in Fig. 21.8. Note in part B how the limbs have attachment points on either side of the pectoral (anterior) and pelvic (posterior) girdles. Forward movement is achieved by extension, placing, and thrust of the limbs, in coordination with the swimming movements of the body.

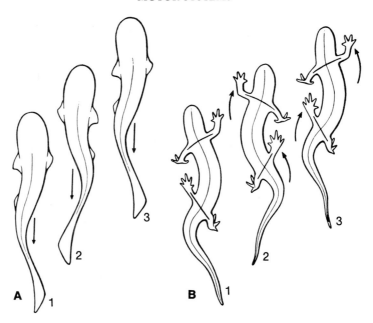

Fig. 21.8. Comparison between swimming movements of a fish (**A**) and primitive walking movements of a salamander (**B**). (From Romer and Parsons, 1977)

The diagrams of Fig. 21.8B might seem to imply that limb movements and their neural control in amphibians are relatively simple, but experimental investigations have shown that they are actually rather complicated. George Szekely inserted fine recording wires into individual muscles of the forelimb of the newt, and recorded the EMG activity during normal walking. The results are illustrated in Fig. 21.9. Alternating bursts of activity are present, but it can be seen that each of these eight muscles has a rather complicated pattern of activity during the stepping cycle, and no two muscles or muscle groups have the same pattern. Also, cocontraction of two or more muscles is common at any given point in the cycle. These patterns are found to persit even after deafferentation by transection of the dorsal roots, showing that they are due to a central rhythm generator in the spinal cord. The half-center model, with similar activity patterns in extensors and flexors (see Fig. 21.3A), is too simple to account for the individualized activity patterns, and

Szekely therefore proposed a network of inhibitory connections (Fig. 21.3B) to account for the findings.

Amphibians and reptiles are constructed such that the limbs are attached laterally to the trunk, whereas in birds and mammals the legs support the body from underneath. The lateral placement has the advantage of a low center of gravity and more stable equilibrium. The vertical placement, however, is regarded as more efficient for the purposes of locomotion. In general this is so; nonetheless, some reptiles are capable of moving very swiftly indeed. Outstanding in this regard are the lizards. The little basilisk lizard can skitter along at rates up to 7 m per sec (about 10 miles per hour). It does this by tucking in its forelimbs and running on its hindlimbs, with the heavy tail helping to maintain balance (see Fig. 21.10). The lizard thus runs with a *bipedal* gait. Several other animals, besides man, have developed a bipedal gait (for example, kangaroos), which illustrates the principle of convergent evolution.

Control of Walking in the Cat. Because of its convenient size and generalized body form, the domestic cat has been a favorate subject for studies of neural mechanisms of locomotion in higher vertebrates. The patterns of movements of the feet during normal locomotion of the cat are illustrated in Fig. 21.11. The stepping sequence is: left hind leg, left front leg, right hind leg, and right front leg. Watch your cat the next time you have a chance, and see if you can identify this sequence—without the help of a photographic analysis! It has been found that this is the basic pattern for most vertebrate species, as well as for fast moving invertebrates like the cockroach (see figure). The reason for this prevalence is that the pattern seems to provide for the best *stability,* which of course is increasingly important in the longer-legged animals.

As the cat moves forward at increasing speeds, the steps are faster, but the same progression is maintained. However, different combinations of legs are on or off the ground at the same time as the speed

Fig. 21.9. Walking in the newt. *Above,* activity of eight forelimb muscles, recorded in the electromyograph (EMG) in the freely moving animal. *Middle,* movement of limbs during locomotion. *Below,* positions of forelimb muscle. (From Szekely et al., 1969)

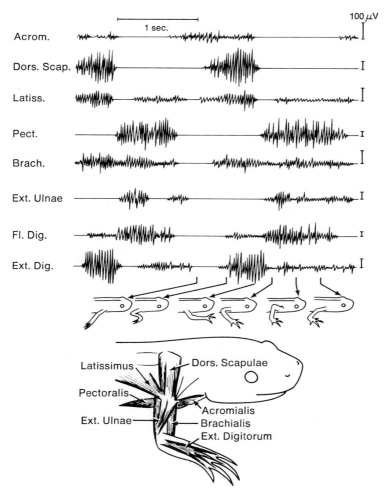

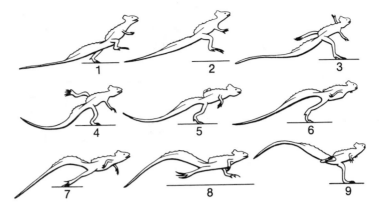

Fig. 21.10. Running of the basilisk lizard. (From Gray, 1968)

Fig. 21.11. Comparison of the stepping movements of the cockroach and the cat for different gaits characteristic of the two species. Open bars, foot lifted; closed bars, foot planted. (Adapted from Pearson, 1976)

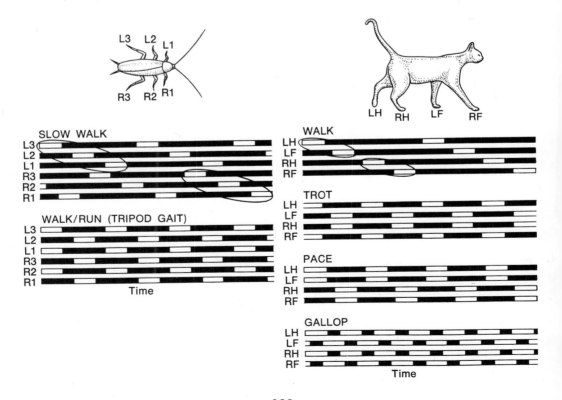

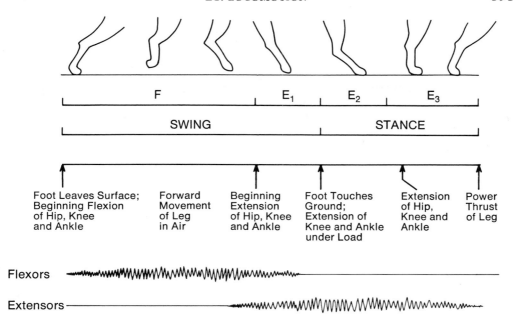

Fig. 21.12. The step cycle, showing phases of leg flexion (F) and extension (E) and their relation to the swing and stance. *Below,* electromyograph (EMG) recordings. (Adapted from Wetzel and Stuart, 1976)

increases, and these combinations are expressed as different *gaits.* The cat has several gaits, for moving to higher speeds, just as a car has several gears; these are illustrated in Fig. 21.11. For comparison, the locust has just one fast-moving gait. The cat can change relatively smoothly from one gait to the next (*gait conversion*), whereas the cockroach shifts more abruptly from the one to the other.

A closer analysis of the movement of one leg through a step cycle is illustrated in Fig. 21.12. As we have seen, a step consists of two phases, swing and stance. During the *swing* phase, the leg is lifted and brought forward, mainly by action of the leg flexor muscles (F). At the end of the swing phase (E$_1$), the extensors become active, and the combined activity of flexors and extensors stiffens the leg as it is planted. During the *stance* phase, extensor activity becomes dominant (E$_2$, E$_3$), providing the force that thrusts the animal forward. These phases of muscle activity seem to be quite gen-

eral, and apply to our own bipedal steps as well as to quadrupeds.

If we examine again the different gaits as depicted in Fig. 21.11, we see that the total time for a step cycle decreases as the speed goes up, but the decrease is almost entirely taken in the stance phase; the duration of the swing phase stays relatively constant. Thus, speed of locomotion comes about mainly by faster and quicker thrust. There is presumably an economy in having the swing phase be relatively stereotyped, so that the central motor circuits can change gaits by controlling muscle activity mainly during the stance phase.

The different gaits and how they are controlled brings us back to the questions originally posed by Muybridge and his photographs. We have seen how Graham Brown's studies led to the idea of "half-centers" in the spinal cord, with intrinsic rhythmic activity controlling flexor and extensor motoneuron pools. Further analysis awaited more refined methods, in which there could be experimental control of locomotor behavior under well-defined conditions. This was first achieved by the Russian physiologists, Shik, Severin, and Orlovsky, in Moscow. The experimental setup is illustrated in Fig. 21.13. The cat is decerebrate, rendered so by a transection between the superior and inferior colliculi in the midbrain to isolate the spinal cord and lower brainstem from higher brain centers. The animal is held rigidly in a holder, and its paws placed on a treadmill. Stepping movements of the paws on the treadmill can be initiated by various procedures, such as electrical stimulation of different parts of the brainstem below the transection, or by injection of substances into the bloodstream.

In the next chapter we will discuss some of the effects of stimulating brainstem centers. Here we will mention the effects of injection of *l*-DOPA into the bloodstream. One of the descending pathways from the brainstem consists of noradre-nergic fibers arising from cells in the locus ceruleus and nearby reticular system (see Chap. 13). The terminals of these fibers in the spinal cord can be stimulated to release NA (noradrenaline) by injection of the precursor *l*-DOPA into the bloodstream. A detailed analysis of the effects of *l*-DOPA was carried out by Anders Lundberg, Elzbieta Jankowska, Sten Grillner, and their colleagues in Göteborg in the late 1960's. They showed that *l*-DOPA produces prolonged excitatory and inhibitory effects on the interneurons in the pathways that mediate the flexion reflex (see previous chapter, Fig. 20.12). Their results are summarized in Fig. 21.14. To begin with, NA fibers have an inhibitory action on a population of interneurons labeled Ⓐ in the figure. This suppresses activation of motoneurons through these interneurons. However, interneurons Ⓐ have connections to other interneurons which inhibit transmission through the interneuron population labeled Ⓑ. In this way, NA inhibition of population Ⓐ at the same time

Fig. 21.13. Experimental set up for studying neuronal activity during treadmill walking in the decerebrate cat. **A.** General view. **B.** Inset showing rigid holding of vertebrae. Numbers identify the following components: 1, cat; 2, treadmill; 3, belt tachometer; 4, stereotaxic head holder; 5, electrode holder; 6, clamps to hold spine; 7, electrodes for recording unitary activity; 8, skin flap forming oil bath; 9, spinal cord; 10, detectors of longitudinal displacement of limbs; 11, joint angle detectors; 12, implanted electrodes in muscle. (From Severin et al., in Wetzel and Stuart, 1976)

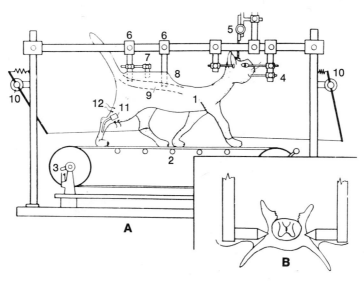

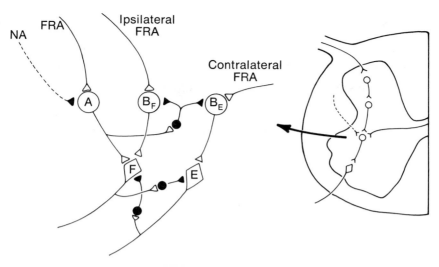

Fig. 21.14. Schematic diagram of the circuit for generating rhythmic stepping movements in the cat lumbosacral cord, showing the postulated site of input of NA fibers. NA, noradrenergic fibers; FRA, flexor reflex afferents; A, B, interneuronal populations; F, flexor motoneuron population; E, extensor motoneuron population. Excitatory connections shown by open terminals, inhibitory connections by filled terminals. (Based on Jankowska et al., in Wetzel and Stuart, 1976)

leads to release of inhibition, and hence facilitation, of population Ⓑ. This arrangement accounts for the alternating activation of motoneurons that is the basis for the alternating stepping movements of the limbs in the cat injected with *l*-DOPA. Of course a circuit model such as that in Fig. 21.14 involves a number of speculative points, but it represents a reasonable and testable mechanism by which NA fibers normally modulate locomotor activity at the spinal level.

REFERENCES

Barrington, E. J. W. 1979. [Chap. 1].

Burrows, M. 1980. The control of sets of motoneurones by local interneurones in the locust. *J. Physiol. 298:* 213–233.

Bentley, D. and M. Konishi. 1978. Neural control of behavior. *Ann. Rev. Neurosci. 1:* 35–59.

Friesen, W. O., M. Poon, and G. S. Stent. 1976. Oscillatory neuronal circuit generating a locomotor rhythm. *Proc. Natl. Acad. Sci. 73:* 3734–3738.

Gray, J. 1968. *Animal Locomotion.* New York: Norton.

Grillner, S. 1975. Locomotion in vertebrates: central mechanisms and reflex interaction. *Physiol. Rev. 55:* 247–304.

Muybridge, E. 1957. *Animals in Motion.* New York: Dover. (from *Animal Locomotion,* 1887).

Pearson, K. 1976. The control of walking. *Sci. Am. 235:* 72–86.

Romer, A. S. and T. S. Parsons. 1977. [Chap. 3].

Smith, D. S. 1965. The flight muscles of insects. *Sci. Am. 212:* 76–88.

Szekely, G. 1968. Development of limb movements: embryological, physiological and model studies. In *Ciba Fndn. Symp. on Growth of the Nervous System* (ed. by G. E. W. Wolstenholine and M. O'Connor). London: Churchill. pp. 77–93.

Wetzel, M. C. and D. G. Stuart. 1976. Ensemble characteristics of cat locomotion and its neural control. *Progr. Neurobiol. 7:* 1–98.

Additional Reading

Dagg, A. I. 1977. *Running, Walking and Jumping. The Science of Locomotion.* New York: Wykeham.

Delcomyn, F. 1980. Neural basis of rhythmic

behavior in animals. *Science 210:* 492–498.

Friesen, W. O. and G. S. Stent. 1978. Neural circuits for generating rhythmic movements. *Ann. Rev. Biophysics and Bioengr. 7:* 37–61.

Grillner, S. 1975. Locomotion in vertebrates: central mechanisms and reflex interaction. *Physiol. Rev. 55:* 247–304.

Stein, P. S. G. 1978. Motor systems, with specific reference to the control of locomotion. *Ann. Rev. Neurosci. 1:* 61–81.

Sukhanov, V. B. 1974. *General System of Symmetrical Locomotion of Terrestrial Vertebrates and Some Features of Movement of Lower Tetrapods.* New Delhi: Amerind. Publishing Co.

22
Command Neurons and Motor Hierarchies

The four preceding chapters have introduced the major elements of the motor apparatus: the glands and muscles themselves, the motoneurons that innervate them, the simplest neural networks for generating rhythms and fixed action patterns to drive the motoneurons, and the simplest reflex pathways involving sensory inputs. For the most part, all of this neural machinery is at the segmental level of the nerve cord in invertebrates, and the spinal cord and brainstem in vertebrates.

We now come to the question: what are the neural mechanisms for operating this segmental apparatus, so that it serves the whole organism in meaningful ways? There are two aspects to this question. One concerns the anatomy of the pathways and the physiological mechanisms by which the segmental apparatus is controlled. This is the focus of the present chapter. The second aspect concerns the nature of the motor control within the context of the whole organism. For example, is a given movement voluntary or involuntary, purposive or automatic? What is the adaptive value of a given type of movement for the individual and for the species? These questions will arise in the final section of the book, which elaborates the central sys-

tems, but it is important at this stage to realize that the most profound students of motor function, such as Charles Sherrington, always regarded individual motor mechanisms from a perspective of their significance for the behavior of the whole organism.

In the analysis of motor control systems, two concepts have been particularly useful. One is the *command neuron,* a single cell or fiber that can activate a piece of behavior. The other is the idea that motor systems have a *hierarchical organization,* with lower centers under control of higher centers. It will be useful to review briefly the origins of these concepts before considering examples of actual systems.

Command Neurons

This concept arose from the work of C. A. G. "Kees" Wiersma, at California Institute of Technology, on motor systems in the crayfish. Beginning in the 1940's, this work was focused on the giant fiber system that controls the escape response, and also the circuit that controls the rhythmic beating of small abdominal appendages called phyllopodia, or *swimmerets.* Wiersma realized that large, identifiable fibers in the connectives to the segmental ganglia can be selectively stimulated and their individual effects on the motor output determined. In 1964 he and Kazuo Ikeda showed that the endogenous bursting of the segmental motoneurons that innervate the swimmeret muscles can be turned on and off by stimulation of specific interneurons in more rostral ganglia and connectives. They introduced the term "command fiber" for the fibers they stimulated. The details of the swimmeret system were worked out subsequently by Paul Stein at Washington University in St. Louis and by Donald Kennedy and his colleagues at Stanford. A summary of the circuit is shown in Fig. 22.1.

The terms *command fiber* and *command neuron* quickly found application to a variety of systems in which similar neural elements and functional properties were found. Although there is not complete agreement on a definition, the following by David Bentley and Mazakuzi Konishi is representative and workable:

> Command (neurons) can be defined as interneurons whose activation alone suffices to elicit a recognizable fragment of behavior through excitation and/or inhibition of a constellation of motoneurons.

Within this definition, command neurons have a number of properties:

1. Command neurons are neither sensory receptors nor motoneurons; hence, the usual designation as "interneurons".
2. Most command neurons are identifiable, each cell body or fiber having a characteristic size, shape, and position within a ganglion or nerve cord.
3. They range widely in size, from small to very large.
4. They are small in number; of all interneurons in the crayfish nerve cord, command neurons probably constitute less than 1%.
5. Activation of a single command neuron produces a unique motor effect; in calling forth this effect, the temporal pattern of the impulses is usually not

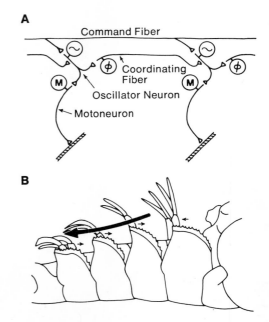

Fig. 22.1. **A.** Rhythm generator circuits for control of swimmerets in the crayfish. Two neighboring hemiganglia are shown, connected by a coordinating fiber. In each hemiganglion, there is an oscillator neuron that receives its input from a nonrhythmic command fiber. (From Stein, in Wetzel and Stuart, 1976) **B.** Movements of swimmerets. The most anterior appendage, at right, is completing the power stroke, while the others are in successive phases of their return strokes, in the direction shown by the arrows. Movement of water is indicated by large heavy arrow. (From Davis, in Kennedy, 1976)

critical. However, the frequency of impulse firing may be important; firing at increasing frequencies may produce a shift in the effects produced.

6. The effect is a coordinated motor pattern; the command neuron achieves this pattern by connecting directly or indirectly to many motoneurons (from a few up to several hundred).
7. Related command neurons produce overlapping effects, which together provide for the entire range of a particular movement pattern.
8. The basic pattern generator for the movements elicited by a command

neuron resides in the motoneurons and their immediate premotor neurons; the function of the command cell is to initiate, terminate, or modulate this pattern. The command neuron is thus a "higher-order" neuron.

What kind of movements are elicited by command neurons? In order to answer this question, it is useful to recognize that movements can be grouped into several main categories: *postures, episodic* (one time only) movements, *repetitive* (rhythmic) movements, and *progressive* sequences of movements. In the crayfish, in which most of the early work was carried out, single neurons have been found that elicit movements in all of these categories. Command neurons have also been found in annelid worms, insects, and molluscs. In vertebrates, Mauthner cells in the brainstem of fish appear to fulfill most of the above criteria.

Examples of movements under control of command neurons have already been discussed in previous chapters. It will be recalled that the heartbeat of the crayfish is generated by a system of interneurons in the cardiac ganglion; these interneurons are in turn under control of command neurons from higher centers (see Fig. 19.3). Identified neurons also control the myogenic heartrate of *Aplysia*, and coordinate it with the movements of the gill and stomach (see Fig. 19.4). The escape responses of invertebrates and vertebrates are mediated by giant fibers, which are among the clearest examples of the command neuron concept (see Chap. 20). Our discussion of locomotion distinguished between motoneurons, pattern generator interneurons, and descending pathways, the latter representing elements mediating command functions (Chap. 21).

It may be noted that many of the types of movement cited above fall into the category of fixed-action pattern, as defined in Chap. 20. The function of the command neuron in these cases is to elicit or control the pattern. Command neurons that elicit

a motor pattern that outlasts the stimulus are called *trigger* cells; the giant fibers are examples of this type. Neurons that require continuous stimulation to elicit or modulate a motor pattern are termed *gating* neurons; these cells commonly control postural or rhythmic motor activity. Examples of more complicated fixed-action patterns, underlying manipulating, communication, feeding, and mating, will be discussed in later chapters.

Decision Making. The identification of command neurons raises the question of how the command neuron is itself commanded; in other words, how does the nervous system decide to activate a given neuron or set of neurons, with its associated behavior pattern, rather than another? In some cases, the activity is obligatory and ongoing (such as the heartbeat), and the problem is simply to modulate it appropriately in relation to different activity levels. In other cases, however, particularly those involving locomotion, there has to be some kind of *decision-making* function that selects one behavior (such as a tail flip or a jump) rather than another (such as walking or feeding). In the case of the giant-fiber escape system, we have already noted that the reflex pathway has a relatively high threshold for activation. Thus, the threshold alone can serve the decision-making function; if sensory stimulation is below threshold, there is no tail flip; above threshold, there is a tail flip. However, the threshold itself is affected by a number of factors, such as whether, in the case of the crayfish, the animal is in or out of the water, or whether it has been injured. This reminds us that sensory pathways are very important in activating or modulating a motor pathway; potentially, this may occur at all levels, from motoneurons up to command neurons, and also at the cells that control the command neurons.

Several systems have been analyzed in which the decision-making mechanism is more complicated. One example is the movement detector-jump system in the locust. The visual detector part of the system has already been described in Chap. 17. On the motor side, W. J. Heitler and Malcolm Burrows showed that the motor program for the jump actually has three distinct stages. First is flexion of the leg; second is cocontraction of extensor and flexor muscles; third, there is sudden relaxation of the flexors, giving rise to the jump. The sequence is shown schematically in Fig. 22.2. Thus, rather than a sin-

Fig. 22.2. The mechanism of the locust jump. **A.** The sequence of events involves cocking of the leg (initial flexion), crouching (co-contraction), and jumping (kick). The impulse activity in different neuronal populations is shown diagramatically, in relation to the different stages of movement of the tibia, the state of arousal, and the action of the central trigger. **B.** Simplified diagram of the neuronal circuit for the jump. The cock stage involves initial activation (mediated by central sensory pathways) of flexor motoneurons followed by extensor motoneurons (dashed lines). The crouch stage involves heightened co-activation of the flexor and extensor motoneuorons by the central pathways, aided by feedback from leg receptors. At this stage the leg is held in extreme flexion by co-contraction and by a locking mechanism which serves to store energy in the elastic and cuticular elements of the knee joint. Proprioceptive feedback also is directed to an interneuron (M), depolarizing it near its threshold for impulse firing. The jump stage is triggered by sudden sensory input (as from DCMDs—see Chap. 17) to interneuron (M), which inhibits the flexor motoneurons; the contracting extensor muscles pull the knee joint out of its locked position, and the stored energy is released in a ballistic kick. (A modified from Heitler and Burrows, 1977; B from Pearson et al., 1980)

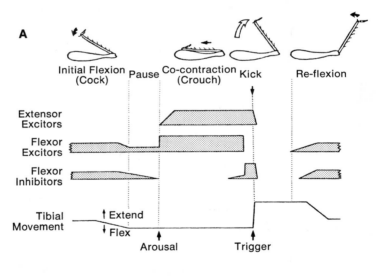

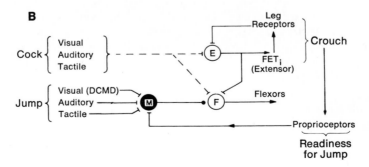

gle neuron or gate, there is a sequence of gates; at each stage, the decision to proceed depends on the presence of several factors, including the intensity of specific sensory stimulation, the coincidence of other sensory stimuli, the state of arousal, and activity in other motor systems. These results suggest that a given behavior is not mediated by a single command neuron, but rather by a network of such cells providing for multiple state-dependent gates.

Motor Hierarchies

Closely allied to the command neuron is the concept of hierarchical control.

Historically, the idea that motor systems are organized in a hierarchical fashion has a long and distinguished lineage. The idea was formulated in the latter part of the nineteenth century by the great English neurologist, John Hughlings Jackson (1835–1911). Jackson, the son of a farmer, had a limited education and medical training. His genius lay in the meticulousness of his observations of patients with neurological diseases, combined with a philosophical cast of mind which enabled him to recognize the principles implied by the observations. One of his main studies was of epileptic seizures, particularly those which involve restricted parts of the body musculature, a type now known, in his honor, as Jacksonian seizures. A tragic footnote is that his profound insights into this disease drew on his wife, who suffered from these seizures and died at an early age from cerebral thrombosis.

Jackson's study of the motor derangements associated with seizures convinced him that there are successive levels for motor control in the nervous system. In evolution, he deduced, there has been a progression from automatic toward purposive movements, and this is reflected in the nervous system in the control of automatic movements by lower levels and purposive movements by higher levels. He reasoned that the higher levels normally exert control over the lower levels, and that this control can be either excitatory or inhibitory. When upper-level function is interrupted or destroyed by disease, lower centers are "released" from higher control, and the result may be hyperactivity (such as exaggerated reflexes) if the normal descending control was inhibitory. Although knowledge of anatomy was limited in Jackson's time, he postulated that the lowest level for motor control is in the spinal cord and brainstem, the next (middle) level is in the cerebral cortex along the central (Rolandic) fissure, and the highest level is in the frontal lobe.

These concepts have influenced all subsequent workers, and today they still provide a useful evolutionary framework for thinking about the organization of motor systems. A recent update of this framework is depicted in the schema of Fig. 22.3. The reader may wish to compare this with the diagrams of Figs. 20.1 and 21.2, which were mainly concerned with representing the lowest, segmental level of organization in the spinal cord. Figure 22.3 shows the immediate control of the spinal apparatus by specific motor regions of the brainstem and cerebral cortex, representing Jackson's "middle level" of control. These regions, in turn, are under the combined control of several areas, including the cerebellum and the basal ganglia (rather than exclusively the prefrontal cortex, as Jackson thought).

Several additional points may be made in reference to Fig. 22.3. One is that motor control is not, in fact, strictly hierarchical. The hierarchical sequence descending from "projection areas" to "segmental motor programs" to "motoneurons" is bypassed by some direct pathways from the projection areas to the motoneurons. In other words, there are parallel pathways as well as serial ones. This recalls the studies of sensory systems, in which recent findings have emphasized the presence of both serial and parallel pathways. Thus, it appears that in both sensory and motor systems, greater adaptability and process-

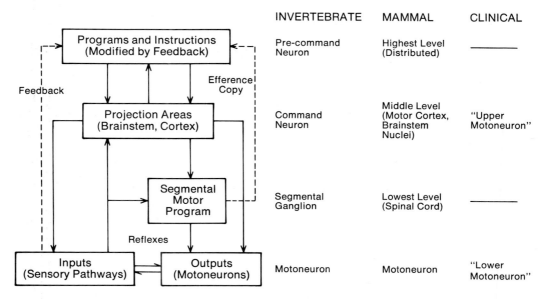

Fig. 22.3. Hierarchical organization of motor control. (Modified from Phillips and Porter, 1977)

ing power is obtained by building in both types of pathways (see also below).

A second point is that there are feedback connections from every level of the motor system. Some of this feedback is from sensory pathways, conveying information from the periphery, information that alerts the animal, or tells it the effect of its motor actions on the environment. The sensory pathways themselves are under the influence of the motor outflow. In addition, the motor pathways not only carry information to the motoneurons, but send a copy of that information back to the higher levels. This internal feedback is known by various names, such as *re-afference, corollary discharge,* or *afference copy.* Through it, higher levels are kept informed of what lower levels are doing. It seems to express a principle of good management, that presidents and generals should not put their trust entirely in their vice-presidents and colonels, but see for themselves what is actually happening in the offices, factories, and battlefields.

A final point is that this schema for the vertebrate brain is general enough to be quite accurately applicable to the inverte-brate nervous system as well. Thus, as indicated on the left, the command neurons of invertebrates are at a level equivalent to the projection areas of vertebrates, and the highest level in both cases contains the *programming instructions.*"

Brainstem Centers

It will be helpful to keep Fig. 22.3 in mind as our discussion moves to higher control of motor function in the vertebrate nervous system. First, the projection areas will be identified (middle level). These include the regions that are sources of descending fibers that terminate in the spinal cord. The main regions are shown in Fig. 22.4.

Reticular Nucleus. The reticular system is distributed diffusely through the brainstem. As we learned in the discussion of sensory systems (Chaps. 11–17), it receives collaterals from sensory projection pathways, and has as one of its functions the mediation of states of arousal. This involves fibers that ascend toward the thalamus, and descend toward the spinal cord. The functions of the reticular system, considered as part of central systems, are discussed in Chaps. 25 and 27.

The descending motor fibers are of concern here. In fish and amphibians, a few cells in the reticular substance of the medulla are differentiated into *giant cells,* with large dendrites, and a long axon which descends into the spinal cord to make synaptic connections with segmental interneurons and motoneurons. These are known as *Mueller cells* (6–8 cells in lamprey, for example) or *Mauthner cells* (a single pair, as in many teleost fish, and amphibians).

From a phylogenetic viewpoint, the significance of these large, reticular neurons appears to be mainly in relation to control of the *tail.* In most vertebrates the tail is an important motor organ. It serves as an organ of locomotion, and it is also used in maintaining balance (as in fish swimming or lizards running: see Fig. 21.9). Part of the importance of the tail lies in the power it can generate; this is why it is so important in escape and startle responses. As we discussed in Chap. 20, the Mauthner cell, with its giant axon, provides a fast pathway for initiating quick and powerful

Fig. 22.4. Principal regions of the human brain involved in immediate motor control through descending fibers to motoneurons.

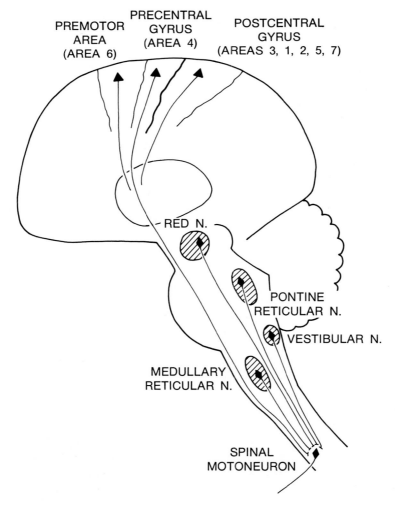

movements of the body and tail, and we noted that its function in this respect is closely analogous to that of giant fiber systems in invertebrates.

In higher vertebrates, reticular neurons in the medulla and in the pons also send fibers to the spinal cord. Some of these fibers come from giant cells, though the cells are not uniquely identifiable. A variety of studies has indicated that the reticulospinal neurons constitute the main brainstem system for immediate control of the segmental spinal apparatus as it is employed in standing and stepping. We will discuss more details of this control below.

Vestibular Nucleus. The vestibular nuclear complex is closely associated with the reticular nuclei. This nucleus receives the afferents from the vestibular canals (Chap. 15) and also fibers from the cerebellum, and in turn provides one of the main inputs to the Mauthner cell in lower vertebrates (Chap. 20). Of the four main parts of the vestibular complex (see Fig. 15.12) in the mammal, the *lateral nucleus* is the main source of fibers to the spinal cord. The lateral nucleus contains *giant cells,* named *Deiter's cells* after the early German histologist who first described them in 1865; the nucleus is accordingly referred to as *Deiter's nucleus.*

The *vestibulospinal tract,* composed of fibers from the giant cells as well as other cells of the lateral nucleus, descends the length of the spinal cord. The lateral nucleus is organized somatotopically, and this order is maintained in the projections to different levels of the cord. Electrical stimulation of the lateral nucleus produces polysynaptic EPSPs in *extensor* motoneurons of the limbs. This has suggested that, through the vestibulospinal tract, the cerebellum exerts a facilitatory control over muscle tone in the extensor limb muscles involved in standing.

It may be noted that the *medial vestibular nucleus* sends fibers to the upper part of the spinal cord by way of the *medial longitudinal fasciculus.* The role of these fibers in the control of eye movements has been discussed in Chap. 15. The *inferior* and *medial vestibular nuclei* project fibers to the cerebellum (see below). Through all these connections the signals from the vestibular canals are widely dispersed throughout the brainstem and spinal cord.

Red Nucleus. The red nucleus is a prominent structure in reptiles, birds, and mammals. It has a slightly pinkish color in fresh specimens, hence its name. Part of the nucleus contains *giant cells*; these, as well as cells of other sizes, project their axons to brainstem centers and to the spinal cord. In higher mammals, including man, there are fewer giant cells, and the spinal tract is less prominent; other connections (see below) become more important.

Electrical stimulation of the red nucleus in the cat causes *flexion* of the limbs. Intracellular recordings have shown that such stimulation produces polysynaptic EPSPs in flexor motoneurons, and polysynaptic IPSPs in extensor motoneurons to the limbs. The excitatory effect may be mediated through segmental interneurons, or by activation of gamma motoneurons and the gamma loop (Chap. 14). The facilitative effect of the red nucleus on limb flexion thus contrasts with the facilitative effect of the vestibular nucleus on limb extension.

The significance of the three brainstem centers discussed above for the control of walking has been assessed by G. N. Orlovsky of Russia, who used the preparation of the cat depicted in Fig. 21.13. Some of his results are summarized in Fig. 22.5. Chief among the three centers in the control of walking is the reticular formation. In unit recordings, the reticulospinal cells increase their discharge in order to facilitate flexor motoneurons, as is necessary to bring the foot up and forward during the swing phase of stepping. After removal of the cerebellum, the spontaneous activity of reticulospinal neurons falls precipitously, associated with a loss of muscle tone and loss of coordination of the limbs. From

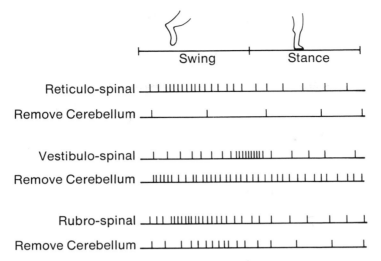

Fig. 22.5. Single-cell activity in brainstem motor centers in relation to stepping. (Based on Orlovsky, in Wetzel and Stuart, 1976)

these results it has been concluded that the maintained discharge of reticulospinal neurons is involved in "switching on" the stepping generator, and the modulated discharge facilitates flexor activity in the swing phase. In contrast, vestibulospinal neurons show peak firing that phase-leads the onset of the stance phase, thereby facilitating extensor motoneurons as the limb is extended to support the body against gravity. Finally, the activity of rubrospinal neurons resembles that of reticulospinal neurons in facilitating flexor motoneurons during the swing phase. Neither the vestibular nor the red nucleus is essential for stepping; their roles thus appear supportive in relation to the reticular formation.

From these and related studies it has been concluded that brainstem centers control the spinal rhythm generator by two mechanisms: a *generalized activation* by means of ongoing spontaneous discharge, and *modulated discharges* that facilitate specific phases of the stepping cycle. The level of activation appropriate for switching on the generator depends exquisitely on the cerebellum, while modulation is due to sensory feedback from the limbs relayed through the cerebellum. As expressed by Mary Wetzel and Douglas Stuart of Arizona:

. . . afferent modulation of efferent output by way of the cerebellum provides for selection from a larger array of corrective signals than if the modulation was achieved by directly ascending tracts, such as the spinoreticular and spinovestibular systems. The cerebellum's importance is becoming evident in the building of large-scale neural ensemble activity from stepping signals that arrive from many different parts of the nervous system.

Cerebellum

It is obvious from the foregoing remarks that a key center for sensorimotor control at the level of the brainstem is the cerebellum. The cerebellum lacks direct connection to the spinal cord, and thus stands higher in the motor hierarchy than the middle level, as indicated in Fig. 22.3. However, it is so intimately involved in brainstem mechanisms that it is appropriate to consider it here.

The cerebellum is an outgrowth of the pons. It arises early in vertebrate phylogeny. In the series of brains of different species depicted in Fig. 3.13, the cerebellum can be seen to vary from a mere nub-

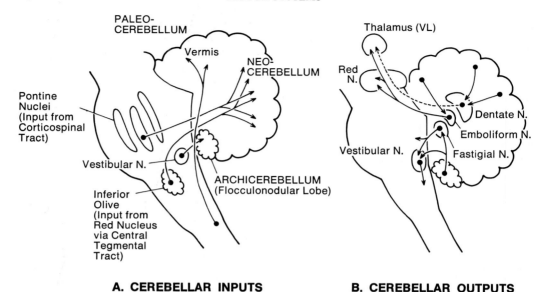

Fig. 22.6. Main input and output pathways of the mammalian cerebellum.

bin in some species to a large, much convoluted structure in others. It is often stated that the cerebellum increases in size during phylogeny, but, as we noted in Chap. 3, there are numerous exceptions to this generalization. Most notable is the enormous expansion in certain species of electric fish, which contrasts with the generally small size in most amphibians and reptiles. The large size in mammals is believed to be related to several important functional roles. Three roles have traditionally been identified; they involve contributions to the control of: 1. *muscle tone*; 2. *balance*; and 3. *sensorimotor coordination*. Let us consider the organization of the cerebellum in terms of its input and output connections, and see how they relate to these functions.

Like Caesar's Gaul, the cerebellum is divided into three parts, which reflect its phylogenetic history. First is the *archicerebellum,* consisting of the small flocculonodular lobe. Next is the *paleocerebellum,* consisting of the anterior lobe. Third is the *neocerebellum,* formed by the great expansion of the lateral hemisphere.

The *inputs* to the cerebellum are specific for these three parts. As shown in Fig.

22.6A, *vestibular fibers* make connections to the flocculonodular node. Fibers from the *spinal cord* ascend in the spinocerebellar tract and terminate mainly in the anterior lobe. The ventral portion of this tract is present as early as fish, but the dorsal tract is present first in reptiles. These fibers carry information from muscle receptors. Finally, input to the neocerebellum comes mainly from large masses of cells in the *pons,* and from the *inferior olivary nucleus* in the medulla.

The *output* fibers from the cerebellar cortex project to the midbrain in fish and urodelen amphibians; the midbrain in these animals is one of the main centers for sensorimotor coordination. In higher vertebrates, however, the output from the cortex goes to a set of *deep cerebellar nuclei* (which may represent specializations of the more primitive midbrain center). The relations between cortex and deep nuclei are somewhat more complicated that the simple tripartite division mentioned above. Thus, as shown in Fig. 22.6B, the *fastigial* nucleus receives fibers from the midline, vermal zone of the cortex, and projects in turn to the lateral vestibular nucleus; there is also a direct connection to this nucleus as well. The *emboliform* nucleus receives fibers from a strip of cortex next to the midline; it projects in turn to the red nucleus, and also has some terminals in the ventrolateral nucleus of the thalamus. The *dentate* nucleus is by far the largest of the deep nuclei, reflecting the fact that it receives the output fibers of the large cerebellar hemisphere. The dentate projects some fibers to the red nucleus, but in higher mammals most of them go to the ventrolateral nucleus of the thalamus.

The connections to the vestibular nucleus account for the powerful control exerted by the cerebellum on mechanisms of balance, and the connections to the red nucleus and reticular nucleus mediate control over reflexes and muscle tone, through the projections of these nuclei to the spinal cord. The role of the lateral cerebellar hemisphere→ dentate→ ventrolateral thalamus circuit in sensorimotor coordination is more subtle; it is expressed through the cerebral cortex, as we will see below.

We have identified the main cerebellar pathways, and the overall effects they mediate, but what actual operations are carried out within the cerebellum itself? For this we must consider the microanatomy and microphysiology of the cerebellar cortex. When we do, we find that this is one of the most astonishing pieces of cellular machinery in the animal body. It consists of a convoluted sheet, divided into a deep and a superficial layer. The deep (granule) layer is packed with tiny "granule" cells; the best estimates put their numbers at 10–100 billion, which is more than all the other cells in the nervous system combined! The granule cell axons ascend to the superficial (molecular) layer and bifurcate into two "parallel fibers" which run for several mm in opposite directions. The molecular layer also contains the large *Purkinje cells,* of which there are about 7 million. Each has a widely branching dendritic tree, that is flattened into a two-dimensional plane and oriented at right angles to the parallel fibers. These relations are diagrammed in Fig. 22.7. The Purkinje cell dendrites are covered with *spines,* which are the sites of

Fig. 22.7. Neuronal organization of the cerebellar cortex. Inputs: mossy fibers (MF) and climbing fibers (CF). Principal neuron: Purkinje cell (P), with recurrent collateral (rc). Intrinsic neurons: granule cell (Gr); stellate cell (S); basket cell (B); Golgi cell (Go). Histological layers are shown at the right; molecular layer (MOL), Purkinje cell body layer (PCL), granule layer (GrL). (From Shepherd, 1979)

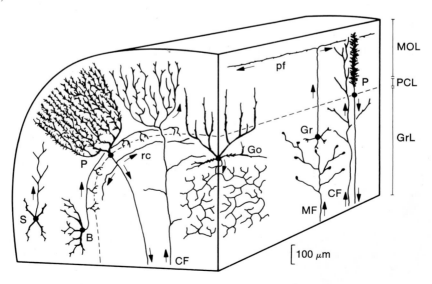

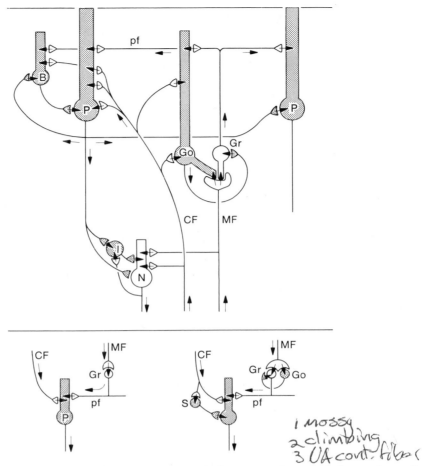

Fig. 22.8. Basic circuit diagram for the mammalian cerebellum. Note deep cerebellar nuclear cells: principal neuron (N) and intrinsic neuron (I). Other abbreviations in Fig. 22.7.

synapses from the parallel fibers as they pass through successive Purkinje cell dendritic arbors. The Purkinje cell axons carry the output of the cerebellar cortex to the deep cerebellar nuclei.

There are three main types of fiber that carry inputs to this neuronal machinery. One type is the *mossy fiber*, which arises from the pontine nuclei, as well as several other sites, and terminates on granule cell dendrites in large endings that, to some early anatomists, seemed to have a "mossy" appearance. This input is relayed through the granule cells to the Purkinje cells, and in so doing is subjected to considerable convergence and divergence, due

to branching of the parallel fibers and overlap of their connections. The second type is the *climbing fiber*, which arises mainly from the inferior olivary nucleus. This fiber ends in an extensive arborization which literally climbs over the Purkinje cell dendritic tree and makes synapses onto it. This input thus has a one-to-one, direct relation to the Purkinje cell. A third type of fiber ramifies widely throughout the cortex; this has been identified as a *noradrenaline*-containing fiber arising from the locus ceruleus (see Chap. 25).

The basic circuit put together from anatomical and physiological studies is summarized in Fig. 22.8. It shows that the direct input pathway, through the climbing fibers, and the indirect pathway, through the mossy fiber→granule cell→parallel fiber relay, are both excitatory. All other connections, by the various types of interneurons present (Golgi, basket, stellate), are inhibitory. So also are the connections of Purkinje cell axons onto their target neurons in the deep nuclei. This was surprising when first discovered, and it means that one of the basic input–output operations of the cerebellar cortex is to convert its excitatory inputs into inhibitory outputs. The deep nuclei, as shown in Fig. 22.8, also receive inputs from the climbing and mossy fibers, so another function of the cerebellar cortex is to act as a highly sophisticated interneuronal system in controlling the input–output operations of the deep nuclei. Finally, both deep cerebellar neurons and Purkinje cells have high rates of resting discharge (50–100 impulses per sec). One function of this high rate is to act as a high *set point,* so that the cerebellum will be maximally sensitive to both decreases and increases in firing rate caused by changes in input activity.

The way in which the cerebellum contributes to central motor programs is discussed in Chap. 25.

Motor Cortex

We discuss now the last component of the middle level of motor control, the *motor cortex.* The identification of the motor part of the cerebral cortex is one of the most dramatic chapters in the history of neurophysiology. During the American Civil War in the early 1860's, Weir Mitchell, a Philadelphia neurologist, noted that one side of the brain appeared to be related to the opposite side of the body. In the Prusso-Danish War of 1864, the German physician Theodor Fritsch observed, in dressing a head wound, that irritation of the brain caused twitching in the opposite side of the body. He took this information to Eduard Hitzig, then in medical practice in Berlin, and they set about to test this finding experimentally. According to the legend (Haymaker, 1953):

At that time there were no laboratories available at the Physiological Institute in Berlin for work on warm-blooded animals, and as a consequence Hitzig and Fritsch did their first studies on dogs in Hitzig's home, operating on Frau Hitzig's dressing table.

This was one of the great discoveries in neurobiology, for it demonstrated both the *electrical excitability of the brain* and the *localization of motor function* in the cerebral cortex. The importance of the finding of localization was not lost on David Ferrier of London, who proceeded in the 1870's to map very thoroughly the excitable cortex in a variety of mammals, including monkeys. One of his aims was "to put to experimental proof the views entertained by Dr. Hughlings Jackson". Ferrier found that the most excitable area for eliciting movements in the monkey is a strip of cortex on the precentral gyrus, the gyrus of Rolandi (where Jackson had expected it to be). He showed an orderly progression of focal areas along the gyrus for eliciting movements of the leg, hand, and face. This was dramatic confirmation indeed of Jackson's postulate that there must be an orderly sequence of discharging foci in the cortex to explain the "march of spasm" of the muscles that is so characteristic of focal epileptic convulsions (the kind now known as Jacksonian seizures).

Studies of localization in the motor cortex were extended to the great apes by Sherrington in the early 1900's, and finally to humans by Wilder Penfield, a student of Sherrington's, in the 1930's. Penfield, with his colleagues at the Montreal Neurological Institute, focally stimulated the cortex of patients during neurosurgical operations. They found, as had many workers before them in other species, a great deal of overlap between the areas for different parts of the body (see Fig. 22.9A). The areas for the hand and face had the lowest thresholds and widest fields (A and

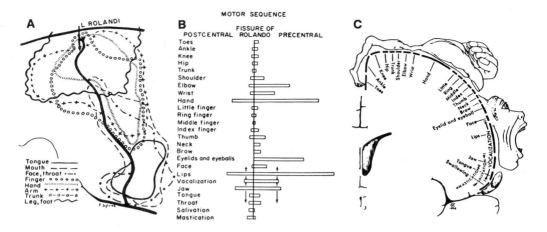

Fig. 22.9. **A.** Lateral view of the surface of the human brain, in the region of the Rolandic sulcus. Outlines show areas from which electrical stimulation elicited movements in different body parts, in the series of patients explored by Penfield and Boldrey in 1937. Anterior surface is to the left. **B.** The relative proportions of movements elicited by stimulation anterior and posterior to the central (Rolandic) sulcus in the series of patients of Penfield and Rasmussen, 1950. **C.** The motor homunculus of Penfield and Rasmussen. (From Phillips and Porter, 1977)

B). Penfield and his colleagues summarized their findings in a homunculus, as shown in Fig. 22.9C. This is the motor counterpart to the sensory map of the body surface previously shown in Chap. 13.

These findings left little doubt that the precentral gyrus (cytoarchitectonic area 4 of Brodmann) is the cortical region most closely involved in immediate control of motoneurons in the spinal cord. This control is mediated by the *corticospinal tract,* which provides a direct connection between the cortex and the spinal cord. Because its fibers are funneled through the pyramids on the ventral surface of the medulla in the brainstem, it is also called the *pyramidal tract.* The traditional view, that this tract mediates voluntary control of movement, seemed to many to be almost self-evident. However, this view concealed several difficult problems that have required many years of work to resolve, and have led to a much expanded view of "motor cortex".

The first problem was: which cells give rise to the fibers in the pyramidal tract? The fibers arise from pyramidal-shaped

neurons in cortical layer V, which is an obvious source of terminological confusion; it must be remembered that the pyramidal tract derives its name from the fact that it passes through the medullary pyramids, not because its fibers arise from pyramidal shaped neurons! The layer V cells include some giant neurons, called Betz cells after their discoverer (see Fig. 22.10). For many years it was thought that all corticospinal fibers arise from Betz cells, but now it is known that only about 3% of the tract fibers can be accounted for on this basis. Betz cells are found mainly in the leg area, and thus their large size appears to be correlated with the greater length of axon they send to caudal parts of the spinal cord. Nonetheless, it is of interest that, like the brainstem centers, the motor cortex of the middle level of the motor hierarchy exerts some of its control through giant neurons.

A second problem has been whether the corticospinal tract arises only from area 4. Both anatomical and physiological studies have shown that area 6 (just anterior to area 4) and the postcentral gyrus (3, 1, and

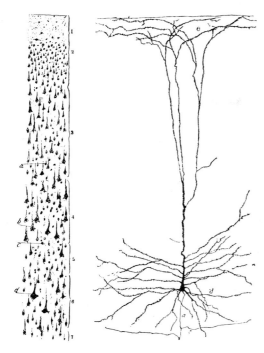

Fig. 22.10. *Left,* Histological laminae of the human motor cortex. *Right,* Single Betz cell of the motor cortex, impregnated by the Golgi method. (From Cajal 1911)

neurons. In mammals like the cat the tract reaches most of the cord, but the fibers make synaptic connections only onto segmental interneurons, which provide a polysynaptic pathway onto motoneurons. It is only in primates that a monosynaptic pathway from the tract fibers to spinal motoneurons exists. The nature and significance of this direct connection for the motor capacities of primates, including humans, will be discussed in the next chapter.

Parallel Motor Pathways

We will conclude this chapter by summarizing the main types of motor centers and their descending pathways, with the help of Fig. 22.13. First are the brainstem centers. The reticular, vestibular, and red nuclei were discussed as representative of these, to which can be added others such as the superior colliculus and its tectospinal tract. These are present in all higher vertebrates, and constitute the middle-level

2 of the somatosensory area) also contribute fibers. Thus, as shown in Fig. 22.4, the corticospinal tract arises from extensive areas of cortex. Movements elicited from area 6 (also called the premotor area) and areas 3, 1, and 2 by electrical stimulation are less precise and have higher electrical thresholds than those elicited from the motor strip in area 4. There is thus *multiple representation* of the motor map in the cerebral cortex (Fig. 22.11).

A third question is whether the corticospinal tract mediates direct (monosynaptic) control of motoneurons. Phylogenetic comparisons provide a useful perspective on this question (see Fig. 22.12). In lower mammals, such as the rabbit, the corticospinal tract barely reaches the anterior segments of the spinal cord, so that further connections within the cord have to be by propriospinal inter-

Fig. 22.11. The motor areas of the monkey cortex. MI, precentral motor area (equivalent to areas 4 and 6 of the human cortex); M II, supplementary motor area; S I primary somatic sensory area. All these areas send fibers to pyramidal tract as well as extrapyramidal centers. Also shown are the secondary somatic area (S II) and the primary visual area (V I). (From Woolsey, in Henneman, 1980)

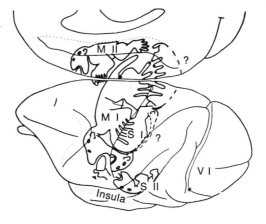

mechanisms that set the main patterns of control of motor behavior. This is referred to as the *extra-pyramidal system*, because the fibers all lie outside the medullary pyramids.

In mammals this middle level gets an added component, the motor cortex. Because the cortex is at a higher anatomical level, it also assumes a higher-level function relative to the brainstem. The corticospinal fibers not only project directly to the spinal cord, but also give off collaterals to the brainstem centers. In addition to these inputs, there are fibers from other cortical cells which terminate only in the brainstem, and do not proceed further. Many of these connections have been established by making HRP injections into subcortical nuclei and identifying the labeled cells in the cortex. These studies, in addition, have shown that the fibers to

these nuclei arise from neurons in layer V. In contrast, motor cortical cells projecting to other areas of cortex arise from several layers. This is summarized in Fig. 22.13.

Traditionally it has been believed that the corticobulbar cells are found in the premotor and postcentral areas, as mentioned above. Recent experiments, however, have shown that the origin of these fibers is much more extensive. For example, when HRP injections are made into the superior colliculus, retrogradely labeled cells are found in the visual and auditory cortex, as well as somatosensory. The cells are pyramidal-shaped cells in layer V, the same as the motor cells of the motor cortex. The superior colliculus, in turn, has direct connections to the spinal cord through its tectospinal tract, as well as indirect connections through other brainstem connections.

Fig. 22.12. Comparison of pyramidal tract pathways and terminations in the spinal cord of a primitive mammal (opossum), a higher mammal (cat), and a primate. Dashed lines indicate small uncrossed portion of the tract.

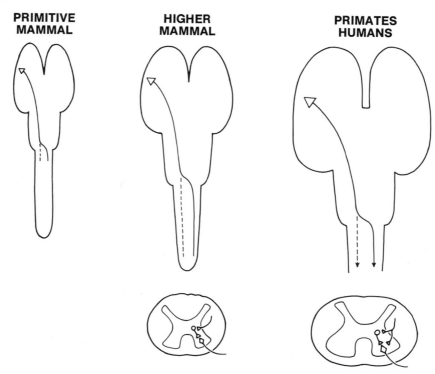

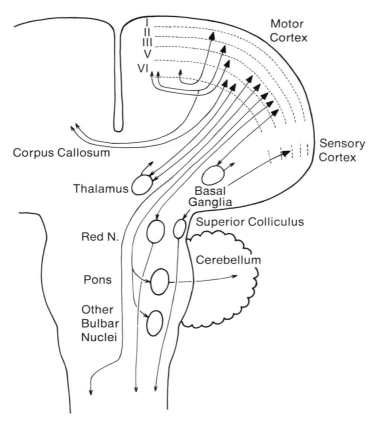

Fig. 22.13. Summary view of descending pathways, showing multiple projections and different laminar locations of cortical output neurons. (Based in part on Jones, 1981)

These findings suggest several important conclusions regarding the organization of motor control. First, the pyramidal and extrapyramidal systems provide to some extent separate and parallel pathways for the control of the spinal cord. Second, the two systems are interrelated by interconnections at all the main levels: cortex, brainstem, and spinal cord. Third, the extrapyramidal centers in the brainstem are influenced by connections from extensive areas of cortex. Together, these form what has been termed the *cortically originating extrapyramidal system*, to distinguish it from the *cortically originating pyramidal system*. Finally, if the primary sensory cortical areas are part of descending motor systems, how do we define motor cortex? Does it include sensory areas

as well? The moral of this story is that electrical stimulation is an artificial and selective tool, that has revealed to us only part of the distributed systems that are engaged in motor control. Here, as elsewhere in the central nervous system, we need to draw on the results of many methods in order to understand functional organization.

REFERENCES

Bentley, D. and M. Konishi. 1978. [Chap. 21].

Cajal, Ramon Y. 1911. [Chap. 5]

Grillner, S. 1975. [Chap. 21].

Haymaker, W. 1953. [Chap. 1].

Heitler, W. J. and M. Burrows. 1977. The locust jump. 1. The motor programme. *J. Exp. Biol.* 66: 203–219.

Henneman, E. 1980. Motor functions of the cerebral cortex. In *Medical Physiology* (ed. by V. B. Mountcastle). St. Louis: Mosby. pp. 859–891.

Jones, E. G. 1981. Anatomy of cerebral cortex: columnar input-output organization. In *The Organization of the Cerebral Cortex* (ed. by F. O. Schmitt, F. G. Worden, G. Adelman, and S. G. Dennis). Cambridge, Mass.: MIT Press. pp. 199–235.

Kennedy, D. M. 1976. [Chap. 20].

Pearson, K. G., W. J. Heitler, and J. D. Steeves. 1980. Triggering of locust jump by multimodal inhibitory interneurons. *J. Neurophysiol 43:* 257–278.

Phillips, C. G. and R. Porter. 1977. *Corticospinal Neurones. Their Role in Movement.* London: Academic.

Shepherd, G. M. 1979. [Chap. 4].

Stein, P. S. G. 1978. [Chap. 21].

Wetzel, M. C. and D. G. Stuart. 1976. [Chap. 21].

Additional Reading

Carpenter, M. B. 1977. [Chap. 15].

Eccles, J. C., M. Ito, and J. Szentagothai. 1967. *The Cerebellum as a Neuronal Machine.* New York: Springer.

Kupfermann, I. and K. R. Weiss. 1978. The command neuron concept. *Behav. Brain Sci. 1:* 3–39.

Llinas, R. and M. Sugimori. 1980. Electrophysiological properties of in vitro Purkinje cell somata in mammalian cerebellar slices. *J. Physiol. 305:* 171–195.

23

Manipulation

The success of an animal in thriving and procreating depends on more than simply moving about in its environment; what matters is its ability *to operate on the environment,* to extract from it the means of sustenance, to attack or defend itself, and to find mates and engage in cooperative behavior with others of its kind. These abilities usually depend on special organs suited for the purpose, and the ecological success of a species often is a direct function of the complexity of these special organs. Complex organs, in turn, require complex nervous systems to operate them. Thus, the more complex the organ, the more complex the nervous system, though this is a generalization that does not do justice to the complex organs found in some of the simpler animals. Conversely, simple organs may be put to complex uses if guided by complex nervous circuits. In general, however, the organs that an animal uses to operate on the environment are complex, and require nervous control by more complex mechanisms than those mediating locomotion.

Some representative animals with their specialized motor organs are portrayed in Fig. 23.1. It can be seen that these organs generally take one of two forms: they are either modifications of the *limbs* (usually the forelimb), or they are modifications of the *head* (usually the face). The arm commonly has, as an elaboration of its distal part, an apparatus for *grasping,* that may take the form of *claws* or *hands.* The facial apparatus is characteristically elaborated in relation to the mouth, and consists mainly of a set of jaws, or a quite elongated and complicated *snout* or *proboscis.* These various organs can carry out a range of operations, and it is difficult to find one word to characterize them all; somewhat arbitrarily we will class them all as one form or another of *manipulation,* to distinguish them from forms of locomotion.

The motor mechanisms we have considered up to now have mainly involved repetitive events, such as the heartbeat or stepping, or single events, such as a tail flip. Specialized organs for manipulation involve more complex sequences of events. Although this heightens our interest in the nervous mechanisms involved, we are forced to recognize that our knowledge of any mechanism depends on selecting simple systems for carrying out the analysis, while most organs of manipulation involve complex systems. For this reason,

413

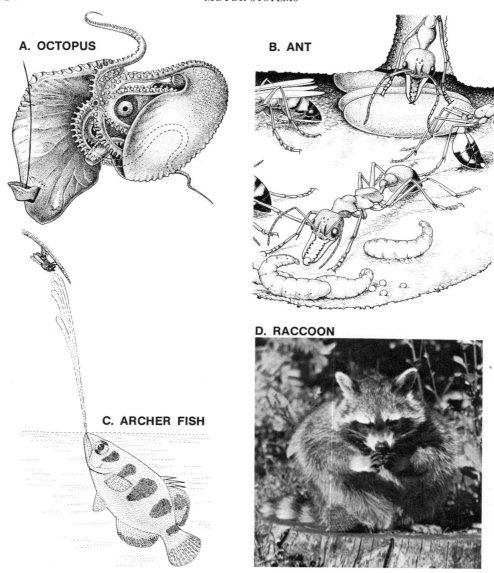

A. OCTOPUS

B. ANT

C. ARCHER FISH

D. RACCOON

Fig. 23.1. Animals with different specialized motor organs. The octopus (**A**) performs manipulations with its tentacles, which are modified limbs, the ant (**B**) with its pincers, which are modified jaws (mandibles). The archer fish (**C**) "manipulates" water with its mouth and pharynx, in order to shoot droplets of water at airborne insects; this actually represents a form of tool-using. The raccoon (**D**) performs dextrous manipulations of foodstuffs with its hand-like forepaws. (A from Young, 1964; B from Wilson, 1975; C from Alcock, 1981)

our knowledge of these systems is much more limited than our knowledge of the nervous control of locomotion. At this stage, what we can do is acquaint ourselves with some of the organs themselves, and identify some of the principles under-lying the operation of those systems that have been studied best.

Invertebrates

Invertebrates have evolved many kinds of organs for carrying out a variety of manipulative functions. As previously noted, the invertebrate has achieved its flexibility in this regard by virtue of the fact that the manipulative appendages evolved independently of the limbs for locomotion, and could therefore be individually adapted to their specific tasks. Table 23.1 gives at least a partial idea of the range of tasks carried out by limbs and facial organs.

Table 23.1 Various specialized motor operations

Limbs (legs, arms)	Face (proboscis, jaws)
grasping	grasping
pinching	pinching
tearing	tearing
clasping	clasping
holding	holding
squeezing	squeezing
crushing	crushing
exploring	exploring
feeling	feeling
	sucking
	grinding
	beating

What are the lowest species on the evolutionary scale capable of carrying out manipulative operations on their environment? One might think that such operations are only possible in the higher invertebrates—the tentacles of the octopus, for example, or the pincers of the crayfish. It is true that these are among the best examples, but a moment's thought reminds us of the arms of coelenterates, such as the *Medusa,* which function to entrap food and bring it to the mouth. This movement is controlled by the simplest kind of nervous organization, the *nerve net.* This type of manipulative function is even found in the plant world, as the Venus fly trap well exemplifies. However, the rigidly stereotyped nature of the response of the fly trap tentacles to a stimulus reflects the limitation of not having a nervous system. Thus, it is not motor organs that are the key to the complexity of manipulative functions so much as the nervous mechanisms for controlling them.

With this as a background, let us con-

sider two types of manipulative organs that illustrate both the complexities and limitations of nervous control mechanisms in invertebrates.

Octopus Tentacles. The motor apparatus of the octopus consists of muscles controlling *gland cells* (chromatophores for protective color changes, and cells for discharging ink), *muscles for rapid movements* (jet propulsion and giant fiber systems), and muscles for moving the arms, or *tentacles.* The tentacle is one of the most versatile manipulative organs devised by Nature. It is used to catch prey (either while the octopus is lurking quietly among the rocks and crannies of the seafloor or while swimming by jet propulsion); to convey the prey to the mouth; to explore the environment and test possible sources of food or danger by means of tactile and chemosensitive receptors in the arms; and to defend against predators.

Although one tends to think of the tentacle as being like an arm, it actually differs markedly from its vertebrate counterpart. The lack of bones and joints is an obvious difference; the advantage gained is that the muscle movements have great degrees of freedom, but this places heavy demands on their neural control mechanisms. The octopus has evolved a hierarchy of nervous centers for this purpose. At the lowest level are the motoneurons that innervate the muscles that move the individual suckers, and the muscles that move the arm. These motoneurons are located in ganglia within the arm. Chemosensory and tactile receptors located within the skin or the suckers, as well as muscle receptors, send their axons to these ganglia, and establish connection with motoneurons and interneurons (see Fig. 23.2). By this means, reflex pathways for exploratory feeling or for withdrawal are present within the arm itself. A severed arm continues to show coordinated, purposeful movements such as conveying food in a mouthward direction, and, similarly, in animals whose brains have been removed,

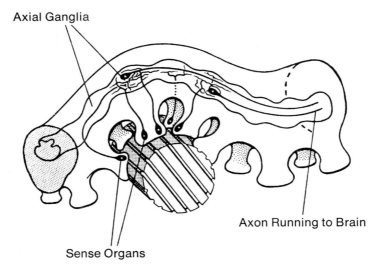

Fig. 23.2. Diagram of part of an arm of an octopus touching a plastic cylinder. The pathways from the receptors are inferred from physiological and degeneration experiments. (After Wells and Wells, in Barrington, 1979)

the tentacles still perform movements of grasping or withdrawal.

The tentacle thus contains its immediate motor control mechanism, and in this respect the nerve ganglia of the tentacle are analogous to the axial nerve cords of annelids and arthropods, and the spinal cords of vertebrates. It is as if the Octopus has attached to it 8 wormlike appendages, each with its self-contained motor ganglia for carrying out simple movements. There is thus a *decentralization* of motor control. The degree of this decentralization is dramatically reflected by the fact that, of the total of about ½ million nerve cells in the octopus nervous system, over half of them (300,000) are found within the ganglia of the tentacles.

Some limitations of this degree of decentralization in the motor control hierarchy have been revealed in behavioral tests. The experiment illustrated in Fig. 23.2 shows that the octopus can distinguish between different amounts of roughness of the surface of a cylinder, but is poor at distinguishing patterns or shapes. Other experiments showed an inability to learn to discriminate between

objects with different weights. These limitations appear to be due to the fact that sensory information is largely confined to local reflex pathways within the arm; it is not made sufficiently available to the rest of the nervous system to serve as a basis for more sophisticated spatial discriminations, or learning. Martin Wells, of England, who carried out these studies, has suggested that all of this is a consequence of the completely flexible nature of the cephalopod body and tentacles, and the enormous amounts of sensory information about limb positions that this generates. It is more economical of nervous tissue to monitor this sensory information through peripheral circuits, but this limits the learning capacity that can only be obtained through central associative pathways. Thus, the tentacle as a manipulative organ attains its extraordinary flexibility at the price of limitation in discrimination abilities, and the inability of the organism to learn new manipulations (see Chap. 30).

The ganglia in the arms are connected to a region of the brain called the *subesophageal* ganglia, which can be regarded as *intermediate* motor centers. The lobes and cords within the brain are very complicated, and were represented in simplified form in Chap. 2 (Fig. 2.12). Many connections between the different lobes have been identified, and a summary is shown in Fig. 23.3. According to the studies of J. Z. Young and Brian Boycott in London, above the intermediate centers are *higher* motor centers, located in the *supraesophageal* ganglia. Above this, as indicated in the figure, are the *optic* and associated lobes, which function as *sensory* analyzers and *memory* stores, and the *frontal, vertical,* and *subfrontal* lobes, which are the main substrate for *motivation* and *reward* systems. We shall have more to say about these highest levels in Chap. 30.

Proboscis of the Fly. One of the main functions of manipulative organs is to ob-

tain food. The problem is to get food to the mouth, and there are two general strategies for doing this. One is to bring the food to the mouth: this is the function performed by the octopus tentacles. The other strategy is to bring the mouth to the food. A sophisticated organ for doing this is the proboscis of the fly.

A schematic view of the proboscis and its relation to the head and thorax is shown in Fig. 23.4A. The distal end of the proboscis is modified into an enlargement called the *labellum.* As the diagram indicates, the mouth is situated in the labellum. We may note in passing that this means the situation is quite different from the proboscis of the elephant, in which the trunk is a modification of the nose: the elephant's trunk thus represents the other strategy, of conveying food to the mouth (Fig. 23.4B).

Fig. 23.3. Schematic diagram showing neural connections between different lobes, and their relation to the hierarchical organization of motor control and learning in the octopus. (Adapted from Wells, 1968)

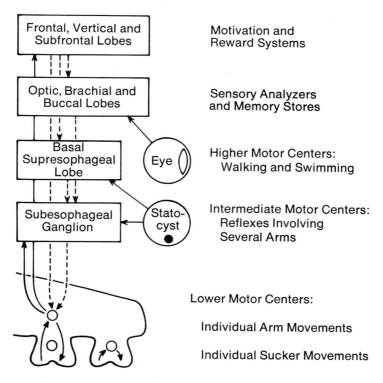

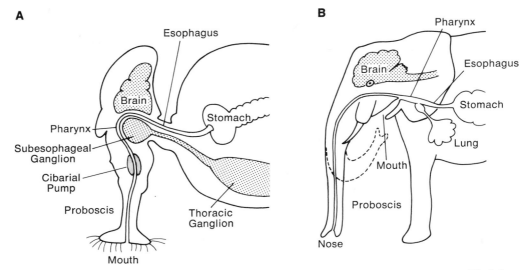

Fig. 23.4. Comparison between the proboscis of the fly (**A**) and elephant (**B**). (A modified from Dethier, 1976)

The proboscis of the fly is far more than a simple extension from the head. As shown in Fig. 23.5A, it contains a complex and delicate system of muscles and joints. There are, in general, two main types of movement, extension and retraction. *Extension* occurs in response to stimulation by food substances of taste receptors in the labellum (see Chap. 12). The proximal part, the *rostrum,* is extended by the pumping of air into its air sacs. The intermediate part, the *haustellum,* is extended by coordinated contractions in a set of five pairs of muscle. *Retraction,* on the other hand, can occur slowly by elastic recoil, or rapidly by contractions in another set of five pairs of muscle. Some of these muscles and their relations to skeletal elements are indicated in the diagram.

The labellum is a complex organ in its own right. The diagram in Fig. 23.5B shows its rich innervation. The sensory fibers come from chemoreceptors in the labellar hairs and skin, tactile receptors, and muscle proprioceptors; there are also motor fibers to the intrinsic muscles. Unlike the octopus tentacle, the sensory receptors do not establish reflex connections within the proboscis; the fibers make these con-

nections in the subesophageal ganglia of the brain (see Fig. 23.4), where the motoneurons are located. There is thus centralization, or encephalization, of reflex and motor control of the proboscis.

The key properties of the labellum are that it is *flexible,* and that it is under close nervous control. The *flexibility* allows it to adapt to a variety of surfaces (see Fig. 23.5C). Thus, it can be set to *filter* particulate suspensions through the teeth surrounding the mouth; *scrape* solid food matter from the surface, with the teeth everted; or *suck* up fluids with the mouth completely everted. These may be regarded as the manipulative functions of the proboscis, and they are obviously essential to the effectiveness of the fly in being able to feed and survive in so many different habitats. These delicate adjustments are all under nervous control, through the wealth of information arriving by means of the sensory receptors and central motor commands. Once inside the mouth and moistened with saliva, the food is conveyed by the pumping action of an internal organ called the *cibarium* to the stomach (see Fig. 27.4).

The coordination of all these delicate

adjustments of the labellum with the extension and retraction of the proboscis and the pumping of the cibarium is the province of the nervous system. The coordination is the outcome of the different information arriving by means of sensory receptors, and control by motor commands from the brain. The extraordinary sensitivity of this sensorimotor apparatus has already been noted (Chap. 12). Stimulation of a single sensory receptor cell in a hair of the labellum is sufficient to elicit extension of the proboscis (Fig. 23.6A). This involves much more than a simple muscle twitch; as Dethier has pointed out, the information must pass from the axon of the single receptor to the subesophageal ganglion, and activate interneurons there that control motoneurons to five sets of

ipsilateral extensor muscle and five sets of contralateral muscles. Peter Getting at the University of California carried out experiments on the neural basis of this behavior in which he stimulated single sugar-sensitive receptor cells in the labellum and recorded the activity of their axons and of the axon to an extensor muscle. Figure 23.6B shows the impulse discharge when two receptors are stimulated individually (upper two pairs of traces) and simultaneously (bottom pair). The upper pairs of traces show the ability of the single receptor to elicit responses in the motoneurons, and the bottom records show that the inputs from receptors can summate to elicit stronger motor responses. These experiments represent a first step in correlating the motor behavior of the proboscis with

Fig. 23.5. Proboscis of the fly. **A.** Front view of the head, showing the structure and some of the muscles of the proboscis. **B.** The nerve supply to the aboral region of the labellum; open circles show positions of hairs. **C.** Diagrammatic view of a cross section of the labellum in a position to take up surface fluids by cupping and filtering. (From Dethier, 1976)

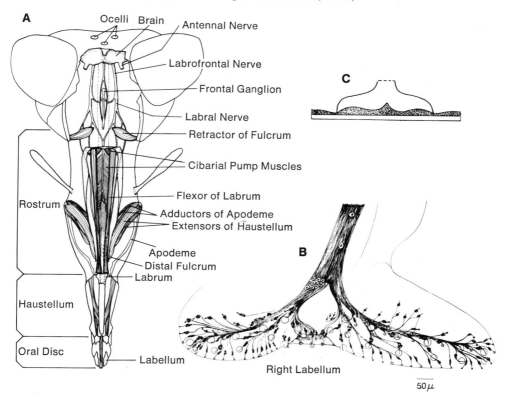

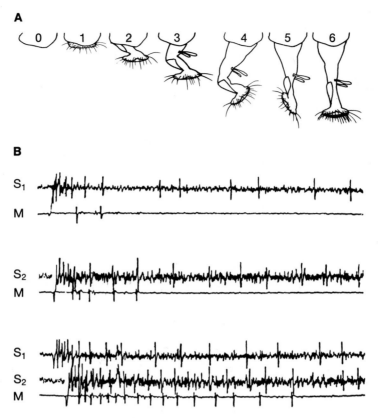

Fig. 23.6. A. Different positions of the proboscis of the fly during extension. These positions are used by investigators to quantify the motor response to sensory stimulation, and the effects of different behavioral states (hunger vs. satiety) on the feeding behavior of the fly. **B.** Sucrose stimulation of two individual hairs, S_1 and S_2 (upper traces), and the effect on activity of a single motor fiber to the proboscis (M). Separate stimulation of S_1 and S_2 in upper pairs of traces. Concentration of sucrose was 100 mM; fly had been starved for three days. Time bar: 100 msec. (From Getting, in Dethier, 1976)

dynamic properties of the sensorimotor central circuits. We shall have more to say about feeding behavior of the fly in Chap. 27.

The Hand

In our discussion of locomotion in the previous chapters we noted the change that occurred when vertebrate animal life became adapted from aquatic to terrestrial environments. Some of these changes involved a relatively direct adaptation of preexisting structures and functions. Such, for example, was the elaboration of two pairs of limbs, the forelimbs from the pec-

toral girdle and fins, the hindlimbs from the pelvic girdle and fins. Such also was the adaptation of the segmental neural apparatus for generating rhythmic alternating activity in the limbs, coordinated with the undulatory movements of the trunk, and their descending control by higher centers.

These adaptations reflect the economical tendency in phylogeny toward adaptation of a preexisting structure (which results in different functions in a new environment) rather than remodeling entirely anew. However, some changes have been more radical, and among these were the development of elongated *limbs,* and the development of complicated distal appendages. These changes are illustrated in the diagrams of the skeletal elements in Fig. 23.7. Our interest here is in the forelimbs, because they gave rise to the *arm* and the *hand,* which were crucial in the evolution of the primates. The hand is one of the most effective and adaptable appendages to emerge along the phylogenetic scale, and its manipulative abilities were crucial to the emergence of the primate. The nervous mechanisms involved in the control of the primate hand are the subject of the rest of this chapter.

The control of the hand is not simply a matter of controlling the distal digits. For most functions, many major muscle groups are brought into play. First are the muscles of the trunk that insert on the humerus, and move the whole arm at the shoulder joint. Second are the muscles that arise from the humerus and insert on the radius and ulna; these move the lower arm and the elbow. Third are the muscles that arise from the lower humerus and insert in the hand; these flex or extend the whole hand or the individual digits. Fourth are the intrinsic muscles of the hand that spread or close the fingers; of those, the muscles that enable the thumb to oppose the fingers are especially important. Although individual functions can be assigned to individual muscles (for example, the abductor policus moves the thumb toward the fingers), *a given muscle always functions as a part of the whole ensemble of muscles.* It can be readily appreciated, for example, that swinging a hammer or a tennis racquet involves coordinated activity of all of the muscle groups mentioned above.

Fig. 23.7. Evolution of the bony structure of the forelimb. (A–G from Romer and Parsons, 1977; H from Warwick and Williams, 1973)

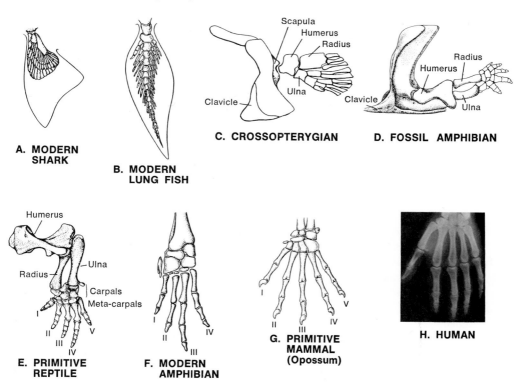

One of the main manipulative functions of the hand is *prehension,* that is, the ability to *grasp.* One sees this as a primitive reflex in a human baby; a finger placed in the baby's hand is always immediately enclosed by warm tiny fingers. One sees it revealed also in disease in the adult; a stroke commonly damages motor cells or fibers in the cortex, resulting in "release" of reflexes from their normal descending inhibitory control. Stretch reflexes become hyperexcitable, and more primitive reflexes such as the grasp reflex may be revealed. As previously noted, Jackson's study of these release phenomena was important for the development of his concepts of motor hierarchies.

In our normal, everyday activities we tend to take it for granted that the manipulative positions of the hand are infinitely variable. However, to some extent they all involve some degree of either power or precision. A *power grip,* for example, is used by a monkey to swing from one branch to another, or when we swing a tool or weapon, or lift a heavy object. A *precision grip,* in contrast, is used by a raccoon when it is cleaning and eating its food, or when a monkey picks up seeds or grooms its mate, or when we are writing with a pencil. Most manipulations involve degrees of both power and precision (Fig. 23.8). And most express the principle stated above, that any given movement depends on the complicated action of an ensemble of muscles. For example, we know from our own experience that a power grip requires not only flexion of the digits but also extension of the hand itself (remember the childhood trick of making someone drop an object by pressing down their hand?); thus, it is the synergy of finger flexion plus wrist extension that gives the greatest power. Similarly, threading a needle involves a delicate counterpoise between extensor and flexor muscles at every level of the hand, arm, shoulder and, indeed, the whole body.

Neural Mechanisms. The axial and proximal limb muscles that contribute to

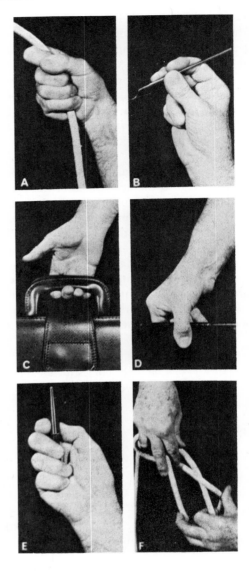

Fig. 23.8. Examples of different kinds of manipulative functions of the human hand. **A.** Power grip. **B.** Precision grip. **C.** Power (Hook) grip. **D.** Power (pinch) grip. **E.** Combined power and precision grip. **F.** Complex posture and manipulation. (From Warwick and Williams, 1973)

movements of the hand are the same as those that take part in maintaining posture and providing for locomotion. Our attention here is rather on the muscles of the distal forearm and hand, and the neural mechanisms that relate to their control.

Table 23.2   Neural mechanisms for fine motor control of the hand

Cortical
1. Large cortical representation of movements of hand and individual digits
2. Low threshold for cortical activation
3. Complex intracortical organization
4. Transcortical sensory feedback loops

Spinal
1. Strong corticospinal projection to spinal cord
2. Convergence of many fibers onto motoneurons
3. Monosynaptic connections to motoneurons
4. Facilitation of repetitive synaptic potentials

The neural mechanisms that are used in the fine control of the hand are summarized in Table 23.2. We have already discussed some of them in the previous chapter, such as the importance of the direct connection between the cortex and the spiral cord through the corticospinal tract. The physiological properties of this connection have been studied extensively in the monkey by Charles Phillips and his colleagues at Oxford. They have recorded intracellularly in the cervical region of the cord from motoneurons that send their axons into the median nerve of the forearm and thence to muscles controlling the hand (see Fig. 23.9). These motoneurons respond to stimulation of the peripheral IA fibers from the muscle spindles with monosynaptic EPSPs, which remain at about the same amplitude during a repetitive train (Fig. 23.9B). They also respond with a monosynaptic EPSP to cortical stimulation; but with repetitive stimulation the EPSPs quickly undergo a marked *facilitation* of their amplitude (Fig. 23.9C,2,4). This property of facilitation is not unique to the corticospinal synapses; it is also seen with stimulation of the rubrospinal pathway, for example, or with activation of polysynaptic pathways through segmental interneurons. This means that when any of these inputs is activated, the higher the frequency and the longer the burst, the more potent that input becomes in com-

Fig. 23.9. A. Experimental set up for intracellular recording of responses of motoneurons to stimulation of input pathways in the baboon. B. Nonsummating EPSPs elicited by a train of six volleys in IA afferents. C. Facilitating EPSPs elicited by 1, 2, and 3 shocks to the hand area of the motor cortex. Each trace is the average of 156 repetitions. The trace in 3 was obtained by subtracting 1 from 2, showing the facilitation of the second response compared with the first. (From Muir and Porter, in Phillips and Porter, 1977)

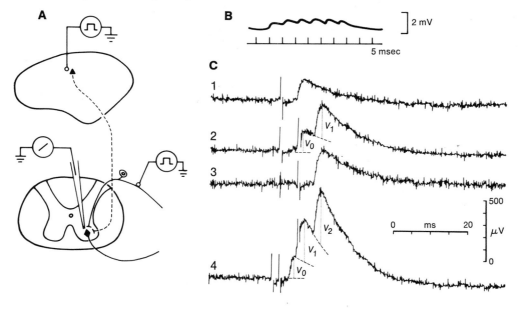

manding the motoneurons. Also, as Phillips and Porter observe in their definitive monograph on *Corticospinal Neurones* (1977), this enables the corticospinal tract "to adjust, by alteration in frequency, the power of its excitatory action on targets." It is interesting to recall that a similar dependence of muscle activity on impulse frequency occurs in the crayfish, but in the periphery, at the neuromuscular junction (see Fig. 18.8).

What of the neural mechanisms at the cortical level? The maps of cortical representation (Fig. 22.9) are the starting point for investigation at this level. One of the most interesting questions is whether the intracortical circuits at a given site are organized on the basis of *modules* similar to those of the glomeruli, barrels, and columns of sensory cortex (see Chaps. 12, 13, and 17). A motor cortex module has been extremely difficult to define; to begin with, there is no highly ordered thalamic input, which imparts to sensory cortex much of its modular structure. The technique of *intracortical microstimulation* has given some insight into this problem. This technique, introduced by Hiroshi Asanuma of the Rockefeller University, involves very selective stimulation of corticospinal neurons through a microelectrode introduced into the cortex. The results have provided evidence that corticospinal neurons activated along a given electrode track through the cortex tend to be related to the same muscle, and to receive inputs from the corresponding part of the limb. This has suggested that there is a radial organization within the cortex for input–output function related to the same muscle. It is possible that this provides the basis for columnar modules. In fact, anatomical studies have shown that, after HRP injections into lower motor centers, the retrogradely labeled output cells in the cortex are grouped in clusters (see Fig. 23.10). However, the physiological studies to date indicate that the modular organization is less distinct than its sensory counterpart; there is variation in the sizes of modules,

and overlap of neighboring modules. This probably reflects the point we stressed at the outset of this section, that muscles are not controlled in isolation, but always as part of an ensemble of muscles with complementary or antagonistic actions.

A summary of the circuits that link the cortical and spinal levels in control of the hand is given in Fig. 23.11. Voluntary movements begin with central programs ① which activate, in appropriate pattern and sequence, the modules of the motor cortex. The corticospinal fibers ② activate the motoneurons to the muscles ③, by the mechanisms we have discussed. Through collaterals, the corticospinal fibers also activate central sensory pathways and other ascending central systems ④ that feed back information to the cortex about the signals that have been sent; this is the "re-afference", or "corollary discharge", mentioned previously (Chap. 22). Sensory input from the muscles ⑤ provides information about the state of contraction of the muscles and the extent of movement that has actually taken place. Some of this information reaches the motor cortex through direct connections from the somatosensory relay nuclei in the thalamus (see Chap. 13), while some is relayed from the somatosensory cortical areas. Connections beween the somatosensory and motor areas thus provide for a "transcortical reflex loop", that can function as part of a servomechanism by which the nervous system can assess errors in accuracy of movements and correct them.

The figure also indicates the information that flows in from other somatosensory receptors in the skin and tissues of the hand and fingers ⑥. This flow contributes to control of motor performance, but it also has an additional significance. As we discussed in Chap. 13, the fingers have a high density of sensory receptors. This is correlated with their large cortical representation, which parallels that for the muscles that move the fingers. We employ this sensory capacity to gather information about the environment, such as the

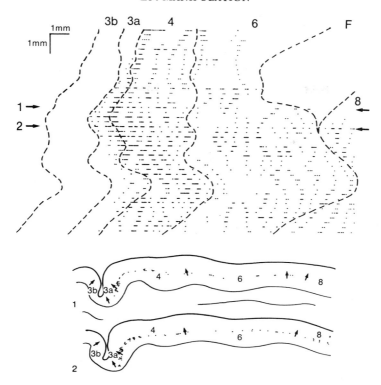

Fig. 23.10. Cross sections (below) and surface map (above) of the monkey cortex, showing clustering of corticospinal neurons as revealed by injection of HRP into the red nucleus. Arrow to left of map indicates location of the cross sections. HRP injections into other subcortical motor centers, including the spinal cord, give similar results. (From Jones and Wise, 1977)

shapes of small objects or the texture of surfaces. This use of the hand is called *active touch* (see Chap. 13). It reminds us that the hand is a sense organ, as well as a motor organ.

The diagram in Fig. 23.12 indicates the direct, corticospinal pathway to the spinal cord, but it should be emphasized that the corticospinal fibers have collaterals to all the brainstem motor nuclei we have mentioned earlier in this chapter (reticular, vestibular, red). These are involved in the control of all the axial and proximal muscles during movements of the hand. In addition, motor control involves pathways through the cerebellum (in the brainstem) and basal ganglia (in the telencephalon). We will discuss the contribution of the basal ganglia to motor control in Chap. 25.

Voluntary Movements

The motor cortex is only at an intermediate level in the hierarchy of motor control as we have seen. It is, nonetheless, at the highest level to which we can trace pathways that can be labeled "motor". Above this, the inputs to the motor cortex come from central systems, to which the terms "motor" and "sensory" do not apply. It is these central systems that provide the "central programs" (see ① in Fig. 23.11) that control the motor cortex.

At present we are only beginning to understand the nature of these central motor programs. Part of the answer will come from more precise mapping of complex central circuits. But higher motor control in humans is not just more complex than in other animals; its essence lies more in

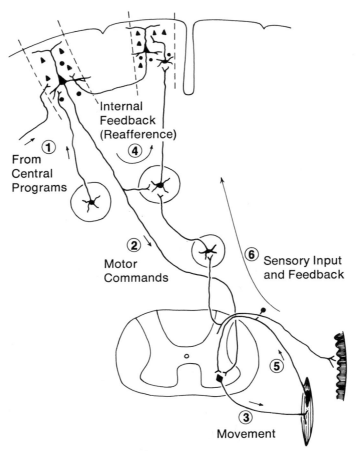

Internal
Feedback
(Reafference)

(1)

(4)

From
Central
Programs

(2)

Motor
Commands

(6) Sensory Input
and Feedback

(5)

(3)

Movement

Fig. 23.11. Summary of some of the circuits and functions involved in voluntary control of movements of the hand.

the fact that what we do seems "voluntary", and is performed with "purpose". We cannot ethically study this dimension of motor control in humans at the cellular level with present techniques, but we can approach it through experiments on awake, behaving monkeys. The results of these experiments have given us insights unobtainable by other means.

This approach to the study of motor behavior was pioneered by Edward Evarts at the National Institutes of Health in the 1960s. A typical experimental setup is illustrated in Fig. 23.12. A monkey is first prepared for chronic recording by placement of a closed recording chamber over an opening in the skull. For the behavioral

study, the animal sits under light restraint in a chair and performs a task. A microelectrode inserted into the motor cortex records the activity of a single cell in relation to performance of the task.

In the example of Fig. 23.12, the task was first to hold a handle in a given position for a few seconds. Then either a red or green lamp was lit. A red light meant "get read to pull" on the handle, a green light meant "get ready to push". The handle was then displaced automatically, and the task of the monkey was to give it either a pull or a push, depending on what the instruction had been. The results are shown in Fig. 23.12B. The impulse discharge of this neuron is displayed for the period of one second before and one second after the onset of the red or green light (arrow). As can be seen, the cell increased its discharge after the instruction to pull, but decreased it after the instruction to push. These changes in cell activity occurred in advance of the actual motor response to the displacement of the handle.

From these kinds of results Evarts has concluded that the warning light "set up preparatory states for a particular direction of centrally programmed movement". This state is reflected in the specific activity of a single cortical cell. Remarkably, this motor activity is entirely internal, as far as the behavior is concerned; there is no overt motor movement during the warning period, and no EMG discharge in the muscles. Thus, the central motor program drives the cortical motor cells, but the motor output stays within the brain. States of readiness, such as this, can also

be detected as "readiness potentials" in the electroencephalogram, recorded by gross electrodes on the scalp (see Chap. 26). These methods thus bring us a step closer to the study of motor output in terms of central circuits which control the state of the organism and the voluntary and purposive nature of motor acts. We will have more to say about the contribution of the cerebellum and basal ganglia to central programs in Chap. 25. The use of metabolic techniques to reveal internal motor states in the human brain will be discussed in Chap. 31.

REFERENCES

Alcock, J. 1979. *Animal Behavior. An Evolutionary Approach.* Sunderland, Mass.: Sinaver.

Asanuma, H. 1981. Functional role of sensory inputs to the motor cortex. *Progr. Neurobiol. 16:* 241–262.

Fig. 23.12. A. Experimental setup for recording from single cells in the monkey motor cortex during visual pursuit tracking. Movements of the handle produced shifts in the lighting of the lower (tracking) row of lamps. The task was to keep the tracking lamp aligned with changing positions of the target lamps. B. Discharge of a corticospinal neuron 1 sec before and 1 sec after the appearance of a red light (signaling "get ready to pull") and a green light (signaling "get ready to push"). *Top,* histograms of number of impulses in 40 msec bins; *bottom,* raster displays of occurrences of impulses in successive trials, see text. (From Tanji and Evarts, in Evarts, 1981)

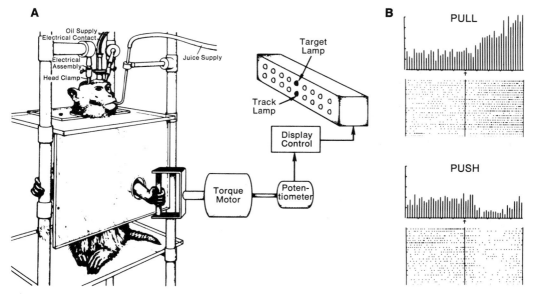

Barrington, E. J. W. 1979. [Chap. 1].

Dethier, V. G. 1976. [Chap. 10].

Evarts, E. V. 1981. Functional studies of the motor cortex. In *The Organization of the Cerebral Cortex* (ed. by F. O. Schmitt, F. G. Worden, G. Adelman, and S. G. Dennis). Cambridge, Mass: MIT Press pp. 199–236.

Jones, E. G. and S. P. Wise. 1977. Size, laminar and columnar distribution of the efferent cells in the sensory-motor cortex of monkeys. *J. Comp. Neurol. 175:* 391–438.

Phillips, C. J. and R. Porter. 1977. [Chap. 22].

Romer, A. F. and T. S. Parsons. 1977. [Chap. 3].

Warwick, R. and P. L. Williams. 1973. [Chap. 12].

Wells, M. 1968. [Chap. 2].

Wilson. E. O. 1975. [Chap. 12].

Young, J. Z. 1964. *A Model of the Brain.* Oxford University Press.

Young, J. Z. 1978. *Programs of the Brain.* Oxford: Oxford University Press.

Additional Reading

Bell, C. 1833. *The Hand.* London: Pickering.

Goldman, P. S. 1976. Maturation of the mammalian nervous system and the ontogeny of behavior. In *Advances in the Study of Behavior,* Vol. 7 (ed. by J. S. Rosenblatt, R. A. Hinde, E. Shaw and C. Beer). New York: Academic. pp. 1–90.

Jones, E. G. 1981. [Chap. 21].

Napier, J. 1979. The evolution of the hand. In *Human Ancestors* (ed. by G. Isaac and R. E. F. Leakey). San Francisco: W. H. Freeman. pp. 43–49.

Phillips, C. G. 1971. Evolution of the corticospinal tract in primates with special reference to the hand. In *Proc. Third Intn. Congr. Primat., Zurich 1970,* Vol. 2. Basel: Karger. pp. 2–23.

24

Communication and Speech

In the preceding chapters we have assembled most of the mechanisms for controlling the motor behavior of the organism. Beginning with internal glands and muscles, we have proceeded to build up the mechanisms, beginning with posture and simple reflexes, through the various kinds of locomotion, to manipulation. Each mechanism seemed more important, more essential to the adaptive success of the organism. However, we have still one more type of motor mechanism to consider, and that is the means by which animals communicate with each other.

Communication is an essential element for any kind of organization. We saw this at the level of the cell, in terms of the molecular signals and messengers that are needed for accomplishing cellular functions. The same is true of the organization of individual organisms into functional groupings, through their ability to send signals to each other. Many types of communication involve the whole organism, and draw on virtually all the motor mechanisms we have discussed thus far: for example, animals communicate with each other through different postures, different forms of walking, or by specific gestures. In contrast are the types of communica-

tion that depend on specific signals, such as pheromones or tactile stimulation.

In this chapter we will consider a type of communication which depends on special organs designed specifically for that purpose. This is communication by *sound*. Since special organs are necessary for making sound, communication by this means is limited to larger or more complex organisms, similar to the case for manipulation. Communication by sound is particularly important in certain orders of insects, in birds, and in mammals. We have already discussed the sensory mechanisms for reception of sound signals in these organisms in Chap. 16, where we also discussed briefly the importance of this mode of communication for humans.

In this chapter we will consider the motor mechanisms for generating sound signals in insects, birds, and humans. A few remarks may be appropriate at the outset. Insect and bird song are both active fields. Many recent advances have been important for understanding neural mechanisms at all levels of the motor hierarchy, from muscles up to central programs; however, these results have perhaps received less general notice than work on locomotion. With regard to vocalization in mammals, there has been surprisingly little interest shown by neurobiologists. Indeed, apart from the identification of the speech area of the human cortex, the subject of mammalian vocal mechanisms does not even exist as far as most textbooks are concerned. This is partly explained by the fact that the neural mechanisms seem to be too complex for successful experimental analysis, compared to those for insects and birds. However, vocalization and speech are much too important to humans to allow us to ignore them. In fact, we shall see that considerable information is available on some aspects of the mechanisms, and comparison with the studies of insects and birds provides some valuable perspectives on the properties that have been important for the evolution of speech as a mechanism for human communication.

Insect Song

Most rapid movements produce sound, some of which may have a signaling value. Among higher invertebrates, crustacea and insects produce various kinds of noises. However, as specific signals these sounds are of relatively limited value, because of their relatively coarse nature, and the fact that, as we discussed in Chap 16, many of these organisms appear to lack specialized auditory sensory cells. Among insects, however, certain species have specialized organs for producing and receiving specific types of sound. Best studied are crickets and grasshoppers (order Orthoptera) and cicadas (order Cicadidae).

The general mechanism for producing sound in insects is by scraping two parts of the exoskeleton against each other. The technical term for this is *stridulation* (meaning to scrape). It is the mechanism that a violinist uses in drawing a bow over the strings of a violin. The mechanism in the cricket is illustrated in Fig. 24.1. Across the dorsum of each wing is a structure called an *elytron,* originally a vein that has been transformed into a row of teeth, like

a file. Under the median edge of each wing is a ridge, called a *pectrum.* When one wing is drawn across the other, the pectrum of one wing scrapes the file of the other, as shown in Fig. 24.1A, and induces vibrations of the wing, which make sound.

The sound produced depends on the rate of movement and the resonant properties of the wing. In some crickets, the teeth are small, the movement rapid, and the wing thin and flexible. In this case, each tooth impact produces an undamped oscillation, and the tooth impact rate during the wing excursion produces a sound at a frequency near the natural resonant frequency of the wing. This is called *resonant sound emission.* The frequency spectrum is narrow, in the range of 2–6 kHz for different species. In other crickets, the teeth are larger, the wing movement slow, and the wing relatively stiff. In this case each tooth impact produces a heavily damped, rapidly decaying wave transient containing high-frequency oscillation. The slow wing excursion, with its slow tooth impact rate, produces a series of these individual complex wave forms. This is referred to as *nonresonant sound emission.* The two mechanisms are illustrated in Fig. 24.1B,C.

Sounds produced by these two mechanisms thus differ in their frequency characteristics, in terms of both the resonant frequencies and the rates of wing beating. The main method for using these sounds to send information is by periodic interruptions of the wing beats, so that the sounds are sent in groups, called *chirps.* By this means, a cricket is able to signal several types of behavioral states. There is a general *calling* song, a song signifying hostility or *aggression,* and a *courtship* song. These are illustrated in Fig. 24.2.

What are the neural mechanisms for generating these motor output patterns? These have been analyzed in electrophysiological studies at several levels of the motor hierarchy. As illustrated in Fig. 24.3, recordings have been made from the

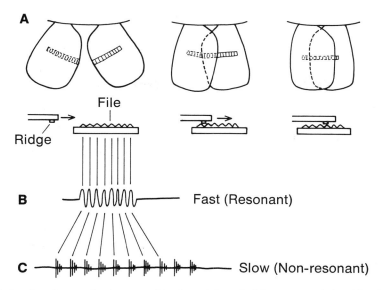

Fig. 24.1. Mechanism for producing sound in the cricket. **A.** Movement of the ridge (elytron) over the file (pectrum). **B.** Fast movement producing resonant sound. **C.** Slow movement producing nonresonant sound.

Fig. 24.2. Different types of cricket song. In this experiment the brain was stimulated at different sites in and around the highest centers (mushroom bodies: MB); at a given site, one or more song patterns could be elicited by applying electrical shocks at different frequencies. Two such sites are illustrated in the diagram. Sites that elicited calling or rivalry song are shown by (●); calling or courtship (+); calling only (○); calling, courtship or rivalry (*); song suppression (□). Abbreviations: P, pons; CB, central body; DC, deutocerebrum; TC, tritocerebrum; SCo, connective to subesophageal ganglion. (From Otto, in Elsner and Popov, 1978)

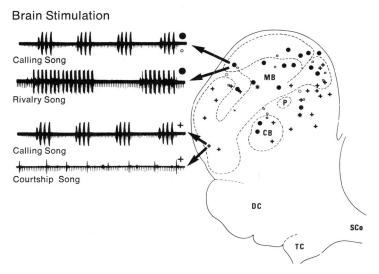

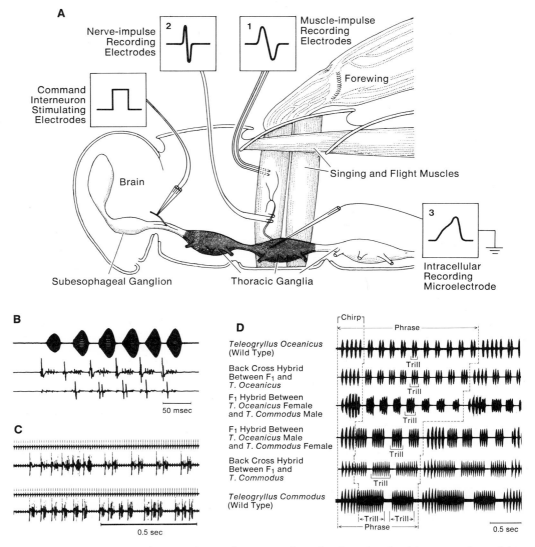

Fig. 24.3. **A.** Experimental set up for studying neural mechanisms involved in generating cricket song. **B.** Relation of chirp sounds in the cricket to impulse activity in the wing-opening muscle (middle trace) and wing-closing muscle (bottom trace). **C.** Prolonged repetitive electrical stimulation of command interneuron fiber (upper trace) elicits intermittent chirping pattern of impulse discharge in motoneuron fibers to the muscles (lower trace). **D.** Song patterns of two wild cricket species (top and bottom traces), and of their hybrid offspring. (From Bentley and Hoy, 1974)

muscles ①, motor nerves ②, and thoracic ganglion ③. Recordings from all of these sites have shown that activity in the nerves to the wing muscles is closely correlated with the chirps of the cricket song; an illustration of recordings from the muscles themselves is shown in Fig. 24.3B. These studies have shown that synchronous volleys of impulses alternate between the nerves to the antagonistic muscles that close and open the wing. These volleys in the motoneurons arise within the thoracic ganglion; their rhythmic alternating character is relatively unaffected if the ganglion is isolated from all proprioceptive input from the muscles, and all intersegmental or descending input from other ganglia or from higher levels. There is thus a stable motor pattern generator within the thoracic ganglion that is responsible for the wing movements that produce sound.

It thus appears that communication by sound utilizes the principle of a rhythm generator at the segmental level, which is the same as that involved in generating the rhythmic movements underlying locomotion. This, in fact, is no surprise when we realize that the muscles that move the cricket's wings to produce sound are the same ones that move the wings during flight. In both cases the wing beat is neurogenic (see Chap. 21). The difference is that, during flight, the opener and closer muscles are changed in their orientation by other muscles so that they function as depressors and elevators of the wings.

The hierarchical control of the song generator follows the same principles we have discussed for flight and other forms of locomotion. For example, stimulation of command fibers turns on chirping, and maintains it throughout the period of stimulation (see Fig. 24.3C). In turn, the command neurons are under control of higher centers in the insect brain. A schematic representation of the elements involved in higher control is shown in Fig. 24.4. The most important elements are sensory inputs, hormonal effects, and central feedback. In different species, singing is evoked by specific *sensory* cues such as a certain temperature of the air, or amount of light or dark, or the sight or song of another member of the species, or by tactile stimulation. Song production is also under close *hormonal* control; in most species only the males sing, and usually only when sexually mature, or when carrying a spermatophore prior to copulation.

The distinctiveness of the songs for a given species, and their resistance to environmental effects, are strong indications of the importance of genetic factors in de-

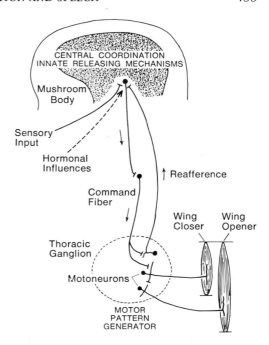

Fig. 24.4. Hierarchical control of song generation in the cricket.

termining the song pattern. This has been investigated by making crosses between males of one species and females of another. The pioneering experiments by David Bentley and Ronald Hoy at Berkeley are illustrated in Fig. 24.3D. The results show that each genotype is associated with a distinctive song, that differs from the others in its intervals between pulses within a chirp or trill, and the intervals between chirps or trills. Further experiments have indicated the intertrill interval is controlled by genes in the X chromosome. Because of the gradual way in which the characteristics of the song patterns change with different hybrid crosses, Bentley and Hoy have concluded that "The genetic system that specifies the neuronal network accounting for cricket song is therefore a complex one, involving multiple chromosomes as well as multiple genes."

Why are cricket songs so stable, so genetically dominated? Part of the answer appears to lie in the fact that there is little overlap in generations of many singing species, so that the young have no opportunity to learn the song of their species from their parents (see Fig. 28.1).

This account gives only a brief introduction to the field of insect song communication. The stable nature of the song pattern makes this an important field for analyzing the neural basis of specific motor behavior; it is thus an important meeting place for neurobiologists and neuroethologists.

Bird Song

We have seen that in insects the structures for producing sound were adapted from the structures for locomotion. [We may recall in passing that this contrasts with the evolution of flight, which in insects took place, not by the adaptation of limbs as wings, but simply by the adding on of wings (see Chap. 21)]. In vertebrates, locomotion, as we have seen, depends on the adaptation of four limbs to a variety of locomotory skills, and manipulative organs have evolved as adaptations of the limbs. In contrast to insects, in vertebrates, specific organs for communicating by sound have evolved independently of the organs for locomotion. This has freed them from the evolutionary pressures on the limbs for locomotion, which is a factor limiting the complexity of song production by insects.

In fish, primitive kinds of sound communication occur in some species by muscular thumping of the swim bladder. In terrestrial vertebrates, however, the key strategy has been to adapt the respiratory apparatus, by expelling air from the lungs through a constricted orifice in the respiratory tract. The production of sound by this means is referred to as *vocalization*. Although some amphibians and reptiles produce sounds by vocalization, it is not until the birds that we see a sophisticated use of acoustic signals comparable to that in the insects.

In birds the organ for producing sound

is the *syrinx*. This is located at the site where the two bronchi arise from the trachea, and is, in fact, a modification of the walls of these structures. Note that the syrinx is distinct and quite separate from the larynx, which is also present, but in birds serves merely to regulate overall air flow. The mechanism of sound production by the syrinx is illustrated in Fig. 24.5. Within the syrinx, the bronchial walls are modified into thin *tympaniform* membranes, surrounded by air sacs. Contractions of muscles attached to the syrinx set the amount of tension on the membrane. As shown in Fig. 24.5B, when air is pressed out of the air sacs and tension is relatively slack, the tympaniform membrane bulges inward, and air flow through the bronchi sets the membranes into high-frequency oscillations.

With this relatively simple mechanism, birds are able to produce an astonishing range of songs. These serve a variety of functions, many of them similar to those in insects. Thus, there are sounds of alarm, distress, or warning. These are usually referred to as *calls*. They are usually simple in structure, and may be made by any member of the species. Contrasting with those are the elaborate vocalizations we refer to as *songs*. These are characteristically made only by males during the breeding season. The song identifies the singer and conveys information that he is defending his territory and is ready to mate. In many species females also vocalize; these include alarm calls and songs related to mating and nesting. In contrast to insect songs, bird songs have a rich tonal structure (as we all know from comparing the chirp of a cricket to the song of a robin), in which the different frequency components are important in conveying information.

The songs of birds are distinct for a given species, and they have therefore been analyzed for the relative importance of genetics and environment in determining their pattern. We can surmise, to begin with, that, unlike insects, the generations

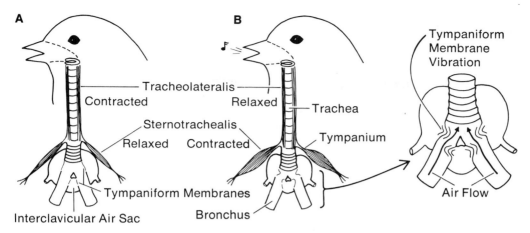

Fig. 24.5. Sound production by the syrinx in birds. **A.** The tracheolateralis muscles are contracted, while the sternotrachealis muscles are relaxed. Under this condition, the syringeal membranes are taut, and the bore from bronchi to trachea is maximally open; air flow through the syrinx generates low-frequency sounds or no sound. **B.** Tracheolateralis muscle relaxed and sternotrachealis contracted. The syringeal membranes bulge inward, and the bore leading from bronchi to trachea is maximally reduced; air flow through the syrinx generates high-frequency sounds. (From Hersch, in Nottebohm, 1975)

overlap; parents care for their young, and thus some degree of learning by the young is possible. The degree to which this takes place is illustrated in Fig. 24.6, which summarizes the results from several workers. In the wild (A of the figure) the songs of the three species are distinct. After rearing in isolation (B), the song of the song sparrow retains most of its structure; the songs of the other two lose some of their species-specific structure, though retaining some aspects of vocal control. However, when the young are deafened (C), their vocalizations as adults are coarse and scratchy, lacking in structure and species-specificity.

From these results it has been concluded that there is a sensitive period, between 10 and 50 days for the male white-crowned sparrow, during which auditory stimulation with the appropriate song pattern is necessary for the development of the ability to produce that song. This has suggested that sensory stimulation with the song pattern sets up an *auditory template* in the central auditory nerve circuits, that not only provides the means for

recognition of the species-specific song pattern, but also for *generation* of the motor output for producing the song itself. Since the sensitive period for auditory learning precedes by several weeks the time when the bird actually begins to sing; it is as if the bird sings from memory. As a young male bird begins to sing, it makes an ever closer match between its template and its performance. Thus, genetics, sensory stimulation, sensory feedback, and, probably, internal corollary feedback, all are necessary in the ontogeny of song.

A final factor involved in this developing control is the effect of hormones. As noted above, singing during courtship is characteristically done only by males. It has been shown that this ability in the male Zebra finch is dependent on male sex hormones; castrated males do not sing, but singing can be reinstated by administration of androgens. Injections of androgens do not induce singing in females, but they do if the females were treated at birth with testosterone metabolites (dihydrotestosterone or estradiol). Even when reared in isolation, these females are able to pro-

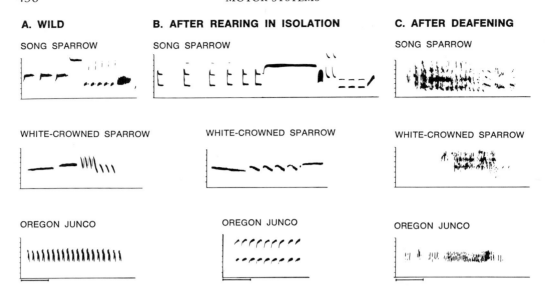

Fig. 24.6. Contributions of genetics and environment to the development of songs in three closely related members of the sparrow family. (From several authors, in Marler, 1976)

duce a song that is very similar to that of the male (see Fig. 24.7A).

Studies of the brain have begun to reveal the neural basis for these hormonal effects. Previous stimulation and ablation studies had permitted identification of several levels in the motor hierarchy: these include the vagal motoneurons to the syringial and chest muscles, located in the brainstem; a center in the midbrain; and several centers in the telencephalon (see Fig. 24.7B). Arthur Arnold, Fernando Nottebohm, and Donald Pfaff at Rockefeller University showed that nerve cells in several of these centers are able to bird injected and radioactively labeled testosterone or its metabolites. The cells in the male are larger than in the female; they are thus *sexually dimorphic*. Recently, Mark Gurney and Mazakazu Konishi have shown that the ability of hormone-treated females to sing is closely correlated with enlargement of brain centers in the song-producing pathways. An example of one of the centers, and the effects of hormones, is shown in Fig. 24.7C. These studies thus give evidence of the powerful

ability of hormones to act as *organizers* of neuronal circuits (see Chaps. 9 and 28).

In addition to sexual dimorphisms, the vocal pathways in birds also demonstrate bilateral asymmetries. Each half of the syrinx is supplied by a right or left branch, respectively, of the twelfth (hypoglossal) cranial nerve. Nottebohm cut each branch separately, and found that cutting the left syringeal nerve branch severely affected the ability to sing, whereas cutting the right branch had very little effect. The basis for this difference is still not completely understood; it appears to be correlated with the fact that a greater portion of the air expired during singing comes through the left bronchus from the left lung. From this work emerged the concept of left hypoglossal dominance in song production. It is somewhat surprising to realize that at the time of its discovery, around 1970, it was the only asymmetry in neural function known in a vertebrate, other than man. Among invertebrates, there are several well-known asymmetries, such as the pincer and crusher claws of lobsters, and in recent years a number of behavioral asymmetries have been discovered in vertebrate species. We will return to this theme in discussing human speech (below and Chap. 31).

Human Speech

Vocalization plays a prominent role in communication among members of most mammalian species. As in birds, this is correlated with a keen sense of hearing (Chap. 16). That some of this keenness is used to respond to intraspecies signals is indicated by the complexity of many of the sounds produced. In fact, the more this question has been investigated, the more complex appear the vocalizations, their neural control, and the behavior they mediate. For example, the purring of a cat involves precise timing between contractions of laryngeal muscles and the diaphragm (see Fig. 24.8A). It is also of inter-

Fig. 24.7. Neural pathways controlling singing in birds, and their dependence on sex hormones. A. The pathways for vocal control in the canary. Dots indicate sites of binding of systemically injected 3H-testosterone. Shading indicates areas more highly developed in males than in females (Area X is present only in the male). HVc, nucleus hyperstriatum ventrale, pars caudale; INT, nucleus intercollicularis; MA, nucleus magnocellularis anterior (neostriatum); RA, nucleus robustus archistriatalis; XII, twelfth cranial nerve. B. Diagrammatic representation of experiment with hormones in the finch. Normally, male finches sing but females do not (upper two rows). However, females treated at hatching with estradiol (E) and subsequently with androgens (A) as adults, are able to sing and show other male behavior. Relative size of the HVc is shown by the shaded circles. C. Histological sections, showing the HVc in normal male (upper), hormone-treated female (middle), and normal female (lower). (Diagram A from Nottebohm, 1980; B from Miller, 1980; C from Gurney and Konishi, 1980)

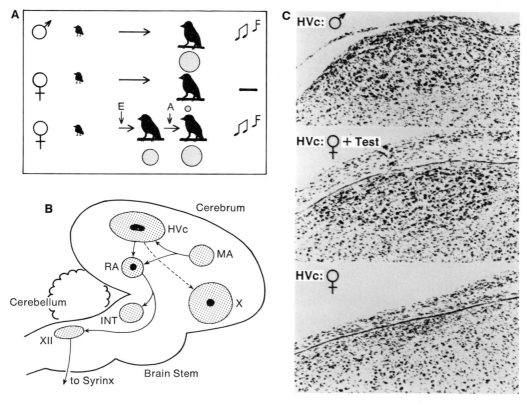

A. CAT PURRING

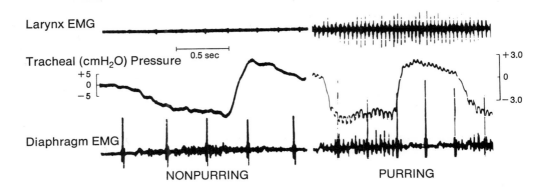

NONPURRING   PURRING

B. SONG OF THE HUMPBACK WHALE

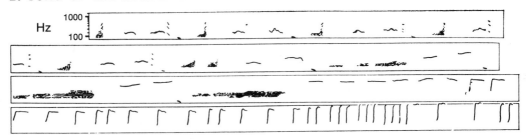

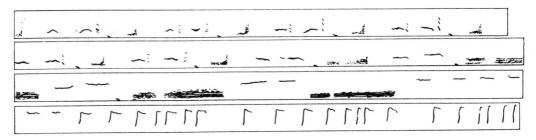

Fig. 24.8. A. Purring of a cat. Upper trace, electromyograph recordings from laryngeal muscles; middle trace, pressure in the respiratory tract; lower trace, electromyograph (EMG) recordings from the diaphragm. Note correlation between impulses in EMGs and oscillations in pressure during purring. **B.** Sonograms of the song of the hunchback whale, obtained from an animal in the vicinity of Bermuda. Top four strips are from a song that lasted over 10 min; bottom four strips are from a subsequent repeat of the song by the same animal. (A from Remmers and Gautier, in Doty, 1976; B from Payne and McVay, in Wilson, 1975)

est that purring is largely under central control; the purring rhythm continues in the motoneuronal discharge despite deafferentation or removal of the muscles. Figure 24.8B illustrates sonograms of the

song of the humpback whale. The entire song lasts for 7–30 minutes; each whale sings its own song, which it repeats faithfully, as indicated in the figure. The ability to repeat a message of this complexity testifies to considerable powers of memory and motor read-out. It has been said that this may be the most elaborate single behavioral display in any animal species.

These considerations indicate that a sophisticated apparatus for vocal communication has emerged in the course of mammalian evolution. Let us see how this apparatus has been adapted in humans for producing speech.

Although we commonly think of speech as emanating from the larynx, our vocal apparatus is a good deal more complicated than that. Sound production is based on the principle of forced air. This requires three main components: a source of *pressure*, a set of *vibrating* elements, and a system of *resonators* and *articulators*. As shown in Fig. 24.9, each of these is a carefully coordinated system of subcomponents. *Pressure* arises by taking air into the lungs (inhalation) and expelling it (expiration). This depends on the *respiratory* muscles, principally the diaphragm, the

Fig. 24.9. Schematic representation of the mechanical elements involved in sound production in humans.

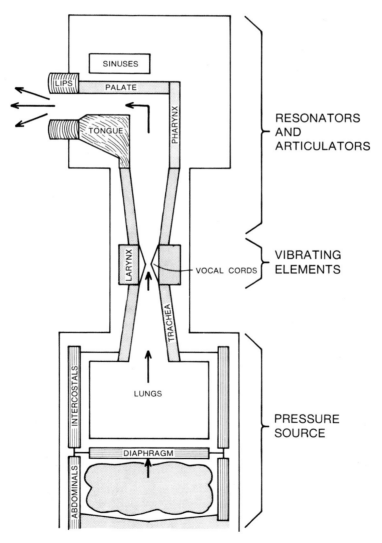

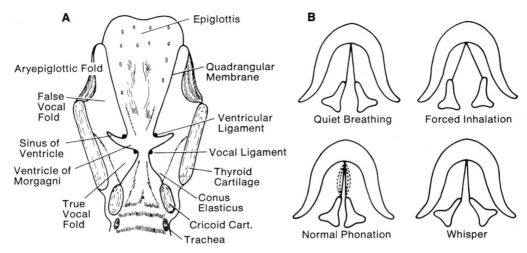

Fig. 24.10. **A.** Longitudinal section through the human larynx. **B.** Configurations of the glottis under different conditions. (from Zemlin, 1968)

intercostal muscles, and the abdominal muscles. The *vibrating* elements are the *vocal cords* within the *larynx;* they are controlled by a complicated set of *laryngeal* muscles. The larynx converts the rush of air through the trachea into a buzzing sound with many frequency components. The *resonators* and *articulators* are composed of the structures of the *upper respiratory tract;* these include the pharynx, mouth, tongue, lips, sinuses, and related structures. These provide for resonance chambers and filters that transform the laryngeal buzz into sounds with specific qualities.

These same main components are present in birds and in other mammals, except that in birds there is a syrinx instead of a larynx. This illustrates that the location of the buzz-producing element and its relation to the resonators is moveable. Still another location is used when we play a musical instrument of the horn or wind family, such as a trumpet. When we blow a trumpet, we supply the pressure with our lungs; the buzz comes, not from the larynx, but from our lips pressed to the mouthpiece. The tone is formed by the resonance chambers within the tubes of the instrument.

The vibrating elements that generate the laryngeal buzz are the *vocal folds.* These are two folds of muscle tissue that have a tough ligament at their free edge and a mucous membrane cover (see Fig. 24.10). They are housed within the *thyroid* cartilage, which forms a protective shield around them. The *cricoid* cartilage forms a ring around the base of the larynx; it supports the thyroid cartilage and provides surfaces of articulation for the *arytenoid* cartilages. These are two small triangular cartilages, each of which is attached at its apex to a laryngeal fold. The base has a complex articulation with the cricoid cartilage, which allows it to rock, rotate, or slide. These movements are brought about by contractions of the intrinsic laryngeal muscles. These include the *thyroarytenoid* (which constitutes the main mass of the vocal cords); *cricoarytenoid; interarytenoid;* and *cricothyroid.*

The individual actions of each of these muscles are too complex to detail here; suffice it to say that they provide for delicate and precise adjustments in the length, tension, and separation of the vocal cords. Figure 24.10B indicates some of the positions of the vocal folds and the way they are brought about by movements of the arytenoid cartilages. The *pitch* of the laryngeal buzz is set by the length, tension, and separation of the folds; the folds then vibrate at that frequency. The buzz is *louder* if more pressure is applied, though the muscles must counteract the pressure precisely in order to maintain pitch.

How is this buzz converted into intelligible vocal signals? This is the task of the resonators and articulators. Each of the structures of the upper respiratory tract plays an important role, as becomes apparent when any one of them is compromised. Thus, a stuffy nose markedly changes the quality of the voice. Also, just try to say anything at all while holding the tip of your tongue! In human speech the tongue is the most important of the organs of articulation. Its complex arrangements of muscle fibers make it a most versatile motor organ, and the high density of innervation is matched by the large representation of the tongue in the motor cortex (see Chap. 22). We should also note the importance of the tongue as an organ for manipulation and mastication of food in this regard.

All of these properties render the tongue well suited to the function of making finely graded adjustments in the configuration of the resonant chamber of the mouth. These configurations are most critical in the production of *vowel* sounds; in fact, each vowel sound is produced by a specific position of the tongue, and there is a systematic shift in these positions for the sequence of vowels (see Fig. 24.11). Consonants, in contrast, result from obstructing the air passage through the vocal tract, at the lips, teeth, hard palate, soft palate, or glottis. In English, these produce sounds that are called stops (t,p), fricatives (f,s), nasals (m), or glides (l). If you place your fingers on your face or neck while producing any of these sounds, it will become obvious that speech involves coordination of activity in most of the muscles in these regions.

We have concentrated on the muscular control of the vibrating elements and the resonators and articulators, but we must not give the impression that the pressure source acts merely as a crude bellows. In a classic study in 1959, M. H. Draper, P. Ladefoged, and David Whitteridge in Edinburgh investigated the activity of different respiratory muscles during vocalization. In addition to the EMGs of the muscles, recorded with needle electrodes, they monitored the volume of air in the lungs and the intratracheal pressure. Figure 24.12 shows the results in an experiment in which the subject took a deep breath and slowly counted to 32. It can be seen that there is a very precise sequence of activity in these widely different muscle groups during this period of phonation. The results show that the diaphragm is relaxed through most of expiration and phonation, and that maintenance of the appropriate subglottic pressure is due to activity in the intercostal, abdominal, and latissimus dorsi muscles. Much the same sequence takes place during the singing of a single note. As Donald Proctor of Johns Hopkins has observed:

. . . the production of a tone of any given intensity requires the appropriate subglottic pressure. This is accomplished by the exact blending of inspiratory and expiratory muscle effort with the elastic force associated with the lung volume at the time. This blending is largely produced through a balancing of the abdominal muscles against or with those of the chest wall across a relaxed diaphragm, occasionally supplemented by accessory expiratory muscles.

When the "appropriate subglottic pressure" is controlled by a trained and gifted singer, one of the transcendent artistic experiences of human life is produced, as illustrated in the following description of the great tenor, Enrico Caruso (Scala recording 825):

. . . his voice floated on a deep and perfectly controlled column of air—something beautiful beyond description.

The delicate balancing of activity indicated in Fig. 24.12 suggests that the mo-

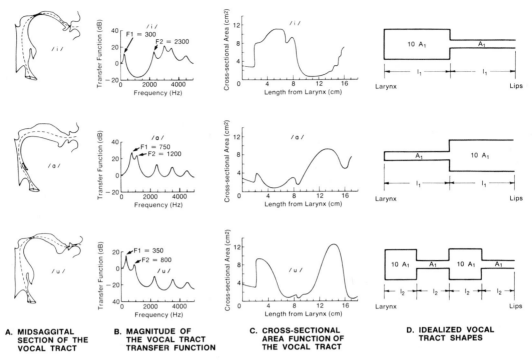

Fig. 24.11. Some principles in the production of human speech. **A.** Positions of the tongue for forming the vowel sounds "ee" (/i/), "ah" (/a/), and "oo" (/u/). There is evidence that these are basic phonemes present in all human languages, and that other vowel sounds are variations on these. **B.** Specific frequency patterns of the different vowel sounds. **C.** Cross-sectional areas of the supralaryngeal speech-producing spaces, from the larynx (0) through the pharynx and mouth to the lips (16), for the three different vowel sounds. **D.** Simplified computer simulations of the supralaryngeal spaces in (C). Note that the considerable length of the space means that the pharyngeal and oral segments can be independently manipulated by the tongue. This is crucial for the formation of the vowels, and hence for human speech. It has been shown that the pharyngeal space is diminished or absent in chimpanzees and Neanderthal man, as well as in the human newborn. (From Lieberman et al., 1972)

toneurons to these muscles are under close control by descending motor pathways. In fact, it has been found that the intercostal motoneurons receive monosynaptic inputs from corticospinal fibers. These findings remind us that it is not only the muscles of the hand that are involved in fine motor performance; muscles as different as those of the tongue and chest and abdomen may accomplish equally delicate maneuvers.

We can think of all the muscles of the abdomen, chest, larynx, head, and neck as being coordinated together to perform complex *manipulations of air* as it is ex-

pelled from the lungs. What are the nervous mechanisms involved in this coordination? We can begin by identifying the motoneurons involved (Fig. 24.13). For the muscles of the *pressure* apparatus, the motoneurons are located in the spinal cord: the motoneurons to the diaphragm are in cervical segments 3–5; those to the intercostals are in thoracic segments 2–5; and those to the abdominal muscles in thoracic segments 6–12. For the larynx, the intrinsic muscles are supplied by the vagus (X) and accessory (XI) nerves. The main branch to the larynx is the recurrent laryngeal nerve, which supplies all of the

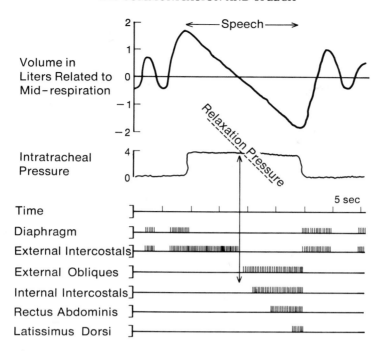

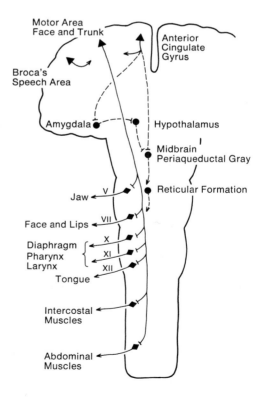

Fig. 24.12. In this experiment, a human subject took a deep breath and counted slowly from 1 to 32. The recordings show the changes in air volume in the lungs, intratracheal pressure, and impulse activity in different muscles. (From Draper et al., in Zemlin, 1968)

intrinsic muscles except the cricothyroid. This nerve is thus crucial to human speech; loss due to injury or infection leaves one able to speak only in a whisper. The *resonators* and *articulators* are controlled by nerves to the muscles of the pharynx (XI, X, VII), tongue (XII), and lips and face (VII). Other cranial nerves also contribute, as indicated in Fig. 24.13.

It can be seen that the motoneurons involved in vocalization constitute a complex array that is distributed along a considerable extent of the neuraxis, from the metencephalon (pons) to the lower tho-

Fig. 24.13. Motor circuits and motor hierarchy involved in control of vocalization in humans. Pathways involved in precise motor control are shown by continuous lines; pathways involved in mediating emotional aspects of vocalization are shown by dashed lines. (Based in part on Hollien, 1975, and Jürgens and Ploog, 1981)

racic levels of the spinal cord. The voluntary control over this array is mediated by descending fibers in the corticospinal tract. These originate in the face, neck, and trunk areas of the motor cortex (see Fig. 23.9) and make either monosynaptic or polysynaptic connections onto the motoneurons. Thus, as in the case of manipulation, the "intermediate" level of the motor hierarchy is in the motor cortex. The mechanism of control by the motor cortex is virtually unknown, though it seems likely that it involves circuits through the basal ganglia and cerebellum, as in the case of control of manipulation. The highest level of speech contol in the human includes Broca's area; the nature of the relation between Broca's area and the motor cortex in the control of speech will be discussed in Chap. 31.

REFERENCES

Bennet-Clark, H. C. 1975. Sound production in insects. *Sci. Progr. Oxf. 62:* 263–283.

Bentley, D. and R. R. Hoy. 1974. The neurobiology of cricket song. *Sci. Am. 231:* 34–44.

Chapman, R. F. 1977. *The Insects. Structure and Function.* New York: American Elsevier.

Doty, R. W. 1976. The concept of neural centers. In *Simpler Networks and Behavior* (ed. by J. C. Fentress). Sunderland, Mass: Sinauer. pp. 251–265.

Elsner, N. and A. V. Popov. 1978. Neuroethology of acoustic communication. In *Advances in Insect Physiology* (ed. by J. E. Treherne, M. J. Berridge, and V. B. Wigglesworth). New York: Academic. pp. 229–355.

Gurney, M. E. and M. Konishi. 1980. Hormone-induced sexual differentiation of brain and behavior in zebra finches. *Science 208:* 1380–1383.

Jürgens, U. and D. Ploog. 1981. On the neural control of mammalian vocalization. *Trends in Neurosci. 4:* 135–137.

Lewis, D. B. and D. M. Gower. 1980. [Chap. 16].

Lieberman, P., E. S. Crelin, and D. H. Klatt. 1972. Phoenetic ability and related anatomy of the newborn and adult human, Neanderthal man, and the chimpanzee. *Amer. Anthropol. 74:* 287–307.

Marler, P. 1976. Sensory templates in species-specific behavior. In *Simpler Networks and Behavior* (ed. by J. E. Fentress). Sunderland, Mass: Sinauer. pp. 314–329.

Miller, J. A. 1980. A song for the female finch. *Sci. News. 117:* 58–59.

Nottebohm, F. 1975. Vocal behavior in birds. In *Avian Biology,* Vol. V (ed. by D. S. Farner and J. R. King). New York: Academic. pp. 287–332.

Nottebohm, F. 1980. Brain pathways for vocal learning in birds: A review of the first 10 years. In *Progr. Psychobiol. Physiol. Psychol.* (ed. by J. M. Sprague and A. N. Epstein). New York: Academic. pp. 86–125.

Proctor, D. F. 1980. *Breathing, Speech and Song.* New York: Springer.

Wilson, E. O. 1975. [Chap. 12].

Zemlin, W. R. 1968. *Speech and Hearing Science. Anatomy and Physiology.* Englewood Cliffs, N.J.: Prentice-Hall.

V
Central Systems

25

Introduction:
the Nature of Central Systems

In previous sections of the book, discussions of specific sensory and motor systems have followed the circuits into the central nervous system and then, just when things were getting interesting, have broken off with the excuse that the story belongs to the province of "central systems". We have finally arrived at that point, and this last section will identify these systems, and attempt to explain how they provide the neural substrates for behavior.

Before beginning it is well to be reminded that the analysis of sensory and motor systems has depended on the fact that they consist of localized circuits and pathways accessible to the investigator; they can be activated discretely and they give a precise and quantifiable output. In central systems, most of these advantages are lost. The systems are deep within the central nervous system and thus relatively inaccessible to the investigator. The cells and circuits form systems that overlap and are difficult to localize, thus making selective activation difficult or impossible. The output from such systems may be too widespread to record or characterize adequately. To this should be added the fact that, in the temporal domain, many of the actions of central systems last for days,

months, or years. Small wonder, then, that although behaviors generated by central systems can be observed and classified, their neural substrates are extremely difficult to identify. It is, in fact, a testimonial to the power of modern methods in neurobiology that much of the experimental evidence for the cellular elements and specific circuits of central systems has become available within the past generation or so.

The possibility of understanding the central neural substrates that govern behavior is exciting not only because it deepens our understanding of humans and of all animal life, but also because it holds the promise that we may someday be able to correct imbalances in behavioral functions or restore functions lost by disease. However, it is important to realize that making correlations between specific neural substrates and specific behaviors is one of the most difficult challenges in all of biology, and the history of endeavors in this area is a record of many deceptions and discouragements. Thus, any apparent correlation or claim must be regarded with healthy skepticism. This is all the more important in a book of this nature, in which accounts of many very complex subjects must necessarily be brief.

With this as a background, let us begin.

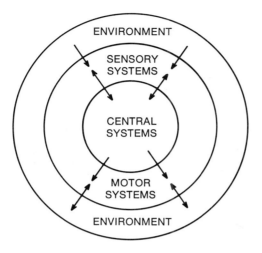

Fig. 25.1. Relation of central systems to sensory and motor systems.

Central systems may be defined as *cells and circuits that mediate functions necessary for the coordinated behavior of the whole organism.* By definition, they are not systems that communicate directly with the external environment. Although central circuits are thus not primarily or exclusively parts of sensory or motor systems, they may overlap with elements of these systems (see Fig. 25.1).

It can be seen that this definition begins with cells and ends with behavior; in be-

tween are several levels of organization, a point already made in Chap. 1. Figure 25.2 indicates one way to think about these levels and how they relate to each other in central systems. At the most fundamental level are the properties of the *nerve cell,* and the local and long-distance processes that a cell sends out. From these elements are made *circuits,* which are of several types, depending on the nature of the cells and their connections. Different circuits, organized together, form *systems.* The systems mediate different functions, such as reflexes and fixed action patterns. Finally, the coordination of different systems results in specific *behaviors.* The items listed at each level are only examples, and other properties can be added where appropriate.

It used to be thought that central neurons are connected as in reflex pathways—linked together in chains. We now know that this is not the only way to hook up neurons. As indicated in Fig. 25.3, there are several ways. One is based on the *neuroendocrine cell* (A), and its communication through blood-borne factors. A second is the *local circuit* (B) within a region of the CNS. Then there are the *long-distance circuits* (C), connecting two or more regions. These may be either specific

Fig. 25.2. Levels of organization of central systems.

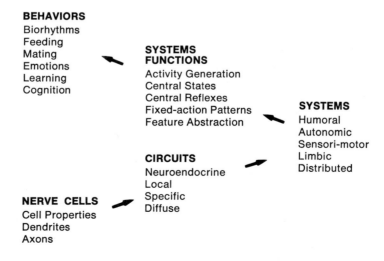

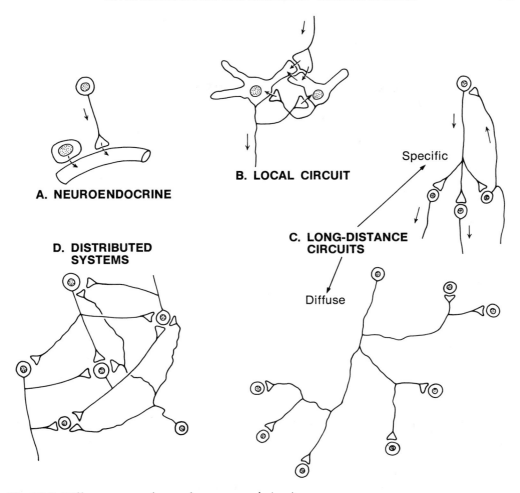

A. NEUROENDOCRINE

B. LOCAL CIRCUIT

Specific

C. LONG-DISTANCE CIRCUITS

Diffuse

D. DISTRIBUTED SYSTEMS

Fig. 25.3. Different types of central neurons and circuits.

or diffuse. Finally, there are complicated systems which involve combinations of circuits of one type or another; these are located in different parts of the brain, and connected hormonally or by long tracts; they are referred to as *distributed systems* (D).

In this chapter we will discuss the four main types of central circuits, with the objective of understanding how they provide the basis for central systems. In subsequent chapters, the discussion will center on how the different levels of organization contribute to the behaviors listed in Fig. 25.2.

Neuroendocrine Circuits

As we have seen, hormones are used in a variety of ways in the body. Those peptides and hormones that are secreted by central neurons, under central nervous control, and with actions that affect the coordinated behavior of the entire organism, may be considered to be parts of central systems.

Invertebrates. Our previous discussions have emphasized the large role played by neurosecretory cells among invertebrates. The grouping of neurosecretory cells and

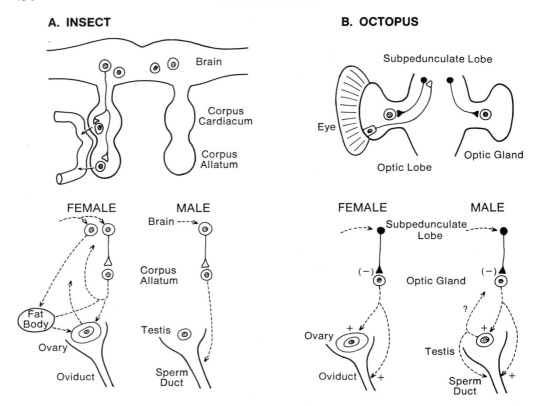

Fig. 25.4. Neuroendocrine systems for control of reproduction in the insect (**A**) and octopus (**B**). Diagrams above show the neural parts of the system; diagrams below show how they interact through circulating hormones with body organs, in both male and female. (Adapted from Gordon, 1970)

terminals into neurohemal organs is a common finding in many phyla, notably annelids, arthropods, and molluscs.

In Chap. 10 we discussed the control of metamorphosis in insects through central neuroendocrine cells and the corpora allata. The same types of mechanisms are used for the control of reproductive processes in the insect, as shown in Fig. 25.4A. The neural part of the circuit consists of the neuroendocrine cells and the central fibers which control them. These in turn are parts of larger circuits, in which there is transport in the circulation of the peptides and hormones released from the terminals, and the substances released from the target organs which act on each other and back on the central neurons. Thus, our concept of a central "circuit" needs to be broadened to include these blood-borne

connections throughout the body. Together these circuits form the neuroendocrine system for control of reproduction. Note, in this case, the more elaborate actions and feedback controls in the female as compared with the male.

In the crayfish, (not shown in the figure) the neuroendocrine control of molting is mediated by a system that is attached to the eyestalk. This consists of an *X-organ* containing the cell bodies of neurosecretory cells, and the *sinus gland,* a neurohemal organ where the terminals of these cells discharge their secretions into the bloodstream. This eyestalk system controls the so-called *Y organ,* located in the antennal or maxillary segments of the body, which in turn controls molting. There is an obvious parallel between the Y organs and their control in crustacea, and the thoracic glands and their control in insects. The fact that the molting hormone in crustacea is a steroid molecule (β-ecdysone, or crustecdysone) closely related to the α-ecdysone of insects, indicates the close similarity between the two systems.

For comparison, the neuroendocrine control of sexual differentiation in the octopus, the best studied mollusc in this respect, is illustrated in Fig. 25.4B. Light stimulates a pathway that projects to neuroendocrine cells in the *subpedunculate lobe*. These cells project to the *optic gland,* which is attached to the eyestalk, and is normally inhibited by the neurosecretory cells; they are active therefore in the dark, when they secrete their hormone, which promotes sexual differentiation. Note in this case the more elaborate interactions in the male than in the female.

An important aspect of these interactions is their long time course. The latency of action of a hormone may be hours or days, and the processes may last days or weeks. Much of this time, as we have seen, is taken up by the cellular events induced by the hormone: the action on the genome, the activation of enzymes, the synthesis of protein, and the remodeling of the cell (see Chap. 9). This stands in contrast to the rapid transmission and processing of information that takes place in many nervous pathways, where the time scale of action is on the order of milliseconds and seconds. Some of the conversion from rapid to slow events takes place in the neuroendocrine cells themselves, as well is in related neurons; there is evidence that this conversion may depend on Ca^{2+}-modulated protein phosphorylation, as discussed in Chap. 9. Neuroendocrine systems thus embrace a broad time scale of actions, and one of the challenges of current research is to understand how these actions are coordinated.

Vertebrates. Vertebrates also have a master neurohemal organ, the pituitary gland. It has been traced back in phylogeny to the tunicates, the earliest chordates (see Chap. 3), where it is believed to be represented by a ciliated pit organ. An interesting fact about this pit organ is that it seems to be sensitive to pheromonal signals from other tunicates; furthermore, these pheromones have a molecular structure similar to steroid sex hormones. J. B. S. Haldane, the great English biologist, speculated that the hormonal system of internal messengers may thus have originated from the pheromonal system of external messengers.

The pituitary consists of an endocrine and a neural part. The endocrine part (anterior pituitary, or adenohypophysis) is derived embryologically from an outpouching of the pharynx, while the neural part (posterior pituitary, or neurohypophysis) is derived from an outpouching from the diencephalon. Both parts are under the control of the hypothalamus, but by different means. The *neurohypophysis* contains the terminals of axons from specific nerve cells in the hypothalamus (see Fig. 25.5). From these terminals are secreted two peptide hormones: *oxytocin,* which promotes contraction of smooth muscle in the uterus and mammary glands, and *vasopressin* (also called antidiuretic hormone, or ADH), which acts on kidney tubule membrane to promote retention of water, and on smooth muscle in arterioles of the body to raise blood pressure. We shall discuss these actions further in Chaps. 27 and 28. These hormones also have actions within the nervous system outside the hypothalamus (see below).

The *endocrine* pituitary system, from its sites of neural control in the hypothalamus to its actions in the body, is summarized in Fig. 25.5. The identification of the pituitary hormones and our understanding of their actions on target organs was largely achieved by 1950, and forms the body of classical endocrinology. The work of Geoffrey Harris and his colleagues in England thereafter showed that the anterior pituitary is controlled by the hypothalamus by means of factors transported in the hypophyseoportal system. As Har-

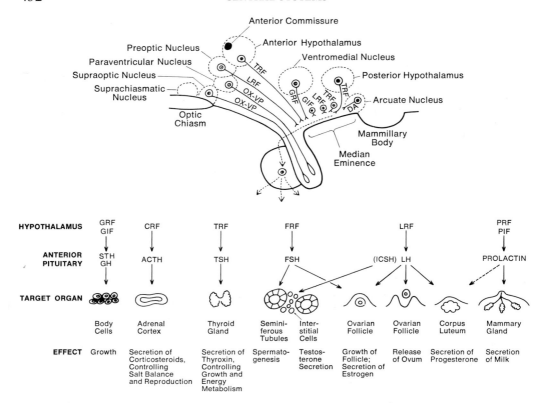

Fig. 25.5. The hypothalamic-pituitary system for neuroendocrine control in the mammal. ACTH, adrenocorticotrophic hormone; CRF, corticotropin releasing factor; FRF, follicle-stimulating hormone releasing factor; FSH, follicle-stimulating hormone; GIF, growth hormone release inhibiting factor (somatostatin); GH, growth hormone; GRF, growth hormone releasing factor; ICSH, interstitial cell stimulating hormone; LH, luteinizing hormone; LRF, luteinizing hormone releasing factor (also called LHRH, luteinizing hormone releasing hormone); PIF, prolactin release inhibiting factor; PRF, prolactin releasing factor; STH, somatotrophic hormone; TRF, thyroid hormone releasing factor; TSH, thyroid stimulating hormone. (Modified from Mountcastle, 1980)

ris wrote in his monograph *Neural Control of the Pituitary Gland* in 1955:

> . . . it seems likely that nerve fibres in the hypothalamus liberate some humoral substance into the primary plexus of the vessels, and that this substance is carried by the vessels to affect anterior pituitary activity. . . . If the hypothalamus . . . regulates the rate of secretion of the anterior pituitary hormones, are there as many humoral mechanisms involved as there are hormones?

This set the stage for an eager search for these substances, in which biochemists prepared extracts of hypothalamic tissue and identified compounds which either promote or inhibit the release and synthesis of pituitary hormones. By 1973 three of these compounds—luteinizing hormone releasing hormone (LHRH), thyrotropin releasing hormone (TRH), and somatostatin, or somatotropin-release-inhibiting factor (SRIF)—had been isolated and synthesized. These releasing factors are all peptides; their molecular structures are given in Chap. 9 (Fig. 9.9).

While this work was proceeding, other studies aimed at identifying the mechanisms for release of these factors. By electrical stimulation and local injections of hypothalamic extracts into the hypothalamus, it was possible to localize the neuroendocrine cells producing the factors. Some of these sites are indicated in Fig. 25.5. The general pattern is that the cells in different regions all send axons to the median eminence, on the floor of the hypothalamus. The peptides are stored in the axon terminals, which rest on the vessels of the portal system. Discharge of the factors is controlled by neural activity within the cell, and by circulating hormones. The factors act quickly (within minutes) before being inactivated in the blood. The actions on pituitary cells are to stimulate immediate release, as well as induce long-term synthesis of hormones. Like other peptide hormones, the releasing factors act on the pituitary cells through membrane receptors and cyclic AMP, as previously discussed in Chap. 9.

Since Harris' time it has been clear that the nervous system is not only involved in controlling the pituitary, but is itself the target of actions of circulating hormones. This is illustrated in Fig. 25.6. If we take the case of the gonadotropins, these stimulate the production of sex hormones in the gonads, either testosterone or estrogen. These hormones induce the secondary sex characteristics of males and females, as well as stimulate the maturation of sperm and eggs, respectively. The levels of circulating gonadotrophins are controlled by several factors; primary among them are sensory stimuli to the nervous system, eventually reaching the hypothalamus, and negative feedback by the circulating hormones onto pituitary cells and central neurons. Thus, although specific details are different, the principles of organization of the central neuroendocrine control system in the vertebrates are similar to those in the invertebrates.

This scheme for the pituitary system will be complete when we have identified all the central neural connections made by the neuroendocrine cells in the hypothalamus. Studies to that end have been carried out by Leo Renaud and his colleagues in Montreal. They have recorded from single

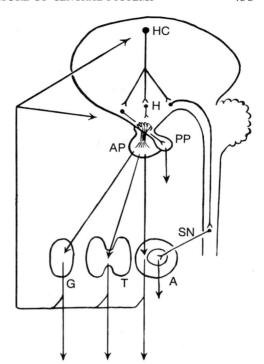

Fig. 25.6. Original diagram of Geoffrey Harris illustrating his postulate of the reciprocal relationship between the central nervous system and endocrine system. A, adrenal gland; AP, anterior pituitary; G, gonad; H, hypothalamus; HC, higher centers; PP, posterior pituitary; SN, splanchnic nerve; T, thyroid gland. (From Harris, 1955)

hypothalamic cells that project to the median eminence (as determined by antidromic backfiring) and thus presumably secrete releasing factors. These cells can also be backfired from a number of other sites, including the thalamus, preoptic area, amygdala, anterior hypothalamic area, and periventricular nucleus (see Fig. 25.7). Synaptic inputs, on the other hand, have been identified by orthodromic firing; these inputs have been found to arise in the amygdala, preoptic area, and hippocampus. To complete the picture on the input side, the neuroendocrine cells receive copious innervation from dopamine-containing neurons (see below). The cells are also subject to feedback regulation by

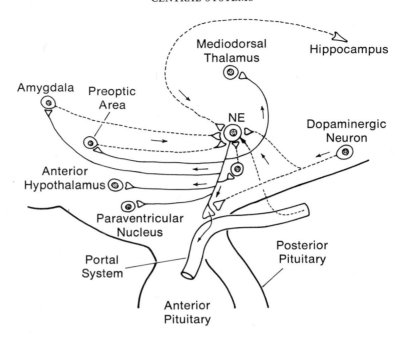

Fig. 25.7. Multiple connections of a single neuroendocrine (NE) cell in the hypothalamus. The cell and its output axon and branches are shown in continuous lines; inputs to the cell are shown in dashed lines. (After Renaud, 1977)

local circuits. Finally, they are regulated by levels of circulating hormones and other humoral factors.

The picture that emerges in Fig. 25.7 is of a neuroendocrine cell that is under extensive control by both neural and humoral mechanisms. Through the neural connections, inputs from many central regions, including the cerebral cortex and limbic systems, reach the hypothalamus. By this means, a variety of behavioral states, such as arousal, stress, and sexual maturation, all have their influence in setting the level of discharge of releasing factors and thus the control of pituitary function.

Central Neural Circuits

In previous discussions of sensory and motor systems and of neuroendocrine circuits, we have seen that in most cases our knowledge of invertebrates runs roughly parallel with that of vertebrates. With central systems, however, the balance tips toward the vertebrates. This is because the big brains of the higher vertebrates seem especially adapted for the elaboration of circuits and systems whose connections are entirely central. Studies of recent years have yielded an enormous amount of data about these systems; some of these results have shed light on the neural basis of behavior, but much of it is so new that we are only beginning to grasp its significance. In order to deal with this great variety of studies, the discussion will be organized around the identification of neurons by neurochemical properties and the different types of neurons and circuits.

In Chap. 9 the biochemistry of putative neurotransmitter substances was discussed. These biochemical techniques have enabled neuroscientists to localize the substances in different neuronal populations. When combined with previous information about fiber connections and Golgi-impregnated neurons, biochemical procedures have yielded chemical maps of the brain. Here we will discuss each of the main substances, and the neuronal types in which it has been found.

Acetylcholine. Acetylcholine (ACh) is quickly hydrolyzed and inactivated by the enzyme acetylcholinesterase. The presence of ACh is therefore sometimes inferred from the presence of this enzyme. However, this gives many false positive results, because the enzyme is widely distributed in the brain and the body, as if on guard to chew up any stray molecules of this transmitter. The better method is to identify the presence of the enzyme choline acetyltransferase, which synthesizes ACh. To this has recently been added other methods, such as the ability to identify ligand binding sites by radioimmunoassay.

The locations of ACh neurons are shown in A of Fig. 25.8. Among central systems, ACh is specific for two cell populations in the limbic system, the septal-hippocampal and habenulo-endopeduncular projection neurons, and a cell population in the caudate-putamen nucleus, which is involved in motor coordination (see below). ACh acts on either nicotinic receptors (producing brief synaptic potentials) or muscarinic receptors (producing slow synaptic potentials) (see Chap. 9). It produces EPSPs by both these actions on Renshaw interneurons in the spinal cord. In the hippocampus, it produces both slow excitatory and inhibitory responses on pyramidal cells (see Chaps. 8 and 31). In the caudate, it is believed to be the transmitter of short-axon cells and of axon collaterals that are involved in local circuits. Degeneration of these cells occurs in certain neurological diseases in which there are uncontrollable jerky movements (Huntingdon's chorea) and dementia.

In summary, ACh is the transmitter of motoneurons to glands, muscles, and ganglia in the periphery. Centrally, it is found in a few specific cell populations, where its actions may be brief or sustained, excitatory or inhibitory, and distant or local.

Dopamine. Dopamine (DA) is the first neuroactive substance in the synthetic pathway for catecholamines (refer back to Fig. 9.6). It is visualized in neurons by treating tissue sections with formaldehyde vapors or glyoxylic acid, which causes DA and its sister monoamine compounds to fluoresce with characteristic colors. This method was introduced in the 1950's by Eränkö of Finland, developed in the 1960's by Falck and Hillarp of Sweden, refined in subsequent years, and supplemented recently by immunohistochemistry and other biochemical methods.

The locations of DA neurons are shown in B of Fig. 25.8. There are two main populations of projection neurons, located within the midbrain (mesencephalon). One consists of the output cells of the substantia nigra, which project to the caudate-putamen (striatum). In Parkinson's disease these cells degenerate, and the resulting loss of DA synapses in the striatum is believed to be a primary cause of the movement disorders, such as limitation of movement and the resting tremor of the hands, that are characteristic of this disease. The therapy of high doses of the compound *l*-DOPA, the precursor of DA, is aimed at correcting this deficiency, and is successful in some, but unfortunately not all, patients.

The other main population of projection neurons is located in the ventral tegmental area (VTA) of the mesencephalon. These cells project to a number of sites in the forebrain, including the amygdala, olfactory tubercle, septal area, nucleus accumbens, and frontal cortex. Since these regions are part of what is called the limbic system, this is called the mesolimbic projection. The limbic structures served by this pathway are implicated in such functions as emotion and aggression (Chap. 30), and the frontal cortex is crucial for some of our highest cognitive functions (Chap. 31). It is likely, therefore, that the mesolimbic pathway plays a role in coordinating these functions. There is also evidence that schizophrenia may be associ-

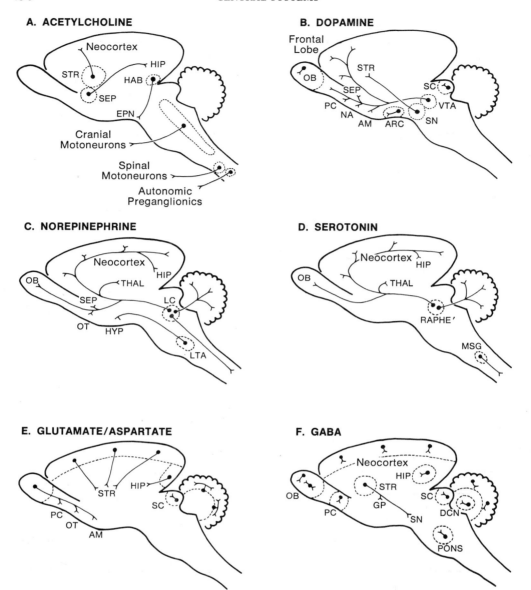

Fig. 25.8. Summary diagrams showing locations of neurons containing different neurotransmitter substances in the mammalian brain. See Fig. 25.9 for abbreviated terms. (Modified from Angevine and Cotman, 1981)

ated with derangements of DA metabolism and DA synaptic transmission, possibly within the mesolimbic pathway.

In addition to these projection tracts, there are also short-axon DA cells in several regions. In the hypothalamus, DA cells

send axons to the median eminence, to modulate the output of releasing factors by neuroendocrine cells there (see above). Intrinsic DA cells in the retina, olfactory bulb, and optic tectum take part in local circuits in those structures. Finally, there is a system of DA cells around the fourth ventricle, extending within the core of the brainstem to the hypothalamus.

Noradrenaline. Noradrenaline (NA), or norepinephrine, is synthesized from DA by the enzyme dopamine-β-hydroxylase. Like DA, NA is found especially in clusters of cells in the midbrain. One of these is called the locus ceruleus, and it is certainly one of the most extraordinary cell populations in the entire nervous system. There are only a few hundred neurons in the locus ceruleus, yet they send axons to almost every region in the central nervous system (see C in Fig. 25.8). In order to do this, each axon branches repeatedly. There are relatively few terminals within any region, but the NA branches and terminals achieve their effects by secreting NA diffusely onto synaptic terminals in the surrounding neuropil. As noted in Chap. 9, these actions are believed to be neuromodulatory in nature. Because of their widespread ramifications and diffuse actions, the NA cells are well suited for setting levels of central neural activity underlying different behavioral states. In this respect they may act somewhat like a central autonomic nervous system, to complement the peripheral autonomic system, and function in parallel with the adrenal medulla and its release of adrenaline into the bloodstream. We will discuss cellular mechanisms involved in NA function below and in Chap. 26.

Complementing the locus ceruleus is a nearby cluster of NA cells in the lateral tegmental area (LTA). These projections overlap those of the locus ceruleus, but are directed mainly to the hypothalamus, where they are believed to participate in the regulation of releasing factors.

Adrenaline. Adrenaline is synthesized from noradrenaline in the catecholamine pathway. As noted above, it is an important hormone of the peripheral autonomic system, where it is liberated from the adrenal medulla and is crucial in preparing the body for action and stress (see also Chaps. 3 and 18). In the central nervous system it is present in a few clusters of cells in the lower brainstem (medulla), which project anteriorly as far as the diencephalon, and posteriorly to the spinal cord. Terminals are found particularly in the dorsal motor nucleus of the vagus (cranial nerve X) and the nuclei of the tractus solitarius (cranial nerves VII, IX, and X), where adrenaline may have a role in modulating motor control of the viscera and taste information from the tongue, respectively.

Serotonin. Serotonin, or 5-hydroxytryptamine (5HT), is a monoamine, because it has a single terminal amine group, but it has a two-ring indole structure that differentiates it from the single-ring catecholamines. It is synthesized from the precursor tryptophan (see Fig. 9.6). Serotonin is present throughout the body, especially in blood platelets and the intestines. In the brain, it is found mainly in the midbrain, in clusters of cells called the raphé, and in the medulla. As shown in D of Fig. 25.8, the fibers of these cells project widely to the forebrain, cerebellum, and spinal cord, in a pattern that resembles that of the NA fibers. Thus, like the NA system, the 5HT system appears to exert a widespread influence over arousal, sensory perception, emotion, and higher cognitive functions.

The first evidence for these effects came from experiments with the hallucinogenic agent lysergic acid diethylamide (LSD) in the 1950's. LSD was found to block 5HT receptors in muscle membranes, and it was suggested that the disastrous effects of LSD on mental states could therefore be attributed to blocking of 5HT receptors in the brain. However, as Cooper, Bloom, and Roth have wisely observed:

. . . none of these data could be considered particularly pertinent since all the research was done on the peripheral nervous system and all the philosophy was applied to the central nervous system.

In molluscan neurons, ionophoretic application of 5HT causes excitatory depolarization, whereas in the vertebrate brain, where the experiments are much less precise, both excitatory and inhibitory effects have been reported. Recent studies indicate that agents such as LSD and drugs such as tricyclic antidepressants have complex actions, both presynaptic and postsynaptic, on the serotonin system. There is evidence that serotonin levels in the brain are depressed in depressed patients. In the next chapter we will discuss the involvement of the raphé pathways in waking and sleeping.

Glutamate and Aspartate. We next consider some neurotransmitters that are amino acids. One of the main representatives of this type is glutamic acid, or glutamate, and its close relative, aspartate. These compounds are widespread constituents of intermediary metabolism in the body and the brain, and thus might seem to be unlikely candidates for the specific actions required at synapses. However, beginning with the studies of van Harreveld and Mendelson in 1959, glutamate has been established as the transmitter at the crustacean neuromuscular junction (see Chap. 18). Although experiments as definitive as these cannot be carried out in the brain, there is considerable evidence for glutamate and/or aspartate as the transmitter, mediating brief excitatory actions, at several types of projection neuron in the brain. These are shown in E of Fig. 25.8.

Of particular interest are the granule cells of the cerebellum. The granule cells are a type of short-axon projection neuron, linking the two layers of the cerebellar cortex. Because of their large numbers (10 to 100 billion, as noted in Chap. 22), we can say that there are more glutaminergic cells than all other cells combined in the nervous system! Other projection tracts using these substances include the olfactory bulb input to olfactory cortex, the entorhinal cortex input to the hippocampus and dentate fascia, and the cortical input to the caudate. At all these sites, glutamate and aspartate have excitatory actions. An intriguing note is that the mitral cells of the olfactory bulb not only project to the olfactory cortex, but also take part in dendrodendritic synapses within the microcircuits of the olfactory bulb. According to Dale's law (Chap. 9), one might expect the transmitter at the dendritic synapses also to be glutamate or aspartate, and there is in fact evidence to support this.

Gamma-aminobutyric acid (GABA). In mammals, GABA is found almost exclusively in the brain, where it is a constituent of intermediary metabolism. Its role as a neurotransmitter was first established in the crayfish, where it was shown to be the transmitter of the inhibitory axon to the stretch receptor cell (Chap. 8) and at the neuromuscular junction (Chap. 18). Localization of this neurotransmitter in the brain has been aided by immunocytochemical methods for identifying the synthesizing enzyme, glutamic acid decarboxylase (see Chaps. 5 and 9).

GABAergic neurons are shown in F of Fig. 25.8. It is interesting that, apart from the short projection tracts from striatum to substantia nigra and from cerebellar cortex to deep cerebellar nuclei, most GABAergic neurons are intrinsic neurons, in such regions as cortex, olfactory bulb, hippocampus, cerebellum, and retina. Within these regions, GABA is present in high concentrations, of the order of μmoles/g of frozen tissue, which is about 1000 times the concentrations of the monoamines. This is in accord with the powerful and specific actions of the GABAergic neurons in these regions. The predominant action of GABA is inhibitory, by increasing Cl$^-$ conductance, though other types of actions are beginning to come to light, too. These actions are exerted at both axonal and dendritic output synapses, and are usually directed at controlling the output neurons. The inhibitory actions are important for many functions, such as sensory processing, negative feedback, gating of rhythmic discharges, and timing and coordination of motor output. Drugs like picrotoxin and bicuculline, which block GABA receptors (see Chap. 9), cause seizures, which has suggested that dysfunctions of GABAergic interneurons in the cortex may be critical in the development of epilepsy.

Glycine. Glycine has been localized mainly to the brainstem and spinal cord. In the spinal cord, it is believed to be an inhibitory transmitter of interneurons onto motoneurons. Ionophoresis experiments have found little evidence for any action of glycine on neurons above the brainstem.

The above substances include those traditionally associated with specific neurotransmitter actions. We next consider substances whose actions are more appropriately termed neuromodulatory (see Chap. 9). Among these, the most prevalent (at least as viewed through our present-day spectacles) are the peptides.

Substance P. Substance P has the distinction of being the first neuroactive peptide isolated from the brain. In 1931 Ulf von Euler of Sweden and John Gaddum of England showed that this compound, present in both brain and gut, has a stimulating effect on smooth muscle. Around 1970, Susan Leeman and her colleagues at Harvard isolated a compound from the hypothalamus that stimulates the salivary gland, and named it a sialogog (sialo= saliva, gog= factor). When they synthesized this compound, it turned out to be identical to substance P isolated some 40 years previously (see structure in Fig. 9.7). Substance P is found in several specific short projection tracts, as shown in A of Fig. 25.9. Its presence in the striatonigral pathway has suggested that it is a transmitter in these fibers, and is therefore important in the motor functions of the basal ganglia (see next section). In the spinal cord, it is present in dorsal root ganglion cells. Although it is 200 times more potent than glutamate in depolarizing motoneurons when applied ionophoretically, its slow time course of action contrasts with the rapid discrete transmission of input signals in many dorsal root fibers. This is consistent with the idea that substance P has a slower modulatory action, but so far it has not been proven.

Somatostatin. This compound derives its name from its action in inhibiting the secretion of growth hormone (somatotropin) from pituitary cells. It is a tetradecapeptide (14 amino acids) (see Fig. 9.7). Like so many neuroactive peptides, it is found in autonomic fibers and other nonneural cells in the visceral organs (see Chap. 18). Within the nervous system, it is found in dorsal root ganglion cells, and, centrally, in cells of the hypothalamus, amygdala, and cerebral cortex (see B in Fig. 25.9). When injected into the cerebral ventricles, it has a depressant effect on motor activity. Like several other peptides, it has a slow inhibitory action when ionophoresed onto single neurons (see Fig. 25.10).

Endorphins. Among the peptides generating the most interest in recent years are the endorphins and enkephalins. This work began in 1975 with the finding of Hans Kosterlitz and Robert Hughes in Scotland that extracts of brain contain a compound which competes with opiates in assay systems, and is blocked by opiate antagonists such as naloxone. The short-chain pentapeptides (5 amino acids) are called enkephalins, while the longer-chain compounds (16–31 amino acids) are called endorphins. Since the enkephalin chain is contained within the endorphin chain, the term *endorphin* may be used to refer to both in general. The synthesis of these compounds from the larger precursor molecule β-lipotropin was discussed in Chap. 9.

Cells containing endorphins are located

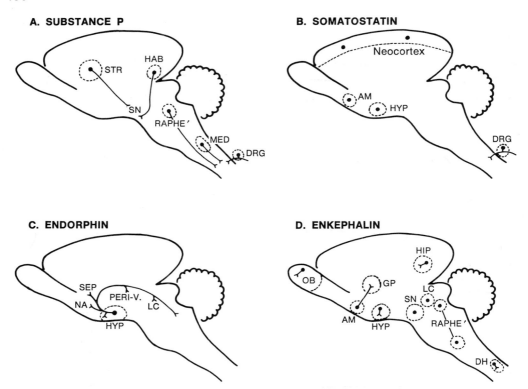

Fig. 25.9. Summary diagrams showing locations of neurons containing different neuropeptides in the mammalian brain. Abbreviations for Figs. 25.8 and 25.9 as follows: AM, amygdala; ARC, arcuate nucleus; DCN, deep cerebellar nuclei; DH, dorsal horn; DRG, dorsal root ganglion; EPN, endopeduncular nucleus; GP, globus pallidus; HAB, habenula; HIP, hippocampus; HYP, hypothalamus; LC, locus coeruleus; LTA, lateral tegmental area; MED, medulla; MSG, medullary serotonin group; NA, nucleus accumbens; OB, olfactory bulb; OT, olfactory tubercle; PC, pyriform cortex; PERI-V., periventricular gray; SC, superior colliculus; SEP, septum; SN, substantia nigra; STR, striatum; THAL, thalamus; VTA, ventral tegmental area.

almost exclusively in the hypothalamus. As shown in C of Fig. 25.9, their fibers project to different nuclei within the hypothalamus, and to several regions outside the hypothalamus, including the septal area and amygdala, and reach as far as the higher brainstem, where they innervate monoamine cells of the locus ceruleus and raphé nuclei. Most of the termination sites are in the core of the brain, around the ventricles.

From the moment of their discovery, it has seemed that the endorphins might act like opiate drugs, and thus function as an internal mechanism for opposing or modulating pain sensations. Part of the interest in analyzing this mechanism lies in the hope of developing a more natural substitute for morphine that is free of addictive properties and side effects. In addition, there has been much speculation on the natural functions in which the endorphins may be involved. In their enthusiasm, people have implicated them in almost every behavior imaginable, from temperature regulation to our sense of self. It is becoming clear, however, that much more work is required to establish the precise contributions of endorphins to specific behaviors.

Enkephalins. Enkephalin-containing neurons are widespread in the nervous system, with a distribution that is quite distinct from that of the endorphins. The main regions in which they are found are shown in D of Fig. 25.9. In the peripheral nervous system, enkephalin is found in the adrenal medulla and in fibers that innervate the smooth muscle of the gut. In the central nervous system, enkephalins are characteristically found in intrinsic neurons; in this respect they resemble GABAergic interneurons. In these cells, the enkephalin is in a position to modulate the processing of information by local circuits. A prime example is the dorsal horn of the spinal cord, where it is believed that enkephalin neurons modulate the processing of input arriving over pain fibers (see Chap. 13). In addition, enkephalins are implicated in most of the functions ascribed to endorphins, as discussed above.

Other Peptides. These are only a few examples from the list of neuroactive peptides in Fig. 9.9. The list continues to grow, and the work that is necessary to characterize the functions of each peptide has only begun. We will discuss further examples in subsequent chapters of this section.

A Central System: the Basal Ganglia

In order to appreciate better the way that the different kinds of circuits are combined to build a central system, let us consider the basal ganglia as an example.

The forebrain includes all of the nervous system above the diencephalon. It consists of two kinds of structure, the outer layer, called the cortex, and an inner mass, called the basal ganglia (basal, because they seem to be within the base of the cerebral hemispheres, and ganglia because this was the term applied by nineteenth-century histologists to large groups of neurons).

The positions of the basal ganglia are shown in Fig. 25.11. Of the several ganglia, the caudate is an elongated extension of the putamen; the two have a similar neuronal structure, and together are called the *striatum* (this term comes from the fact that there are bands of fibers passing through which produce a striated appearance). As indicated in the diagram, the striatum receives widespread inputs from

Fig. 25.10. Depressant actions of three peptides on different central neurons. **A.** Recording of impulse discharge from a cell in the ventromedial nucleus of the thalamus. **B.** Cell in parietal cortex. **C.** Cell in cerebellar cortex. (From Wilbur et al., in Renaud, 1977)

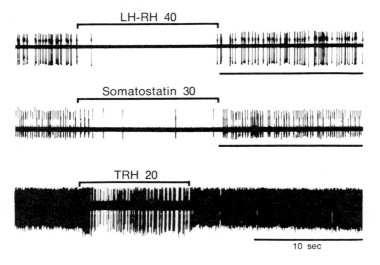

LH-RH 40

Somatostatin 30

TRH 20

10 sec

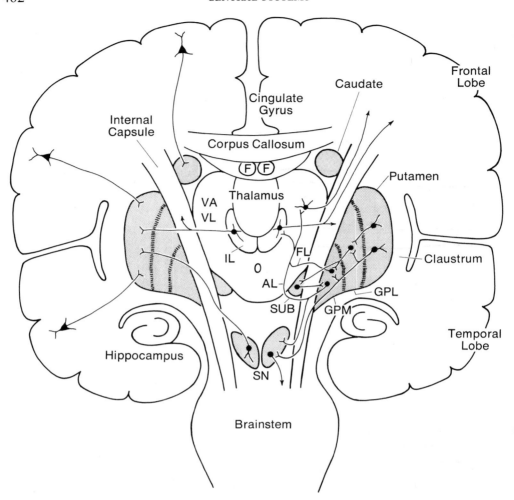

Fig. 25.11. Schematic frontal section of human brain, showing main connections and relations of the basal ganglia (shaded). Globus pallidus, lateral segment (GPL); medial segment (GPM). SUB, subthalamic nucleus; SN, substantia nigra; AL, ansa lenticularis; FL, fasciculus lenticularis. Thalamic nuclei: VA, ventral anterior; VL, ventral lateral; IL, interlaminar nucleus. Connections of caudate are similar to those shown for putamen. (Modified from Shepherd, 1979)

the cerebral cortex; its output, in turn, is directed to another of the basal ganglia, the *globus pallidus,* and to the *substantia nigra.* The substantia nigra is actually located in the midbrain, but its main connections are with the striatum and globus pallidus, and it is therefore functionally linked with the basal ganglia. The output of the globus pallidus is directed to the thalamus, to the same nuclei which receive inputs from the cerebellum and pro-

ject widely to the cerebral cortex. The output of the substantia nigra is directed both to the thalamus and back to the striatum. These conections can all be traced in Fig. 25.11.

Until the 1960's, almost nothing was known about the functions of these large masses of cells; they were the great silent interior of the cerebral subcontinent. The only clues were that pathological changes were found in these regions in patients with certain striking movement disorders. Lesions in the putamen and globus pallidus were associated with slow writhing movements (athetosis). Degeneration of cells in the striatum was found in patients with Huntington's chorea, characterized by involuntary jerking movements. Lesions of a small region called the subthalamic nucleus were associated with violent flinging movements of the extremities (ballismus). The most interesting correlation was the finding of degeneration of the dopaminergic input from the substantia nigra to the striatum in patients with Parkinson's disease. This was established in the 1960's, and was the first correlation of

a neurotransmitter deficiency with a neurological disease. It provided the basis for the use of l-DOPA to treat these patients, as mentioned above. It has also provided the precedent for hoping that other diseases, such as schizophrenia, may also be linked to a defect in a specific transmitter or substance.

All this work indicated that the basal ganglia are crucially involved in the control of movement and in sensorimotor coordination. Spurred by these findings, neuroscientists have directed their attention to the cellular properties and microcircuits within each region. Figure 25.12 illustrates some of these results. In the

Fig. 25.12. Synaptic organization and interactions in the basal ganglia. **A.** Caudate-putamen, showing the profuse dendritic tree of an HRP-filled neuron. To the right, the schematic diagram shows some possible synaptic actions of dopaminergic fibers from the substantia nigra. Thick arrow, brief synaptic action; dotted arrow, slow synaptic action; other arrows, actions of dopamine on autoreceptors and on other synaptic terminals. **B.** Substantia nigra, showing, on the right, two dopaminergic output neurons. On the left, some possible actions of dopamine, analogous to those in (A). (HRP-filled neuron in (A) is from Kitai (1981). Diagrams are based on Aghajanian and Bunney, 1976; Nowycky and Roth, 1978; and Groves et al., 1979)

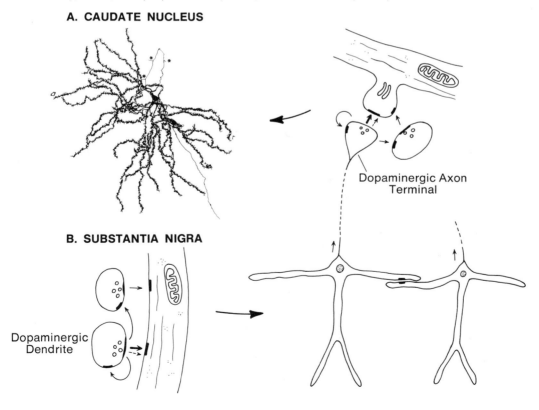

A. CAUDATE NUCLEUS

Dopaminergic Axon
Terminal

B. SUBSTANTIA NIGRA

Dopaminergic
Dendrite

striatum, Stephen Kitai and his colleagues at Michigan State University have injected single cells with HRP and shown that most have dendrites covered with spines (A). The axon gives off an enormous number of collateral branches, providing for multiple local circuit conections to neighboring neurons. On the input side, neuroanatomists have found that fibers from the cortex, thalamus, and substantia nigra make synapses onto the spines. Most of these synapses have a type I morphology (see Chap. 5), suggesting an excitatory action. However, the action of the input fibers has been a matter of keen debate. For the case of the dopaminergic fibers, some studies have suggested a rapid, brief excitatory action, while others have suggested a slower, inhibitory action. Biochemical studies have identified a dopamine-sensitive adenylate cyclase in the striatum, presumably activated by the dopaminergic fibers. In addition to its specific synaptic action, DA may act by diffusing from varicosities to postsynaptic sites, and it may also act on presynaptic terminals (A).

These studies indicate that a single type of fiber secreting a single transmitter can have several kinds of actions at several sites. This is in accord with similar results obtained under more precisely controlled conditions in invertebrate neurons. At each site, a specific combination of cellular properties is brought into play, to integrate information, transmit it to neighboring sites, and exert local feedback and modulatory control, actions that in addition may be use-dependent and lead to plastic changes. It is interesting to note that these functional properties of a site within a synaptic circuit have their analogies with the functions and controls of an enzyme in a metabolic pathway; in other words, this may be viewed as the expression of cellular properties at a circuit level.

Similar results have been obtained in the substantia nigra. Phillip Groves and his colleagues in San Diego have postulated that the output firing of the dopaminergic cells is controlled by feedback of DA similar to the presynaptic control in the stria-

tum. DA is contained within the dendrites of these cells; when released, it may act on autoreceptors in the same dendrites, or diffuse to receptors on neighboring dendrites, or act at dendrodendritic synapses; such synapses have been identified in the electron microscope (see Fig. 25.12B).

To complete the picture of organization, we need to consider the basal ganglia as a system, and the way it relates to other systems. The basal ganglia feed into two thalamic nuclear groups, the ventral lateral–ventral anterior group, and the intralaminar group. These, in turn, project to the cortex, and thus complete a loop through cortical cells back onto the striatum. This loop is shown in Fig. 25.13. This organization into closed loops is one of the outstanding characteristics of basal gan-

Fig. 25.13. Distributed system formed by the loop circuits through basal ganglia, cortex, thalamus, and cerebellum. Putative transmitters: DA, dopamine; GABA, gamma aminobutyric acid; GLU, glutamate; SP, substance P.

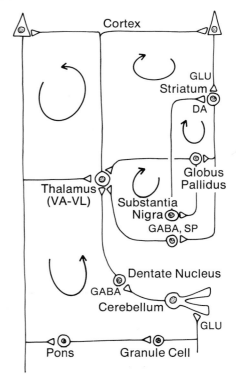

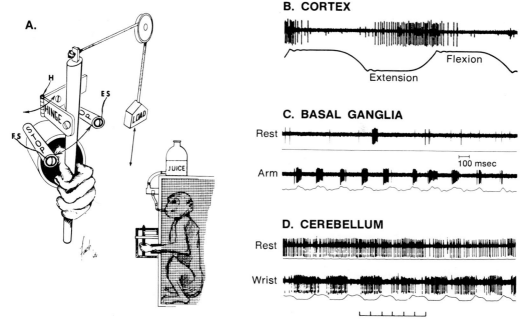

Fig. 25.14. Correlations of central neuron activity and movement in the awake behaving monkey. A. Experimental setup for training a monkey to perform an extension or flexion of the wrist; it received a reward of fruit juice if the movement was performed within a brief specified period of time (400–700 msec). B. Activity of a single pyramidal tract neuron in the motor cortex in relation to movement. This unit was active prior to and during flexing of the wrist to a steady flexed position (but not during the maintained flexion). It increased its activity when flexion was performed against a flexion load (as in A), but was silent when flexion was performed against an extension load; this indicates that the motor cortex encodes force of movement as well as direction, displacement, and speed. C. Activity of a single neuron in the globus pallidus. The unit showed regular bursting in relation to push–pull movements of the arm, but not in relation to similar movements of the leg. Note the low rate of impulse firing at rest. D. Activity of a single Purkinje cell in the cerebellum. This cell showed regular bursting in relation to alternating extension and flexion of the wrist. Note the high rate of firing at rest, compared with the low rate of the basal ganglia cell in C. Time bar: 100 msec divisions. (A, B from Evarts, in Phillips and Porter, 1977; C from DeLong and Georgopoulos, 1981; D from Thach, in Brooks and Thach, 1981)

glia circuits, at all levels: it is seen in the several forms of feedback in microcircuits, in the reciprocal relations between striatum and substantia nigra, and in the loop through thalamus and cortex. In the thalamus, the input from the basal ganglia is integrated with input from the cerebellum. The cerebellum is embedded in its own loop, through thalamus to cortex and back through the pons (see Chap. 22). The organization of these circuits into loops apparently confers the advantages of tight feedback at all levels in the control of movement. It appears also to have the disadvantage of uncontrollable oscillations when any part is damaged, as in the disorders seen in neurological diseases.

The extensively related circuits shown in Fig. 25.13 involve many regions of the brain, and are a good example of what we have termed a *distributed system*. In order to gain insight into how activity throughout this system is coordinated, single-unit recordings have been made in several of the regions, using the methods of Evarts described in Chap. 23. Figure 25.14 summarizes the results obtained from three regions—cortex, basal ganglia, and cerebellum—in relation to specific movements performed by awake monkeys. These experiments have shown that in both the cerebellum and the basal ganglia, single cells begin their discharges in advance of the onset of a volitional movement. Furthermore, cerebellar cells have been found to change their activity in advance of cortical cells during the state of "readiness" that precedes a motor act, as discussed previously in the experiment of Fig. 23.12.

From these results, the remarkable conclusion emerges that the distributed system that contains the highest motor programs includes centers that are anatomically at lower levels. This means that when we try to formulate concepts of central control, we need to free ourselves of the idea that higher functions are lodged exclusively in the cortex. The cortex is the necessary instrument of higher function, but it is an instrument played by programs fashioned from the interactions between centers throughout the central nervous system. The multiple interconnections between centers both provide for the higher levels of abstraction underlying volition and purpose, and ensure that those functions emerge from the fabric of the organism as a whole.

REFERENCES

Aghajanian, G. K. and B. S. Bunney. 1976. Dopamine "autoreceptors": pharmacological characterization by microiontophoretic single cell recording studies. *Naunyn-Schmiedeberg's Arch. Pharmacol. 297:* 1–7.

Angevine, J. B. Jr. and C. W. Cotman. 1981. *Principles of Neuroanatomy.* New York: Oxford.

Brooks, V. B. and T. T. Thach. 1981. Cerebellar control of posture and movement. In *Motor Control.* Vol. 2 of *Handbook of Physiology,* Sect. 1: *The Nervous System* (ed. by V. B. Brooks). Bethesda, Md.: American Physiological Society. pp. 877–946.

DeLong, M. R. and A. P. Georgopoulos. 1981. Motor functions of the basal ganglia. In *Motor Control.* Vol. 2 of *Handbook of Physiology,* Sect. 1: *The Nervous System* (ed. by V. B. Brooks). Bethesda, Md.: American Physiological Society. pp. 1017–1061.

Gordon, M. S. 1972. [Chap. 16].

Groves, P. M., D. A. Staunton, C. J. Wilson, and S. J. Young. 1979. Sites of action of amphetamine intrinsic to catecholaminergic nuclei: catecholaminergic presynaptic dendrites and axons. *Progr. Neuro. Psychopharmacol. 3:* 315–335.

Harris, G. W. 1955. *Neural Control of the Pituitary Gland.* London: Edward Arnold.

Kitai, S. T. 1981. Anatomy and physiology of the neostriatum. In *GABA and the Basal Ganglia* (ed. by G. Di Chiara and G. L. Gessa) New York: Raven. pp. 1–21.

Mountcastle, V. B. (ed). 1980. [Chap. 9].

Nowycky, M. C. and R. H. Roth. 1978. Dopaminergic neurons: role of presynaptic receptors in the regulation of transmitter biosynthesis. *Progr. Neuro-Psychopharmacol. 2:* 139–158.

Phillips, C. G. and R. R. Porter. 1977. [Chap. 22].

Renaud, L. P. 1977. TRH, LHRH, and somatostatin: distribution and physiological action in neural tissue. In *Soc. for Neurosci. Symp,* Vol 2 (ed. by W. M. Cowan and J. A. Ferrendelli). Bethesda, Md.: Soc. for Neurosci. pp. 265–290.

Shepherd, G. M. 1979. [Chap. 4].

Additional Reading

Barrington, E. J. W. 1979. [Chap. 2].

Bell, P. R. (ed.). 1959. *Darwin's Biological Work.* Cambridge: Cambridge University Press.

Brooks, V. B. (ed.). 1981. [Chap. 22]. See especially articles on cerebellum, basal ganglia, and cerebral control mechanisms.

Cooper, J. R., F. E. Bloom, and R. H. Roth. 1982. [Chap. 9].

Evarts, E. V. 1981. [Chap. 23].

McGeer, P. L., J. C. Eccles, and E. G. McGeer. 1978. *Molecular Biology of the Mammalian Brain.* New York: Plenum.

Rakic, P. 1976. [Chap. 4].

26
Biorhythms

Although motor activity is one of the cardinal features of animal life, animals are not ceaselessly in motion. Characteristically, periods of activity alternate with periods of inactivity. The inactivity can take many forms, such as simply sitting, lying, or standing still; sleeping; hibernating; or passing through stages of larval development. Underlying these periods are fluctuations in the secretions of glands, and fluctuations in many cellular functions, such as the synthesis of RNA, protein, and other molecules. Cyclical activities are thus basic characteristics of animal life, and we may refer to them collectively by the term *biorhythms*.

Any cyclical activity is usually defined initially in terms of its *period,* that is, the time it takes to complete one full cycle of activity. A cycle that lasts a day, such as the sequence of waking and sleeping, is said to have a period that is *circadian* (circa: approximately; die: day). Longer periods (less frequent) are called *infradian* (infra: less), while shorter periods (more frequent) are called *ultradian* (ultra: more). Some representatives of these types are listed in Table 26.1. These biorhythms almost always involve in some way, directly or indirectly, the nervous system, and many are directly under nervous control. We have, of course, already encountered ultradian rhythms in the discussion of impulse discharge, heart and locomotion rate; an illustration of infradian control of developmental processes was given for the case of eclosion in the moth in Chap. 10.

In this chapter, we will focus on circadian rhythms, and the cellular mechanisms that lead to their generation. We will attempt to gain an understanding of the

Table 26.1 Main categories of rhythmic activity, with some examples

Infradian (longer than one day)	Circadian (approx. one day)	Ultradian (shorter than one day)
menstrual cycle	waking–sleeping	feeding
seasonal variations	body temperature	respiration
lifetime	body electrolytes	heart rate
	various hormones	nerve impulse discharge

baseline they provide for the centrally controlled behaviors to be discussed in the following chapters.

It might be thought that the obvious relations of many plant and animal activities to day and night would have invited close study even in ancient times. However, it appears that the facts were simply too familiar. It was not until 1729 that the French geologist de Mairan did the simple experiment of placing a plant under constant temperature and illumination, and observed that its normal daily period of fluctuations still persisted. This showed that periodic behavior could be a function of the organism itself. Although this finding aroused some interest, people still didn't quite know what to make of it; there were suspicions that the experiment might be affected by some undetectable rays or forces.

It was not until the 1930's that biologists began to make the connection between photoperiodicity (the changing illumination during the day) and bodily rhythms. A breakthrough came in 1950, in the work of two German biologists, Gustav Kramer and Karl von Frisch. Kramer showed that birds could use the sun as a compass by virtue of the fact that they have an "internal clock" which, in effect, tells them the time of day and how much to correct for the position (azimuth) of the sun in the sky. Von Frisch came to a similar conclusion for bees. A number of biologists then initiated the search for the cellular basis of the "internal clock", a search that has continued to the present. The importance of circadian rhythms has grown in parallel with the increasing understanding of their mechanisms, and the increasing realization of how pervasive they are in the life of the organism. As Colin Pittendrigh (of Stanford University), one of the early pioneers, has put it:

. . . a circadian oscillation assumes a unique phase relationship to the 24-hour light/dark cycle that entrains it . . . The functional significance of this is many-sided: It permits *initiation* of events in *anticipation* of the time at which their culmination most appropriately occurs, and it permits timing that cannot be entrusted to control by conditions for which the system has no adequate modality.

From the extensive work that has been carried out on circadian oscillations, we will focus on three examples: studies of simple cells and small systems in Aplysia and birds, and studies of multiple systems controlling waking and sleeping in mammals, especially humans.

Circadian Rhythms in Invertebrates

Cellular Mechanisms. In our earlier discussions of rhythmic behavior (for example, heart rate or locomotion), we saw that there are two basic types of mechanism: one can have a pacemaker cell, which imparts its rhythmic output to other cells, or one can have a rhythmic cell group or network, in which no one cell has an intrinsic rhythmic property, but which gives a rhythmic output by virtue of its interconnections. The same two alternatives apply in the analysis of mechanisms of circadian oscillation.

The sea hare *Aplysia* has been a useful system for studying circadian mechanisms; it was introduced for this purpose by Felix Strumwasser of the California Institute of Technology in 1965. Like most animals, *Aplysia* shows a circadian rhythm of locomotor activity; in general, it is active during the day and inactive at night. Since we do not know whether an invertebrate animal like *Aplysia* ever "sleeps", in the same sense that we apply that term to mammals, it is best to refer to the inactive periods as simply periods of *rest*. We then say that there is a *basic rest-activity cycle* that characterizes the overall behavior of an animal through a 24-hour day. Some animals, like *Aplysia*, are active during the day, but of course many animals, particularly warm-blooded predators, are active at night.

An *Aplysia* that has been entrained to a normal dark-light cycle and is then exposed to constant illumination or constant dark, still shows its basic rest-activ-

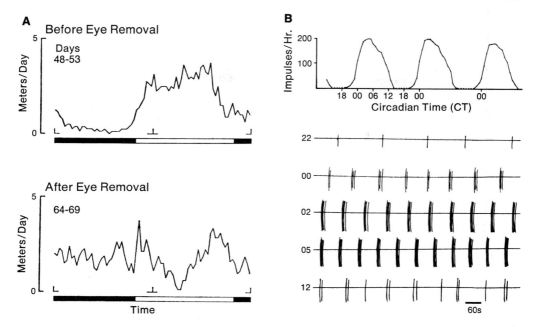

Fig. 26.1. A. The average locomotor activity (monitored with a video camera) of a sea hare, *Aplysia,* before (top) and after (bottom) removal of both eyes. Each trace represents the average of six days' observations. The observations for the bottom trace began 3 days after eye removal. (From Strumwasser, 1974) **B.** Circadian rhythm in the frequency of extracellularly recorded action potentials of the optic nerve. Top, graph of discharge frequency (in impulses per hour), plotted against circadian time (CT). Bottom, representative recordings, at times indicated. (From Jacklet, 1981)

ity cycle for several days. This showed that the circadian rhythm persists in the absence of inputs from the environment, or from other ganglia. The rhythm of the ganglion maintained under constant conditions is referred to as the *free-running rhythm.* The free-running period is not quite precisely 24-hours (hence the general term circadian); we say therefore that in the intact animal the rhythm is *entrained* by the 24-hour light-dark cycle.

This result indicates that the rest-activity cycle has a circadian generator somewhere within the nervous system. The generator is not the large bursting neuron, R15, in the abdominal ganglian; removal of the ganglia has no effect on the free-running cycle. However, removal of both eyes does abolish the locomotor cycle, in both normal and maintained conditions (Fig. 26.1A). Correlated with this is the

finding that the eye of an animal maintained in constant darkness shows a free-running rhythm in the amount of spontaneous impulse activity that can be recorded from the optic nerves. A similar rhythm can be recorded from the isolated eye (see Fig 26.1B). These experiments have therefore indicated that the neuronal mechanisms that drive the circadian rhythm of locomotor activity in *Aplysia* are found within the eye itself.

The search for those mechanisms has involved several methods, including application of pharmacological agents known to block impulse generation, chemical synapses, and electrical synapses. Full agreement has not yet been reached on the local neuronal circuits within the eye that are responsible for generating the circadian rhythm. A tentative circuit is shown in Fig. 26.2. It appears that there are two

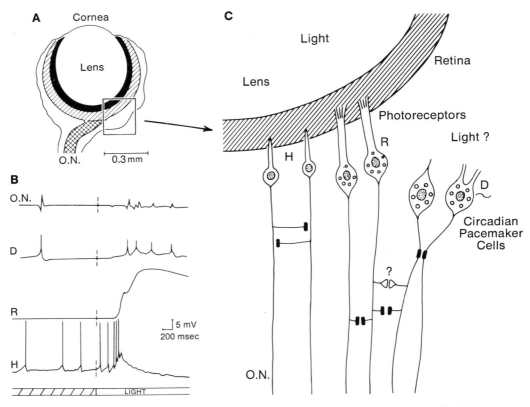

Fig. 26.2. **A.** Structure of the eye of *Aplysia*. **B.** Types of responses to light stimuli: O.N., extra-cellular recording of impulses in the optic nerve; D, intracellular recording from a secondary cell that gave a depolarization and impulse discharge (note the correspondence with the impulses in O.N.); R, intracellular recording from a photoreceptor cell that responded with a large graded receptor potential; H, intracellular recording from a photoreceptor cell that gave a depolarization followed by a hyperpolarization. **C.** Local circuits of the eye. Electrical synapses are indicated by short bars. (A, B from Jacklet, 1976; C based on Strumwasser, Audesirk, and especially Jacklet, Schuster, and Rolerson, 1982)

basic types of cell in the eye, photorecep-tors and secondary neurons. The photo-receptors are additionally divided into two types: the R type gives a nonspiking, graded response to light stimulation, whereas the H type gives a spike response followed by a hyperpolarization (see Fig. 26.2B). The secondary neurons, called D cells, give a depolarization and burst of spikes to a light flash; the spikes are cor-related with the spike discharge recorded from the nerve, suggesting that the D cells are primarily responsible for the nerve im-pulse activity that expresses the circadian rhythm of the eye (as in Fig. 26.1B). The

diagram in Fig. 26.2C summarizes most of these results; note the apparent impor-tance of electrical synapses in mediating the interactions between the different types of cell.

What mechanisms within the D cells are responsible for their special pacemaker properties? Three sites have been pro-posed: the membrane, cytoplasm, and nu-cleus. Among cytoplasmic mechanisms, there is increasing evidence for the role of protein syntheis. This can be conveniently studied by observing the effects of a pro-tein synthesis inhibitor. An experiment of this nature is illustrated in Fig. 26.3; it can be seen that in the continued presence of the inhibitor at higher concentrations, impulse activity is still present in the nerve but the rhythm is lost. When a pulse of the substance is introduced in the bathing medium, the subsequent cycles are delayed, an effect referred to as phase-shifting. It will be recalled (Chap. 4) that protein synthesis occurs at polyribosomes; in the presence of anisomycin, the polyribosomes are intact; peptide formation is initiated, but it cannot proceed because anisomycin binds to the 60S subunit of the ribosome, possibly acting specifically on peptidyl transferase. According to Jon Jacklet of Albany, "these findings imply that the daily synthesis of protein is a general requirement for circadian clocks." Further experiments are needed to define a more specific role, and correlate it with the control of impulse firing.

In *Aplysia,* the circadian rhythm of the eye is thus generated within the eye itself. In *Limulus,* in contrast, the ommatidium of the eye undergoes changes in structure, pigmentation, and sensitivity that are imposed by centrifugal activity from a central generator. The centrifugal fibers fire faster during the night than during the day, and this is correlated with a higher frequency of impulse response to a flash of light (Fig. 26.4A). This in turn is correlated with the behavioral observation that this animal is more active at night. Intracellular recordings from retinular cells have shown that the centrifugal activity is associated, at night, with a decrease in spontaneous quantum responses to light, thereby making the membrane potential less noisy, while at the same time there is enhancement of the response to a flash of light, thus making the receptors more sen-

Fig. 26.3. Rhythmic impulse discharges in the optic nerve of *Aplysia* are reduced and abolished by anisomycin at three concentrations, introduced into the bathing medium at the times indicated by the arrows. N, noon time; ▲, peak activity. (From Jacklet, 1981)

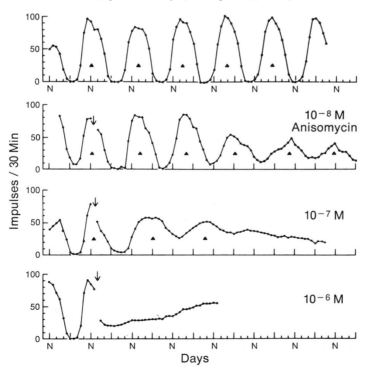

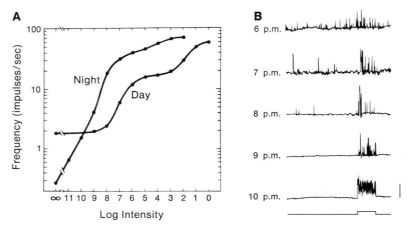

Fig. 26.4. **A.** Frequency of impulse response of a single *Limulus* optic nerve fiber to a standard test flash of light. Note the increase in sensitivity during the night. **B.** Intracellular recordings from a *Limulus* retinula cell at different times indicated at left. In each trial, a 20 sec recording period preceded the 5 sec test flash. Calibration bar, 10 mV. (A from Barlow et al., in Jacklet, 1981; B from Kaplan and Barlow, 1980)

sitive. Both of these effects increase the signal-to-noise ratio of the response during the night, when greater visual sensitivity is needed. These experiments show how a central circadian system can have affects on the earliest stages of transduction and excitation in a sensory pathway.

Circadian Rhythms in Vertebrates

As in invertebrates, the basic rest-activity cycles are closely linked to the day-night cycle in most vertebrates. As noted, animals vary in whether they are active principally during the day or night, or at specific times such as dawn or dusk. This obviously reflects the strategy of a particular species in finding food or sexual mates with the greatest success, while at the same time minimizing the risks of being preyed upon. From this perspective it can be seen that the circadian clock or clocks within an organism are essential components of the apparatus for survival, and for carving out the ecological niche of the species. The niche may in fact be very narrow in a temporal sense, requiring very strict timing of specific activities during the day-night cycle. This is seen in the fact that many species have only a

few hours a day for foraging for food, and it is also seen in the exquisite coordination in timing of male and female activities at specific hours of the day or night, to bring about mating in many species.

The changing illumination that occurs during the day-night cycle is as important in entraining circadian rhythms in vertebrates as it is in invertebrates. In Chap. 17 the visual pathways involved in visual perception were discussed; here we will become acquainted with the pathways that mediate this other very important visual function. As far as is known, this function is an unconscious one; this reflects the fact that sensory information may have essential roles in nervous and body functions that are separate and distinct from their roles in perception, discrimination, and consciousness. Visually entrained circadian rhythms depend simply on levels of illumination rather than on the discrimination of any particular visual pattern.

The visual pathways that are involved in control of circadian rhythms in the vertebrate are shown in Fig. 26.5. The key pathway is made up of a small bundle of fibers which emerges from the optic nerve and terminates in a small group of cells at the anterior border of the hypothalamus. In the 1960's Curt Richter of John Hopkins showed that the anterior hypothalamic region was essential for circadian rhythms in rats. Then, in the early 1970's, a small cell group in this region was identified by independent studies of Robert Moore and V. B. Eichler at Chicago, and F. K. Stephen and Irving Zucker at Oregon. Because of its position just over the optic chiasm, this cell group is called the *suprachiasmatic nucleus* (SCN). A number of studies since then, using autoradiographic tracing methods, have permitted the anatomical identification of the *retinohypothalamic tract,* made up of retinal ganglion cell axons that terminate in the suprachiasmatic nucleus.

Many studies have provided evidence for the functional properties of the SCN in relation to circadian rhythms. For example, ablation of the SCN bilaterally results in disruption of circadian rhythms of

Table 26.2   Circadian rhythms disrupted by lesions of the suprachiasmatic nucleus in rats or hamsters

---

Locomotor activity (wheel running)
Drinking
Sleep–wake rhythms
Adrenal corticosteroid levels
Estrous periods and ovulation
Temperature
Pineal N-acetyltransferase

Adapted from Menaker et al. (1978)

many nervous and bodily functions; some of them are summarized in Table 26.2. The term "disruption" is carefully chosen; in general, the free-running rhythms are not totally abolished, and some degree of visual entrainment may persist. This has suggested that the other main subcortical structures in the visual pathway, the lateral geniculate nucleus and the superior colliculus, make some smaller contributions to the maintenance and entrainment of rhythms.

Fig. 26.5. Some pathways and related regions involved in the control of circadian rhythms in vertebrates. HAB, habenula; LGN, lateral geniculate nucleus; LH, lateral horn containing autonomic (sympathetic) motoneurons; MFB, medial forebrain bundle; SC, superior colliculus; SCG, superior cervical ganglion; SCN, suprachiasmatic nucleus; S–P–H, septal, preoptic, and hypothalamic regions.

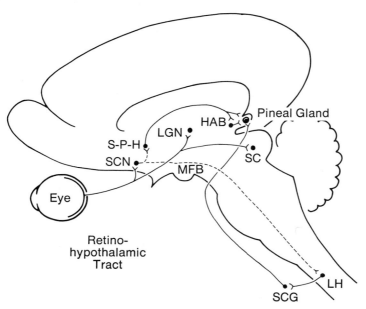

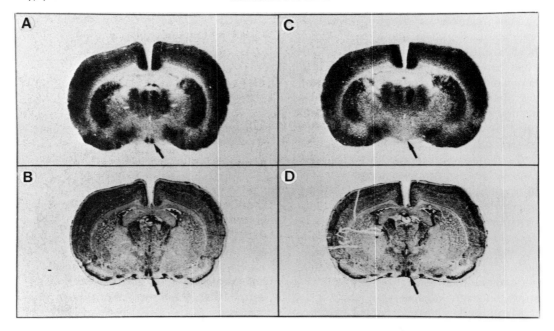

Fig. 26.6. Correlation of activity in the suprachiasmatic nuclei (SCN) with the day–night cycle in rats, using the 2-deoxyglucose (2DG) method. **A.** Autoradiogram of 14C-2DG patterns, showing localization of 2DG in the SCN during the day. **C.** Autoradiogram showing lack of 2DG localization in SCN at night. The circadian rhythm shown in A and C persisted even when the rats were maintained continuously in the dark. **B,D.** histological sections used for obtaining the autoradiograms in A and C, stained with cresyl violet, to confirm the location of the SCN. (From Schwartz and Gainer, 1977)

One of the clearest bits of evidence for the functions of the SCN has come from application of the 2DG method (Chap. 9). William Schwartz and Harold Gainer at the National Institutes of Health injected 14C-2DG into rats during either the day or night, and examined the autoradiographs of sections through the brain. As shown in Fig. 26.6, the SCN's showed a marked circadian rhythm, with low levels of 2DG uptake indistinguishable from neighboring regions during the night (when the rats, being nocturnal animals, were most active), and high levels during the day (when the rats mostly slept). Since 2DG uptake is a tag for the glucose uptake needed for energy metabolism (Chap. 9), the changes in uptake presumably reflect widely differing levels of activity in the SCN during the day-night cycle. How this is related to the regions of the nervous sys-

tem controlled by the SCN is not yet known.

In discussing visual control of circadian rhythms, we should also mention the *pineal gland*. It is, embryologically, an outpouching from the dorsal part of the diencephalon. In lower vertebrates (such as sharks, frogs, and lizards) it forms a third eye in the dorsal cranium, and functions to detect changes in levels of illumination. In birds it is present only as the pineal gland, which may retain some photoreceptive properties. However, in birds, and especially in mammals, it is more important as a gland that secretes a hormone called *melatonin*. Melatonin is one of the indole family, and arises from metabolism of serotonin (5-hydroxytryptamine). Synthesis of melatonin has a marked circadian rhythm, as shown in Fig. 26.7. The rate-limiting enzyme is N-acetyltransferase. In mammals (though not in birds), this enzyme is controlled by norepinephrine from the fibers of the sympathetic nervous system that innervate the pineal gland. The superior cervical ganglion, the source of the fibers, is believed to be influenced by fibers ultimately arising from the SCN, because lesions of either the SCN or the median forebrain bundle (containing fibers from the SCN) block the rhythm of N-acetyltransferase activity. The norepi-

nephrine is believed to act on a beta-adrenergic receptor, which in turn activates adenyl cyclase to increase the concentration of cyclic AMP, according to the sequence we discussed in Chap. 9. The linkage between the second-messenger cyclic AMP and the changes in N-acetyltransferase is not yet known.

We thus see that many body functions have circadian rhythms, and that these are entrained by the daily light-dark cycle,

Fig. 26.7. Circadian rhythms in indole metabolism in the rat pineal gland. The pathway from 5-hydroxytryptamine (serotonin) to melatonin is shown at left. The variations in concentrations of metabolites and activities of enzymes are shown at right, in relation to dark (shaded) and light periods of the day. (From Klein, 1974)

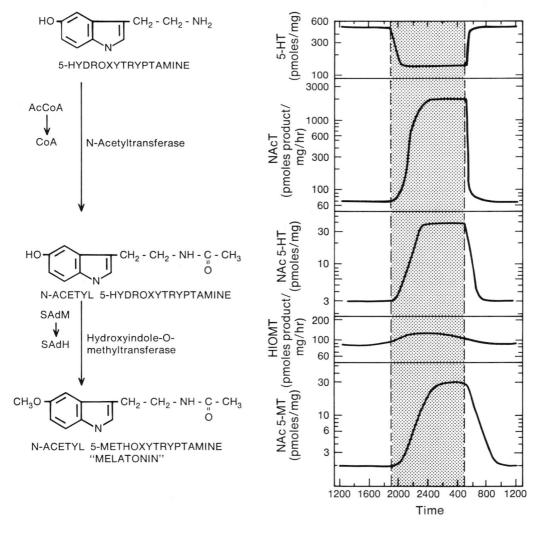

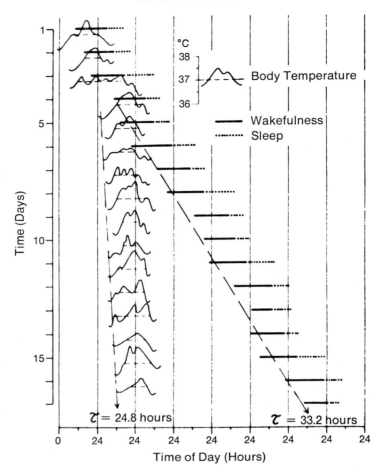

Fig. 26.8 Separate circadian rhythms of body (rectal) temperature and activity (sleep-wakefulness) of a human subject who lived in an isolation chamber without time cues for 17 days. Consecutive periods are charted below each other; precise 24-hour rhythms would appear exactly below each other; the two rhythms shown are longer than 24 hours, and therefore are successively displaced to the right. (From Aschoff, in Block and Page, 1978)

acting through the visual pathway. The most important center in this pathway is the SCN, but there are other centers that also contribute to maintaining and modulating the rhythms. From this and related work has emerged the concept that circadian systems are composed of *multiple oscillators*, each with properties to some extent specific and distinct from the others. The oscillators may not only have distinct properties but also different intrinsic rhythms. This was demonstrated in a clas-

sic experiment by Jürgen Aschoff of Germany in 1969, illustrated in Fig. 26.8. This was a human subject who lived in an isolation chamber, deprived of any time cues. After several days, he fell into a circadian sleep-wake cycle of approximately 33 hours, while his temperature cycle had a period of only about 25 hours. This suggests that there are two different oscillators controlling these functions, and that normally they are entrained to the single 24-hour rhythm of night and day. Multiple oscillators may be considered to form *distributed systems,* in the sense discussed in Chap. 25.

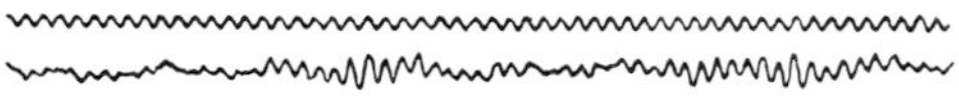

Fig. 26.9. Illustration from Berger's original report, showing recording of electrical waves (electroencephalogram) below, time marker above. (From Berger, in Brazier, 1970)

Waking and Sleeping

The circadian rhythms we have discussed so far concern variations in bodily functions and locomotor activity that provide a kind of baseline for the organism during the 24-hour day. During the period of activity we say we are "awake" and "aroused"; during the period of rest we fall into a state we refer to as "sleep". Within the awake period our levels of activity and alertness vary widely, as any student sitting a warm lecture room after eating a large lunch well knows! Similarly, sleep is a process that contains within it alternating periods of deep and light sleep, the light sleep correlated with dreaming and with a modified state of arousal. Our next task is to understand the neurobiological mechanisms which are responsible for the waking and sleeping states, and, within the sleeping state, for the periods of arousal and dreaming.

The Electroencephalogram

The study of sleep has drawn on many disciplines. A useful starting point for our discussion is the discovery that different patterns of brain activity are related to different levels of consciousness. Richard Caton of England had shown as early as 1875 that waves of electrical activity can be recorded from the surface of the brains of animals, but this finding lay unnoticed until the work of Hans Berger, of Germany, in the 1920's. Berger was a psychiatrist, and also served as Rector of the University of Jena. His main research interest was determining what he called the physical basis of psychic functions. In pursuing this interest, he was led to place electrodes on the scalp of human subjects and attempt to record the electrical activity of the brain. Although the electrical activity of the heart had been recorded from skin electrodes for many years, Berger's report in 1929 that electrical waves could be recorded from the scalp (the first published recording, obtained from Berger's young son, is reproduced in Fig. 26.9), and his interpretation that they represented the activity of the brain, were greeted with incredulity and even derision.

The evidence for the nervous origin of "Berger's waves" included the demonstration that the regular rhythms present in a subject resting quietly with eyes closed are replaced by low-amplitude random waves when the subject opens his eyes. Within a few years disbelief gave way to acceptance as many leading neurophysiologists, including Edgar Adrian of Cambridge, confirmed and extended the findings. In analogy with the electrocardiogram (ECG) recorded from the heart, "Berger's waves" came to be called the electroencephalogram (EEG).

These early studies established that the dominant rhythm in the resting subject is 8–13 cycles per sec, and is most prominent when the recording leads are over the occipital lobe of the brain (where the primary visual cortex is located; see Chap. 17). This is called the *alpha rhythm*. The replacement of these waves during arousal was termed *alpha blocking*. It was surmised that the alpha rhythm is due to populations of brain cells acting periodically in *synchrony,* and that the low-voltage fast waves during alpha blocking are due to *desynchronized* activity, as different cells become active in different ways during waking.

Subsequent work has enabled researchers to identify several types of EEG

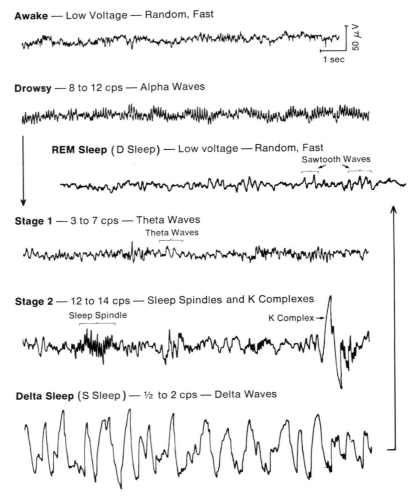

Fig. 26.10. Stages of sleep, as recorded in the electroencephalogram of the human. (Modified from Hauri, 1977)

rhythms and correlate them with different levels of awakeness and sleep. Some characteristic patterns are shown in Fig. 26.10. Note that the largest amplitude synchronous waves are present during deepest sleep. By EEG criteria, therefore, we refer to deep sleep as *S sleep* (for synchronous or slow-wave), and light sleep as *D sleep* (for desynchronous). A desynchronized EEG can also signify *arousal* or *waking*. Thus the EEG patterns are clues to fundamentally different levels of activity of the brain as they relate to waking and sleeping. Since observation of an animal is often not suf-

ficient to characterize its levels of consciousness, the EEG has served as an overall monitor of brain states, especially in animals subjected to various experimental procedures.

The cellular basis of the EEG has been the subject of intense study. The first interpretation was that the waves represent the envelope of summed impulses of many cells in the region of the cortex beneath a recording electrode. However, beginning in the 1950's, evidence began to accumulate for the importance of synaptic activity, and it was suggested that the waves represent mostly the contributions of summed synaptic potentials in the apical dendrites of the cortical cells.

Another line of investigation was aimed at elucidating the mechanism for generating the rhythms. A useful hypothesis to explain this was put forward by S. Andersson of Sweden and Per Andersen of Norway in 1968. They suggested that the cortical cells are driven by cells of the thalamic nuclei, and that the basic rhythm generator resides within the thalamic circuits.

A final question concerns how the activity of cells within the brain can give rise to electrical potentials detectable on the surface of the scalp. The explanation is somewhat similar to the interpretation of the electrocardiogram. The rhythmic contractions of the heart are brought about by a sequence of impulses in the muscle cells and conducting fibers. Each impulse

discharge is so powerful and so synchronous that it gives rise to electric current that not only flows through the heart itself, but also throughout the tissues of the body. A similar argument applies to the EEG waves, except that they are much smaller in amplitude (50 μV compared with 1 mV) and have faster and more irregular rhythms. These differences reflect the fact that the populations of cells giving rise to the EEG waves are much more diverse than the muscle cells in the heart.

Figure 26.11 represents an attempt to summarize these various lines of evidence regarding the cellular basis of the EEG waves. The thalamic nucleus below contains a rhythm generator which provides for rhythmic output of the thalamocortical cells projecting to the cortex. The rhythms may arise either by an intrinsic pacemaker property of cells within the nucleus, or from a network of excitatory and inhibi-

Fig. 26.11. Model for the synaptic organization underlying generation of EEG waves. The model depicts the local circuits of the thalamus, which generate a rhythmic output to the cortex. Within the cortex, the model depicts synchronous EPSPs (shaded) in the distal dendrites of cortical pyramidal cells P_1 and P_2. This generates pathways of electrical current flow as indicated by the arrows. The flow of extracellular current past electrodes 1 and 2 generates a voltage drop which is recorded as a potential difference between the two electrodes, resulting in the EEG.

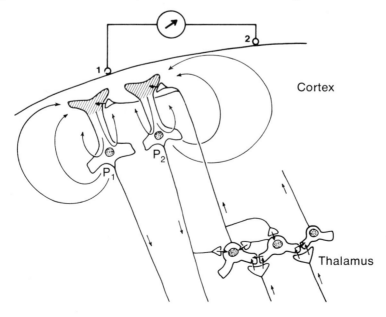

tory synaptic connections, along the lines we have discussed for other rhythm generators in the nervous system (see above, and Chap. 21). This brings about rhythmic synaptic depolarization (EPSPs) of the apical dendrites of cortical pyramidal cells. This gives rise to current flows within the dendrites (the electrotonic spread of the EPSPs toward the cell bodies, to affect impulse generation). It also gives rise to flows of extracellular current, some of which follow a return path just outside the dendrites. The more synchronous the activity and densely packed the dendrites, the more return current will be pushed out into the surrounding tissue, including the cranium and scalp. It is the difference between the amount of current flowing past recording electrode 1 compared with recording electrode 2 that is registered as a voltage deflection in the EEG. If pyramidal cell P1 and cell P2 are both active in synchrony, their currents will summate, and the waves will be large. This is the situation in S sleep, and also applies to alpha rhythms and other prominent waves. On the other hand, if the thalamic nucleus drives cell P1 in a way different from that of P2, the two cells will be asynchronous in their activity and their currents will not summate. This would be the situation during arousal or during D sleep.

This schema should be regarded as a working hypothesis for bringing together the main elements contributing to EEG waves, as an aid for understanding the application of the EEG to the study of waking and sleeping in the following section.

Early Studies of Sleep and Arousal

Like circadian rhythms, sleep invited no close study until very recently. The first experimental investigations of brain mechanisms were carried out by the Belgian neurologist Frederic Bremer, in the 1930's. He performed transections at many different levels of the brainstem in cats. Such lesions had been made for many years to produce different degrees of pa-

ralysis and hyperexcitability of spinal reflexes, but Bremer turned his attention to their effects on the head end of the animal. He found that with low transections, through the medulla and pons, a cat shows normal waking and sleeping cycles, but with high transections, through the midbrain, permanent somnolence ensues. These experiments pointed to the importance of the midbrain-pontine region for mechanisms of arousal.

Arousal and sleeping are behaviors involving the whole animal. As mentioned in the previous chapter, such behaviors require a central system with widespread connections. The first evidence for this came from experiments in which stimulating electrodes were placed in different parts of the thalamus. Stimulation of the specific sensory relay nuclei produced responses restricted to the appropriate sensory areas of the cortex. However, stimulation of other sites produced responses which were widespread throughout all cortical regions, and which increased in amplitude during repetitive stimulation. These sites were identified as the *nonspecific thalamic nuclei*, and the responses were termed *recruiting responses*.

The brainstem system and its linkage to the thalamic system were discovered by Guiseppi Moruzzi of Italy and Horace Magoun of Los Angeles in 1949. They mapped the brainstem using electrical shocks, and showed that high-frequency stimulation in the core of the brainstem produces arousal responses in the cortex. The sites of stimulation were correlated in general with the *reticular formation*, extending from the medulla to the diencephalon, as indicated in the well-known diagram of Fig. 26.12. Further experiments showed that lesions of the reticular formation produce a state of deep sleep, and that they also block the arousal that is usually produced by somatosensory stimulation. It was known that specific sensory fibers send collaterals to the brainstem reticular–nonspecific thalamus region. These studies thus suggested the

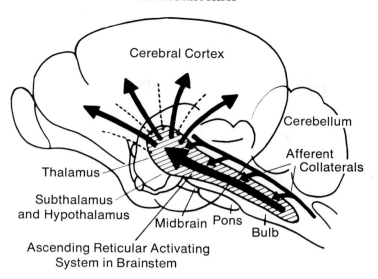

Fig. 26.12. Simplified diagram of ascending reticular activating system in the cat brain. (From Starzl et al., 1951)

very attractive hypothesis that arousal is mediated by the *reticular activating system,* stimulated by sensory collaterals, and activated through the nonspecific thalamic nuclei.

The idea that sleep is a simple state involving only a lack of arousal was soon disproven, however. In a classical study in 1953, Edward Aserinsky, a graduate student, and Nathaniel Kleitman, who had spent almost a lifetime amassing data on sleep, did a very simple experiment: they recorded the eye movements of sleeping subjects. This may seem a strange thing to do, but they explained the rationale at the outset of their paper in 1955:

One is led to suspect that the activity of the extra-ocular musculature and the lids might be peculiarly sensitive indicators of CNS changes associated with the sleep-wakefulness cycle. The disproportionately large cortical areas involved in eye movements, the well-defined secondary vestibular pathways to the extra-ocular nuclei, and the low innervation ratio of the eye muscles point to at least a quantitative basis for their reflection of general CNS activity. A more specific relationship . . . is suggested by anatomical proximity of the oculomotor nuclei

to a pathway involved in maintaining the waking state . . .

The reader may wish to review some of these points of anatomy in Chaps. 15, 17, and 23.

People had previously observed that the eyes rotate upwards and outwards, and that there are eye movements, during sleep. However, no one had studied the eye movements carefully and correlated them with the depth of sleep throughout an entire night. It is another of those experiments which could have been done, to some extent, by the ancients, but had to wait until modern times. Aserinsky and Kleitman found indeed that, after falling into deep sleep, subjects went through alternating periods of *light sleep* and *deep sleep;* that light sleep is associated with *rapid eye movements,* and that subjects awakened at these times reported that they had been *dreaming.* These findings showed that sleep contains alternating periods of light and deep sleep, and that light sleep is associated with a modified state of *arousal,* in which the heart rate increases, but skeletal muscles seem paralyzed. They showed that dreams occur during light sleep, and

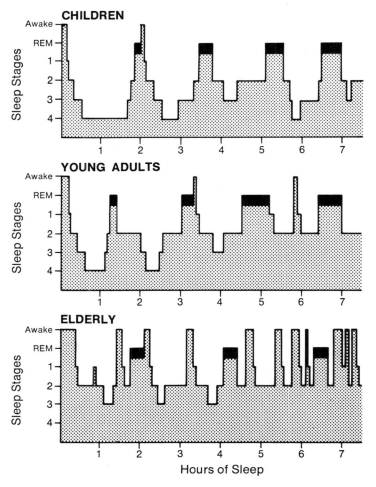

Fig. 26.13. Normal sleep cycles of humans at different ages. Dreaming episodes indicated by black bars. Note deeper sleep of children, more frequent periods of waking in the elderly. Sleep stages judged by EEG criteria. (From Kales and Kales, 1974)

suggested that "the rapid eye movements are directly associated with visual imagery in dreaming."

These findings were soon independently confirmed by William Dement, then at Chicago. Dement and Kleitman together then carefully characterized the different stages of the EEG and correlated them with the levels of sleep, as already indicated in Fig. 26.10. They could then follow the EEG patterns through a night of sleep, and relate them accurately to the occurrence of rapid eye movements, body move-

ments, and dreaming. A typical correlation is shown in Fig. 26.13. Of special interest are the findings that sleep always begins with an initial period of deep sleep, the deepest sleep of the night; that there then ensues a sequence of light and deep sleep, in which deep sleep becomes less deep and light sleep becomes more prolonged; and that rapid eye movements are invariably associated with light sleep and a stage I EEG. The terminology for light and deep sleep has evolved to reflect the associated changes in the EEG, eye movements, and other behavior. Thus, deep sleep is referred to as *S sleep* (for slow-wave EEG activity). Light sleep is referred to as *D sleep* (for desynchronized EEG activity; also for dreaming). Light sleep also has other names; *REM sleep* (for its associated rapid eye movements); *emergent stage I sleep* (because it emerges in the wake of deep sleep); and *paradoxical sleep* (because the EEG activity resembles that in the awake state, but the individual is hard to arouse).

Neuronal Systems Controlling Sleep and Waking

These studies in humans showed that sleep has a complicated internal structure which includes periods of arousal that share some properties with arousal during waking. It became clear that sleep involves more than a simple turning off of arousal, and likely involves the interaction of several neuronal subsystems. A great number of animal experiments (mostly in cats) ensued in the 1960's and 1970's in the attempt to identify these subsystems. Michael Jouvet in France, in particular, carried out an extensive series of studies on the effects of lesions of specific brainstem structures. These and other studies have combined assays for different transmitter substances, and the effects of transmitter agonists and antagonists. Other experiments have involved stimulation of specific brainstem and basal forebrain regions, and unit recordings from cells in these regions.

To review adequately all these studies would take an entire chapter in itself. Instead, we will summarize them in relation to Fig. 26.14. This diagram depicts the main regions that have been shown to be involved in either arousal or sleep. Let us review each region briefly.

Arousal Regions. High-frequency electrical stimulation is most effective in bringing about arousal and D sleep when applied to the *pontine reticular formation* (Pons, in Fig. 26.14) as in the experiments

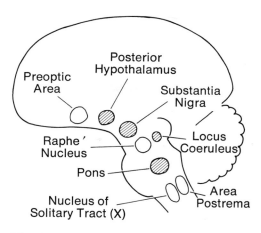

Fig. 26.14. Summary diagram showing regions of the brain that have been reported to be involved in controlling arousal or sleep. Arousal centers indicated by shaded areas, sleep centers by open areas.

of Moruzzi and Magoun. The most effective sites are in the gigantocellular tegmental fields (FTG), whose neurons branch widely throughout the brainstem. A second arousal area is the *locus coeruleus* (LC). As discussed in Chap. 25, this nucleus contains the noradrenergic neurons whose axons branch widely and innervate most of the forebrain, cerebellum, and spinal cord. Jouvet showed that destruction of the locus coeruleus selectively eliminates D sleep in cats. A third center related to arousal is the dopaminergic system of fibers arising in the *substantia nigra* (SN) and nearby midbrain. Lesions of these fibers in cats render the animals comatose. However, EEG arousal can still be elicited by sensory stimulation, and the effect of the lesions is not seen in rats, suggesting that the dopaminergic fibers may be more involved in the initiation of locomotor activity than with arousal itself. Finally, there is evidence that the *basal forebrain* also contributes to arousal mechanisms; stimulation in the hypothalamus is very effective in producing arousal, and ablations of the posterior hypothalamus, as first reported by Walle Nauta in Holland in 1946, produce prolonged

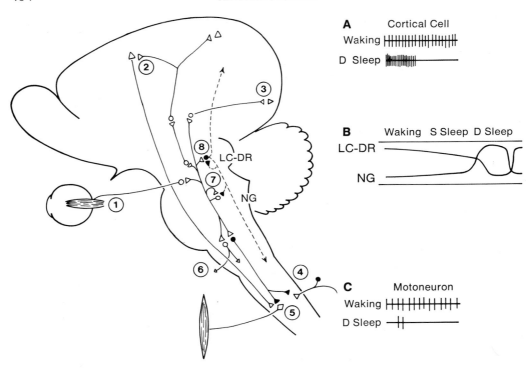

Fig. 26.15. Central circuits and neural activity believed to be involved in mediating D sleep in the cat. The key element is the giant reticular neuron of the pons (in nucleus gigantocellularis, NG). The numbers in the diagram indicate the systems which it controls or affects to bring about the state of D sleep. ①, phasic activation of motoneurons to the extraocular muscles produces rapid eye movements (REM); ②, generalized activation of the forebrain through the reticular formation produces bursting activity in forebrain neurons (see recordings in **A**); this may be associated with the production of dream images; ③, phasic activation of the visual pathway by means of PGO spikes (pons–lateral geniculate–occipital cortex) possibly contributes to visual imagery; ④, inhibition of sensory input raises the threshold for arousal; ⑤, inhibition of motoneurons raises the reflex threshold and suppresses internally generated movements by cortical and brainstem motor centers (see recordings in **C**), ⑥, activation and inhibition of various brainstem neurons produces: phasic fine movements of facial muscles (possibly expressing the emotional content of dreams); tonic autonomic contraction of the bladder and rectal sphincters; intermittent bursts of activity in the cardiovascular, respiratory, and other parts of the autonomic nervous system.

The cyclic relation between waking, S sleep, and D sleep is believed to involve interactions between the NG neurons and neurons of the locus coeruleus (LC) and dorsal raphé (DR). In the model of Hobson and McCarley, NG neurons are reexcitatory to themselves ⑦, and they also excite LC–DR neurons ⑧. The LC–DR neurons are in turn inhibitory to themselves, and to the NG neurons. With appropriate time delays in the onset and buildup of activity in these two neuronal populations, the activity in the two populations alternates in relation to the different stages of waking and sleeping, as indicated in the graph in **B**. (From Hobson and McCarley, 1977, and other sources)

somnolence. However, these effects may be due in part to the fibers of the median forebrain bundle, particularly the fibers in this bundle which connect brainstem nuclei and the forebrain.

Sleep Regions. A number of studies have pointed to the importance of the serotonergic cells of the brainstem *raphé nuclei* in mediating deep sleep. Destruction of the raphé nuclei produces cats that cannot sleep (i.e., insomnia). A parallel pharmacological experiment consists of blocking serotonin synthesis with the drug p-chlorophenylalanine (PCPA), which inhibits tryptophan hydroxylase. This also produces insomnia, an effect which is alleviated by administration of serotonin. A second brainstem region is the *nucleus of the solitary tract*, which receives sensory fibers from the taste buds of the tongue (Chap. 12) as well as other visceral inputs. Stimulation of this region promotes a synchronization of the EEG. A related region is the *area postrema*. This area is special in that it has no blood-brain barrier, and thus can be stimulated directly by substances in the blood; toxic substances that enter the bloodstream elicit vomiting by acting on the cells in this region. Serotonin applied to this area modulates the influence of the nucleus of the solitary tract on sleep. The mechanisms of these two regions are not understood, but they may mediate some of the effects of feeding, metabolism, and visceral activities in inducing sleep. Finally, in the *basal forebrain*, lesions of the *preoptic region* produce insomnia, and electrical stimulation of this region induces EEG synchrony and drowsiness leading to sleep. Bremer in 1970 showed that preoptic stimulation reduces the arousal induced by stimulation of the reticular activating system.

Neuronal Mechanisms: a Synthesis

The foregoing account is far too brief to indicate the numerous controversies that have arisen in attempting to assess the contributions of each of these regions to the control of sleeping and waking. At the very least we can say that the regions depicted in Fig. 26.14 form a distributed system involved in this control. In this system, the three brainstem centers, each using a specific transmitter, seem to be of special importance. It is attractive to suggest, as Jouvet and others have done, that arousal is associated with activity in the noradrenergic fibers, and deep sleep is associated with activity in serotonergic fibers. A coherent proposal to explain how these centers interact with each other has been put forward by Allan Hobson and Robert McCarley at Harvard. As shown in Fig. 26.15, the cholinergic NG cells are thought to provide the main rhythmic driving force. During waking LC cells are active; they activate the cortex, but suppress the NG cells through inhibitory synapses.

It is important to realize that this system has its effects not only on the thalamocortical system, but on other brainstem centers and on the spinal cord as well. This reminds us that sleep involves not only control of consciousness, but also sensory and motor pathways. The diagram in Fig. 26.15 summarizes how pervasive these controls are during just one phase of sleep, the D phase.

REFERENCES

Block, G. D. and T. L. Page. 1978. Circadian pacemakers in the nervous system. In *Ann. Rev. Neurosci. 1:* 19–34.

Brazier, M. A. B. 1970. *The Electrical Activity of the Nervous System*. London: Pitman.

Hauri, P. 1977. *The Sleep Disorders*. Kalamazoo, Mich.: Upjohn Co.

Hobson, J. A. and R. W. McCarley. 1977. The brain as a dream state generator: an activation-synthesis hypothesis of the dream process. *Am. J. Psychiat. 134:* 1335–1348.

Jacklet, J. W. 1976. Dye marking neurons in the eye of *Aplysia*. *Comp. Biochem. Physiol. 55A:* 373–377.

Jacklet, J. W. 1981. Circadian timing by endogenous oscillators in the nervous system: toward cellular mechanisms. *Biol. Bull. 160:* 199–227.

Jacklet, J. W., L. Schuster, and C. Rolerson. 1982. Electrical activity and structure of retinal cells of the *Aplysia* eye: I. secondary neurones. *J. Exp. Biol.* (in press).

Kales, A. and J. D. Kales. 1974. Sleep disorders. *New Engl. J. Med. 290:* 487–499.

Kandel, E. R. 1976. [Chap. 2].

Kaplan, E. and R. B. Barlow Jr. 1980. Circadian clock in *Limulus* brain increases response and decreases noise of retinal photoreceptors. *Nature 286:* 393–395.

Klein, D. C. 1974. Circadian rhythms and indole metabolism in the rat pineal gland. In *The Neurosciences: Third Study Program* (ed. by F. O. Schmitt and F. G. Worden). Cambridge, Mass: MIT Press. pp. 509–515.

Menaker, M., J. S. Takahaski, and A. Eskin. 1978. The physiology of circadian pacemakers. In *Ann. Rev. Physiol. 40:* 501–526.

Pittendrigh, C. S. 1974. Circadian oscillation in cells and the circadian organization of multicellular systems, in Schmitt and Worden (op. cit.), pp. 437–458.

Schwartz, W. J. and H. Gainer. 1977. Suprachiasmatic nucleus: use of 14C-labeled deoxyglucose uptake as a functional marker. *Science 197:* 1089–91.

Starzl, T. E., C. W. Taylor, and H. Magoun. 1951. Collateral afferent excitation of the reticular formation of the brain stem. *J. Neurophysiol. 14:* 479–496.

Strumwasser, F. 1974. Neuronal principles organizing periodic behaviors. In *The Neurosciences: Third Study Program* (ed. by F. O. Schmitt and F. G. Worden). Cambridge, Mass: MIT Press. pp. 459–478.

Additional Reading

Andersen, P. and S. A. Andersson. 1968. *Physiological Basis of the Alpha Rhythm.* New York: Appleton-Century-Crofts.

Aserinsky, E. and N. Kleitman. 1953. Two types of ocular motility occurring during sleep. *J. Appl. Physiol. 8:* 1–10.

Dement, W. and N. Kleitman. 1957. Cyclic variations in EEG during sleep and their relation to eye movements, body motility, and dreaming. *Electroencephal. Clin. Neurophysiol. 9:* 673–690.

Flicker, C., R. W. McCarley, and J. A. Hobson. 1981. Aminergic neurons: state control and plasticity in three model systems. *Cell. Mol. Neurobiol. 1:* 123–166.

Hartman, E. L. 1973. *The Functions of Sleep.* New Haven: Yale.

Jouvet, M. 1974. Monoaminergic regulation of the sleep-waking cycle in the cat. In *The Neurosciences: Third Study Program* (ed. by F. O. Schmitt and F. G. Worden). Cambridge, Mass: MIT Press. pp. 499–508.

27
Visceral Brains: Feeding

Among the many types of behavior in which animals engage, two in particular stand out: feeding and mating. Feeding is necessary for the survival of the individual organism, and mating is necessary for the reproduction and propagation of the species. A good proportion of other types of behavior, such as predation and flight, or grooming and courtship, have their significance as preludes or consequences of these two fundamental activities.

One of the basic distinctions between animal and plant life is that animals procure their food and find their mates by *active* rather than passive means. Thus, much of the sensory apparatus is tuned to receiving stimuli from sources of food or mates, and much of the motor apparatus is adapted for moving the animal to those sources and ingesting food or copulating with a mate. The motor behavior thus has two phases, an *appetitive* phase, during which the animal has an appetite for something and seeks to find it, and a *consummatory* phase, in which the goal is achieved and the appetite is satisfied. These phases, in fact, can be recognized in even the simplest kinds of motor acts; Sherrington, for example, in studying the scratch reflex, noted that the cat first brings the leg to the site that itches (the appetitive phase) and then carries out the scratching (the consummatory phase). In the cases of complex behaviors like feeding and mating, the sensory and motor mechanisms for the two phases are of course quite different, and the temporal sequence may be quite prolonged. Although it is impossible to generalize adequately across all species, the sequence usually includes such activities as waiting or search, collection or capture, acceptance or rejection, and finally ingestion.

Ingested food typically enters an intestinal tract, where it is digested and the nutrient substances absorbed into the bloodstream, in order to satisfy the needs of the body for hydration, mineral balance, and nutrition. These factors are kept in balance within the body by homeostatic mechanisms which maintain the "constancy of the internal milieu", one of the basic principles of body function first formulated by the great French physiologist, Claude Bernard, in the nineteenth century. The ingested foodstuffs provide the raw materials and sources of energy for these mechanisms. The whole sequence of feeding, from search to absorption, is under close control at every stage by a combination of nervous and hormonal mechanisms, and the parts of the central nervous system that mediate this control may be referred to as the "visceral nervous system" or "visceral brain". The activities of the visceral brain are coordinated with the rest of the nervous system by a variety of centers which, in vertebrates, is called the limbic system. The relations between these systems have been indicated in Chap. 3, and will be discussed further in subsequent chapters in this section.

The fact that feeding is crucial for survival and requires a complicated series of actions means that each link in the chain is subject to the forces of natural selection. Each link can be adjusted for the greatest efficiency and advantage for a particular species, and the whole chain can undergo endless permutations in different species. Therefore, when we study feeding, we are dealing with nervous mechanisms that, perhaps more than any others in the brain, most directly and vividly reflect the forces of evolution acting in the daily life of the animal.

The diversity of nervous mechanisms, which we have so often noted, is therefore nowhere more evident than in the control of feeding behavior. Animals have explored a wide range of food sources, and have devised the most clever strategies for catching and consuming them. In this chapter we will consider examples that have been particularly well studied, and

illustrate some of the more general principles of nervous control by central systems.

INVERTEBRATES

In introductory biology, we learn that the great chain of life begins with the simple plantlike microorganisms called phytoplankton, unicellular algae that float in the sea, and are capable of capturing the energy of light and using it to manufacture organic compounds, the process called photosynthesis. The phytoplankton are present in enormous numbers in most bodies of water, and form what has been called an aquatic pasture. The simplest animals, the amoebalike zooplankton, feed on this pasture. The higher animals, the metazoans, thus have three possible sources of food. One is the nutrient-rich fluids secreted or contained within other organisms; these animals are called *fluid-feeders*. Another is the microorganisms of the sea; animals that feed on them are said to be *microphagous*. Alternatively, larger animals may feed on each other, in which case they are said to be *macrophagous* (see Table 27.1).

One of the most effient methods for microphagous feeding is to let seawater flow through the animal so that the plankton can be filtered out. This method is appropriately called filter feeding. In many invertebrates the microorganisms are trapped in secretions and moved to the

Table 27.1 Types of feeding by animals

Fluid feeding	Microphagy (small particles)	Macrophagy (large particles)
Bacterial Planktonic Scavenging (some nematodes) Predatory (some arachnids; some insects, such as flies and mosquitoes)	Filter feeding (some sponges; some arthropods) Deposit feeding (some annelid worms)	Herbivores (cows, horses) Carnivores (predators such as many molluscs, arthropods, vertebrates)

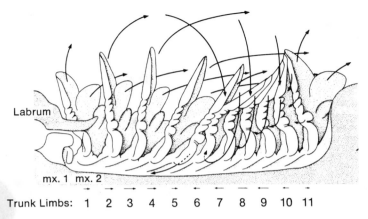

Labrum

mx. 1 mx. 2

Trunk Limbs: 1 2 3 4 5 6 7 8 9 10 11

Fig. 27.1. Currents of water created by swimming and feeding movements of the swimmerets of a crustacean *Branchinella*. Arrows below show direction and relative strength of limb movements; in this example, limb 5 is just completing its backward stroke, while limb 6 is just beginning to move forward. Hair-like setae on surface of limbs are not shown. The motor mechanisms controlling swimmeret movements are discussed in Chap. 21. (From Cannon, in Barrington, 1979)

digestive tract by ciliary motion. In small aquatic arthropods, which generally lack cilia, filter feeding is achieved by an ingenious use of the limbs. As shown in Fig. 27.1, the swimming motions of the limbs create currents which cause the water to circulate through the limbs and over the opening of the mouth, before passing backwards to propel the animal forward. The food is trapped by fine hairlike setules, and then passed forward to be filtered out by the mucus-covered setae around the mouth.

This provides a very nice example of how motor mechanisms serve multiple uses. We previously described the neural mechanisms for generating the orderly beating of the crustacean swimmerets in Chap. 21. This metachronal rhythm is equally efficient for moving food and for propelling the animal. As E. J. W. Barrington has pointed out

. . . the mechanisms involved (in filter feeding) are unexcelled for the precision and beauty of their adaptive organization. . . . The animal economically employs the limbs simultaneously for feeding as well as locomotion, while their delicate structure enables them also to serve for respiratory exchange.

Stomatogastric Nervous System of the Lobster

Filter feeding is widespread among small aquatic animals, especially crustacea and molluscs. It has been estimated that an oyster may filter up to 40 liters of water in an hour, from which it obtains less than a tenth of a gram of nutrients. Larger animals obviously need more ample sources of nourishment, and many species acquire this by consuming other large animals. This sets up one of the fundamental polarizations of animal life—the predator and its prey. Successful predation requires adequate size, speed, strength, and other capabilities, and therefore has been one of the main pressures leading to complex behaviors mediated by complex nervous systems. Since animals do not particularly enjoy being eaten, the same pressures work on animals that are prey. The behaviors must be almost evenly matched, in order to maintain the ecological balance that is necessary between predators and their food supply.

Feeding on large bodies is called macrophagy. It is well-exemplified by our old friend, the lobster, and its freshwater

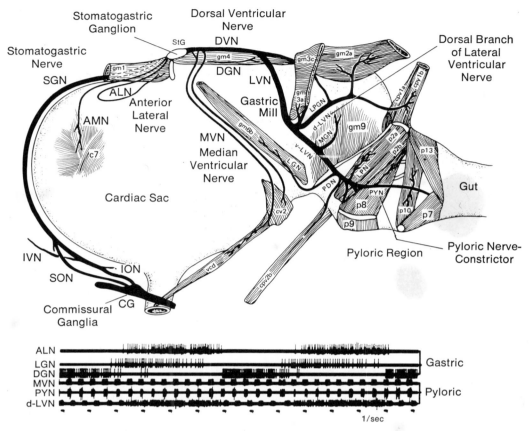

Fig. 27.2. The main regions of the lobster stomatogastric system, together with their nerve supply and some of the muscles. Recordings from nerves labeled in the diagram are shown in the traces below. These are extracellular recordings in the deafferented stomatogastric ganglion of impulse activity in motoneurons supplying their respective nerves. (Modified from Selverston, 1976)

cousin, the crayfish. The claws of the lobster are specialized for grasping, cutting, and crushing prey, and bringing the pieces to the mouth. The food is thus highly variable in its composition, containing many hard parts as well as soft tissue. The foregut is adapted for dealing with this mixture of ingested material. As shown in Fig. 27.2, the stomach is divided into three parts. Foodstuff passing through the esophagus first enters the *cardiac sac*, which is mainly a large storage area. From here it passes to the *gastric mill*, which contains three calcified ossicles which function like sharp teeth. Muscles of the gastric mill wall move the teeth, to grind,

macerate, and chew the food. In this way, the gastric mill functions like the vertebrate jaw. The food then passes to the *pyloric region*, where it is further churned by muscular contractions, squeezed between platelike ossicles, and subjected to the actions of digestive enzymes, before passing into the remainder of the gut where the nutrients are absorbed into the bloodstream and the waste materials are eliminated.

The muscles of the gastric mill and pyloric region are under control of nerves that originate in neurons of the *stomatogastric ganglion*. This ganglion has an unusual location, being plastered against the inside wall of the nearby ophthalmic artery that runs to the eye. There seems to be no special significance to this location, other than that it is near the stomach. Experimentally, the ganglion can be exposed by making a slit in the artery from above, removing the wall beneath the ganglion, and dissecting away the periganglionic sheath. Under the dissecting microscope the nerve cell bodies can be seen to be quite large, between 40 and 90 μm in diameter; like so many invertebrate ganglia, many of the cells are identifiable by size and location, and can be recorded from using intracellular electrodes.

The attractiveness of this preparation for studying the nervous control of the stomach rhythms was recognized by Don Maynard, and has been exploited by Allan Selverston and his colleagues at San Diego to the extent that it is one of the best understood of all invertebrate neuronal systems. The synaptic connections between neurons within the ganglion have already been mentioned in Chap. 5; as discussed there, the connections include microcircuits between neighboring dendrites that are similar to those seen in other systems, including the vertebrate retina and olfactory bulb.

There are two main rhythms in the stomach, related to the gastric mill and the pyloric region. Recordings from the nerves to the gastric mill muscles show slow prolonged impulse discharges lasting several seconds, and occurring at intervals of 6–8 seconds. The discharges to antagonist muscles controlling the teeth alternate with each other, as shown in Fig. 27.2. In contrast, the nerves to pyloric muscles fire in briefer bursts of impulses, at intervals of less than a second.

The main focus of experimental work has been on understanding the nature of these rhythms. With regard to the *gastric mill,* it has been found that there are 10 motoneurons and 2 interneurons within the stomatogastric ganglion that are involved in generating the slow rhythm of impulse firing and muscle contractions. In

completely isolated ganglia, the rhythmic firing is usually abolished, indicating that it is normally dependent on excitatory input from sensory fibers. Intracellular analysis has enabled the main functional connections between the 12 cells to be identified. No spontaneous bursting cell has been found, suggesting that the gastric rhythms are a property of the whole network, of the type that we discussed in Chap. 21.

The neural system controlling the *pyloric muscles* is composed of 13 motoneurons and one interneuron. Two cells innervate the pyloric dilator muscles, and are called PD neurons. These show a prominent spontaneous bursting discharge. As shown in Fig. 27.3, when a PD cell is blocked by hyperpolarizing injected current, other cells, such as the pyloric neurons (PY) to which it is connected, are released from rhythmic driving. In contrast, when a PY cell is blocked, there is no effect on the PD neuron. These and many other results have indicated that PD is an endogenous burster, that drives the rhythm of the other motoneurons. A circuit diagram to explain these results is shown in Fig. 27.3. This is a much simplified circuit, in which two cell types, PD and AB, are combined because they are tightly linked by electrical synapses. Note the prevalence of inhibitory synapses, which, as in so many other systems we have studied, provide the main basis for the rhythmic alternations of activity in the different cell populations. Thus, the same principles of organization of pacemaker systems that we discussed in Chap. 21 for locomotion are also applicable to the pyloric rhythms of the stomatogastric system.

Feeding in the Blowfly

One of the best understood species with respect to feeding behavior is the blowfly. Taste receptors in the blowfly have been discussed in Chap. 12, and the motor control of the proboscis was discussed in

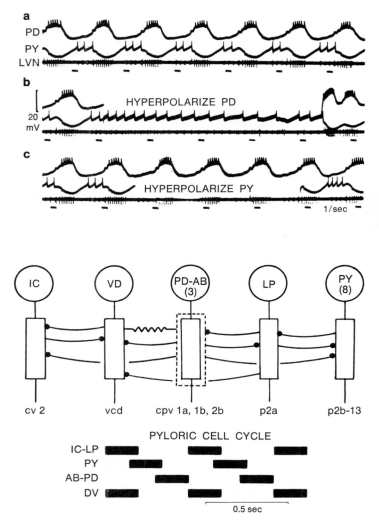

Fig. 27.3. *Upper traces,* dominant role of PD cells in maintaining the pyloric rhythm is shown in these intracellular recordings from a PD and PY cell, together with extracellular recording from output fibers in the LVN. **a.** PD and PY show normal alternating activity, characteristic of the isolated ganglion. **b.** hyperpolarizing current injection into PD blocks PD discharge, converts PY from rhythmic tonic discharge, and eliminates output in LVN. **c.** hyperpolarization of PY blocks PY discharge, but has no effect on PD or LVN rhythmic activity. *Below,* neuronal circuit for generating the pyloric rhythm. The large circles represent neuronal cell bodies; the rectangles represent the combined neuropil branches of each cell. Black dots are chemical inhibitory synapses, and the resistor symbol is an electrotonic junction. The dashed line around the PD–AB cells indicates that this group is electrotonically coupled and functions as a unit. The muscles innervated by each cell are indicated at bottom, and can be seen in Fig. 27.2. The symbol "F" signifies a functional connection not yet proven to be monosynaptic. The sequential firing pattern for the bursts of activity generated by these neurons is shown in the diagram at bottom. For the synaptic organization of the PD cell within the stomatogastric ganglion, see Fig. 5.11. (From Selverston, 1976)

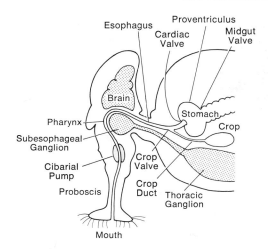

Fig. 27.4. The digestive system of the blowfly. (Modified from Dethier, 1976)

Chap. 23. The blowfly obtains all its nutrients by sucking them in through the labellum (see Fig. 27.4). The pharynx is lined with muscles which form what is called the cibarial pump. The ingested fluid is moved through the pharynx and into the esophagus by rhythmic contractions of the cibarial muscles. These contractions are controlled by a neuronal rhythm generator located in the brain. The food passes by peristalsis from the esophagus into both the midgut and the crop, a storage region. As food is absorbed from the midgut into the blood, it is replenished by movement of stored fluid from the crop through the crop valve and cardiac values into the midgut.

What are the mechanisms that initiate feeding behavior? This has been studied in flies that are starved for several days. This deprivation generally enhances the locomotor activity of the fly, and it engages in bursts of activity (flying about in search of food) alternating with periods of rest. This is presumed to represent a balance between maximizing the chances of finding food and the need to conserve the dwindling energy stores. When food, such as a sugar solution, is encountered, excitation of chemoreceptors on the legs (tarsae) stimulates proboscis extension, and exci-

tation of chemoreceptors on the labellum of the proboscis stimulates sucking movements. These chemosensory stimuli are believed to be the sole excitatory inputs driving feeding behavior.

What are the mechanisms involved in terminating feeding? In order to identify these factors, many experiments have been carried out in which nerves to different parts of the gut have been cut, and in which nutrients have been placed directly in different parts of the gut or removed through artificial fistulae. The outcome of these experiments appears to be that feeding is inhibited by activity arising from three factors: first, the amount of peristalsis in the foregut, as sensed by stretch receptors in the gut wall; second, distention of the crop, as sensed by stretch receptors in the crop wall; and third, the amount of locomotor activity mediated by limb motoneurons in the thoracic ganglion. These factors have the effect of raising the central threshold for incoming chemosensory stimuli, so that they become less and less effective in eliciting proboscis extension and sucking. Some of these factors, and their interrelations, are indicated in Fig. 27.5.

The surprising result emerging from these studies has been summarized by Vincent Dethier in the following way:

> At no stage in ingestion does the nutritive value of food regulate intake. . . . The initiation of feeding depends on stimulating properties; the termination of feeding depends on mechanoreceptors; the emptying of the crop is regulated by osmotic properties. In the laboratory each one of these can be varied independently of the other and of caloric value. In nature the different properties tend to be correlated.

VERTEBRATES

Vertebrates show interesting similarities and differences in their feeding behavior among various species. Fish, for example, move about in a medium that contains their food; thus, their feeding is more or

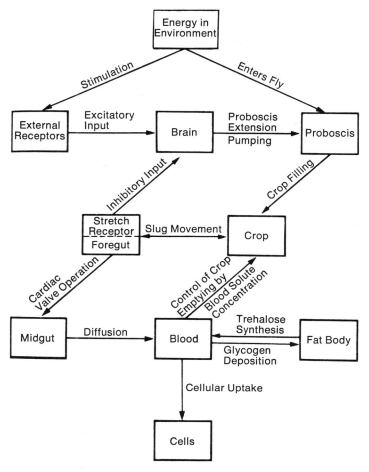

Fig. 27.5. Multiple mechanisms for regulating feeding behavior and metabolism in the blowfly. (From Gelperin, in Dethier, 1976)

less continuous. Some terrestrial animals have similar habits; herbivores like cows, for example, have their food literally under their noses all the time, and spend much of their waking hours ingesting or chewing. The cow munching its way through its terrestrial pasture seems rather similar to a crustacean or mollusc filter-feeding on its aquatic pasturage. In the case of the cow, the almost continuous eating makes it difficult to characterize its feeding behavior in terms of *meal size* and *meal frequency,* two of the variables we are most familiar with in our own daily lives. Nor does a third variable, *food preferences* or *aversions,* appear to be very rel-

evant; it seems that the cow, who consumes enormous quantities of plant material in the course of a day, may simply dilute any noxious or poisonous plants to the level of harmlessness, without needing to pick and choose the way we do. Like many other terrestrial animals, especially carnivores, humans eat only intermittently, and meal size, meal frequency, and food preferences are important variables in our eating habits; indeed, they largely determine the rhythm of daily life.

Among vertebrates, no species has been studied more intensively with regard to all aspects of feeding behavior than the laboratory rat; in fact, the studies of the rat probably outnumber those of all other species combined. Much of this is due to the possible implications of the rat as a model for mammals in general, and humans in particular. In the practical realm, the laboratories of drug companies and government agencies test rats for the possible harmful effects of food additives or substitutes, under the premise that the effects will be relevant to humans. At the research level, psychologists for almost a century have focused their concepts (and controversies) about drives and motivation on behavioral studies of the rat, much of it in relation to feeding. Over the past 30 years, neuroscientists have exerted considerable efforts to identify the main nervous pathways and mechanisms involved. We will summarize some of this evidence first, and then discuss some implications for motivated behavior.

Feeding in the Infant Rat

Although most attention has traditionally been given to the adult, a new field of interest concerned with the development of feeding in the infant rat has emerged in recent years. This work is significant for several reasons. First, it has shown that the infant is not simply a small adult; it is a very special creature, living in a very special world, during the first few weeks of life. Second, the change from the infant to the adult pattern gives insight into processes of development and learning that provide the basis for adult feeding behavior and their neuronal mechanisms. Third, suckling at a mammary gland is the defining characteristic of all the animals we call mammals, and is therefore important for understanding this class of animals. Finally, studies in subprimates may contribute to better understanding of suckling and infant–mother relations that are so crucial in the first days and weeks of human development.

The baby rat, called a pup, is born after about three weeks gestation. At birth the mother occupies herself with a complex series of interrelated behaviors that create the transitional environment from womb to outside world. She consumes the placenta, licks her ventrum and its nipples, and also vigorously licks the infants. Her behavior has two main functions. It imprints her nipples with olfactory substances in her saliva, and it serves to warm, protect, and arouse the infants. The aroused infants search for and find the nipples, and begin sucking.

The act of sucking involves an extraordinary close relation between mother and infant. As shown in Fig. 27.6, the nipple fills the mouth, and milk is ejected deep into the pharynx. Although the muscles for posture and locomotion are weak and poorly coordinated, the facial and neck muscles involved in suckling are well developed at birth; it is, in fact, the one coordinated motor act that the infant can perform on its environment. In some mammals the suckling contractions are so strong that the infants remain attached despite locomotion of the mother, an obvious advantage if the mother has to flee from danger. The rat pup suckles virtually continuously throughout the first two weeks of life, and intermittently for the next week or two until weaning occurs. It could well be asserted that suckling must be among the most intimate and sustained (to say nothing of beneficial) relations between two organisms to be found in the animal world.

The odor link in suckling behavior. The close proximity of the nose to the mouth suggests that the sense of smell may be an important factor in suckling, and this has been found to be the case in many species. Ablation of the olfactory bulbs at birth in rats and kittens eliminates suckling. This suggests that the infants must be able to smell some odor in order to suckle. Following this lead, Elliott Blass and Martin Teicher at Johns Hopkins University washed the nipples of lactating mothers and found that this too eliminated suckling of the nipples by the pups. Dabbing

A. RAT PUP
B. HUMAN INFANT

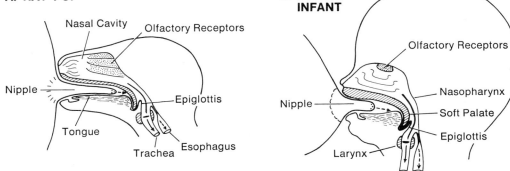

Fig. 27.6. Suckling in the rat pup (A) and in the human infant (B). Note that in both cases, the tip of the soft palate drops behind the back of the tongue and is held there by the epiglottis. This permits air flow between nose and trachea, while milk passes laterally around the epiglottis and into the esophagus. By this means, both the rat pup and the human infant can breathe while suckling. The high position of the larynx is maintained in the adult rat, an obligate nose breather. In the human, during infancy and childhood the pharynx grows in length and the larynx descends to its position in the neck in the adult. This elongation of the pharynx is crucial to our ability to form the different vowel sounds in human speech, as discussed in Chap. 24. (Diagram A based in part on J. Alberts, P. E. Pedersen, J. Laitman, and E. S. Crelin, personal communications; B adapted from Crelin, 1976)

the washing fluid back on the nipples reinstated suckling, as did samples of the amniotic fluid and the mother's saliva, but not saliva of virgin females. This suggests the presence of a substance in the saliva that is dependent on the hormonal status of the mother. After suckling has begun, the pups' own saliva contains the odor cue necessary to maintain suckling.

The vital link in establishing and maintaining suckling in the rat pup is thus an odor cue on the nipple. In order to analyze the kind of activity in the olfactory pathway that mediates this response, we injected radioactively labeled 2-deoxyglucose into suckling pups and obtained autoradiographs of the olfactory bulbs by the Sokoloff method (see Chap. 9). As shown in Fig. 27.7, the most characteristic activity pattern in these olfactory bulbs was a small focus at the extreme dorsomedial margin of the main olfactory bulb, near its junction with the accessory olfactory bulb. Closer examination revealed that this is a site where the usual small, round glomeruli of the bulb are replaced

by a large, irregular complex of glomeruli, an anatomically distinct region that had not previously been recognized.

These experiments have therefore suggested the hypothesis that the odor cue essential for suckling is processed by a distinct part of the olfactory pathway. There is an analogy in this regard with the macroglomerular complex in the antennal lobes of insects, which is involved in processing male responses to female sexual attractant odors (Chap. 28); in both cases, a crucial olfactory-mediated behavior appears to have its own "labeled line" to the brain.

Mother–infant interactions. Although the rat pup suckles continuously in the first two weeks, it does not receive milk continuously; milk is ejected from the nipple only intermittently. This process is called *milk letdown.* It is under control of the hypothalamus. Neurons in the paraventricular and supraoptic nuclei synthesize *oxytocin,* an undecapeptide hormone (see Chap. 9) and transport it through their axons to their terminals in the posterior lobe of the pituitary. Single-cell recordings from PV cells in lactating mother rats show a background spontaneous discharge. Periodically, the neurons fire bursts of impulses, followed some 10–15 seconds later by ejection of milk (see Fig. 27.8). These results indicate that sensory inputs to the PV cells lead to depolarization and in-creased impulse generation; that the impulses invade the terminals in the posterior pituitary and cause release of oxytocin stored there; and that oxytocin acts on the smooth muscle of the mammary gland after a delay due to the time for circulation of the hormone through the blood circulation, from pituitary to nipple. Parts of this circuit are depicted in Fig. 27.8.

Fig. 27.7. Mapping of 2-deoxyglucose uptake in the olfactory bulb of the suckling rat pup. **A.** This 10-day-old pup was injected with 14C-2-deoxyglucose and allowed to suckle for 45 minutes. The autoradiogram (2) shows a focus at one site in the olfactory bulb; the histological correlation (1,3) shows that the site is a modified glomerulus adjacent to the accessory olfactory bulb. **B.** Computerized image analysis of an autoradiogram of 2DG uptake in the olfactory bulbs of another suckling rat pup, age 6 days. Note the bilateral foci (arrows), shown by histological correlation to be located in the modified glomerular complex. **C.** Higher-power view of the modified glomerular region in the olfactory bulb of a 12-day-old rat pup. Arrows indicate two glomeruli within the modified complex. Accessory olfactory bulb (AOB) is to the left, layers of the main olfactory bulb are to the right. Abbreviations: G, granule layer; M, mitral cell body layer; EPL, external plexiform layer; GL, glomerular layer. Bouin's fixation, stained with cresyl violet. Bar is 85 μm. (A from Teicher et al., 1980; B,C from Greer et al., 1982)

A. 10 DAY OLD-SUCKLING

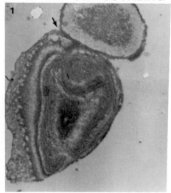
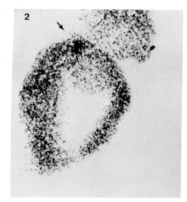
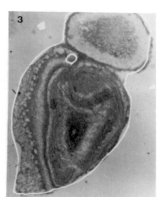

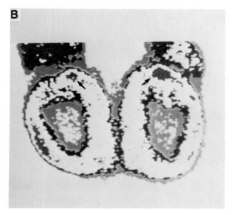
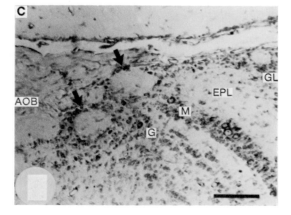

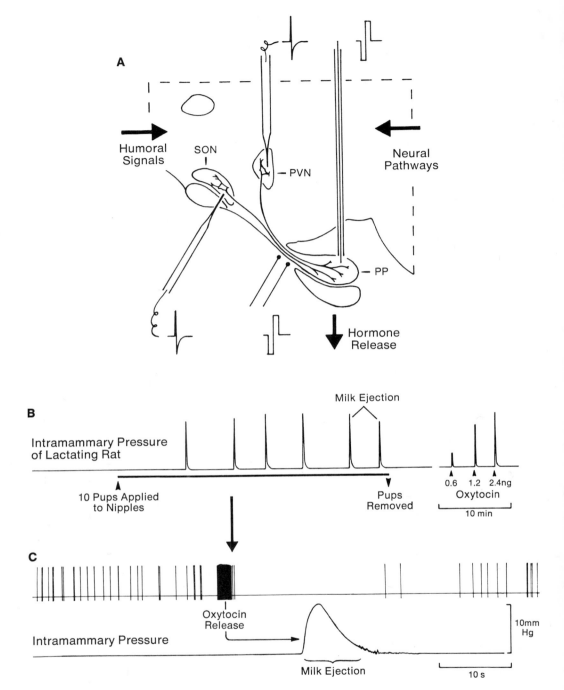

Fig. 27.8. Milk letdown in the lactating mother rat. **A.** Neurons in the paraventricular nucleus (PVN) and supraoptic nucleus (SON) in the hypothalamus and their connections to the posterior lobe (PP) of the pituitary. **B.** Intermittent pattern of milk ejection, as shown by recordings of intramammary pressure. The slow, long-duration trace shows milk ejections by an anesthetized mother rat in response to suckling by her litter. The slow, short-duration trace shows the mammary response to intravenous pulse injections of increasing concentrations of oxytocin. **C.** Unit activity recorded from a PVN neuron, showing the correlation of intense burst activity, oxytocin release, and subsequent mammary response and milk ejection. Note the much faster trace speed in C than in B. (Courtesy of D. W. Lincoln; see also Wakerly and Lincoln, 1973)

For their part, the rat pups are not just passive receptacles for the ejected milk. Letdown lasts only a few seconds, and the pup must be able to detect the engorgement of the nipple and respond with vigorous sucking. From these considerations it has been realized that the state of arousal of pups is very important in their ability to thrive. It appears that nipple attachment and ingestive control are exquisitely dependent on the level of arousal; a deprived pup with an empty stomach is more alert than a satiated pup, and therefore is more responsive to nipple engorgement and more active in sucking. This importance of arousal in initiating feeding appears to be similar to the higher activity levels of the adult blowfly after food deprivation, discussed earlier in this chapter. If rat pups are persistently aroused by experimental manipulation, they ingest milk beyond the normal capacity of the stomach. It is not until the age of 15 days that adultlike controls of ingestion begin to appear, and the rat begins to adjust intake to need.

Feeding in the Adult Rat

There was no clear idea about the neural pathways involved in adult feeding until Anand and Brobeck showed in 1951 that small, bilateral lesions in the lateral hypothalamic area (LHA) cause a rat to stop eating (aphagia) and stop drinking (adipsia), leading to death within a few days. The lesions did not appear to interrupt specific sensory or motor pathways. These workers suggested that the LHA could therefore be regarded as the center for the control of feeding (and drinking) behavior. The location of this area is shown in the drawing of Fig. 27.9. The cross-sectional view in (A) indicates the insertion of the lesioning electrode in this area. The diagrams in (A) and (B) bring out the point that the LHA lies within, and is traversed by, fibers of the medial forebrain bundle (MFB), the massive and complex population of fibers which serves as the

main conduction pathway linking many areas of the brainstem–hypothalamus–basal forebrain into a common system. The diagram in (A) also illustrates that the LHA–MFB area has no clear boundaries, and lesions thus commonly involve or affect neighboring areas, such as the subthalamus, endopeduncular nucleus, and medial part of the internal capsule.

In 1954, Phillip Teittlebaum and Eliot Stellar, at the University of Pennsylvania, showed that lesioned rats do not die if they are tube fed, and that they subsequently recover and are able to regulate their food and water intake. Figure 27.10 shows the time course of changes in food and water intake, and in body weight, in these experiments. As indicated in Fig. 27.10, the recovery process could be divided into four stages. In stage I, the animals are profoundly aphagic and adipsic. In stage II, the animals begin to accept wet, highly palatable food, but still will not drink. In stage III, the animals are less finicky: they eat a wider variety of food, and will drink sweetened water with a meal. In stage IV, the animal regulates its food intake, though it ingests water only with a meal.

These general results have been replicated many times in the intervening years, with many variations practiced on the exact sites and extents of lesions, the means of producing them, and the relations of other parts of the brain to the LHA-MFB. In addition, experiments in which the LHA has been stimulated electrically have generally shown increased eating. Unit recordings from the LHA have shown increased impulse firing under conditions of deprivation. From all these results it seems clear that the LHA-MFB is intimately involved in control of feeding behavior, but there has been much disagreement on the actual pathways involved and the nature of the control.

Despite the many controversies that have arisen, two major themes have emerged. The first theme is that, despite the remarkable recovery that can take place, LHA-lesioned animals show a

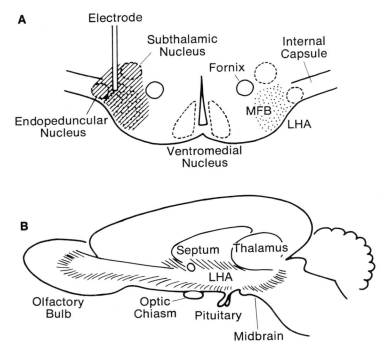

Fig. 27.9. A. Diagram of a cross section through the rat hypothalamus. Fibers of the medial forebrain bundle (MFB) are shown by dots. Note the electrode used to make electrolytic lesions. Sites of lesions of the lateral hypothalamic area (LHA) indicated by shading. **B.** Sagittal section of the rat brain, to emphasize the extent of the MFB, and its relation to the LHA. (A after Epstein, 1971; B after Clark, in Teitlebaum, 1971)

Table 27.2 Long-lasting deficits in feeding behavior of rats after bilateral ablation of LHA or destruction of catecholamine-containing neurons by injection of 6-hydroxydopamine

	LHA ablation	6-HDA
Ingestive behaviors		
No feeding response to glucopriva-tion (insulin or 2-deoxyglucose)	+	+
Lower body weight set point	+	+
Depressed drinking response to dehy-dration	+	+
Depressed salivary reflexes	+	−
Depressed feeding response to so-dium deficiency	+	−
Depressed taste aversion learning	+	−
General behaviors		
Depressed arousal	+	+
Motor impairment	+	+
Depressed affect	+	+
Depressed tolerance for stress ("central sympathectomy")	+	+

500

number of permanent deficits, not only related to feeding behavior but also profoundly affecting general behavior. Some of these effects are summarized in Table 27.2. Under *Ingestive Behavior* it can be seen that the recovered rat, though able to survive, is far from normal. These defects all place serious limitations on feeding behavior; the depression of salivation, for example, could by itself explain much of the inability of an animal to eat after lesioning. (It may be noted that electrical stimulation of the LHA causes, on the contrary, copious salivation.) Under *General Behavior* it can be seen that the lesion has serious consequences, leaving an ani-

Fig. 27.10. Time course of the lateral hypothalamic syndrome. Graphs show effects of bilateral LHA ablations on food and water intake, and on weight. Stages of recovery indicated below. (Adapted from Teitlebaum and Stellar, in Teitlebaum, 1971 and Epstein, 1971)

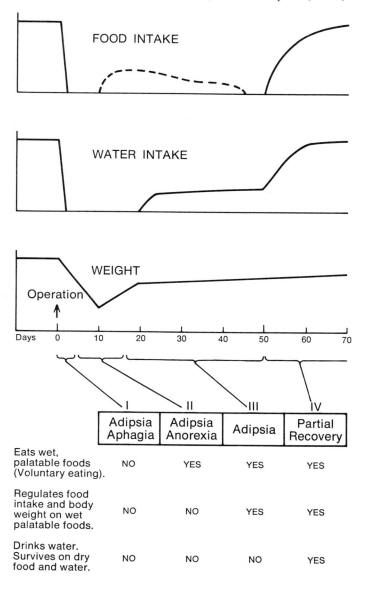

	I	II	III	IV
	Adipsia Aphagia	Adipsia Anorexia	Adipsia	Partial Recovery
Eats wet, palatable foods (Voluntary eating).	NO	YES	YES	YES
Regulates food intake and body weight on wet palatable foods.	NO	NO	YES	YES
Drinks water. Survives on dry food and water.	NO	NO	NO	YES

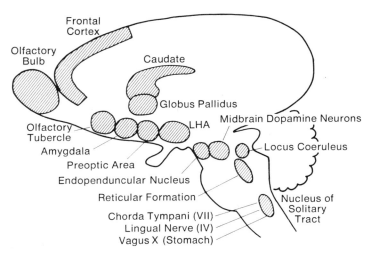

Fig. 27.11. Brain centers involved in initiating and maintaining feeding behavior in the rat.

mal that is lethargic, generally akinetic, emotionally depressed, and with limited tolerance for stress. These effects obviously contribute to the depression of feeding.

A second theme, related to the first, is that many systems, not just an isolated one, are affected by an LHA lesion, and, conversely, that many parts of the nervous system have inputs to and effects on the LHA. The LHA-MFB is simply a locus, a common path, for many *overlapping distributed systems,* as we defined them in Chap. 25. Recent work has suggested that these systems include the ascending DA and NA pathways from the brainstem. As shown in Table 27.2, intraventricular injections of 6-hydroxydopamine, which selectively destroys catecholamine-containing neurons, produces a syndrome very similar to that of the LHA-lesioned animal. Parts of the syndrome can also be produced by selective lesions or cuts at various places in the brainstem, at the borders of the hypothalamus, and in the basal ganglia, cortex, and olfactory pathway.

The diagram in Fig. 27.11 is an attempt to summarize some of the areas that have been shown to be involved in mediating feeding behavior. It can be seen that many of them are found within the midbrain–

hypothalamus–basal forebrain axis, and are thus part of a core system bound together by the medial forebrain bundle. This system includes the pathways for arousal that we discussed in the previous chapter, and it forms the core for systems mediating aggressive and emotional behavior, as we will see in Chap. 29. Finally, it includes the sites at which electrical stimulation has rewarding effects; rats readily learn to press a bar to receive electrical stimulation in these central areas, as first shown by James Olds and Peter Milner in 1954. This phenomenon of self-stimulation has been demonstrated in many species, including even humans; neurosurgical patients receiving electrical stimulation in these regions report feelings of pleasure and euphoria. All of this evidence indicates that the core regions interconnected by the medial forebrain bundle are parts of distributed systems concerned with coordinating neural activity underlying arousal, feeding, and emotion in complex ways.

Thus far, we have discussed the possible neural substrates that activate feeding. Feeding ceases when "satiety" is reached; what substrates and mechanisms are responsible for this? The first evidence was obtained by Brobeck and his colleagues in the 1940's. They found that bilateral lesions in the ventromedial nucleus of the hypothalamus (VMH) produce an animal that grossly overeats and becomes enormously obese. Subsequent work has indicated that the VMH is under the influence of several neural pathways: olfactory, amygdala, and sensory input from the mouth and stomach. It is also sensitive to circulating levels of glucose and insulin. These factors are summarized in Fig. 27.12.

From these various studies the hypothesis has emerged that feeding is under dual control, by a "feeding center" in the LHA and a "satiety center" in the VMH. According to this hypothesis, LHA activity instigates feeding; as this progresses, VMH becomes active, and, through inhibitory connections onto LHA cells, brings about cessation of LHA activity and feeding (see Fig. 27.12). Although this is an attractive hypothesis, it has remained an unproven formal concept, because direct evidence of the postulated connections and interactions between the two regions is lacking, and properties of VMH cells have not been described. One of the main stumbling blocks is that, as we have seen, neither VMH nor LHA are really centers; rather, they are loci within overlapping distrib-

uted systems. Stimulations or ablations at these loci are therefore complex in their effects; in line with this, recent investigators have noted a number of endocrine and metabolic dysfunctions induced by VMH lesions.

To conclude this discussion, it is appropriate to quote Jacques LeMagnen of Paris, a pioneer in the physiological and behavioral analysis of feeding, and a wise observer of both laboratory animals and his fellow countrymen:

> Food intake is not . . . separately regulated. . . . This field . . . represents perhaps the most advanced point in the study of a multifactorial physiological regulation. . . . A multifactorial system of regulation, in which the play of a network of positive and negative feedback mechanisms enables a body of variables to be simultaneously causes and effects, requires from the experimenter a kind of new mental program for collecting and processing data, and yet difficult to build and handle.

Drinking

Closely allied to feeding is drinking. Cells universally contain water, and metazoan animals universally consist of cells bathed in extracellular fluid. Maintenance of the fluid composition of both cells and extracellular fluid is therefore basic to animal

Fig. 27.12. Brain centers involved in terminating feeding ("satiety centers").

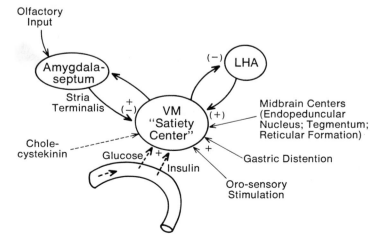

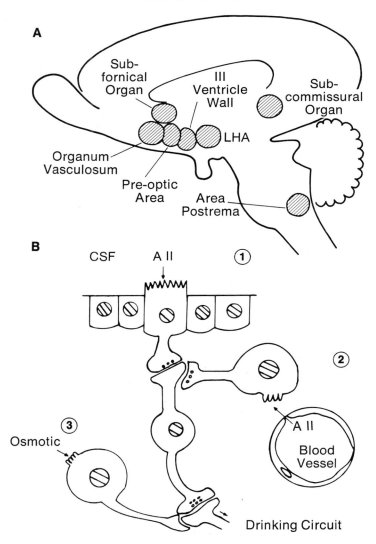

Fig. 27.13. **A.** Brain centers involved in control of drinking. **B.** Microcircuit of central receptors for angiotension. Site 1, receptor in the wall of the cerebral ventricle. Site 2, receptor in circumventricular organ, where there is no blood–brain barrier. Site 3, osmoreceptor in the hypothalamus. Drinking circuit includes cells projecting to the neural lobe of the pituitary, where vasopressin (antidiuretic hormone) is released. (B from Phillips et al., 1977)

life. As animals evolved from aquatic to terrestrial environments, homeostatic mechanisms became necessary for ensuring adequate fluid intake to offset dehydration and excretion. The need for intake is expressed as thirst, and is met by drinking.

In an animal deprived of water, the extracellular fluid begins to become more concentrated, and one says it is hyperosmotic; since the extracellular and intracellular compartments are in equilibrium across the cell wall, the cell cytoplasm also becomes hyperosmotic. In 1953, Bengt Andersson in Sweden showed that injections of hyperosmotic solutions into the hypothalamic region of goats induces drinking, suggesting that there are osmo-

receptors, sensitive to cellular dehydration, in that region. This is a logical place to expect such receptors, near the location of the cells to the posterior pituitary that secrete antidiuretic hormone (ADH), which stimulates the kidney to retain water. Subsequent experiments by Elliott Blass and Alan Epstein at the University of Pennsylvania showed that the osmoreceptors are distributed rather widely throughout the hypothalamus, especially in the preoptic and lateral hpothalamic areas (see Fig. 27.13). These and other workers have found that microinjections of mildly hypertonic saline into these areas readily induces drinking, as do injections into the carotid arteries which supply these areas; conversely, lesions of these areas impair drinking behavior.

In addition to cellular dehydration, a loss of extracellular fluid volume is also a stimulus to drinking. This involves the *angiotensin* system. Knowledge of this system began with the finding that a reduction of blood volume stimulates cells of the kidney to release the enzyme renin into the bloodstream. Renin acts on a circulating peptide, angiotensinogen, to make angiotensin I, which in turn is converted to angiotensin II (A II) (see Fig. 27.13). In 1970, Epstein and his colleagues made microinjections of A II into the hypothalamus, and showed that this is a powerful stimulus for drinking. Subsequent experiments have shown that all the components of the renin–A II system are also present in the hypothalamus. The preoptic area is particularly sensitive to A II, as are several sites along the cerebral ventricles; these are indicated in Fig. 27.13.

What are the relative contributions of osmoreceptors and A II receptors to normal drinking? In experiments carried out by Barbara Rolls, Ed Rolls, and Roger Wood at Oxford, it was found that about 65% of the drinking following water deprivation is due to cellular dehydration, and about 25% is due to blood volume reduction. This is in the rat; in the monkey, the proportions were 85% and 5%, respectively. These and other experiments have supported the idea that the osmoreceptors

Fig. 27.14. Does motivation play a role in human feeding and drinking behavior? This artist thinks so! (With kind permission of the New Yorker magazine and S. Koren)

"We're very good eaters."

are most important, and that the A II receptors are supplementary, perhaps acting as an emergency system invoked under conditions of extreme deprivation or blood loss.

Water deprivation is an easy variable for the experimenter to manipulate. An animal deprived of water has a strong *drive*, or *motivation*, to correct the deficit by drinking. In behavioral experiments, the drive can be quantitated by testing how hard the animal will work, or how intense the aversive shocks it will sustain, in order to obtain water and correct the deficit. Water deprivation is thus a convenient variable for studying both physiological and behavioral mechanisms. However, among humans, much of our water intake in daily life is actually guided by other factors. We drink fluids with our meals; we drink coffee because it is time for a coffee break; we drink at cocktail hour to be sociable; we drink when our mouths feel dry; we drink because it tastes good. These activities depend on different kinds of receptors: taste receptors in the mouth and pharynx; somatosensory receptors in the mouth, pharynx, and esophagous; stretch receptors that sense the amount of distention in the stomach and duodenum; stretch receptors and osmoreceptors in the hepatic portal veins that return blood from the liver to the heart. There is thus a complex array of signals that determines the pattern of normal drinking. This pattern is shaped by our learned habits, habits that in effect anticipate need, and keep our bodies well hydrated so that we do not have to respond in situations of need or emergency.

REFERENCES

Barrington, E. J. W. 1979. [Chap. 1].

Blass, E. M., W. G. Hall, and M. N. Teicher. 1979. The ontogeny of suckling and ingestive behaviors. In *Progr. Psychobiol. Physiol. Psychol.* 8: 243–300.

Blass, E. M. and A. N. Epstein. 1971. A lateral preoptic osmosensitive zone for thirst in the rat. *J. Comp. Physiol. Psychol.* 76: 378–394.

Crelin, E. S. 1976. Development of the upper respiratory system. *Clin. Symp. CIBA,* vol. 28, No. 3.

Dethier, V. G. 1976. [Chap. 12].

Epstein, A. N. 1971. The lateral hypothalamic syndrome: its implications for the physiological psychology of hunger and thirst. *Progr. Psychobiol. Physiol. Psychol.* 4: 263–317.

Epstein, A. N., J. T. Fitsimons, and B. J. Rolls. 1970. Drinking induced by injection of angiotensin into the brain of the rat. *J. Physiol.* 210: 457–474.

Greer, C. A., W. B. Stewart, M. H. Teicher, and G. M. Shepherd. 1983. Functional development of the olfactory bulb and a unique glomerular complex in the neonatal rat. *J. Neurosci.*

LeMagnen, J. 1971. Advances in studies on the physiological control and regulation of food intake. *Progr. Psychobiol. Physiol. Psychol.* 4: 203–261.

Phillips, I. M., D. Felix, W. E. Hoffman, and D. Ganten. 1977. Angiotensin-sensitive sites in the brain ventricular system. In *Soc. for Neurosci. Symp.* vol. 2 (ed. by W. M. Cowan and J. A. Ferrendelli). Bethesda, Md.: Society for Neuroscience. pp. 308–339.

Selverston, A. 1976. A model system for the study of rhythmic behavior. In *Simpler Networks and Behavior* (ed. by J. C. Fentress). Sunderland, Mass: Sinauer. pp. 82–98.

Stricker, E. M. and M. J. Zigmond. 1976. Recovery of function after damage to central catecholamine-containing neurons: a neurochemical model for the lateral hypothalamic syndrome. In *Progr. Psychobiol. Physiol. Psychol.* 6: 121–188.

Teicher, M. H. and E. M. Blass. 1980. Suckling. *Science* 210: 15–22.

Teicher, M. H., W. B. Stewart, J. S. Kauer, and G. M. Shepherd. 1980. Suckling pheromone stimulation of a modified glomerular region in the developing rat olfactory bulb revealed by the 2-deoxyglucose method. *Brain Res.* 194: 530–535.

Teitlebaum, P. 1971. The encephalization of

hunger. *Progr. Psychobiol. Physiol. Psychol. 4:* 319–350.

Wakerly, J. B. and D. W. Lincoln. 1973. The milk-ejection reflex of the rat: a 20–40-fold acceleration in the firing of paraventricular neurones during oxytocin release. *J. Endocrinol. 57:* 477.

Additional Reading

Hofer, M. A. 1981. *The Roots of Human Behavior.* San Francisco: Freeman.

Fitsimons, J. T. 1979. *The Physiology of Thirst and Sodium Appetite.* London: Cambridge.

28

Visceral Brains: Mating

As mentioned at the beginning of the previous chapter, mating is the function that is necessary for the propagation of the species. The object of mating is characteristically a copulatory union which brings the sexual organs of male and female together, so that fertilization of the female's egg or eggs by the male's sperms can occur. This requires proper maturation of the gonads and the copulatory organs, and proper timing of the preparedness of the male and receptivity of the female. In those animals in which fertilization occurs within the female, a series of internal body changes then takes place during gestation, leading up to birth. The diagram in Fig. 28.1 shows the relation of mating to those other phases in the reproductive cycle of a social insect and a mammal.

Mating, like feeding, takes place under a combination of nervous and hormonal control. Much of this control is mediated by parts of the nervous system within the visceral brain. In the case of feeding we saw that this part of the brain is responsible for a variety of different control mechanisms. Similarly, in the case of mating, the visceral brain mediates the most delicate and ingenious mechanisms for bringing about copulatory unions and the

mixing of genes. This part of the brain also is involved in controlling other aspects of the reproductive cycle shown in Fig. 28.1, such as the maturation of gonads, and behavior related to maternal care. In this chapter we will focus on the functions of mating, and mention these related functions where relevant.

To begin with, let us get a perspective on the mechanisms of sexual reproduction. In some organisms, each individual is a hermaphrodite, which means it contains both male and female sexual organs. This has the advantage that any two individuals can meet and reproduce. Examples include the earthworm, the sea hare (*Aplysia*), and, among vertebrates, a number of species of fish. In these cases, nervous mechanisms appropriate for both male and female mating behavior must be present. This obviously puts a limitation on the degree of specialized sexually related behavior that is possible, which may be part of the explanation for why this form of sexual reproduction is not more widespread.

Among vertebrates, the potential for hermaphroditism is expressed in the ability of certain species to undergo sex reversal. For example, Robert Goy and Bruce

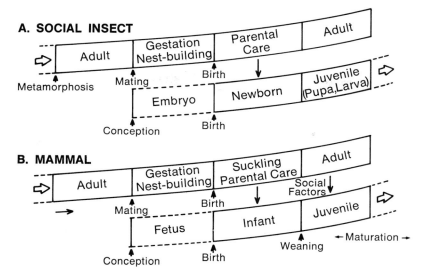

Fig. 28.1. Life cycles of a social insect and a mammal, with emphasis on events related to reproduction.

McEwen, in their book on *Sexual Differentiation of the Brain* (1980), cite studies in which genetically female fish, frogs, or salamanders grown in water containing testosterone develop into males that mate with normal females, and, conversely, males grown in water containing estradiol develop into females that mate with normal males. Even more amazing are studies of certain species of fish which live in social groups; all the members of the group develop as females, and only a few differentiate into males. If an adult male is lost, within a week or two one of the adult females differentiates into a male to take its place! A contrasting species of fish is also known, in which a group has a single female; if this female is lost from the group, a male differentiates into a female to take its place. These studies have thus provided evidence for the ability of social factors to control the differentiation of sexes, presumably through effects on nervous mechanisms and the organizational actions of sex hormones.

Among higher invertebrates and vertebrates, the common pattern is for sexual differentiation to occur early in develop-

ment, and for the male and female forms to be stable throughout life. This presumably reflects the adaptive advantages to be gained from specialization of each sex for its role in the reproductive behaviors revolving around courtship, mating, and care of the young. We have already mentioned an example of specialized nervous mechanisms in the pathways for control of singing in male birds (Chap. 24), and we will discuss several further examples below. We will also discuss the mechanisms for development of these differences and will see that they involve a series of changes under control of the organizational effects of hormones.

INVERTEBRATES

Given the importance of reproduction for the species, mating is not an activity that is entirely left to chance. As indicated already in connection with Fig. 28.1, it requires a careful orchestration in the development of the male and female partners. During development and maturity, animals of course spend much of their time looking for food and trying to avoid being eaten themselves. As a general rule, mating is not a part of this daily business of survival. Instead, it takes place at very prescribed times. The time is set by the biorhythm generators, the maturation and readiness of the gonads and secondary sex organs, and the differentiation of the parts of the neural pathways for controlling the appropriate behavior. These are basic principles that apply more or less to all animals, invertebrates and vertebrates.

A crucial task for the neural apparatus is the control of an appropriate series of behaviors that will bring the male and female together. A basic problem is that in their daily business of survival, animals spend much of their time engaging in behaviors that are either aggressive or defensive. In order to mate, the male and female must overcome these attitudes and, at least briefly, trust each other. Furthermore, there must be an opportunity for each of the partners to test the other for its attractiveness as a source of sound genes; it is a waste to mate with a partner that is sick, weak, or maladapted, but an advantage to combine one's genes with those of a partner that is healthy, strong, and with optimal abilities to survive and flourish.

For these reasons, it is common for mating to involve a sequence of interactions between the prospective partners, during which the aggressive and defensive instincts are subdued, and attractiveness as partners is tested. Many species are every bit as meticulous in this process of choosing mates as humans are. Since we view this through human eyeglasses, we call it "courtship". Ethologists have studied these sequences in many species, and have developed flow charts for representing them. An example of the mating behavior of the cockroach is shown in Fig. 28.2. Each one of the behaviors can be identified as a distinct entity—one that is a necessary prelude to the behavior that follows it. Each requires a response from the partner. Each gives rise to a sensory stimulus or a set of stimuli that call forth the next response. The whole sequence involves a number of specific motor acts and sensory stimuli that, taken together, are specific for this species, and ensure the suitability of the partners.

In the language of ethologists, a sequence such as that in Fig. 28.2 is called a *reaction chain*. Each behavior in the sequence is thought to be activated or "released" by a set of neuronal centers and their connections, called an *innate releasing mechanism*. The stimuli that activate these mechanisms are called *releasing stimuli*, or *releasers*. It can be further realized that each behavior has the character of a *fixed-action pattern* (FAP), that is, a particular pattern of postural attitude, glandular secretion, or motor activity, such as that discussed in Chap. 20. Each of these motor acts in turn generates the stimuli which release the next act in the chain. The details of each step in the sequence are summarized in Fig. 28.3.

A reaction chain such as that in Fig. 28.2 involves a prescribed sequence of behaviors, but it should be emphasized that any given step is a probabilistic, not a rigidly determined, event. This, in fact, is the whole point of the sequence: any given step serves as a test for whether conditions are just right, so that the next step can take place. This is the means for assuring optimum gene transmission, as described above.

The releasing stimuli for a given behavior act on sensory receptors which in turn set up input in sensory pathways, as already discussed in previous chapters in sensory systems. In some cases it is the whole pattern of stimulation that is important, such as visual recognition of a partner or a prominent marking in a partner. In other cases, it is a conjunction of two or more sensory modalities, such as tactile and chemosensory stimuli in the cockroach in Fig. 28.2. In many cases it involves stimulation only of a specific type of receptor, as in tactile stimulation of specific parts of the body in the cockroach.

A dramatic example of a specific sen-

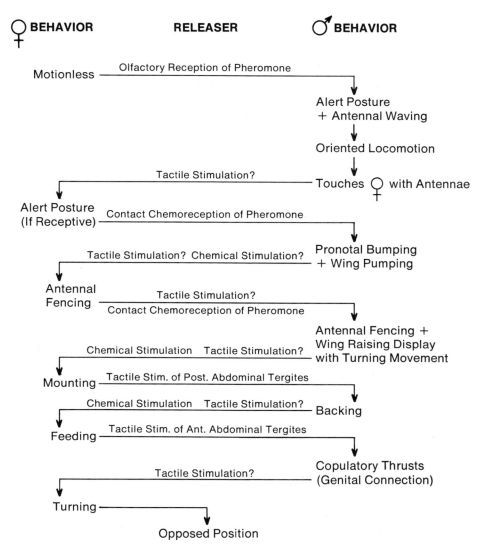

Fig. 28.2. Reaction chain underlying mating behavior of the cockroach. Behaviors of male and female are shown in outside columns; releasing stimuli shown in center columns. (After Barth, in Gordon, 1972)

sory pathway involved in mating behavior is found in the insect olfactory system. As can be seen in Fig. 28.2, many of the steps leading to mating in the cockroach depend on chemical cues, a very general finding in many species. Such cues are mediated by pheromones (Chap. 8). The narrowly tuned responses of certain receptor cells in the male silk moth to the pheromone bombykol, emitted by the female,

were described in Chap. 12. Recently it has been discovered that these special receptors make connections to a special part of the antennal lobe. Careful studies by Jurgen Boeckh and his colleagues in Germany have shown that this part consists of a distinctive complex of glomerular structures, termed a macroglomerulus or macroglomerular complex (Fig. 28.4). Steve Matsumoto and John Hildebrand at Harvard

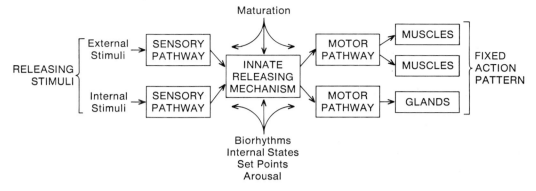

Fig. 28.3. Details of one step in a reaction train. (Adapted from Tinbergen, 1951)

have succeeded in recording intracellularly from antennal lobe cells and marking them with HRP injections. They have found cells that respond preferentially to bombykol; these cells are present only in the male; and they always have neurites which connect to the macroglomerulus. An example of this type of cell is shown in Fig. 28.4. The central connections of antennal lobe cells have not yet been determined; possible targets are the higher interpretive centers in the mushroom bodies (see Chap. 12) or other central neurons that command motor output to the wing motoneurons.

The involvement of pheromones and other chemical cues in mating and other types of behavioral reaction chains reflects the fact that they provide for very sure means of identification of individuals between and within species. In addition, the olfactory sensory pathways characteristically have direct access to parts of the visceral brain that contain innate releasing mechanisms. We will meet these same principles again in the mating and maternal behavior of vertebrates.

An important aspect of mating behavior is the crucial role played by the neuroendocrine systems in preparing the body and the nervous system. As indicated in Fig. 28.3, the actions of nervous centers and pathways are contingent on internal factors such as maturation and internal state, and these are typically under neuroendocrine control. This control also involves a sequence of carefully orchestrated actions.

An overall scheme for the control of reproduction in insects is shown in Fig. 28.5. The sequence begins with sensory stimuli ① which activate neurosecretory cells in the brain. This causes the corpora allata ② to release their gonadotropin hormone. Gonadotropin promotes yolk formation in the ovum and stimulates the accessory sex glands ③. The ovary containing its maturing eggs releases ovarian hormone ④, which suppresses secretion of gonadotropin from the corpora allata, and also stimulates neurosecretion from the corpora cardiaca ⑤. The neurosecretion from the corpora cardiaca promotes ⑥ oviposition (the movement of the eggs into position for fertilization), possibly by acting through the central nervous system. This terminates the cycle, and the animal is ready to begin anew.

Of course the details in this sequence vary in different insects. Also, the hormones have actions on other parts of the body economy not shown in the diagram, such as metabolism; neurosecretions from the corpora cardiaca, for example, contribute to the preparation for mating by regulating the metabolism of fat tissue, so

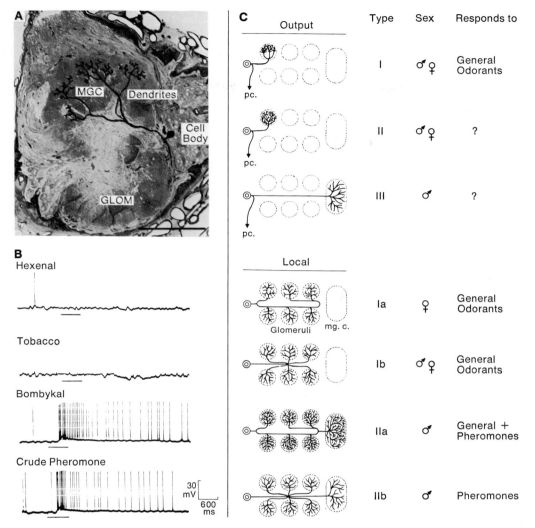

Fig. 28.4. Mediation of responses to sex pheromones by the specific pathway through the macro-glomerulus in insects. **A.** Antennal lobe of a male Saturniid moth *Antheraea*. An olfactory neuron has been stained after injection of cobalt from an extracellular electrode. The tracing of the stained neuron is here superimposed on a corresponding histological section. The dendrites of this neuron connect to the macroglomerulus (above), but not to the common glomeruli (below). This unit responded to stimulation by the sex attractant pheromone emitted by the female. **B.** Intracellular responses recorded from a neuron in a male hawkmoth *Manduca*. Note the specific response to bombykal, a major component of the sex pheromone emitted by the female, and to the pheromone itself. **C.** Correlation between the responsiveness of antennal lobe neurons and their dendritic connections, as revealed by intracellular HRP staining of recorded neurons. The antennal neurons pictured here all receive inputs in the glomeruli from the antennal receptor cells; the output cells project to the mushroom bodies and other central regions, as described in Chap. 12. Abbreviations mg. c., macroglomerular complex; p.c., corpora pedunculata. (A from Boeckh and Boeckh, 1979; B, C from Matsumoto and Hildebrand, 1981)

513

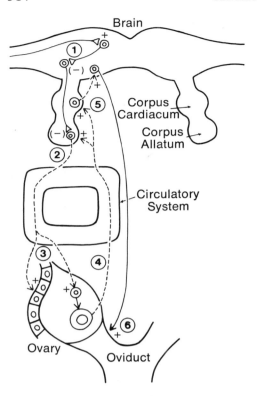

Fig. 28.5. General scheme for control of reproduction. Sequence of actions (1–7) is described in text. (Adapted from Tombes, 1970)

that proteins and other nutrients are provided for the developing oocyte. It should also be noted that the control of reproduction by the corpora allata in the adult follows in sequence the control of development through pupal stages to the adult by this same organ. It is of considerable interest in this regard that juvenile hormone and gonadotropin hormone in fact appear to be the same, or very similar, molecules. This suggests an economy in having different effects depend on the stage of development of receptor molecules in target organs, rather than requiring the added job of synthesizing a different hormone at each stage. This expresses a principle of *multiaction hormonal effects in temporal sequence,* which is complementary to multiple actions of a given hor-

mone on more than one target at the same time (Chap. 9).

VERTEBRATES

Most of the principles underlying mating behavior in invertebrates apply also to vertebrates. Thus, mating requires proper maturation of the reproductive organs and the nervous and neuroendocrine mechanisms for controlling them. Mating in vertebrates is characteristically preceded by courtship maneuvers every bit as complicated as that depicted in Fig. 28.2. The sequences of behavior can be conceived to involve fixed-action patterns, released by innate neural mechanisms under appropriate endogenous conditions and external stimulations as depicted in Fig. 28.3.

Our knowledge of neural mechanisms mediating mating behavior in vertebrates draws on work in many fields. There is a long tradition of biochemical work, beginning early in this century, on isolation and characterization of the hormones secreted by the reproductive organs and the hypothalamopituitary region. There is an enormous literature on the behavioral effects of removal of these organs in experimental animals, and the effects of diseases of these organs in human patients. In recent years, the identification of hypothalamic releasing factors and the localization of these and related peptides in many parts of the nervous system has greatly extended our concepts of the extent of neural systems involved in control of reproductive processes. Neuroanatomical studies have revealed a number of sites at which the organizational effects of hormone actions bring about sexually dimorphic regions. Neurophysiological studies have begun to reveal the time course and mode of action of nerve cells that mediate reproductive control.

Against this background of multidisciplinary studies, let us consider first the ways by which male and female animals achieve their final adult forms, and then

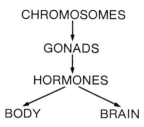

CHROMOSOMES
↓
GONADS
↓
HORMONES
↙   ↘
BODY   BRAIN

Fig. 28.6. Steps involved in sexual differentiation.

consider examples of mating in several species.

Sexual Differentiation

Sexual differentiation is brought about by a sequence of steps. As summarized in Fig. 28.6, the general scheme is that the chromosomes carry the code for male or female, which determines the type of gonad, male or female. The gonad synthesizes and secretes hormones which organize the secondary sex characteristics. In addition, the hormones act on the brain to organize or modify circuits for appropriate nervous control of the sex organs and related behaviors.

An important generalization for understanding sexual differentiation is that, in higher vertebrates at least, all individuals will develop as one sex unless the chromosomal condition for the opposite sex is present and is expressed during a critical period on development. In birds, the sex chromosomes of the male are ZZ, whereas in the female they are ZO; hence birds are regarded as basically male, unless one of the sex chromosomes is missing. It is believed that ZZ inhibits the primordial ovary, allowing the testes to develop; in the case of ZO, the ovary develops while suppressing the primordial testis. In contrast, in mammals the sex chromosomes of the female are XX, whereas in the male they are XY; hence, mammals are regarded as basically female, unless the Y chromosome is present.

The differentiation of the sexes begins early in fetal life. We can illustrate the sequence of changes for the rat, a well-studied vertebrate (Fig. 28.7). The rat has a gestation period of about 21 days. By day 11, a genital ridge has formed in the lower abdomen (A). Germ cells, male or female, which have been lurking in the wall of the gut, migrate into this ridge, and bring about a proliferation of cells to form a primitive though undifferentiated gonad (B). The germ cells are grouped here into clusters, called *primary sex cords*. At about 13 days, the gonad begins to differentiate. In a genetic female, the primary sex cords migrate to the inner, medullary part of the gonad and degenerate. They are replaced in the outer, cortical part by secondary sex cords, which give rise to the egg cells (*oocytes*) (D). In the genetic male, the primary sex cords give rise to the seminiferous tubules, which contain in their walls the germ cells which give rise to spermatozoa (C).

As soon as the male gonad begins to differentiate into a testis, interstitial cells within the testis begin to synthesize and secrete the hormone testosterone. Synthesis has been detected as early as day 13. The levels of testosterone in the blood reach their peak around day 18 and decline gradually through the first ten days after birth. This burst of testosterone defines what is called a *critical period*, during which the message of the genetic sex is carried to the body; the testosterone acts on intracellular receptors as discussed in Chap. 9, and causes the development of male secondary sex organs, and the differentiation of certain parts of the brain responsible for male behavior patterns. Experimental manipulations, such as castration or hormone injections, have profound and enduring effects on both the sex organs and the brain if carried out during the critical period, up to about day 5 postnatal; after this, they have little effect. This critical period is relatively brief in the rat; in species with longer gestation periods, such as the guinea pig (67 days) or monkey (160), the critical period may be longer, and occur mostly before birth.

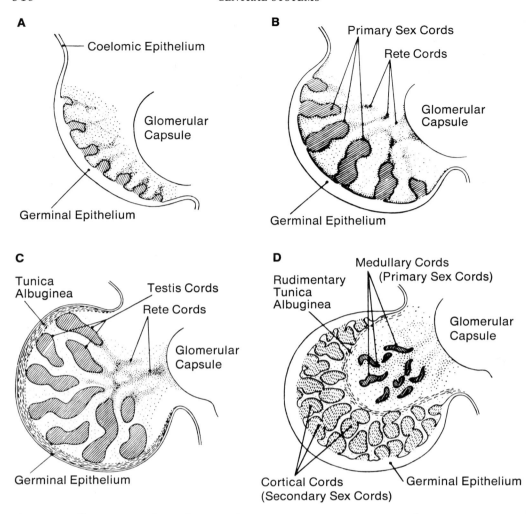

A

Coelomic Epithelium

Glomerular Capsule

Germinal Epithelium

B

Primary Sex Cords

Rete Cords

Glomerular Capsule

Germinal Epithelium

C

Tunica Albuginea

Testis Cords

Rete Cords

Glomerular Capsule

Germinal Epithelium

D

Medullary Cords (Primary Sex Cords)

Rudimentary Tunica Albuginea

Glomerular Capsule

Cortical Cords (Secondary Sex Cords)

Germinal Epithelium

Fig. 28.7. Differentiation of gonads in vertebrates. (From Burns, in Romer and Parsons, 1977)

In some species the end of the critical period occurs at about the time postnatally when the eyes open, which has been taken to indicate that sexual differentiation takes place before neural pathways in the brain are fully functional, and hence still more readily modifiable.

As already mentioned, the basic body plan is female, with maleness imposed by the action of testosterone. Although this remains a useful generalization, the situation is much more complicated than that. For instance, Fred Naftolin and his colleagues, then at McGill, showed in 1975

that much of the masculinization effects produced by testosterone are actually due to conversion of testosterone to estradiol. The conversion involves, biochemically, the aromatization of the hormone molecule (Fig. 28.8), and one says therefore that estrogen can act as an androgen through aromatization. Another example is the finding that during the critical period, circulating testosterone levels are nearly as high in the female as in the male, with only a peak at day 18 in the male to distinguish clearly between the sexes.

These and other results have made it

necessary to postulate additional bio-chemical mechanisms that contribute to sex differentiation. For example, the testosterone peak may have a "primary effect," of inducing estrogen receptors in cell nuclei, or aromatizing enzymes in cell cytoplasm, so that these cells would be more sensitive to further testosterone actions in the male. In addition, the several pathways for metabolizing testosterone (Fig. 28.8) yield a variety of active metabolites with the target cell. As Goy and MacEwen point out, this may be viewed

. . . as a means to diversify the action of a single hormone by producing . . . agents able to interact at different points in intracellular metabolism. It may provide a mechanism for achieving high concentrations of specific metabolites at discrete sites and for modulating hormone action through the regulation of the activity of the metabolizing enzymes. Not surprisingly, the CNS may prove to be the target

Fig. 28.8. Metabolic pathways for sex hormones. (Modified from Keele and Sampson, in Gordon, 1972)

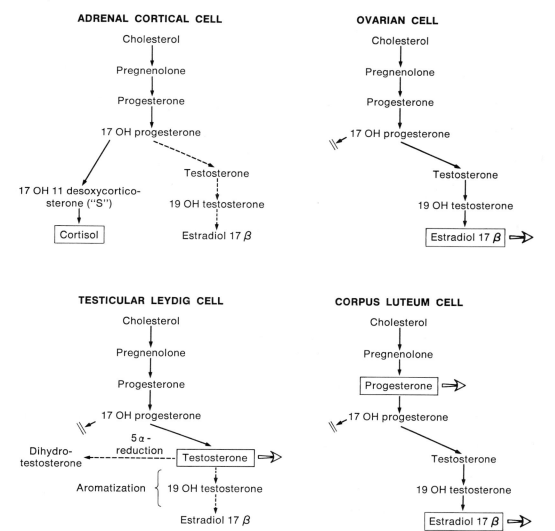

organ in which these possibilities are most extensively exploited.

These mechanisms provide means not only for diversifying the effects of testosterone, but also of protecting the male embryo from circulating estrogens from the mother.

Sexual Dimorphisms

The previous section indicates that there is considerable biochemical evidence for sexual differentiation of the brain. We next consider how this produces differences in brain structures and behavior.

The behaviors of male and female organisms are necessarily different during mating. The earlier idea (the "peripheral hypothesis") was that these behaviors reflect the differences in the sexual organs and their hormonal control through the pituitary. In this view, the decrease in male sexual behavior induced by castration of a newborn male rat, for example, is due to the underdeveloped penis rather than any effects on the brain. The first evidence for differences in brain mechanisms in the two sexes (the "central hypothesis") was obtained by a closer examination of the behaviors of young animals.

It is typical of many mammalian species that the young engage in rough-and-tumble play amongst themselves. This play includes attempts at *mounting,* and receptive displays involving downward bending of the back and exposure of the bottom, termed *lordosis.* Both sexes engage in these behaviors, but normally males tend to be more active in mounting, and females in showing lordosis.

In 1959, Charles Phoenix and his collaborators at the University of Kansas reported studies in which they injected a small dose of testosterone into pregnant guinea pigs, and observed a reduction in lordotic behavior in the female progeny. This they interpreted as a *defeminizing* effect of the androgenic hormone on central brain mechanisms. In addition, guinea pigs

ovariectomized at birth and subsequently injected with testosterone showed more mounting behavior, which was interpreted as a masculinizing effect of the hormone on the brain. Since that time, numerous studies have confirmed the generality of these two types of effects of male hormones on behavior patterns (see also Chaps. 29 and 31).

If behavior is mediated by the brain, then it should be possible to find differences in brain structure in the centers and pathways that mediate male or female behavior. At first the possibility of identifying such differences seemed remote, but the pioneering work of Geoffrey Raisman and Pauline Field, then at Oxford, in the early 1970's, showed that such differences could be found, and at the level of resolution of the electron microscope. They studied the preoptic nucleus, a region in the basal forebrain that is involved in control of biorhythms, including the estrous cycle (see Chap. 26). The nucleus receives inputs from the amygdala, a structure in the limbic system (see next chapter) as well as from other sources. After placing lesions in the amygdala, they found more non-amygdalar nondegenerating synapses on dendritic spines in the nucleus of females than in males. These results are summarized in Fig. 28.9A. This study thus showed a difference in synaptic connections in males and females, a difference that depends on exposure to sex hormones early in life. The preoptic area is involved in control of the surge in secretion of LH that underlies the estrous cycle in females (see below), and the differences in synaptic connections may be related to this control.

Stimulated by these results, research workers have looked for and found differences between males and females in several other parts of the brain. These differences in brain structure are referred to as *sexual dimorphisms.* We have already mentioned the differences in binding of sex hormones and in the size of certain centers in the pathways controlling singing in male

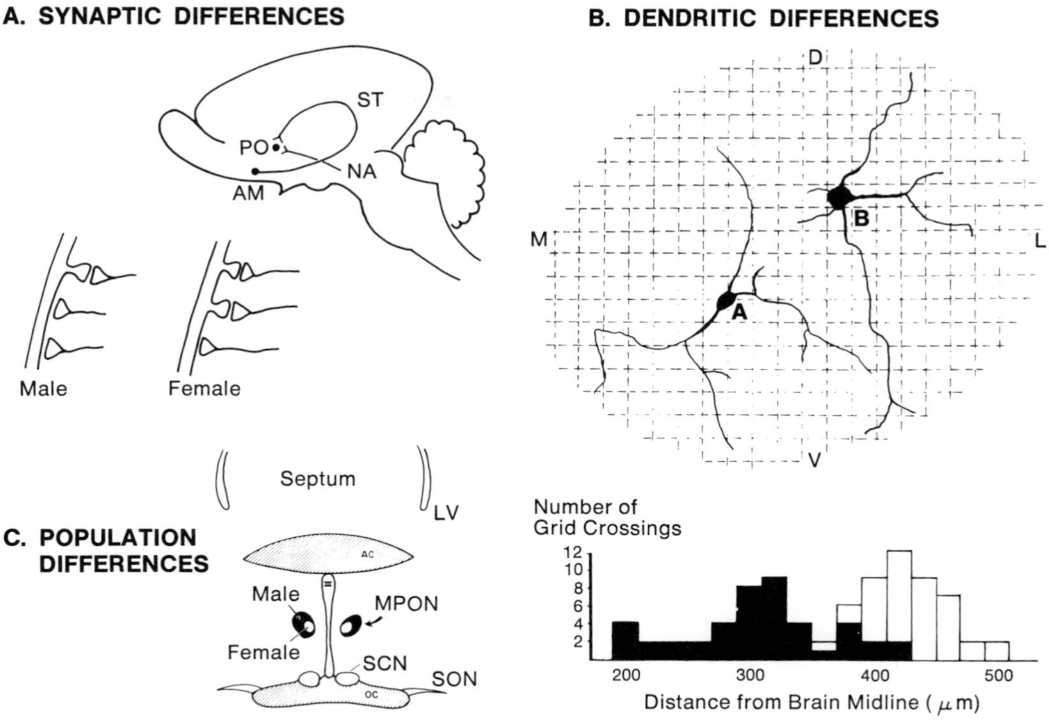

A. SYNAPTIC DIFFERENCES

B. DENDRITIC DIFFERENCES

C. POPULATION DIFFERENCES

Fig. 28.9. Sexual dimorphisms in the mammalian brain. A. Summary of experiments in the rat, showing that nonamygdalar (NA) fibers make more synapses on dendritic spines in the preoptic (PO) nucleus of females than males. AM, amygdala; ST, stria terminalis. B. Two Golgi-impregnated neurons in the preoptic area of hamster brain, illustrating that neurons in males (A) have dendrites more oriented toward the center of the area, whereas in females (B) the dendrites tend to be oriented toward the periphery. C. Medial preoptic nucleus (MPON) on the rat, showing that this region is larger in the male than in the female. AC, anterior commissure; LV, lateral ventricle; OC, optic chiasm; SCN, suprachiasmatic nucleus; SON, supraoptic nucleus. (A based on Raisman and Field, 1971; B from Greenough et al.; C from Gorski et al., in Goy and McEwen, 1980)

song birds, in Chap. 24. In the mammal, various nuclei of the hypothalamus show differences in cell size and sex hormone binding. Study of Golgi-impregnated neurons in the preoptic area of the hamster has suggested that neurons in the male have dendrites more oriented toward the center of this area, while in the female they are more oriented toward the periphery (see Fig. 28.9B). In another part of this area, there is a nucleus of cells that is up to eight times larger in males than in females (Fig. 28.9C). In addition to these structural dimorphisms, differences in functional properties of neurons have also

been found; for example, amygdalar stimulation is more effective in driving preoptic cells in males than in females.

There is thus ample evidence that the brains of males and females are different in certain very specific ways. Let us next examine how their differences relate to specific mating behavior.

Brain Mechanisms in Mating

Among the behaviors that are essential for mating to occur in many vertebrates are *mounting* by the male and *lordosis* by the female. Recent studies have begun to

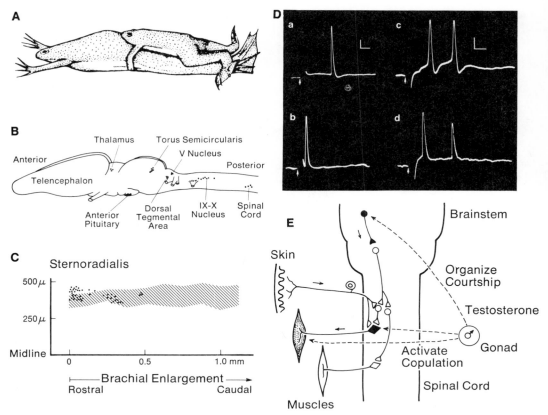

Fig. 28.10. Neural mechanisms mediating the clasp reflex of the male frog *Xenopis laevis*. **A.** Diagram of male clasping the female. **B.** Sites of binding of dihydrotestosterone to neurons in the central nervous system of the male frog. Binding in the auditory pathway (torus semicircularis) and the motor pathway controlling the larynx (dorsal tegmental area and IX–X nucleus) is related to mate calling during courtship. **C.** Localization of testosterone binding in the spinal cord. The shaded area indicates the distribution of the entire population of motoneurons innervating the sternoradialis muscle of the forelimb; dots indicate androgen-concentrating cells within that population. **D.** Intracellular recordings from a single sternoradialis motoneuron. a, b, Responses in spinal cord of castrated male to single stimulus delivered to dorsal root (a) and sternoradialis nerve (b). c, d, Responses in spinal cord of a clasping male. **E.** Neural circuit mediating the male clasp reflex, showing sites of organizational and activational actions of androgen hormones. (A from Russell, 1964; B from Kelley, 1980; C, D from Erulkar et al., 1982. See Erulkar et al. for references)

identify the specific nervous pathways that are involved in the control of these behaviors.

Mounting by the Male Frog. Mating in the frog takes place in the following manner. After suitable courtship preliminaries, the sexually mature male mounts the receptive female from behind so that their pelvises come together and fertilization can

occur, a position known as amplexus (see Fig. 28.10A). The transfer of sperm takes many hours, which puts the male at risk, because other males may come along and try to dislodge him, and the female may try to throw him over for more attractive paramours. In order to maintain his position, the male clasps the female firmly with his forelimbs. This clasp is a remarkable reflex, which can be maintained for up to

30 hours. The spinal nature of the reflex is shown by the fact that after decapitation a male may continue to clasp for several hours, an experimental observation that was first made in the eighteenth century. Very recently, a team headed by Darcey Kelley at Princeton and Sol Erulkar at the University of Pennsylvania has carried out a multidisciplinary study of the spinal circuits. The results may be summarized as follows:

Anatomy. The main muscles used by the male in clasping are the sternoradialis and flexor carpi radialis of the forelimbs. HRP injections into these muscles showed their motoneurons to be localized in the brachial enlargement of the spinal cord.

Steroid Uptake. Castrated males were injected with dihydrotestosterone (DHT), one of the active metabolites of testosterone (see above). In addition to uptake in cells of the hypothalamus, uptake was found in cells of the spinal cord, among the motoneuron populations that mediate the clasp reflex (Fig. 28.10B,C).

Facilitation of Motoneuron Activity. Intracellular recordings were obtained from sternoradialis motoneurons in males induced to clasp by injection of gonadotropin, and compared with recordings from these motoneurons in castrated males. As shown in Fig. 28.10D, in clasping males the responses showed larger EPSPs and multiple spiking. This effect of androgens may be due to facilitation of transmitter actions, or to increased excitability of the membrane. Related experiments showed that the facilitation is blocked by cyclohexamide, a protein inhibitor, suggesting that the androgen action is mediated through protein synthesis.

Enzyme Localization. The criteria for identifying neuroactive hormones parallel those for neurotransmitters (see Chap. 9). One of the criteria is the presence of appropriate enzymes. A search was therefore carried out for the presence of 5 *α-reductase,* the enzyme which converts testosterone to DHT (see above). Segments of the spinal cord were homogenized and incubated with tritiated testosterone. Thin-layer chromatography showed substantial 5 *α-reductase* activity in the spinal segments innervating the clasping muscles. The results are consistent with the idea that testosterone may affect clasping motoneurons by conversion to DHT.

Muscle Types. Recent studies are aimed at characterizing the types of muscle fibers in clasping muscles by observing the binding of antibodies to fast myosin (present in fast twitch muscles) and slow myosin (present in slow twitch muscles). The proportion of slow myosin increases in males during the breeding season. This may be due in part to a direct action of androgens on the muscles, but Erulkar and his colleagues speculate that the changes induced in motoneuron activity by the binding of androgen, as described above, may be the main determinant of the myosin type in the muscles which these motoneurons innervate.

A summary of the neural and hormonal elements involved in male clasping behavior is shown in Fig. 28.10E. Note the two main neural targets of androgens, one in the hypothalamus to prepare the male for courtship behavior, the other in the spinal cord to prepare for clasping and copulation. In this way the spinal circuits are primed for mediating the clasp reflex; in ethological terms, the fixed-action pattern (clasping) is released by appropriate releasing stimuli (tactile stimulation). Clasping behavior is thus programmed into the spinal circuits, much as we have seen to be the case with motor activities related to posture and locomotion. The circuits thus appear to be constructed along the same principles as those controlling other motor behavior.

Lordosis in the Female Rat. Mating in the rat also involves mounting by the male, but copulation, in contrast, is extremely rapid: the entire sequence of mounting, thrusting, ejaculation, and release may take less than a second! The female's co-operation is critical, and the main motor activity which she must coordinate with mounting is lordosis. It has been known since the pioneering experiments of Frank Beach, then at Yale, in the 1940's, that lordosis is under control of female go-nadal hormones. Recently, the neural circuits which mediate lordosis have been extensively studied by Don Pfaff and his collaborators at Rockefeller University. This work has also demonstrated the use-fulness, indeed the necessity, of a multi-disciplinary approach. The results will be summarized briefly, with reference to Fig. 28.11.

Lordosis is a reflex response to tactile stimulation by the male's body against the female's rump region ①. The main tactile receptors are believed to be Ruffini end-ings, responding to pressure stimulation with a slowly adapting barrage of im-pulses in the sensory fibers to the spinal cord.

Since lordosis does not occur if the spinal cord is transected (in contrast to frog clasping discussed above), the reflex requires supraspinal connections. The as-cending information is carried in fibers in the anterolateral columns ② to three sites: the lateral vestibular nucleus, and the medullary and midbrain reticular forma-tions.

Lordosis depends on estrogen; fully de-veloped lordosis normally occurs only in mature females adequately primed by es-trogens. The estrogens are primarily in neurons in the ventromedial hypothala-mus and related regions (③; see also next section). The effect on these cells is to raise the level of tonic impulse activity, thereby facilitating the midbrain neurons to which these cells project.

When adequately facilitated by hypo-thalamic inputs, the midbrain neurons re-spond to the sensory inputs. Through a relay in the medullary reticular formation,

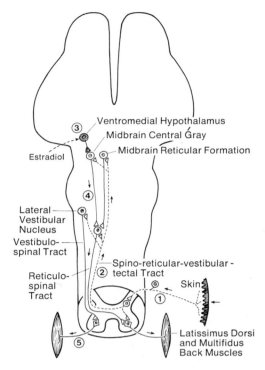

Fig. 28.11. Neural circuits mediating lordosis in the female rat. Sequence of actions (1–5) is described in text. (After Pfaff and Modianos, in Pfaff, 1980)

this descending pathway ④ completes the reflex pathway to the spinal cord. The de-scending excitation is combined with sen-sory inputs to control the muscles of the back that execute lordosis ⑤. The lateral vestibular nucleus contributes to this con-trol by raising the tone of postural mus-cles.

In this system we see again the principle of hierarchal organization; the basic cir-cuit for controlling the pattern of motor activity is present at the spinal level, and is modulated, gated, or activated by the higher centers. It is also worth pointing out that lordosis involves primarily axial mus-cles; thus, as in the case of respiratory and vocal activity, a delicate control of axial muscles is necessary, that rivals that of fine control of the extremities.

Neural Control of Gonadotropin Secre-tion in the Female Rat. It remains to con-

DIAGRAM OF FOUR DAY ESTROUS CYCLE IN RAT

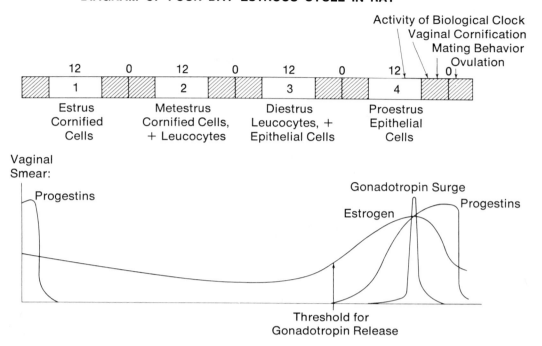

Fig. 28.12. The estrous cycle in the laboratory rat. (After Gordon, 1972)

sider the neural factors which affect the hormonal status of the female, and its preparedness for mating.

In mammals, most females upon reaching maturity undergo cyclic changes in their preparedness to mate and produce offspring. This is termed the *estrous cycle.* It reflects changes in the levels of the gonadal hormones, estrogens, and progestins, secreted in the ovary, which in turn reflect changes in stimulation of the ovary by gonadotropin (FSH and LH) secreted by the pituitary. The way these levels change during the estrous cycle of the rat is shown in Fig. 28.12. Mating behavior must be critically timed in relation to the cycle; as indicated in the figure, mating must occur within several hours after the LH surge, and several hours before the actual time of ovulation.

The estrous cycle is thus one of the most important of the biorhythms we discussed in Chap. 26. Its duration varies considerably in different mammals. In contrast to rats, for example, are species in which the cycle lasts a year. Many primates are intermediate; in the case of humans, of course, the cycle lasts approximately 28 days, and is called the menstrual cycle.

The cyclic changes in gonadotropin secretion from the pituitary are determined by changes in levels of releasing factors secreted in the hypothalamus, as we discussed in Chap. 24. What then determines the secretion of these factors? Part of the answer lies in the gonadal hormones themselves, which, as we have seen, are taken up and bound by specific cells in the hypothalamus. A kind of negative feedback control is achieved in this way: increased hormone uptake suppresses production of releasing factors, decreasing the level of hormone, which in turn means less suppression and increased hormone levels, and so on. Part of the answer lies in the suprachiasmatic nucleus, which plays its role as the master oscillator in the brain; removal of the SCN abolishes the estrous

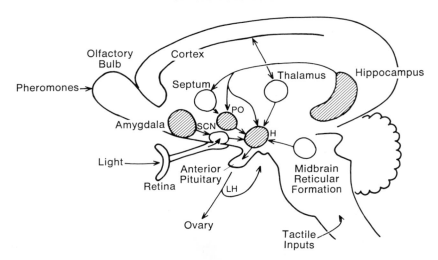

Fig. 28.13. Brain centers involved in the control of gonadotrophin secretion and the estrous cycle in the female rat. Shaded areas indicate regions showing sexual dimorphism. H, hypothalamus; LH, luteinizing hormone; PO, preoptic area; SCN, suprachiasmatic nucleus. (Adapted from Harlan et al., 1979)

cycle. In addition, many other regions of the brain make their contributions. These areas have been identified by a variety of studies. One approach is to stimulate electrically different regions, and observe the effects on blood levels of LH; conversely, the effects of ablation of different regions can be observed. Biochemical analysis of different regions has been carried out. Localization of sex hormones has been studied using intracerebral implants of hormones, and sites of steroid uptake and steroid receptors have been identified by autoradiography. Finally may be added studies of sexual dimorphisms.

The results of these various studies are summarized in Fig. 28.13. These regions and the pathways that connect them may be said to form a distributed system, as we defined it in Chap. 25, for the neural control of the estrous cycle. At the heart of the system is the median eminence where the releasing factors are secreted (see Fig. 25.5). Feeding into this are the mamillary body, preoptic area (PO), the dopamine neurons of the median eminence, and the SCN (see Fig. 25.5). Next are regions of the limbic system such as the amygdala, septal region, thalamus, hippocampus, and mesencephalic reticular formation (see Chap. 29). Finally are the sensory pathways, especially olfactory, tactile, and visual, that have inputs to different regions. Within this distributed system, different regions are more or less closely related to the final control of releasing factors, and thus provide multiple ways in which nervous influences can be integrated and can have an influence on circulating hormonal levels. In some species, as in the rodent, the neural controls may be relatively powerful. In other species, such as the primate, they are less powerful, and hormonal levels are more dominated by pituitary–gonadal interactions.

Variety and Adaptability of Nervous Controls

No species better illustrates the powerful influences that the nervous system can exert on reproductive processes than the common house mouse. This is one of the most adaptable and opportunistic of all mammalian species, as attested by its distribution throughout the world. A key to this dispersion is the tendency of male mice to be aggressive toward each other, an aspect of behavior which we will discuss further in the next chapter. For now, we note that the result of this aggressiveness is for dominant mice to establish their territories, and for subordinate mice to be forced to seek elsewhere for mates.

One of the main ways through which mice interact is through odor cues. When you put a mouse into a new cage, the first thing it does is to go around and mark it everywhere with urine. Figure 28.14 illustrates how this can be documented by simply taking a photograph under ultraviolet light. The urine carries odor cues (pheromones) that are like a fingerprint of that mouse, conveying specific information about its species, sex, sexual maturity, and social rank. By this means, a dominant male establishes his territory. The amount of pheromone in the urine is directly dependent on the high levels of circulating androgen that are present in a dominant male. The biochemical identity of the pheromone substance is still unknown.

The development of timing of ovulation in the female is critically dependent on the pheromones in the urine. The way this comes about is summarized in Fig. 28.15. Urine deposited by other females has an inhibiting effect on the development of puberty in a young female. This is viewed as a protection against pregnancy while the females are crowded and still growing, and before there is maximal opportunity for dispersion. In contrast, mature male urine odors act as powerful priming pheromones, which accelerate and indeed, help to organize the processes of puberty, ovulation, mating, and pregnancy. The direct stimulatory effect on LH secretion is indicated in the figure. This ability of males to bring a female into ovulation is obviously an important adaptive advantage in ensuring the success of mating. It is also known that female urinary pheromones can stimulate the secretion of LH and testosterone in males. This effect is indepen-

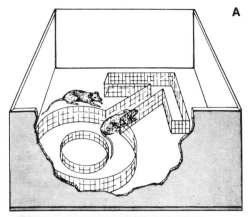

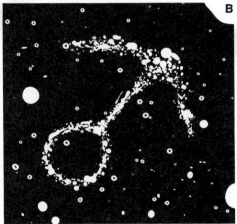

Fig. 28.14. A. Demonstration of urine marking by the house mouse. Diagram shows cage containing fence in the form of the male symbol. Male mouse is inside cage, female mouse outside. B. Photograph of cage taken with UV light; white areas are sites of urine deposit. Picture was taken after mice had been in cage for 20 minutes. (From Bronson, 1979)

dent of the reproductive status of the female. By this means there is a positive feedback loop between the two sexes that ensures the greatest chances for ovulation and reproduction.

These experiments thus attest to the powerful effects of pheromones in regulating mating and reproductive behavior. These effects are found, to a greater or lesser degree, in most mammals. Many of the effects require or are enhanced by other

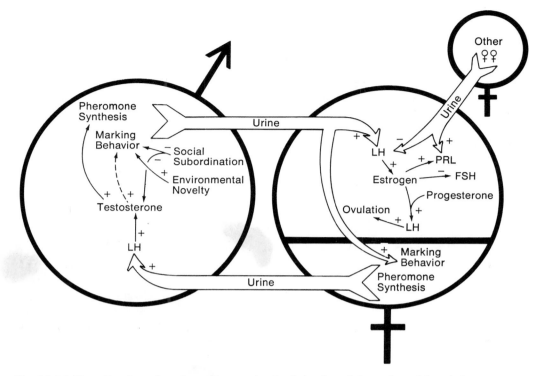

Fig. 28.15. Coordination of mating and reproductive behavior of the male and female house mouse through pheromones in the urine. FSH, follicle-stimulating hormone; LH, luteinizing hormone; PRL, prolactin; +, stimulation; −, inhibition. (From Bronson, 1979)

factors, such as appropriate tactile stimulation by other animals, or adequate nutrition, or the ambient temperature.

It should be stressed that most of our information comes from studies on laboratory animals living in crowded conditions, and the mechanisms of reproduction may be much modified compared with conditions in the wild. This has been stressed by Frank Bronson, of Texas, one of the main contributors to the above account:

. . . we really have no idea whether or not the estrous cycle that has been so well delineated in the laboratory ever occurs with any regularity in the field. . . . house mice in natural populations (may) not routinely ovulate every fourth or fifth day . . . They may ovulate only when the probability of a successful, ensuing pregnancy is high. Thus ovulation may be a relatively rare event in the life of a mouse . . . It may be more adaptive for wild animals

to concentrate on survival rather than reproduction unless the time for reproduction is truly propitious.

The fact that ovulation may be a relatively rare event in the mouse under some natural conditions has an interesting parallel among humans. Throughout most of human history, in many societies women have typically spent most of their childbearing years either pregnant or breastfeeding. Under these conditions, a woman ovulates only at irregular intervals, perhaps no more than a few dozen times in her entire lifetime. An interesting example of this is seen in the present-day 'Kung tribe in Africa, in which the mother breastfeeds her babies for several years. Suckling stimulates the release of prolactin from the pituitary, which not only stimulates lactation but also suppresses ovulation. Prolactin thus acts as a natural contraceptive, and a 'Kung woman may become pregnant only a few times. Roger Short of Edinburgh, who has studied the 'Kung people, points out that we should consider infrequent and irregular ovulation and menstruation as just as normal as the modern belief in uninterrupted regular cycles. Thus, in humans as well as other mammals, there is evidence of the adaptability of the reproductive apparatus, and its ability to be shaped and modified by social and cultural factors mediated through the brain.

REFERENCES

Beach, F. A. 1971. Hormonal factors controlling the differentiation, development, and display of copulatory behavior in the ramstergig and related species. In *The Biopsychology of Development* (ed. by E. Tobach, L. R. Aronson, and E. Shaw). New York: Academic. pp. 249–298.

Boeckh, J. and V. Boeckh. 1979. Threshold and odor specificity of pheromone-sensitive neurons in the deutocerebrum of *Antheraea pernyi* and *A. polyphemus* (Saturnidae). *J. Comp Physiol.* 132: 235–242.

Bronson, F. H. The reproductive ecology of the house mouse. *Q. Rev. Biol. 54:* 265–299. 1979.

Erulkar, S., D. B. Kelley, M. E. Jurman., F. P. Zemlan, G. T. Schneider, and N. R. Krieger. 1981. Modulation of the neural control of the clasp reflex in male *Xenopus laevis* by androgens: a multidisciplinary study. *Proc. Nat. Acad. Sci. 78:* 5876–5880.

Gordon, M. S. 1972. [Chap. 16].

Goy, R. W. and B. S. McEwen. 1980. *Sexual Differentiation of the Brain.* Cambridge, Mass: MIT Press.

Harlan, R. E., J. H. Gordon, and R. A. Gorski. 1979. Sexual differentiation of the brain: implications for neuroscience. *Rev. Neurosci. 4:* 31–61.

MacLusky, N. J. and F. Naftolin. 1981. Sexual differentiation of the central nervous system. *Science 211:* 1294–1303.

Matsumoto, S. G. and J. G. Hildebrand. 1981. Olfactory mechanisms in the moth *Manduca sexta:* response characteristics and morphology of central neurons in the antennal lobes. *Proc. Roy. Soc. B. 213:* 249–277.

Pfaff, D. W. 1980. *Estrogens and Brain Function.* New York: Springer.

Phoenix, C. H., R. W. Goy, A. A. Gerall, and W. C. Young. 1959. Organizational action of prenatally administered testosterone propionate on the tissues mediating behavior in the female guinea pig. *Endocrinology 65:* 369–382.

Raisman, G. and P. M. Field. 1971. Sexual dimorphism in the preoptic area of the rat. *Science 173:* 731–733.

Romer, A. S. and T. S. Parsons. 1977. [Chap. 3].

Short, R. 1980. quoted in *New Scientist, Apr. 24:* p. 209.

Tinbergen, N. 1951. [Chap. 14].

Tombes, A. S. 1970. *An Introduction to Invertebrate Endocrinology.* New York: Academic Press.

Additional Reading
Alcock, J. 1979. [Chap. 23].

29

Emotion

Human beings have speculated about the nature of their emotions since earliest recorded history. The Pythagorian philosophers of ancient Greece believed that the universe is composed of four elements: fire and water, earth and air. Hippocrates and his followers deduced that the body is similarly composed of four corresponding humors: blood and phlegm (mucous discharge), black bile and yellow bile. A person's temperament was believed to express an excess of one or more of these humors. Thus, an excess of blood rendered a person sanguine: ruddy-complexioned, courageous, hopeful, amorous. An excess of phlegm made a person phlegmatic: dull, cold, even-tempered. An excess of black bile made a person melancholic and sad, while an excess of yellow bile made a person choleric, or angry. These ideas were so believable that they lasted until the seventeenth century.

Even though we regard this scheme now as a prescientific fairy tale, it is nonetheless sobering to realize that these terms are still used to describe human emotions. And when we try to define emotions, we find that we have made little progress, despite all our science. Shakespeare never used the word *emotion;* Hamlet, for example, praised his friend Horatio as a man

> . . . whose blood and judgment
> are so well co-mingled . . .

Today we would say that Horatio's thoughts and emotions were in good balance, but what have we gained?

According to the Oxford English Dictionary, the word *emotion* is derived from the French word *mouvoir,* to move, and came into use in the seventeenth century to describe mental feelings (pain, desire, hope, etc.) that are distinct from thoughts, or cognitions. Within this broad and rather vague definition are three types of emotion, which are illustrated in Fig. 29.1. First are *complex behaviors* of an animal, such as predation, feeding, copulation, and related actions, which appear to us, through our human eyes, to express an emotion, but which may actually have no emotional component for the animal itself. Second are specialized motor actions— *emotional expressions*—in lower animals as well as humans which seem to express directly some inner feeling or emotion. Third are *inner emotions* which are entirely felt or perceived within us, and therefore known only to humans.

The neurobiological study of these three types of emotions has been rather limited. On the one hand, most complex behaviors

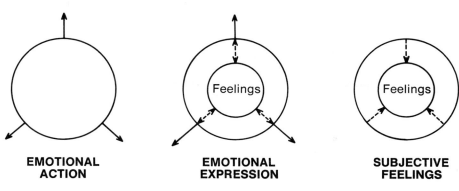

EMOTIONAL   **EMOTIONAL**   **SUBJECTIVE**
 ACTION   **EXPRESSION**   **FEELINGS**

Fig. 29.1. Types of emotional behavior.

are simply too complex to analyze, particularly when their emotional component is not obvious. On the other hand, our inner emotions are known only to ourselves. Most scientists rule out such subjective phenomena as objects of scientific study. That leaves us with only emotional expression as the type of emotion that is observable and amenable to precise analysis.

The subject of emotional expression was begun as a scientific study in 1806 by Sir Charles Bell of England, the same remarkable man responsible for the discovery of the sensory functions of the spinal nerves (Chap. 13), and for one of the first monographs on the structure and function of the hand (Chap. 23). In his book *Anatomy and Physiology of Expression,* he discussed the detailed relations between the facial muscles and many different expressions, such as laughter or grief. Various nineteenth century authors added their observations, but the subject was little more than popular science, a branch of phrenology, until Charles Darwin published his book *The Expression of Emotions in Man and Animals,* in 1872:

Sir C. Bell's view (wrote Darwin), that man had been created with certain muscles specially adapted for the expressions of his feelings, struck me as unsatisfactory. It seemed probable that the habit of expressing our feelings by certain movements, though now rendered innate, had been in some manner gradually ac-

quired . . . expressions, such as the bristling of hair (during terror), or the uncovering of teeth (during rage), can hardly be understood, except on the belief that man once existed in a much lower and animal-like condition. . . . He who admits . . . that the structure and habits of all animals have been gradually evolved, will look on the whole subject of Expression in a new and interesting light.

Darwin based much of his study on comparisons between humans and domestic animals, and he analyzed the expressions of these animals as meticulously as he had the beaks of finches. One of his conclusions was that opposite emotions, such as hostility or affection, may be expressed by oppositely directed movements, and the illustration of Darwin's dog displaying these two attitudes (Fig. 29.2) has been often reproduced.

After Darwin there could be little doubt that humans express emotions by motor and muscular mechanisms that have evolved out of similar mechanisms present in ancestral forms and exemplified in present-day vertebrates, most particularly domesticated mammals. This provided the necessary rationale for scientific exploration of the neurobiological basis of emotions, using animals as experimental subjects. The techniques for doing these experiments did not become available until the 1920's and 1930's, and much of our present understanding of brain mechanisms had its origins in that era. Before

Fig. 29.2. Darwin's dogs, displaying the contrasting expressions of hostility and affection (the latter to a somewhat abject degree). Can you tell which is which? (From Darwin, 1872)

discussing this work in mammals, however, we need first to discuss the interesting question of whether emotions occur in invertebrates and lower vertebrates.

Invertebrates and Lower Vertebrates

The question of whether lower animals have, or express, emotions, has been the subject of lively debate. The view prevailing until the nineteenth century was well-summarized by Bell: ". . . with lower creatures there is no expression but what may be referred, more or less plainly, to their acts of volition or necessary instincts." Note that Bell was willing to grant lower creatures volition while denying them emotions! These acts or instincts fall into our first category of emotional behavior (see Fig. 29.1).

In contrast, Darwin was quite willing to extend his view of emotional expression in animals to lower forms. He wrote that "Even insects express anger, terror, jealousy, and love by their stridulation." Now, in Chap. 24 it was noted that insects use stridulation to communicate with each other, with songs that signal "calling," "hostility," and "courtship." But whether or not these are accompanied by emotions, in the sending or receiving insect, remains unanswerable.

One test for the presence of an emotion is whether a given perception or motor act is accompanied by changes in the auto-nomic nervous system, such as faster heart beat or increased perspiration. This, for example, is the basis for the lie detector used to test whether suspects in a legal proceeding are telling the truth. It was stated in Chap. 19 that invertebrates have nerve ganglia that innervate their visceral organs, but that this innervation is relatively simple compared to that of vertebrates. The contrast has been summarized by Alan Epstein:

. . . like all other invertebrates (the molluscs) do not have an autonomic nervous system with which so much of affective expression is achieved. They do employ the same or very similar biogenic amines in their nervous systems and their viscera is innervated by peripheral ganglia, but this is hardly an autonomic nervous system which is an anatomically widespread and highly reactive system that provides duplex and functionally antagonistic innervation to the viscera, smooth muscles, and glands, and is complemented by an adrenal gland.

Epstein notes the observation of Wells, that during sexual arousal and copulation, the octopus shows no changes in heart rate.

Later in this chapter it will be shown how important the vertebrate autonomic nervous system is for the expression of emotions in mammals.

Another feature of arthropods is their rigid exoskeleton, which limits their ability to express inner states by local muscular movements on their body surface. Nonetheless, arthropods do express different behavioral states in their displays and actions related to courtship, predation, and territory. An example of a fierce struggle for dominance between two male spiders is depicted in Fig. 29.3A. However, these are signals conveyed by whole body movements; there is no associated specialized system for conveying the emotional intensity or tone behind the actions. Nor is it entirely due to the limitations of an exoskeleton; frogs engaged in a struggle for territory similarly reveal little of the intensity of their efforts in their facial expressions (Fig. 29.3B).

We must conclude that a complex innervation of the internal viscera, and a complex set of muscles which can independently signal autonomic and other internal states, are two components that are necessary for the expression of emotion in animals. These two components are almost entirely lacking in invertebrates and lower vertebrates. Therefore, although these animals can express behavioral states through whole body actions, they lack the ability to express emotions, as we generally understand that term.

Mammals

The fact that the expression of emotion seems to be a special ability of mammals is a clue that it may play an important role in the development of higher nervous functions in mammals. Let us consider the evidence for the neural basis of emotions, and then discuss its implications, particularly with regard to motivated behavior.

Hypothalamic Mechanisms. The success of Ferrier and his contemporaries in mapping out the motor areas of the cortex in the late nineteenth century (see Chap. 22) prompted others to investigate the effects of electrical shocks to deep structures of the brain. This early phase culminated in the demonstration by W. R. Hess of Zurich in 1928 that attack behavior, including expressions of rage, and defensive behavior, including expressions of fear, can be elicited in cats by stimulation within the hypothalamus (see Fig. 29.4). At about this time, Walter Cannon and his student Philip Bard, at Harvard, carried out a complementary series of studies in which they examined the behavior of cats after transections of the brain at different levels. They

Fig. 29.3. Displays of aggressive behavior. **A.** Fight between two male hercules beetles for dominance and access to female in lower left. **B.** Fight between two male frogs (*Dendrobates*) for possession of a territory. (A by Sarah Landry; B from Duellman, in Wilson, 1975)

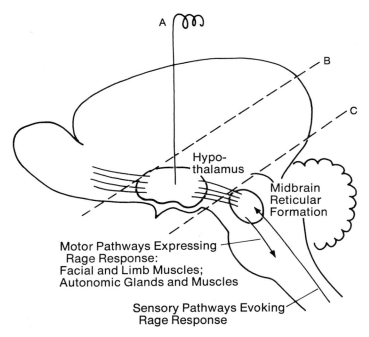

Fig. 29.4. Diagram of brain illustrating experimental demonstrations of various emotional behaviors in the cat. Electrode (A) used to stimulate hypothalamus and produce expressions of rage or fear. Transection (B) removing the forebrain and leaving the hypothalamus (hypothalamic animal) produces sham rage; transection (C) below hypothalamus results in animal which does not display sham rage.

found that removal of the forebrain (cortex and basal ganglia + thalamus, but sparing the hypothalamus), yields an animal that is irritable, and can be triggered into a display of rage (baring of teeth, hissing, clawing) at the slightest provocation (see Fig. 29.4). The display is accompanied by autonomic changes, such as increased heart rate and bristling of the fur. However, because of its low threshold, and uncoordinated and undirected nature, the display lacks the conscious dimension of normal attack behavior, and it was therefore termed "sham rage." This is a useful concept; after all, it is reasonable to expect a certain emptiness of meaning in the behavior of a cat that lacks its entire forebrain! When the transection occurs just below the hypothalamus, the sham rage response is lost (see Fig. 29.4).

These two lines of evidence thus firmly established the importance of the hypothalamus for the expression of emotional behavior. This importance is seen both with respect to the somatic component (control of facial and limb muscles) and the visceral component (control of glands and muscles in the autonomic nervous system). With regard to the autonomic responses, the displays of intense emotional behaviors are one of the best ways to bring out the actions of the sympathetic, as compared with the parasympathetic, divisions, as was first described by Cannon. Thus, displays of rage or fear are accompanied by increased levels of epinephrine and norepinephrine; in addition to increased heart rate and piloerection, blood is shunted to the muscles and the brain, the eyes dilate, and so forth. These changes bring the animal to the highest level of alertness, and prepare it for the most extreme levels of physical action which may be necessary for ensuring its survival.

Subsequent studies have added some details to this general picture. An important advance was the series of studies which John Flynn and his associates at Yale initiated in the 1960's. By selective stimulation of sites in the hypothalamus of awake, behaving cats, combined with careful behavioral observation, they were able to distinguish between emotional and unemotional attack behaviors. The behavioral test was to put a cat and a rat into a cage and test the effects of hypothalamic stimulation on the cat. Stimulation could induce two basic types of attack. In *affective attack* (see Fig. 29.5), the animal displays most of the signs of sympathetic arousal, emotional excitement, and rage. The cat attacks the rat, with clawing and hissing, though it does not usually proceed to biting the rat unless stimulation is prolonged. In contrast, in *quiet biting*, the cat makes no sound nor shows any emo-

Fig. 29.5. Two types of aggression shown by a cat toward a mouse. **A.** Affective attack. **B.** Quiet biting. (From Flynn, 1967)

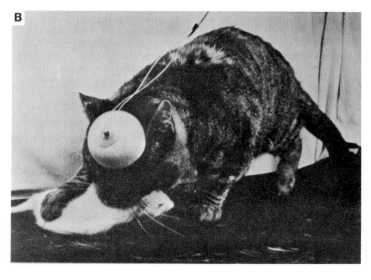

tion, but proceeds to capture the rat and bite it (see Fig. 29.5). This is actually similar to the normal predatory behavior of the cat. If you have seen films of cheetahs stalking and pursuing Thomson's gazelles in the Serengeti of Africa, you will recall the similar lack of emotional expression as they go about their business.

It thus appears that one can distinguish between *predation,* which has autonomic activation but may proceed without the expressive components, and *aggressive displays,* in which some of the components of predatory behavior are displayed in heightened form and used as threats to achieve dominance or defend territory.

We have previously seen that the hypothalamus contains neural elements and mechanisms that are involved in several types of behavior: feeding, thirst, sexual activities, and hormonal and autonomic functions. To this we now can add mechanisms that are essential for the expression of emotions. To some extent it is logical for these mechanisms to be closely related to emotions. Behaviors may be accompanied by emotions (such as attack accompanied by rage), may lead to emotions (such as eating leading to satisfaction or dissatisfaction), or emotions may be the primary motivating force leading to the behaviors (such as fear leading to flight) (see below). However, it should be emphasized that the mechanisms are to some extent distinct; thus, animals stimulated to attack and bite prey do not also eat the prey. Close analysis of these relations is difficult, because of the close proximity of different centers within the hypothalamus, and the many systems of fibers that pass through it, as we have previously noted.

The "limbic" system. For the expression of emotion, we can therefore consider the hypothalamus as one center, or group of centers; in our previous terminology, it is one node, or collection of nodes, in a distributed system. Let us now consider the rest of that system.

The most closely related region to the hypothalamus for the expression of emotion is the *midbrain,* just posterior to it (see Fig. 29.4). Attack behavior elicited by hypothalamic stimulation is blocked by lesions of the midbrain. Midbrain stimulation by itself can elicit attack behavior, even after surgical isolation of the hypothalamus from the rest of the brain. These results have indicated that much of the neural mechanism for the control of aggressive actions is present in the midbrain and lower levels. In line with the hierarchial view of motor organization, it appears that the motor control mechanisms are delegated to the brainstem and the spinal cord, and the hypothalamus may be mainly involved in initiating and coordinating these mechanisms. The close relations of the hypothalamus and midbrain in these respects suggested to Walle Nauta, then at Walter Reed, that this part of the neuraxis has a functional unity in mediating visceral and emotional behavior. He has termed it the *"septo-hypothalamic-mesencephalic-*continuum" (see Chap. 25). It is virtually identical with the regions embraced by the medial forebrain bundle.

What are the relations of this core system with other parts of the brain? The only coherent scheme of these numerous and complicated relations was put forward by James Papez of Chicago in 1937. We will discuss this scheme first, before reviewing more recent studies.

Papez was a neurologist who had noted reports of emotional outbursts in patients with damage to the hippocampus and to the cingulate gyrus. He carefully considered the known anatomy of the brain, and came up with a brilliant hypothesis for the neural circuit underlying emotions. The circuit starts with the hypothalamus as the site of output for expression of the emotions (see Fig. 29.6). Collateral fibers pass to the anteroventral nucleus of the thalamus, where they connect to cells that project to an area of the cerebral cortex known as the cingulate cortex. Here it was proposed that conscious, subjective emo-

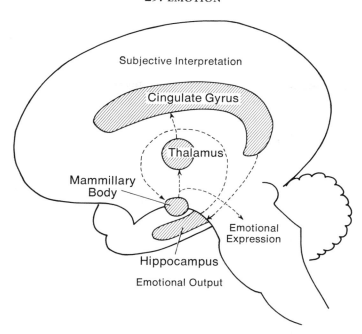

Fig. 29.6. Schematic diagram illustrating the Papez circuit for emotions.

tional experience arises; the cingulate gyrus was considered to be the cortical receptive region for emotional input relayed through the thalamus, in analogy with the visual cortex as the receptive region for visual input relayed through the thalamus. The cingulate gyrus, in turn, projects to the hippocampus. The hippocampus was proposed to combine this and other inputs and organize this information for output to its main projection site (it was believed), the mammillary bodies in the hypothalamus, thus completing the circuit. The pathway from cingulate to hippocampus to hypothalamus provided a means whereby the subjective experiences at the cortical level could be combined with the emotional content of the hypothalamic output.

No one had previously conceived of how these structures of the brain might be meaningfully related, and the Papez circuit was taken up with great enthusiasm and became a powerful stimulus to further research. An attractive feature was that it gave an interesting function to the

hippocampus, which up to then had been considered to be part of the rhinencephalon (nose brain) and related in some unknown way to olfaction. It was soon recognized that Papez's circuit was reminiscent of "The Great Limbic Lobe" of Broca. In 1879, Paul Broca, the great French neurologist, had noted how the cingulate gyrus and hippocampus seem to encircle or border the base of the forebrain. He imagined that this border, "placed at the entrance and exit of the cerebral hemisphere", was like the threshold of a door; hence, the term limbic, the Latin for threshold being "limen". He imagined that this limbic lobe is the seat of lower faculties, in comparison with the higher faculties in the rest of the cerebral cortex. In 1952, Paul MacLean, then at Yale, and one of the foremost workers on the visceral functions of the brain, suggested the term "limbic system" for Papez's circuit and the other regions related to it, and the term stuck.

The idea that there is a distinct "limbic system" for emotions, just as there is a visual pathway for visual perception, is of course very attractive. However, after 30 years, it increasingly appears that this is a case of a beautiful theory at the mercy of some stubborn facts. Studies have indeed upheld the role of the hypothalamus and the cingulate gyrus in emotional behavior. But the essential roles of the remaining two regions in the Papez circuit, the thalamus and the hippocampus, remain uncertain. Ablation or stimulation of these regions has given variable or conflicting results in different species. In addition, several other regions have been shown to have powerful effects on emotional behavior. Foremost among these regions is the amygdala.

The *amygdala* is a complex of related cells located in the cortex, at the base of the forebrain in lower mammals, and on the medial wall of the base of the temporal lobe in higher mammals In the same year that Papez published his circuit, Heinrich Klüver and Paul Bucy at Chicago reported the results of experiments in which they bilaterally removed the temporal lobe in higher mammals. In the same effects on behavior (see Fig. 29.7). They noted five main effects:

1. Overattentiveness: the animals are restless; they have an urge to orient toward or respond to all stimuli.
2. Hyperorality: the animals compulsively examine all objects by putting them in their mouths.
3. Psychic blindness: the animals see but do not understand; they indiscriminately approach and examine objects even though they are harmful (such as a lighted match).
4. Sexual hyperactivity: the animals increased their sexual activity, also indiscriminately, even toward inanimate objects.
5. Emotional changes: monkeys previously wild and aggressive are rendered tame and placid, and can be handled easily.

This complex of features has come to be known as the *Klüver-Bucy syndrome*. The psychic blindness has subsequently been shown to be due to loss of temporal lobe neocortex (see Chap. 31). The hyperactiv-

ity may be due in part to discharging neurons on the borders of the lesion. The sexual hyperactivity (which originally was one of the most sensational aspects of the syndrome) seems to be so undirected as to be part simply of the general hyperactivity of these animals. Finally, the emotional changes in the Klüver-Bucy syndrome have been especially linked to the amygdala. However, the changes vary, depending on the species; cats, for example, are rendered savage after amygdala destruction. Some research has connected the hypersexuality with the increased aggression in these cases. However, ablation is such a crude tool, and there are so many uncertainties about the extent of damage in different studies, that no firm conclusion can be reached.

Another approach in the study of the amygdala has been to use focal electrical stimulation. Some typical results are summarized in Fig. 29.8. Although these effects are quite dramatic, and seem relatively localized to the amygdala, a number of uncertainties limit the interpretation. For example, repeated shocks are often delivered over many seconds, or even minutes, to elicit these responses, raising questions about how much spread of seizure activity there is within the brain. Or the site stimulated may actually be suppressed by excessive currents, with activity being elicited only in surrounding areas.

In order to understand the functions of the amygdala, we need to know what it is connected to. By studying transport of HRP and radioactively labeled amino acids, neuroanatomists have shown that the amygdala has connections with a number of brain regions. These results are summarized in Fig. 29.9. There are, first, projections from the two parts of the olfactory pathway (see Chap. 12). Then, starting from the forebrain, we have connections to the cerebral cortex (frontal lobe and cingulate gyrus), the thalamus (mediodorsal nucleus), the septal region, the hypothalamus (through a long, looping tract, the stria terminalis, as well as short, direct

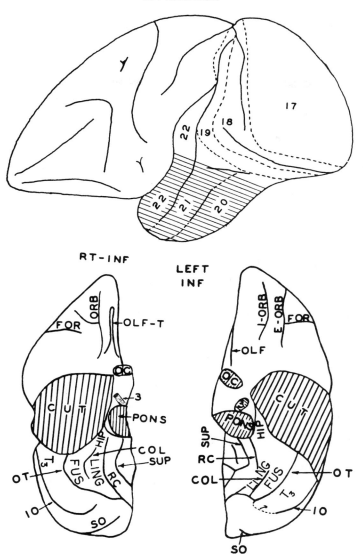

Fig. 29.7. Area of monkey temporal lobes removed (bilaterally) to produce the Klüver-Bucy syndrome. (From Bucy and Klüver, 1955)

ventral fibers), and numerous sites in the brainstem (fibers from the taste pathway—see Chap. 12—and from the raphé and locus ceruleus). Many of these connections are reciprocal, so that the amygdala gets feedback information from the sites it projects to. It should be emphasized that the amygdala is actually a complex of a number of nuclei (see Fig. 29.8). The *cortical and medial nuclei* form one

main division, concerned with olfactory and taste information. As we have learned in Chap. 28, this information is used in the control of feeding, by the connections of the amygdala to the hypothalamus. The other main division of the amygdala, the *basolateral group of nuclei*, is much expanded in higher mammals. It seems likely that the connections of this division to the cortex and thalamus, as well as those to

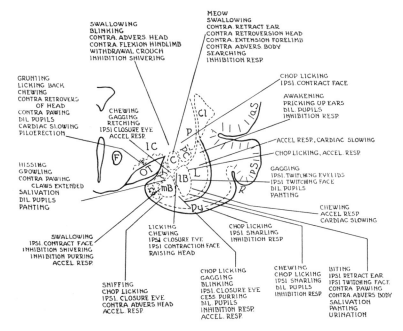

Fig. 29.8. Behavioral effects produced in the awake monkey by focal electrical stimulation at the sites shown. (From MacLean and Delgado, 1953)

the "septo-hypothalamo-midbrain continuum," are involved in the expression of emotional behavior. Finally, it is likely that the microcircuits within different amygdaloid nuclei mediate special modes of local processing that the amygdala provides to the systems for emotional behavior.

Similar studies have been carried out on other regions of the limbic system. The results of studies on the *cingulate gyrus* are summarized in Fig. 29.10. These results have fully confirmed the input pathway from the mamillary bodies through the anterior-ventral nucleus of the thalamus, and the output to the hippocampus, as postulated in the Papez circuit. However, they have shown further that the cingulate gyrus has connections to many other structures. Particularly important are connections to the amygdala, the subiculum (a cortical region neighboring the hippocampus), the septum, and several sites within the midbrain (the superior colliculi, for example, and the locus ceru-

leus). In addition, there are connections to other areas of cortex, in the frontal, parietal, and temporal lobes. Many of the relations are reciprocal. From these results it appears that the cingulate gyrus may well have connections to a greater variety of subcortical and cortical structures than any other region in the brain. What is the significance of this great variety? Why should there be connections, for example, to the superior colliculus, which is involved in the precise sensori-motor coordination of visual tracking, as well as to the nearby locus ceruleus, whose diffuse projections throughout the brain are believed to be involved in biorhythms and mechanisms of consciousness (Chap. 26). We do not know why, but part of the answer may be that emotional expression requires extensive coordination of both visual and somatic behavior, and the cingulate gyrus is a center for this coordination.

In conclusion, we may attempt to summarize present concepts of the limbic sys-

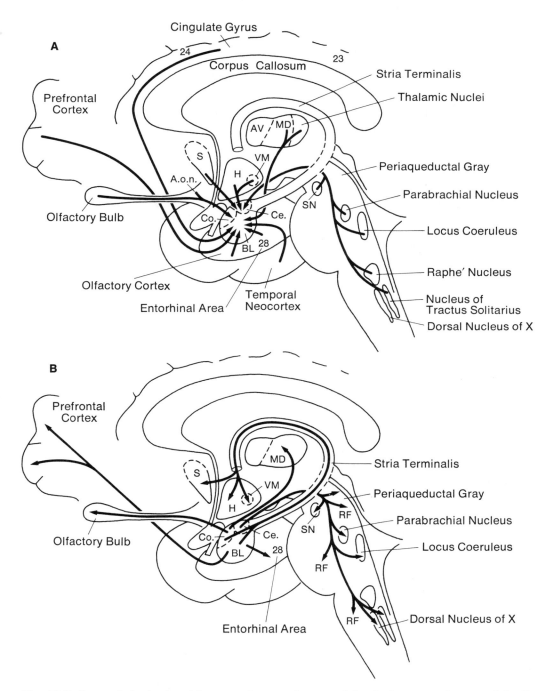

Fig. 29.9. Parts of the brain with connections to the amygdala. **A.** Inputs to the amygdala. **B.** Outputs from the amygdala. Abbreviations: A.o.n., anterior olfactory nucleus; AV, anteroventral thalamic nucleus; BL, basolateral amygdaloid nucleus; Ce., central amygdaloid nucleus; Co., cortical amygdaloid nucleus; H, hypothalamus; MD, dorsomedial thalamic nucleus; RF, reticular formation; S, septum; SN, substantia nigra; VM, ventromedial hypothalamic nucleus. (From Brodal, 1981)

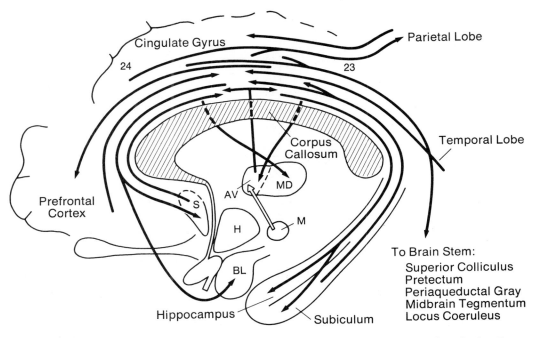

Fig. 29.10. Parts of the brain with connections to the cingulate gyrus. M, mammillary body. (From Brodal, 1981) For other abbreviations, see Legend of Fig. 29.9.

tem in the following manner. There is a series of structures, extending from the midbrain through the hypothalamus and into the basal forebrain, a phylogenetically ancient core system following the route of the medial forebrain bundle, that is concerned not only with visceral motor functions but also with related displays of motor behavior expressing emotion. These displays require the coordinated action of other brain centers. Some of these, such as the amygdala and the cingulate gyrus, are closely related to this core system. Others, such as the hippocampus and parts of the thalamus and midbrain, are related in limited, though specific, ways. Each of these regions acts as a nodal point in a distributed system, processing unique combinations of inputs and sending this information to unique combinations of output sites. By this means is achieved the coordination of visceral and somatic motor output to the whole body that is required for the expression of emotional behavior. Thus, it is still useful to think of a limbic system in terms of a core with many internal and outlying integrative centers; however, the borders of this system are not sharp, and the system overlaps with many other systems in the brain. In Chap. 31 we will discuss the particular contribution of the cerebral cortex to this system.

Dermal Muscles

Most of the observations derived from studies of mammals appear to apply to the control of emotional behavior in humans as well. However, we would not want to leave the subject without discussing further the special motor apparatus that we humans have for expressing emotions, the muscles of the face. These have an interesting phylogenetic history. Snakes have small muscles that insert into their scales, and can hold the scale at different angles to help regulate how smoothly it moves; birds similarly have small muscles that regulate the angle of the feathers. Most mammals have a relatively loose skin, and there is characteristically a sheet of *dermal muscles* that inserts into the skin over most of the body. When a horse twitches the skin of its back to shake off the flies, it is using dermal muscles. The dermal muscles in the face are called *facial muscles,* and they serve a variety of obvious functions, such as moving whiskers (vibrissae) on the snout, pricking up ears, assisting in the forming of different sounds, or moving the mouth during oral exploration or eating.

In higher mammals, such as the dog, and especially in primates and humans, the facial muscles have become adapted for the expression of emotions. This was recognized by the earliest writers on the subject, and the diagram in Fig. 29.11 shows the detailed picture from Bell's book of these muscles that had been obtained by anatomists by the nineteenth century. If, as Darwin put it, "expression is the language of the emotions," then movements of the facial muscles provide the vocabulary for that language. Although whole body movements and gestures are important in the expression of many emotions, the facial muscles represent a special apparatus for this function.

The degree of fine control exercised by the brain over these muscles is reflected in the large extent of their representation in the map of the motor cortex. It will be recalled from Chap. 22 that, in the homunculus of the body surface, the area of cortex involved in control of the facial muscles is greater even than the area for fine control of the hand. The pathways for this control are shown in Fig. 29.12. The fibers arising from pyramidal neurons in the facial area of the cortex connect bilaterally to the facial nuclei in the brainstem, there making monosynaptic and polysnaptic connections onto motoneurons that innervate the facial muscles through cranial nerve VII.

For the display of emotions by humans, we must therefore add this motor pathway to our limbic system. Detailed studies

Fig. 29.11. Dermal muscles of the human face, as portrayed by Bell and Henle, in Darwin, 1872. A, Occipito-frontalis, or frontal muscle; B, corrugator muscle; C, orbicular muscle of the eyelid; D, pyramidal muscle of the nose; E, medial lip-raising muscle; F, lateral lip-raising muscle; G, zygomatic muscle; H, malaris muscle; I, little zygomatic muscle; K, mouth depressor muscle; L, chin muscle; M, cheek muscle.

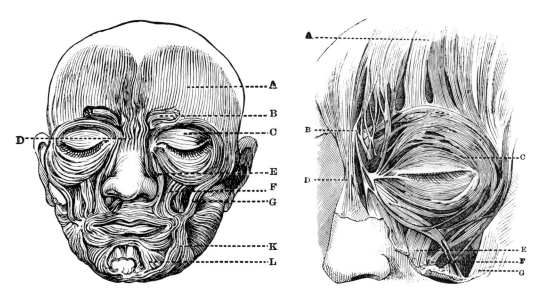

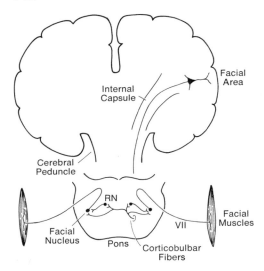

Fig. 29.12. Neural circuit mediating control of the dermal muscles of the face.

have shown that certain facial signals can be traced from primitive mammals through primates to humans. An example is shown in Fig. 29.13, for the baring of teeth combined with vocalization.

Emotion and Motivation

In our previous discussion of motivation (Chap. 27) we noted that the behavior of most animals, certainly of higher animals, is not governed simply by reflex responses to deficits or immediate needs. We saw that most behavior starts with the internal generation of behavior patterns by the brain itself. This intrinsic activity of nervous centers produces instinctual patterns of behavior, that may be triggered or guided by appropriate environmental cues and feedback circuits. The intensity of these patterns varies by a complex set of factors, that include habits, incentives and rewards, learning and experience, as well as actual bodily needs. This set of factors is thought of as determining the amount of drive, or motivation, behind a given behavior pattern.

To this set of factors we now can add

emotion. Emotion can be seen to be one of the key variables determining the kind of motor activity we engage in, and the strength or intensity of that activity. It is one of the primary factors responsible for the individuation of responses, for bringing out individual differences in behavior patterns among members of a species. We have seen that many of the neural mechanisms involved in the mediation of emotional behavior are found in the visceral part of the brain, and in the limbic system which coordinates visceral with somatic activities. Although we tend to think of these as lower functions, compared with higher functions such as learning or cognition, from an evolutionary point of view these mechanisms are among the most crucial to the success of individuals of a species, and for the adaptive survival of the species. This importance of emotions for motivated behavior has been eloquently stated by Alan Epstein:

Motivated behavior is laden with affect and its performance is accompanied by overt expressions of internal affective states. Affect is expressed by very young animals, is often full-fledged when first exhibited, and is typically species-specific . . . it does not depend on learning . . . These are not simply changes in limb movement or in the intensity of locomotion, but are true displays, organized into recognizable patterns, and sufficiently diversified to express a variety of internal states . . . in other words, motivated behavior is hedonic. . . . It arises from mood, is performed with feeling, and results in pleasure or the escape from pain, and although the moods, feelings, and satisfactions themselves are private and beyond our reach as scientists, their overt expression is a necessary characteristic of motivation.

The "hedonic" properties of behavior, mentioned above, are those that relate to our conscious judgments about whether a given sensation or action gives us pleasure or pain. How does the limbic system provide for this? Papez presumed that it depends on the cingulate gyrus. Modern

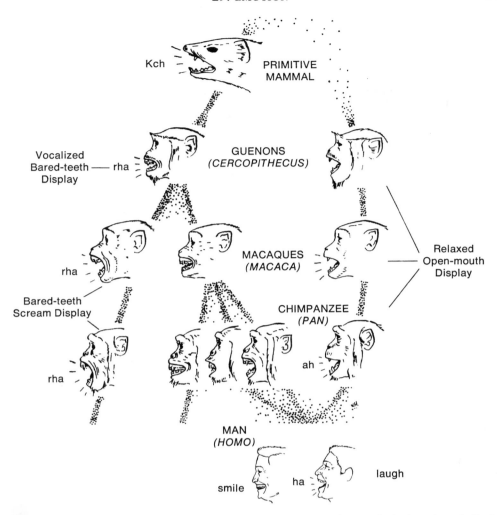

Fig. 29.13. Comparison of human expressions of smiling and laughter with the bared-teeth displays of lower primates and primitive mammals. (From van Hooff, in Wilson, 1975)

concepts include the contributions of other regions, especially of the cerebral cortex, as we shall see in Chap. 31.

REFERENCES

Bard, P. 1934. On emotional expression after decortication with some remarks on certain theoretical views; Parts I and II. *Psychol. Rev. 41:* 309–329, 434–429.

Bell, P. R. (ed). 1959. [Chap. 25].

Brodal, A. 1981. [Chap. 14].

Bucy, P. C. and H. Klüver. 1955. An anatom-ical investigation of the temporal lobe in the monkey (*Macaca mulatta*). *J. Comp. Neurol. 103:* 151–252.

Cannon, W. B. 1929. *Bodily Changes in Pain, Hunger, Fear, and Rage.* New York: Appleton.

Darwin, C. A. 1872. *On the Expression of the Emotions in Man and Animals.* London: Murray.

Epstein, A. N. 1980. A comparison of instinct and motivation with emphasis on their differences. In *Neural Mechanisms of Goal-Directed Behavior and Learning* (ed. by R. Thompson and L. Hicks). New York: Academic. pp. 119–126.

Flynn, J. P. 1967. The neural basis of aggression in cats. In *Neurophysiology and Emotion* (ed. by D. C. Glass). New York: Rockefeller. pp. 40–69.

Kluver, H. and P. C. Bucy. 1937. "Psychic blindness" and other symptoms following bilateral temporal lobectomy in rhesus monkeys. *Am. J. Physiol. 119:* 352–353.

MacLean, P. D. and J. M. R. Delgado. 1953. Electrical and chemical stimulation of frontotemporal portion of limbic system in the waking animal. *EEG Clin. Neurophysiol. 5:* 91–100.

Nauta, W. J. M. 1972. The central visceromotor system: a general survey. In *Limbic System Mechanisms and Autonomic*

Function (ed. by C. H. Hockman). Springfield, Mass.: C. C. Thomas. pp. 21–38.

Papez, J. W. 1937. A proposed mechanism of emotion. *Arch. Neurol. Psychiatr. 38:* 725–743.

Wilson, E. O. 1975. [Chap. 12].

Additional Reading

Bennett, T. L. 1977. *Brain and Behavior.* Belmont, Calif: Wadsworth.

Kolb, B. and I. Q. Whishaw. 1980. *Fundamentals of Human Neuropsychology.* San Francisco: Freeman.

Schiller, F. 1979. *Paul Broca: Founder of French Anthropology, Explorer of the Brain.* Berkeley, Calif. University of California Press.

30

Learning and Memory

Thus far we have assembled most of the major components needed by a central system to mediate behavior. A very rough idea of how these components vary across phyla is conveyed by Fig. 30.1. It can be seen that reflexes and instincts govern the lives of most invertebrates and lower vertebrates, with increasing contribution of motivated behavior in more complex vertebrates. We now consider an additional ability, and an essential one for most animals, the ability to learn, and remember what is learned. We shall discuss first the nature of learning and memory, and then consider what is known thus far about mechanisms, in invertebrates and vertebrates.

The word "learning" shares with other words we have used, like "instinct" and "motivation", the problem of being a term in wide daily use. S. A. Barnett, the well-known ethologist, has maintained that "colloquial terms with many . . . definitions, such as learning, are useful only as labels for general . . . categories of phenomena. . . . On this view it is inappropriate to ask what is the essence or the definition of learning." This valid criticism notwithstanding, neurobiologists go right ahead and work on what they believe to

be the problem of learning, so we need an appropriate definition for what they are working on.

A very broad definition would state that *learning is an adaptive change in behavior caused by experience.* For the neurobiologist, the usefulness of this statement lies in a careful definition of each of the terms within it:

Adaptive: adaptive indicates that the change must have some *meaning* for the behavior of the animal and the survival of the species.

Change: by change we mean that there must be a measurable *difference* between the behavior before and after some identifiable or imposed event. The change must be *selective* for the parts of the nervous system mediating the specific behavior, not just some general change in the animal, like increased metabolism or growing bigger. By the same token it must be independent of ongoing *development* or *maturation*. It should not be simply a reflection of *fatigue, damage,* or *injury,* or the normal *adaptational* properties of receptors and nerves.

Behavior: the behavior must involve control by *central* systems of the whole organism. It should not be confined to a

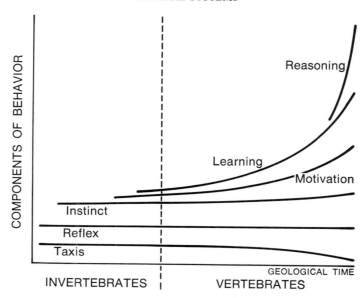

Fig. 30.1. Schematic portrayal of the relative development of different modes of adaptive behavior in phylogeny. (Modified from Dethier and Stellar, 1964)

part of the peripheral nervous system, or a point in a sensory or motor pathway.

Although these qualifications may seem unduly burdensome, we shall see that each one has meaning when we come to the experimental analysis of mechanisms.

Closely allied to learning is *memory*. Memory may be defined as *the storage and recall of previous experiences.*

This is a definition that applies as easily to computers as to animals. Memory is necessary for learning; it is the mechanism whereby an experience is incorporated into the organism, so that it can later cause the adaptive change in behavior. In lower organisms, the mechanism for storage of information may involve almost any cellular or neuronal process that can be perturbed by experience or actions of the environment. In higher vertebrates, and especially humans, we usually think of memories as those experiences that are subject to conscious recall. In many cases these recollections may be of the nature of impressions of the passing world, and bear no obvious relation to learning. In this sense, memory may include more than the mechanisms

specific for learning, as we have defined it.

Although everyone agrees that the mechanisms for learning and memory are found in the nervous system, there has been considerable debate about whether one could ever learn anything about them. Many psychologists, for example, believe that theories about learning and memory should be self-consistent, without recourse to neuronal mechanisms. In this view, psychologists and physiologists should each have their own theories, and not try to join the two; it can only result, in the opinion of B. F. Skinner, in "bad physiology and bad psychology." For most neurobiologists, this view is a bit outdated, and one of the goals of modern research is indeed to join the two levels into a coherent explanation.

A more powerful voice in the debate was that of the psychologist Karl Lashley. In 1950 he published a paper entitled "In search of the engram." Engram is another word for memory trace; Lashley had spent most of a lifetime carrying out experiments designed to reveal the presence of memory traces in different parts of the brain. He concluded that engrams do not exist; that memories are not localized in any one structure within the brain, but are distributed diffusely throughout the brain. In a way, this was the reticular theory reincarnated with a vengeance. Just as the reticular theory made rational investigation of neuronal organization seem hopeless, so the idea of functions spread diffusely throughout the brain seemed also to deny that they could be experimentally revealed. Lashley even observed, only half humorously that, after a lifetime of studying learning, he was beginning to doubt it could exist! Lashley's famous essay had a powerful influence on the field, and it took a generation to reveal the shortcomings of his experiments and interpretations, and supplant them with a more optimistic view based on modern techniques.

The conceptual framework for the approach of modern neurobiologists to the study of the neuronal mechanisms underlying learning and memory was laid down by two other psychologists, Donald Hebb of Montreal and Jerzy Konorski of Poland, in the late 1940's. Both drew on notions dating back to Cajal that learning and memory must involve changes in nervous circuits. Hebb, in his book on *The Organization of Behavior,* hypothesized that a psychological function, like memory (or emotion or thought), is due to activity in a *cell assembly,* in which the cells are connected together by specific *circuits.* He suggested that when a cell is active, its synaptic connections become more effective. This effectiveness may be a relatively short-lived increase in excitability, as in short-term memory, or it may involve some long-lasting structural *change in the synapse,* as in long-term memory. Konorski's ideas were similar. The concept that brain functions are mediated by cell assemblies and neuronal circuits has become widely accepted, as will be obvious to the reader of this book, and most neurobiologists believe that plastic changes at synapses are the underlying mechanisms of learning and memory.

In the last 30 years there has been an outpouring of work by anatomists, biochemists, and electrophysiologists, each searching for clues to the postulated changes in synapses. Some of the main types of approaches that have been used are summarized in Table 30.1. We cannot review all this work here, and for further information the student will want to refer to textbooks and reviews in behavior, psychobiology, and physiological psychology. However, we may note that much of this work was carried out before modern methods of cell biology were available. Also, many of the most sensational results have been found, on reexamination, to require more modest, or alternative, interpretations. A prime example is the recognition of the crucial importance of arousal. When an animal is tested in a learning task, its level of arousal, attention, motivation, and distraction are critical determinants of its performance. For example, many of the findings in studies of interanimal transfer of learning (see item 2 under Biochemical in Table 30.1) have been attributed to non-specific effects of the injected extracts on arousal, rather than on specific pathways in learning. Similar interpretations apply to several of the items under Electrophysiological in the table. This identification of the pervasive role of arousal and attention in learning is itself a valuable result, and is in accord with the importance we have placed on these functions for many aspects of behavior. With regard to specific mechanisms of learning, most of the approaches listed in Table 30.1 may be regarded mainly as a historical background. For the remainder of this chapter we will focus on modern research of the last few years, which has shown that the postulated mechanisms of plastic changes at snyapses can indeed be investigated at the cellular and molecular level. Thus, the field of learning and memory holds out some of the best prospects for understanding how cells and synaptic circuits provide the basis for behavior.

Table 30.1   Historical overview of some of the experiments that have provided evidence for mechanisms of learning and memory

Anatomical	
1. Environmental enrichment leading to bigger brains, dendrites, and synapses	Bennett et al., 1964
2. Effects of use on synapses	many authors, 1960's to present
Biochemical	
1. Increased neuronal activity leading to increased RNA	Hyden, 1959
2. Memory transfer between animals	
A. Cannabalism in Planaria	McConnell, 1962
B. Injections of brain extracts from trained animals into untrained animals	Babich et al., Fjerdingstad et al., Reinin et al., 1960's
3. Susceptibility to antimetabolite drugs (memory consolidation requires protein synthesis)	Flexner et al., 1960's
4. Cellular biochemistry of effects of use on synapses	many authors, 1960's to present
Electrophysiological	
1. Resistance to electroconvulsive shock	Duncan, 1949
2. Changes in EEG activity with learning	
A. Changes in hippocampal theta rhythms	Adey, 1960; Grastyan, 1966
B. High-frequency EEG rhythms in forebrain	Sheer, 1970
C. Slow potentials related to arousal or attention	Rowland, 1968
3. Changes in single neuron activity with learning	
A. During self-stimulation reinforcement	Olds and Olds, 1961
B. In relation to hippocampal theta rhythms	Ranck, 1973
C. In relation to amygdala and reward vs. aversive training	Fuster and Uyeda, 1971
4. Cellular electrophysiology of membrane properties at synaptic terminals	many authors (see Table 30.3)

For references, see Bennett (1977)

Types of Learning and Memory

Since behavior takes a variety of forms, it should not be surprising that there are a number of different types of learning and memory. Table 30.2 lists some of the main categories. The plan of this chapter is to consider each of these types in turn. We will illustrate each type with examples drawn from both invertebrates and vertebrates. One of the main accomplishments of recent research has been to show that each type of learning has its counterpart in invertebrates as well as vertebrates.

Table 30.2   Main categories of learning and memory

Types of learning	Types of memory
Simple	immediate
habituation	short term
sensitization	long-term
	specific
Associative	
passive (classical)	
operant (instrumental)	
one-trial (aversion)	
Complex	
imprinting	
latent	
vicarious	

SIMPLE LEARNING

Nerve cells have a number of properties that change with stimulation. For example, sensory receptors adapt, as already mentioned; their response tends to fade with continued or repeated stimulation (Chap. 11). Similarly, on the motor side, repeated stimulation of a motor nerve may cause a muscle to give either stronger (facilitation) or weaker (depression) responses. As we learned in Chap. 18, these

Table 30.3 Historical overview of some of the experiments that provided first evidence for molecular and membrane properties of synapses as a basis for plastic changes underlying learning and memory

Post-tetanic potentiation at neuromuscular junction	Feng, 1941
Post-tetanic potentiation in sympathetic ganglion	Larrabee and Bronk, 1947
Post-tetanic potentiation in spinal cord	Lloyd, 1949
Quantal release of transmitter correlated with post-tetanic potentiation and depression at the neuromuscular junction	del Castillo and Katz, 1954
Heterosynaptic interactions and presynaptic modulation	Dudel and Kuffler, 1961
Voltage dependence of transmitter release	Hagiwara and Tasaki; Takeuchi and Takeuchi, 1958–62
Calcium dependence of transmitter release; voltage dependence of calcium channels	Katz and Miledi, 1967
$[Ca^{2+}]$ (internal) and synaptic plasticity	Rahamimoff, 1968
I_{Ca} and synaptic plasticity	Zucker, 1974
Membrane potential effects of synaptic potential	Shinnahara and Tauc; Nicholls and Wallace; Erulkar and Weight, 1970's

For reference, see Klein et al. (1980)

changes are due to differences in the mobilization and release of the neurotransmitter at the neuromuscular junction. Table 30.3 lists some of the many studies of peripheral synapses that have laid the foundation for our understanding of the plastic changes that occur at synapses as a consequence of activity.

This raises an interesting question: do we say that the neuromuscular junction "learns" or has "memory"? The answer lies in the way we qualified our definitions in the previous section. Thus, plastic changes may occur at many sites in the nervous system; these changes may contribute to learning and memory, and may serve as valuable models for their mechanisms. However, learning and memory are basically properties of *central systems* that control the behavior of the whole organism, and it is therefore within the central nervous system that we must ultimately seek our answers.

Habituation

Closely related to the properties we have just discussed are habituation and sensiti-zation. Habituation is defined as *the decrease in behavioral response that occurs during repeated presentation of a stimulus*. It may be seen that inclusion of the term *behavioral* helps to make this response fit our definition of learning. However, habituation is such a universal phenomenon, and the term gets applied to so many isolated components of behavior, that it can overlap considerably with the properties discussed above. In addition, habituation involves only a change in the intensity of a response, not in the nature of the response itself, and some workers, particularly psychologists, therefore do not consider it to be real learning. However, habituation seems in so many cases to be of adaptive value that it is valid to consider it as a very elementary form of learning.

Habituation is usually observed as a change in the strength of a reflex response. Reflexes, as we have seen, are readily amenable to experimental analysis. Much of the early work on habituation was carried out on reflexes in mammals. This work showed that habituation (and its opposite, sensitization) occurs in a num-

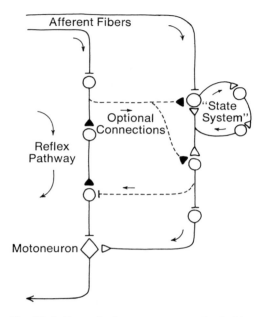

Fig. 30.2. Formal scheme to account for habituation and sensitization in a neural system, as
exemplified by the mammalian spinal cord.
Nonplastic synapses are indicated by bar terminal, habituating synapses by open terminals.
(Modified from Groves and Thompson, 1970)

ber of neural systems. Some of the best
studied were spinal reflex pathways in the
cat, and the reticular system of the brainstem. From these studies, Phillip Groves
and Richard Thompson at the University
of California elaborated a general scheme
that accounts for the neuronal circuits that
underlie habituation and sensitization, and
delineates the way the two processes are
related. As shown in Fig. 30.2, it is envisaged that habituation is a property of relatively specific neural pathways, whereas
sensitization involves a separate and more
extensive set of connections which includes mechanisms for setting the "state"
of the system. In Chap. 25 we discussed
the significance of central systems with this
property, and we shall see that this has
provided a useful framework for considering sensitization in invertebrates as well
as vertebrates.

In order to extend the studies summarized in Table 30.3 to habituation of cen-

tral systems, what one wants ideally is a
very simple response, a carefully controlled stimulus, and a neuron along the
central pathway that can be analyzed with
intracellular recordings. These conditions
are most closely met in simple organisms
with large, identifiable neurons.

The use of *Aplysia* for this purpose has
been brilliantly exploited by Eric Kandel
and his colleagues at Columbia University. They have studied the defensive withdrawal reflex of the siphon and gill (Fig.
30.3). The stimulus is a jet of water that
activates tactile receptors in the siphon and
gill and causes their reflex withdrawal.
With repeated stimulation there is less
withdrawal, and with sufficient repetition,
this depression of responsiveness may last
for several weeks (A). Thus, both short-
term and long-term habituation appear to
occur.

For electrophysiological analysis, the
sensory neuron mediating this response
was stimulated electrically, while intracellular recordings were obtained from the
motoneuron to the gill muscles (B). These
experiments showed that the EPSP elicited
in the motoneurons by the sensory synapse underwent a decrease in amplitude
with repeated stimulation that paralleled
the habituation of the reflex. By analyzing
the miniature EPSPs, it was found that the
decrease in EPSPs with repeated stimulation was due to a decrease in the number
of transmitter quanta released by the synapse; the response of the postsynaptic
membrane to each quantum was unaffected.

What causes the decrease in number of
transmitter quanta released? We know that
Ca^{2+} is a critical factor controlling release
at the neuromuscular junction, but how
can one examine this at central synapses,
which are too small to record from directly? Mark Klein and Kandel used the
clever tactic of analyzing the Ca^{2+} channels of the cell body of the sensory neurons, and, by careful consideration of indirect evidence, inferring the properties of
the Ca^{2+} channels in the synaptic terminal

A. THE REFLEX BEHAVIOR

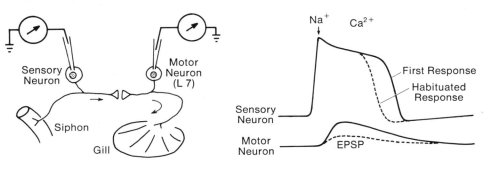

Gill

Water
Jet

Siphon

Mantle

1. Normal, Unstimulated

2. Initial Withdrawal

3. Withdrawal after
   Habituation

B. ELECTROPHYSIOLOGICAL ANALYSIS

Sensory
Neuron

Motor
Neuron
(L 7)

Siphon

Gill

Experimental Set-up

Na^+ Ca^{2+}

First Response

Habituated
Response

Sensory
Neuron

Motor
Neuron

EPSP

Recordings Before and After Habituation

C. CONCEPTUAL MODELS

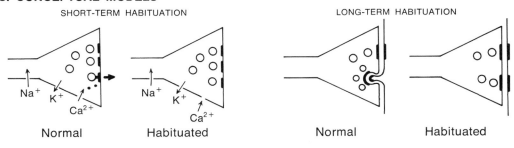

SHORT-TERM HABITUATION

LONG-TERM HABITUATION

Na^+ K^+ Ca^{2+}

Normal

Na^+ K^+ Ca^{2+}

Habituated

Normal

Habituated

Fig. 30.3. Summary of studies of habituation of the gill withdrawal reflex in *Aplysia*. **A.** The observed behavior. **B.** Intracellular recordings showing shortening of sensory action potential and decrement in motoneuron EPSP with repeated stimulation of sensory input. **C.** Left, simplified model of synapse to account for habituation by depression of inward calcium current at the terminal. Right, changes in structure of synaptic terminals during long-term habituation. (Adapted from Kandel, 1979)

of this neuron. They blocked the Na^+ channels with TTX in the medium bathing the sensory ganglia, and showed that the TTX-insensitive part of the action potential, presumably mediated by Ca^{2+}, decreased in amplitude in parallel with the habituation. They concluded that depression of the Ca^{2+} current plays a critical part in short-term habituation. Their model for this mechanism is depicted in C of Fig. 30.3.

Additional changes were found to be related to long-term habituation. In this case it was found that a large proportion of sensory neurons produce no detectable EPSPs in motoneurons, as if a functional disconnection had occurred. In electron microscopic studies it has been found that after repeated stimulation the structure of the synapses differs from that of normal synapses (see C). This may be produced by vesicle fusion with the terminal membrane, or by action of contractile proteins; in both cases, the mechanisms are dependent on Ca^{2+}. These hypotheses are now under active investigation.

Sensitization

Sensitization may be defined as *the enhancement of a reflex response by the introducing of a strong or noxious stimulus.* Although it appears to be the opposite of habituation, it differs in several respects. It depends on a stimulus different from that which elicits the reflex in question. Any strong stimulus activates general arousal mechanisms (Chaps. 25, 26), and so do noxious stimuli (Chap. 13). Thus, sensitization involves activation of general arousal systems, which affect the intensity of reflex response. For example, if you are startled by a loud noise, you are more sensitive to a subsequent soft sound. It is a widespread phenomenon; it alerts animals to predators and other potentially harmful stimuli, and thus is of important adaptive value.

The cellular basis for sensitization has also been investigated in the gill withdrawal reflex of *Aplysia*. Noxious stimulation can be produced by delivering a rain of strong electrical shocks to the skin of the animal. The effect of this stimulation is to restore partially the original amplitude of a habituated gill withdrawal reflex response (Fig. 30.4A,B). Analysis of the quantal EPSPs shows that the restoration results from an increase in the number of transmitter quanta released by each impulse in the sensory terminal.

The nociceptors activated by these shocks make connections onto the presynaptic terminals of the sensory neurons in the gill reflex pathway. In a variety of studies by James Schwartz and Kandel and colleagues, evidence has been obtained that the nociceptor fibers are serotonergic, and that their action on the sensory terminals is to activate a serotonin-sensitive adenylate cyclase. This leads to protein phosphorylation, by the steps discussed in Chap. 9. It has been postulated that this causes increased Ca^{2+} current by phosphorylation of a Ca^{2+} channel protein; alternatively, there may be phosphorylation of a K^+ channel, that decreases K^+ current, increasing the duration of the action potential and thereby the influx of Ca^{2+} (see C in Fig. 30.4).

Thus, sensitization works in a manner that is opposed to habituation, to increase the amount of neurotransmitter released by each impulse in the circuit, one can say. Taken together, these studies provide one of the best examples of excitable channels that are controlled by multiple factors, a topic that was introduced in Chap. 9.

Sensitization also occurs in the neural circuits that control feeding and heart rate in *Aplysia*, as well as in a variety of other invertebrate preparations. The three systems are similar in that sensitization appears to be mediated by serotonergic fibers, acting through cAMP to control voltage-dependent Ca^{2+} conductances. However, the points at which sensitization occurs are different in the three sys-

A. EXPERIMENTAL SET-UP DEMONSTRATING SENSITIZATION

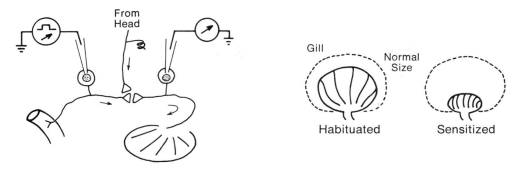

B. ELECTROPHYSIOLOGICAL ANALYSIS

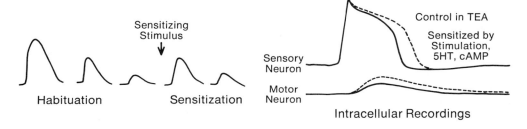

C. CONCEPTUAL MODELS

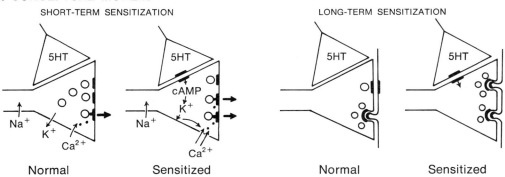

Fig. 30.4. Summary of studies of sensitization of the gill withdrawal reflex in *Aplysia*. **A.** Intracellular recordings from gill motoneuron, showing habituation to sensory input and sensitization by stimulation of nociceptors from the head. **B.** Left, amplitude of the gill response during habituation and sensitization. Right, broadening of the sensory action potential and facilitation of the motoneuron EPSP during sensitization of gill reflex. **C.** Left, simplified model of the synapse to account for sensitization (see text). Right, model of structural changes underlying long-term sensitization. (Adapted from Kandel, 1979, and Shapiro et al., 1980)

553

tems. The serotonergic fibers function to mediate arousal, and the different sites of connection are believed to reflect the differing significance of arousal for short-term sensitization, and for long-term plastic changes underlying learning in the case of the gill withdrawal and feeding reflexes. These arousal systems in *Aplysia* have their counterparts in vertebrates, as we discussed in Chaps. 25 and 26.

From these results, Kandel has postulated that

. . . Ca²⁺ current modulation may prove a general mechanism for learning and memory. The changes in Ca²⁺ influx can control the instantaneous level of transmitter release. . . . modulation of Ca²⁺ channels . . . (might) be capable of contributing to long-term memory . . . by producing simple geometric changes in the shape of the synaptic apposition.

Similar mechanisms of synaptic modification have been proposed by others to underlie the changes that occur during neuronal development (see Chap. 10), and Kandel has speculated whether in this light one ". . . can conceive of learning as being a late . . . stage in neuronal differentiation?" Thus, Cajal's belief that development and learning share common processes of neuronal remodeling seems a step nearer realization.

The work on habituation and sensitization therefore illustrates very nicely how neurobiologists, by isolating for study a very simple and elementary function, can progress through a series of experiments to arrive at results of considerable general interest. Much more work remains, of course, in applying these concepts to the behaving animals. Despite these results showing synaptic plasticity, the learning abilities of *Aplysia* in behavioral tasks are in fact rather limited. We shall consider this question further below.

ASSOCIATIVE LEARNING

In associative learning, an animal makes a connection through its behavioral re-

sponse between a neutral stimulus and a second stimulus that is either a reward or punishment. The best known example is the way a dog, which normally salivates when presented with a piece of meat, will salivate at the sound of a neutral stimulus like a bell, after the bell has been paired with the presentation of the meat. This is called a *conditional reflex*. It was discovered in the early 1900's by Ivan Pavlov. By force of tradition it has come to be called *classical conditioning*.

In classical conditioning the animal is a passive participant. In contrast, an animal may be asked to learn a task or solve a problem, such as escaping from a box, or pressing a lever, or running a maze. This experimental method was introduced by Edward Thorndike in 1898. Since the animal learns to solve the problem and get the reward (or avoid the punishment) by operating on its environment, it is called *operant conditioning, or instrumental conditioning;* since the animal usually makes mistakes before learning the task, it is also called *trial-and-error learning*.

In both classical and instrumental conditioning, the strength of the response depends on the amount of reward or punishment. Particularly in the case of instrumental conditioning, the strength of the response can be used as a measure of the animal's "drive" to obtain the reward or escape the punishment. These experiments have thus provided the basis for studies of motivation, as discussed in Chap. 27.

One of the most surprising results of these studies has been the ability to condition single neurons in the brain by operant techniques. This was first demonstrated by James and Marianne Olds at Michigan in 1961 (see Table 30.1). Figure 30.5 illustrates such an experiment on neurons in the motor cortex of the monkey, conducted by Eb Fetz and Mary Ann Baker of the University of Washington. The recordings were made using implanted microelectrodes in awake animals. The rate of impulse firing was registered

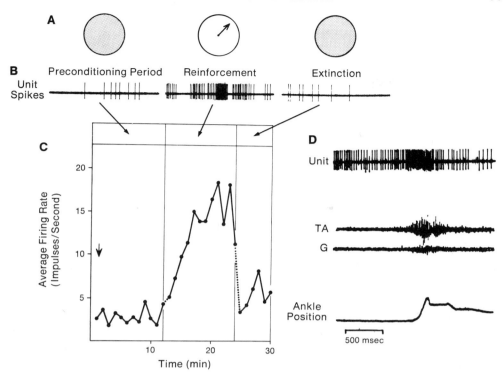

Fig. 30.5. Operant conditioning of a single neuron in the motor cortex of an awake behaving monkey. **A.** Meter registering rate of impulse firing; when firing rate exceeded a preset level, dial became illuminated, and food reward was given. **B.** Representative records of impulse activity. **C.** Graph of impulse firing rate during successive experimental periods. **D.** Relation of muscle activity (EMG of tibialis anticus (TA) and gastrochemius (G) muscles) and ankle movement to operant impulse burst of a reinforced motor cortical neuron. (Modified from Fetz and Baker, 1973)

on an illuminated dial, and when the rate exceeded a preset level, a few drops of tasty fruit juice were given as a reward. During the training period the increase in activity took the form of bursts of impulses; as conditioning proceeded, the bursts became more frequent and more intense. When the reward was withheld, the rate of firing fell rapidly to its former level, a property called extinction. Occasionally, two units could be recorded from the same electrode; in some cases the firing patterns were similar, indicating coactivation; in other cases they were inversely correlated, indicating differential control of neighboring cortical cells. The relation of the neuronal activity to muscle movement was studied by recording the electrical activity of the muscles (electromyograph) and

muscle movement. As shown in Fig. 30.5D, the impulse bursts tended to precede slightly the onset of muscle activity and muscle movement, suggesting that the bursts were part of the motor activity initiating motor performance during reinforcement, rather than simply a result of sensory feedback to the cortex from the moving muscles. The student should review Chaps. 13, 23, and 25 to appreciate the sensory, motor, and central circuits involved in this motor activity.

With regard to membrane mechanisms underlying associative learning, progress has been slow. It is not easy to find complex systems that can be isolated for experimental study. In mammals, studies of cortical neurons have shown that conditioning is accompanied by an increase in

Table 30.4 Some model systems in which associative learning has been studied

EEG alpha blocking	Jasper and Shagass, 1941
	John, 1967
Flexion reflex	Buchwald et al., 1965
Auditory tones	Woody, 1972
Single neurons	Olds and Olds, 1961
Motor cortex neurons	Fetz, 1961
Nictitating membrane response	Thompson, 1962
Leg position in cockroach	Horridge, 1960's
Electrical stimulation of the brain	Olds and Milner, 1954
Heart rate in pigeon	Cohen, 1969
Sensory stimulation in Hermissenda	Alkon, 1975

For references, see Groves and Schlesinger (1979)

the sensitivity of single neurons to direct electrical stimulation through the recording microelectrode. This indicates that conditioning involves an increase in the excitability of at least some cells, but these experiments do not reveal the nature of the underlying mechanisms. In invertebrates, it has been possible to demonstrate that associative learning does occur (see Table 30.4), but these systems have also proved difficult to tackle experimentally.

One promising preparation has been the mollusc *Hermissenda,* a sea slug. Daniel Alkon and his colleagues at Woods Hole have found that the movement of this animal toward a light source is markedly reduced after repeated pairing of the light with rotation of the animal. This behavior thus meets some of the main criteria for associative learning, in that it involves a specific response (phototaxis) modified by pairing of two different sensory stimuli, light and rotation. The neuronal systems involved in this learning model are illustrated in Fig. 30.6 (we discussed the statocysts of *Hermissenda* in Chap. 15). Intracellular recordings have shown that the type B photoreceptors are depolarized by light and the hair cells of the statocyst are depolarized by rotation, and when these stimuli occur simultaneously the response of the photoreceptor is enhanced. It is believed that this increased and long-lasting depolarization may be mediated by changes in Ca^{2+} and protein phosphorylation. The type B cell inhibits the type A photoreceptor, reducing the overall phototaxic response of the animal.

This preparation has the attractions of a simple system for analysis at the molecular and membrane level. At the same time it is limited because the systems mediating the associative processes are peripheral, and lack the complexity of central systems in higher vertebrates. This is a good illustration of how our understanding of associative processes must be built up by a careful correlation of results from many different systems, each with its particular advantages and disadvantages for experimental analysis.

Aversion Learning

For most of this century, classical and operant conditioning have dominated our concepts of how learning may occur. Each seemed to have such obvious value to an animal that it was impossible for most behavioral scientists to conceive of any other mechanism. However, it has become clear that there are indeed other very important forms of learning. The problem first is to recognize them, and then to figure out how to study them experimentally.

An excellent example of this is aversion learning. In the 1960's John Garcia and Robert Koelling were interested in how

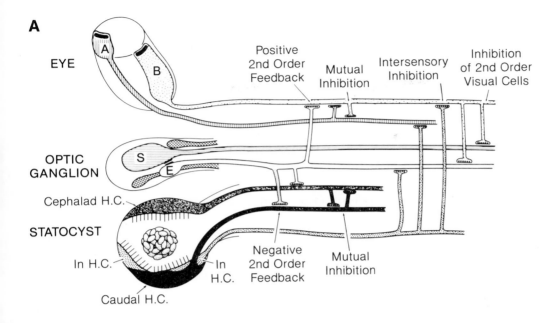

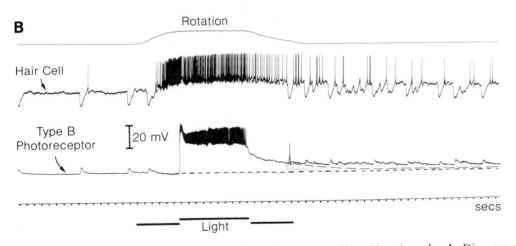

Fig. 30.6. Model of associative leaning in the nudibranch mollusc *Hermissenda*. **A.** Diagram of sensory neurons and interconnections. The eye has type A and B photoreceptors; the optic ganglion has E cells (which give rise to EPSPs in type B photoreceptors) and S cells (physiologically silent, but electrically coupled to E cells; the statocyst contains hair cells (H.C.) in three locations. **B.** Intracellular recordings from a caudal hair cell (above) and type B photoreceptor (below) to simultaneous rotation and visual stimulation. After stimulation, the IPSPs in the hair cell are larger, and the EPSPs and long-lasting depolarization in the photoreceptor are larger (line of long dashes indicates control level). (From Alkon, 1979)

557

rats learn to associate tastes with sickness. They used the fact that strong X-irradiation of an animal damages the gastrointestinal tract and induces sickness after a period of several hours. The rats were given distinctively tasty solutions of water to drink, paired with X-irradiation. After recovering from the sickness, the rats refused to drink the tasty water. This is a laboratory demonstration of a phenomenon we all recognize: when we suspect that a food has made us sick, we lose our "taste" for the food and avoid it. In field studies of animals it is called "bait-shyness." Because it requires only one episode of sickness, it is also called "one-trial learning."

Although the pairing of an unconditional stimulus (sickness) and a conditional stimulus (taste) satisfies the criteria for associative learning, there are several differences from the situation in classical conditioning. In classical conditioning, many trials are needed for transfer from the unconditional to the conditional response, and the unconditional and conditional stimuli must be timed very closely together, usually within a second or two, or else the animal cannot make the association between the two. In contrast, in aversion learning, only one trial is necessary, and the association between taste and sickness is made after a delay of several hours. These differences are so dramatic that at first few psychologists would even believe the results; one of them has been quoted as commenting "These findings are no more likely than bird droppings in a cuckoo clock!" (quoted in Chance, 1979).

By now the basic findings have been repeatedly documented and extended to many different species. It has been found that many agents can serve as the unconditional aversive stimuli; these include lithium chloride solutions, psychoactive drugs like amphetamine and apomorphine, and certain poisons. However, many agents are surprisingly ineffective; these include toxic substances like strychnine, and general factors such as stress. Electric shocks, which are so effective for classical or operant conditioning when paired with visual and auditory stimuli, have little effect. Parallel studies of the conditional stimulus have shown that one-trial learning can be demonstrated only by using stimulation of the tongue. The learning is strongest when the inputs come from the taste buds, but aversion can also by demonstrated with tactile stimulation of the tongue.

Many fascinating questions are raised by these findings, but we will consider only two here. First, what are the neural pathways for aversion learning? The taste part of the system was discussed in Chap. 12, and is reproduced in Fig. 30.7. The other pathway, mediating the aversive input, is more difficult to specify, because of the diversity of agents that may serve as unconditional stimuli. However, it is believed that much of this input is carried in visceral afferent fibers. These fibers convey sensory input from the intestines and other internal organs to the brainstem, through the tenth cranial nerve (see Chap. 3). Among the sites of termination within the brainstem is the nucleus of the solitary tract, the main sensory relay nucleus in the taste pathway. The explanation of aversion learning requires a site, or sites, at which the taste and aversive pathways meet, and the nucleus of the solitary tract appears to be a likely candidate.

In addition to the two pathways mediating the sensory inputs, a variety of other brain regions has been found to have an influence on aversion learning. These have been identified by ablation and stimulation experiments, which, as we have emphasized, are rather crude tools. Some of the main regions identified by these means are shown in Fig. 30.7. The diversity of these regions is remarkable. Note that many of them have been encountered before, as nodal points in limbic systems involved in mediation of feeding, arousal, and sexual functions. Each region is an integrative center that makes its special contribution to these different functions. Thus,

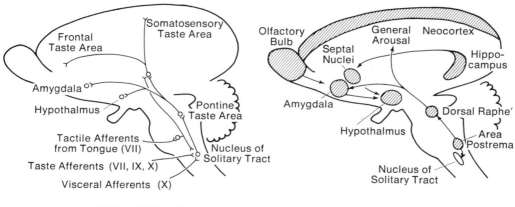

A. PATHWAYS FOR TASTE INFORMATION

B. PATHWAYS FOR CENTRAL MODULATION

Fig. 30.7. Neural pathways mediating taste aversion learning in the mammal. (Based in part on Ashe and Nackman, 1980)

the nucleus of the solitary tract is itself significant not only as the convergence point for taste and visceral inputs, but also as a region involved in arousal, as discussed in Chap. 26. As another example, lesions of the amygdala produce deficits in several types of learning. In the case of aversion learning, the rats seem to have difficulty in recognizing the significance of different taste stimuli, which has been interpreted as a perceptual deficit. In addition, animals with amygdalar lesions are unable to orient normally, which is believed to represent deficits in motivation.

From these considerations, the study of the neural circuits involved in aversion learning has led to a much broader perspective on learning processes in general. This new view has been expressed by John Ashe and Marvin Nachman in the following way:

When an animal undergoes an experience, learning is only one of a wider complex of physiological responses that may occur. Arousal, attention, stress, and motor responses are (also) . . . initiated, and it is . . . likely that these responses are coupled to associative mechanisms . . . One of the major by-products of learned taste aversion research has been the reemphasis on the importance of understanding the total animal in elucidating prin-ciples of associative formation. In neurobio-logical terms . . . stimuli that initiate internal consequences that are smoothly coupled to the on-going physiology of the animal should re-sult in robust learning and thus the animal will appear to be especially "prepared" for the acquisition of this learning.

It can thus be seen that considerable progress has been made toward understanding the neural circuits involved in aversion learning. In contrast, we know almost nothing about the cellular mechanisms that mediate these remarkably long-lasting effects. As a working hypothesis, one can speculate that the mechanisms that have been invoked for long-term changes in habituation and sensitization may be involved—that is, metabolic changes at synapses involving protein phosphoryla-tion. It will, of course, be advantageous to analyze such mechanisms in a simple system. It is of interest in this regard that Alan Gelperin at Princeton has found that the land slug *Limax* can show one-trial aversion learning that lasts for periods of up to three weeks. Recently he and his colleagues have demonstrated this phenome-non in an isolated preparation of the *Li-max* nervous system. It is, hoped that further studies of this and other prepara-tions will provide some leads into the molecular events taking place during aversion learning.

COMPLEX LEARNING

The types of learning we have discussed thus far are those that have received the greatest attention from behaviorists and that have been most amenable to experimental analysis by neurobiologists. In order to have an adequate perspective, it is necessary to recognize that these by no means exhaust the types of learning that occur. As indicated in Table 30.2, several additional types may be grouped under the general heading of *Complex Learning*.

Imprinting is the process whereby a young animal forms a behavioral attachment to a parent. It was discovered by ethologists, who found that the attachment usually depended on some special stimulus, such as the shape of the parent's body, or a particular colored spot on the plummage. A young animal can often be induced to form its attachment to an individual or object that sufficiently resembles the specific stimulus; hence, the famous picture of young geese following Konrad Lorenz on his daily walk. Imprinting usually occurs during some early *critical period* in the young animal's life, and if it does not occur, the subsequent normal development of behavior is irretrievably lost. Thus, songbirds fail to learn their song (see Chap. 24), and animals fail to develop their adult social and sexual behaviors. Imprinting is thus an essential kind of learning in many species.

Some evidence for the brain mechanisms that are involved in imprinting has been obtained by Gabriel Horn and his colleagues at Cambridge. They have studied young chicks, which become attached to a visually conspicuous object (normally the mother hen) early in life. Experimentally the chicks can become attached to a rotating disc. In animals trained in this manner, it was found that the incorporation of radioactive uracil into RNA was selectively increased in a part of the fore-

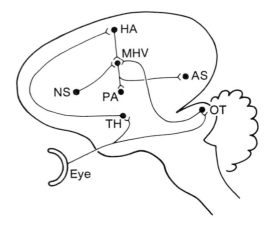

Fig. 30.8. Neural connections in the brain of the chick that are believed to mediate visual imprinting early in life. Abbreviations: AS, archistriatum; HA, hyperstriatum accessorium; MHV, medial part of hyperstriatum ventrale; NS, neostriatum; OT, optic tectum; PA, paleostriatum augmentatum; TH, thalamus. (Based on Horn, 1979)

brain called the medial part of the hyperstriatum ventrale (MHV) (Fig. 30.8). This could reflect a growth of synaptic boutons in this region, requiring synthesis of proteins and increased RNA. Electron microscopic measurements of the synapses in the MHV showed an increase in the area of contact of about 20% over controls. Studies in other laboratories have shown changes in 2DG uptake in this region during training. Thus, several lines of evidence suggest that increases in synaptic activity and synaptic effectiveness are associated with processes of imprinting in this species.

Another type of complex learning occurs when an animal is introduced to an experimental environment, like a maze, and allowed to run about in it without being trained or rewarded. Although there is no evidence of learning at the time, the animal later learns an operant task in the maze much faster than an unexposed animal. This effect of experience is called *latent learning*. Although there have been no experiments explicitly aimed at the neural mechanisms of this phenomenon, there is evidence that experiences such as maze running or social interactions with other animals lead to larger brains, and increases in the numbers of cortical dendritic branches and spines, and even the sizes of individual synapses (Table 30.1). These findings recall the observations of Darwin on the larger brains of wild compared with domesticated animals (see Chap. 31).

In the light of the perspective taken above with regard to aversion learning, familiarity with a training apparatus could facilitate learning through various ways, including alleviating stress, reducing fear, and enhancing attention and orienting mechanisms; in other words, we learn better in comfortable surroundings.

The final type of learning we will mention is called *vicarious,* or *observational, learning.* This occurs when an animal observes another animal performing a task, and then learns the task more rapidly. This is obviously extremely important in humans; it covers the way we imitate and follow examples, learn from experiences of others, and follow symbolic directions to achieve skills and attain goals. It is more difficult to demonstrate in other mammals, and, in fact, for a long time behaviorists denied that vicarious learning occurs in subhumans. There is no evidence that observational learning takes place in lower vertebrates or invertebrates. It is believed by many behaviorists that observational learning goes beyond associative conditioning, and involves *cognitive* processes: attention, retention, and thinking. Behaviorists are only beginning to form a coherent view of these processes, and it may be hoped that neurobiologists may be able to contribute their information about neural mechanisms to these emerging concepts.

MEMORY

As mentioned in the preceding section, memory, the capacity to store and recall information, is a necessary component of learning. Animals as low on the evolutionary scale as the flatworms (*Planaria*; see Table 30.1) can show classical conditioning, which implies that there is a memory mechanism present. Whether this is distributed throughout the peripheral nerves or body cells of this animal, as some of the more sensational experiments imply, is still a controversial question. In higher invertebrates and vertebrates it is clear that memory mechanisms related to behavioral experiences depend on the brain.

Invertebrates

The octopus has been a particularly attractive subject for the study of memory. As we learned in Chap. 2, it has the largest brain among the invertebrates. It also has highly developed eyes and a highly developed tactile system in its tentacles. J. Z. Young and his colleagues in London have shown that the octopus can readily learn visual discrimination tasks, such as distinguishing between vertical and horizontal lines. By making ablations of different parts of the brain, they showed that visual memory is stored in the vertical lobe (see Fig. 30.9). Octopuses can also learn tactile discriminations with their tentacles (though, as we discussed in Chap. 23, they cannot learn proprioceptive discriminations). It was found that tactile memories are stored in the inferior frontal and subfrontal lobes. Thus, as indicated in Fig. 30.9, the visual and tactile memory systems are mostly separate, though there is some overlap in the vertical lobe. This separation of memory systems is more distinct than is the case in vertebrates, at least as far as is known at present. The vertical lobe is packed with millions of very small neurons; many of these lack axons, and thus appear to form microcircuits by means of dendrodendritic interactions (see Chap. 4). Young has hypothesized that these "microneurons" are crucial for memory; during learning they inhibit unwanted pathways, leaving others open to

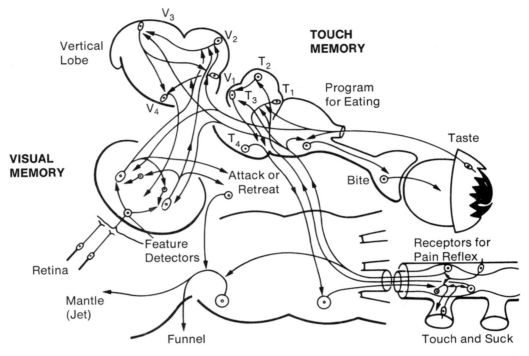

Fig. 30.9. Some of the pathways involved in the octopus memory systems. Fibers sending signals from the eyes (vision), suckers (touch), lips (taste), and skin (pain) make local connections to operate reflex circuits and then connect to central circuits where memories are stored. The visual input passes through four centers (V_1–V_4), and the other inputs merge to pass through a similar sequence of four centers (T_1–T_4). (From Young, 1978)

be used selectively in the learned task. This is an interesting hypothesis that deserves further study.

Vertebrates: the Hippocampus

The brain structure that has attracted most attention as a possible repository of memories in the vertebrate is the hippocampus. This was first dramatically demonstrated by the accidental discovery that removal of the hippocampus in neurosurgical operations results in almost total loss of recent memory in humans. Complementing this was the finding that brief electrical shocks applied to the hippocampal area elicit fleeting memories in awake patients undergoing neurosurgical operations for the relief of epilepsy.

The hippocampus is certainly one of the most intriguing regions in the brain. It ful-

fills all our criteria for a central system: a well defined region, remote from specific sensory and motor pathways. What does it do, and how is it related to memory?

The hippocampus derives its name from its curving shape, which reminded some early neuroanatomist of a sea-horse (and others of a ram's horn). This is an ancient part of the brain; as one of the first areas of the wall of the forebrain to become differentiated in primitive vertebrates, it is called the archicortex (see Fig. 30.10A). Its functions are unknown, but they appear to depend on the nearby septum, to which it is closely connected. As the forebrain expanded during evolution, the hippocampus got pushed and dragged around. It got particularly attached to the temporal lobe, and so as this lobe enlarged, the hippocampus got pulled along in a loop through the dorsal forebrain to the temporal lobe (B), and eventually ended up entirely within that lobe (C) in primates, snuggled up against the amygdala. It retains its primitive connection with the septum through a thick tract called the fornix, whose graceful arc describes the evolutionary trajectory.

The hippocampus is one of those regions, like the cerebellum and olfactory bulb, whose internal circuits are organized in a highly distinctive manner. This by itself is an interesting fact: stereotyped microcircuits and local circuits are not used just for processing sensory information, but also for processing information related to higher brain functions. The circuits in the hippocampus have been described in Chap. 8. There we learned that the inputs are excitatory, as are two pathways (the mossy fibers and Schaffer collaterals) for internal transfer of information. Pitted against this in the control of the output neurons are local inhibitory interneurons. A delicate balance is thus set up between excitation and inhibition, a balance that can be upset by too much excitation or too little inhibition, either of which leads to uncontrolled discharges which become manifest in humans as certain kinds of epileptic seizures.

If the hippocampus is to have a role in memory, one would expect these synapses to have properties that change with use, and in fact this has turned out to be one of the outstanding characteristics of this region. In 1973, Tim Bliss and Terje Lømo in London reported studies in the intact, anesthetized rabbit, in which they recorded the field potentials evoked in the dentate fascia by a shock to the entorhinal cortex (which activates pathway ① in Fig. 8.14). If they stimulated at high frequency (tetanically) for several seconds, and then tested with a single shock at various intervals after that, they found that the part of the recording due to the synaptic response of the granule cells grew to a much greater amplitude than normal (Fig. 30.11). This phenomenon is similar to the post-tetanic potentiation that is seen at the neuromuscular junction (Chap. 18). In the dentate cells, this potentiation persists for a surprisingly long time; as shown in Fig. 30.11, it characteristically lasts for several hours, and can even be demonstrated over periods of days and weeks.

Fig. 30.10. Evolution of the hippocampus, as exemplified in a lower vertebrate (shark), a mammal (rat), and the human. Above, longitudinal views; below, cross-sectional views. (Based on Sarnat and Netsky, 1981)

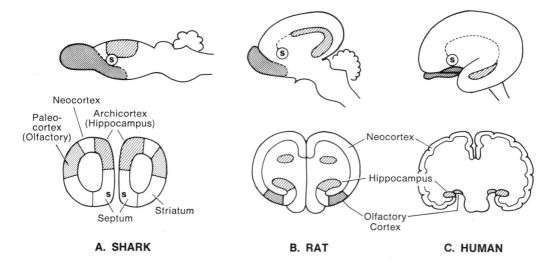

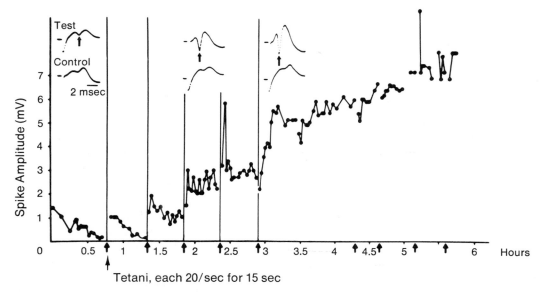

Tetani, each 20/sec for 15 sec

Fig. 30.11. Long-lasting potentiation of the granule cell response of the dentate fascia. Electrical stimulation was applied to the perforant fibers, at a rate of 20 per sec for 15 sec; this was repeated at times marked by arrows in the graph. The amplitude of the sharp wave in the field potential (due to granule cell responses) grew, as shown in insets (arrows); the time course of the increase over a period of 6 hours is plotted in the graph. (From Bliss and Lømo, 1973)

Bliss and Lømo suggested several possible mechanisms for this potentiation, such as increased release of transmitter by the input synapses, or increased postsynaptic response. It can be seen that these are the types of mechanisms implied in Hebb's and Konorski's original concepts of the effects of use on neural circuits. In the hippocampal slice preparation (see Chap. 8), Per Andersen and his colleagues in Norway have obtained evidence that the potentiation is associated with increased transmitter release, giving a larger postsynaptic potential response in the hippocampal cells. Under the electron microscope, morphologists have obtained evidence that potentiation is associated with increases in the sizes of the dendritic spines of the hippocampal cells, and in the microstructure of the synapses.

The plasticity inherent in hippocampal circuits is also expressed in the response to loss of an input pathway. Normally, the dentate fascia is innervated by several types of fibers, each of which has its special level of termination in the granule dendritic tree. When the predominant input, the perforant pathway, is removed on one side, there is massive degeneration of its synapses in the outer three-quarters of the granule cell dendrites. This is followed after several weeks by the appearance of new synapses on the dendrites. A series of experiments by Gary Lynch and Carl Cotman and their colleagues in California has shown that these new terminals result from sprouting and migration of other types of fibers, which take over the vacated synaptic sites (see Fig. 30.12). The hippocampus is not unique in this respect; we have had ample opportunity to note the astonishing abilities for plasticity of connections in many parts of the nervous system. However, the hippocampus is certainly a favorable site for demonstrating these properties.

If the hippocampus has properties at the cellular level appropriate for playing a role in memory, what evidence is there for this role at the behavioral level? The most dramatic evidence was provided in 1953 by

William Scoville and Brenda Milner at the Montreal Neurological Institute. They reported that one of their patients, a 27-year-old skilled mechanic known as H.M., in whom bilateral hippocampal removal had been performed for relief of epilepsy, had lost the ability to remember recent events, without any significant impairment of other intellectual abilities. Needless to say, this operation was never performed again. H.M. has become perhaps the most studied patient in history. In a recent thorough reexamination 28 years after the operation, Suzanne Corkin and her colleagues in Boston report:

He still exhibits a profound anterograde amnesia, and does not know where he lives, who cares for him, or what he ate at his last meal.

. . . Nevertheless, he has islands of remembering, such as knowing that an astronaut is someone who travels in outer space. . . . A typical day's activities include doing crossword puzzles and watching television.

Corkin's studies have shown that H.M. cannot recall words that are presented to him verbally, but he can show improvement in the ability to solve puzzles and acquire perceptual skills in repeated trials. This has contributed to a variety of evidence that memory is not just one global entity, but rather consists of many subsystems. Other interesting results in the recent studies are that H.M. has a diminished perception of pain, a lack of feelings of hunger or satiety, and an inability to identify different odors.

Fig. 30.12. Plasticity of synaptic connections onto dentate granule cells after a lesion of the ipsilateral entorhinal cortex, destroying the perforant fibers. Note the sprouting and migration of the fibers from the contralateral entorhinal cortex, the septal nucleus, and the commissural-associational projection. (Modified from Cotman and McGaugh, 1980)

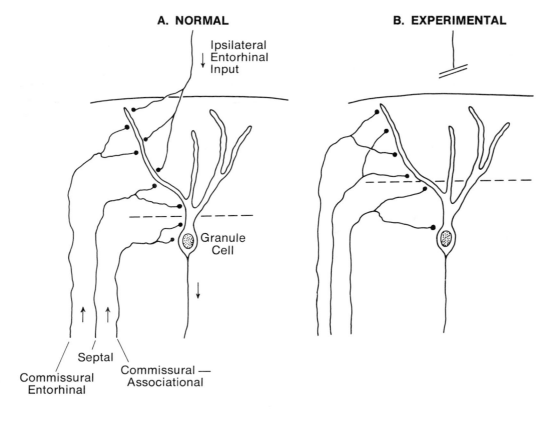

It would seem that this case clearly establishes the role of the hippocampus in memory. The situation, however, is far more complicated. For example, it has been argued that the effects seen after such an operation may be due not to removal of the hippocampus per se, but rather to damage to tracts that supply the surrounding temporal lobe cortex. Severe memory deficits are seen in various clinical states, such as Korsakoff's psychosis, which mainly involve degeneration of neurons in midline structures of the thalamus, and spare the hippocampus. In animal experiments, bilateral removal of the hippocampus in monkeys and rats does *not* result in the relatively complete loss of memory seen in humans. Instead, there are more selective deficits. These include an inability to terminate a given motor response (perseveration), and an inability to chain together a sequence of motor behaviors, such as in gathering food or caring for young. These results have been interpreted as indicating that there are different kinds of memory; for example, remembering when it is appropriate to terminate a motor act, and remembering sequences of motor acts in complex behaviors.

The most reasonable conclusion from all this work is that the hippocampus may have a role in memory, but it is not an all-embracing or exclusive one. We have seen that plasticity is a very general cell property, and it is possible that memory is correspondingly a widely distributed function. According to the principle we have seen expressed so often in the nervous system, the contribution of the hippocampus is likely to depend on its multiple interconnections with other centers. Among them, the connections with the nearby temporal lobe are important, as are those with the cingulate gyrus. Modern workers are beginning to recognize that the overall term "memory" includes many different specific sub-types; each is probably a product of a particular distributed system, and the different systems probably over-

lap to a considerable extent. That leaves the specific contribution of the remarkable piece of neuronal machinery contained within the hippocampus still to be determined.

Peptides and Memory

Recent work has disclosed the presence of neuroactive peptides in so many regions that it is not surprising that they should be implicated in memory mechanisms. It has been shown, for example, that removal of the pituitary gland in rats causes, in addition to specific endocrine effects, several types of behavioral disturbances, including deficits in learning. The learning deficits can be restored by treatment with peptides, such as ACTH or vasopressin or fragments of these compounds which lack any other observable physiological action. This kind of result has led some workers to the postulate of "one peptide, one behavior", a claim not supported by the evidence. As pointed out by de Wied and Gispen, the surgical interventions in the hypothalamic area interrupt ascending systems involved in arousal and motivation, and the effects of treatments with peptides are similarly widespread. For example, injections of ACTH or ACTH fragments have been found to activate cells in many parts of the nervous system, including the hippocampus. Until the specific memory functions can be satisfactorily identified independently of the arousal and motivational states of the animal, the roles of peptides will remain intriguing but conjectural.

REFERENCES

Alkon, D. L. 1979. Voltage-dependent calcium and potassium ion conductances: a contingency mechanism for an associative learning model. *Science 205:* 810–816.

Andersen, P. et al. 1977. [Chap. 8].

Ashe, J. H. and M. Nackman. 1980. Neural mechanisms in taste aversion learning.

Progr. Psychobiol. Physiol. Psychol. 9: 233–262.

Barnett, S. A. 1981. *Modern Ethology: The Science of Animal Behavior.* New York: Oxford.

Bennett, T. S. 1977. [Chap. 29].

Bliss, T. V. P. and T. Lømo. 1973. Long-lasting potentiation of synaptic transmission in the dentate area of the anaesthetized rabbit following stimulation of the perforant path. *J. Physiol. 232:* 331–356.

Boring, E. G. 1950. [Chap. 1].

Chance, P. 1979. *Learning and Behavior.* Belmont, Calif: Wadsworth.

Chang, J. J. and A. Gelperin. 1980. Rapid taste aversion learning by an isolated molluscan central nervous system. *Proc. Natl. Acad. Sci. 77:* 6204–6206.

Cotman, C. W. and J. L. McGaugh. 1980. *Behavioral Neuroscience.* New York: Academic.

Corkin, S., E. V. Sullivan, R. E. Twitchell, and E. Grove. 1981. The amnesic patient. H.M.: clinical observations and test performance 28 years after operation. *Soc. for Neurosci. Absts. 7:* p. 235.

Dethier, V. G. and E. Stellar. 1964. *Animal Behavior: Its Evolutionary and Neurological Basis.* Englewood Cliffs, N. J.: Prentice-Hall.

Fetz, E. and M. A. Baker. 1973. Operantly conditioned patterns of precentral unit activity and correlated responses in adjacent cells and contralateral muscles. *J. Neurophysiol. 36:* 179–204.

Garcia, J. and R. A. Koelling. 1966. Relation of cue to consequence in avoidance learning. *Psychonomic Sci. 4:* 123–124.

Groves, P. M. and K. Schlesinger. 1979. *Introduction to Biological Psychology.* Duguque, Ia: Wm. C. Brown.

Groves, P. M. and R. F. Thompson. 1970. Habituation: a dual-process theory. *Psychol. Rev. 77:* 419–450.

Hebb, D. O. 1949. *The Organization of Behavior.* New York: Wiley.

Horn, G. 1979. Imprinting- in search of new mechanisms. *Trends in Neurosci. Sept:* 219–222.

Kandel, E. R. 1979. Cellular insights into behavior and learning. *Harvey Lectures 73:* 19–92.

Klein, M., E. Shapiro and E. R. Kandel. 1980. Synaptic plasticity and the modulation of the Ca^{2+} current. *J. Exp. Biol. 89:* 117–157.

Kolb, B. M. and I. Q. Whishaw. 1980. [Chap. 29].

Lashley, K. S. 1950. In search of the engram. *Symp. Soc. Exp. Biol. 4:* 454–482.

Olds, M. E. and J. Olds. 1961. Emotional and associative mechanisms in the rat brain. *J. Comp. Physiol. Psychol. 54:* 120–126.

Sarnat, H. B. and M. G. Netsky. 1981. [Chap. 3].

Scoville, W. B. and B. Milner. 1957. Loss of recent memory after bilateral hippocampal lesions. *J. Neurol. Neurosurg. Psychiat. 20:* 11–21.

Shapiro, E., V. F. Castellucci, and E. R. Kandel. 1980. Presynaptic inhibition in *Aplysia* involves a decrease in the Ca^{2+} current of the presynaptic neuron. *Proc. Natl. Acad. Sci. 77:* 1185–1189.

Young, J. Z. 1978. *Programs of the Brain.* Oxford: Oxford University Press.

de Wied, D. and W. H. Gispen. 1977. Behavioral effects of peptides. In *Peptides in Neurobiology* (ed. by H. Gainer). New York: Plenum. pp. 397–448.

31

The Cerebral Cortex
and Human Behavior

The trend toward a larger brain and more elaborate cerebral cortex culminates in the human. In previous chapters we have noted many areas of the mammalian cortex given over to specific functions related to sensory processing, control of motor outputs, and integration of centrally mediated behaviors. The diagram in Fig. 31.1 provides a summary view of the human. Specific areas are present in lower mammals, and are further elaborated in primates and humans. While these specific areas are important in the evolution of human attributes, it is the other parts of the cortex that have undergone the greatest expansion. Some idea of this expansion can be grasped by realizing that the area of the cortex of a cat is about 100 cm^2, or about ¼ the size of this page, whereas that of the human is about 2400 cm^2, or about 6 times the size of the surface of this page. The specific areas discussed thus far account for only a small part of this total. It is therefore to these vast tracts of neural landscape, with billions of neurons and hundreds of billions of synapses, that we now turn to identify the circuits and mechanisms that make us uniquely human.

It is appropriate to begin by asking:

Table 31.1 Human characteristics

1. Locomotion on hind legs: forelimbs free for other functions
2. Prehensile hand: making of tools and development of technology
3. Enlargement of brain relative to body size
4. Development of speech and language
5. Development of social interactions and culture: prolonged youth; division of labor in society; controls on sex and aggression
6. Individual artistic and spiritual expression

Modified from Isaac and Leakey (1979)

what is it that makes humans unique? The attributes that are commonly regarded as distinctive of humans are listed in Table 31.1. The erect posture and walking on hind legs allowed the forelimbs to be free for other functions. It is amusing to recall that locomotion by the minimum number of legs expresses a trend present also in the invertebrates, as discussed in Chap. 21. The important thing was that the forelimbs did not become dedicated to other obligatory tasks, like flying in birds or swinging through trees in monkeys, but rather were free to work on the environment in new and novel ways. The most crucial way was provided by the prehensile hand, which led to tools and technology. The parallel development of speech

568

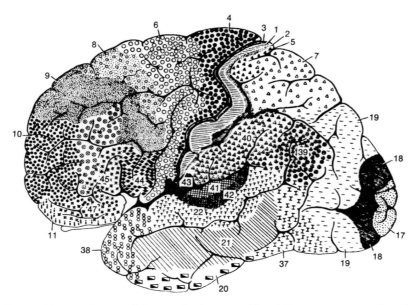

Fig. 31.1. Cytoarchitectural map of the cerebral cortex. The different areas are identified by the thickenss of their layers and types of cells within them. Some of the most important specific areas are as follows. Motor cortex: motor strip, area 4; premotor area, area 6; frontal eye fields, area 8. Somatosensory cortex: areas 3, 1, 2. Visual cortex: areas 17, 18, 19. Auditory cortex: areas 41 and 42. Wernicke's speech area: approximately area 22. Broca's speech area: approximately area 44 (in the left hemisphere). (From Brodmann, in Brodal, 1981)

and language gave rise to more adaptable modes of communication, and ultimately to symbolic thought. These attributes involved changes in the musculoskeletal system, and associated adaptations in neural systems for sensorimotor control of posture, locomotion, throwing, grasping, vocalization, and related activities. In addition, a prolonged childhood provided the basis for complex social organization and an enduring culture. Finally, human beings express themselves as individuals. The ingredients in this include emotion, motivation, and imagination; their testing ground is play; they realize themselves to the fullest in the supremely human qualities of artistic expression and spiritual experience.

Phylogeny of Cerebral Cortex

The human attributes listed in Table 31.1 depend on the cerebral cortex. In order to gain insight into how the human cortex

has evolved, we need to consider the phylogeny of the vertebrate forebrain.

As histological stains for visualizing nerve cells and fiber tracts became available around 1900, neuroanatomists applied them across the vertebrate spectrum and attempted to identify corresponding centers and pathways in the brains of different species. This work culminated in 1936 in the monumental tome by Kappers, Huber, and Crosby entitled *The Comparative Anatomy of the Nervous System of Vertebrates, Including Man.* The view emerging from this survey was of a gradual "linear" increase in size of the forebrain and differentiation of the cortex as one ascends from fish to mammals. In fish, it seemed that the cortex was very primitive, devoted mainly to olfactory inputs (paleocortex) and higher-order olfactory processing (archicortex). In amphibians, and especially in reptiles, a new cortex (neocortex) appeared; in reptiles and birds, other sensory systems began to

Table 31.2 Evolution of the forebrain (telencephalon):a comparison of old and new ideas

Old ideas	New ideas
1. Linear increase in size through the vertebrate series	1. Independent increases in size among several radiations
2. Early olfactory dominance and later dominance by ascending thalamic inputs	2. Early restricted olfactory inputs plus early restricted thalamic inputs
3. Lower vertebrates have only a primitive cortex	3. Main divisions of cortex are present in all vertebrates
4. Lower vertebrates lack long descending tracts from cortex	4. Long descending tracts are present in all vertebrate groups
5. Functionally specific tracts are stable across different groups	5. The same function may be mediated by different tracts in different species ("phylogenetic plasticity"). There is no truly "typical" tract or center for a given function.
6. Similar structures in different groups are homologous (evolved from a common ancestral form)	6. Similar structures in different groups are often homoplastic (they evolved independently: convergent evolution)

Based on Northcott (1981) and others

project to the cortex through a thalamus. In mammals the neocortex, together with its thalamic inputs and closely related basal ganglia, greatly expanded. This sequence was supposed to mirror the events that lay behind the evolution of the primate cortex. It was a satisfying view, and is summarized in Table 31.2 under "Old Ideas".

So satisfying was this view that the comparative anatomy of the nervous system came to be regarded as a rather stodgy subject, like an old exhibit in a museum. It is only in the last decade or so that neuroanatomists have returned in force to rejuvenate this whole field by new studies. The surprising outcome is that most of the old ideas have had to be discarded, in the face of new evidence that significantly alters the interpretation of the evolution of the forebrain. One of the most important new findings is that the forebrain and cortex have not undergone a gradual, linear increase, but rather there have been independent offshoots of forebrain expansion at several stages; examples of this are certain fish, and the dolphin. This phenomenon should not be surprising to the reader

of this book; we have already noted in Chap. 22 the enormous expansion of the cerebellum in certain species of electric fish. Similar but independently evolved structures are referred to as "homoplastic", in contrast to similar structures in a linearly evolved series, which are referred to as "homologous". The case of the dolphin illustrates that cortical enlargement by itself confers only limited adaptive abilities; it is the whole constellation of adaptations in Table 31.1 that is necessary for human behavior.

Another important finding has been that olfactory projections to the forebrain are much more specific than formerly believed, and that other sensory modalities are represented already in fishes by projections through thalamic relays. In studies of the visual pathway from the retina through the thalamus to the cortex, considerable variation has been found among lower vertebrates; according to R. Glenn Northcutt of Michigan, the visual pathway may project ipsilaterally or bilaterally, through different central tracts, to different cortical sites, in different species.

This may be regarded as a kind of "phylogenetic plasticity", reflecting in part the flexibility of the nervous system in its routing of information through central pathways. The "New Ideas" emerging from these and related studies are summarized in Table 31.1. The phylogeny of the three main types of cortex was indicated diagrammatically in Fig. 30.10, and will be further discussed below in relation to the temporal lobe.

Ontogeny of Cerebral Cortex

In Chap. 10 we discussed the stages involved in the development of the nervous system, and we can now apply those principles to the specific case of the cortex.

Neurons characteristically migrate from their site of birth (the last mitosis) to their final position, and the neocortex is no exception. The precursor cells are located in the proliferative zones that line the surface of the cerebral ventricles. As shown by studies in which animals are sacrificed shortly after radioactively labeled thymidine injections, all of the final mitoses take place in the proliferative zones. The neurons must therefore migrate to the primitive cortical plate. They are guided in this by a special type of cell, the radial glia, which spans the distance between the proliferative zone and the cortical plate. This mechanism has been elucidated by the elegant studies of Pasko Rakic, at Harvard and at Yale, and is illustrated in Fig. 31.2. The neurons are all generated within a period of about 60 days in the monkey (100 days in the human), and the migration is complete in the monkey by day 100 (gestation lasts 165 days). Within the cortex, the first neurons are laid down in the deepest layers, with later neurons migrating to more superficial layers; hence, there is an "inside-out" sequence of cortical development. Thus, according to the timing of its last mitosis, each neuron appears to be destined as a specific cell type in a specific layer. According to Rakic:

The redistribution of such a vast number of cells during development undoubtedly provides opportunities for establishment of essential relationships and key contacts that eventually determine the radial and tangential coordinates of each neuron in the 3-dimensional map of the neocortex. Thus, the separation of proliferative centers from the final residence of neurons is of great biological significance.

Within the cortex, the larger pyramidal neurons (projection neurons) mature first, followed by the smaller interneurons (local circuit neurons). In comparison with the relatively brief period for cell birth, maturation is a much more prolonged process. An indication of this is given in Fig. 31.3. Note the small sizes of the cells in the newborn and their limited dendritic branches, and the subsequent growth and differentiation of the cells. It is apparent from this evidence alone that early childhood is a time of rapid and profound maturation of the cells in the cortex. The rates differ in different parts of the cortex; for example, motor areas tend to develop before sensory areas, and lower sensory centers tend to develop before their corresponding cortical areas.

The maturation of cortical neurons is associated with a maturation of cortical circuits. This can be documented and quantitated by staining the synapses with a special stain and counting them. The best data have been obtained in the rat, where a sevenfold increase in the number of synapses was calculated to occur in the parietal cortex between the twelfth and twenty-sixth day after birth (see Fig. 31.4). A similar tremendous increase in synaptic connections occurs in the primate and human after birth. At the same time, various degrees of cell death and synaptic remodeling are also taking place.

Maturation does not occur in a vacuum; in addition to the timetable prescribed by the genetic program, a neuron reaches its final form under the influence of its environment. The old debate of nature vs. nurture has been rendered obso-

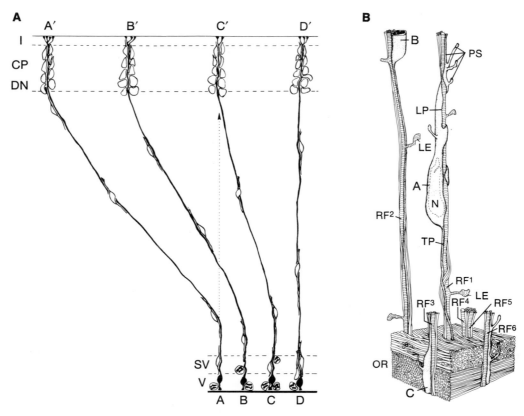

Fig. 31.2. A. Diagram showing how radial glia provide guides for the migration of neurons (N) from ventricular (V) and subventricular (SV) zones to the cortical plate (CP). Within the CP, the new neurons migrate past deeper neurons (DN) to layer I (I). Note that despite shift of cortical position (A′–D′) relative to proliferative zones (A–D), the radial glia preserve the topographical relations. **B.** Relations between migrating neuron and radial glia fiber, based on electron microscopy. Six radial fibers (RF[1–6]) are shown traversing the packed fibers of the optic radiation (OR). Three neurons (A–C) are shown at various stages of migration. Neuron A is shown with nucleus (N), leading process (LP), and pseudopodia (PS). (A from Rakic, 1981; B from Rakic, in Jacobson, 1978)

lete, and we now recognize that both shape the neuron. To speak of one without the other is like asking what is the sound of one hand clapping. Furthermore, the question is not just whether a neuron by itself will mature, but whether it will survive in the competition for available nutrients, synaptic connections, and functional validation. Thus, the competition of organisms for survival in the external world mirrors a competition in the inner world among neurons to fashion the circuits that will be most effective in the ex-

ternal world. We shall see clear evidence of the relations between the two worlds when we discuss the organization of cortical circuits.

We may summarize this section by noting that ontogeny, like phylogeny, is not a simple linear process. It involves a series of stages, in which the organism at one stage gives rise to the next stage through the complex interaction of a number of factors. This is evident at the cellular level in the development of the cortex, and it is also evident in the behavior of the devel-

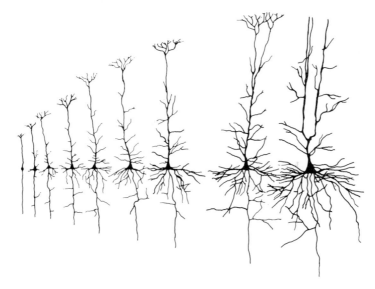

Fig. 31.3. Growth and differentiation of the dendritic trees and axon collaterals of cortical pyramidal cells in the human, from fetus to adult. (Courtesy of P. Rakic)

oping fetus and child. This has been summarized elegantly by Myron Hofer of Albert Einstein College of Medicine as follows:

Development is characterized by transformations in which certain functional patterns come into being that are not found in previous or even in subsequent stages. Functionally as well as structurally, it is not the same creature

Fig. 31.4. Increase in number of synapses per cubic millimeter during early life in the parietal cortex of the rat. (From Aghajanian and Bloom, 1967)

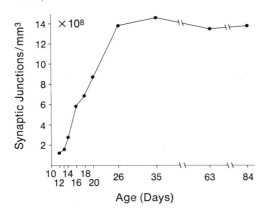

at two different stages of its own development. The differences between stages of development in a single animal are almost as profound as those between species of vertebrates. The implications of this fact are difficult for adults to fully grasp, accustomed as we are to relative stability in our remembered past experience. It means that we cannot generalize about the mechanism of an action, the effect of a stimulus, or the long-term impact of an experience from one stage of development to another. We have to understand exactly how the developing infant interacts with its environment separately at each age.

Levels of Cortical Organization

We are now in a position to tackle the key question: What are the cortical mechanisms that underlie our uniquely human abilities? The nineteenth-century idea was that ideas and other human mental faculties actually reside in the cortex, and constitute a kind of supreme executive which hands down orders to its neural minions. These faculties were believed to be embedded in some fashion in the billions of cells distributed throughout the cortex. It should be obvious to the reader of this book that the modern view is radically different. Rather than being like a self-contained college of bishops and cardinals, the cortex actually contains many areas that function at middle levels of signal processing, within specific sensory and motor systems. Furthermore, there is increasing evidence that higher functions are mediated by distributed systems, in which the cortex is only one part. Thus, the significance of any given region in the cortex is to be found in the internal organization of its synaptic circuits, and its external organization in terms of its connections to a set of other regions, cortical and subcortical. The synaptic circuits generate particular functional properties, and the external connections determine the contributions of these properties to the distributive systems of which they are a part. These are the principles that apply to the organization of all central systems, as discussed in Chap. 25.

It is clear, then, that the significance of the cortex for human attributes lies in the organization of its synaptic circuits. In recent years it has been possible to identify several levels of circuit organization, and relate them to global aspects of primate and human behavior. In considering these correlations we draw on everything we have learned about cellular mechanisms and synaptic circuit.

Microcircuits. At the finest level of circuit organization is the individual synapse and its associated pre- and postsynaptic structures. Although one may think of a single synapse as a simple link, or circuit element, we have seen that it is a complex functional unit in its own right, with a variety of time- and use-dependent controls. This is demonstrated vividly by synapses in the cortex, especially those made onto the dendritic spines of pyramidal cells. The increase in cortical synapses during development is largely associated with spines; as shown in Fig. 31.5, the spines in a seven-month-old human fetus are few in number and irregular in shape, whereas the stouter

dendrite of even an 8-month-old infant is bristling with well-formed lollipop-shaped spines. Each of these spines is the site of a synapse, usually a type I synapse (see Chap. 5) with an excitatory action.

Cortical synapses have been shown to be extraordinarily sensitive to a number of environmental influences. In the visual cortex, the number of spines on dendritic shafts of deep pyramidal cells is reduced following removal of one eye in newborn rodents. This could be due to several factors, including loss of spines already formed, or failure of dendrites to mature. A reduction in visual experience, caused by raising animals in the dark, also leads to a reduction in numbers of synapses in visual areas, and to reduction in sizes of individual synapses. Even more dramatic results are seen in experiments comparing the cortices of animals raised in enriched environments, containing lots of toys to play with and mazes to run in, with those raised in barren cages. The animals raised in enriched environments have thicker cortices, and bigger synaptic contacts. Similarly, the cortex may be up to one-third thicker in wild animals compared with those that have been domesticated. The fact that the brain is reduced in size in domesticated animals was actually first noted by Darwin. Finally, we may note that dendritic spines are affected in certain kinds of neurological diseases that produce mental retardation; the derangements of spines that occur in Patau's syndrome and in mongolism are shown in Fig. 31.5A.

The fact that cortical synapses, and especially those on spines, are sensitive to environmental influences, should not be surprising. Spines in the lateral geniculate nucleus are also sensitive to visual deprivation, as shown in Fig. 31.5B, and many examples could be cited in other systems. What is special about the cortex is the way the spines are organized in dense linear arrays along the dendrites, so that unique contributions of inputs from many sources can interact. Each spine can be conceived of as creating a microenvironment,

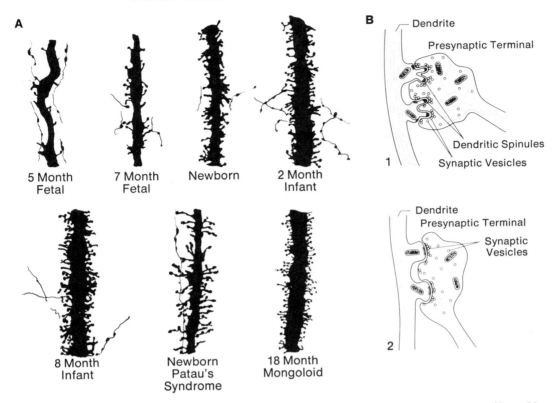

A

5 Month Fetal   7 Month Fetal   Newborn   2 Month Infant

8 Month Infant   Newborn Patau's Syndrome   18 Month Mongoloid

B

Dendrite

Presynaptic Terminal

Dendritic Spinules

Synaptic Vesicles

1

Dendrite
Presynaptic Terminal

Synaptic Vesicles

2

Fig. 31.5. **A.** Increase in number of spines on apical dendrites of large pyramidal neurons of layer V of human cortex, at five different ages before and after birth. In a disease known as Patau's syndrome, the spines are fewer, elongated, and irregular in form. In mongolism, the spines are thin and tiny. **B.** Effects of deprivation on spines in the lateral geniculate nucleus of the dog. 1, normal; 2, animal reared in the dark. (A from Marin-Padilla, in Lund, 1979; B from Hamori, in Hofer, 1981)

wherein the postsynaptic response is modulated by use, and exerts its first and most immediate effects on its neighbors. Each spine thus acts as a miniature input–output unit, whose properties depend on its history, its metabolic machinery, its inputs, and its interactions with its neighbors.

Local Circuits. As in every other region in the brain, the synaptic circuits in the cortex are built up out of the triad of neural elements: input fibers, output neurons, and intrinsic neurons. By combining methods for intracellular staining and recording with cellular identification of transmitters, it has been possible to begin to construct the basic circuits that characterize each of

the three main types of cortex. We have had occasion to discuss each of these in previous chapters: olfactory cortex (Chap. 12), hippocampus (Chaps. 8 and 30), and neocortex (sensory regions in Chaps. 13–17, motor cortex in Chaps. 22 and 23).

Since the neocortex is the main instrument for human qualities, we want to know what is unique about the organization of its local circuits. This is one of the most intriguing questions in all of neurobiology. In order to answer it, we must draw on everything we have learned about the organization of invertebrate and vertebrate neural circuits.

In invertebrates, circuits tend to be organized either in ganglia, in which there is a grouping of input–output connections,

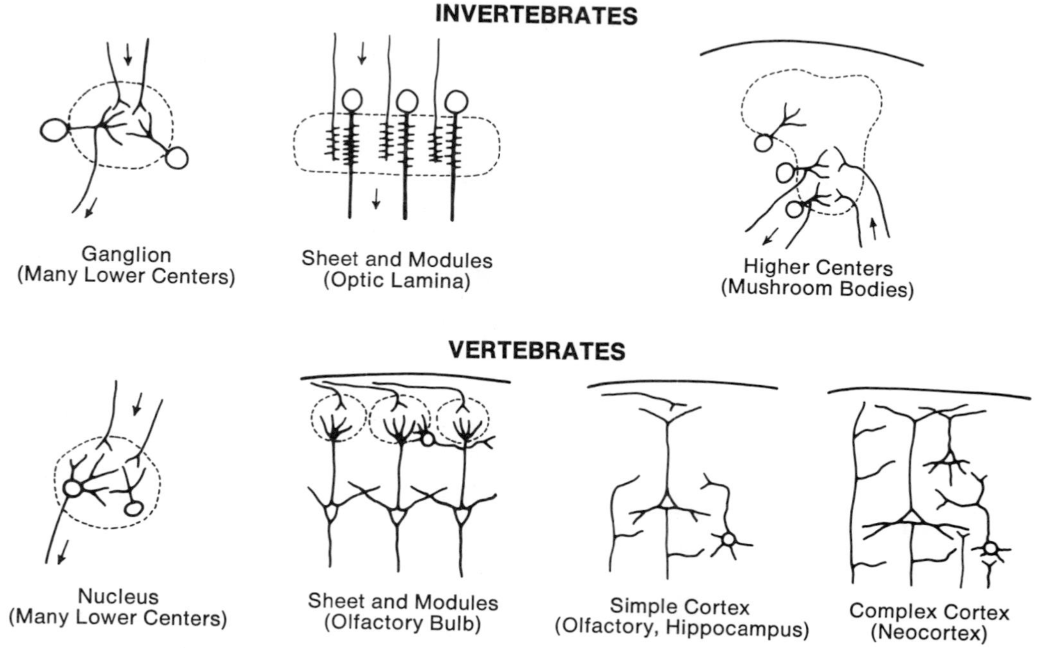

INVERTEBRATES

| Ganglion
(Many Lower Centers) | Sheet and Modules
(Optic Lamina) | Higher Centers
(Mushroom Bodies) |

VERTEBRATES

| Nucleus
(Many Lower Centers) | Sheet and Modules
(Olfactory Bulb) | Simple Cortex
(Olfactory, Hippocampus) | Complex Cortex
(Neocortex) |

Fig. 31.6. Comparison between the neural organization of lower centers and higher centers in invertebrates and vertebrates. For simplicity, the local circuits within the centers are omitted.

or in laminae, which provide for a two-dimensional linear array of input–output connections (see Fig. 31.6). These provide the means whereby specific operations are carried out in different sensory and motor pathways. These regions characteristically are polarized; the input comes in from one side and the output exits from another. The internal operations through local circuits and interneurons tend to be devoted to the sequence of operations necessary to process the specific input and generate a specific output.

Higher levels of integration occur in centers like the mushroom bodies of the insect brain. Although we as yet know little about the internal organization of these centers, we can guess that, despite the multimodal nature of the operations, the basic input–output format probably still applies. Increased complexity can also be achieved by increasing the extent of the center, but here the rigid exoskeleton and very small body size are serious limitations. Centers like the mushroom bodies

remain buried within the brain substance, instead of being spread out on the surface where there would be opportunity for expansion.

In vertebrates there is the same tendency to organize neural circuits within ganglialike clusters (such as olfactory glomeruli or cortical barrels), spread out in linear sheets. Also, many centers located within the brain substance expand in phylogeny by becoming convoluted, resembling the mushroom bodies in this respect. The new feature in the vertebrates, however, is the organization of neurons within sheets that lie on the surface of the brain, sheets that we call cortex. Phylogenetically, the first center to take advantage of this opportunity was the cerebellum, which, as we have seen, is enormously expanded in certain electric fish, and is large in birds and mammals. Why doesn't the cerebellar cortex become an instrument of higher mental function? Part of the answer seems to lie in the fact that it is an outgrowth of the brainstem; because of this, it is forever bound to the operations involved in coordination of inputs and outputs at this lower level. The most primitive cortical area in the forebrain, the olfactory cortex, remains tied closely to the olfactory input, remote from access by other sensory modalities. The olfactory inputs arrive at the surface of this cortex, and the outputs exit from the depths, giving a functional polarization similar to that of many other centers.

We can now begin to get a perspective on the properties that are special about the neocortex. First, it is placed where it is accessible to every major sensory input, arriving either directly (from the olfactory cortex) or relayed from below through the brainstem and thalamus. Second, it is a layered structure doubled back on itself, so that inputs arrive from the depths and outputs exit through the depths. This leaves the cells in every layer potentially accessible to every input. When the local circuits through collaterals and interneurons are added to the picture, the potential ways by which information can be integrated, stored, and recombined become enormous. Such a structure is no longer dominated by the operational sequence demanded of a particular input or output. Third, rather than there being one type of

output cell, as is common in so many centers, there are several types. In fact, each layer is the source of output fibers; some fibers go only to other layers (such as outputs from layer I and IV), others go to different distant targets (such as outputs from layers II, III, V, and VI). As a result, each layer, in effect, acts as a semi-independent unit, defined by its particular inputs, outputs, intrinsic connections, and relations to its neighboring layers. Finally, give this structure the chance to expand, through some property of its not-quite-rigid braincase, and one has the opportunity to go on enlarging individual areas, or adding on new ones, in order to combine information from new combinations of inputs or control different combinations of output targets.

An interesting example that illustrates some of these principles is provided by recent work on peptides in the cortex. Using immunocytochemical methods, P. C. Emson and S. P. Hunt of Cambridge University have localized two peptides, cholecystokinin (CCK) and vasoactive intestinal polypeptide (VIP), as well as GABA, in neurons of different cortical regions. Figure 31.7 summarizes their findings. In primitive cortex (paleocortex and archicortex), immunoreactive terminals for

Fig. 31.7. Diagrams summarizing the localization of neurons and terminals in different types of cortex, as shown by immunocytochemical staining methods for the peptides, cholecystokinin (CCK) and vasoactive intestinal polypeptide (VIP), and glutamic acid decarboxylase, the enzyme that synthesizes GABA. (Adapted from Emson and Hunt, 1981)

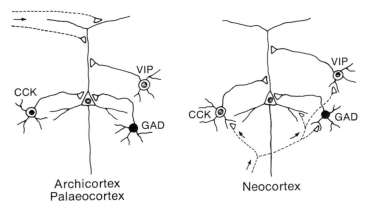

Table 31.3   Modules in cerebral cortex

Hippocampus	transverse lamellae
Somatosensory cortex	modality-specific columns
	glomeruli (barrels)
Visual cortex	ocular dominance columns
	orientation columns
	hypercolumns
Motor cortex	colonies
	"columns"
Entorhinal cortex	glomeruli
(fetal human)	
Frontal association cortex	columns

References in Shepherd (1979), Goldman (1981), and Kostovic (personal communication)

both CCK and GAD were found on the cell bodies of large pyramidal (output) neurons, whereas terminals positive for VIP were found on the apical dendrites. The results in neocortex were similar for GAD and VIP, but CCK terminals were found predominately on the proximal portions of apical dendrites. In interpreting their results, Emson and Hunt noted that the main excitatory input through specific afferents connects directly to the apical dendrites of the pyramidal (output) neurons in primitive cortex, but is mostly relayed indirectly through interneurons in neocortex (see Fig. 31.7). They speculated that "The altered position of the CCK terminals on the neocortical neurons may reflect the altered role of the CCK neuron from providing a *parallel* excitatory input, for example to the hippocampal pyramidal neurons, to providing the *principal* excitatory input to certain neocortical neurons."

Local Circuit Modules. In our studies of nervous systems, both invertebrate and vertebrate, we have seen that local circuits tend not to be arranged diffusely, but rather in discrete clusters, or modules. The ganglia of invertebrates, and the discrete regions of neuropil called glomeruli in the vertebrate olfactory bulb, are perhaps the clearest anatomical expressions of this modularization. In the cortex, modulari-

zation is expressed in many ways; some of them are summarized in Table 31.3.

Modules are not static, hard-wired entities. We have noted that individual neurons and synapses must compete for functional validation and survival, and it should not be surprising therefore to learn that the same applies to the aggregates within modules. This has been seen most clearly in the visual cortex.

In the monkey, the fibers from the two lateral geniculate nuclei first project during development in a diffuse and overlapping manner to the visual cortex; as Rakic has shown, it is only about two weeks before birth that segregation into columns dominated by input from one or the other eye is first seen. This process of establishment of ocular dominance columns is complete in the monkey by about three to six weeks after birth (Fig. 31.8A). Hubel and Wiesel showed in the early 1960's that if one eye is closed at birth, the ocular dominance columns of the normal eye expand. This was first demonstrated with unit recordings, and has recently been documented by injecting radioactively labeled amino acids into the spared eye and making autoradiographs of the distribution of the transported material in the cortex. As shown in Fig. 31.8B, the terminal fields of the fibers from the normal eye have expanded, at the expense of the neighboring fields from the deprived eye.

Moreover, the fact that this can be demonstrated with deprivation beginning at 5½ weeks, when the normal adult ocular dominance columns are already established, suggests that the expansion of the fields from the normal eye involves an actual sprouting of the fibers. Recently, T. Kasamatsu and Jack Pettigrew at California Institute of Technology have obtained evidence that this plasticity after monocular deprivation depends on noradrenaline being present in the cortex, with the implication that this might be one of the "state-setting" functions of the NA fibers from the brainstem to the cortex. This problem is currently under active investigation by several laboratories.

Plasticity in cortical modules has also been suggested for the orientation selectivity of cells in the visual cortex. In kittens exposed only to a pattern of vertically oriented stripes, the recordings from the cortex show units that tend to respond maximally only to stimulation with vertically oriented stripes. This implies that the circuit connections within orientation columns are dependent to some extent on visual experience.

Areas and Lobes. Modules of local circuits are repeated throughout a given region of cortex, to give that region certain specific operational capacities in relation to a set of input connections and a set of output connections. At the borders of the region, all three of these components change, and neighboring regions have some modification of local circuits and the sets of input and output connections. The early anatomists who studied the cortex were limited to methods that stained only cell bodies; they saw that the cell bodies are arranged in different layers, and that the layers differ in many parts of the cortex. On this basis, they divided the cortex into a number of areas, as shown in Fig. 31.1. Since then, many additional methods have been developed, which have led to new ways to characterize the cortex: by

intrinsic circuits; by input and output connections; by particular functional properties; by neurochemical constituents. Although these classifications have introduced many new aspects to our concepts of cortical organization, the extent to which they still can be incorporated in the old areas has been nonetheless surprising. We therefore think of each of these areas as a kind of local region, differentiated to perform some set of functions within the distributed systems of which it is a part, and differing from its neighboring regions, each having its own distinctive functional properties and system connections. Those areas we understand best are related to specific sensory and motor systems, and have been discussed in previous chapters.

At the next higher level of organization are lobes. The mammalian cortex is divided into four main lobes: occipital, parietal, frontal, and temporal. These terms are already familiar. You already know that the occipital lobe receives visual input, the parietal lobe receives somatosensory input, the temporal lobe receives auditory input, and the frontal lobe is the origin of many motor pathways.

The areas of each lobe that are not directly related to a specific sensory or motor function have traditionally been termed association areas. Since these are the areas that have undergone greatest expansion in the human brain, it has been commonly assumed that they have a large role to play in the attributes that are distinctly human. Three main functions have been ascribed to these association areas. First, a surprisingly large expanse of what appeared to be "association" cortex is actually given over to multiple representations of sensory or motor fields. This was a common theme in our discussion of visual, somatosensory, auditory, and motor cortex. Second, increasingly complex processing takes place within sensory areas; this is seen clearly, for example, in the abstraction of visual information in the occipital lobe. Third, some areas are concerned with multimodal integration of information from other lobes. The capacity to integrate higher-order sensory information and use it to control different kinds of motor outputs must lie near the basis of at least some of our higher cognitive functions. We will return to this theme in discussing certain of these functions below.

Closely allied to the differentiation of structure and function within a lobe is its neurochemical composition. The concentration and turnover of neuroactive substances are not the same throughout the cortex. A recent study of monamines by Patricia Goldman and her colleagues at the National Institutes of Health is instructive in this regard. They analyzed a number of areas of monkey cortex, as shown in Fig. 31.9A. The results for noradrenaline and dopamine are illustrated in B and C. Although NA is distributed throughout the cortex, in accord with the diffuse ramifications of the ascending fibers from the brainstem, there is a peak concentration in somatosensory cortex. This suggests a special role for NA in mediating our tactile perceptions. Drugs like cocaine, that potentiate the action of NA, cause tactile hallucinations; perhaps this reflects a direct action on somatosensory cortex. The normal function of NA at this site is yet unknown; perhaps it is related to the kind of plasticity revealed by the experiments on visual cortex mentioned above.

In contrast to NA, the highest concentrations of DA are in the most anterior parts of the frontal lobe, in what is termed the prefrontal area (see Fig. 31.9C). This is in accord with other studies showing the projection of the mesolimbic part of the brainstem DA system to the frontal lobe. Here, DA is believed to be involved in several types of higher brain functions, as will be discussed further below.

Hemispheres: Laterality and Dominance. All of the lobes together constitute a hemisphere, and the whole forebrain thus consists of two hemispheres. Just as each hemisphere is differentiated into lobes, so are the two hemispheres differentiated from each other in mediating the highest levels of cerebral function. The first evidence that the hemispheres are different came from the French neurologist Paul Broca; in 1863 he described a patient with the inability to speak (aphasia), who turned out to have a tumor in the left frontal lobe. Broca deduced that this is the area of cortex that controls speech; in his words, "we speak with the left hemisphere". In 1875, Carl Wernicke, a 26-year-old German neurologist, reported that aphasia can also be caused by a lesion in the temporal lobe. He showed the difference between sensory aphasia, the lack of ability to formulate words due to temporal lobe damage, and motor aphasia, the inability to produce words (speak) due to

Fig. 31.8. **A.** Summary of establishment of ocular dominance columns in the developing rhesus monkey. The five diagrams start at embryonic day 78 and end with the adult. For each age, a monkey had been injected with radioactively labeled amino acids into one eye 14 days previously; the amino acid was incorporated into protein by the ganglion cells in the retina of that eye and transported by axonal transport to the lateral geniculate, where interneuronal transfer took place to geniculate cells that projected to the visual cortex. The diagrams show how the pattern of termination within the cortex changed from diffuse (E 91) to columnar (E 144 and adult). Cortical layers 1–6 are indicated at the side. IZ, intermediate zone; SP, subplate layer; OR, optic radiation; WM, white matter. **B.** Experiments showing effects of long-term monocular deprivation on ocular dominance columns at different ages in the rhesus monkey. Deprivation was begun at 2 weeks (a), 5½ weeks (b), 10 weeks (c), and in the adult (d). In each case, the normal (nondeprived) eye was injected with radioactive amino acids. In the photomicrographs, the sites of label appear white. Note the expansion of the terminal fields of the geniculate input from the nondeprived eye up to 5½ weeks. (A from Rakic, 1981; B from LeVay et al., 1981)

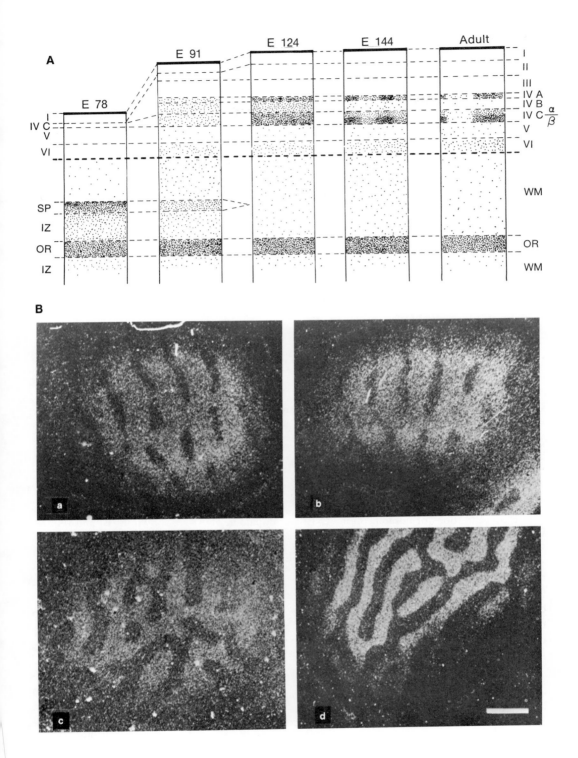

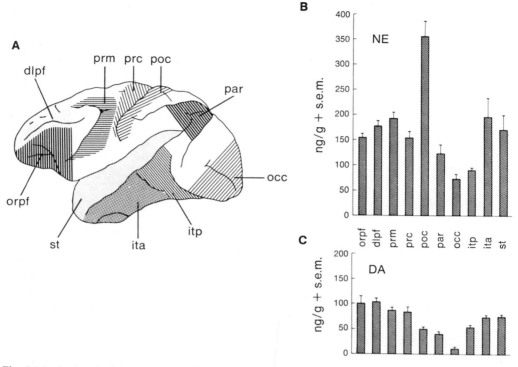

Fig. 31.9. A. Cortical areas examined for monoamine content. The abbreviations for the different areas are as follows:

orpf, orbital frontal cortex   par, posterior parietal cortex
dlpf, dorsolateral prefrontal cortex   occ, occipital cortex (visual area)
prm, premotor cortex   itp, inferior temporal gyrus
prc, precentral gyrus (motor strip)   ita, anterior inferior temporal gyrus
poc, postcentral gyrus (somatosensory cortex) st, superior temporal gyrus

Tissue concentrations of norepinephrine (NE) and dopamine (DA) are shown in (B) and (C), respectively, for the different cortical areas. (From Brown et al., 1979)

frontal lobe damage. His diagram of the way these two regions are involved in the control of speech (Fig. 31.10) was one of the first attempts to identify the brain circuits underlying specific behavioral functions.

This work thus clearly established that the left hemisphere is "dominant" for a specific function, speech. And there the matter rested. Until the 1950's this stood as an isolated exception to what appeared to be the general equivalence of the two hemispheres in all their other functions, sensory and motor. Then R. D. Myers and Roger Sperry carried out a series of ele-

gant experiments in which they cut the corpus callosum, the thick band containing millions of fibers that connect the two hemispheres. Until that time, no significant function had been ascribed to these fibers. When visual stimuli were presented to both eyes, the animals behaved as competently as normal cats. However, when the decussating fibers in the optic chiasm were cut and each eye was tested separately, it was found that each hemisphere functioned independently; visual learning in one hemisphere was not transferred to the other hemisphere.

Sperry and Michael Gazzaniga then ex-

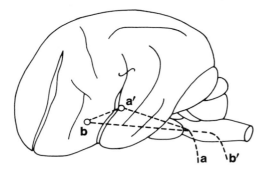

Fig. 31.10. Wernicke's original drawing in 1874, illustrating his concept of the brain circuits involved in language. Sounds received in the ears are converted into neural signals and transmitted through the auditory pathway (a) to the brain, where the sound "images" are stored in Wernicke's area (a'). These neural images are transferred to Broca's area (b) where they activate the descending pathway for motor control of speech (b'). The diagram indicates how lesions in (a') give rise to sensory aphasia (an inability to understand spoken words or organize words coherently), whereas lesions in (b) give rise to motor aphasia (an inability to articulate spoken words). (From Kolb and Whishaw, 1980)

amined a series of human patients in whom the callosum had been cut to prevent spread of epileptic seizures. These studies confirmed that, with independent visual input to one hemisphere or the other, the hemispheres also functioned and learned independently of one another. This work, which earned Sperry the Nobel Prize in 1981, led to our present concepts of the laterality of higher functions in the human brain: The left hemisphere is dominant for control of speech, language, complex voluntary movement, reading, writing, and arithmetic calculations. The right hemisphere is specialized for mainly nonlinguistic functions: complex pattern recognition in vision, audition, and the tactile senses; the sense of space, spatial shapes, and direction in space; the sense of intuition (see Fig. 31.11).

There have been many attempts to read

a lot into these differences, such as the idea that the left hemisphere is scientific whereas the right is artistic. It seems safe to conclude at present that the left hemisphere is specialized for certain kinds of motor output, whereas the right is more specialized for global relations of the body in space, something akin to the perceptual Gestalt referred to in Chap. 11. In this view, neither hemisphere is "dominant" in the absolute sense; one can conceive that each constellation of functions is of adaptive value, and the human brain attempts to optimize both by letting the hemispheres specialize in these two directions.

In recent years, lateralization of function has been found in a number of species, invertebrate as well as vertebrate; we have noted several instances in this book. It may well be that it is an inherent tendency in an animal with bilaterally organized body and brain.

Distributed Cortical Systems

In the foregoing section we have built up the organization of the cortex, from the single synapse to the lobes of an entire hemisphere. It would be convenient if each lobe subserved one of the higher mental functions, but it should already be evident that this is not the case. Each lobe contains centers for certain specific functions, such as the reception of visual input in the occipital lobe. However, our functional abilities are not compartmentalized in terms of these centers. For example, in a simple behavior, such as picking up an object with out fingers, visual information is used to direct and coordinate the movements of the arm and fingers. This requires connections from the visual cortex in the occipital lobe to the source of motor outflow in the parietal and frontal lobes. In addition, there must be connections to the eye fields in frontal cortex to mediate voluntary control of eye movements as we follow our fingers visually. All of these connections have in fact been demonstrated in anatomical studies (Fig. 31.12).

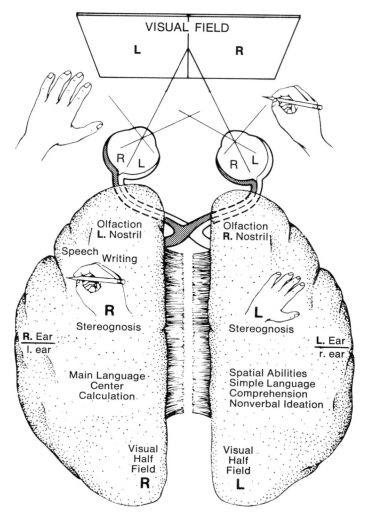

Fig. 31.11. Schematic representation of the brain, showing the relative specialization of the two hemispheres and their relations to sensory inputs and motor outputs. Cutting of the corpus collosum is shown in the midline. (From Sperry, 1974)

In addition, the diagram shows that there are connections from visual cortex to the inferior temporal lobe. Behavioral studies have shown that the temporal lobe is of crucial importance for visual discrimination learning, as first suggested by the "psychic blindness" of animals with the Klüver-Bucy syndrome (Chap. 29).

From these considerations it can be seen that even a simple act requires active participation by large areas of cortex distributed in different lobes and coordinated between the hemispheres. Thus, the old idea that cerebral functions are organized in terms of lobes is giving way to the new idea that cerebral functions are organized in terms of distributed systems. A given function is presumed to be subserved by some combination of centers, cortical and subcortical. Each center contributes the special operational properties mediated within its local circuits, the centers being tied together by multiple long tracts, collateral branches, and feedback connec-

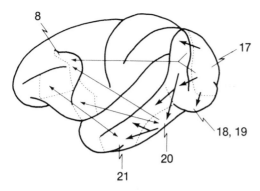

Fig. 31.12. Schematic diagram showing relations of the visual cortex to other cortical areas in the monkey. Based on anatomical studies in which a lesion was first placed in area 17, which produced degenerating fibers and terminals in areas 18 and 19. Lesions in these areas produced degeneration in areas 20, 21, and 8. Other connections demonstrated by this method are also indicated. (After Jones and Powell, 1970, in Poggio, 1980)

tions. A crucial feature is that different areas of the cortex are accessible to each other, so that there are maximal opportunities for the areas to interact. Within each area there is maximal opportunity for different inputs to tap or utilize specific properties of the local-circuit machinery, as we have already described above.

Analysis of the cellular basis of distributed systems requires single neuron recordings from many areas, combined with dye injection and neurochemical manipulations. That task has only barely begun, and the necessary procedures are not even possible, for the most part, in humans, for obvious ethical reasons. Thus, most of our knowledge of distributed cortical systems at present is based on results of ablation studies in monkeys, and of neurological diseases in humans. This kind of material has considerable limitations for interpreting neuronal circuits and mechanisms, as has often been remarked in this book. However, it has provided a wealth of fascinating data on some of the areas that must be involved in higher brain functions. An excellent summary may be found

in Kolb and Whishaw's *Fundamentals of Human Neuropsychology*. We have previously discussed the circuits involved in such higher functions as memory and emotion, and will finish here by considering briefly cortical systems for complex space and for language.

Complex Space. In order for our visual and tactile perceptions of space to be coordinated, as in the simple motor act of picking up an object described above, there must be a site or sites where the information from these two modalities is integrated. This was already recognized centuries ago: philosophers in the eighteenth century postulated a "sensorium commune" where sensory information comes together to form a coherent representation of our perceptual world. For visual and tactile space, an important site appears to be in the posterior parietal cortex (see Fig. 31.13).

Vernon Mountcastle and his colleagues have succeeded in recording from units in this area in awake, behaving monkeys. Most of these neurons responded to one or another submodality of muscle, joint, or skin stimulation, similar to neurons in the primary somatosensory cortex (see Chap. 13). However, some units showed complex properties. One type was active only when the animal performed a movement of the arm or a manipulation of the hand; in other words, movement in the immediate extrapersonal space. Another type was active only when the animal visually fixated on an object in which it had an obvious interest, such as an item of food when the monkey was hungry. The activity continued even when the object was moved in space. These experiments thus gave evidence of higher levels of abstraction, in which the mutual effects of location in space of a limb, location in space of an object, and the motivational state of the animal, combine to specify the activity of a single cortical cell. The tuning of the cell to multiple contingencies is one of the defining characteristics of higher abstrac-

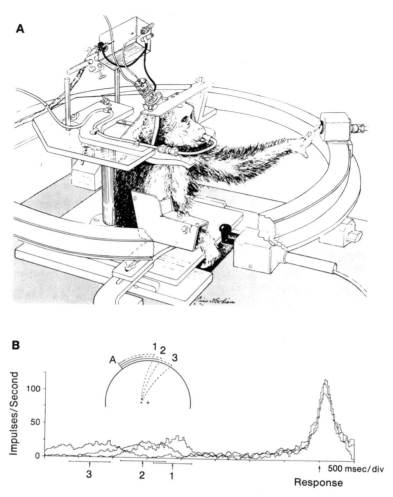

Fig. 31.13. Activity of higher-order cells in posterior parietal association cortex related to control of purposive movement. **A.** Monkey sitting in recording and test apparatus. The small box containing a signal light moves along the circular rail. The monkey starts by resting its left hand on the signal key (see black knob), then releases and projects the hand to touch the moving signal light when it is illuminated, as shown. **B.** Activity of an arm projection neuron. In this experiment, the signal light moved through three different arcs (inset); solid lines show the movement before, dashed lines the movement after, the signal came on. The trajectories of the hand, from the starting position (+) to the final points (1–3) at which the finger contacted the signal light, are also shown by dashed lines. Histograms of the firing frequency of this neuron are superimposed in the graph, aligned on the instant at which the finger touched the signal light (Response). Horizontal bars (1–3) below the abscissa indicate the detection times for the different trials. The similar firing patterns of this neuron during different arm trajectories indicate that the activity of this neuron is related to command signals for this type of purposive movement, rather than to detailed instructions for individual muscle contractions. (From Mountcastle et al., 1975)

tion. It was concluded that this kind of sensory integration is concerned with spatially orienting the animal toward behavioral goals.

A different aspect of space has been revealed by studies of the hippocampus. Here, single-unit recordings, as well as EEG recordings from depth electrodes inserted into the hippocampus, in awake, behaving animals show that pyramidal neurons are tuned to fire impulses when the animal is in a particular location in its environment. Thus, the cell may be active when the animal is in a certain corner of its cage, but not in any other location. Moreover, this activity occurs only when the animal itself has actively moved to this location; the cell is silent if the animal is passively placed there by the experimenter. From experiments of this type, J. O'Keefe and L. Nadel of London have hypothesized that the hippocampus contains a "cognitive map", in which are stored spatial memories relating to experiences in the animal's life. This expands the memory functions of the hippocampus, as discussed in Chap. 30, to the combining of information about space, time, active movement, and emotional content.

Finally, space and time also come together in the frontal lobe. As was first shown in 1936 by Carlyle Jacobson in John Fulton's laboratory at Yale, monkeys with lesions of the frontal lobe lose the ability to remember the location of a test object over brief intervals of time. This loss of "delayed response" learning is quite specific; the performance on other complex learning tasks is unaffected. With single-unit recordings it has been possible to show that there are neurons which are selectively active during the delay period of the task. Recently, Goldman-Rakic and her colleagues tested the hypothesis that this ability depends on the fact that the frontal lobes are rich in dopamine (DA). They made microinjections of 6-hydroxydopamine (which selectively depletes DA) into the frontal cortex, and found an impairment of performance on a spatial delayed task nearly as severe as that caused by surgical removal of the frontal lobe. This effect could be reversed pharmacologically by injections of DA agonists such as l-DOPA and apomorphine. These results provide further evidence that both spatial orientation and memory depend on distributed systems that embrace many cortical (as well as subcortical) areas. They further indicate how one type of neuron—the dopaminergic neuron—may be critically important for a specific cognitive function involving space and time.

Dopaminergic systems are important not only for their role in normal cognitive functions, but also because of the possibility that malfunctions in dopaminergic circuits may underlie or contribute to the major psychotic illnesses, depression and schizophrenia. The experiments and theories that bear on this question are summarized in Kolb and Whishaw, and in appropriate medical texts.

Language. The simple circuit first proposed by Wernicke as the basis for cortical mechanisms in language still holds, but it has been considerably elaborated by recent studies. An important finding has been the discovery that there is an anatomical asymmetry associated with the functional asymmetry of language in the human brain. This simple fact had escaped most neuroanatomists and neuropathologists, in their examinations of the brains of humans obtained postmortem, until 1968. In that year, Norman Geschwind and W. Levitsky at Harvard reported that measurements of the right and left temporal lobes showed a striking difference. In most brains, an area called the "planum temporale", located on the upper border of the temporal lobe and extending deep into the Sylvian fossa, is considerably larger on the left. This is shown diagrammatically in Fig. 31.14. The planum temporale contains Wernicke's speech area. It is tempting to conclude that the larger speech

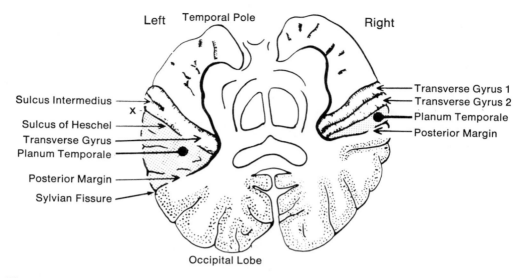

Fig. 31.14. Diagram of a horizontal section through the human brain, showing asymmetry of the temporal lobe upper surface, and the larger area called planum temporale on the left. (From Geschwind and Levitsky, in Geschwind, 1981)

area on the left is correlated with left-hemispheric dominance for language in most humans. This, of course, does not explain how Wernicke's area mediates language, but it indicates that one of the mechanisms for obtaining greater complexity of information processing, that of

increasing the number of neurons and extent of local circuits, has been utilized in this case.

An expanded view of the distributed system for language is shown in Fig. 31.15. This is based on the results from electrical stimulation of speech areas in

Fig. 31.15. Summary of the main pathways believed to be involved in seeing an object and saying its name. **A.** Lateral view of left hemisphere. **B.** Overhead view of both hemispheres. AF, arcuate fasciculus; CC, corpus callosum. (A from Popper and Eccles, 1977; B modified from Geschwind, 1980)

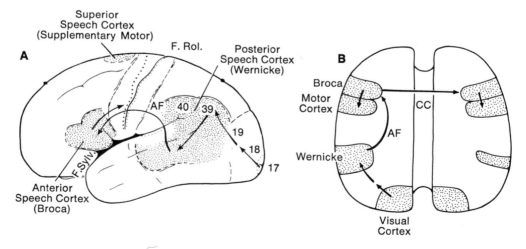

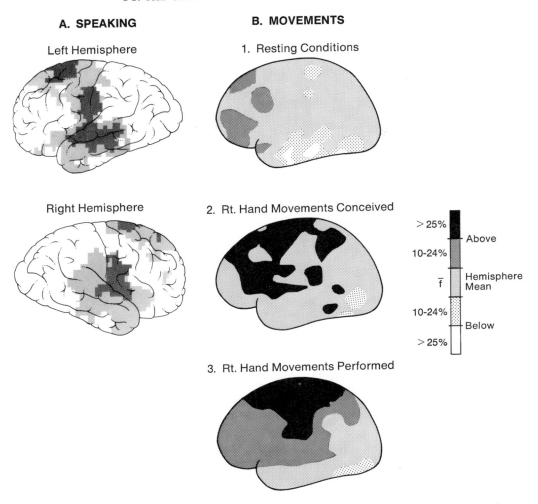

A. SPEAKING

Left Hemisphere

Right Hemisphere

B. MOVEMENTS

1. Resting Conditions

2. Rt. Hand Movements Conceived

> 25%
10-24%
$\bar{f}$
10-24%
> 25%

Above

Hemisphere
Mean

Below

3. Rt. Hand Movements Performed

Fig. 31.16. Computerized images of differences in regional blood flow in the human brain during different behaviors. **A.** Regions active during speaking. These images represent averages from nine different subjects. Squares indicate the resolution of the multiple detector array aimed at the side of the head. Regions of high blood flow (and increased cortical activity) are indicated by darkest shading; regions of light shading indicate background levels; unshaded regions indicate below-average activity. **B.** Comparison between regions active during the conceptualization of a motor act and the performance of that act. 1, resting condition (note activity in frontal poles). 2, the subject was asked to imagine rhythmic clenching movements of the right hand (note active regions in frontal, parietal, and temporal lobes, but largely sparing the motor strip along the central sulcus). 3, when the movements were actually performed, activity was centered over the motor strip. Drawings are adapted from data plots like those in (A); results were from six subjects. (A from Lassen et al., 1978, in Kolb and Whitshaw, 1980; B from Ingvar and Phillipsson, in Yarovsky and Ingvar, 1981)

human patients, as well as on anatomical studies in monkeys and humans. The diagram emphasizes the connections involved in one language task: naming a seen object. Visual information is first received in area 17, and elaborated in areas 18 and 19. From here, the perceptual image of the object is transferred to a large "posterior speech area", which includes area 39 (of parietal cortex) as well as the classical

Wernicke's area. Area 39 transfers the visual representation of the object to its auditory representation in area 22. From area 22, the information is transferred to Broca's speech area, where the motor programs for speech are located. These programs are then "read out" to the face area of the motor cortex, where they control the complex spatiotemporal coordination of the muscles of speech, so that the name of the observed object can be articulated.

This circuit, inferred from the traditional methods of anatomy and physiology, has been directly visualized by new methods for mapping cerebral function. We have previously described the Sokoloff method for mapping brain activity by autoradiography. A related method is based on the fact that when different cortical regions are active, they receive an increased blood flow, much as does a muscle when it is active. By injecting into the bloodstream a substance (xenon $_{133}$) whose concentration can be monitored by radioactivity detectors placed on the skull, the activity of different cortical regions can be mapped in awake subjects while they perform specific mental tasks.

In the example in Fig. 31.16A, the subject was asked to speak. The peaks of activity occur over the mouth-tongue-larynx area of the motor and somatosensory cortex, the supplementary motor area in the frontal lobe, and the auditory cortex, including Wernicke's area. There is considerably more activity in the left hemisphere than in the right, as expected for the left hemisphere being dominant for speech. Figure 31.16B shows that these methods can reveal not only the patterns associated with performance of a motor task, but also those associated with the conceptualization of that task.

Results such as these confirm the general postulates regarding the contributions of different areas to specific higher functions. When combined with single-cell recordings and neurochemical analysis, these new methods should provide a firm foundation for analyzing cortical systems at the cellular level. An understanding of the nature of cortical function, and the nature of our own being, seems a bit closer to our grasp; our progress, as always, will depend on our ingenuity in devising new methods, our imagination in interpreting the results, and our wisdom in maintaining a balanced view of mankind among the creatures of this planet.

REFERENCES

Aghajanian, G. K. and F. E. Bloom. 1967. The formation of synaptic junctions in developing rat brain: a quantitative electron microscopic study. *Brain Res.* 6: 716–727.

Brodal, A. 1981. [Chap. 14].

Brown, R. M., A. M. Crane, and P. S. Goldman. 1979. Regional distribution of monoamines in the cerebral cortex and subcortical structures of the rhesus monkey: concentrations and in vivo rates. *Brain Res. 168:* 133–150.

Emson, P. C. and S. P. Hunt. 1981. Anatomical chemistry of the cerebral cortex. In *The Organization of the Cerebral Cortex* (ed. by F. O. Schmitt, F. G. Worden, G. Adelman, and S. G. Dennis). Cambridge, Mass: MIT Press. pp. 325–345.

Geschwind, N. 1980. Some special functions of the human brain. In *Medical Physiology* (ed. by V. G. Mountcastle). St. Louis: Mosby. pp. 647–665.

Goldman-Rakic, P. S. 1981. Development and plasticity of primate frontal association cortex. In *The Organization of the Cerebral Cortex.* (op.cit.), pp 69–97.

Hofer, M. A. 1981. [Chap. 27].

Isaac, G. and R. E. F. Leakey (eds.). 1979. *Human Ancestors.* San Francisco: W. H. Freeman.

Jacobson, M. 1978. [Chap. 10].

Kasamatsu, T., J. D. Pettigrew, and M. Ary. Restoration of visual cortical plasticity by local microperfusion of norepinephrine. *J. Comp. Neurol. 185:* 163–182.

Kolb, B. and I. Q. Whishaw. 1980. [Chap. 29].

Kostovic, I. (personal communication).

Lassen, N. A., D. H. Ingvar, and E. Skinhoj. 1978. Brain function and blood flow. *Sci. Am. 239:* 62–71.

LeVay, S., T. N. Wiesel, and D. H. Hubel.

1981. The postnatal development and plasticity of ocular dominance columns in the monkey. In *The Organization of the Cerebral Cortex* (op. cit.), pp. 29–46.

Lund, R. D. 1978. [Chap. 10].

Mountcastle, V. B. et al. 1975. Posterior parietal association cortex of the monkey: command functions for operation within extra-personal space. *J. Neurophysiol.* 38: 871–908.

Northcutt, R. G. 1981. Evolution of the telencephalon in non-mammals. *Ann. Rev. Neurosci.* 4: 301–350.

O'Keefe, J. and L. Nadel. 1978. *The Hippocampus as a Cognitive Map.* Oxford: Oxford University Press.

Poggio, J. F. 1980. Central neural mechanisms in vision. In *Medical Physiology* (op. cit.), pp. 544–585.

Popper, K. R. and J. C. Eccles. 1977. [Chap. 17].

Rakic, P. 1976. [Chap. 4].

Rakic, P. 1981. Developmental events leading to laminar and areal organization of the neocortex. In *The Organization of the Cerebral Cortex* (op. cit.), pp. 7–28.

Sarnat, H. B. and M. G. Netsky. 1981. [Chap. 3].

Shepherd, G. M. 1979. [Chap. 4].

Sperry, R. W. 1974. Lateral specialization in the surgically separated hemispheres. In *The Neurosciences: Third Study Program* (ed. by F. O. Schmitt and F. G. Worden). Cambridge, Mass: MIT Press. pp. 5–19.

Yarowsky, P. J. and D. H. Ingvar. 1981. Neuronal activity and energy metabolism. *Fed. Proc.* 40: 2353–2362.

Index

593

Hippocampus (*Continued*)
isolated preparations of, for studying synaptic
circuits, 137–38
in memory, 562–66
spindle synapses of, 79
Histogenesis, definition of, 165
Hodgkin-Huxley model of nerve impulse, 105–8
Homologous structures, definition of, 570
Homoplastic structures, definition of, 570
Hormone(s)
in bird song generation, 435–36
eclosion, in molting process, 179–80
juvenile, in molting process, 178–79
in neuron interactions, 72–73
and peptides, binding of, 39
pituitary, 451–54
plasma membrane as site of action of, 52
polypeptide, in large vesicles, 78–79
steroid, actions of, on nucleus, 54
thoracotropic, in molting process, 178
Horseradish peroxidase
in identification of synaptic connections, 82
intracellular transport of, 62
in study of CNS pathways, 58–59
"Hot spots" on dendrites, impulse spread and,
117–18
Humans
behavior of, cerebral cortex and, 568–90
characteristics unique to, 568–69
Hydrostatic pressure, 90
5-Hydroxytryptamine in central neural circuits,
457–58
Hyperpolarized membrane potential, 93
Hyperpolarizing response of synaptic potential, 128
Hypothalamus
in emotion, 531–34
in neuroendocrine system, 39
neurons of, large synapses in, 78

Immunological methods for identification of
neuroactive substances, 152–53
Impedance matching in mammalian ear, 292
Imprinting, 560
Impulse
functions of, 118
generation of, 192–94
spread of, mechanisms for, *117*
Infradian rhythms, definition of, 467
Inhibiting factors in hormone secretion control, 39
Inhibition
command-derived, of crayfish escape response, 369
presynaptic
decreased, by pain, 241
increased, by tactile stimulation, 241
Inhibitory postsynaptic potential (IPSPs), 125
and excitatory postsynaptic potentials, interaction
of, 125–26
Ink gland of Aplysia, 26
Innate releasing mechanism in mating of invertebrates, 510
Innervation
polyneuronal, 343
reciprocal, of muscles to joint in vertebrates, 372
Inorganic anions of squid giant axon, 88
Inorganic ions of squid giant axon, 88

Inputs in synapses, 83
Insects
compound eye of, 313–15
gross morphology of, 21–23
metamorphosis of, 177–80
nervous organization controlling flying in, 385–87
olfactory system of, in mating behavior, 510–12
social, 23
song of, neural mechanisms controlling, 430–34
Instrumental conditioning, 554–56
Integration, synaptic, 125–26
Integrative organization of nerve cell, 129–34
Integument. *See also* Skin
functions of, 227t
Intensity of sensory response, receptor and, 194
Intermembranous particles in type I chemical
synapse, 77
Internal chemoreceptors, 205–6
Interneuron(s), 68–69
in spinal cord, 35–36
in synaptic circuit, 84
of visceral muscles of invertebrates, 352
Interoceptors, 189
Intracellular recording of membrane potentials,
92–93
Intrafusal fibers of vertebrates, 257
Intrinsic neuron synapses, 83
Invertebrates, 13–27
auditory receptors of, 286–88
autonomic functions of, 350–53
autonomic nervous systems of, organization of,
349
chemical sense of, 206–14
circadian rhythms in, 468–72
emotions in, 530–31
feeding in, 488–93
fixed action patterns of, 364–70
hearing in, 286–89
kinesthesia in, 252–56
locomotor systems in, 382–87
manipulation in, 414–20
mating in, 509–14
memory in, 561–62
muscle sense in, 252–56
muscles of, motor function of, 342
neuroendocrine circuits of, 449–54
olfactory system of, 210–14
origins of, 14–15
reflexes of, 364–70
sense of balance in, 269–73
sensory hairs in, neuronal differentiation and,
169–70
somatic senses of, 228–31
taste system of, 206–10
vision in, 308–16
Ionic currents in synaptic potential production,
126–27
Ion channels, voltage-dependent, 112t
Ion conductances, different, in neurons, 111–13
Ions
concentrations of, in vertebrate cell, 88t, 89
inorganic, of squid giant axon, 88
of nerve cells, 87–89
organic, of squid giant axon, 87–88
Isethionate as organic ion of squid giant axon, 87